advantage

Dear Valued Customer,

We realize you're a busy professional with deadlines to hit. Whether your goal is to learn a new technology or solve a critical problem, we want to be there to lend you a hand. Our primary objective is to provide you with the insight and knowledge you need to stay atop the highly competitive and ever-changing technology industry.

Wiley Publishing, Inc., offers books on a wide variety of technical categories, including security, data warehousing, software development tools, and networking — everything you need to reach your peak. Regardless of your level of expertise, the Wiley family of books has you covered.

- For Dummies® – The ***fun*** and ***easy*** way™ to learn
- The Weekend Crash Course® – The ***fastest*** way to learn a new tool or technology
- Visual – For those who prefer to learn a new topic ***visually***
- The Bible – The ***100% comprehensive*** tutorial and reference
- The Wiley Professional list – ***Practical*** and ***reliable*** resources for IT professionals

The book you now hold is part of our new *60 Minutes a Day* series which delivers what we think is the closest experience to an actual hands-on seminar that is possible with a book. Our authors are veterans of hundreds of hours of classroom teaching and they use that background to guide you past the hurdles and pitfalls to confidence and mastery of Visual Basic .NET in manageable units that can be read and put to use in just an hour. If you have a broadband connection to the Web, you can see Bruce introduce each topic — but this book will still be your best learning resource if you download only the audio files or use it strictly as a printed resource. From fundamentals to security and Web Services, you'll find this self-paced training to be your best learning aid.

Our commitment to you does not end at the last page of this book. We'd like to open a dialog with you to see what other solutions we can provide. Please be sure to visit us at www.wiley.com/compbooks to review our complete title list and explore the other resources we offer. If you have a comment, suggestion, or any other inquiry, please locate the "contact us" link at www.wiley.com.

Finally, we encourage you to review the following page for a list of Wiley titles on related topics. Thank you for your support and we look forward to hearing from you and serving your needs again in the future.

Sincerely,

Richard K. Swadley
Vice President & Executive Group Publisher
Wiley Technology Publishing

15 HOUR WEEKEND CRASH COURSE

Visual

Bible

FOR DUMMIES

Wiley Publishing, Inc.

more information on related titles

Wiley Going to the Next Level

Available from Wiley Publishing

60 Minutes a Day Books...

- Self-paced instructional text packed with real-world tips and examples from real-world training instructors
- Skill-building exercises, lab sessions, and assessments
- Author-hosted streaming video presentations for each chapter will pinpoint key concepts and reinforce lessons

0-471-43023-4

0-471-42548-6

0-471-42314-9

0-471-42254-1

Wiley Publishing, Inc.

Available at your favorite bookseller or visit www.wiley.com/compbooks

Visual Basic .NET™ in 60 Minutes a Day

Bruce Barstow
Tony Martin

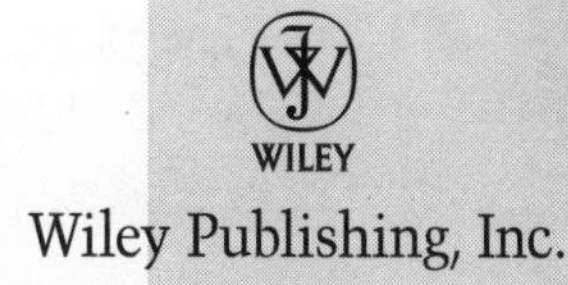

Wiley Publishing, Inc.

Executive Publisher: Robert Ipsen
Vice-President & Publisher: Joseph B. Wikert
Senior Editor: Ben Ryan
Editorial Manager: Kathryn A. Malm
Development Editor: Jerry Olson
Production Editor: Vincent Kunkemueller
Media Development Specialist: Travis Silvers
Text Design & Composition: Wiley Composition Services

For general information on our other products and services please contact our Customer Care Department within the United States at (800) 762-2974, outside the United States at (317) 572-3993 or fax (317) 572-4002.

Wiley also publishes its books in a variety of electronic formats. Some content that appears in print may not be available in electronic books.

Library of Congress Cataloging-in-Publication Data:

ISBN: 0-471-42548-6

Printed in the United States of America

10 9 8 7 6 5 4 3 2 1

A Note from the Consulting Editor

Instructor-led training has proven to be an effective and popular tool for training engineers and developers. To convey technical ideas and concepts, the classroom experience has been shown to be superior when compared to other delivery methods. As a technical trainer for more than 20 years, I have seen the effectiveness of instructor-led training firsthand. *60 Minutes a Day* combines the best of the instructor-led training and book experience. Technical training is typically divided in short and discrete modules, where each module encapsulates a specific topic. Each module is then followed by "questions and answers" and a review. *60 Minutes a Day* titles follow the same model: each chapter is short, discrete, and can be completed in 60 minutes a day. For these books, I have enlisted premier technical trainers as authors. They provide the voice of the trainer and demonstrate classroom experience in each book of the series. You even get an opportunity to meet the actual trainer: As part of this innovative approach, each chapter of a *60 Minutes a Day* book is presented online by the author. Readers are encouraged to view the online presentation before reading the relevant chapter. Therefore, *60 Minutes a Day* delivers the complete classroom experience—even the trainer.

As an imprint of Wiley Publishing, Inc., Gearhead Press continues to bring you, the reader, the level of quality that Wiley has delivered consistently for nearly 200 years.

Thank you.

Donis Marshall
Founder, Gearhead Press
Consulting Editor, Wiley Technology Publishing Group

To Tamra, Brian, and Alyssa: my children and my teachers.

—Bruce Barstow

To Nico, Alex, Hanna, Joy, Daniel, Kate, Christina, Alex P., Jonathan, and all of the other kids in my life.

—Tony Martin

Contents

Acknowledgments

Bruce would like to thank Tony Martin for his help on this project. Tony provided key chapters that demonstrate his broad-reaching experience and unique insight.

Thanks to Tamra, Brian, and Alyssa, who waited patiently for me to finish this project, and to God for giving them to me. Thanks to my wife, Jody, for her unbelievable patience and crucial support on the book. Additionally, thanks to my mom for pushing me to run in directions I would not have walked.

Thanks to J. W. (Jerry) Olsen for being so incredibly patient and for sharing his wisdom and energy. Also, thanks to Donis Marshall and Wiley Technology Publishing for the privilege of writing a book. Of all the mentors I have had in my life, a few shaped who I am and provided me with examples I will never forget. Of these, I would like to thank James Kilbourne of CTI, Barbara Straw of Autodesk, Steve Busse, Karen Wildblood, and James Yoder (wherever you are).

To my friends Sean, Major, Ken, Billy, and Mark, thanks for the Saturdays of laughter and mayhem that make the weeks less stressful. Sean has been my personal version of Peter Norton and has frequently been a great sounding board.

In these changing times I want to thank the brave men and women of our space program that reach beyond the stars to the freedom of space and for those who fight for our freedom here on Earth. May God keep you close.

—Bruce Barstow

Tony would first like to thank Bruce for allowing him to work on this project. Though intense, it was fun and educational. Bruce is a sharp programmer and he always had something new to impart. Additionally, thanks to Kathryn Malm, who, as an editor and friend, was always willing to share advice about writing and dealing with people and the process (not to mention dropping my name to others so I could work on this book). Thanks to J. W. (Jerry) Olsen and Donis Marshall, who brought me onto this project and moved it forward.

Friends are always a big help on projects like this even though they don't write a single word. Dominic Selly, an author I've worked with before, helped me out with a database connection problem while I was writing my parts of this book. But the most heroic people are those who allowed me to talk endlessly about the book as it was being written and yet remained my friends. So, a big thanks to friends and family, including Mom, my sister Lise and her family, Poppop, Warren, David, Susan, Cheryl, Mike, Betsy, Mary, Curtis, Otto, Ann, and others who, though they realized I was going to tell them how the book was doing, listened anyway without running at top speed in the opposite direction. All of you are priceless.

Finally, thanks to Dan Castellaneta, Julie Kavner, Hank Azaria, Harry Shearer, Nancy Cartwright, Yeardly Smith, Phil Hartman, Pamela Hayden, Tress MacNeille, Maggie Roswell (who did a stunning Sherry Bobbins!), Russi Taylor, Marcia Wallace, Matt Groening, James L. Brooks, Al Jean, Conan O'Brien, and all the writers, producers, and others that came together to create one of the most intelligent, clever, funny, and inspiring television shows to grace our planet. Your efforts over the last 14 years helped me to get through this book and other life events. Thanks!

—Tony Martin

About the Authors

Bruce Barstow has been writing software since Atari 2600 and TIAs (Television Interface Chips). Through more than 10 years in the military and aerospace industry, Bruce contributed software and systems engineering support for projects including the American Launch system, The Soyuz Assured Crew Return Vehicle, The Mars Project, The National Launch System, and the Space Shuttle programs.

A professional instructor and consultant for about 15 years, Bruce has programmed in more languages than he'll admit but still avidly develops in and teaches C++, Visual Basic, Visual Basic .Net, and C#. He has delivered lectures or provided consulting in almost every state and in nine countries. A long-time advocate of Microsoft development tools, Bruce holds several Microsoft certifications and a degree in Computer Science, and was lucky enough to present Microsoft technologies at TechEd '96 overseas. With a dynamic style and on-the-fly adaptation to the customer's needs, Bruce is most often found assisting development teams in the design, architecture, and implementation of enterprise solutions with .Net technology.

When Bruce isn't attached to a keyboard, he enjoys spending time with his three children and other adults who act like children. He enjoys making people laugh and sharing his love of technology.

Tony Martin has been a programmer for about 22 years. He started in 1981 with such tools as CP/M and DOS. He has been involved in many aspects of software development and has special interests in the software development process, user interface design and implementation, and Web development. However, like most programmers, he will code anything he can get his hands on. He works regularly with Visual Basic, Visual C++, and Visual Basic .NET. Tony works for Best Software, Inc., a commercial software company that creates fixed-asset accounting solutions and other software (such as Act and Peachtree Accounting) for small- to medium-sized businesses. He teaches programming courses in-house as well as being a full-time programmer and software project leader. Tony has written two other books on enterprise programming with Visual Basic and Visual Basic .NET.

When not programming, Tony is likely to be found romping through the woods, camera in hand, photographing the natural beauty around him. He might also be spending time with friends and family, which are near and dear to his heart. When his editors are able to talk him into it, he might also be writing programming books.

Introduction

Overview of the Book and Technology

This book is part of a new, classroom-in-a-book approach to learning. Each book in the series is written by experienced trainers with years of real-world experience as industry consultants and architects. Each chapter includes in-depth technology overviews, tips, step-by-step labs, and chapter assessment reviews. Integrated question and answer sessions with questions from actual Visual Basic .NET students help to provide a classroom environment.

Visual Basic .NET is much more than a new version of Visual Basic; it is the most exciting and empowering system of development around. This book will help you quickly grasp the important concepts surrounding .NET while mastering many new technologies previously lacking in Visual Basic.

How This Book Is Organized

I separated the book into four major sections. The first section, "The .NET Experience," introduces you to the world of .NET development, where you'll see how Visual Basic .NET has become a first-class citizen in a development environment in which languages are, more or less, equal. You'll learn how to build Windows applications with the power and flexibility of C++, the elegant simplicity and abstraction of Visual Basic, and many features similar to Java development.

In the second section, "Middle-Tier Development in .NET," you will be guided through the massive capabilities offered by true object-oriented development. You'll discover how to understand and master the power of inheritance, the lure and grace provided by polymorphism, and the power of multithreaded applications.

In the third section, "Web Technologies in .NET," you will see the ease of integrating business systems through the use of SOAP and XML Web services, the amazing new features and execution speed in ASP.NET Web development and the seamless integration and power of XML in .NET.

Finally, in the fourth section, "Distribution and Interoperability in .NET," interoperability, distribution, migration, localization, and deployment are discussed in detail, with step-by-step procedures for performing each task. In addition, The Mobile Internet Toolkit is described and demonstrated with real-life examples of this exciting new area of development.

Who Should Read This Book

The book best targets those experienced in previous versions of Visual Basic. Because of the dramatic changes to development from Visual Studio 6 to Visual Studio .NET, Visual Basic .NET will provide more of a level playing field than you might think for people of varying backgrounds. Because of the classroom style approach, readers with little programming experience may find this book quite useful. Every attempt has been made to aid experienced Visual Basic developers in their migration of self and code to this exciting new environment.

Tools You Will Need

.NET development in general requires Visual Studio .NET and the Windows Component Update CD. The labs in this book as well as the book's Web site do not provide these tools. Appendix A, "Installing .NET," details installation and setup requirements.

What's on the Web Site

The companion Web site for this book, at www.wiley.com/compbooks/60minutesaday contains many examples, tools, and other developer resources used or referenced throughout the book. These examples will be updated as technology changes and will reflect changes to the emerging versions of Visual Basic .NET. Purchase of this title allows you access to all material as it is added to the site.

Conventions in This Book

This book employs conventions found in the many computer books that no doubt are already on your bookshelf, but we won't bore you by explaining that a Tip set off from the rest of the text is intended as a helpful tip and so forth.

The one point we want to observe is that code listings throughout the book often contain highlighted phrases. When code provides a syntactical example of language structure or implements key components in the preceding discussion, we put the keywords and language components in highlight so that you can focus directly on how these keywords and language components are used.

Summary

We sincerely believe that this book will significantly reduce your learning curve as you explore this amazing development environment and prepare yourself for today's ever more connected world. If you ever wanted to sit through a course and wish you could just turn the instructor off and on as needed, sit back, and enjoy the ride.

The .NET Experience

CHAPTER

1

Nothing but .NET

The more I develop in .NET, the more I can't believe that this isn't the way things were always done. Although the environment looks similar to Visual Basic 6, the underlying changes are vast and quite impressive.

This chapter explains the various high-level features related to .NET development and the tools necessary to get a Visual Basic programmer up to speed with Visual Basic .NET. Getting lost in the changes to the way Microsoft applications are developed can be confusing. With that in mind, this chapter attempts to introduce each of the primary benefits of .NET to get an idea of what .NET is before going deeply into the low-level detail. The major features of .NET are introduced in the chapter and expanded on throughout the book.

This part, "The .NET Experience," focuses on the .NET fundamentals and the creation of .NET Windows applications. As we progress through future chapters, we will build the various components of an enterprise application using Visual Basic .NET Windows applications, class libraries, ASP.NET applications, and XML Web services.

What Is .NET?

To explain what .NET is as a concept requires an understanding of why it was created in the first place. Several fundamental problems faced the development community as a whole, and Microsoft created some things simply to improve its own business model. Whatever the reason behind each of the features, it is a daunting change in the way we develop applications.

Microsoft had many reasons for creating .NET. Among them are:

- The world wanted a generic language that would enable portability to different operating systems and a specification was created. This specification became known as the Common Language Specification (CLS). The CLS is the standard to which .NET languages must adhere.
- Microsoft's remote model for communicating between two components (DCOM) was too tightly coupled, meaning that the client had to be a Microsoft client. Although the development of Simple Object Access Protocol (SOAP) and Extensible Markup Language (XML) Web services solved this issue for both Microsoft and Java development, those concepts had never been integrated into the Microsoft development environment prior to .NET. With XML Web services, any XML-sentient programmer anywhere on any operating system (OS) can use remote components.
- C++ as the object-oriented programming (OOP) standard had some things to fix, such as the removal of multiple implementation inheritance, syntax changes known to cause infamous issues in code, the addition of a realistic level of type safety to the language—the list is not small. Java, Visual Basic, and C++ each had something to offer, and the result is the best of all three. All .NET languages are equally object oriented and built from the ground up using the same foundation.
- Windows developers prior to .NET not only expected that their code would not run on multiple operating systems but also expected serious issues just trying to raise an exception (error) between two languages on the same operating system. .NET has exactly one way of raising an exception (System.Exception), and it is known by all .NET languages.

Classroom Q & A

Q: You mentioned that Microsoft wanted to compete with the J2EE initiative, and I realize that the fact that they both use Web services resolves the tight coupling issue, but how is my code supposed to run on Linux, Unix, or the "any OS" you mentioned earlier?

A: Much like Java's byte code, .NET uses an intermediary language (IL) that can be ported to other operating systems, where it can be compiled to native machine code. This requires those operating systems to have a compiler that can do this, just as operating systems need a Java Virtual Machine (JVM) to run Java code.

Q: Do these .NET or IL compilers exist on other operating systems?
A: Yes. Microsoft has opened up the common language runtime and the C# specification to the standards organization, ECMA, so vendors other than Microsoft can build .NET applications for their platforms. Several efforts were being thrown around as buzzwords in 2001, including Ja.NET, iNet, dotGNU, and Xamian-Mono, but the Mono Project as a Linux common language runtime seems to be the strongest player now. The Mono Project even added ASP.NET support. The URL for the Mono Project is www.go-mono.com.

Q: After the code is on another operating system, does it have to run from its IL representation or can it be compiled to native code?
A: .NET code is compiled to IL, and on Windows we can use the ngen .exe utility to compile it for our specific Windows architecture. Different operating systems have or will have similar utilities. Code can be run in its IL form and compiled on the fly or compiled to native form before execution.

The .NET Infrastructure

Visual Basic .NET, C# (pronounced "see sharp"), J#, and any other .NET language is, in a sense, just a bunch of keywords that map back to a core set of underlying code called the .NET common language runtime class libraries. Common language runtime is responsible for controlling literally *everything* that happens to or in a .NET application. Where C# uses an int keyword, Visual Basic programmers still use the familiar Integer keyword. Regardless of which is used, after compilation to IL, they are both changed to the underlying type: System.Int32. This data type, which exists in the core set of libraries, is then further mapped to something specific to the operating system on which it runs when the application is further compiled to native code. Figure 1.1 depicts this relationship.

Microsoft refers to this infrastructure as the .NET Framework. Although the Framework is more complicated than shown, Figure 1.1 helps explain how things are accomplished in .NET. The reference in Figure 1.1 to a common language runtime base type indicates that virtually all things in .NET are done explicitly or implicitly by referencing some class or interface in those common language runtime libraries. How those libraries actually accomplish their task is up to the operating system. In Microsoft operating systems, the Win32 API is still the powerhouse behind the scenes.

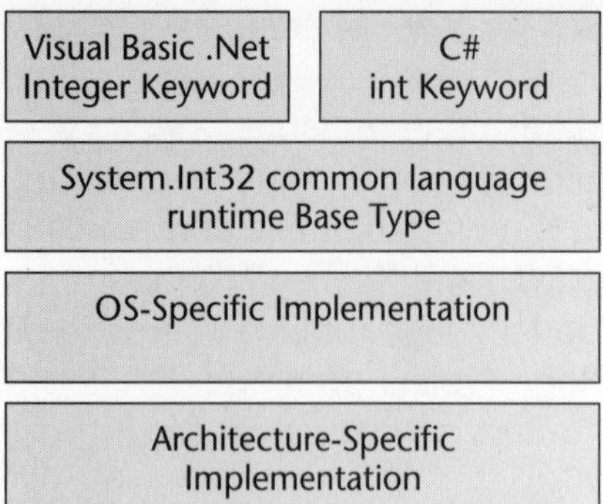

Figure 1.1 .NET languages use types that map to types in the common language runtime libraries that are implemented in an OS-specific way.

The Common Language Runtime

The common language runtime refers to the engine that controls every aspect of .NET. Its file implementation is mscoree.dll and can normally be found in the System32 folder under the Windows or winnt folders. Nothing happens in .NET without the common language runtime making it happen. It's a *common* runtime because all .NET languages use it. This contrasts with the fact that in Visual Basic 6 we used a runtime dynamic link library (DLL) that was used specifically for Visual Basic and even specific for each version of Visual Basic.

The Common Development Environment

We should spend little time discussing the environment and more time seeing what it can do. Not only is the environment almost identical to Visual Basic 6, it is a single Integrated Development Environment (IDE) that is shared for all .NET languages and all .NET project types. You can create a Windows application, class library, Web service, ASP page, or your own custom controls and services all in one environment, and they can all be written in different languages.

Creating New Projects

Let's start with the New Project window, which can be used to create any of the project types in any installed .NET language. After installing J# (the .NET Java equivalent from Microsoft), it would also appear in the Project Types list in the New Project window (see Figure 1.2).

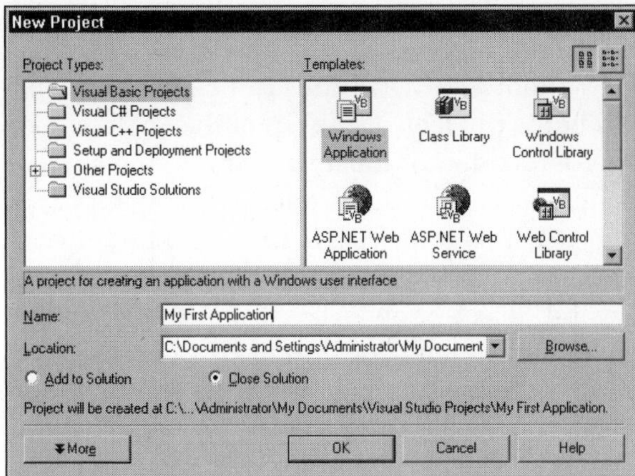

Figure 1.2 The New Project window adds a project to the current solution.

After selecting Visual Basic Projects for the Project Type and Windows Application for the template, a veteran Visual Basic programmer will find a thankfully familiar environment. Beneath the scenery, things are built using the best features of C++ and Java, but the interface is built mostly of features found in Visual Basic 6 and Visual Interdev. Figure 1.3 provides a look at the Visual Studio .NET IDE with a new Windows application project loaded.

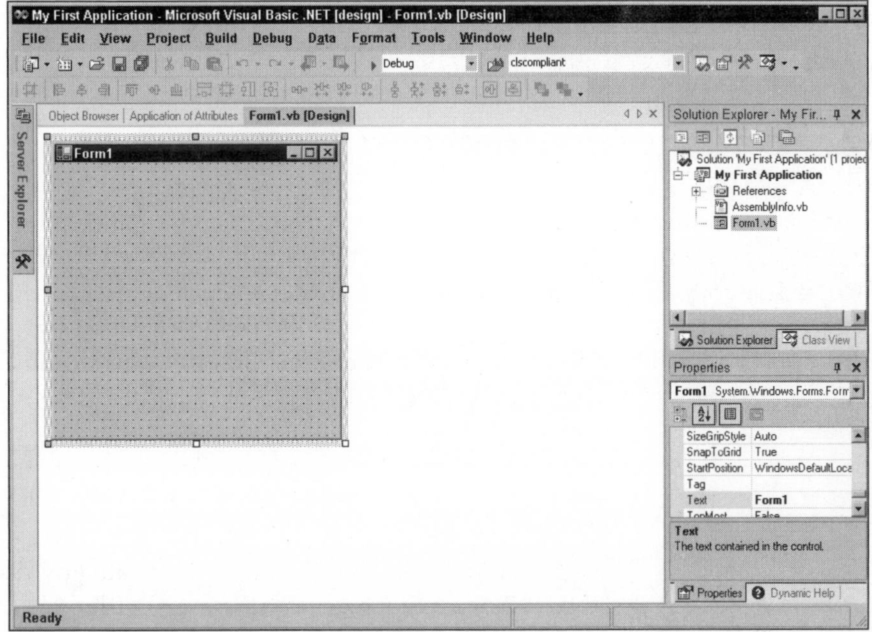

Figure 1.3 The Visual Studio .NET development environment is shared by all .NET languages.

The Toolbox

The Toolbox containing all your standard .NET controls can be made permanently visible or hidden by clicking the pin icon at the top of the Toolbox. You will find the Toolbox in the upper-left corner of the IDE the first time you use the Visual Studio .NET IDE. Code that is copied into memory will appear in the Toolbox tab, Clipboard Ring, which is only visible in code view. Several tabs don't appear in the Toolbox by default. To make the additional tabs appear, right-click the Toolbox and select Show All Tabs. Although right-clicking the Toolbox also gives you an option to sort the items in a tab, new tabs can be added to hold your favorite or custom controls by right-clicking the Toolbox and selecting Add Tab. Controls can be moved between Toolbox tabs by dragging them. In the code view, highlighted code can even be dragged directly to a Toolbox tab for later use. The sorely missed ability in Visual Basic 6 to do a simple drag of a control from the Toolbox to a form has been added to the IDE (see Figure 1.4).

The Solution Explorer

The Project Explorer from Visual Basic 6 becomes the Solution Explorer in .NET and displays not only a list of files used by the application but also any references made to other components and information required to build the current application into a .NET assembly (discussed later). The Show All Files button views files not normally displayed, such as the code-behind module associated with an ASP.NET page (see Figure 1.5).

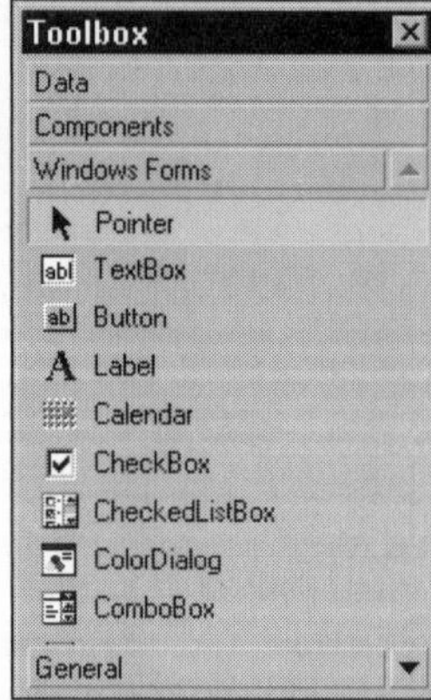

Figure 1.4 The Toolbox contains controls for customizing forms.

Figure 1.5 The Solution Explorer displays all projects, files, references, and resources in the current solution.

The Properties Window

The Properties window displays the properties of the selected item or items, but many of the properties for objects have changed in Visual Basic .NET. For instance, instead of a Caption property, all controls have a Text property. Instead of using Left, Top, Width, and Height, .NET controls use a Location property to indicate their relative position on the form. The Properties window is deceiving to a Visual Basic 6 programmer. The properties listed do not display some properties that were left in the language for backward compatibility. These additional properties can still be accessed programmatically. The Properties Window is shown in Figure 1.6.

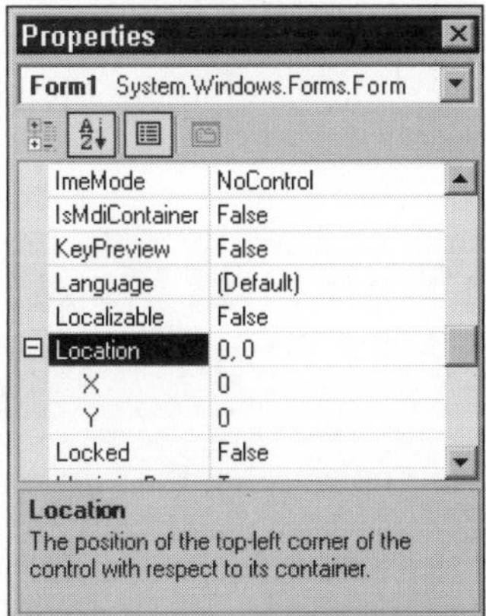

Figure 1.6 The description of the selected property appears at the bottom of the Properties window. Not all properties of an object appear in the Properties window.

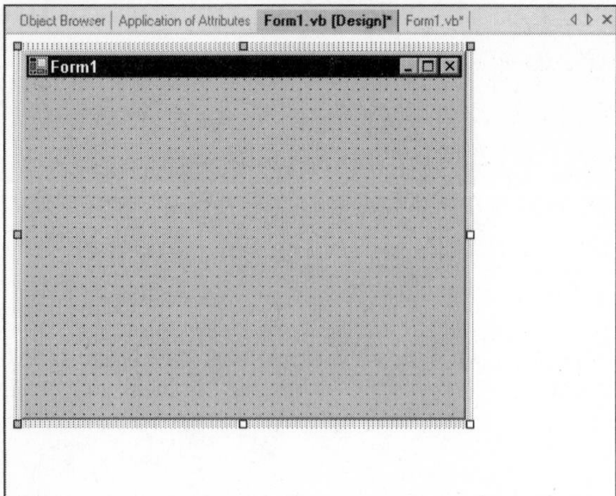

Figure 1.7 The Design area acts as a container for forms and code during development.

The Design Area

The Design Area contains the forms used in your applications. As in Visual Basic 6, the Form object represents the basic window in a Windows application. The Form object in .NET inherits its functionality from a common language runtime Base Type called System.Windows.Forms.Form. The Design Area in .NET has included tabbed controls directly above the design space for ease in switching between code, design view, and things like the Object Browser. Although the default view in the Design area is tabular, this can be changed to an MDI view by selecting the MDI environment option button under Tools, Options, Environment, Settings. Figure 1.7 shows a tabular view of the Design area.

Lab 1.1: Your First Visual Basic .NET Application

As our first Visual Basic .NET program, this lab demonstrates that for most tasks in Visual Basic .NET, there is a .NET approach to performing the task and a Visual Basic 6 approach. Although .NET provides a structured error-handling approach, users can still use err.raise [instead of Throw(system.exception)] to create an error, and Visual Basic .NET will faithfully create a System.Exception out of the raised error. The point is that for migration purposes, the Visual Basic 6 way of doing things has been preserved in many cases, but the code looks rather foreign when compared to other .NET languages. By writing code using .NET-specific features and libraries, we will become much more proficient as .NET developers and produce code that can be easily migrated between .NET languages. Perform the following steps:

1. Start a New Visual Basic Windows application. Selecting File, New, Project from the menu opens the same window depicted in Figure 1.2.
2. Drag three TextBox controls and a Button control from your Toolbox to Form1. Line up all four controls vertically.
3. Change the text on Button1 to Add by changing the Text property for Button1 in the Properties window. Selecting the control causes its properties to appear in the Properties window. If this window is not available, you can press F4 or select the Properties window from the View menu.
4. Double-click the Button control to open the Code Editor window. We'll be adding the contents of the first two text boxes and placing the value into the third text box by writing code within the Click event of our button.

   What you should see is:

   ```
   Public Class Form1
   Inherits System.Windows.Forms.Form
   Private Sub Button1_Click(ByVal ...)...
   End Sub
   End Class
   ```

   Here is the code explanation:

   a. Form inherits its functionality from a common language runtime base class called System.Windows.Forms.Form. Here, we see how that inheritance of functionality is indicated in code, using the Inherits statement. This is a fundamental object-oriented principal known as *implementation inheritance* that was missing in Visual Basic 6. You may notice a code section in every form labeled Windows Form Designer Generated Code. This section is for the behind-the-scenes code we would never see in Visual Basic 6. For now, we'll pretend we still don't see it.

5. Add the following line of code to the Button1_Click event:

   ```
   TextBox3.Text = TextBox1.Text + TextBox2.Text
   ```

6. Run the application by pressing F5, by selecting Start from the Debug menu, or by clicking the blue triangle in the Visual Basic .NET toolbar.
7. Enter numbers into the first two text boxes and click the Button control. The result is only a concatenation of the numbers when we might have hoped for a sum.

8. Stop the application by clicking the Stop icon (the blue square in the toolbar), selecting Stop Debugging from the Debug menu, or closing Form1 as you would any window in an application.
9. There are two ways (at least) to fix the concatenation problem: the Visual Basic 6 way and the Visual Basic .NET way. Whether you choose one or the other really doesn't matter because after .NET code is compiled, things will end up the .NET way (IL) anyway.
   a. The Visual Basic 6 way: Replace the code in the Button1_Click event with this line and test the application again using numbers in the first two text boxes. Here, we see the integer conversion functions used to convert the contents of the first two text boxes to numeric values prior to performing the addition. This works as expected.

   ```
   TextBox3.Text = CInt(TextBox1.Text) + CInt(TextBox2.Text)
   ```

   b. The .NET way: Replace the code in the Button1_Click event with this line and test the application again using numbers in the first two text boxes:

   ```
   TextBox3.Text = System.Convert.ToInt32(TextBox1.Text) + _
   System.Convert.ToInt32(TextBox2.Text)
   ```

The .NET way is to consistently use something in the common language runtime Base Libraries to perform the task at hand. That doesn't mean it's necessarily better. If programmers are learning Visual Basic .NET from a Visual Basic 6 point of view, the fact that their code still works (there are certainly some exceptions to that) allows them to focus on fundamental differences in the environment without getting lost in syntax changes or drowning in thousands of types residing in the common language runtime Base Libraries. The second style, however, would work in any other .NET language. The purpose of this simple exercise was primarily to convince you that your familiar environment is still around and that our process for developing applications using forms and controls works much the same way in Visual Basic .NET as it did in Visual Basic 6.

Classroom Q & A

Q: I tried the line of code from the lab in C# and it didn't compile the way you said it would. Did I do something wrong?

A: Well, I meant that the code wouldn't change when used in other .NET languages, but other languages might have syntactical differences that append to the code. In C#, C++, and Java, you must add a semicolon to the end of every statement.

Q: Are Visual Basic .NET and C# equal?
A: Ahh, the inevitable question. C++ code uses a concept called pointers. A *pointer* is a variable that holds an address of something in memory. These pointers and the ability to directly access memory give C++ much of its famed speed—and infamous potential for disaster. Because most C++ code uses pointers, C# programmers who migrate from C++ have had to have a mechanism to access them from .NET. This is the one fundamental difference between Visual Basic .NET and C#, but technically pointers are not a .NET feature. Visual Basic .NET does have access to something similar.

Q: But they run at the same speed?
A: Absolutely, with the exception of code that uses pointers, Visual Basic .NET and C# are both compiled to the same IL, which produces the same native code. There are differences, but when a C# programmer does something that's not available in the base class libraries, it's not portable to other operating systems.

Q: What if my boss tells me I need to call a C++ function that uses pointers?
A: That question is getting way ahead of the current topic, but for now let's just say that we could write a wrapper function that uses C# to quickly call the C++ function and then call the C# function from Visual Basic .NET.

The Common Type System

The Common Type System (CTS) is really just a reference to the fact that all "things" in .NET are in a common place. I have been referring to the base class libraries as the official name of where those types are defined. A type can be a rectangle, an integer, a string, or any type of object. In .NET all types are defined centrally and shared by all languages. Even an Error is a type (System.Exception). Although Visual Basic cannot officially declare an unsigned integer, it is still legal to Dim a variable of type System.Uint32. Whether that declaration is portable to another operating system is a topic for later. Portability of types is a matter of adherence to the CLS. The CTS is covered in more detail in Chapter 3, "Examining Visual Basic .NET."

Structured Exception Handling (SEH)

Even within the different flavors of C++, programmers could not agree on what an exception (what Visual Basic 6 calls errors) should look like. Visual Basic had its own strange way of handling errors that nothing but Visual Basic could understand. In all of .NET there is absolutely one way of creating or raising an exception. The syntax that Java and C++ use for exceptions was adopted in .NET. Chapter 4, "Debugging and Exception Handling," covers debugging and exception handling. For now, consider the following code in Visual Basic .NET:

```
Private Sub SEHExample()
        Dim num1 As Integer = 1
        Dim num2 As Integer = 0
        Try 'code that may cause an exception
            MsgBox(num1 / num2)
        Catch ex As Exception When num2 = 0   MsgBox(ex.Message)
        End Try
End Sub
```

The Try keyword encapsulates code that could cause an exception. If an exception occurs, an exception object is thrown to the adjacent Catch block, where it is handled or thrown again as a new exception. Because all .NET languages see an exception as an object of type System.Exception, there are no cross-language issues among the .NET languages.

Assemblies and the Global Assembly Cache

In Visual Studio 6 you distributed EXE and DLL files separately. In .NET there is a concept of packaging these files intro groups called *assemblies*. When an assembly is installed on a user's machine, all the DLLs and types inside those DLLs are also installed.

The .NET system of development uses a repository for assemblies known as the Global Assembly Cache (GAC) that is completely independent from the Windows registry. The GAC is located in the assembly folder beneath the Windows or winnt folders.

Figure 1.8 depicts the GAC as it appears when attempting to view the folder c:\winnt\assembly in Windows. To get a better view of what is really in this location, open a command window to view the contents of c:\winnt\assembly\GAC. Although the GAC view provided in Windows shows little information, the view provided via a command window reveals that each installed assembly contains copies of all DLLs that the assembly contains.

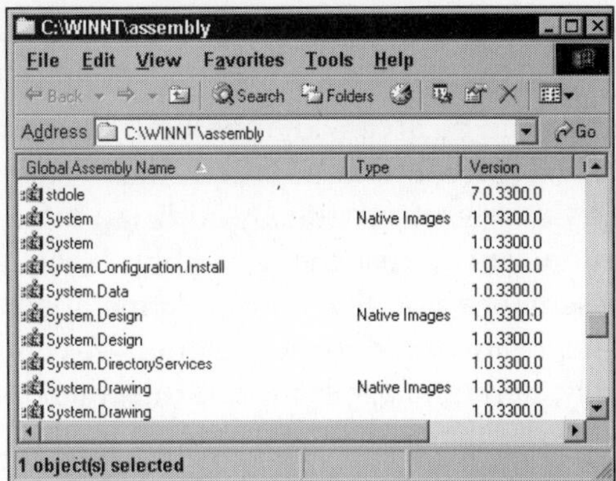

Figure 1.8 The GAC contains all public assemblies.

Metadata and Attributes

Our assemblies are completely described using a concept known as metadata. Every type and member within those types defined in or referenced by our assembly is described within metadata. When the common language runtime loads a .NET executable, the metadata is also loaded into memory. Everything about an assembly is stored in metadata, including its name, version, types, security context information, and dependencies. Each piece of metadata is referred to as an attribute. Opening the AssemblyInfo.vb file in the Solution Explorer window shows some of the standard metadata attributes associated with an assembly, as shown here:

```
<Assembly: AssemblyTitle("")>
<Assembly: AssemblyDescription("")>
<Assembly: AssemblyCompany("")>
<Assembly: AssemblyProduct("")>
<Assembly: AssemblyCopyright("")>
<Assembly: AssemblyTrademark("")>
<Assembly: CLSCompliant(True)>
<Assembly: Guid("45339FE5-01F8-4A41-8842-1870B17FCE18")>
<Assembly: AssemblyVersion("1.0.*")>
```

This attribute listing from a project's assemblyinfo.cs file is the set of attributes that describe the assembly as a distributable unit. Other attributes describe individual classes or even methods. In a Web service, the WebMethod attribute is used to indicate that a method is to be exposed to the Web as a member of a Web service.

Reflection

Reflection is a process by which metadata can be accessed, modified, or even dynamically created. The objects used by Reflection are found in the System .Reflection assembly referenced in the AssemblyInfo.vb file. By adding a reference to System.Reflection in an application, you can use the Assembly object to load assemblies and walk through the assemblies modules, types, and members.

You can even use Reflection to make anonymous invocations on objects. That is to say that I can load an assembly, iterate to a specific module, then to a specific type, then to a specific method, and then call invoke on that method using the MethodInfo.Invoke method. The following code loads the ADO.NET assembly into memory and displays the DLLs used by that assembly:

```
Dim Assy As System.Reflection.Assembly
Assy = System.Reflection.Assembly.LoadWithPartialName("ADODB")
Dim modulex As System.Reflection.Module
Dim modules As Object
modules = Assy.GetModules
For Each modulex In modules
   MsgBox(modulex.ToString)
Next
```

Lab 1.2: Examining an Assembly

This lab familiarizes you with tools to answer many questions related to .NET assemblies and types. This lab introduces the IL Disassembler (ILDASM) utility to display code in its IL form and the Object Browser to show the contents of an assembly's types.

Perform the following steps:

1. Open an Explorer window and navigate to the obj\debug folder under your project directory. We'll focus on the EXE file in this folder that was created when we ran the application. The name of the project in the file system should be identical to the project name used in the Solution Explorer window. For now, back up one folder level so that you're looking at the contents of the obj folder. All you should see is the debug folder name. Keep the Explorer window open to the obj folder.
2. Using the Windows Start button, navigate to Programs, Microsoft Visual Studio .NET, Visual Studio .NET Tools, Visual Studio .NET Command Prompt.

3. At the Visual Studio .NET Command Prompt, type *cd* followed by a space.
4. Drag the debug folder that you left open to the command prompt so that you have a command that looks something like this:

```
cd "C:\My First Application\obj\Debug"
```

5. Press Enter to navigate to the location of your executable file.
6. Type *ILDASM* to open the IL disassembler.
7. Open your executable using the File, open menu in ILDASM, and browse the various objects in your application.

   An assembly can contain one or more EXE and DLL. We can see a reference to manifest in Figure 1.9. A manifest is a section in an assembly that lists all the components needed to make up that assembly. One component (a single EXE or DLL) in the assembly is responsible for maintaining the assembly manifest and acts as an assembly representative.
8. Leave ILDASM open and return to your project in Visual Basic .NET.
9. Open the Code Editor window again by double-clicking Form1.
10. Add a public variable named x to the Form1 class between the Windows Form generated code and the Button Click event:

```
Public x As Integer
```

11. Run your application to build the project and determine if you have any syntax errors. The process that creates your files and builds the underlying assemblies is referred to as a build or building an application. To build the application without running it, we could use one of the options under the Build menu.

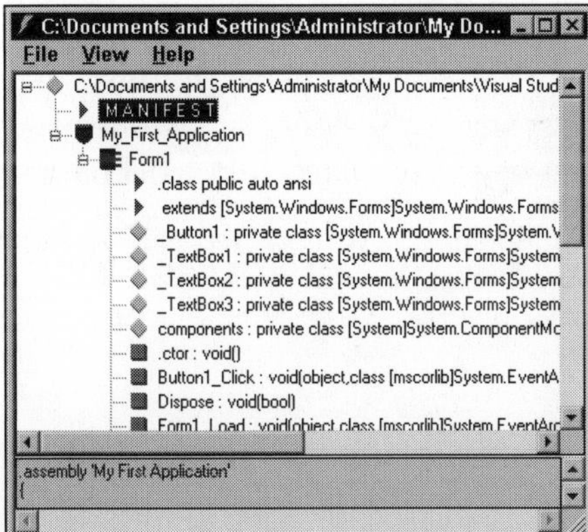

Figure 1.9 The ILDASM is used to view assemblies in IL form.

12. Return to ILDASM and reload your executable.
13. Expand your application and Form1 in ILDASM.
14. One of the members listed for Form1 is the variable x, but notice in Figure 1.10 that after the code was compiled, the variable declaration of Integer was changed to Int32!
15. Return to Visual Basic .NET.
16. Click the Object Browser tab located just above the Design area. Alternatively, select Object Browser from View, Other Windows.
17. Find your application in the Object Browser and expand it as far as you can.

    Form1 inherits from System.Windows.Forms.Form, but you will find that there is quite a lot of inheritance going on farther up the object hierarchy, as indicated by Figure 1.11. Understanding what we're seeing will be much easier when we see more information regarding inheritance in Chapter 8, "Implementation Inheritance."
18. Click the Form1.vb* tab above the Design area to switch from the Object Browser to Form1's code view.
19. Right-click the word *Integer* from your earlier declaration and select Go To Definition. This should jump directly to Int32 in the Object Browser. Right-clicking an int in C# would jump to the same location.

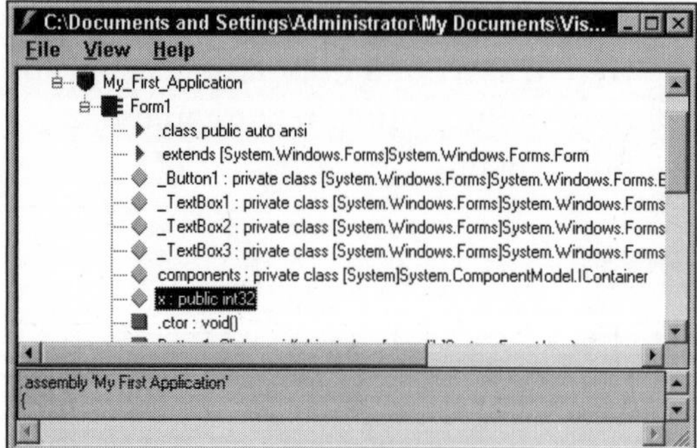

Figure 1.10 The ILDASM utility shows that the Integer keyword is represented as its underlying type, Int32, after the assembly is compiled to IL form.

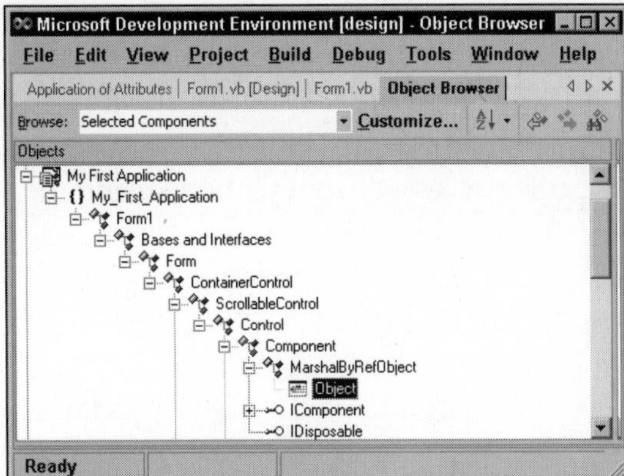

Figure 1.11 The Object Browser shows an extensive object hierarchy associated with the Form class.

The purpose of this lab was to introduce you to the tools that I will be using to explain almost every feature in .NET. Understanding the relationship between types later in this class would be almost impossible without the Object Browser. For now, let's just say that everything in .NET is an object, that objects have things such as properties, methods, and events, and that each object has a type. An object type may be Employee, Form, Int32, or an endless number of other possibilities, but in .NET there is one ultimate type: System.Object. It is from System.Object that all things inherit their basic functionality. Objects are explained in Chapter 6, "Building Class Libraries in .NET."

Interoperability

Interoperability refers to the ability of one thing to work with another. Chapter 16, "Interoperability," explores many topics related to interoperability and .NET. This section briefly introduces this aspect of .NET. The main areas of interest related to interoperability in Visual Studio .NET include the following:

- ActiveX controls can be used in .NET by adding them via the Project, Add Components menu.
- ActiveX DLLs can be used in .NET by referencing them via the Project, Add Reference menu.
- All Calls to ActiveX/COM DLLs or controls from .NET assemblies are marshaled to the registry by the common language runtime.

- COM components can access .NET assemblies once the assemblies are installed into the GAC and then exported as types to the Windows registry. The common language runtime handles the marshaling of calls between COM (registry) and Assemblies (GAC).
- C++ code that uses pointers can be accessed from C# code using the unsafe keyword.
- P/Invoke calls, such as directly calling the Win32API, are possible, although this bypasses the base class libraries. The Win32API, is Windows-specific and is not portable as IL.

ASP.NET

Active Server pages (ASPs) have been Microsoft's solution to server-side Web scripting for years, but ASPs were interpreted and built around technology that was too connection-oriented. The ASP.NET Web development features added to .NET greatly outperform ASP:

- ASP.NET pages are written with all new ASP.NET controls that can actually run on the server.
- ASP.NET pages are compiled and boast approximately four times the execution of ASP Pages.
- ASP.NET, like all of .NET, is built on a connectionless system to support the XML features found in every aspect of .NET and today's development standards (most of which involve XML as the means for a connectionless world).
- ASP.NET can be written in any .NET-compliant language. The benefit is that you never have to change languages to build different pieces of your enterprise applications if you don't want to. In ASP, switching between HyperText Markup Language (HTML), JavaScript, and VBScript on the same page was common.

ASP.NET offers many improvements over ASP and represents an enormous performance gain over previous technologies. Chapter 13, "ASP.NET," provides a strong overview of Web development using ASP.NET.

Web Services

Web services allows anyone, anywhere to invoke methods on components using the Web as a medium. The requirements for calling XML Web services are simple: The client must be able to send HTTP requests over Internet Protocol (IP) and have a programmer on the receiving end who knows what to do with the XML data that Web services return. Web services are an essential part of both the .NET and J2EE architectures and are becoming the standard for remote communication for developers. Prior to .NET, many Visual Basic and C++ Windows developers had already replaced DCOM with XML Web services. XML Web services can be created in Visual Studio .NET using an ASP.NET Web service project type. Chapter 15, "XML Web Services," is dedicated to XML Web services and the related technologies of SOAP, Universal Discovery, Description, and Integration (UDDI), and Web Service Description Language (WSDL).

ADO.NET

ADO.NET represents the latest data access technology in the Microsoft Data Access Components (MDAC) family of libraries and offers some exciting changes to the way we view data. ADO.NET is built on an XML framework, with XML only a method call away when using the new DataSet objects. ADO.NET is built around a connectionless ideology and therefore has many design changes, which are discussed in Chapter 10, "Data Access in .NET." SQL 2000 users gain such a performance benefit from switching to ADO.NET from ADO that this gain alone may warrant a move to .NET. The older version of ADO allowed for disconnected record sets, but with no built-in support for XML, making it quite difficult to work with large client-side record sets.

Garbage Collection

In Visual Basic 6, we destroy objects referenced by public variables by setting the reference to nothing. In .NET, the Garbage Collection (GC) System is responsible for the destruction of objects. By carefully designing our classes in Visual Basic .NET, we can avoid issues such as memory leak. The GC system is controlled by the common language runtime and manages memory for all .NET applications on the system. Chapter 11, "Memory Management and Performance Monitoring," describes the GC System in detail.

Getting Help

Online help in .NET help comes in a lot of ways. For example, searching in .NET online help for the word *walkthrough* points you to approximately 400 "labs" built into .NET. Walkthroughs are step-by-step exercises describing the process for writing your own Web controls, Windows services, data-aware applications, and almost any fundamental topic in .NET.

Classroom Q & A

Q: Is there a good resource to stay up to date with .NET releases and related topics as they emerge from Microsoft? I keep hearing about new technologies surrounding the use of .NET, and once I learn .NET, I'd like to keep current.

A: There is one reference that is exactly what you're looking for. It's called The .NET Show. The URL is http://msdn.Microsoft.com/theshow, and it has postings of informative recorded interviews with the project managers and developers that built .NET. It also does an excellent job of introducing the related technologies as they're released.

Q: Are there .NET sample applications in .NET?

A: Microsoft added an incredible amount of samples to .NET. Search for the StartSamples.htm file, located in the Samples directory of the .NET Framework Software Development Kit (SDK) after installing .NET and follow the instructions there. You will be happy with what you find after you install the samples and Quickstart tutorials.

Q: Is there a quick reference for tools in .NET? Earlier we used the ILDASM tool and you mentioned the ngen.exe utility. What else is there?

A: Although it doesn't list every tool, the starttools.htm file lists and describes many of the tools such as ILDASM that we'll be using. This file is installed as part of .NET.

Summary

.NET brings a lot to the table, but so far we've seen only the highlights of what it can do. With impressive changes provided by a complete rebuild and rethink of everything Microsoft had traditionally placed in its application architecture, .NET offers a great deal. Future chapters focus on these benefits and features until you find yourself suddenly building multitier applications with an ease that makes Visual Basic 6 look like machine code. Although the existence of thousands of underlying types and the introduction of more advanced OOP principles may seem daunting at first, you quickly will find that the benefits are well worth the investment in time.

Review Questions

1. Why can an exception be thrown from one .NET language and handled in another?
   a. The common language runtime performs disparate exception transformations between languages as a service.
   b. The common language runtime base libraries provide mappings between the various implementations of exceptions in each .NET language.
   c. Each language in .NET creates all exceptions as implementations of System.Exception.
   d. They can't be handled in this way. Functions should return error codes instead of raising exceptions when multiple languages are involved.
2. .NET is an entire system of developing applications. True or False?
3. XML Web services were first developed for .NET to solve the problem of tight coupling in distributed systems. True or False?
4. What controls the execution of code in .NET?
   a. The CLS
   b. Mscoree
   c. The GAC
   d. The language-specific runtime for the executing code
5. What specification describes what IL should look like?
   a. MSIL
   b. CLS
   c. ILDASM
   d. XML
6. When writing Visual Basic .NET code, is it better to use a Visual Basic-specific feature or the .NET equivalent?
7. How is .NET code compiled?
   a. .NET code is first compiled into native code and then broken down into IL when exported to a different architecture for further development.
   b. .NET code is first compiled to IL and then transformed to native code using the ngen utility prior to exporting the code to a different architecture.
   c. .NET code is first compiled to IL and then transformed to native code on the target architecture by an architecture-specific compiler that generates native code for that architecture.
   d. .NET code is first compiled to native machine code and then transformed to IL for portability, using the ngen utility.

8. XML Web services replace which Microsoft technology?
   a. COM
   b. DCOM
   c. COM+
   d. ASP
9. What is the distributable unit in .NET?
   a. An assembly
   b. A module
   c. An attribute
   d. A DLL or EXE file
10. Where are .NET assemblies installed?
    a. All assemblies must be installed into the GAC before they can be used.
    b. Assemblies must be installed into the directory of the client and registered in Windows.
    c. Public assemblies must be registered in Windows where private assemblies must be in the directory of the client.
    d. Private assemblies can simply be copied to the directory of a client and executed, but public assemblies must be installed into the GAC.
11. How are objects destroyed in .NET?
    a. The GC is responsible for freeing heap-based memory in .NET.
    b. For all objects that are created using the New keyword, we must destroy them using the Delete keyword.
    c. The programmer must explicitly invoke object destructors.
    d. Objects are retained for just-in-time object brokering and are destroyed when the application is terminated.
12. What is the underlying type behind a Visual Basic integer?
    a. System.Int
    b. System.Integer
    c. System.Int32
    d. System.Int64

13. .NET components can be used by COM components by directly accessing the GAC and referencing the component's assembly. True or False?
14. What are some benefits of using .NET to develop applications?
15. What .NET feature allows for the dynamic discovery and creation of assemblies?
    a. Reflection
    b. The common language runtime
    c. Metadata
    d. Attributes

Answers to Review Questions

1. **c.** An exception can be thrown from one .NET language and handled in another because all .NET languages implement exceptions as System.Exception.
2. True. .NET is an entire system of developing applications.
3. False. .NET makes XML Web services easier to use than ever before, but they were developed long before .NET. Web services to solve the problem of tight coupling in distributed systems.
4. **c.** Mscoree is the file implementation of the common language runtime. The common language runtime controls virtually everything in .NET. The GAC is where assemblies are registered for public use.
5. **b.** The CLS is the specification that describes what IL should look like. MSIL is Microsoft-specific IL. ILDASM is a utility for viewing IL. XML is a markup language for manipulating data.
6. Whether you use the Visual Basic-specific features or the underlying types is up to you, and which is better is completely subjective. If the reason for using Visual Basic .NET is to build solid systems with a low learning curve, one could argue for doing "what we've always done."
7. **c.** .NET code is first compiled to IL and then transformed to native code on the target architecture by an architecture-specific compiler that generates native code for that architecture.
8. **b.** XML Web services replace DCOM in Microsoft's architecture.
9. **a.** An assembly is the distributable unit in .NET. Modules (EXE and DLL files) make up an assembly and are described with attributes.
10. **d.** Private assemblies can simply be copied to the directory of a client and executed, but public assemblies must be installed into the GAC. Assemblies are not registered in the Windows registry.
11. **a.** The GC is responsible for freeing heap-based memory in .NET. .NET languages do not provide an explicit means of destroying objects.
12. **c.** System.Int32 is the underlying type behind a Visual Basic integer. System.Int and System.Integer are fictitious. System.Int64 is the underlying type for a Long integer.
13. False. .NET components can be used by COM components once the .NET components have exported type libraries loaded into the registry in Windows and only by using the common language runtime as a proxy messenger. The common language runtime marshals all calls to and from .NET assemblies.

14. Some of the major benefits of .NET are a standardized development environment, common everything, portability, incredibly organized and well thought out system of types, garbage collection, structured exception handling, cross-language and cross-platform interoperability, massive speed increases for Web applications, easy access to XML Web services, built-in XML support everywhere, and impressive performance increases provided by the SqlClient library in ADO.NET. The list is quite impressive.

15. **a.** Reflection allows us to create, modify, or access assemblies at runtime.

CHAPTER

2

Building Visual Basic .NET Windows Applications

Windows Application is really inappropriate as a project title, considering that it has the ability to be compiled to IL and ported to another operating system where it can be natively compiled. We'll use this term only because it's the name of the project type in .NET.

Rather than attempting to demonstrate every feature related to developing Windows applications in Visual Basic .NET, we will use key features and tools that will help you see the object-oriented nature of .NET as you work with the standard design components in the Visual Studio .NET IDE. The main focus of this chapter is to introduce you to some key concepts related to .NET development using forms and controls, while looking at their underlying implementation in .NET. In Chapter 5, "Advanced .NET Windows Applications," we will build applications with a wider range of features.

Working with .NET Forms and Controls

The basic unit of development in a .NET Windows application is (still) a form. Each form represents a single window in a running application. We add controls from the Toolbox to enhance a form's user interface.

The .NET version of a form has many new features. In .NET, all languages create a form based on the System.Windows.Forms.Form class in the common language runtime libraries. When I say "based on," I am actually referring to an OOP concept known as *implementation inheritance*, which allows one type to establish a relationship to another type for the purpose of inheriting functionality. Look at it this way: Visual Basic has always had forms, but we have never had to design into them the ability to be resized or minimized or to display a blue title bar, and so on. All that functionality was inherited from a generic Form object when we added the form to our project. Even in Visual Basic 6 we could declare a variable of type Form, and a new object would be created in memory that had its own Name, hwnd, caption, and so on. Even the first piece of code you see in Visual Basic .NET requires that you have some understanding of Inheritance, as you can see in the Visual Basic .NET code that follows. This code shows the relationship between a form and its immediate base class:

```
Public Class Form1
    Inherits System.Windows.Forms.Form
End Class
```

Forms Are Objects

Visual Basic has always created forms as objects, but until Visual Basic .NET we had not seen any underlying code to prove that. Quite possibly the biggest change in Visual Basic .NET is that all the underlying details of how things are done are no longer abstracted away from us. Although classes are formally discussed in Chapter 6, "Building Class Libraries in .NET," for now you need to understand two basic points. The first point is that all things in .NET are objects. The second point is that all objects are based on a template that a programmer built using code. The most common template for an object is called a class. The description for an *object* in this chapter will be limited to a self-contained entity that has properties to describe it, methods that provide behaviors, and events that allow it to respond to messages.

Form1 is actually a class called Form1 and at runtime, any number of actual Form1 objects can be created based on that class. This chapter focuses on many aspects of designing Windows applications, but as we're using different forms, controls, and other objects, I need you to remember that all these things are built using these object templates.

A Change of Events

Events in Visual Basic .NET are very different from what they were in Visual Basic 6. Event names, the way they are used, and their sheer number have understandably changed in .NET because all controls in .NET were built from the ground up.

For example, the event for a Visual Basic 6 text box that occurred as the user typed into that text box is called the Change event. In .NET, that event is now implemented as the TextChanged event. Besides the name change, the next major difference is that this event now takes sender and e arguments. In Visual Basic we used control arrays when multiple controls needed to share code. In Visual Basic .NET we map two events to the same event handler. Finally, the keyword Handles is used to indicate that a subroutine is to handle the TextChanged event for the text box txtFirstName. Although we might think from our prior experience with Visual Basic that this isn't necessary, keep in mind that the things we're using to build our applications in .NET are based on the CLS and a solid object-oriented foundation. The more you learn about the underlying foundation of .NET, the easier it will be to understand why some things are so different from Visual Basic 6. The following examples contrast the difference between the Change and TextChanged events.

Here is an example in Visual Basic 6:

```
Private Sub Text1_Change()
End Sub
```

Here is an example in Visual Basic .NET:

```
Private Sub txtFirstName_TextChanged(ByVal sender As System.Object, _
ByVal e As System.EventArgs) Handles txtFirstName.TextChanged
End Sub
```

Classroom Q & A

Q: If the .NET version of this code says that it handles the TextChanged event for txtFirstName, could I name this subroutine anything I want?

A: In Visual Basic we just write the code in the event and don't differentiate between the event and event handler. Here, we have a predefined set of events that can be raised in an object and we need to write custom handlers to handle those events. We can name it whatever we want.

Q: So, I take it that sender is kind of like the index parameter from Visual Basic?

A: Well, in a way. It is used to identify which object received the event that caused the event handler to execute. By accessing properties of the sender object, we can find out exactly which control received the event.

Q: How do we make it so that more than one control can use the same event handler?

A: You just append more information to the Handles part of the event handler declaration. Lab 2.1 demonstrates that process.

Lab 2.1: Working with Event Handlers

This lab demonstrates the association between events and event handlers. We will create three text boxes. The first two contain the first and last names of an individual. As either the first or last name is changed, the third text box will dynamically display the resulting email address. To start, we will use separate TextChanged events for capturing changes to the first and last names but will quickly change our implementation to a more efficient event handler.

Perform the following steps:

1. Start a new Visual Basic Windows application.
2. Drag three TextBox controls and three Labels to the form.
3. Change properties for controls by selecting them at design time and entering a new value for the desired property in the Properties window. Change the following properties for the six controls you just added to Form1.P: txtFirstName_TextChanged to txtLastName_TextChanged and test the application again. This time the results were correct, but the method we used to obtain those results used redundant code.
4. Remove the entire txtLastName_TextChanged event handler.
5. Change the name of the txtFirstName_TextChanged event handler to Names_TextChanged.
6. Add the following code to the end of the declaration for Names_TextChanged so that the same event handler handles the TextChanged events for both text boxes.

   ```
   , txtLastName.TextChanged
   ```

   What you should see is:

   ```
   Private Sub Names_TextChanged(ByVal sender As System.Object, _
   ByVal e As System.EventArgs) Handles txtFirstName.TextChanged, _
   txtLastName.TextChanged
       txtEmail.Text = txtFirstName.Text & "." & txtLastName.Text &
   _
   "@somecompany.com"
   End Sub
   ```

7. Run the application again. Functionally, it still works the same but with half the code. This event-handling process uses a concept known as delegation, discussed in Chapter 7, "Extending Visual Basic .NET Classes."

For now, let's just view our Names_TextChanged event handler as a method of the Form1 class that handles the TextChanged event for two text boxes. The next step will be to get used to the different controls and events used in building Windows forms.

The Controls Collection

Each form has a collection called Controls, which contains all the controls on that form. The Contains method (not specific to a form) returns a boolean value that indicates whether one control is contained in another.

```
Dim i As Integer
For i = 0 To Me.Controls.Count - 1
If Me.Controls(i).Contains(mycontrol) Then
   MessageBox.Show(Me.Controls(i).Name)
End If
Next I
```

Most of the standard controls used on Windows forms are part of the System.Windows.Forms assembly in System.Windows.Forms.dll.

Familiar Controls or Just Familiar Looking?

Many controls that look identical to their predecessors act quite differently in .NET. Let's take the scrollbar controls as an example. The first thing you'll see regarding scrollbars in .NET is that instead of having a single control with an orientation property, the .NET Toolbar has separate vertical (VScrollBar) and horizontal scrollbar (HScrollBar) controls. The scrollbars have Minimum and Maximum properties that are typically mapped to the target range they are used to scroll through. These properties used to be Min and Max in Visual Studio 6. The following exercise demonstrates much more than scrollbars. In Lab 2.2 you're going to use HScrollBar controls to see how even the simplest of tasks have changed for Visual Basic programmers.

Lab 2.2: Controls in .NET

.NET controls are smarter than their predecessors. They can adapt to their surroundings. We'll be using three HScrollBar controls to control the background color of the current form by individually setting the red, green, and blue values (RGB) of a Color object.

Perform the following steps:

1. Start a new Visual Basic Windows application.
2. Drag a GroupBox (used to be called a Frame control) to Form1.
3. Drag three HScrollBar controls inside the GroupBox.
4. Because each of these HScrollBar controls will be setting the RGB values, we need to set their Minimum and Maximum values to match the possible values for RGB. For each control, set the Maximum property value to 255 and leave the Minimum property value at 0. The HScrollBar1 control will change the red, HScrollBar2 will change the green, and HScrollBar3 will change the blue value of a Color object. Because RGB values are always in red, green, blue order and have values ranging from 0 to 255, a value of 0,0,255 indicates pure blue.
5. Add the following event handler to handle the Scroll event for all three HScrollBar controls:

```
Private Sub ScrollAll(ByVal sender As System.Object, ByVal e As
System.Windows.Forms.ScrollEventArgs) Handles HScrollBar1.Scroll,
HScrollBar2.Scroll, HScrollBar3.Scroll
Me.BackColor = Color.FromArgb(HScrollBar1.Value,
HScrollBar2.Value, HScrollBar3.Value)
End Sub
```

Color is a class defined in System.Drawing. If you look at the References section in the Solution Explorer, you will see that our application has a reference to the System.Drawing assembly. That is why we can use the Color class.

6. Run the application. Use the scrollbars to change the BackColor of Form1, but watch the GroupBox controls color! The GroupBox has the inherent ability to change the color of its border in relation to its immediate container, as shown in Figure 2.1. We deduce from this that there is an event that notifies the GroupBox that such a change was made. The System.Windows.Forms.Form and System.Windows .Forms.Control classes have many events we're not used to seeing

yet, such as ForeColorChanged and BackColorChanged that make features like this possible. All of our controls and forms are based on (inherited from) these two classes.

If you're starting to believe that I'm trying to get you used to the object-oriented nature of .NET, you're right! If the objects, classes, and inheritance are all still confusing, don't be discouraged. We haven't even formally explored those concepts yet. By the time we get to a discussion on classes and objects, you will have quite a few examples to fall back on. For now, understand that we are in a pure object-oriented environment and nothing is abstracted away from us as it was in Visual Basic 6. These two truths will drive your application development in .NET more than you may realize at this point, but be excited; with this environment comes a developmental power and elegance previously lacking in Visual Basic.

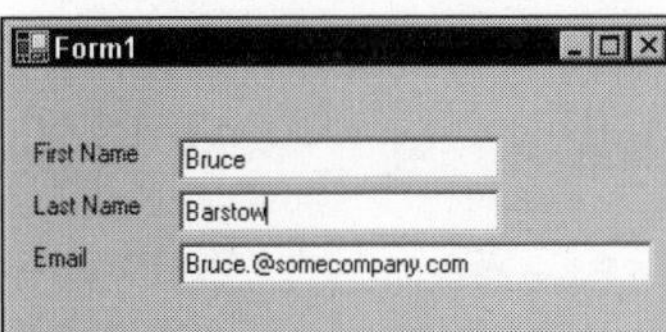

Figure 2.1 The GroupBox control dynamically adjusts to its parent's BackColor property by changing the color of its own border.

Classroom Q & A

Q: I have used quite a lot of objects in the past, but I'm a little confused by the syntax used with the Color object. I don't see how we have a copy, *instance* I think you called it, of the Color object and yet we are calling a method on it.

A: First of all, FromARGB() is a static method in the base class Color. You should remember that Form1 inherits many methods and properties from the Form class and can redefine what those methods (like Load) do for each specific form we create. That makes Form the *base class* for Form1. Well, Color is the base class for a new Color object, but the Color base class has functionality that doesn't make much sense to be overwritten in each of the colors created based on the Color class. FromARGB() is an example of such a method and is referred to as a static method. *Static* methods are not called as object.methodname, but rather, as baseclass .methodname.

Q: Is this explained further in this book?

A: Yes, I talk about this more in Chapter 6. We just haven't had to learn a lot of these concepts in Visual Basic because it was focused on being a very friendly, productive environment with a lot of the detail abstracted away. Now we have the friendly environment with all the power of an object-oriented language. Think of it as changing your tools in your Toolbox. We just got rid of our Toolbox and replaced it with a roomful of the latest power tools. By showing you what's new while I'm using a concept like scrollbars, text boxes, and labels that have hardly changed at all, we can use what *is* familiar to us as an anchor for our OOP learning process.

Locations and Size in .NET

In Visual Basic 6, we used the Move method or the Left, Top, Width, and Height properties to move things to the desired location. In .NET we do things (of course) a little differently.

The older Left and Top properties *seem* to have been replaced with the more universally correct representation of an x- and y-axis value pair known in .NET as the Location property. The Left and Top properties still exist, but they are not in the Properties window. To move a control to the upper-left corner of a form we could set the control's Location property using the values of 0 and 0.

```
Button1.Location = New Point(0, 0)
```

Here, I've created a new Point object and initialized it by setting both its x- and y-axis to zero. If you look at the IntelliSense in Figure 2.2, you will see that the Location property is very clear about needing a Point object instead of just two numbers.

Setting Width and Height

Setting the Width and Height properties also offers a small surprise. If you set these two Integer values thinking about the twip unit of measurement from Visual Basic, you'll have some huge controls. The default unit of measurement is expressed in pixels in .NET.

```
Button1.Width = 100  'pixels
Button1.Height = 40  'pixels
```

Double their size:

```
Button1.Width *= 2   'equivalent to Button1.Width = Button1.Width * 2
Button1.Height *= 2  'using C++-style shorthand
```

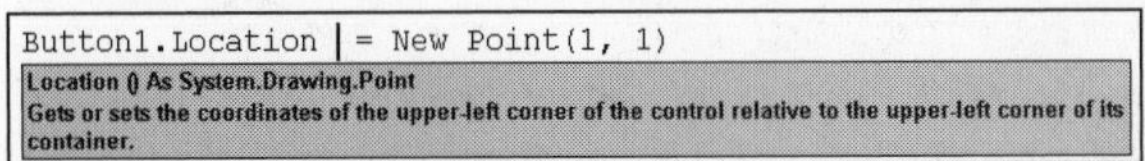

Figure 2.2 Pay attention to what IntelliSense is telling you in .NET. The IntelliSense here indicates that the Location property requires a Point object.

Setting the Form Size Using the Size Property

Setting the Size property requires the assignment of a Size object. Restated, that means that the Size property is a property of type Size. The following code creates a new Size object to be used in the assignment:

```
Me.Size = New Size(100, 100)
```

Strangely enough, when the form is maximized, this code will apparently do nothing, but when the form is back in Normal mode, it will have a width of 100 and a height of 100.

Controlling How Large or Small a Form Can Be

The Form object uses the MaximumSize and MinimumSize properties to limit how small or large a form can be. These values have no effect on the ability to maximize or minimize the form using the minimize and maximize buttons. These values control how small or large the form can be by using the handles to expand and contract the form's borders.

The SystemInformation object can be used to determine not only the minimum window size, but also things such as the user name, the domain the user is logged into, whether the user has a network card, how many buttons the user's mouse has, and even the system boot mode.

Docking and Anchoring

Controls have a Dock property that enables them to be permanently fixed to different sides of a container. The Anchor property for a control is used to ensure that the anchored edges maintain a position relative to the edges of the container. Figure 2.3 shows the result of setting the Dock property for Button1 to Top.

Affecting Visibility

Forms can be manipulated with the standard Visible property and the Hide and Show methods from Visual Basic 6, but there are some new features to note.

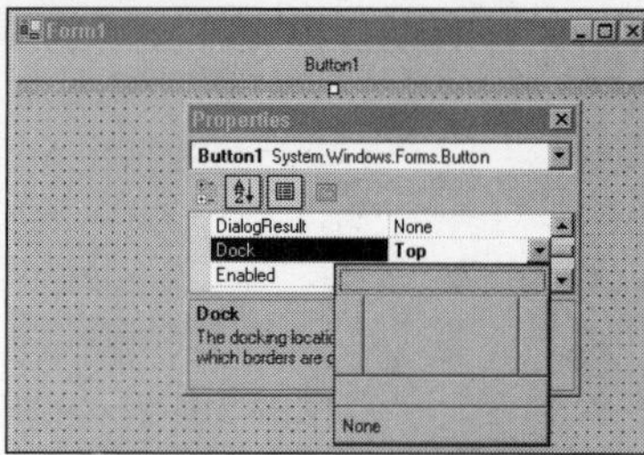

Figure 2.3 Controls are anchored using the Dock property.

Keeping a Form on Top

The TopMost property of a form can be used to ensure than no matter what is displayed, the TopMost form will always be on top of any other form. The following code creates a new form beneath the current form:

```
Me.TopMost = True
Dim myform As New Form()
myform.Show()
```

Changing a Form's Opacity

A form can be made partially visible (or partially invisible for you pessimists) by using the Opacity property. This property normally has a value of 1 to indicate that it appears normal (that is, opaque not transparent). The Opacity value of 0 indicates that the form is completely transparent. The following code causes the current form to fade away and then return. Figure 2.4 shows a form at 50 percent (.5) transparency.

```
Dim i As Double
For i = 1 To 0 Step -0.01
     Me.Opacity = i
Next
Me.Opacity = 1
```

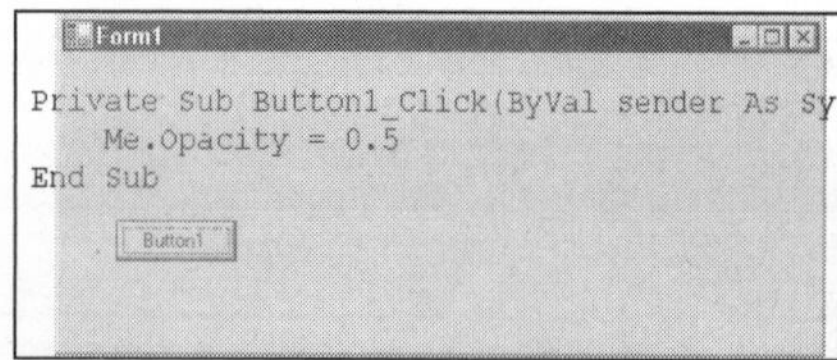

Figure 2.4 A form with an Opacity setting of .5. is exactly half visible.

The standard For loop used here iterates through its code between the possible values for opacity from 1 to 0, decrementing by –0.1 until the current form is completely transparent. For loops have an incremental Step value of 1 when not specified.

.NET Controls

This section is not intended to show you every control in .NET. Actually, my only intention is to get you familiar with the environment and how different things really are beneath the surface of controls that seem like old friends. Now that we have some of the basic principles in our skill set, we can start working with a few traditional controls, look at what's new in them, and progress to some of the controls that are unique to .NET. All the following code applies to the ListBox, ComboBox, and other list-related controls in .NET.

The ListBox Control

Every Windows programmer has used a ListBox control before, but the changes to the ListBox in .NET have a lot to do with what is underneath the control. Many objects have collections of things such as images, buttons, controls, or the Items collection in a ListBox. In .NET, collections aren't created differently for each object but rather inherited from a common collection interface.

The Items Collection

Any object that has a collection in .NET will most likely inherit its methods from ICollection and IList. These two things are known as interfaces in the common language runtime libraries. By having all collections inherit a defined set of methods from these interfaces, we can expect any collection in .NET to have an expected interface.

The interface for a car usually doesn't vary from car to car for its basic, expected functionality, although each car can have extended features. We expect to enter all cars via a door, we expect to start all cars with an ignition key, we press an accelerator to make the car go, and we press a brake pedal to make the car stop. The point is that by having an *expected interface* for every example of a given type, the user of each item (type) can use it intuitively. Doing something unexpected in the design, such as putting the brake pedal on the right, could mean that the user of the vehicle might never want to attempt using that model again.

In .NET collections, this translates to every collection having an Add method, a Remove method, a Count property, and an Item Property that we instinctively look for as programmers using those objects. As a matter of fact, after a very short while as a .NET programmer, you will quickly become agitated by programmers who reinvent the wheel instead of supporting a standard interface.

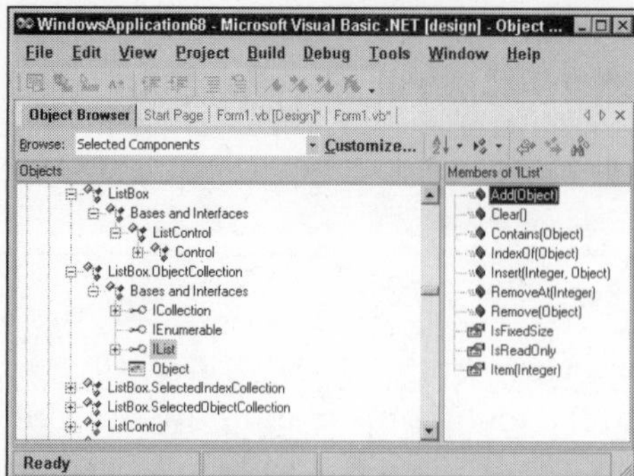

Figure 2.5 ListBox.Items is actually based on the class ListBox.ObjectCollection that implements the ICollection and IList interfaces.

Looking at the Object Browser in Visual Basic .NET, we can see on what classes and interfaces each of our objects are based. Figure 2.5 shows the classes and interfaces implemented by a ListBox. The right panel in Figure 2.5 shows the methods and properties of the IList interface.

The Items collection represents the items stored in the ListBox. To add values to any collection that is based on these well-known interfaces, we use the Add method as shown in the following code:

```
ListBox1.Items.Add("Azure")
ListBox1.Items.Add("Crimson")
ListBox1.Items.Add("DarkOrchid")
ListBox1.Items.Add("DodgerBlue") 'yes that is actually a built-in color
```

Common Collection Methods and Properties

All Collections have at least the properties and methods listed in Table 2.1.

Changing the Selected Item in a ListBox

In earlier forms of Visual Basic we would use the Click event to write code to capture the newly selected item. In .NET we write an event handler for the SelectedIndexChanged event of the ListBox. The SelectedIndex property can be used to pinpoint which item was selected. The following code shows an example of a SelectedIndexChanged event handler:

```
Private Sub ListBox1_SelectedIndexChanged(ByVal sender
As System.Object, ByVal e As System.EventArgs) Handles
ListBox1.SelectedIndexChanged
     Me.ListBox1.ForeColor =
     Color.FromName(ListBox1.Items(ListBox1.SelectedIndex))
End Sub
```

Table 2.1 Collection Properties and Methods

PROPERTY OR METHOD	DESCRIPTION
The Count property	Represents the number of items in the collection
The Add method	Add items to a collection
The Remove method	Remove items from a list
The Item property	Used to refer to a specific item in a collection

When an item is selected, the text value in the ListBox is used as the argument for the FromName method on the Color class to set the ForeColor on the ListBox as shown in Figure 2.6.

Taking Advantage of the Collection Interfaces

Although showing you the underlying interfaces and classes of .NET may seem premature, knowledge of the underlying common language runtime class libraries will be the single most defining factor in your mastery of .NET. We can already take advantage of the knowledge we have by looking at the AddRange method of a ListBox. The AddRange method for a ListBox takes an ObjectCollection as its only argument. Because we know that the Items Collection is an example of an ObjectCollection, we should be able to add the contents of one ListBox to another by passing the Items collection of one ListBox to the AddRange method of another ListBox as shown here using Visual Basic .NET:

```
ListBox1.Items.Add("Test Data1")
ListBox1.Items.Add("Test Data2")
ListBox2.Items.AddRange(ListBox1.Items)
MessageBox.Show(ListBox2.Items(0).ToString())
```

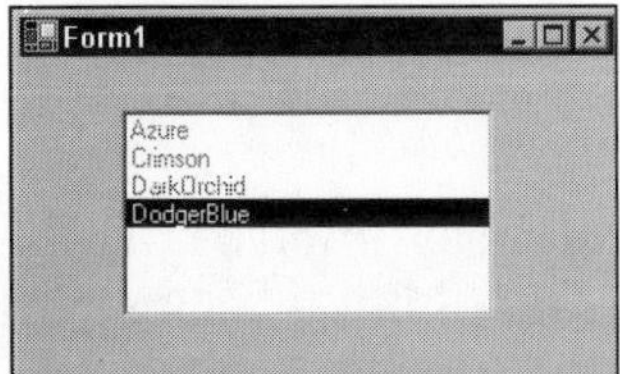

Figure 2.6 Clicking on a ListBox item causes the SelectedIndexChanged event.

Classroom Q & A

Q: How many classes and interfaces are there in .NET?

A: I have no idea, but there are many. We end up using more and more as we build broader applications. We are going to use more than you will remember after reading these chapters, but you will have learned a certain set of behaviors and patterns related to the libraries that will make using them much easier and intuitive. Don't worry if it seems intimidating now; we haven't even officially introduced the concept of an interface yet.

Q: In your last example, why did you need to use ToString in the last line of code?

A: You need to be sure what you are sending to a method is the right type. MessageBox.Show needs a String, so make sure you treat the value at Items(index) as a String using the ToString method.

Q: When I tried it without the ToString method, it still worked.

A: It's good to experiment and you're right; it does work without the ToString() method, but Visual Basic doesn't always do things for you. My first two golden rules of programming are always be explicit and never let a compiler do you a favor. It is considered a better programming practice to indicate explicitly how values are to be treated in an expression.

The CheckedListBox Control

The CheckedListBox control is new to .NET. Each item in the control appears with a check box preceding it. Much of the code we use for other list-related controls still applies. but we'll need to look at a few new methods, events, and properties to make use of this new control.

Adding Items to a CheckedListBox

Because the Items collection for this control also indirectly implements the IList interface, it has an Add method for adding items. But implementing an Add method is done differently for different objects. This particular Add method has three versions we could use. Different versions of a member with the same name are referred to as *overloaded methods*, which we will discuss later. Figure 2.7 shows how the most common version of the Add method, which takes an object followed by a boolean value, controls whether the new item's check box should be selected. That shouldn't be too hard to code because object is actually a reference to System.Object, which applies to every type in .NET and a boolean value is just True or False.

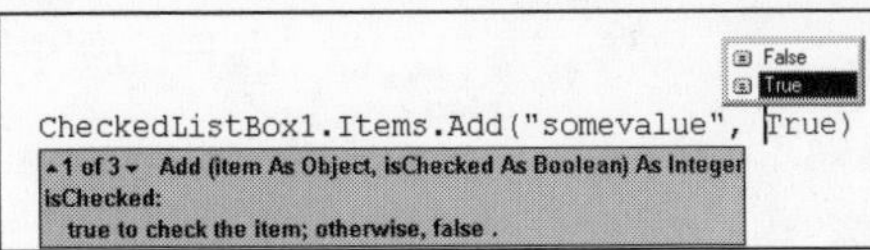

Figure 2.7 Version 1 of 3 for the CheckListBox.Add() method.

In Visual Basic 6, any nonzero value was True. That is not the case in .NET. Only True is True and only False is False.

The following code shows how items can be added to a CheckedListBox control named clb1 with the first three values checked and the last value unchecked:

```
clb1.Items.Add("Architect", True)
clb1.Items.Add("Consultant", True)
clb1.Items.Add("Trainer", True)
clb1.Items.Add("PogoStick Champion", False)
```

As with all collections in .NET, the first position (or index) is zero and the collection has *Count* number of items.

Determining Which Items Are Checked

The CheckedItems property procedure returns an object of type CheckedItem-Collection. We can iterate through unfamiliar collections in a very generic way using an iterator of type Object (see Figure 2.8). It is always more efficient to use an iterator of an appropriate type for the given collection, but an item is actually a property that returns a generic object.

```
Private Sub btnGetCheckedItems_Click(ByVal sender As System.Object,
ByVal e As System.EventArgs) Handles btnGetCheckedItems.Click
   Dim o As Object
   Dim msg As String
   For Each o In clb1.CheckedItems
      msg += o.ToString & Convert.ToChar(13) 'chr(13), vbcrlf still work
   Next o
   MessageBox.Show(msg, "By Item:")
End Sub

Private Sub btnGetCheckedIndices_Click(ByVal sender As System.Object,
ByVal e As System.EventArgs) Handles btnGetCheckedIndices.Click
   Dim o As Object
   Dim msg As String
   For Each o In clb1.CheckedIndices
      msg += o.ToString & Convert.ToChar(13)
   Next o
   MessageBox.Show(msg, "By Index:")
End Sub
```

Figure 2.8 Items in a CheckedListBox can be interrogated for their checked status by Index or by Item.

Changing the Click/Checked Behavior

I was pleasantly surprised to find that I could cause the items to be checked by a single click instead of the default. The following Visual Basic .NET code causes an item to be checked on a single click:

```
checkedListBox1.CheckOnClick = True
```

Sorting

Even though a property seems to be similar to a property we might have become used to in Visual Basic 6, take nothing for granted. Some things are more flexible and some are more restricted. The Sorted property of the ListBox type of controls in Visual Basic 6 was read only at runtime, but the same property can be set at design or runtime in .NET as shown here:

```
checkedListBox1.Sorted = True
```

Other Useful Properties and Methods

Many properties for the ListBox line of controls simply didn't exist as features before .NET. The properties and methods in Table 2.2 are particularly useful.

Table 2.2 ListBox Controls in .NET

PROPERTY OR METHOD	DESCRIPTION
The ClearSelected method	Clears selection without affecting checked status.
The Contains method	Determines if a control is in this container.

Table 2.2 *(continued)*

PROPERTY OR METHOD	DESCRIPTION
The FindString method	Searches for partial match to Item data; second overload for this method allows searching to start at a specific index. FindString("Train") would return the index of "Trainer" in our example.
The FindStringExact method	Searches for exact match of item data. FindStringExact("trainer") would return the index of "Trainer," but FindStringExact("Train") would return a value of –1.
The SelectedIndex property	Returns the index of the selected item.

Dialog Controls

In Visual Studio 6 we typically used a single Common Dialog control to handle all our dialog needs. This created a control that had far too many methods and properties that weren't related to the task we were performing at the time. In .NET we have separate controls for each of the standard dialogs. Table 2.3 shows examples of the separate dialog controls in Visual Studio .NET.

Using the Dialog Controls

The ColorDialog control is activated for display by using the ShowDialog() method. The ColorDialog window is shown in Figure 2.9.

Table 2.3 Dialog Controls in Visual Studio .NET

DIALOG	ALLOWS THE USER TO
ColorDialog	Pick a color from a color palette
FontDialog	Choose a font and apply formatting
OpenFileDialog	Locate a file to be opened
PageSetupDialog	Display page formatting dialog box
PrintDialog	Control and start printing
PrintPreviewDialog	Preview print jobs
SaveFileDialog	Indicate a file and path for saving

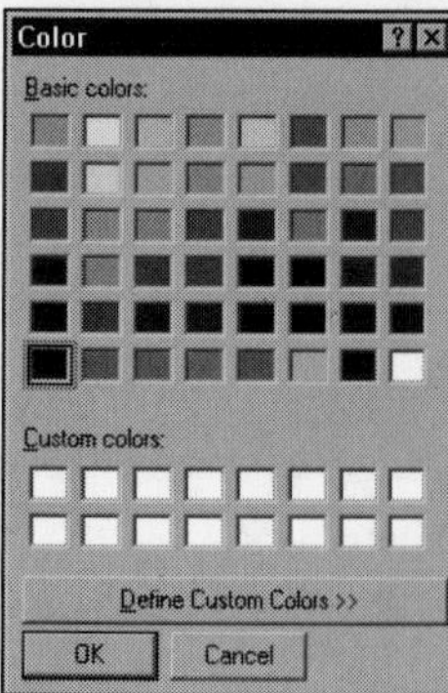

Figure 2.9 The ColorDialog control's Color property is set when the dialog box closes.

After the user selects a color and closes the ColorDialog window, the control's Color property holds a valid Color object. Printing this Color object with ToString()reveals that some colors have proper names such as Chartreuse, whereas others have ARGB values:

```
Color[A=255, R=255, G=0, B=128].
```

The Color property can be used as expected:

```
ColorDialog1.ShowDialog()
Me.BackColor = ColorDialog1.Color
```

Each dialog control sets different values when they are closed. For the SaveFileDialog control, the FileName property is set to the file indicated by the user inside the Save dialog window.

The DataGrid Control

The DataGrid control allows us to view and modify records from a database. Chapter 5, "Advanced .NET Windows Applications," expands on data access in .NET; here we will focus on the DataGrid control and some controls that support its use. Lab 2.3 demonstrates the use of this control.

Lab 2.3: Using Data Access Controls in .NET

This lab demonstrates the use of the DataGrid control and several underlying objects associated to data access. This lab requires a database from the .NET QuickStart samples to be installed. The objective of this lab is to introduce you to the DataGrid control and expose you to the concepts of the Data Adapter, DataSet, and Connection objects.

Perform the following steps:

1. Start a new Visual Basic Windows application.
2. Add a DataGrid control from your Toolbox to Form1. This control is used to display records from a database.
3. On the Toolbox, you should see several tabs: Windows Forms, Components, General, and Data. Select the Data tab on your Toolbox.

   The Data tab contains objects that represent objects in the System.Data and System.Data.SqlClient assemblies. These controls make data access easy by abstracting the details of data access.

If you cannot see the tabs I described in step 3, change your current view to Designer view by selecting Designer from the View menu.

4. Add an OleDbDataAdapter control from the Data tab of the Toolbox to Form1. The control appears in the Control Tray underneath the current form. Unlike Visual Basic 6, controls that are not visible at runtime don't reside on the form surface at design time in .NET.
5. In the Welcome to the Data Adapter Configuration Wizard screen, click Next.
6. When confronted with the Choose Your Data Connection screen, click the New Connection button to display the Data Link Properties window. We are using the Microsoft Jet provider to indicate that we are working with a Microsoft Access database (see Figure 2.10).

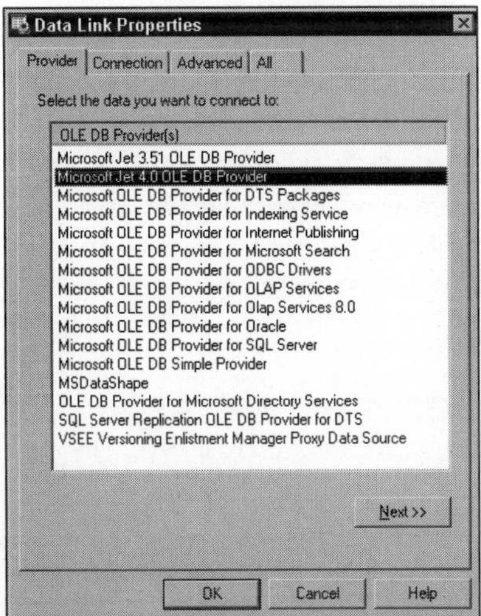

Figure 2.10 Select the Microsoft Jet provider when working with Microsoft Access databases.

7. From the Provider tab of the Data Link Properties window, select Microsoft Jet 4.0 OLEDB Provider.
8. Click Next to move to the Connection tab or just select the Connection tab on the Data Link Properties window.
9. Assuming you have installed the Quickstart samples, use the button to the right of the Select or Enter a Database Name text box to browse for and select the grocertogo.mdb database. This database will be buried quite a few levels deep, so use the search tool in windows to find the database.
10. Click OK to return to the Choose Your Data Connection window.
11. Click Next to advance to the Choose a Query Type window.
12. Click Next to accept the default of Use SQL Statements and to advance to the Generate the SQL Statements window.
13. Type Select * From Products into the only text box on the Generate the SQL Statements window.

The Query Builder button can be used to experiment with the Structured Query Language (SQL) and to build more complex queries. SQL has become the standard language for communicating with relational databases.

14. Click Finish to end this Wizard. A new object should have appeared in your control tray beneath Form1. OleDbConnection1 is an object that represents a connection to a database.
15. Select the OleDbConnection1 object and view its ConnectionString property using the Properties window. This property has most of the information needed to locate and connect to your database.
16. Be sure you are in Designer view (as opposed to code view). Use the View menu to change between the two views if necessary. Switching to Designer view causes the Data menu to appear in Visual Studio .NET.
17. Choose Generate DataSet from the Data menu.
18. Nothing needs to be changed on the Generate DataSet window, so click OK. This creates yet a third type of control in the control tray that represents a DataSet.

The underlying objects we're using are as follows:

Connection object. Represents a database connection.

Data Adapter object. Uses a connection and a command to fill a DataSet with Records.

DataSet. Represents a set of records that were requested using a command. Our command was Select * from Products, which asks for all records (*) from the Products table.

To associate the set of records returned from our SQL query with the DataGrid control we have to set the DataSource property. Establishing an association between a control and a database is referred to as *binding* a control to data.

Continue on and bind the DataGrid control to the DataSet.

19. Select the DataGrid control and set its DataSource property to DataSet11.Products as shown in Figure 2.11.
20. Double-click Form1 to open the Code Editor window, focused on the Form1_Load event handler. Enter the following code for form's Load:

```
OleDbDataAdapter1.Fill(Me.DataSet11)
```

21. Run the application, and your DataGrid control should display all the records from the Products table (see Figure 2.12).

Navigation, modification, addition, and deletion of records are possible with this control. You'll be sadly disappointed if you attempt to code the Click, Navigate, or KeyDown event to respond to the user clicking on different fields or using the arrow keys to move from one record to the next. Theses events don't do a very good job of detecting user interaction. Chapter 5, "Advanced .NET Windows Applications," introduces you to the underlying concepts surrounding data access in .NET.

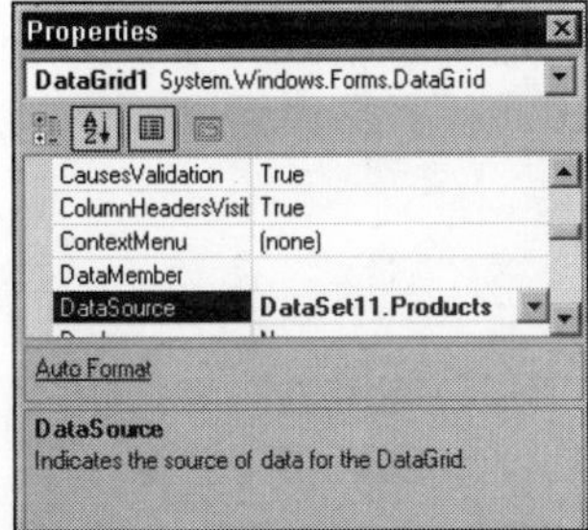

Figure 2.11 Use the arrow next to the DataSource property to select from valid data sources on the current form.

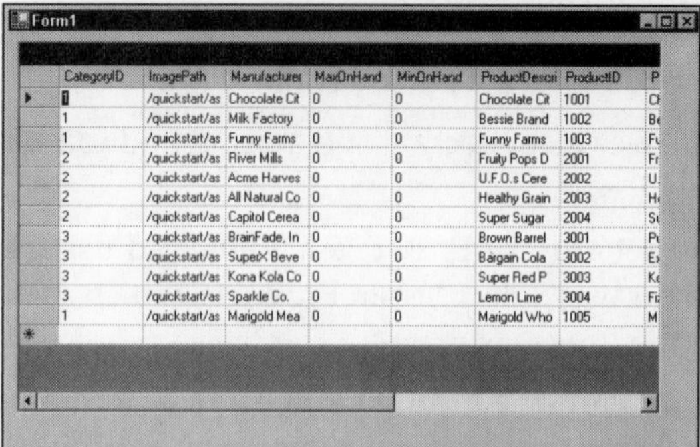

Figure 2.12 The DataGrid control displays records based on its DataSource.

The Panel Control

The Panel controls are dockable containers in .NET. They work like frames in HTML development. These panels are used as viewing panels (or panes if you like) to separate sections of our user interface. Figure 2.13 shows a form with a single panel whose BorderStyle property has been set to Fixed3D and whose Dock property has been set to Left. Panels are invisible, by default, at runtime.

The DateTimePicker and MonthlyCalendar Controls

The DateTimePicker is possibly the simplest of the controls. To use it, just place it on a form. Users are presented with a drop-down calendar from which they can choose a date. The MinDate and MaxDate values can be used to define a valid range of dates. After a date has been chosen, the Value property of the control will contain that date. The Format property can be set to Long, Short, Time, or Custom to change the format in which the date or time is stored and displayed. The MonthlyCalendar control displays a calendar page for the current month with the current day circled and special dates in boldface type. The DateTimePicker control is used to select a date, whereas the MonthlyCalendar control is used to display the date via a calendar page.

Figure 2.13 Panel controls allow you to separate or even hide sections of a user interface.

Dynamically Adding Controls

Adding controls at runtime (dynamically) is a little different than it was in Visual Basic 6. The following code creates a control, but it never appears:

```
Dim mybtn As New Button()
mybtn.Location = New Point(10, 10)
mybtn.Show()  'DOES NOTHING
mybtn.Visible = True 'DOES NOTHING
Me.Controls.Add(mybtn) 'This is what we want!
```

Controls must be associated with a container and added to the container's control collection. To add a control dynamically to a panel named Panel1 on Form1, use the following code:

```
Me.Panel1.Controls.Add(mybtn) 'bingo!
```

That method works for all controls that have a Controls collection. In the first example, the attempts to use the Show method and the Visible property do nothing and should be omitted.

Scrollable Forms

If we keep running the code in the previous example and add a little code to make each successive button appear underneath its predecessor, eventually we will have controls that cannot be displayed on the form. That was always a point of contention many people have had with Visual Basic forms. In .NET, however, we have only to set the AutoScroll property for a form to resolve that issue. I wanted to see just how far the form would scroll if I kept creating controls.

First I changed the AutoScroll property for the form to True. Then I created a private variable inside Form1 to keep track of the next control's y-value:

```
Private y As Integer = 10
```

Next, I added a button with the following code:

```
Private Sub Button1_Click_1(ByVal sender As System.Object,
ByVal e As System.EventArgs) Handles Button1.Click
   Dim mybtn As New Button()             'create a new button object
   mybtn.Location = New Point(10, y)     'create 10 pixels down from last
   mybtn.Text = Me.Controls.Count - 1    'number the buttons
   Me.Controls.Add(mybtn)                'display the new button
   y += 30                               'set next button's y value
End Sub
```

Somewhere near 1,000 buttons, things went haywire, the controls stopped displaying, and the scrollbars didn't work as expected. I would recommend keeping your form within some respectable limitations on its size.

As shown in Figure 2.14, if even a portion of a control is off the viewable portion of the form, the appropriate scrollbars appear.

Multiple Forms

In applications such as Word, Excel, and even Visual Studio, we have a container environment that holds our documents in Word, our workbooks in Excel, and our design components in Visual Studio. These *container environments* are actually forms themselves. They are a parent form in which all other forms reside. Yes, what you know to be Microsoft Word is simply a parent form that contains children you know as documents. This type of application is referred to as an Multiple Document Interface (MDI) application. What we are using in this chapter are referred to as Single Document Interface (SDI) applications. We will implement MDI applications in Chapter 5.

Adding New Forms

Adding new forms is similar to Visual Basic 6: Just select Add Windows Form from the Project menu, select Windows form, and click Open. The difference is where to go to set the startup form. One minute you'll see Properties appear as the last menu item in the Project menu, and the next minute it disappears. The trick is that you either have to right-click the project in the Solution Explorer or select the project name and choose Properties from the Project menu. Once in the properties page for the project, set the startup object to the appropriate form.

Properties only appear under the Project menu when a project is selected in the Solution Explorer.

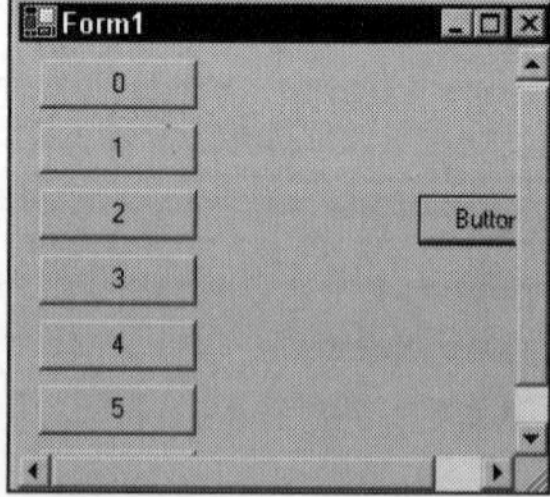

Figure 2.14 AutoScroll adds scrollbars to forms when any control's dimensions are not completely contained in the form's viewable area.

The Anatomy of a Form

By now, I'm sure you've noticed there are things in a form beyond what we've talked about. Most of the information that used to be hidden away in .frm files in Visual Basic 6 appears in our code in Visual Basic .NET. The plus and minus signs allow us to display or hide any section of code. The section, Windows Form Designer generated code, contains all the behind-the-scenes code that controls the creation of our form and the controls on it and is hidden by default.

```
Public Class Form1
    Inherits System.Windows.Forms.Form
      + Windows Form Designer generated code
End Class
```

New()

The first piece of code within that section is a method New. New is a special method for a class called a constructor. In Visual Basic 6, we would think of this as the initialize event for a class. A constructor controls how a class is created.

Dispose()

For those of you who have heard enough about interfaces, Dispose() is used to clean up memory used by the form. For those who want to know more, this method will most likely exist in every class you ever create. Dispose() is part of the IDisposable interface. Objects made from classes that support the IDisposable interface have a much better chance of avoiding delayed recovery or loss of resources.

InitializeComponent()

InitializeComponent represents all the code to define, default, and create your controls on the form. The code here and in the other methods in this section should not be modified directly unless you are very comfortable with what you're doing.

Classroom Q & A

Q: Okay, so you said that Dispose() was a method that was part of the IDisposable interface, but I don't see any reference to this form inheriting that interface.

A: I think proving it will require jumping into the Object Browser, as you might discern from Figure 2.15. You'll notice that the declaration of the Dispose method in Form1 uses the Overrides keyword. That means that the Form class that Form1 inherits from also has a Dispose method, and we are overriding that functionality locally.

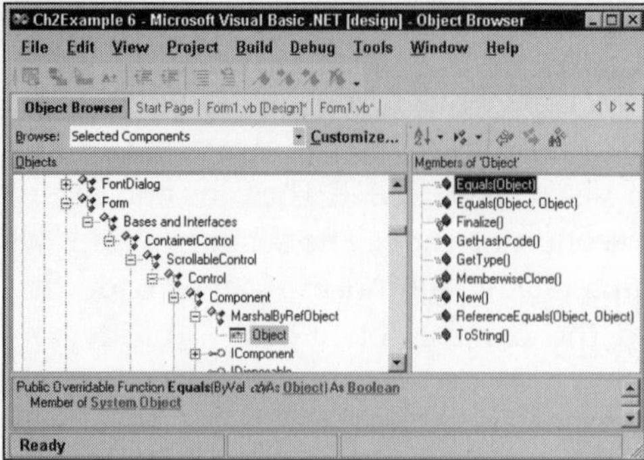

Figure 2.15 The Form class inherits and overrides a Dispose method from a class that is five levels up an object hierarchy.

This is expected in that each object needs to dispose of its own resources in memory accordingly. Figure 2.15 shows how far up the class hierarchy you have to go to see exactly where IDisposable was first inherited.

Summary

This chapter introduced you to more than a few controls and new form tricks. The fundamentals of the relationships between the objects we use in .NET were a strong underlying theme. We will use many more objects and eventually create not only our own controls but also our own libraries of classes. As we progress, use the Object Browser and ILDASM to explore and discover information about the objects you are using.

Review Questions

1. Where does a new form get its default functionality on creation?
2. What keyword is used to map an event handler to a control's event?
3. What happened to the Caption property we used in Visual Basic 6?
4. What is a text box's Change event now called?
5. What method did we use to determine if one control is a parent to another control?
6. Where is the Button class defined?
7. Where is the Color class defined?
8. What property allows you to set an object's *x* and *y* positions?
9. A form's Width and Height can be modified using the Size property. What must be passed to the Size property?
10. How can you set a form to 50-percent transparent?
11. How do you change the startup form in a project?
12. What property can be used to make a Panel visible at runtime?
13. Which of these methods causes a dynamically created control named Button1 to appear on a form?
    a. Me.Container.Add(Button1)
    b. Me.Controls.Add(Button1)
    c. Me.Add(Button1)
    d. Me.Container.Controls.Add(Button1)
14. When will scrollbars appear on a form?
15. What is the purpose of the New() method declared in the Windows Form Designer generated code section of a form?
16. Location is a property of what type?
17. How do you populate a data set with records?
18. What is the property for a control to cause it to be bound to data?
19. Where can you find the OleDbDataAdapter control?
20. What does Select * From Employees return when it is used as the command sent to a relational database?

Answers to Review Questions

1. New forms inherit from the System.Windows.Forms.Form class.
2. The Handles keyword is used to map an event handler to one or more events.
3. Visual Basic .NET uses only the Text property, whereas Visual Basic 6 used Caption for some controls and Text for others.
4. Text boxes in .NET have a TextChanged event to replace the older Change event.
5. The Contains method can be used to determine if a control is a child (contained in) of another control.
6. The Button class is defined in System.Windows.Forms.Button.
7. The Color class is defined in System.Drawing.Color.
8. The Location property allows you to set an object's *x* and *y* positions on the screen.
9. A form's Width and Height can be modified using the Size property by assigning a Size object.
10. A form can be made 50-percent transparent by setting the form's Opacity property to .5.
11. You can change the startup form in a project by right-clicking on the project name in the Solution Explorer, selecting Properties, and changing the startup object to the desired startup form.
12. BorderStyle is one property that can be used to make a Panel visible at runtime.
13. **b.** Me.Controls.Add(button1) will cause Button1 to appear.
14. Scrollbars appear on a form when the form's AutoSize property has been set to True and at least one control is partially outside of the viewable portion of the form.
15. The New() method declared in the Windows Form Designer generated code section of a form is the constructor of the class defining that form. A constructor for a class acts like an initialize event in a sense but is primarily responsible for the actual creation of objects based on that class.
16. Location is a property of type System.Drawing.Point.
17. A DataSet is populated with records by using the Fill method on a data adapter. Although different data adapters can be used, we used the OleDbDataAdapter.
18. The DataSource property is the property we used to cause a DataGrid control to be bound to data. Other properties might be required for different controls we use later.
19. The OleDbDataAdapter control is located on the Data tab of the Toolbox.
20. Select * From Employees returns all fields of all records in the Employees table.

CHAPTER

3

Examining Visual Basic .NET

The language we have always known as Visual Basic is a collection of many keywords and structures that came from the various versions of BASIC that lots of us grew up with. Visual Basic .NET did an interesting thing: It kept a lot of those keywords to make code migration easier, but it mapped them to the underlying structures and types in .NET. This allows us some flexibility: doing some things as we always have, doing some things the .NET way, and being prohibited from using certain Visual Basic 6 features at all.

Over the years with Visual Basic, I slowly learned that certain practices were inherently bad and that certain features in Visual Basic were sources of concern. Those practices are, for the most part, prohibited (or can be) in Visual Basic .NET, and the disconcerting features are self-fixing because they're only keywords that map back to underlying .NET functionality. This chapter takes a look at this latest version of Visual Basic, helping you to see what's new, what's old and okay to use, and what's old and just here for backward compatibility. In addition to the language syntax, control structures, operators, and types, you'll see the underlying .NET CTS and learn about its importance as the foundation for all things in .NET.

The Common Type System and Visual Basic .NET Types

All data type keywords used in .NET languages map back to some data type declaration in the common language runtime types. For instance, the Visual Basic .NET String data type is just an implementation of System.String in the CTS. The following code shows both Visual Basic .NET and C# declarations of strings by using their native keywords and the direct references to the CTS types:

```
'Visual Basic .NET, using Visual Basic .NET keywords:
Dim s1 As New String("Hello")

'Visual Basic .NET, using direct reference to CTS String type:
Dim s2 As New System.String("Again")

'C#, using C# keywords:
string s1 = new string("Hello");

'C#, using direct reference to CTS String type:
System.String s1 = new System.String("Again");
```

The fact that the type system is shared by all .NET languages offers an interesting possibility. Just because Visual Basic .NET doesn't have an unsigned data type doesn't mean we can't use it (like System.UInt32). Be careful in what you use by directly referencing the common language runtime types, because not all data types are CLS compliant. It is the compliance to the CLS that makes .NET code portable.

Variable Declaration in Visual Basic .NET

A *variable* is a named memory location whose contents can change. We use variables to hold data or to refer to an object in memory. Variables that hold data are simple data types such as Integer, Char, Single, and Byte. Variables that refer to more complex things such as forms or controls need much more complex types. These data types dictate how an object is to be stored and treated in memory. Data types must be large and flexible enough to hold the largest and most complex object we intend to store in a variable of that type. For instance, if you created a poker game and the pot was only a 2-byte integer, a player could match a pot at $20,000 and win (supposedly $40,000), only to find out that the net outcome was –$7,233! That is because the range of a signed, 2-byte integer is negative 32768 to positive 32767. The following Visual Basic .NET code shows two methods of variable declarations:

```
'This method uses memory immediately
Dim string1 As New String("Hello")
'This method uses memory on assignment
Dim string2 As String
string2 = "world" 'string is created in memory here
```

Visual Basic .NET Types Mapped to Common Language Runtime Types

Table 3.1 shows all of Visual Basic .NET's data types, their sizes, their correlation to the underlying type system, and their Visual Basic 6 counterparts.

Of the data types listed, two are not like the others. String and Object are both based on classes, whereas the rest of these types are based on a different type of object template called a Structure. Both Class and Structure are keywords in Visual Basic .NET and can be used to create our own types based on these two forms of templates. The concepts of a class and a structure are not new to Visual Basic, but a structure was called a Type in Visual Basic 6.

Table 3.1 Mapping Types

VISUAL BASIC .NET TYPE	BYTES	COMMON LANGUAGE RUNTIME TYPE	VISUAL BASIC 6 TYPE
Single	4	System.Single	Single
Double	8	System.Double	Double
Short	2	System.Int16	Integer
Integer	4	System.Int32	Long
Long	8	System.Int64	-
Boolean	2	System.Boolean	Boolean
Byte	1	System.Byte	Byte
Decimal	16	System.Decimal	Currency(8)
Char	2	System.Char	-
String	(varies)	System.String	String
Date	8	System.DateTime	Date
Object	4	System.Object	Object, Variant

Value Types Versus Reference Types

Understanding the need for both structures and classes requires an awareness of the intentions and uses related to the two. The confusing part is that many people want to say that a class represents an Object template. Although that statement is true, it doesn't exclude that same truth being applied to things built from a Structure template. All things in .NET are objects. That said, let's redefine what an object is. An *object* is a self-contained entity that may or may not contain state (properties), may or may not have behaviors (methods), and may or may not respond to messages (method invocations, events, callbacks). Every Form, Integer, Rat, Apple, Hairdryer, and Point object created in .NET must be directly or indirectly derived (inherited) from System.Object.

Table 3.2 compares the primary differences between the only two high-level data types in .NET: value types and reference types.

You can see the difference in inheritance between a String and an Integer in the Object Browser. Figure 3.1 shows that String inherits directly from System.Object, but Integer (Int32) inherits from System.ValueType, which inherits from System.Object.

By default, Visual Basic .NET classes don't inherit from System.Object until they are compiled unless you explicitly use Inherits System.Object in the class declaration. This explains why the Object Browser might insist that your class does not inherit from System.Object.

Table 3.2 Comparing Value Types and Reference Types

VALUE TYPES	REFERENCE TYPES
Created using a Structure in Visual Basic .NET (struct in C#)	Created using a class in both Visual Basic .NET and C#
Create objects on the stack in memory	Create objects on the heap in memory
Assignment of a Structure-based object creates a copy	Assignment of a class-based object creates a reference
Used when state (data) is key	Used when behavior (functionality) is key
Derived from System.Object, System.ValueType	Derived from System.Object
Cannot be derived from	Can be derived from
Examples include Integer, Date, Byte and Boolean	Examples include Form, DataSet, Button, and String

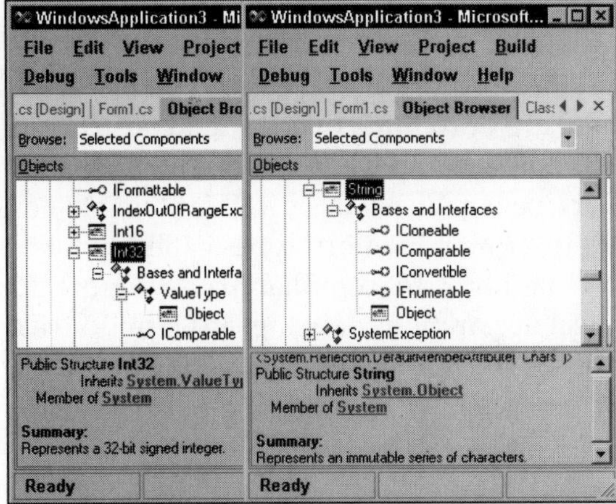

Figure 3.1 String is a reference type and inherits directly from System.Object. Integer (Int32) is a value type and inherits directly from System.ValueType.

Strings in .NET

As previously mentioned, reference types should be used when behavior is key. Well, there are a considerable number of behaviors that are desired for a string.

Unlike a simple numeric value, a string may change in size, need to have its case changed, need to be searched, and may even need to be constructed in memory using a variety of different methods. Because of the expected behaviors of a string, it had to be created as a reference type. It is also important to understand that a variable-length type should not be created on the stack because the stack has limited space.

String Construction

To understand some of the behaviors of a String data type, let's start at its construction. The variations for the construction of an object based on a class are limited to the number of constructors defined in that class. In other words, if you design your own class and want to have people create a new string from a Date object, you need to create a constructor method for that class that accepts a Date object. The following declaration is illegal because there is no string constructor that accepts zero arguments:

```
Dim s As New String()
```

The use of several methods with the same name that take different arguments is referred to as *overloading*. When you create a string in Visual Basic .NET, the Intellisense (the pop-up information that appears as you enter code in .Net) is misleading. It informs you that there are only three overloaded constructors for a new string. If you were to create a new string in C#, it would tell you that there are in fact eight constructors for a string. Visual Basic .NET is lying to you because the remaining constructors use direct-memory types called pointers that are available only in C# and create non-CLS-compliant code. Figure 3.2 shows the difference between identical declarations of strings in C# and Visual Basic .NET with different indications for the number of constructors.

String Concatenation

Concatenation can be done with the concatenation operators or with the Concat method of the String class. All three forms of concatenation used in the following Visual Basic .NET code produce the same string: "Hello, new world."

```
Dim s1 As New String("Hello, ")
Dim s2 As New String("new world")
'+ operator performs addition based on type:
MessageBox.Show(s1 + s2)
'& is the appropriate concatenation operator:
MessageBox.Show(s1 & s2)
 'Uses Concat method of the string class:
MessageBox.Show(s1.Concat(s1,s2)
```

The Join member of a string can be used to join members of a String array for concatenation into a separate string, as in the following Visual Basic .NET code:

```
Dim s() As String = {"one", "two", "three"} 'a string array
Dim s2 As String
'Produces: "one, two, three" as a single string:
s2 = s2.Join(", ", s)
```

The Split method of the String class is the opposite of the Join method. Split takes a string and makes an array out of it. The original string can be split apart using any separation char, including a space.

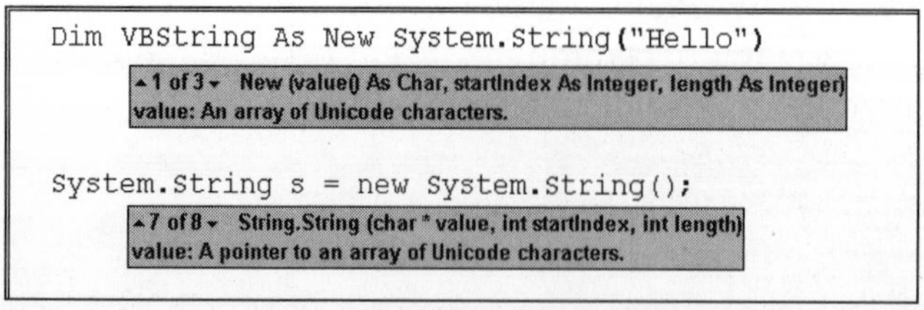

```
Dim VBString As New System.String("Hello")
    ▲1 of 3▼  New (value() As Char, startIndex As Integer, length As Integer)
    value: An array of Unicode characters.

System.String s = new System.String();
    ▲7 of 8▼  String.String (char * value, int startIndex, int length)
    value: A pointer to an array of Unicode characters.
```

Figure 3.2 Although Visual Basic .NET and C# both implement strings as System.String, the C# version has extra constructors hidden from languages that do not support pointers.

Table 3.3 String Comparison Examples

STRING 1	STRING2	USAGE	RETURNS
"Hello"	"Hello"	Compare(String1,String2)	0
"Hello"	"ello"	Compare(String1,String2)	1
"Hello"	"Hello World"	Compare(String1,String2)	-1
"Hello"	"hello"	Compare(String1,String2)	1
"Hello"	"hello"	Compare(String1,String2,True)	0 'ignore case

String Comparison

String comparison can be done with the equality operator (=) or with the Compare method of the String class. The Compare method takes two strings as arguments to compare. The Compare method returns a positive value if the first string is greater than the second string and a negative value if the first string is smaller than the second string. If both strings are equal, a zero is returned. A difference in case between two strings may or may not indicate a difference in equality, depending on which overload of the Compare method you use. Table 3.3 shows the difference in equality seen by two versions of the Compare method.

String comparison using the equality operator acts according to the Option Compare statement in Visual Basic .NET. This statement can appear at the very top of the code section, preceding the declaration of the form itself, and can have values of Text or Binary. If Option Compare is set to Text, comparisons are case-insensitive. If Option Compare is set to Binary, comparisons are case-sensitive. Figure 3.3 illustrates how Option Compare affects string comparisons.

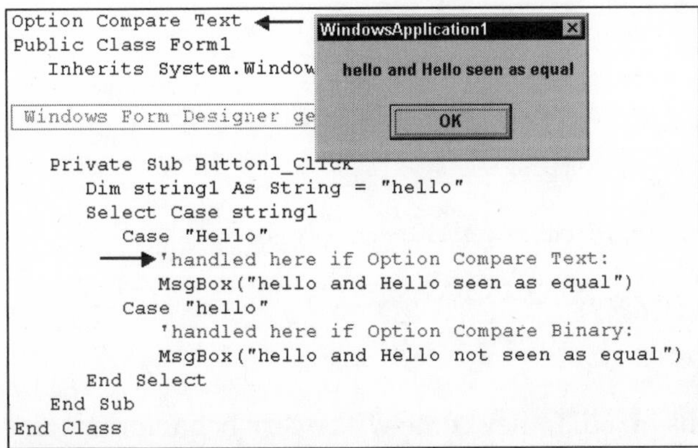

Figure 3.3 Shows the comparisons of two strings that differ only by case and are considered equal because Option Compare has been set to Text.

String Equality

Because strings inherit from System.Object, they inherit an Equals method. The Equals method is not used to determine if strings are equal in the same sense as Compare but rather to determine if two variables of type String refer to the same string data in memory.

Let's discuss the concept of equality in English terms. What would you mean if you asked, "Are Brian and Wendy equal"? You might be referring to their height, age, or even their prowess as software engineers. If we use the example of a class Person as an object type, there is a question about what equality means. Now, let's say we have two numbers, number1 and number2, and they both hold the value of 5. Are they equal? Certainly. Without a doubt, number1 and number2 are equal in English and mathematical terms. Strangely enough, we just described a fundamental difference between a reference type and a value type. Value types are simple, data-centric types. Reference types are more complex objects based on real-life entities such as a person. Because of the ambiguity associated with equality among reference types, the Equals method for value and reference types works differently for the two.

ReferenceType1.Equals(ReferenceType2) determines if both reference types refer to the same address in memory. ValueType1.Equals(ValueType2) only determines if both values are equal.

Recall that value types are copied by value and reference types are copied by reference. If you assign one number to another, you copy the value. If you copy one string to another, you make both string variables refer to the same memory address. Consider the following Visual Basic .NET code:

```
Dim s1 As New String("Hello")
Dim s2 As New String("Hello")
MessageBox.Show(s1.Equals(s2)) 'False, different
                               'memory addresses
s1 = s2  'make s1 refer to what s2 refers to in memory
MessageBox.Show(s1.Equals(s2)) 'True, same memory address
Dim n1 As New Integer()
Dim n2 As New Integer()
n1 = 10
n2 = 10
MessageBox.Show(n1.Equals(n2)) 'True, same value
n1 = 20
MessageBox.Show(n1.Equals(n2)) 'False, different values
```

Other String Operations

Strings are first-class citizens in .NET; they come with every behavior imaginable for a piece of text. Table 3.4 describes the more popular members (properties and methods) of the String class and their proper syntax. For the syntax usage for each of these members, assume a string "Greeting" contained in a String variable named s1.

It's clear from this partial list of String functionality that a String is no simple data type. None of these methods, however, modify the contents of the original string unless you implicitly state that as your intention:

```
'returns a new string: Greetings, s1 is unchanged
s1.Insert(8, "s")
'This will change s1:
s1 = s1.Insert(8, "s") 's1 now holds Greetings
```

You can imagine how confusing it is to a new programmer to call the Sort method of an object only to find that the object itself does not sort. This behavior of returning a new object instead of modifying the original is quite common in .NET, and we merely have to pay attention to each method's behavior.

Table 3.4 String Class Members

MEMBER	DESCRIPTION
Chars	Returns a character at a given index Usage: s1.Chars(2) Returns: e (index 2 of the string "Greeting")
EndsWith	Determines if a string ends with a particular pattern Usage: s1.EndsWith("ing") Returns: True
IndexOfAny	Finds a string and returns its starting index Usage: s1.IndexOfAny("tin") Returns: the value 4 (tin is at indexes 4–7 in Greeting)
Insert, Remove	Inserts or removes a string in another at a given position Usage: s1.Insert(8, "s") Returns: a new string containing Greetings
Length	Returns the length in byte (1 char = 1 byte) of a string Usage: s1.Length Returns: 8, because Greeting has 8 chars
Replace	Replaces every occurrence of one character with another Usage: s1.Replace("e", "i") Returns: a new string containing Griiting
Substring	Returns a portion if a string, given the starting position and the number of characters to return. Usage: s1.Substring(0,5) Returns: a new string containing Greet

Intrinsic Value Types

The discussion of the String data type was lengthy only because it's our only example of a reference type that we can really experiment with prior to Chapter 6, "Building Class Libraries in .NET." Now we look at the simpler intrinsic data types and use Integer as our ValueType representative.

The Integer keyword maps to System.Int32, which derives from System .ValueType, which derives from System.Object. That's a wonderful statement, but what does it really mean? It means that an Int32 object has some inherent members, some that it gains from ValueType, and some that it gains from System.Object.

Because System.Object is the ultimate base class for everything, let's take a look at what members a type gains by being derived from it. Figure 3.4 shows the members that are in System.Object. This inheritance from System.Object is why all objects have ToString, GetType, and Equals methods.

Now that we know where all types get these behaviors, let's look at some substantiation that everything is an object. The following Visual Basic .NET code provides proof that even the most mundane things are indeed objects by the time they exist in memory:

```
'We can call ToString on the value 10!
MessageBox.Show(10.ToString())
```

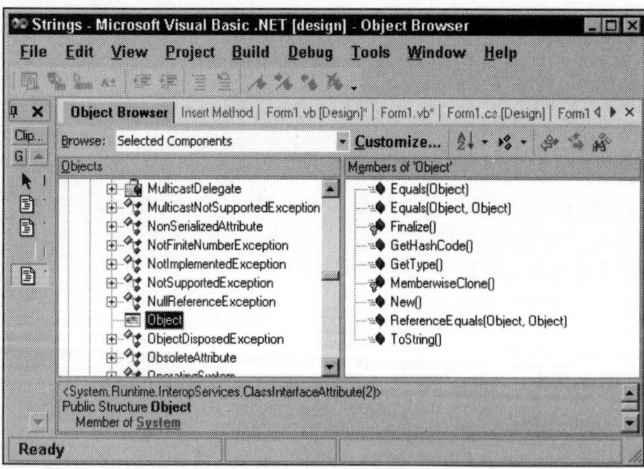

Figure 3.4 System.Object is the ultimate base class from which all types are derived. The Object Browser can be used to display its members.

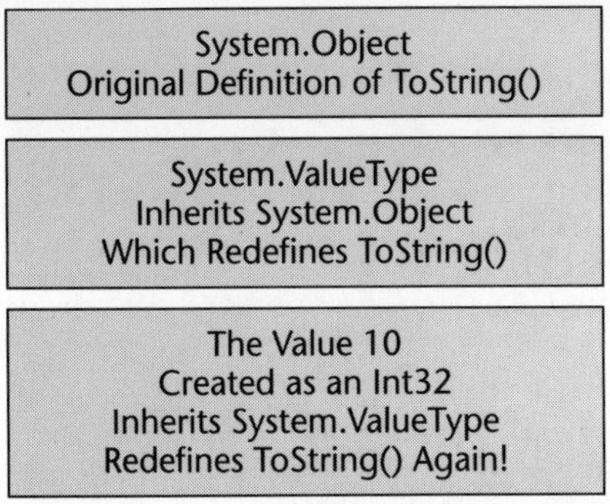

Figure 3.5 Int32 inherits from System.ValueType, which redefines methods that ValueType inherited from System.Object. Int32 further redefines ToString for an Integer.

The value 10 was dynamically converted to an object at runtime. This happens to ensure that no matter what we are using, it has an expected set of behaviors. Furthermore, we know that there are only two basic types in .NET, and the value 10 would most certainly have been further derived from ValueType when it was encountered. It happens that ValueType redefines what Equals and ToString do for value types. That's not all! The Int32 class also redefines what these methods do specifically for Integers. Figure 3.5 shows the relationship between these objects.

Numeric Type Members

Most numeric types (such as Integer, Short, and Long) have a few methods and only two properties. These properties, MinValue and MaxValue, are used to determine the range of a type. The Decimal type, however, has been extended far beyond the functionality sported by those simple numeric types to include methods such as Round() and Truncate().

Dates and the Date Data Type

The Date data type in Visual Basic .NET maps to common language runtime type System.DateTime. The DateTime type extends the functionality of the Data type in Visual Basic 6. The following examples demonstrate common usage variations for constructing and using dates in Visual Basic .NET:

```
'Date declarations
Dim myDate1 As Date
myDate1 = #1/1/2003 12:00:00 PM#
'Or
Dim myDate2 As New Date(2003, 12, 31)
```

```
'Getting current date and time
myDate1 = DateTime.Now
'Creating a Date from a String
myDate1 = DateTime.Parse("9/7/1966") 'Parse date from string
'Determining net 30 from current date
'TimeSpan uses (Days, Hours, Minutes, Seconds)
myDate1 = myDate1.Add(New System.TimeSpan(30, 0, 0, 0))
'Or
myDate1 = myDate1.AddDays(30)
'Useful DateTime operations
MessageBox.Show(DateTime.DaysInMonth(2002, 2)) '28
MessageBox.Show(DateTime.MinValue) '12:00:00 AM
MessageBox.Show(DateTime.MaxValue) '12/31/1999 11:59:59 PM
MessageBox.Show(DateTime.IsLeapYear(Now.Year)) 'False for 2002
MessageBox.Show(myDate1.ToShortDateString) '1/1/2003
MessageBox.Show(myDate1.ToShortTimeString) '12:00 PM
'Wednesday, January 1, 2003:
MessageBox.Show(myDate1.ToLongDateString)
MessageBox.Show(myDate1.ToLongTimeString) '12:00:00PM
```

Char

The Char data type is not the same as a Byte in Visual Basic 6. A Char is a 2-byte variable, capable of holding characters in multinational language sets. Using Chars can be initially confusing when Option Strict is on.

Option Strict On can be placed at the very top of a module to tell the compiler that you don't want it to perform type conversions for you. You should never develop in Visual Basic .NET unless Option Strict has been set for a given module. Having Option Strict on forces you to write code correctly and helps avoid nasty logic errors. Unfortunately, even attempting to assign a value to a Char can be frustrating. The following code provides examples of both correct and erroneous assignments.

```
Option Strict On
Dim c As Char
c = "A"       'FAILS because it's a string
c = 'A'       'FAILS because it's a comment
c = ('A')     'FAILS because it's a comment
c = "A"c      'CORRECT! uses the literal type char c
              'to force a conversion
c = System.Convert.ToChar("A") 'Overkill, but effective
```

Of course, you could never have turned on Option Strict and the conversion would have just happened, but the compiler and other programmers can only guess what your intentions were.

Boolean Mishap?

The Boolean data type holds only the values of True and False. Visual Basic .NET, however, *appears* to be much less restrictive in its view of True and False than C# is. This incongruity can cause problems. It should not be possible in a type-safe system to do the following:

```
Dim x As Integer
x = 10
'sees x as True because it's not zero and prints 10
If x Then MsgBox(x)
```

The ability to be seen as True or False in other .NET languages is limited to Boolean types. In this example, we can see that Visual Basic treats any nonzero value as True. This behavior can and should be avoided by leaving Option Strict On. Adding Option Strict On to the top of a module causes Visual Basic to fail at compile time when code requiring dynamic type coercion is encountered. In the case of treating an integer as a boolean, the integer is being coerced into a boolean value by the compiler. After Option Strict is turned on, any attempt to use types in that manner results in a compilation error similar to "Option Strict on disallows implicit conversions from Integer to Boolean."

Conversions and Casting

Without Option Strict turned on, Visual Basic .NET continually converts anything to anything behind the scenes without telling you there was ever a problem. This can cause some of the most difficult errors to find. Besides, it's just plain lazy and foolhardy to let a compiler perform any type conversion that it wants to. Explicitly performing the conversion yourself also means that other programmers don't have to guess what your intentions were. Table 3.5 lists the basic conversions that exist in Visual Basic .NET.

Table 3.5 Basic Visual Basic .NET Conversions

FUNCTION	CONVERTS ARGUMENT TO
CBool()	Boolean
CByte()	Byte
CChar()	Char
CDate()	Date
CDbl()	Double

(continued)

Table 3.5 *(continued)*

FUNCTION	CONVERTS ARGUMENT TO
CDec()	Decimal
CInt()	Integer
CLng()	Long
CObj()	Object
CShort()	Short
CSng()	Single
CStr()	String

These functions actually convert a copy of their arguments for assignment to the value on the left of the assignment statement without changing the data or type of the original variable. The comments in the following Visual Basic .NET code illustrate this more clearly:

```
Dim x As Integer = 0
Dim s As Single = 10.5
'convert the Single to Integer then assign to x:
'conversion is only for assignment and doesn't change s:
x = CInt(s)
'holds 10, the Integer portion of s:
MessageBox.Show(x.ToString())
'still 10.5, conversion did not affect s:
MessageBox.Show(s.ToString())
'convert the contents of x back to a Single:
s = CSng(x) 'only the value 10 is placed back into s
```

Just because a conversion exists doesn't mean it's valid for every type. Some conversions that work with Option Strict turned off don't work when it's turned on. One such illegal conversion is between a Char and an Integer. There is no direct conversion between a Char and an Integer in Visual Basic .NET, causing the following code to fail:

```
Dim x As Integer = 10
Dim c As Char = "A"c
x = CInt(c) 'FAILS, illegal conversion.
```

Don't get discouraged; there are more ways to force this conversion than you need. The following examples are valid conversions from a Char to an Integer:

```
'Works fine - interprets c as a UNICODE char, value: 65:
x = AscW(c)
'Compiles, but returns zero because "A" isn't a digit:
```

```
x = Val(c)
'Works Fine, converts to value: 65:
x = System.Convert.ToInt32(c)
```

Although it might take a little more code, the System.Convert conversions don't require you to remember relatively obscure functions such as the AscW (ASCII Wide) function. Twenty-three separate conversions are available in System.Convert.

Beyond all these conversion methods is one method, CType, that offers a more generic approach to type conversion. CType can be used on the simple types we have employed so far as well as on more complex, composite data types. We could even use CType to convert an ArrayList as an IList or any of its supported interfaces. The CType conversion method is used in the following Visual Basic .NET code to convert a Char to a String:

```
Dim c As Char = "A"c
Dim s As String = ""
'convert the contents of c to a string and store in s:
s = CType(c, String)
```

Operators

The standard operators from Visual Basic have been extended to include several new ones. What these operators do depends upon their left and right operands because each type must define how these operators affect objects of that type. An arithmetic operator has been defined inside the String class to result in a concatenation of two string operands, whereas the Int32 class performs an Integer addition when an addition operator is used on two Integer operands. Table 3.6 lists the most commonly used operators in Visual Basic .NET.

Table 3.6 Common Operators

TYPE	OPERATOR NAME	OPERATOR
Arithmetic	Addition	+
	Subtraction	–
	Multiplication	*
	Floating point division	\
	Integer division	/
	Exponentiation	^
	Negation	–
	Modulus operator	Mod
	Shorthand operators	^=, *=, /=, \=, +=, -=, &=

(continued)

Table 3.6 *(continued)*

TYPE	OPERATOR NAME	OPERATOR
Comparison	Equality Greater than or equal to Inequality Less than Greater than Less than or equal to	= >= <> < > <=
Logical/bitwise	Negation Conjunction Disjunction	Not And AndAlso (for binary only) Or OrElse (for binary only) Xor
Miscellaneous		AddressOf TypeOf...Is Like

The Eqv operator from Visual Basic 6 was replaced with the = operator in .NET, and the Imp operator is no longer supported.

The TypeOf...Is operator can be used only for reference types. We could iterate through the Controls collection in a form and use the TypeOf operator to do something specific on a certain type as in the following Visual Basic .NET code:

```
Dim ctrl As System.Windows.Forms.Control
For Each ctrl In Me.Controls
  If TypeOf ctrl Is TextBox Then
     MessageBox.Show(ctrl.Name)
  End If
Next
```

The Like operator uses wildcard characters to do yet another comparison of strings. The Like operator uses a question mark (?) as a single character placeholder and an asterisk (*) as a placeholder for 0 or more characters as seen in the following code:

```
Dim s As String
s = "VB.NET"
if s Like "*Net" Then ...   'evaluates to True
If s Like "?B.NET" Then ... 'evaluates  to True
```

We'll be using every one of these operators throughout the book to solve various problems.

Control Structures

Although I expect many of you to have a solid understanding of the control structures that have been in Visual Basic since Ronald Reagan was the President, I include them here for completeness and urge experienced Visual Basic programmers to skip this section entirely.

The If Statement

The If condition is identical in concept to the meaning of the if statement in the English language. When you say, "If you are good to your sister, I'll take you both to the movies," the child can expect one of two results: he or she will or will not go to the movies, depending upon his or her behavior. Programming is much different in the sense that we can't change our minds. If a condition is met (the conditional statement evaluates to True), the associated code for that If condition is executed. We could describe this situation with the following If structure:

```
If good then
     'go to movies
Else
     'don't go movies
End If
```

Whether or not we even need the Else portion depends upon what we plan to do if the condition is False. Sometimes we only want to perform an action if the conditional statement evaluates to True. In this case, good = true is the condition being checked. There is no need to provide an Else section if there is no else action.

If statements don't need to appear on multiple lines. When an If statement appears on a single line, the End If keyword is not necessary. An If statement containing an Else section cannot be written this way:

```
If Loading Then Exit Sub
```

The following complex If statement uses an ElseIf clause to check multiple values of a particular numeric grade and assigns an appropriate letter grade to the variable LetterGrade. Take a look at this use of a complex If statement in Visual Basic .NET before we discuss why it's inefficient.

```
Dim Grade As Double
Dim LetterGrade As Char
Dim x As Object
x = InputBox("Enter grade:") 'ask the user to enter a grade
'convert the entered value to double:
```

```
Grade = System.Convert.ToDouble(x)
If Grade >= 3.9 Then
   LetterGrade = "A"c
ElseIf Grade >= 3.5 Then
   LetterGrade = "B"c
ElseIf Grade >= 3.0 Then
   LetterGrade = "C"c
ElseIf Grade >= 2.5 Then
   LetterGrade = "D"c
Else 'this condition handles all values less than 2.5
   LetterGrade = "F"c
End If
MessageBox.Show(LetterGrade)
```

If the value entered were 2, each of the conditions would be checked sequentially until the final Else statement was encountered. That's horrendous, considering that we might have hundreds of possible values for different scenarios.

The Select Case Statement

The Select Case statement offers a dramatic improvement over sequential ElseIF statements. The Select Case statement is like a complex If statement that looks at an input value and immediately jumps to the appropriate code for that value. Each of the code sections in a Select Case statement is referred to as a Case. Let's replace the logic in the preceding ElseIf structure with a Select Case statement:

```
Dim Grade As Double
Dim LetterGrade As Char
Dim x As Object
x = InputBox("Enter grade:")
Grade = System.Convert.ToDouble(x)
Select Case Grade
Case Is >= 3.9
   LetterGrade = "A"c
Case Is >= 3.5
   LetterGrade = "B"c
Case Is >= 3.0
   LetterGrade = "C"c
Case Is >= 2.5
   LetterGrade = "D"c
Case Else 'if all else fails, use this code
   LetterGrade = "F"c
End Select
```

The possibility still exists that the user could type something into the InputBox to cause an error, but we'll deal with such issues in Chapter 4, "Debugging and Exception Handling."

A Case entered as Case Grade >= 3.9 would be ignored and would not cause a compilation or runtime error. Be careful not to refer to the control variable in a Case clause.

While Loops

The While loop is a precondition loop. That is, it checks a condition prior to entering the code within the While structure. If the condition evaluates to True, the code inside the While is executed. When End While is encountered, the condition is reevaluated before entering the loop again. The following While loop continues to call the GetTransactionFromUser method until TransactionType is set to either iDeposit or iWithdrawal transaction values:

```
Dim TransactionType As Integer
While TransactionType <> iWithdrawal And TransactionType <>
iDeposit
   TransactionType = GetTransactionFromUser()
End While 'used to be called Wend in Visual Basic 6
```

Do Loops

Visual Basic .NET has all four versions of the Do loop from traditional Visual Basic. Although these looping structures exist, they're not all necessary. The difference between a Do...While loop and a Do...Until loop is only a semantic one. Many looping structures exist in Visual Basic .NET more for ease of code migration than an inherent necessity. Each of the following four loops does exactly the same thing:

```
Dim i As Integer
'precondition Do...Until:
Do Until i = 10
   i += 1
Loop
'postcondition Do...Until:
Do
   i += 1
Loop Until (i = 10)
'precondition Do...While:
Do While i < 10
   i += 1
Loop
'postcondition Do...Until:
Do
   i += 1
Loop While i < 10
```

In the case of an ATM machine screen asking you to make a language selection, for example, the screen always displays at least once and continues to display until you select a valid language. In a case where code needs to always run at least once, a postcondition loop is appropriate. Consider the possibility of an ATM card that has the user's preference of Spanish embedded in the card; in that case we would have a valid language preference and never need to display the screen at all. In the latter case, a precondition loop would be appropriate.

For Each Loops

The For Each loop provides a simplistic way to iterate through collections without the use of indexes. In .NET, a collection class must implement the IEnumerable interface for a user of that class to iterate through its elements using a For Each loop. The following For Each loop iterates through a directory structure and fills ListBox1 with the names of the files in that directory:

```
Dim DirInfo As New System.IO.DirectoryInfo("c:\winnt")
Dim Files() As System.IO.FileInfo
Dim File As System.IO.FileInfo
Files = DirInfo.GetFiles() 'GetFiles returns an array of
'FileInfo objects
ListBox1.Items.Clear()
For Each File In Files
   ListBox1.Items.Add(File)
Next
```

Regardless of what objects you are using, For Each syntax is always easier to read and write than For Next syntax but executes at a very slight performance degradation when compared to For Next.

For Next Loops

For Loops (For Next or For Each) are used when you know exactly how many iterations need to be made. The items in an array, the controls on a form, and the files in a directory are all things that have a known number of items and would best be iterated with a For loop. The For loop has an iterator, a starting value, an ending value, and a step value. Every time the For loop executes, the iterator is incremented or decremented using a Step value. The default Step value is 1. The following examples demonstrate both incrementing and decrementing For Next loops:

```
Dim i As Integer
'Loop forward from 0 to 10,
'incrementing i by 1 on each iteration:
For i = 0 To 10 Step 1
```

```
    MessageBox.Show(i.ToString())
Next
'Loop backward from 10 to 1,
'decrementing i by 1 on each iteration:
For i = 10 To 0 Step -1
    MessageBox.Show(i.ToString())
Next
```

In general, the larger the type of the iterator, the slower the execution of a For loop. Comparing execution time of a For loop using an Integer as an iterator to a For loop that uses a Decimal as an iterator shows a readily noticeable difference.

With Statements

The With statement is more of a language optimization than a control structure. Instead of setting several properties for an object with sequential lines of code that continually repeat the object reference, you can use the With statement. The With statement in the following Visual Basic .NET code offers a performance improvement over setting each of these properties individually:

```
With Button1
    .ForeColor = Color.Tomato
    .Location = New Point(0, 0)
    .Enabled = True
    .Visible = True
End With
```

Exit and Exit()

The Do loop, While loop, For loop, Sub routine, and Function all have an Exit statement that prematurely causes them to terminate. Exit Do, Exit While, Exit For, Exit Sub, and Exit Function work on these constructs, but the Application.Exit() method can be used to end the entire application.

Arrays and ArrayLists

A variable is usually described as a named place in memory. Variables come in different types. Normal variables such as the ones we have been using that hold a single value are referred to as scalar variables. No one outside of a textbook would ever use the term *scalar*, but the term *array* is always used to refer to a named place in memory that can hold multiple values.

Arrays Declarations

The syntax for dealing with arrays hasn't changed much from Visual Basic 6. The following examples in Visual Basic .NET show various methods for declaring arrays:

```
Dim myArray1(6) As String '7 element array (positions 0 to 6
Dim myArray2() As String = {"VB.NET", "J#", "C#"}
                            '3 element array
Dim myArray3() As Object 'Size determined later with ReDim
Dim myArray4(2,2) As Object '2 dimensional array of 9 elements
```

Arrays Iteration

Iterating through the elements in an array can be done in quite a few ways. The GetLength property can be used to return the number of elements in an array but requires an array dimension as an argument. For one-dimensional arrays, the only dimension value is 0. The following Visual Basic .NET code uses the GetLength property to create an upper bound for array iteration:

```
Dim i As Integer
For i = 0 To myArray2.GetLength(0) - 1
   MessageBox.Show(myArray2(i))
Next
```

The For Each loop uses an iterator of whatever type the array was based on. For arrays of objects, an iterator of type Object is required. The following Visual Basic .NET code uses a String iterator to display each element in an array of strings:

```
Dim s As String
For Each s In myArray2
     MessageBox.Show(s.ToString())
Next
```

Arrays also have GetUpperBound and GetLowerBound methods that work in a way that is similar to their Visual Basic 6 UBound and LBound counterparts. Two-dimensional arrays are quite common. An Excel spreadsheet and a database table are examples of two-dimensional collections of data. In both of these we need two pieces of information to identify an element: a row and a column. The following code iterates through array elements of a two-dimensional array using the GetLowerBound and GetUpperBound methods in a nested For loop:

```
'Creates ands seeds a random number generator
Dim r as System.Random(32767)
'Fill array1 with random values:
```

```
For i = array1.GetLowerBound(0) To array1.GetUpperBound(0)
   For j = array1.GetLowerBound(1) To array1.GetUpperBound(1)
      'store a new random number
      array1(i, j) = r.Next(99999).ToString()
   Next
Next
'Fill a ListBox with the contents of array1:
For i = array1.GetLowerBound(0) To array1.GetUpperBound(0)
   For j = array1.GetLowerBound(1) To array1.GetUpperBound(1)
      ListBox1.Items.Add(array1(i, j))
   Next
Next
```

Resizing Arrays

Resizing can be done only on dynamic arrays, which are declared with no initial size. To resize an array, you use the ReDim statement with a value indicating the maximum index of the newly resized array. ReDim myarray (1) redeclares the size of myarray to have two positions: 0 and 1. If the Preserve keyword is not used following the ReDim keyword, all data in the array prior to the use of ReDim will be lost.

```
Dim s() As String 'array of strings with no defined size
Dim i As Integer  'to use as iterator
'This loop stores ,,,,,5 in the array s:
For i = 0 To 5    'loop 6 times
   ReDim s(i) 'keep expanding the array, destroy previous data
   s(i) = CStr(i) 'place a string cast of i in each position
Next
'This loop stores 0,1,2,3,4,5 in the array s:
For i = 0 To 5    'loop 6 times
   ReDim Preserve s(i) 'keep expanding the array, preserve data
   s(i) = CStr(i) 'place a string cast of i in each position
Next
```

Using ArrayLists in Visual Basic .NET

Although arrays in Visual Basic .NET are declared and used in much the same way they were in Visual Basic 6, the behavior of Visual Basic .NET arrays is very different than in other .NET languages. An ArrayList is a structure in System.Collections and represents a dynamically resizable structure that is available to all .NET languages. Besides its convenient availability, an ArrayList is easier to use and more flexible than either Visual Basic .NET's or C#'s intrinsic array structures. ArrayLists are collections of type System.Object and can therefore contain any imaginable thing in .NET. The following Visual Basic .NET examples demonstrate the use of ArrayLists:

```
'Declaring an ArrayList:
Dim alist1 As New ArrayList()'Creates a new System.Collections.ArrayList

'Populating an ArrayList:
alist1.Add("Hello") 'Add a System.String (String)
alist1.Add(714) 'Add a System.Int32 (Integer)
'Add a System.DateTime (Date):
alist1.Add(New DateTime(2003, 1, 1))
alist1.Add(#1/1/2003#) 'Add a System.DateTime (Date)
alist1.Add(4.5) 'Add a System.Double (Double)
alist1.Add(4.5F) 'Add a System.Single (Single)
```

Although the array is of type Object and all items in the array are of type Object, the GetType method always gives you the type of the actual element that we placed in the ArrayList. The result of the following code example is shown in Figure 3.6.

```
Dim o As Object
For Each o In alist1
   'add the item data and item type to a ListBox named ListBox1
   ListBox1.Items.Add(o & ": " & o.GetType().ToString())
Next
```

Working with the same data elements shown in Figure 3.6, we can begin to experiment with the well-named members of the ArrayList type. The following attempt to use the Remove method fails to remove an item because the Remove method looks for an object to delete, not an index:

```
alist1.Remove(0) 'Remove first element containing a zero
```

The Remove method would have succeeded in removing the first occurrence of the value 0 if such a value existed. To remove an item at a specific index, use the RemoveAt method as shown here:

```
alist1.RemoveAt(0) 'Remove the first element in the ArrayList
```

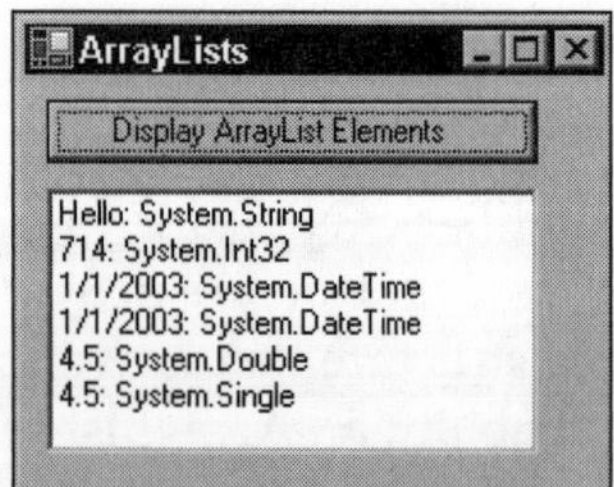

Figure 3.6 Even though these types are stored in an ArrayList of Objects, the GetType method always returns the type of the most derived object.

Remember to look closely at the Intellisense shown for each method you're using to avoid such pitfalls. Besides implementing the methods and properties in the IList and ICollection interfaces, ArrayLists also have extended functionality provided by methods such as Sort and Reverse.

Procedural Code

Procedural code allows an application to be broken down into manageable tasks. Visual Basic .NET offers both subroutines and functions as procedural blocks just as previous versions of Visual Basic did. There are, however, a few changes to the way these procedures are used in Visual Basic .NET. A subroutine is a callable block of code, enclosed by Sub and End Sub, which does not return a value. A function is a callable block of code, surrounded by Function and End Function statements, that does return a value. The following code sample illustrates how subroutine calls are made with the name of the subroutine, followed by parentheses:

```
Private Sub btnTest_Click(ByVal sender As System.Object, ByVal
      e As System.EventArgs) Handles btnTest.Click
   Greet() 'calls the greet subroutine
End Sub
Private Sub Greet()
   MessageBox.Show("Greetings")
End Sub
```

Functions and subs can be called using the Call statement in front of the called procedure name; however, the return value from a function is ignored when the Call statement is used.

Return Values

Functions in Visual Basic 6 return values by setting the name of the function to the value to be returned. You can do the same thing in Visual Basic .NET, but you have an additional option of using the Return statement to return values from a function call. In the following code, the GetNet30Date function returns a string, representing the date 30 days from today:

```
'Call GetNet30Date and display the day 30 days from now:
Private Sub btnTest_Click(ByVal sender As System.Object, _
ByVal e As System.EventArgs) Handles btnTest.Click
   MessageBox.Show(GetNet30Date()) 'Call function, show result
End Sub
```

```
'GetNet30Date adds 30 days to Now and returns a string
Private Function GetNet30Date() As String
   Return Now.Add(New TimeSpan(30, 0, 0, 0)).ToShortDateString
End Function
```

Passing Arguments by Value Versus by Reference

Arguments to Procedures in Visual Basic 6 are passed by reference by default. In Visual Basic .NET, all arguments are passed to procedures by value by default. The declaration of whether these arguments must be passed by value or by reference is no longer optional. If neither the ByVal nor ByRef keyword is used for an argument in a procedure declaration, ByVal is automatically added to the declaration. Passing a value to a procedure by value (ByVal) means that a copy of the original value is given to the called procedure. Passing a value by reference (ByRef) to a procedure enables the procedure to use its local variable to change the original value of the variable passed to it. Figure 3.7 illustrates the difference between the use of the ByVal and ByRef keywords.

Optional Parameters and Default Parameter Values

Parameters in a function's parameter list can be made optional with the use of the Optional keyword. Optional parameters in Visual Basic .NET must be given default values, a restriction that Visual Basic 6 does not have. The following code modifies the GetNet30Date function to accept a date. If a date is passed to the function, it returns net 30 from that date. If no date is passed to the GetNet30Date, it acts as it did before, returning net 30 from the current date.

```
Private Sub btnTest_Click(ByVal sender As System.Object, _
ByVal e As System.EventArgs) Handles btnTest.Click
   MessageBox.Show(GetNet30Date(#1/1/2003#).ToString())
End Sub
Private Function GetNet30Date(Optional ByVal fromDate _
As Date = #1/1/1900#) As String
   If fromDate.Year = 1900 Then 'no date was passed in
      Return Now.Add(New TimeSpan(30, 0, 0, 0)).ToShortDateString()
   Else
      Return fromDate.Add(New TimeSpan(30, 0, 0, 0) _
      ).ToShortDateString()
   End If
End Function
```

Dim x as integer = 100
Call Function1(x)
Call Function2(x)
Function1(ByVal num as Integer)
num is a separate variable that also holds 100.
Function2(ByRef num as Integer)
Num refers directly to x and any change to num will change x.

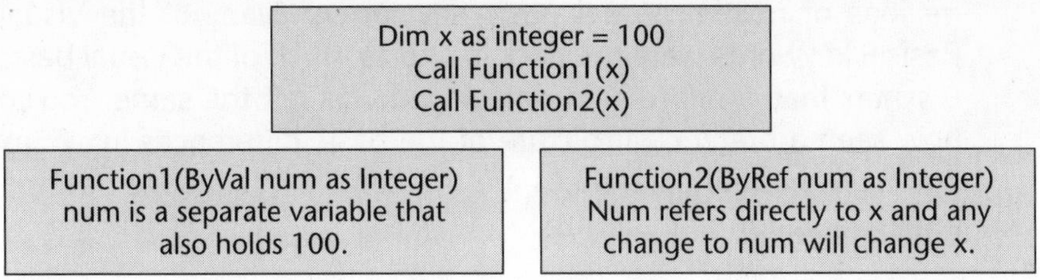

Figure 3.7 Parameters are passed by reference (ByRef) or by value (ByVal).

Classroom Q & A

Q: It looks like Visual Basic .NET has a lot of rules we didn't have in Visual Basic 6. Is there a list of things I can change in my Visual Basic 6 code to make code migrate easier?

A: Chapter 19, "Visual Basic 6 to Visual Basic .NET Migration," provides an exhaustive set of migration tips, tools, and techniques to help with that.

Q: You used the TimeSpan method in your function example but didn't provide any explanation. Could you describe what it's doing?

A: TimeSpan creates an object that represents a range of time. It has several overloads but, in general, has the format of TimeSpan (Days, Hours, Minutes, Seconds, Milliseconds). A TimeSpan object can be added to a DateTime to create a new date.

Q: Is there a time to use subs and a time to use functions?

A: All event handlers are subs by default. When I create my own procedures, I tend to use functions because almost all of my procedural code returns values. Some people use only functions, and return values just to indicate that the function executed successfully. The lone absolute is that only a function can return a value, so if that's what you need, it's the only alternative.

Q: I heard that a lot of the code in Visual Basic .NET was completely stripped away and things like the Select Case statement are much more limited than in Visual Basic 6. It doesn't seem like that is the case, so what were people referring to?

A: In the early stages of .NET development, Microsoft hacked up Visual Basic but underestimated the opposition provided by the millions of existing Visual Basic developers. Many of the Visual Basic 6 keywords were put back in and as much of the Visual Basic 6 syntax that could remain unchanged was left the same. You've now seen a pretty clear picture of the basic differences in syntax and how the real differences are the common language runtime implementation of that syntax.

Lab 3.1: Working with File and Directory Structures

This exercise uses many of the constructs from this chapter but uses them in such a way that even seasoned Visual Basic developers will find the resulting code useful. You'll work with various objects and methods for files and directories using the related common language runtime types.

Perform the following steps:

1. Start a new Visual Basic .NET Windows application.
2. Right-click the project name (not the solution name) in the Solution Explorer and select Properties.
3. Choose Common Properties, Build, Option Strict, On to set Option Strict for all modules, and click OK.
4. Add a Panel control to Form1.
5. Set the Dock property for Panel1 to Left.
6. Add a new Button control inside Panel1.
7. Change the Name property of the new Button control to btnGetFiles.
8. Change the Text property of btnGetFiles to Show Files.
9. Add a new TextBox control to Form1.
10. Change the Name property of the new TextBox to txtPath.
11. Change the Text property of txtPath to c:\winnt. If the winnt directory does not exist for your operating system, use c:\Windows.
12. Add two ListBox controls named lstPrimary and lstSecondary to Form1. Figure 3.8 shows the result of completing steps 1–12.
13. Add the following code to the btnGetFiles_Click event handler:

```
Dim DirInfo As New System.IO.DirectoryInfo("c:\winnt")
Dim Files() As System.IO.FileInfo
Dim File As System.IO.FileInfo
lstPrimary.Items.Clear()
'GetFiles returns an array of FileInfo objects:
```

```
Files = DirInfo.GetFiles()
'add only the files in the directory to lstPrimary:
For Each File In Files
   lstPrimary.Items.Add(File)
Next
```

14. Run the application and test the btnGetFiles. The lstPrimary ListBox should display all files in the folder specified in step 11.
15. Now create a button to be used to find files with a particular extension using the Extension property of the FileInfo object. Add a new Button control named btnFindFileType inside Panel1 and beneath btnGetFiles.
16. Change the Text property of btnFindFileType to Find Type.
17. Add the following code to the btnFindFileType_Click event handler:

```
Dim DirInfo As New System.IO.DirectoryInfo("c:\winnt")
Dim Files() As System.IO.FileInfo
Dim File As System.IO.FileInfo
Dim ext As String
lstPrimary.Items.Clear()
ext = InputBox("Enter extension to filter on: ", _
"Enter Extension", ".exe")
Files = DirInfo.GetFiles()
For Each File In Files
   If File.Extension = ext Then lstPrimary.Items.Add(File)
Next
lstSecondary.Items.Add(lstPrimary.Items.Count & _
" of " & Files.Length & " files matched that extension.")
```

18. Run the application and click the btnFindFileType button. After responding to the InputBox with a valid extension, the lstPrimary ListBox should display only files with that extension. Figure 3.9 shows the results of executing this code, using the default extension of .exe.

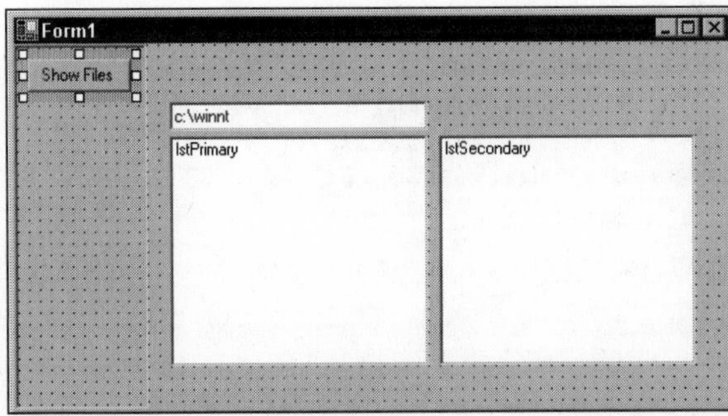

Figure 3.8 Your form should look like this after completing steps 1–12.

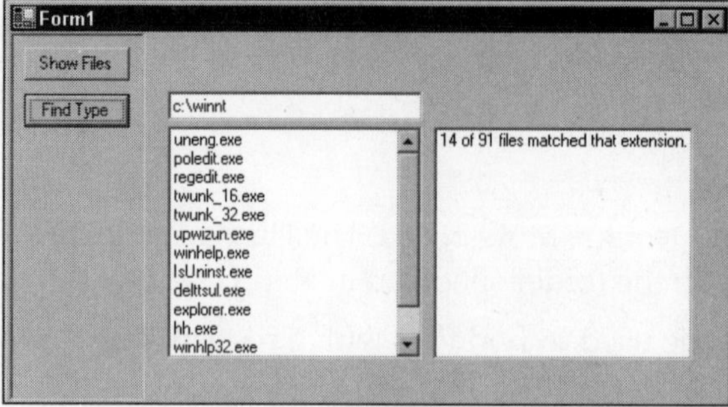

Figure 3.9 Only files matching the given extension are displayed after clicking the btnFindFileType button.

One wonderful feature of a list box is that it retains the types of the objects stored inside it. That is, once these FileInfo objects are stored in the list box, they're not relegated to simple strings that represent a filename. Using that knowledge, we can manipulate the elements of lstPrimary as FileInfo objects. With Option Strict turned on, we would find out that even though the items in the list box are FileInfo objects, they are temporarily cast as System.Object.

First, to prove that the elements in the lstPrimary list box are still FileInfo objects, we could use the following line of code in the lstPrimary_SelectIndexChanged event:

```
'This displays System.IO.FileInfo:
MessageBox.Show(lstPrimary.SelectedItem.GetType().ToString())
```

Next, to treat the elements in the list box as FileInfo objects, we use the CType() conversion function to cast them back to FileInfo objects.

19. Stop the application and add the following code for the lstPrimary_SelectedIndexChanged event handler:

```
Dim fi As System.IO.FileInfo
fi = CType(lstPrimary.SelectedItem, System.IO.FileInfo)
With lstSecondary.Items
    .Clear()
    .Add("Created: " & fi.CreationTime)
    .Add("Resides In: " & fi.DirectoryName)
    .Add("Last Accessed: " & fi.LastAccessTime)
    .Add("Last Modified: " & fi.LastWriteTime)
    .Add("Length: " & fi.Length)
    .Add(fi.Attributes)
End With
```

20. Run the application.
21. Click the btnFindFileType button.
22. Now, click one of the items inside the lstPrimary ListBox to see results, which are similar to Figure 3.10.

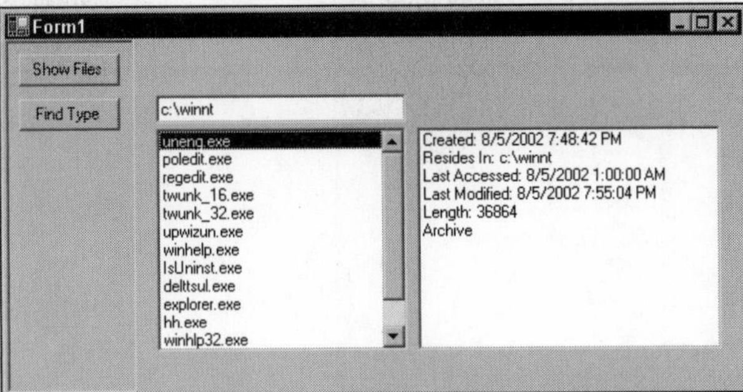

Figure 3.10 Clicking any item in lstPrimary causes the code in the lstPrimary_Selected-IndexChanged event handler to populate the lstSecondary ListBox with the attributes of the selected file.

23. Now we want a button that looks at the subdirectories in the specified directory; it uses the GetDirectories method of the DirectoryInfo object. Add a new button to Panel1.
24. Change the Name property for the new button to btnGetDirectories.
25. Change the Text property for btnGetDirectories to Directories.
26. The Click event handler for btnGetDirectories will use the GetDirectories method if the DirectoryInfo object GetDirectories returns an array of type System.IO.DirectoryInfo. To iterate through all directories in a specified folder and then through all the files in each directory, add the following code to the btnGetDirectories_Click event handler:

```
Dim DirInfo As New System.IO.DirectoryInfo("c:\winnt")
Dim Files() As System.IO.FileInfo
Dim Directories() As System.IO.DirectoryInfo
Directories = DirInfo.GetDirectories()
Dim Directory As System.IO.DirectoryInfo
Dim File As System.IO.FileInfo
lstPrimary.Items.Clear() : lstSecondary.Items.Clear()
For Each Directory In Directories
   lstSecondary.Items.Add(Directory.ToString & "\")
   Files = Directory.GetFiles()
   For Each File In Files
      lstSecondary.Items.Add("---" & File.ToString())
   Next
Next
```

27. Run the application again and test the btnGetDirectories button. You should see lstSecondary populated with directories and files as shown in Figure 3.11.

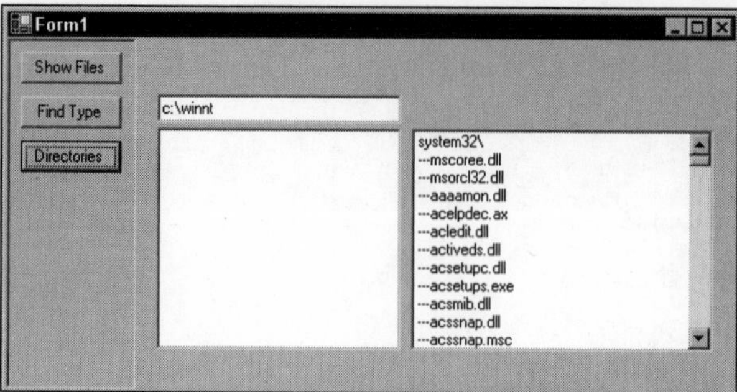

Figure 3.11 The Click event handler for btnGetDirectories uses a nested For Each loop to display all Directories in the current path, and the files contained in those directories.

Besides finding a good use for CType() and implementing a few control structures, you can see that For Each loops come in quite handy for iterating through hierarchical structures. Although we used ListBox controls to display data while we were experimenting with a new object model, the TreeView control is more appropriate for viewing hierarchical relationships like File and Directory structures.

Summary

We've covered a wide range of topics, some of which were not terribly new to Visual Basic programmers and some of which may seem rather foreign. I hope that by now you've begun to see certain patterns and are starting to expect and look for certain behaviors in objects you encounter. Please heed what I said about Option Strict: leave it on. Turning it off may seem to make life easier, but it will make learning .NET rather difficult. As you progress into building your own objects, the information you learned about the relationship between types is crucial in understanding your own objects.

Review Questions

1. How can we turn off the compilers ability to coerce types?
2. What is the largest numeric type?
3. What is the immediate base class for a System.Int32?
4. When would Equals() return True for two strings?
5. When would Equals() return True for two Integers?
6. What effect does the Insert method have on a string?
7. Assuming that Option Strict is on and that c is a Char data type, which of the following will work?
   a. c = "A"
   b. c = System.Convert.ToChar("A")
   c. c = 'A'
   d. c = ('A')
   e. c = "A"c
8. What is the generic type converter?
9. How can a function be exited prematurely?
10. Function return values must be specified with a Return statement in Visual Basic .NET. True or False?
11. What is wrong with the following function declaration?

```
Private Function MyFunction(Optional ByVal num As Integer) As String
End Function
```

Answers to Review Questions

1. The Option Strict On statement disables the compilers type coercion.
2. The largest numeric type is Decimal (System.Decimal).
3. The immediate base class for System.Int32 is System.ValueType.
4. When used on any reference type such as a string, the Equals method returns True only if both reference types refer to the same memory address.
5. When used on any value type such as an Integer, the Equals method returns True only if both values held by those types are equal.
6. None. The Insert method returns a new string that contains what was inserted. The original string would have to be set to that return value to affect any change.
7. **b.** and **e.** Without Option Strict, many conversions are simply performed by the compiler with a significant performance degradation when applied throughout an enterprise project. In this case, choices **a**, **c**, and **d** will produce illegal conversion attempt exceptions if Option Strict is on.
8. The CType statement acts as a generic type converter.
9. Functions can be exited prematurely using the Exit Function statement.
10. False. Return is one of two options for returning values from functions.
11. Optional parameters must be given default parameters.

CHAPTER

4

Debugging and Exception Handling

Debugging and exception handling are different topics, but related. This chapter uses debugging tools and techniques in Visual Basic .NET to locate application errors that can be avoided before an application is executing. Debugging is the art of finding and removing code that causes errors.

Exceptional conditions during execution are unavoidable; maybe the database you were connected to was shut down, maybe the records you were updating were deleted by another user, or maybe the network connection your application was dependent on was severed because the network cable was wrapped repeatedly around your swivel chair. The point is, things happen—things that are *exceptions* to the intended course of desirable execution. Exception handling isn't about avoiding these scenarios. It's about gracefully handling them without dumping a meaningless error number to a user and without being forced to shut down an application in the face of some unforeseen occurrence.

Debugging helps you locate the source of errors and exception handling helps you deal with the executions that you can't avoid.

Structured Exception Handling

Although Visual Basic has retained its On Error coding structures, the standard for error handling in .NET is using SEH. Where Visual Basic 6 programmers typically used the term *error*, Visual Basic .Net consistently uses the term *exception* to indicate an error condition. SEH in .NET guarantees that any piece of code written in .NET can create an exception that can be handled natively in any other .NET language. This is because the only errors that can be created in .NET are derivations of System.Exception.

Trying and Catching

Exception handling in .NET requires any code that could potentially cause an exception be wrapped in a Try...End Try block. If an exception occurs in a Try block, an object of type System.Exception is created and thrown to a Catch block, adjacent to the Try block. It gets more complicated, but let's see the basic structure first. In the following code, the SEH keywords are highlighted to outline the basic structure of an SEH block.

```
Try
   'Place code to test here.
Catch x As Exception 'All errors are System.Exception objects
   'Handle the exception here.
    'Or re-throw the exception using a Throw command
End Try
```

If a user tries to open a .doc file in a TIFF viewer utility, tries to shut down Excel while an application is still remotely automating it, or attempts to save a file to a drive that does not exist, some error will occur. Unhandled, these simple exceptions end applications in rather unpleasant ways. None of these situations is a showstopper, and they can be handled simply as long as we have an exception handler for each potential problem.

Consider a button and a text box. The button contains simple code to set the current form's BackColor property to the color entered in the text box. The code works properly until the user enters an invalid color or misinterprets what is expected. The following code would cause an exception and crash the current application if the contents of TextBox1 did not match a preordained .NET color:

```
Dim c As Color
c = Color.FromName(TextBox1.Text)
Me.BackColor = c
```

Assuming the user entered an acceptable color, all is well, but Figure 4.1 shows the results of entering an invalid value.

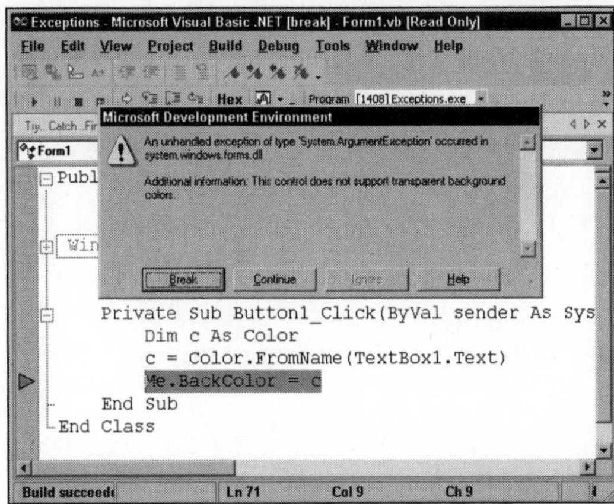

Figure 4.1 When an exception occurs in the development environment, you can click Break to enter Break mode, causing the offending line of code to be highlighted.

I could have written that code on one line, but I wanted to use separate lines to demonstrate that objects handle some exceptions internally. Notice in Figure 4.1 that the highlighted code is the assignment to the Form's BackColor property and not the assignment of the bogus color value to the Color object's FromName method. The FromName method apparently converted the bogus text to some usable value because the error message that was reported on the attempt to set the BackColor property was complaining about a transparent background color. Although it might obfuscate the true source of the exception, that code could be written more efficiently, as follows:

```
Me.BackColor = Color.FromName(TextBox1.Text)
```

Wrapping the offending code in a Try block allows you to catch and handle the exception caused by the illegal color assignment. Before you handle the exception, consider what you want from the user. Can the user help fix the problem? Do you handle the problem and move on? Do you throw up a message box and dump the application? You have to ask yourself questions like these before you handle an exception. In this case, it's easy—tell them it's an invalid color and return the user's focus to the TextBox, as shown in the following Visual Basic .NET code:

```
Try
   Me.BackColor = Color.FromName(TextBox1.Text)
Catch ex As Exception
   MessageBox.Show("Please try another color.", "Invalid Color", _
   MessageBoxButtons.OK, MessageBoxIcon.Exclamation)
   TextBox1.Select() 'sets focus and highlights contents
End Try
```

Here, variable ex is used to handle a generic Exception (actually, System .Exception). When the exception occurs, an exception object is created in memory and thrown to the Catch block. The variable ex in the Catch block then represents the exception object that was generated. In this solution there was no need to use methods on the Exception object because the code is simple enough that it can be handled by telling the user to try another color. Finally, the Select method was used to adjust the user's focus to what caused the problem. The Select method of a text box sets the focus to the text box and highlights the contents. Figure 4.2 shows the custom error message generated in the Catch block.

Finally

The Finally block appears between the last Catch block and before the End Try statement. Whether this is an exception and regardless of whether that exception is handled, the code in the Finally block will execute. The Finally block is useful when the surrounding code consumes resources or leaves things in an unfinished state. In those cases you can use the Finally block to close files, close database connections, and free up other resources before the current procedure ends.

The Exception Object

Sometimes, you might need more information about the exception to deal with it because the offending code has the possibility of producing many different exceptions. Just setting the connection string for a database connection object may fail because the server name is wrong, the database driver specified was missing or incorrect, or maybe there was a typo somewhere else in the string. All these would produce unique exception objects that would be handled differently. In Visual Basic .Net, the Exception object replaces the Err object used in Visual Basic 6 but has similar members. The members of the exception object are shown in Table 4.1.

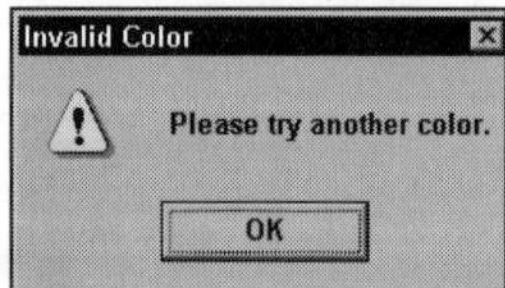

Figure 4.2 Custom error messages should be more informative than extreme if the problem is as simple as entering a new value.

Table 4.1 System.Exception Members

MEMBER	DESCRIPTION
Message	The error description. Similar to Err.Description in Visual Basic 6.
Source	The module where the error occurred. Similar to Err.Source.
GetBaseException	The first error if many occurred.
HelpLink	The Help File associated with this error. Similar to Err.HelpFile.
StackTrace	Provides a stack dump as a string. This string includes the source of the error right down to the line number if in debug mode.
Target Site	The actual method that threw the error.

In .NET, exceptions don't have error numbers. Exceptions are differentiated by the type of the exception and the Message value for that exception. For backward compatibility, Err.Number can be interrogated for an equivalent value.

Figure 4.3 shows the contents of various exception object properties and methods for the illegal color assignment error. In the figure you will notice that the TargetSite of the exception is not a method I wrote but rather an internal method for System.Windows.Forms.Control called set_BackColor.

Throwing Exceptions

The Throw command can be used to throw a new exception. When throwing an exception, you can create a handler for each exception type as well as a generic exception handler to handle any exception. The generic exception handler may do nothing more than rethrow the exception to the calling code or an outer Try block. The following code presents a rather nasty logic error inside an exception handler:

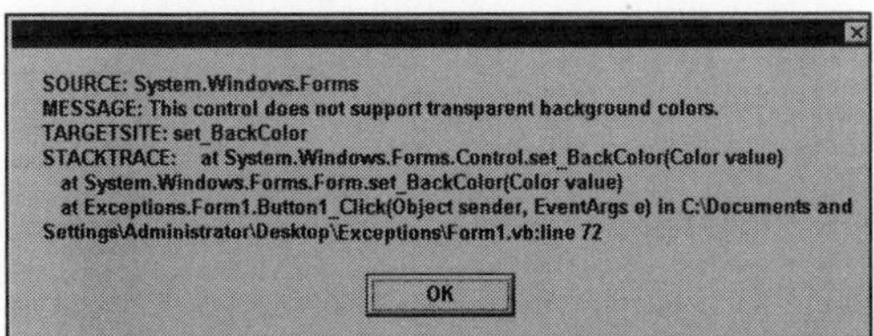

Figure 4.3 The exception object has several methods and properties that extend the functionality of the traditional Err object in Visual Basic.

```
Try
   '...
   Throw New System.DivideByZeroException() 'Creates and throws a new
error
Catch ex1 As Exception 'The error is mistakenly caught but not handled
here
   Select Case ex1.Message
      Case "The method or operation is not implemented."
         'handle System.NotImplementedException
      Case "Attempted to perform an unauthorized operation."
         'handle System.UnauthorizedAccessException
   End Select
Catch ex2 As System.DivideByZeroException 'this code is unreachable
   'This code in unreachable
End Try
```

In the preceding code, a DivideByZeroException is thrown and the first Catch statement encountered receives the exception because it's built to handle any exception. Once inside the Select Case statement, the first and second cases don't match and there is no Case Else clause, so execution jumps right to the End Try block, bypassing the exception handler that was specifically intended to handle System.DivideByZeroException.

If you're going to use a generic As Exception Catch block, place it last among the other Catch blocks to avoid silently ignoring an exception. Furthermore, any Select Case statement should always have a Case Else clause to ensure notification of exceptional cases.

Nested Try Blocks

Try blocks can be nested. When an inner Try block throws an exception from within a Catch block, the exception is thrown up to the outer Try block. The following code demonstrates an inner Try block rethrowing an exception to an outer Try block:

```
Private Sub btnNestedTryExample_Click(...) ...
   Dim s As Short '(System.Int16)
   Try
      Try
         s = System.Convert.ToInt16("100000") '1. Error: overflows s
      Catch ex1 As Exception '2. Exception initially thrown to here
         Throw New System.ArithmeticException() '3. rethrow exception
      End Try
   Catch ex As Exception '4. Exception finally caught here
      Dim msg As String
      msg += "Message: " & ex.Message & vbCrLf
```

```
        msg += "Occurred in: " & ex.TargetSite.Name & vbCrLf
        msg += "Stack Trace: " & ex.StackTrace & vbCrLf
        MessageBox.Show(msg)
    End Try
End Sub
```

From the results for the Nested Try Blocks example, shown in Figure 4.4, we can see that certain information is excellent for us as developers and testers but completely inappropriate for messages intended for users.

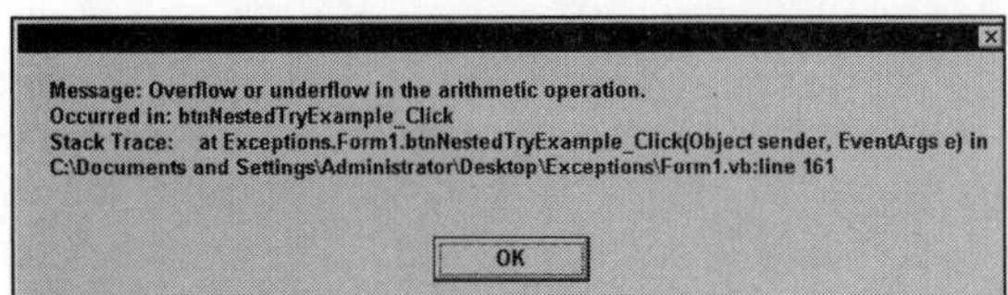

Figure 4.4 The StackTrace and TargetSite members of the exception object offer information that is valuable to developers and testers but may be confusing to users.

Classroom Q & A

Q: I noticed that StackTrace is telling me the line number where the error occurred. Is there an easy way to jump to line numbers?

A: Yes. You can select GoTo from the Edit menu, use Ctrl-G or turn on line numbers by selecting Tools, Options, Text Editor, Basic, Line Numbers Checkbox.

Q: After an exception is rethrown, is there a way of accessing the original exception object's properties?

A: Yes. In an outer exception, the local exception object's InnerException member represents the original exception object.

Q: I'm confused. I don't understand why the compiler wasn't smart enough to figure out that the conversion from 100000 to Int16 would overflow a short. Did you have Option Strict turned off?

A: Option Strict is always on in every code sample I've shown here. This brings up a difference between two of our conversion methods. If we use the CShort method to perform the conversion, it may or may not catch a conversion issue at compile time. If we use the System.Convert.ToInt16 method, we are assured that the conversion issue won't be caught at compile time. The following four examples illustrate that point fairly well:

```
Dim s as Short '(System.Int16)
s = CShort(1000 ^ 5) 'WON'T COMPILE because it's computed at design time
s = CShort("100000") 'Not caught at compile time
s = System.Convert.ToInt16(1000 ^ 5) 'Not caught by at compile time
s = System.Convert.ToInt16("100000") 'Not caught by at compile time
```

Throwing Exceptions to a Client

When a procedure throws an exception that is not handled locally, the exception is received by the calling code. In the following example, Button1_Click calls the SetColor method that causes and throws an exception back in the Button1_Click Event handler:

```
Private Sub Button1_Click(...) Handles Button1.Click
   Try
      SetColor(Color.FromName("Oringe")) '1. Pass in invalid color
   Catch ex2 As System.Exception '5. Exception finally handled here
      MsgBox("Error: " & ex2.Message & vbCrLf _
      & "Occurred in: " & ex2.TargetSite.Name)
   'Displays:
   '   Error: Invalid Color
   '   Occurred in SetColor
   End Try
End Sub
Private Sub SetColor(ByVal c As Color)
   Try
      Me.BackColor = c '2. Error occurs here
   Catch ex As Exception 'exception first caught here
      Throw New Exception("Invalid Color") '3. Exception rethrown here
   End Try
End Sub '4. Subroutine ends and is removed from the Call Stack
```

Custom Exceptions

All things in .NET are objects. Exceptions are reference objects that were created with a Class construct. Each specific exception is a class that inherits from System.Exception and locally redeclares what System.Exception.Message means for that object. All we have to do to create our own custom exceptions is create a class that inherits from System.Exception, redefine what the exception message is and throw our own exception when it's needed. This process is demonstrated in Lab 4.1, "Intralanguage Exception Handling."

Writing Errors to the Application Event Log

Selecting Start, Programs, Administrative Tools, Event Viewer opens the Event Viewer in Windows. This viewer displays information from three log files: Application, Security, and System. Errors produced from our applications should write error information to the Application log (if they log errors at all). The primary log object is System.Diagnostics.EventLog, which is created to target one of the log files. The following Visual Basic .NET code uses the EventLog object and logs an application error in the Application event log. This procedure represents a member within a custom exception class that is responsible for logging the custom exception:

```
Dim e As System.Diagnostics.EventLog
e = New System.Diagnostics.EventLog("Application")
e.Source = "Error Source Here"
e.WriteEntry("Error Message Here", _
   System.Diagnostics.EventLogEntryType.Error)
```

Lab 4.1: Intralanguage Exception Handling

This lab demonstrates the process of raising an exception in one .NET language and handling it in another. To accomplish this task, you'll get a first glimpse of a Class Library project in .NET. Class libraries represent a callable library of objects and are the primary focus of Chapter 6, "Building Class Libraries in .NET." By creating all exceptions as objects that inherit from System.Object, every module in every project in every .NET language can catch and handle an exception without regard for the language that threw the exception.

Perform the following steps:

1. Start a new C# Windows application.
2. Select File, Add Project, New Project, and add a new Visual Basic Class Library Project. Be careful because changing the language type will change any project type you selected back to Windows application.

   Your Solution Explorer window should look like Figure 4.5.
3. Double-click Class1.vb in the Solution Explorer to open the Code Editor window for Class1.
4. Modify Class1 as follows:

```
Public Class MyObjectType
    Public Sub MyMethod()
        Throw New System.InvalidOperationException()
    End Sub
End Class
```

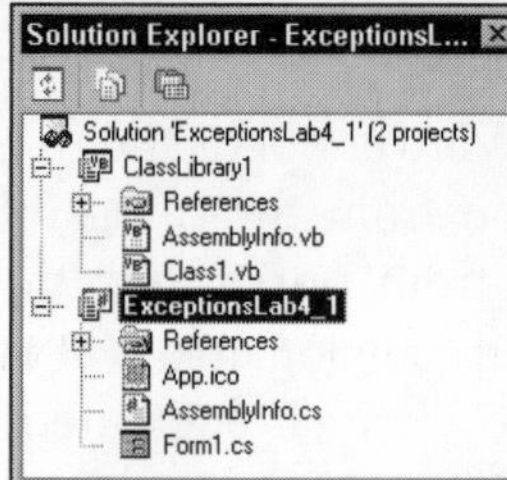

Figure 4.5 Projects written in different languages can reside in the same solution in .NET.

By creating your own class, you are creating a type of object that can be created in memory. Your object will have a single, publicly callable method named MyMethod.

5. Select Build Solution from the Build menu so that your application files are created.

Previously, project files were created for you when you ran your application. A Class Library represents a .DLL type of application, which is not executed like an .EXE. DLLs are loaded into the memory address of a client at runtime.

6. Double-click Form1.cs in the Solution Explorer window to enter the Designer view for Form1 in your C# Windows application.
7. Add a reference to the Visual Basic Class Library. Select Project, Add Reference, and Projects tab; double-click ClassLibrary1 in the Add Reference window; and click OK. Figure 4.6 shows what the Add Reference window should look like prior to clicking OK.

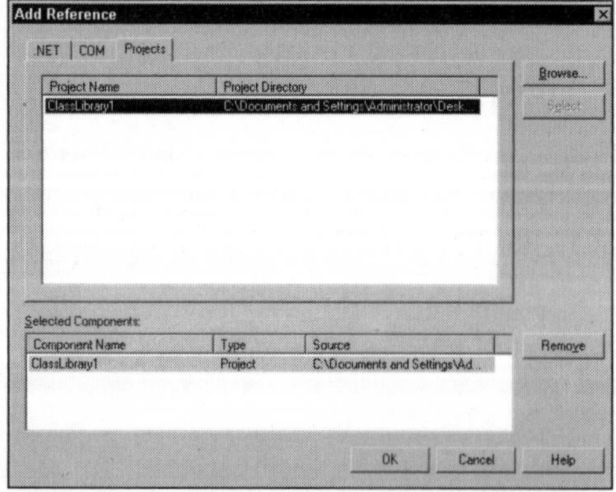

Figure 4.6 Adding a reference to a class library allows a client to create and use objects in that library at runtime.

8. Add a button to Form1 in your C# Windows application.

9. Double-click Button1 to Open the C# Code Editor window and enter the Button1_Click event handler.

   Before you write the following code, we should discuss a few language rules for C#. It uses curly braces around all language constructs (as Begin and End), ends every line with a semicolon, uses lowercase try and catch as keywords, and is always case sensitive.

10. Add the following code for the Button1_Click event handler:

```
private void button1_Click(object sender, System.EventArgs e)
{
   'Create an instance of our very first object:
   ClassLibrary1.MyObjectType myobj = new
ClassLibrary1.MyObjectType();
   try
   {
      myobj.MyMethod(); 'Call our Visual Basic .Net method
   }
   catch (Exception E)  'The Visual Basic Method throws the
                         exception here
   {
      MessageBox.Show(E.Message + ", " + E.Source); 'Handled
                                                     natively
   }
      myobj = null;
}
```

11. Run the application and test the code by clicking Button1 at runtime.

    That's pretty impressive, considering that in Visual Studio 6 there were so many ways to produce errors just in the different versions of C++ (MFC, ATL, STL, and so on) much code was written to return function values instead of raising errors to avoid causing disparate clients to crash.

12. Stop the application.

13. Modify the file containing Class1 to support a new custom exception and throw that new exception to the client using the following code:

```
Public Class MyException
   Inherits System.ApplicationException
   Private m_Source As String
   Public Sub New(ByVal Message As String)
      MyBase.New(Message)
      Me.m_Source = "ClassLibrary1"
   End Sub
```

```
End Class
Public Class MyObjectType
   Public Sub MyMethod()
      Throw New MyException("Unhandled Error in MyMethod")
   End Sub
End Class
```

14. Run the application again to test the new exception object.

This lab demonstrated that for the most part .NET languages are different only in syntactical ways. Beneath their syntax and keywords, they use the same types, objects, and interfaces. The custom exception handler uses a few features that we'll discuss in Chapter 6, "Building Class Libraries in .NET," and Chapter 7, "Extending Visual Basic .NET Classes." It was included here for completeness.

Common Exceptions and the Exceptions Window

Besides the generic exception base class System.Exception, several predefined exceptions exist in the System namespace. These and all other addressable exceptions in .NET are listed in the Exceptions window.

For all exceptions, the default behavior can be changed within Visual Studio .NET. To change the default exception behavior, select Exceptions from the Debug menu to open the Exceptions window. This window provides three options for handling exceptions. Table 4.2 describes the options provided by the Exception Options Window for configuring the default behaviors caused when exceptions occur.

Table 4.2 Exception Window Options

OPTION	DESCRIPTION
Break Into The Debugger	This setting causes the application to enter Break mode immediately on encountering this exception to allow the programmer to manually deal with the exception.
Continue	Execution continues when the exception is encountered.
Use Parent Setting	Every specific exception is subordinate to some parent exception node. When this option is selected, the exception will cause whatever behavior was specified in the parent node.

To change the default behavior for a custom exception, select one of the high-level nodes in the Exceptions window, click Add, enter the name of a custom exception you have created in your application, and set the desired behavior. In Lab 4.1, setting Break Into The Debugger for the exception would act as if there was no error in the client code and give you the familiar Debug/Continue screen in Visual Basic .NET, allowing you to break in the class instead of the client. The benefit of this is that when the exception breaks in the client as it does in Lab 4.1, your object is no longer in memory, and debugging the source of the error is impossible in Break mode.

Debugging Visual Basic .NET Applications

Errors come in three basic varieties. There are syntax errors that Visual Basic .NET is more than happy to tell you about, logical errors that compile and execute properly but just don't do what we want, and runtime errors that, if unhandled, end the application. *Debugging* is the process of locating and fixing avoidable errors in your code. With the capability to simultaneously debug an entire multitier, multilanguage application, without having to compile anything, without using more than one tool, and while using a single solution file, Visual Studio .NET is the most powerful debugging environment around.

Break Mode

Break mode a mode where an application is no longer executing, but all objects and memory used by the application stay loaded in memory. By using this freeze-frame view of an application, Debug mode allows you to follow execution paths and watch variable values as they change.

Entering Break mode

Break mode can be entered in a number of ways, including:

- Execution encounters a Stop statement.
- The Retry response is given following a failed assertion (Debug.Assert).
- The Debug button is clicked when an unhandled error occurs.
- A breakpoint is encountered.
- The Ctrl-Break command is issued.
- A command is entered in the Command window.

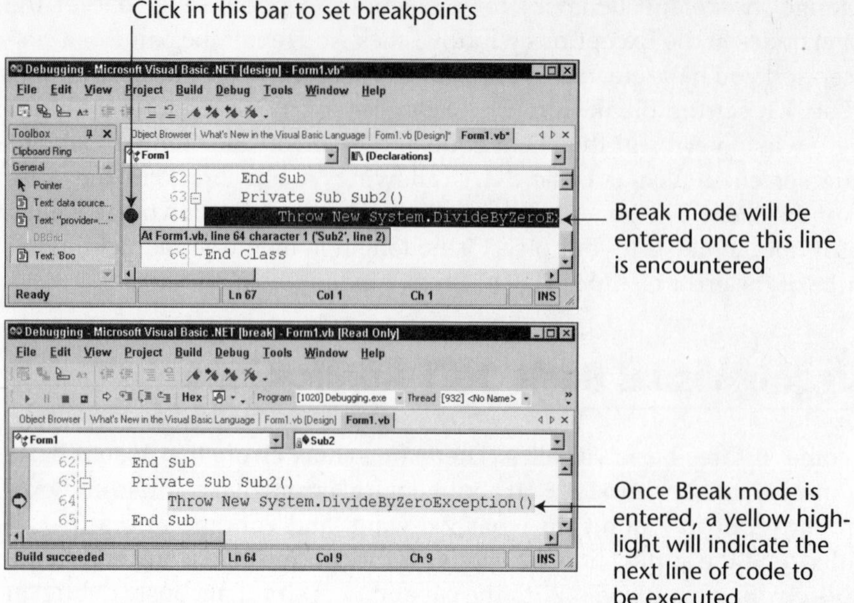

Figure 4.7 When a breakpoint is encountered, the application will cease execution and enter Break mode at the breakpoint. When in Break mode, a yellow highlight indicates the next line of code to be executed.

Setting Breakpoints

Setting a breakpoint on a line of code causes the application to enter Break mode when that line of code is encountered. A breakpoint can be set by selecting New Breakpoint from the Debug menu, by pressing Ctrl-B, or by Clicking in the gray, vertical bar in the left of the Code Editor window as shown in Figure 4.7.

The Call Stack

The Call Stack represents those procedures that are still loaded into memory. If Button1_click calls Sub1, which calls Sub2, which has a breakpoint, the contents of the Call Stack when that breakpoint is encountered will include all three procedures. After a procedure is loaded onto the Call Stack, it cannot be removed (terminated) until all procedures on the Call stack, loaded after that procedure, have terminated. For example:

```
Private Sub Button1_Click(ByVal sender As System.Object, _
ByVal e As System.EventArgs) Handles Button1.Click
    Sub1() '1. Calls Sub1
End Sub
Private Sub Sub1()
    Sub2() '2. Calls Sub2. Sub2 removed from Call Stack on return
    Sub3() '4. Calls Sub3
End Sub
Private Sub Sub2()
    '3. Calls no other subs so it hits End Sub and terminates.
End Sub
Private Sub Sub3()
    '4. Hits breakpoint on following line and enters break mode
    Throw New System.ApplicationException()
End Sub
```

Figure 4.8 shows the contents of the Call Stack when the breakpoint in Sub23 is encountered.

The Call Stack can be viewed only in Break mode. To view the Call Stack in Break mode, select Debug, Windows, Call Stack. Given the state of the Call Stack in Figure 4.8, Button1_Click cannot terminate until Sub1 terminates and Sub1 cannot terminate until Sub3 terminates.

The terms used for placing things on, and removing things from, a stack data structure are *Push* (on) and *Pop* (off) operations.

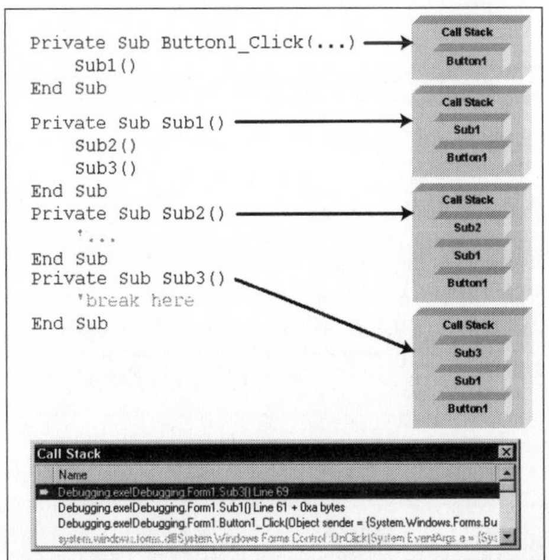

Figure 4.8 The Call Stack shows the procedures that are still resident in memory that led to the execution of the current method where the breakpoint was encountered.

The Locals Window

While in Break mode, the Locals window can be used to view the contents of all objects in the current scope of execution. For a form, this includes the entire Me object (Me is the current form or class instance) and all variables declared at the Form class level. Variables, including the properties of objects, can be viewed or modified in the Locals window.

The Command Window

The Command window, which was called the Immediate window in Visual Basic 6, has Immediate and Command modes. Immediate mode can be used to execute commands and statements, evaluate expressions, and display values of variables while in Debug mode, and it allows you to directly modify the value of most variables.

Immediate mode also lets you enter commands to the development while in Debug mode to allow for simultaneous debugging and interaction with the Visual Studio IDE. Commands in Immediate mode are prefaced with the > symbol. Table 4.3 lists useful commands that are in the Immediate window. Command mode automatically uses the char as a prompt, so for entering commands such as ?Me.Text (to print a form property), you need to switch to Immediate mode by issuing the immediate command. Virtually everything that can be done in the IDE can be accomplished with a command in the Immediate window.

Table 4.3 Command Window Commands

COMMAND	DESCRIPTION
>close	Stops the debugger and closes the current file.
>cls	Clears the contents of the Immediate window.
>Debug.Print *somevalue*	Prints information to the Output window. This works just like Debug.Print in Visual Basic 6. Normally in Visual Basic .NET, we programmatically use Debug .Write or Debug.WriteLine, from the System.Diagnostics namespace.
>Debug.Breakpoints	Opens the Breakpoints window and displays all breakpoints.
>Debug.CallStack	Opens the Call Stack window.
>Debug.Exception	Opens the Exceptions window.
>Debug.StopDebugging	Ends the current debugging session.
>Debug.ListCallStack	Displays the contents of all primary system registers.

Table 4.3 *(continued)*

COMMAND	DESCRIPTION
>Edit.Find "Sub1"	Searches for "Sub1" starting at the beginning of the current module.
>registers	Displays the contents of all primary system registers.
>shell notepad.exe	Shell can be used to launch applications from the Immediate window, in this case, Notepad.exe.
View.ObjectBrowser	Opens the Object Browser window in Visual Studio .Net.
>alias	Temporarily enters Command mode.
>cmd	Switches to Command mode.
immed	Switches back to Immediate mode from Command mode.
?Me.Text	A question mark (?), followed by a statement, causes that statement to be evaluated. The evaluated value is displayed directly to the Immediate window.

The Command window can be used to do much more than this list indicates, including recording and running macros, editing and maneuvering through code, displaying and modifying memory contents, and even navigating to your favorite publisher's Web site: >View.ShowWebBrowser http://msdn.wiley.com /ext.

Stepping Through Code

Stepping is the process, available only in Break mode, that allows you to move through code, executing a single line at a time. As each line is executed, the contents of changing variables can be viewed and process flow determined. Stepping is often the single most valuable tool in Debug mode to determine exactly what is happening while code is executing. Starting an application by pressing F11 enters Break mode on the first line of code encountered, allowing the programmer to step through code, one line at a time by subsequently pressing F11. When a subroutine call is encountered and you do not want to step through the lines of code in that subroutine, Shift-F11 can be used to step over (equivalent to Debug, Step Over) the subroutine and resume Break mode with the line of code following that procedure.

To run an application and only enter Break mode inside a particular method, you would place a breakpoint inside the target method and start the application normally by pressing F5.

The Watch Window

The Watch window is similar to the Locals window in that it allows you to view variables and object properties, but the Watch window also allows you to watch multiple values change as each line of code is executed in Debug mode. Pressing Shift-F9 in the Command window opens the QuickWatch window. The Watch window is demonstrated in Lab 4.2.

Running Without the Debugger

When debugging an application in .NET, the Debugger (debugger.exe) attaches to our processes and enables all our debugging support, such as breakpoints. To run an application without debugger support, select Debug, Start Without Debugging to run the application as if the application's .exe file was double-clicked.

Lab 4.2: Exploring Debugging Tools in Visual Studio

This lab demonstrates some of the things you can do while in debug mode, such as viewing the Call stack, using the Immediate window, using the Locals window, and adding watches.

Perform the following steps:

1. Start a new Visual Basic .NET Windows application.
2. Add a ListBox and a Button control to Form1.
3. Select the list box and press F4 to open the Properties window for ListBox1.
4. In the Properties window, click the ellipsis (...) button inside the Items property for ListBox1 to display the String Collection Editor.
5. Enter data into the String Collection Editor as shown in Figure 4.9 and click OK.

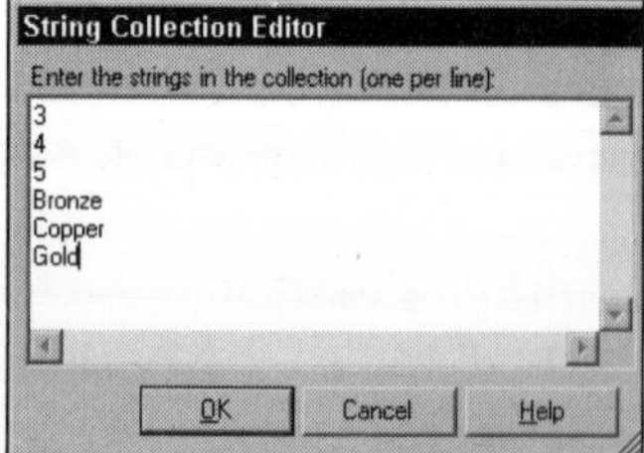

Figure 4.9 The String Collection Editor is used to populate the Items collection for the various list-related controls.

The code in step 9 uses some flawed logic to attempt to remove an item from the list box control. As you progress, you will use various debugging tools and techniques to help find and resolve the errors.

6. Change the Sorted property for ListBox1 to True. The contents of the list box should appear as sorted even at Design time.
7. Change the Text property for Button1 to Test.
8. Open the Code Editor window to the Button1_Click event handler.
9. Add the following code to the Button1_Click event handler:

```
Dim i As Integer
For i = 0 To ListBox1.Items.Count -1
   If ListBox1.Items(i).ToString = "Copper" Then
      ListBox1.Items.RemoveAt(i)
   End If
Next
```

   This code appears to remove all items containing the word *Copper*, but when the button is tested, it crashes inside the For loop.

10. Run the application and test the button. The application should have thrown a System.ArgumentOutOfRangeException.

    You only iterated from 0 to Items.Count –1 to be sure you didn't go past the end of the list box, but you still have an error saying you exceeded array bounds.

11. Stop the application.
12. Set a breakpoint on the first line of the For loop (the line actually containing the word *For*). Click in the gray vertical bar as shown in Figure 4.7 to set the breakpoint.
13. Run the application by pressing F5 and click Button1 to enter Break mode at your breakpoint.
14. On the line where the application entered Break mode, highlight just the variable *i* and press Shift-F9 to open the QuickWatch window and click Add Watch.
15. Add another watch to display the data at the current position in the list box using the following expression:

```
ListBox.Items(i).ToString()
```

16. Add another watch to display the count for the items in the list box, using the following expression:

```
ListBox1.Items.Count
```

    Inside the Watch window, you can see when i is 0, Items(i) is 3, and Items.Count is 6, although these values may be displayed in hexadecimal.

17. Let's force Visual Basic .NET to display things in decimal format instead of hexadecimal. Select Debug, Windows, Immediate to open the Command window.

18. If you don't already have a > prompt in the Command window, enter the command >cmd to enter Command mode.

19. Enter the command Debug.SetRadix 10 to change the display of values to decimal (base 10) from hexadecimal (base 16). The Watch window values should now be displayed in decimal, as shown in Figure 4.10.

20. While still in Break mode, repeatedly press F11 to step through the application one line at a time, while watching the values in the Watch window change, until you reach a point where the application encounters the exception.

    At some point (when Copper was removed) the value of Count for ListBox.Items changed from 6 to 5. When the application crashes, a value of 5 is displayed for *i* as well. The problem is that *i* is a representation of the attempted index into a list box that now has only five items that are indexed from 0 to 4, making an index value of 5 exceed the upper bounds of the list box.

    Some people describe the choice of using a For loop as limited to those situations where the number of iterations is fixed with known, stationary upper and lower bounds. The For loop is faster than the While loops because it doesn't recheck the control variables, but it's this lack of rechecking the ListBox.Items.Count that causes the iteration to go right past it. If we rethink our logic, we can still use a For loop even though it might not seem to be a good match.

21. Use the following code to fix the problem:

```
Dim i As Integer
For i = ListBox1.Items.Count - 1 To 0 Step -1  'Step in reverse
   If ListBox1.Items(i).ToString = "Copper" Then
      ListBox1.Items.RemoveAt(i)
   End If
Next
```

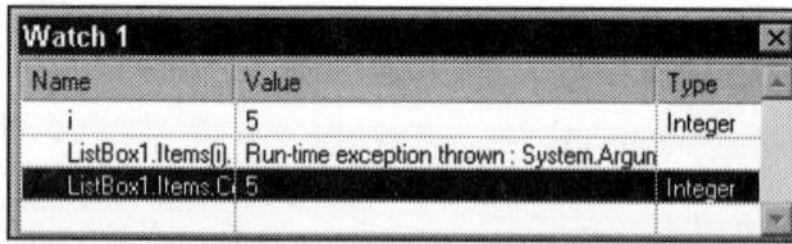

Figure 4.10 The Watch window allows you to view the values of simple variables or complex expressions as you step through an application.

Because 0 is stationary and Items.Count changes, we make the stationary control condition the target by stepping in reverse and all is well. It is quite common for developers, new to .NET, to mistakenly use the Remove method instead of the RemoveAt method. This mistake could have really complicated this example, because two logic errors in the same small block of code can be confounding.

To complete this lab you used several debugging features inside the Visual Studio .NET IDE, including breakpoints, the Watch window, and the Command window. In addition, you saw some alternative thinking regarding the use of a For loop for implementation. Are we done with that code? Well, it should be pointed out that the code you used could have been replaced with the following line:

```
ListBox.Items.Remove("Copper")
```

Printing Debugging Information

The System.Diagnostics.Debug and System.Diagnostics.Trace are the two primary objects used for debugging in .NET. Debug.WriteLine and Trace.WriteLine can be used to send information to the Output window. Debug statements are moved from source code when code is compiled as a release build. Trace statements remain in release builds. Displaying information to the Output window during code execution can be quite informative for debugging and testing. Table 4.4 describes the methods common to both the Trace and debug objects for displaying information to the Output window.

The following code overuses the methods for illustration sake and produces the output shown in Figure 4.11:

```
Dim i As Integer = 0
Dim j As Integer = 0
For i = 0 To 2
   Debug.Write("Entered Outer loop ")
   Debug.WriteIf(i = 0 And j = 0, "for the first time ")
   Debug.WriteLine("I is: " & i)
   For j = 0 To 2
      Debug.Write("   Entered Inner loop ")
      Debug.WriteIf(i = 0 And j = 0, "for the first time ")
      Debug.WriteLine("J is: " & j)
      Debug.WriteIf(i = 2 And j = 2, "It's over!")
   Next
Next
```

Table 4.4 Trace and Debug Methods

METHOD	DESCRIPTION
Write	Send data with no carriage return
WriteLine	Send data, followed by a carriage return
WriteIf	Send data only if the specified condition is met
WriteLineIf	Send data and a carriage return only if the condition is met

To enable tracing in Visual Basic you add this statement: #Const TRACE = True.

Using Asserts

Assert statements are useful to ensure that certain conditions hold true in our code. As with any Debug and Trace statements, Debug.Assert statements are removed when code is compiled for Release and Trace. Assert statements are not. In either case, it's never a good idea to use code inside Assert statements that changes values. The following simplified Assert statement displays a message and enters Break mode if x < 0:

```
Assert(x >=0, "x is < 0")
```

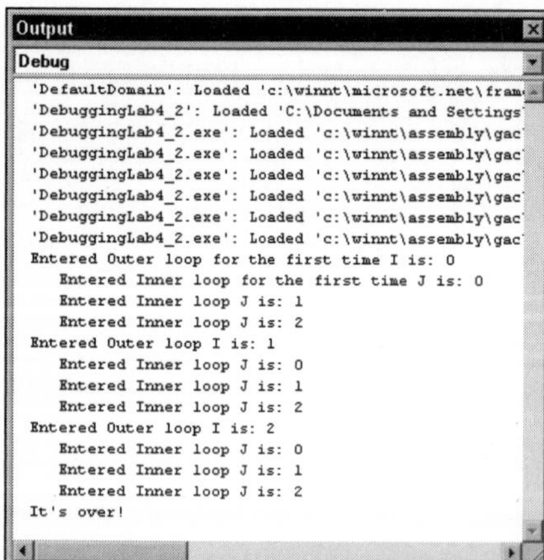

Figure 4.11 The Debug.Write statements are similar to the Debug.Print statements from Visual Basic 6 and display information to the Output window.

When we assert a particular value, it's usually because we want to know when a variable has exceeded some expected control limit or is just not in a range we were expecting, and we want to enter Break mode and find out what happened. The following code uses the string strSQL to issue a SQL statement to a database. If that database query doesn't return any records, the number of rows (records) in table zero of the resulting DataSet will be zero.

```
Private Sub Tester(ByVal strSQL As String, ByVal strCon As String)
    Dim con As New System.Data.OleDb.OleDbConnection()
    Dim odba As New System.Data.OleDb.OleDbDataAdapter(Sqlstring, con)
    Dim ds As New DataSet()
    con.ConnectionString = strCon
    con.Open()
    odba.Fill(ds)
    Debug.Assert(ds.Tables(0).Rows.Count > 0, "No rows returned")
End Sub
```

The preceding code uses the same objects used in Chapter 2, "Building Visual Basic .NET Windows Applications," when you populated a DataGrid control with data. By creating the function with no hard-coded connection or command information (both are passed to this procedure), this function can be called from the Command window or another testing tool to repeatedly send different connection strings and commands to test the results. The Tester procedure enters Break mode when no rows are returned. When an Assert fails, you are presented with options of Abort, Retry, or Ignore. Strangely, selecting Retry enters Break mode. Clicking Ignore in an Assert message silently continues the application, and clicking Abort terminates the application. The results of Assert failure are shown in Figure 4.12.

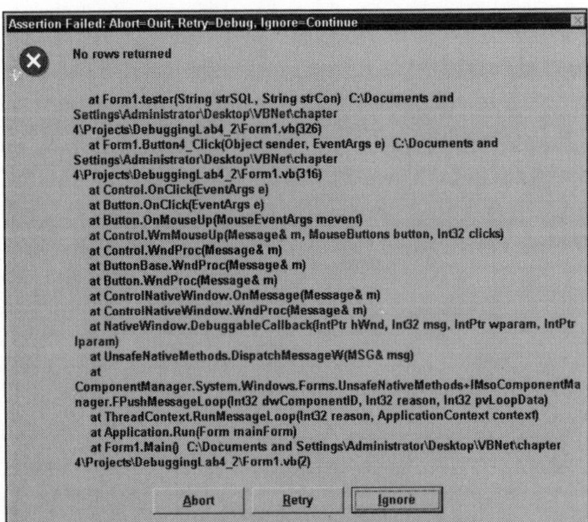

Figure 4.12 Assert statements fail when the assert condition evaluates to False. To enter Break mode for a Debug.Assert, click Retry.

Debug and Release Modes

Your application is separated into Debug and Release builds. Debug builds are filled with information known as debugging symbols, which are maintained and used by the debugger. Symbolic information for .NET applications is maintained in .pdb files and is used only when an application is running in Debug mode. The Debug version of the code is also not optimized as the Build (Release) version is.

The symbolic information maintained in these .pdb files is what allows the debugger to hit a breakpoint, modify variable content at runtime from debug windows, step through applications, and evaluate variables and expressions while debugging. A Debug build represents source code that is still being debugged, whereas a Release build represents a source tree that is being tested for production.

Project Debugging Properties Page

The Debugging Properties page allows you to change your configuration mode between Debug and Release, configure remote debugging, and enable SQL Server debugging. To open the Debugging Property page, select the project to debug in the Solution Explorer, select Properties from the Project menu, and select the Debugging node beneath the Configuration Properties node. The Debugging properties page is shown in Figure 4.13.

To switch between debug and release builds, click the Configuration Manager button in the Debugging properties page and select the appropriate option from Active Solution Configuration drop-down menu.

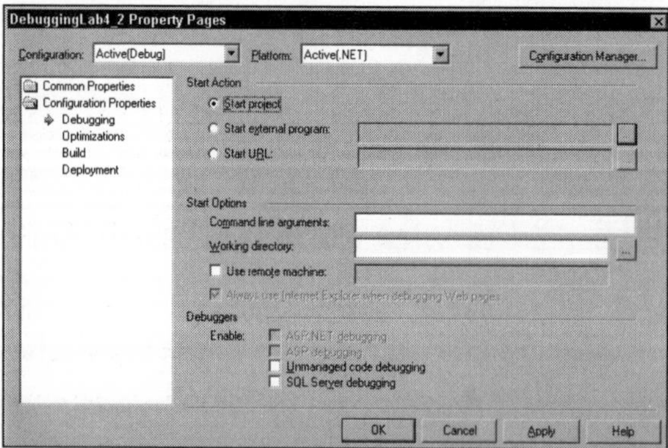

Figure 4.13 The Debugging Properties page allows you to change your configuration mode between Debug and Release, configure remote debugging, and enable SQL Server debugging.

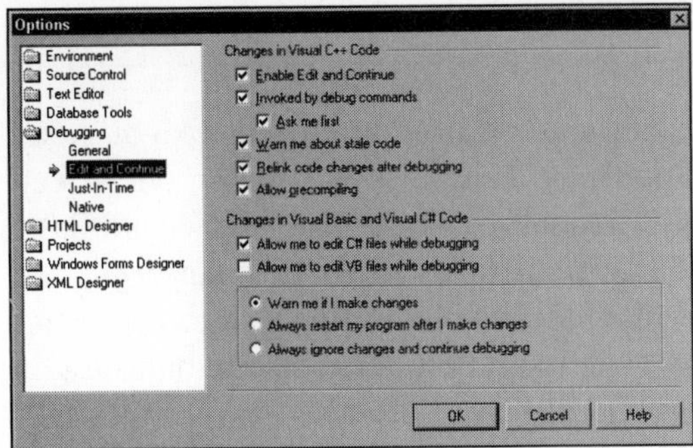

Figure 4.14 The Debugging Options page allows you to configure the debugging behavior for your projects.

Edit and Continue, Debugging Options Page

Even more debugging configuration options exist in Visual Basic .NET and can be accessed by selecting Tools, Options, Debugging folder. Figure 4.14 depicts the Debugging Options page in Visual Basic .NET. You may have noticed that the capability to modify code while in Break mode and simply continue executing from Visual Basic 6 doesn't seem to happen in Visual Basic .NET. The option on the Debugging Options page seems to offer promise, but even when the Allow Me To Edit VB Files While Debugging check box is selected, any change to the code requires that the application exit Break mode, recompile, and reexecute before those changes may be realized.

Classroom Q & A

Q: You keep using objects but never call their Dispose methods, close their resources, or free up anything in memory. Shouldn't we be doing that?

A: Yes, definitely. In Chapter 6, "Building Class Libraries in .NET," we won't be writing code without attention to resource management.

Q: I don't have Visual Studio .NET installed, but I have the .NET SDK. Can I still debug .NET code?

A: There are two utilities that are quite good for debugging .NET code. The Microsoft common language runtime debugger (dbgclr.exe) provides an entire IDE for developing .NET applications outside Visual Studio. The Runtime Debugger (cordgb.exe) uses the common language runtime debug API to debug .NET applications from the command line.

Summary

As we explore increasingly complex topics, the fundamentals of debugging and exception handling will be a valuable skill set. In this chapter, we looked at how SEH works in Visual Basic .NET from the perspective of a Visual Basic .NET Windows application. ASP.NET applications, XML Web services, and class libraries will present more complex issues related to these topics. After having used so many features related to debugging and exception handling in .NET, you're ready for Chapter 5, "Advanced .NET Windows Applications," and more complete solutions.

Review Questions

1. What clause in a Try block is guaranteed to execute, regardless of exception state?
2. What is the base class for exceptions in .NET?
3. What namespaces contain the generic exception classes?
4. What method for a text box immediately gives it the focus?
5. What property for an exception represents the actual procedure that threw the exception?
6. What is on the Call Stack when the following code enters Break mode:

```
Private Sub btnTest_Click(...)
   sub1()
End Sub
Sub sub1()
   sub2()
   Try
      sub3()
   Catch e As Exception
      Stop
   End Try
End Sub
Sub sub2()
   'do nothing
End Sub
Sub sub3()
   Throw New System.ApplicationException()
End Sub
```

7. What type of interoperability code is required to throw and catch exceptions between .NET languages?
8. What Command window command can change the default numeric display in the Output window to hexadecimal?
9. What line of code must be added to a module to enable Tracing?
10. Which of the following commands opens the QuickWatch window?
    a. Shift-F11
    b. Shift-F9
    c. Ctrl-F5
    d. F9
11. What does the following line of code do?

```
Debug.Assert(false)
```

Answers to Review Questions

1. The Finally clause in a Try block is guaranteed to execute, regardless of exception state.
2. The base class for exceptions in .NET is System.Exception.
3. Most of the generic exceptions are located in the System namespace.
4. The Select method for a text box immediately gives it the focus.
5. The TargetSite property for an exception represents the actual procedure that threw the exception. This property is a .NET Reflection object that represents a method at runtime.
6. Looking at the numbered comments added to the following code, follow the contents of the stack up to the point when the breakpoint is encountered. The answer is btnTest_Click, sub1.

```
Private Sub btnTest_Click(...) '1. stack = btnTest_Click
   sub1()
End Sub
Sub sub1() '2. stack = btnTest_Click, sub1
   sub2()
   Try
      sub3() '4. stack = btnTest_Click, sub1
   Catch e As Exception '6. stack = btnTest_Click, sub1
      Stop 'Breakpoint entered here
   End Try
End Sub
Sub sub2() '3. stack = btnTest_click,sub1,sub2
   'do nothing
End Sub
Sub sub3() '5. stack = btnTest_Click, sub1
   Throw New System.ApplicationException()
End Sub
```

7. No operability is required for intralanguage communication in .NET.
8. Debug.SetRadix 16 can change the default numeric display in the Output window to hexadecimal.
9. To enable tracing in Visual Basic .NET, use the following line of code in the beginning of a module:

```
#const Trace = True
```

10. **b.** Shift-F9 can be used to open the QuickWatch window.
11. The command, Debug.Assert(false), enters Break mode unconditionally.

Middle-Tier Development in .NET

CHAPTER

5

Advanced .NET Windows Applications

We've talked about controls, forms, types, and a multitude of the *pieces* of .NET applications, and now we'll look at building applications using design models such as MDI and multipanel applications that incorporate these pieces. Focused on the more advanced features related to .NET Windows applications, this chapter uses an ever-extending set of the common language runtime libraries as you build broader, more complete applications. The graphics library in .NET, known as GDI+ (Graphics Device Interface), is tightly integrated with many other .NET libraries. Even the simplest graphics constructs such as Point and Size are provided via this library. This chapter demonstrates how objects in the GDI+ library, System.Drawing, can be integrated into Windows applications.

Building MDI Applications in .NET

Excel and Word and are two popular examples of MDI applications. In an MDI application, there is a primary container form that holds some sort of child form. In Excel, the child forms are spreadsheets, and in Word, they are documents. From your experience, you may have noticed a few characteristics of these applications, such as closing the parent ends the application; the parent is always maximized; and the menus, toolbars, toolbox, and status bars are all affixed to the parent form.

Another major point of these applications is that the parent form has an expected interface. The expected interface of an MDI application always has an option in the File menu for adding the appropriate child form type and a Window menu with which to arrange the child forms for display. Without hesitation, any Windows user could tell you that the last menu item in a File menu is Exit. For this reason, deviating from this standard interface has a detrimental affect on your application's usability.

Building an MDI Parent and Child

The process of building an MDI application begins with the parent form. To build an MDI parent and child in Visual Basic .NET, we perform the following steps:

1. Add a new form and set its IsMdiContainer property to True, which causes the form to change its appearance to that of an obvious container. This type of form is often referred to as the container form, the parent form, or the MDI parent form.
2. Set the container form's WindowState property to Maximized. All MDI parent environments such as Excel, Word, or Visual Studio are initially maximized. Although this is not a critical step, it follows expected design standards.
3. Make the parent form the startup form if it isn't already. Child forms cannot be loaded unless the parent form is loaded. Attempting to load a child form when no parent is available causes the parent form to load.
4. Add a new child form by selecting Add Windows Form from the Project menu. This new form will not be a child until its MDIParent property is set to a valid MDI parent.
5. Add some code to cause the child form to be bound to and displayed in the parent container environment.

Building an MDI Child Form

A child form in an MDI application is merely a normal form whose MDIParent property has been set to a valid MDI parent form. Normally, the child items are added at runtime by the user via the File menu or by the initialization of the Parent form. In Excel, the initialization process creates a new Workbook (child form), which contains three Worksheet objects. The following code creates and displays four MDI child forms in the parent, Form1, as illustrated in Figure 5.1:

```
Private Sub Form1_Load(...) Handles MyBase.Load
    Dim myform As Form2
    Dim i As Integer
    For i = 1 To 4
        myform = New Form2() 'create a new Form2 in memory
        myform.Text = "Document" & i 'change each form's Title
        myform.MdiParent = Me 'associate child to parent
        myform.Show() 'display the new child form
    Next
End Sub
```

Several things happen when an MDI child is associated with an MDI parent form. Internally, the following things occur when this association is made in .NET:

- The child form can no longer be displayed without the parent.
- The child's IsMDIChild property is set to True.
- The parent form's ActiveMDIChild property is set to the new child form.
- The child form is added to the parent's MDIChildren collection.
- The child form's MdiParent property is set to the MDI parent form.
- The child's lifetime is made dependent upon the lifetime of the parent form. The exception to this is that the child form can ignore the parent's attempt to close by issuing e.Cancel=True in the Closing event handler.

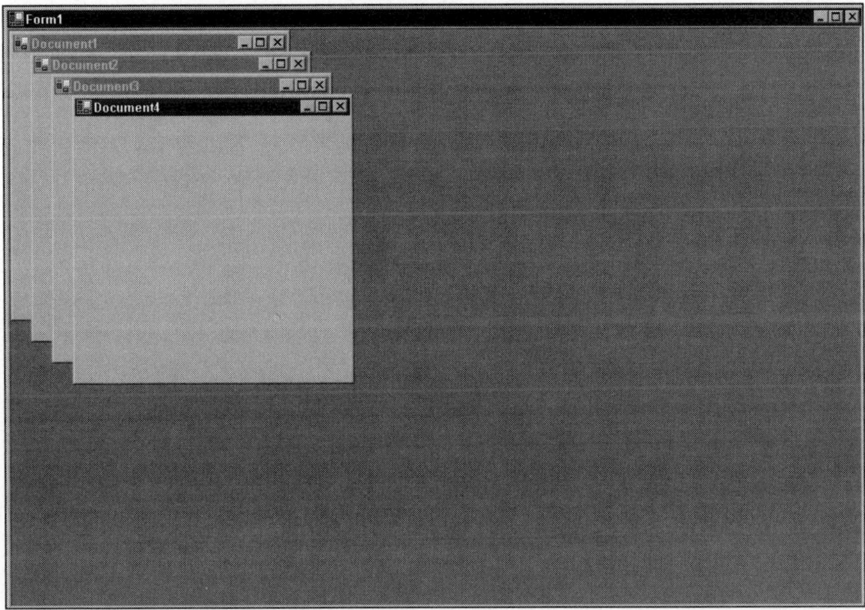

Figure 5.1 MDI child forms are displayed inside the client space of the MDI parent.

IsMdiChild is read-only at runtime.

Adding Menus

Menus are added in Visual Basic .NET in a much more natural way than in Visual Basic 6. To add menus to a form in Visual Basic .NET, you drag a MainMenu control to the form. In MDI applications, menus are added to the parent form. Instead of using the traditional Menu Editor, in Visual Basic .NET, we type the menus directly to the form, as shown in Figure 5.2.

An MDI form typically displays a list of all open MDI child forms at the bottom of the Window menu. You can add this list in Visual Basic .NET by selecting the Window menu item at design time and changing the MdiList property to True in the Properties window.

When menus are added, each menu item becomes a member of the parent form and is addressable as ParentName.MenuItemName.

Using ImageList controls

ImageList controls are used to hold collections of images and are used to support other controls. For instance, the Toolbar control has an ImageList property that points to an ImageList control as a source for images for the buttons in the Toolbar. ImageList controls store images in an Images collection. When supporting Toolbar controls with images, the ImageSize property of the ImageList control should be set to 16x16. To add an image to an ImageList, click the ellipsis (...) button next to the Images property in the Properties window, and use the Add button in the Image Collection Editor.

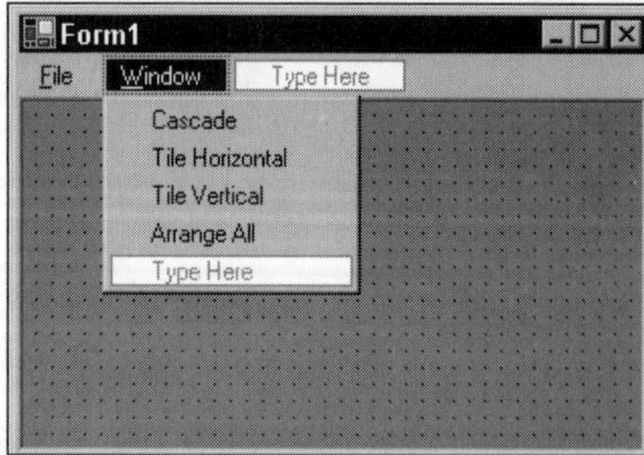

Figure 5.2 Menus are typed directly onto MDI parent forms using MainMenu controls from the Visual Basic .NET Toolbox.

The Images property for a ListBox control is a collection that supports the IList, ICollection, and IEnumerable interfaces. Because it supports the IList interface, we expect Add and Remove methods. Furthermore, because it supports the IEnumerable interface, we know we can use a For Each loop to iterate through it. Support for the ICollection interface means that we can easily transfer its contents to other collections effortlessly as shown in the following code:

```
Dim Pic As System.Drawing.Image
For Each Pic In ImageList1.Images 'iterate through images
   ListBox1.Items.Add(Pic) 'Copy each Picture to a ListBox
Next
```

We can copy the entire Images collection to any other ICollection with the AddRange method:

```
Dim a As New System.Collections.ArrayList() 'Create Arraylist
'Since the Images collection is a Class that implements the
'ICollection interface, the AddRange method can be used to
'copy the entire contents of that collection:
a.AddRange(ImageList1.Images)
```

Adding Toolbars

The Toolbar control in .NET maintains its buttons in a Buttons collection. Buttons are added via the Buttons collection in the Properties window. To assign pictures to buttons on a toolbar, the toolbar's ImageList property must be set to the name of a valid ImageList control on the MDI parent form. Images placed on Toolbar buttons should be iconic 16x16 pixels and use symbols that are as universal as possible to indicate the underlying functionality.

The following code programmatically creates a new ImageList, populates it with an image at Images index zero, creates a new ToolBarButton on the existing ToolBar1, and assigns the image from the ImageList to the new ToolBarButton:

```
Private Sub Button1_Click(sender As System.Object, _
e As System.EventArgs) Handles Button1.Click
   Dim ImageList1 As New ImageList()
   'Following line should use full path.
ImageList1.Images.Add(Image.FromFile("CLSDFOLD.ICO"))
   ToolBar1.ImageList = ImageList1
   Dim tbb As New ToolBarButton()
   tbb.ImageIndex = 0
   Me.ToolBar1.Buttons.Add(tbb)
End Sub
```

A toolbar can be used to create what is commonly referred to as a Toolbox. If you think about it, toolbars and Toolboxes aren't really that different, and most applications don't differentiate between the two. Programming environments like Visual Basic have always had both. Toolbars in applications are not always anchored at the top of the parent object, and they can be floating or hidden. When a toolbar is docked to the left side of the MDI parent and is wider than a single row, some environments such as Visual Basic .NET refer to it as a Toolbox. To perform those changes to a Toolbox in .NET, we just change the toolbar's Dock property to Left and the AutoSize property to False and widen the control. We end up with a Toolbox as in Figure 5.3.

Working with StatusBar Controls

StatusBar controls are traditionally used to display the current time, the Caps Lock status, open applications, the date, or just about anything you want. The Start button in Windows is the first panel in a StatusBar that has a wide range of uses. Browsers typically have a StatusBar at the bottom that displays the status related to the current page being downloaded.

StatusBar controls in .NET are similar to their older counterparts only in appearance and the fact that there is a Panels collection. There are only two styles of panels in StatusBar controls in .NET: Text, which is system-drawn and limited to text in a predetermined font, and OwnerDraw, which can contain pretty much anything we want it to contain, in any font.

StatusBar panels can be added at design time or at runtime. To add panels at runtime for an existing StatusBar, SB1, we could use the following code:

```
SB1.Panels.Add("panel0")
SB1.Panels(0).Style = StatusBarPanelStyle.OwnerDraw
SB1.Panels(0).BorderStyle = StatusBarPanelBorderStyle.Sunken
SB1.Panels(0).AutoSize = StatusBarPanelAutoSize.Contents
SB1.Panels(0).ToolTipText = "Displays File Transfer Status"
SB1.ShowPanels = True
```

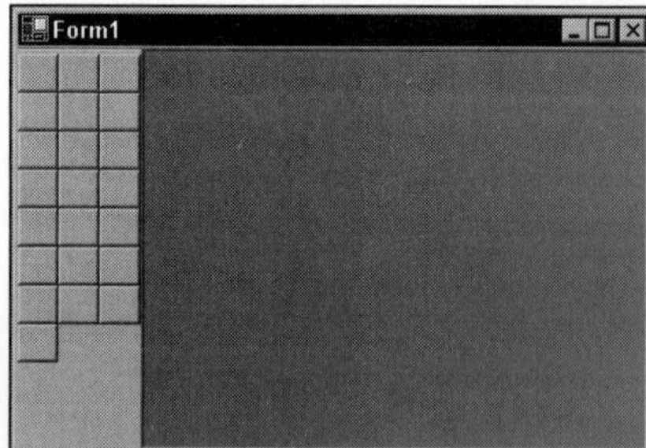

Figure 5.3 A Toolbox in .NET is created with a Toolbar control.

Table 5.1 Customization Properties

STATUSBARPANELSTYLE	DESCRIPTION
Text	Single font, no graphics, system drawn.
OwnerDrawn	User drawn, with ability to graphically enhance.
STATUSBARPANELBORDERSTYLE	**DESCRIPTION**
Sunken	Causes the panel to appear Inset.
Raised	Causes the panel to be raised like the Start button.
None	In the panel, no border will be displayed.
STATUSBARPANELAUTOSIZE	**DESCRIPTION**
Contents	Panel size determined by its contents.
Spring	Panel size determined by sharing the available space with other panels with AutoSize-Spring.
None	Panel size does not change.

If we don't want the panel to be created in memory until we are ready to add the control, we could modify our code as follows:

```
Dim panel0 As New StatusBarPanel() 'create a new panel object
panel0.BorderStyle = StatusBarPanelBorderStyle.Sunken
panel0.AutoSize = StatusBarPanelAutoSize.Contents
StatusBar1.Panels.Add(panel0)
'cause newly added panels to be displayed:
StatusBar1.ShowPanels = True 'If the following code preceded
'the previous ShowPanels statement, it would get cleared:
StatusBar1.Panels(0).Text = "Transfer Status"
```

Table 5.1 describes the possible settings for toolbar panel customization properties.

Lab 5.1: Building an MDI Application

This lab guides you through the process of building an MDI application with menus, multiple template-based documents, and a status bar. We create a simple image viewer that uses PictureBox controls and is populated from System.Drawing.Image objects.

For this lab, leave Option Strict Off. This allows various methods of coding to be used, one of which uses late binding, a feature not allowed by Option Strict On. The lab gradually corrects related issues.

Perform the following steps:

1. Start a new Visual Basic .NET Windows application. In my examples, the solution name is MDILab5_1.
2. Change the Title of Form1 by setting its Text property to Image Viewer.
3. Make Form1 an MDI parent form by setting its IsMdiContainer property to True.
4. Change the name of Form1 to frmIVMain.
5. You may have noticed that the filename appearing in the Solution Explorer doesn't agree with the new name property for frmIVMain. Right-click on Form1 in the Solution Explorer and rename it frmIV-Main.vb.
6. Cause frmIVMain to appear maximized at startup by changing its WindowState property to Maximized.
7. Add a MainMenu control to frmIVMain.
8. Add menus according to Table 5.2 (the & char causes the character immediately following it to be a hot key for that menu).

Table 5.2 Add These Menus

MENU TEXT	MENU NAME
&File	mnuFile
&New	mnuFileNew
E&xit	mnuFileExit
&Insert	mnuInsert
&Image	mnuInsertImage
&Window	mnuWindow
&Cascade	mnuWindowCascade
Tile &Horizontal	mnuWindowH
Tile &Vertical	mnuWindowTV
Arrange &All	mnuWindowArrange

9. You should now have three top-level menus, File, Insert, and Window. Click on the E&xit menu item and press the Insert key to force a new menu position between &File and E&xit.
10. In the new menu position, use a single hyphen for the Text property. This causes separator bar to be created before the E&xit menu.
11. Add a new child form by selecting Add Windows Form from the Project menu in Visual Basic .NET.
12. Change the new form's Name property to frmViewer.
13. Change the filename for frmViewer to frmViewer.vb.
14. Back in the MDI parent, frmIVMain, create a variable to keep track of the next available document number by adding the following code directly beneath the Inherits statement in frmIVMain:

```
Dim NextForm As Integer = 1
```

15. In frmIVMain, double-click on the mnuFileNew menu item to open its Click event handler, and add the following code:

```
Dim myform As New frmViewer()
myform.Text = "Viewer" & NextForm 'modify the new form's Title
myform.MdiParent = Me 'Associate child with parent
NextForm += 1 'Increment the value of NextForm
myform.Show() 'Display the new child form
```

16. The startup object for the application still refers to Form1. Change the startup object to frmIVMain by right-clicking on the project name in the Solution Explorer, selecting Properties and using the Startup Object drop-down ListBox to select frmIVMain.
17. Double-click on mnuWindowCascade to open its Click event handler.
18. Change the name of the Click event handler to ArrangeWindows_Click and add the appropriate handlers for all four menu items under the Window menu as shown in the following code:

```
Private Sub ArrangeWindows_Click( _
ByVal sender As System.Object, ByVal e As System.EventArgs) _
Handles mnuWindowCascade.Click, mnuWindowArrange.Click, _
mnuWindowTH.Click, mnuWindowTV.Click
End Sub
```

19. Now that we've created a single handler to be shared by the four menu items under our Window menu, add the following code to ArrangeCascade_Click to enable these menu items:

```
'This won't work with Option Strict On
'Arrange the open MDI children using the menu index:
Me.LayoutMdi(sender.index) 'sender is the menu selected
```

The LayoutMdi method takes four values, numbered 0 to 3. The menu items were given index values that match the corresponding LayoutMdi functionality indicated by the menu names. Because mnuWindowsCascade has an index of 0 and the LayoutMdi value for Cascade is 0, the code doesn't require a Select Case statement. When multiple events use the same handler, the sender object that is passed to the event handler represents the object that really received the event. In the preceding code, sender.index is the index of the menu item.

20. Select the Window menu item and change its MdiList property to True. This causes all open children to be listed at the bottom of the Window menu at runtime.
21. Run the application. Add three forms using File, New menu, and change the MDI layout to Tile Vertical using Window, Tile Vertical. Your application should look something like Figure 5.4.
22. Stop the application.
23. Modify the mnuFileExit menu item to end the application by adding the following code to its Click event handler:

```
Application.Exit()
```

24. Add a PictureBox control to frmViewer and set its Anchor property to Top, Bottom, Left, Right. Set its BorderStyle to Fixed3D.
25. Drag the edges of the PictureBox control to fill the frmViewer's client area. Once the PictureBox is maximized in this way, the Anchor property maintains the PictureBox's borders as the form is resized.

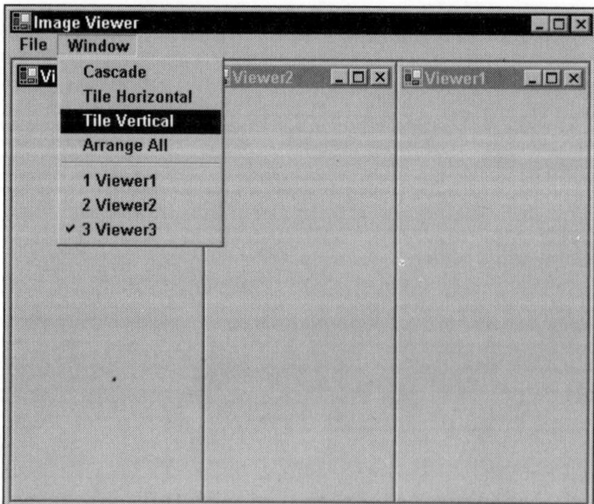

Figure 5.4 MDI child forms displayed after setting LayoutMdi to Tile Vertical view.

26. Set the Modifiers property for the PictureBox to Public so that we can set its Image property from the parent form.

27. Back in the MDI parent, frmIVMain, add an OpenFileDialog control to frmViewer.

28. Add the following code to the mnuInsertImage_Click event handler to enable the user to locate an image for loading into the PictureBox control:

```
Private Sub MnuInsertImage_click(...) ...
    OpenFileDialog1.Filter = _
    "*.gif;*.bmp;*.ico|*.gif;*.bmp;*.ico"
    'set the default extension:
    OpenFileDialog1.DefaultExt = "*.bmp"
     'Use c:\winnt as the default directory:
    OpenFileDialog1.InitialDirectory = "c:\winnt"
     OpenFileDialog1.Title = "Locate Image"
    'Display the Open File dialog:
    OpenFileDialog1.ShowDialog()
    'Exit this procedure if the user cancels:
    If OpenFileDialog1.FileName = "" Then Exit Sub
     Dim o As Object
    Try
       For Each o In Me.MdiChildren 'find the active viewer
          If o.Text = Me.ActiveMdiChild.Text Then
             o.picturebox1.image = _
             Image.FromFile(OpenFileDialog1.FileName)
             'needed later
             o.picturebox1.tag = OpenFileDialog1.FileName
          End If
       Next
    Catch Ex As Exception
       MsgBox(Ex.Message, MsgBoxStyle.OKOnly, _
       "Invalid Selection")
    End Try
  End Sub
```

The OpenFileDialog box protects you from errors such as an invalid filename, and we already took care of the Filename="" issue, but a Try block is necessary in case the user selects a file that is not a valid source type for the PictureBox. Filenames as objects have an Extension property that could be checked prior to the assignment to avoid the exception altogether.

29. If the winnt directory does not exist or does not contain any graphic files, change the InitialDirectory property to point to a folder that does.

30. Test the application by running it and clicking File, New, and then clicking Insert, Image. After you locate an image and close the OpenFileDialog box, the active child form should display an image.

31. Stop the application.
32. Insert Image should be something that happens as we bring up a new viewer window, but we also want the separate functionality so that we can change the image after the initial form load. To cause the initial loading of a new frmViewer to load an image, add the following line as the *last* line of code in the mnuFileNew menu on frmIVMain:

```
Me.mnuInsertImage_Click(sender, e)
```

33. Add a StatusBar control for frmIVMain.
34. Change the StatusBar's Modifiers property to Public.
35. Change the StatusBar's ShowPanels property to True. Leaving this property set to False causes our changes to the status bars not to be displayed.
36. Using the Panels collection property for StatusBar1, add a panel and set the new panel's AutoSize property to Contents.
37. To display the path of the file chosen when inserting an image, add the following line of code to the bottom of the mnuInsertImage_Click event handler in frmIVMain:

```
'Display the selected file in a StatusBar panel:
StatusBar1.Panels(0).Text = OpenFileDialog1.FileName
```

38. If you ran the application now, you would notice that the StatusBar representation of the file path isn't correct if the user switches between open viewers. We've already provided for that when we stored the filename in the PictureBox's Tag property. We'll use that Tag property to fix the problem. Enter the Code Editor window for frmViewer.
39. There are two drop-down list boxes at the top of the Code Editor window. Select Overrides from the left drop-down list box, select OnGotFocus from the right drop-down list box, and create the following event handler. *Warning:* This step causes an intentional error.

```
Me.ParentForm.statusbar1.panels(0).text() = Me.PictureBox1.Tag
```

It sure seems like the code in step 39 should work, but with or without Option Strict On, it doesn't see StatusBar1 as a valid member of Me.ParentForm. If you look in the Output window at the error message related to the attempted code, it indicates that me.ParentForm is an object of type Form, not an object of type frmIVMain. Well, they're both correct, but they won't be until we cast the ParentForm object as an frmIVMain that we'll be able to access the StatusBar1 control on that form.

40. The following demonstrates the correct code for the assignment of the filename to the StatusBar in the parent form and satisfies all conversion requirements for Option Strict On:

```
Protected Overrides Sub OnGotFocus(ByVal e As System.EventArgs)
CType(Me.ParentForm, frmIVMain).StatusBar1.Panels(0).Text =
   _ CType(Me.PictureBox1.Tag, String)
End Sub
```

Figure 5.5 shows what the application should look like when tested at this point. These are pictures taken from my office in Pleasanton, California.

41. To test what you've learned, I'd like you to ignore the next step for now and attempt to fix the code in mnuInsertImage to replace the For loop and use CType to resolve a call to frmViewer's PictureBox properties. When you have solved the problem or want to see one possible solution, go to the next step.

42. To fix the mnuInsertImage code so that it doesn't use late binding (late binding is slower at runtime and cannot be syntax-checked at design time), modify mnuInsertImage as follows:

```
Private Sub mnuInsertImage_Click(ByVal sender As System.Object,
  _ ByVal e As System.EventArgs) Handles mnuInsertImage.Click
        OpenFileDialog1.Filter = _
        "*.gif;*.bmp;*.ico|*.gif;*.bmp;*.ico"
        OpenFileDialog1.DefaultExt = _
        "*.bmp" 'set the default extension
        OpenFileDialog1.InitialDirectory = _
        "c:\winnt" 'look here on startup
        OpenFileDialog1.Title = "Locate Image"
        OpenFileDialog1.ShowDialog() 'Display Open File dialog
        If OpenFileDialog1.FileName = "" Then Exit Sub
        Try
            CType(Me.ActiveMdiChild, frmViewer). _
            PictureBox1.Image = _
            Image.FromFile(OpenFileDialog1.FileName)
            CType(Me.ActiveMdiChild, frmViewer). _
            PictureBox1.Tag = OpenFileDialog1.FileName
        Catch Ex As Exception
            MsgBox(Ex.Message, MsgBoxStyle.OKOnly, _
            "Invalid Selection")
        End Try
        StatusBar1.Panels(0).Text = OpenFileDialog1.FileName
    End Sub
```

In the process of building an MDI application, you experienced several important aspects of application design in Visual Basic .NET. The use of CType to resolve ambiguous references to objects in other forms combined with Public Modifiers setting for those objects will be part of every application you create in .NET. By leaving Option Strict Off, we were able to experiment with code that compiles and seems to do the job, but it was certainly not the most efficient code. The fix for such inefficient code, albeit different from Visual Basic 6, seems to solve quite a lot of problems in Visual Basic .NET. If we can possibly cast an object to the expected type in our code, we should do so instead of letting the compiler perform type coercion at runtime. This is referred to as early binding and allows for syntax checking at design time and faster execution at runtime. Some implementations of late binding are not necessarily bad. For example, the ArrangeWindows_Click event handler provides implementation with a single line of code to handle four menu options by using late binding on the sender object.

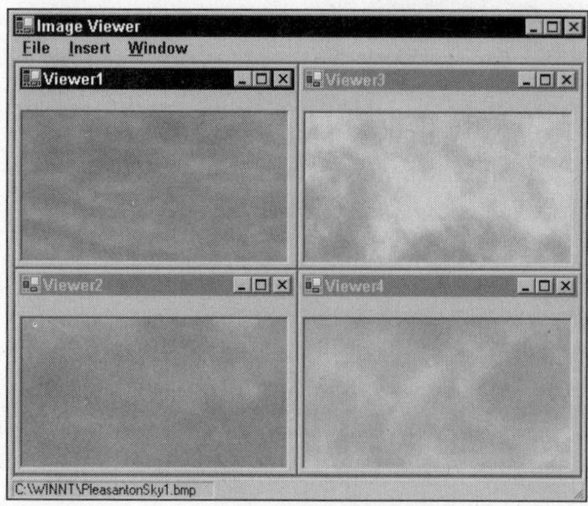

Figure 5.5 Image Viewer application test results following step 40.

Classroom Q & A

Q: Do menu items still have the ability to be checked and disabled?
A: Yes. Actually, they use the same properties (Checked and Enabled) that menus in Visual Basic 6 use.

Q: In Lab 5.1, shouldn't we move the myform.Show() statement beneath the call mnuInsertImage so that the frmViewer doesn't appear until it has a valid image?
A: That would seem to hold with our expectations of how image viewer-type applications should act, but in this case it would cause an error. Because our mnuInsertImage_Click code relies on the

ActiveMDIChild property, the fact that a form cannot become the ActiveMDIChild until it is visible would prevent that design choice. We could modify the way mnuInsertImage works to make that happen, though.

Q: Couldn't we use myform.Activate() prior to calling mnuInsert-Image_Click() and then call myform.Show after the call?

A: No. That method doesn't do much for a form that isn't displayed. We can hide MDI children in .NET, unlike Visual Basic 6, but hidden forms can't receive the focus, which is required to be set to the ActiveMDIChild.

Q: What does CType do?

A: CType is a type casting mechanism that forces objects of a given type to be treated as another type. For instance, in an array of objects that is populated with strings, we can't just index into the array and manipulate the contents of one index as if it were a String. In that case, it is said that the Strings were cast as System .Object to be placed into the array and must be cast back to System.String before they can be used as strings.

Building Multipane .NET Applications

Every explorer window you open in Windows is an example of a multipanel application. These applications are typically used to organize, display, and manipulate hierarchical sets of objects such as XML nodes or file/folder structures. Figure 5.6 uses a standard explorer window to highlight the relationship between the components of the explorer window and the .NET controls we use to create such an interface in .NET. Multipaneled forms use a combination of ListView, TreeView, and Splitter controls. ListView and TreeView controls are typically placed in Panel controls that are separated by a Splitter, as demonstrated in Lab 5.2.

The ListView Control

The most common example of ListView controls is the file explorer window used throughout Windows operating systems. ListView controls can display items as a single item list, as a detailed list, or as large or small icons. If you open a new explorer window by clicking Start, Run and typing Explorer in the Run box, you see a window similar to Figure 5.6.

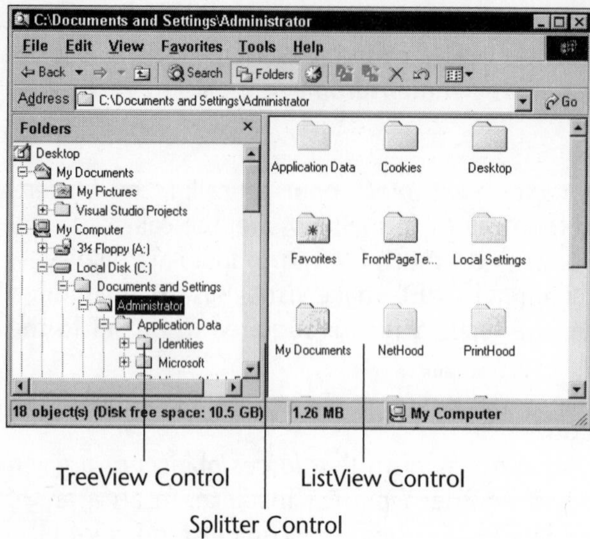

Figure 5.6 Microsoft Windows uses a combination of TreeView, Splitter, and ListView controls for Explorer windows.

ListView Control Collections

The ListView control implements an ICollection interface in its member, Items. Items is actually an example of a ListViewItem collection, which is a class that implements the ICollection, IList, and IEnumerable interfaces. As such, the Items collection has the expected members Add, Remove, and AddRange for populating and depopulating the displayed items.

Adding Items to a ListView Control

Adding items to a ListView control's first column is pretty straightforward, but adding items to subsequent columns might seem strange. This control is more complex than a simple list and contains multiple collections that other, simpler controls do not. The following list describes these collections and their purpose:

Items. Refers to elements in the ListView control. These elements are objects of type ListViewItem.

Columns. Used to refer to individual columns. Columns can be added to a ListView control by using Columns.Add and can be viewed as long as the View property for the ListBox control is set to Details.

SubItems. A ListView control is essentially a collection of ListViewItems, and each ListViewItem is a collection containing data that will be displayed on a single row but spanning multiple columns. The SubItems collection of a ListViewItem is used to add data to the subsequent columns following the first column in a ListView control.

To add new items to a ListView control, we create a ListViewItem, add the data for each appropriate column, and then add the ListViewItem to the ListView control as shown in the following code:

```
Dim MyListViewItem As New ListViewItem(file.Name)
MyListViewItem.SubItems.Add(file.Extension)
MyListViewItem.SubItems.Add(file.Length)
ListView1.Items.Add(MyListViewItem)
```

To display data for more than the first column, we must set the View property for the ListView control to Details and add columns to the ListView control to support the subitems of ListViewItem objects added to the ListView control.

Figure 5.7 is an example of a detailed-view list box and is the result of executing the following Visual Basic .NET code:

```
Private Sub getfiles(ByVal path As String)
   ListView1.Columns.Clear()
   ListView1.Items.Clear()
   ListView1.View = View.Details 'use detailed view
   'Add the columns to be displayed in the ListView control:
   ListView1.Columns.Add("Filename", 100, _
   HorizontalAlignment.Left)
   ListView1.Columns.Add("Extension", 50, _
   HorizontalAlignment.Left)
   ListView1.Columns.Add("Bytes", 50, _
   HorizontalAlignment.Right)
   Dim DI As System.IO.DirectoryInfo = _
   New System.IO.DirectoryInfo(path)
   Dim files() As System.IO.FileInfo = DI.GetFiles
   Dim file As System.IO.FileInfo
   For Each file In files
      Select Case file.Extension
         Case ".jpeg", ".gif", ".bmp", _
              ".jpg", ".tif", ".tiff", ".avi"
            Dim li As New ListViewItem(file.Name)
            li.SubItems.Add(file.Extension)
            li.SubItems.Add(file.Length)
            'Add the ListViewItem to ListView1:
            ListView1.Items.Add(li) End Select
   Next
End Sub
```

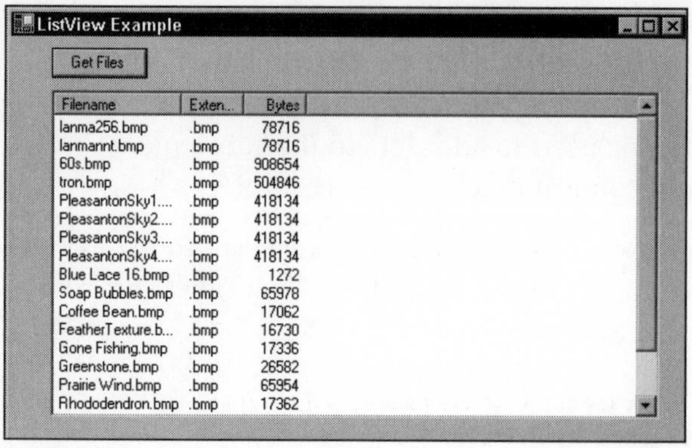

Figure 5.7 File lists are typically displayed in a ListView control. The Details view displays multiple columns of related information for each list item.

The TreeView Control

The ListView control displays multicolumned items, whereas the TreeView control represents a hierarchical collection of containers for those items. In an explorer window, folders are displayed in a TreeView control and files are displayed in a ListView control.

Populating a TreeView Control

A TreeView control is a hierarchical collection of TreeNode objects. Each TreeNode object can contain other TreeNode objects in its Nodes collection. After having seen so many collections, we fully expect by now to add child nodes to a node using an Add method. Figure 5.8 displays the results of executing the following code to demonstrate how nodes can be added to a TreeView control:

```
Private Sub E1_Click(sender As System.Object, _
e As System.EventArgs) _
Handles E1.Click 'ByVal keywords deleted for formatting
    'Using a TreeView control named TreeView1...
    'create new TreeNode named aNode:
    Dim aNode As New TreeNode("The Parent")
    TreeView1.Nodes.Add(aNode) 'add aNode as the root node
    aNode.Nodes.Add("A Child") 'add a subordinate node to aNode
    aNode.Nodes(0).Nodes.Add("GrandChild")
    aNode.ExpandAll() 'Expand all nodes in the tree
End Sub
```

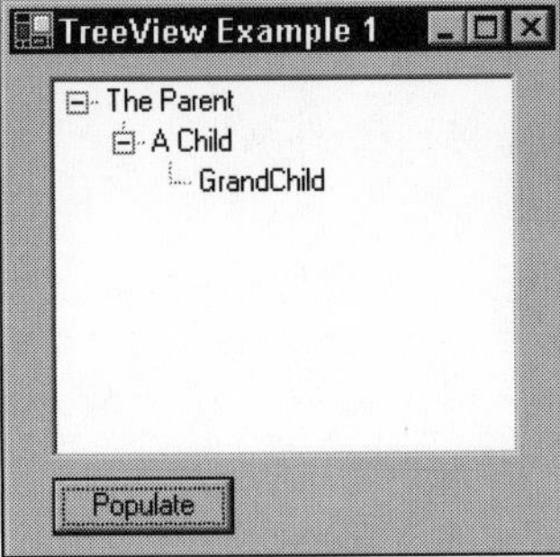

Figure 5.8 You can add subordinate nodes to the Nodes collection of each node in a TreeView control.

What if we want to populate the TreeView control using a prebuilt structure such as a directory structure or an XML file? The process would involve iterating through the prebuilt collection while dynamically creating nodes. The following example uses a directory tree to populate a TreeView control. It uses the winnt directory as the root and populates that root with just the directories immediately subordinate to that folder. The result of executing the following code is shown in Figure 5.9.

```
Private Sub E2_Click(sender As System.Object, _
e As System.EventArgs) _
Handles E2.Click 'ByVal keywords deleted for formatting
   Dim DI As System.IO.DirectoryInfo = _
   New System.IO.DirectoryInfo("c:\")
   Dim directories() As System.IO.DirectoryInfo = _
   DI.GetDirectories()
   Dim directory As System.IO.DirectoryInfo
   Dim rootNode As New TreeNode("c:\winnt") 'create a root node
   TreeView1.Nodes.Add(rootNode) 'add the root node
   For Each directory In directories
      rootNode.Nodes.Add(directory.Name) 'add the child nodes
   Next
   TreeView1.ExpandAll()
End Sub
```

Displaying a Directory Structure in a TreeView Control

Let's say that we want to display the entire contents of the C drive in a TreeView control. Well, you could, but that usually isn't useful to a user. Recursion would solve the issue, but we have to ask ourselves if we want every node in the tree of directories expanded automatically or if we want it to act like a normal explorer window. The expected interface of an explorer window is one in which the user can click a plus sign or a folder icon and have that directory node expand to display its contents.

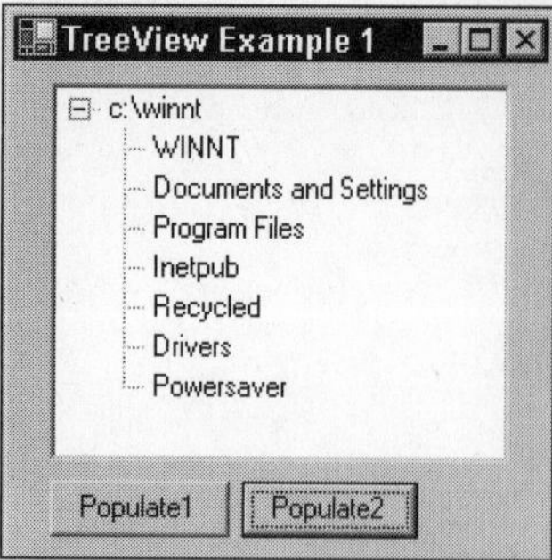

Figure 5.9 TreeView controls can be used to display prebuilt, hierarchical collections such as XML files, directory structures, and manufacturing parts lists.

To solve the problem we need to write an event handler for a TreeView control event, AfterSelect. The AfterSelect event occurs after the user clicks on a node in the TreeView control. Such an event handler dynamically builds a subordinate collection of child nodes for directories in the current directory and has the following signature:

```
Private Sub getDirs(ByVal sender As Object, _
ByVal e As TreeViewEventArgs) _
Handles TreeView1.AfterSelect
```

When the AfterSelect event handler is invoked, the parameter e that is passed into that handler contains a node member representing the node that was selected.

By declaring a subroutine that handles the AfterSelect event, we can populate the directory structure as the user indicates that he or she wants to expand a given directory. When the user clicks the plus (+) sign to the left of the directory node, the following code dynamically adds a child node for each directory under the current directory in the TreeView control:

```
Private Sub getDirs(ByVal sender As Object, _
ByVal e As TreeViewEventArgs) _
Handles TreeView1.AfterSelect
Dim directory As New System.IO.DirectoryInfo( _
e.Node.Tag.ToString())
Dim directories As System.IO.DirectoryInfo()
   directories = directory.GetDirectories()
   For Each directory In directories
      Dim aTreenode As New TreeNode(directory.Name)
      aTreenode.Tag = directory.FullName
      e.Node.Nodes.Add(aTreenode)
   Next
End Sub
```

Modifying TreeView Behavior

The ability to display plus and minus signs next to nodes is one of several properties we can configure for a TreeView control. The following list describes some of the most useful of these properties:

HotTracking. When set to True, this property causes the nodes to act as hyperlinks (blue and underlined) when the mouse pointer is moved over them.

ShowPlusMinus. When set to True, this property causes plus and minus signs to appear next to nodes that have children to facilitate collapsing and expanding those child nodes. The default value for ShowPlusMinus is True.

ShowLines. When set to True, ShowLines displays connecting lines between nodes in the TreeView control. This is a very desirable behavior and helps avoid confusion when using large trees. ShowRootLines causes lines to be drawn between nodes at the root of the tree. Both ShowLines and ShowRootLines are True by default.

Sorted. Setting Sorted to True causes the entire contents (current and future) of the TreeView to be sorted in ascending alphabetical order. Any dynamically added nodes also will be sorted at each level in the tree.

Adding Images to TreeView Items

Typically, windows that use TreeView and ListView controls display different icons for each item, depending on the type and state of the item. Using the BeforeCollapse, BeforeExpand, AfterCollapse, and AfterExpand events for the TreeView control, we can alter the ImageIndex property to adjust a node image appropriately. If the nodes are depicting folders, we can switch between an open or closed folder icon. The steps for associating images to nodes are as follows:

1. Add an ImageList control to the current form.
2. Add the desired images to the ImageList. In .NET, the icons are located in:

   ```
   Microsoft Visual Studio\.NET\Common7\Graphics\icons\
   ```

3. Set the TreeView control's ImageList property to the name of an ImageList control.

4. Use the ImageIndex property for individual nodes to set or change their associated image based on images stored in the ImageList associated with the Treeview control. If an ImageIndex of 0 is used for a node, the first icon stored in the ImageList is used for that node.

OPENFOLD.ICO and CLSDFOLD.ICO are typically used to depict open and closed folders in a TreeView control.

Lab 5.2: Creating a Multipaned User Interface

This lab combines the use of the TreeView, Splitter, and ListView controls to create a multipanel .NET Windows application.

Perform the following steps:

1. Start a new Visual Basic .NET Windows application.
2. Add a TreeView control (TreeView1) to the form.
3. Set TreeView1's Dock property to Left.
4. Add a Splitter control (Splitter1) to Form1.
5. Add a Panel control (Panel1) to Form1.
6. Set Panel1's Dock property to Fill.
7. Drag a ListView control (ListView1) from the Toolbox onto Panel1.
8. Set ListView1's Dock property to Fill. What you should see at this point is shown in Figure 5.10.
9. Add the following code for the form's Load event to create the initial node and configure the TreeView control with some default properties.

```
Private Sub Form1_Load(sender As Object, _
e As System.EventArgs) _
Handles MyBase.Load 'ByVal keywords deleted for formatting
    'display plus and minus signs for nodes:
    TreeView1.ShowPlusMinus = True
    'Sort the TreeView Control:
    TreeView1.Sorted = True
    'Display Connecting Lines Between Nodes:
    TreeView1.ShowLines = True
    'Build The Root Node:
    Dim aNode As New TreeNode("c:\")
    aNode.Tag = "c:\"
    TreeView1.Nodes.Add(aNode)
End Sub
```

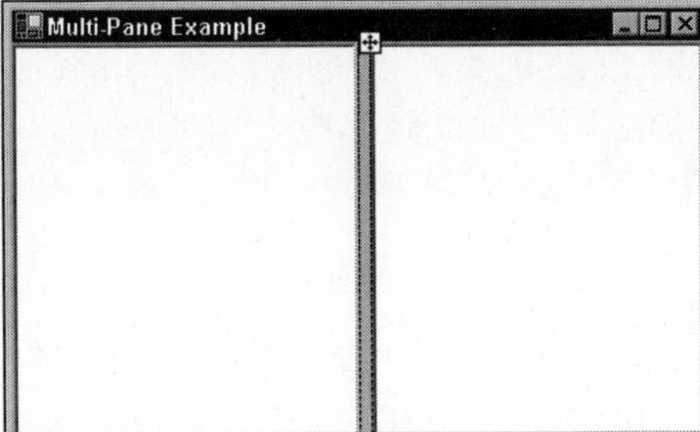

Figure 5.10 A basic multipaneled application shell. The TreeView control (left) is separated from the ListView control (right) by a Splitter control.

10. Add subroutines to dynamically display directories under the current node and the associated files for the selected directory. The following code adds subdirectories, expands the current node to display those subdirectories, and calls a getFiles subroutine to populate the ListView with files from the current folder.

```
Private Sub getDirs(ByVal sender As Object, _
ByVal e As TreeViewEventArgs) _
Handles TreeView1.AfterSelect
   If Not e.Node.Nodes.Count = 0 Then Exit Sub
      Dim directory As New System.IO.DirectoryInfo(_
      e.Node.Tag.ToString())
      getFiles(directory)
      Dim directories As System.IO.DirectoryInfo()
      directories = directory.GetDirectories()
      For Each directory In directories
         Dim aTreenode As New TreeNode(directory.Name)
         aTreenode.Tag = directory.FullName
         e.Node.Nodes.Add(aTreenode)
      Next
   e.Node.Expand()
End Sub
Sub getFiles(ByVal directory As System.IO.DirectoryInfo)
   ListView1.Columns.Clear()
   ListView1.Items.Clear()
   ListView1.View = View.Details
   ListView1.Columns.Add("Filename", 100, _
   HorizontalAlignment.Left)
   ListView1.Columns.Add("Extension", 50, _
   HorizontalAlignment.Left)
   ListView1.Columns.Add("Bytes", 50, _
   HorizontalAlignment.Right)
   Dim files() As System.IO.FileInfo = directory.GetFiles
   Dim file As System.IO.FileInfo
   For Each file In files
      Dim li As New ListViewItem(file.Name)
      li.SubItems.Add(file.Extension)
```

```
        li.SubItems.Add(file.Length)
        ListView1.Items.Add(li)
    Next
End Sub
```

11. Test the application. Your application should look similar to the interface shown in Figure 5.11.

This short example demonstrated a common user interface (UI) style often referred to as an explorer-style or multipaned application. We'd typically add enhancements to enable sorting by individual field columns in the ListView and icons to represent open and closed folders.

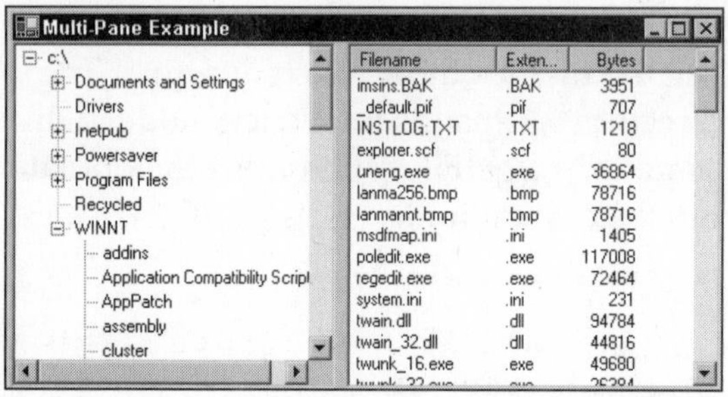

Figure 5.11 Final solution using TreeView, Splitter, and ListView controls.

Using GDI+ in Windows Applications

The graphics system in .NET is embedded into many of the objects we use in every .NET application. A control's Location property is an implementation of System.Drawing.Point, and its Size property is actually a System.Drawing.Size object. .NET provides a rich set of objects for working with graphics that have found their way into many class hierarchies. When working with images in an image viewer, we discovered that the PictureBox control has an Image property that is, of course, a System.Drawing.Image.

The collection of namespaces, classes and interfaces found in the System .Drawing assembly is referred to collectively as GDI+, which replaces GDI and represents our sole option for graphics development using .NET libraries. Rendering images has never been easier. In .NET, GDI has been enhanced for performance and ease of use. By discussing the graphics subsystem in .NET, we can also discover the appropriate use of the Form Paint event.

GDI Namespaces

GDI graphics support is included in several namespaces in the System.Drawing assembly. The following list represents the various namespaces related to GDI in .NET and their intended use:

System.Drawing. The primary GDI namespace. Most of your work with GDI will use objects from this namespace.

System.Drawing.Design. UI-related GDI support. This namespace contains classes to enable the development of extensions to the design-time user interface. It also is used to build custom type converters.

System.Drawing.Drawing2D. Provides support for vector graphics and advanced two-dimensional graphics support. The Matrix class, used to define geometric transforms, is included in this namespace.

System.Drawing.Imaging. Contains advanced GDI+ imaging functionality and classes such as ColorMap, ColorMatrix, and FrameDimension.

System.Drawing.Printing. Provides printing services.

System.Drawing.Text1. Using its FontCollection collection, this namespace provides support for discovery of system-installed fonts and manipulating font families.

The System.Drawing namespace is included in new Visual Basic .NET Windows applications by default. To view the default namespaces in a project, select Project, Properties, Common Properties, Imports. Table 5.3 describes some of the most common members in the System.Drawing namespace.

Table 5.3 Common System.Drawing Namespace Members

MEMBER	DESCRIPTION
Bitmap	An image defined by pixel data.
Brush	Used to fill interiors of shapes.
Brushes	Contains brushes for all standard colors.
Color	An ARGB color object.
Font	Describes a particular text format.
FontFamily	A group of type faces.
Graphics	Represents a GDI drawing surface.
Icon	Represents a Windows icon.

(continued)

Table 5.3 *(continued)*

MEMBER	DESCRIPTION
Image	Creates an image to be used in GDI-capable controls.
ImageAnimator	Animates an image that has time-sequenced images.
Pen	An object used for drawing lines and arcs.
Point	Represents a location expressed as x and y pairs.
Size	Object dimensions expressed as a width and height pair.
Rectangle	Represents a rectangle. Rectangles are a combination of one Point object and one Size object.
SolidBrush	Represents a brush with a single color.
SystemColors	Used to set and get colors for the different Windows display elements such as InactiveBorder and ActiveCaption. SystemIcons and SystemPens are related members within the System.Drawing namespace.

The System.Drawing Enumerations

The System.Drawing namespace also includes several enumerations that are useful when working with GDI objects. Table 5.4 describes these enumerations.

Point and Size Objects

The Point and Size objects represent the simplest of objects in the System .Drawing namespace. The Location property, defined in the Control class from which all controls in .NET inherit, is the most common implementation of a Point object. A Point object consists of an x and a y value, both expressed as integers.

A Size object is a width and height value pair. A Rectangle is a combination of a Point and a Size object. All references to size and dimension are expressed in pixels. The following code demonstrates how Point and Size are related to a common Button control:

```
Dim btn As New Button()
btn.Location = 0,0 'ERROR: will not compile because 0,0 is not
'a Point object. The Point(0,0) would indicate the upper
'left corner however.
btn.Location = New Point(0, 0) 'This is correct
btn.Size = New Size(60, 20)
Me.Controls.Add(btn)
```

Table 5.4 System.Drawing Enumerations

ENUMERATION	DESCRIPTION
ContentAlignment	Used to specify alignment of the drawing content on the drawing surface.
FontStyle	Used to specify text font style formatting.
GraphicsUnit	Represents a graphic object's unit of measurement.
KnownColor	Represents an extensive list of friendly names for all common, and many not-so-common (Dodger Blue), colors.
RotateFlipType	Used to specify the manner in which graphics objects are manipulated in terms of flipping an object on a given axis.
StringAlignment	Used to specify a strings alignment in relation to the drawing surface.
String Trimming	Contains support for trimming strings on a drawing surface. Possible values are None (no trimming), Word (trims at nearest word), and Character (trims at nearest character).
String Unit	Represents a Strings unit of measure.

The Rectangle Object

The Rectangle object is not limited to use in GDI graphics. Many classes that have the basic implementation of a width and height inherit from Rectangle. By creating a Point to hold the upper-left corner of the rectangle and a Size object to determine its dimensions, we can create a rectangle with the following code:

```
Dim r As New Rectangle(New Point(10, 10), New Size(200, 200))
```

The Rectangle object has quite a few useful members with rather intuitive names (Top, Left, Width, Height, Right, Bottom) and a few not-so-intuitive members, which are listed here:

Inflate. Expand a rectangle.

Intersect. Create a new rectangle based on an intersection of two rectangles.

Union. Create a new rectangle based on a union of two rectangles.

Using the Graphics Object to Draw Rectangles

The Graphics object in the System.Drawing namespace controls the actual drawing of GDI graphics in .NET. Before discussing topics such as invalidation and Paint events, let's look at using the Graphics object to draw objects in .NET.

To draw in .NET, we have to have a drawing surface. The following code passes the Windows handle for the current form to Graphics.FromHwnd() to use the current form as the drawing surface for our rectangle:

```
Dim G As System.Drawing.Graphics
G = Graphics.FromHwnd(Me.Handle)
Dim r As New Rectangle(New Point(10, 10), _
New Size(200, 200))
G.DrawRectangle(New Pen(Color.Blue), r)
```

The following code offers a slightly more complex example that draws multiple rectangles with random Size and Point values:

```
Private Sub Btn_Click(sender As System.Object, _
e As System.EventArgs) _
Handles Btn.Click
   Dim rand As New System.Random(Now.Millisecond)
   Dim G As System.Drawing.Graphics
   G = Graphics.FromHwnd(Me.Handle)
   Dim i As Integer
   Dim p As Point
   Dim s As Size
   Dim r As Rectangle
   Dim c As Color
   For i = 0 To 100
      p = New Point(rand.Next(Me.Width), rand.Next(Me.Height))
      s = New Size(rand.Next(100), rand.Next(100))
      r = New Rectangle(p, s)
      c = Color.FromArgb(rand.Next(255), _
      rand.Next(255), rand.Next(255))
      G.DrawRectangle(New Pen(c), r)
   Next
End Sub
```

Drawing Images Inside Rectangles

Drawing Image objects is accomplished with the DrawImage method of the Graphics object. This method has 30 separate overloads and offers some pretty complex variations. One of the more basic overloaded versions of DrawImage is overload 7 of 30, which takes two arguments: an Image and a Rectangle in which to draw the image. The following code demonstrates how we can render an image within a client Rectangle object. The result of executing this code is shown in Figure 5.12.

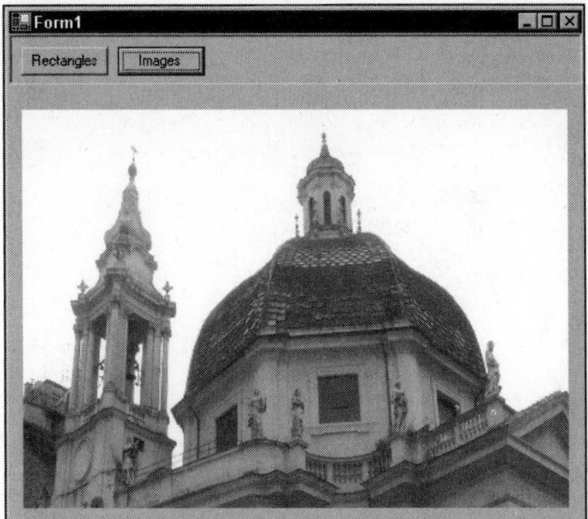

Figure 5.12 Images can be drawn inside any implementation of Rectangle by using the Graphics.DrawImage method.

```
Dim G As System.Drawing.Graphics = Graphics.FromHwnd(Me.Handle)
'Following Line Should Use a Full Image Path.
Dim img1 As Image = Image.FromFile("Rome.JPG")
Dim r As New Rectangle(10, 60, 500, 500)
G.DrawRectangle(New Pen(Color.Black), r)
G.DrawImage(img1, r)
```

If graphics are drawn this way (external to the Paint handler), they will disappear if anything covers the form. Switching between forms causes the image and the rectangle to disappear. This issue is resolved in the *A Painting to Remember* section later in this chapter.

Working with Fonts

System.Drawing contains a FontFamily class that can be used to iterate through the various installed fonts. The following code iterates through every font in the FontFamily collection and draws the name of each font with the associated font style.

```
Dim G As System.Drawing.Graphics = Graphics.FromHwnd(Me.Handle)
Dim yoffset As Integer = 60
Dim aFont As System.Drawing.FontFamily
For Each aFont In FontFamily.Families
   Try
      G.DrawString(aFont.Name, New Font(aFont.Name, 10), _
      New SolidBrush(Color.Black), 10, yoffset)
```

```
            yoffset += 15
        Catch ex As Exception
            'not all fonts support size 10
            End Try
    Next
```

The output for this code is shown in Figure 5.13. The font collection is displayed using the method DrawString in System.Drawing.Graphics.

DrawPie and FillPie

DrawPolygon and DrawRectangle can be used for most charts, but pie charts can be created with System.Drawing.DrawPie and System.Drawing.FillPie. The following example demonstrates the use of both methods and produces output shown in Figure 5.14.

```
Dim G As System.Drawing.Graphics = Graphics.FromHwnd(Me.Handle)
Dim bluebrush As New SolidBrush(Color.Blue)
Dim greenbrush As New SolidBrush(Color.Green)
Dim blackpen = New Pen(Color.Black, 16)
blackpen.Width = 0.2
G.FillPie(bluebrush, 100, 60, 100, 100, 90, 120)
G.FillPie(greenBrush, 100, 60, 100, 100, 210, 90)
G.DrawPie(blackpen, 100, 60, 100, 100, 300, 150)
```

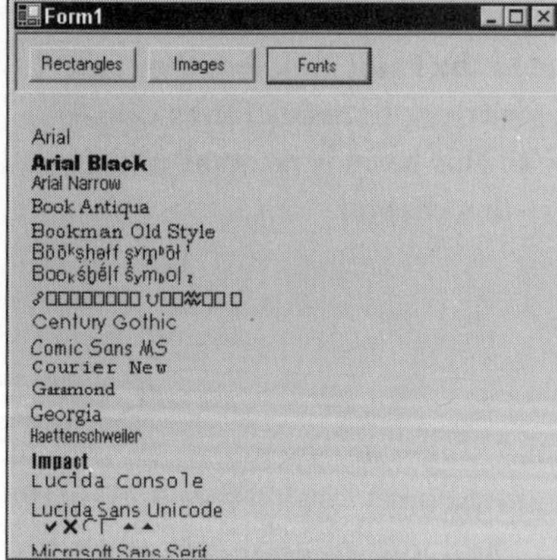

Figure 5.13 System-installed fonts are accessed via the Families collection in a System.Drawing.FontFamilies object.

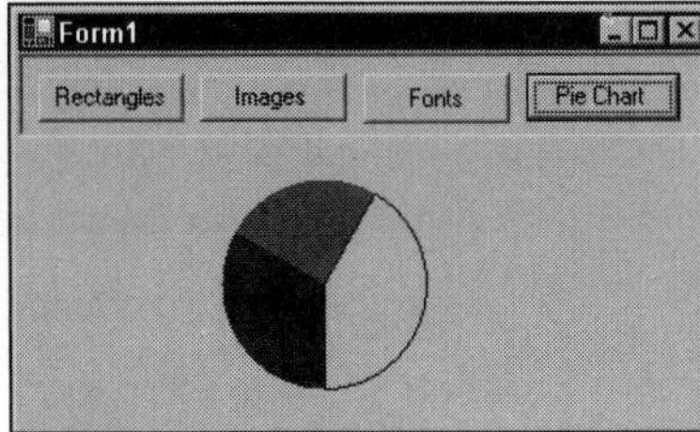

Figure 5.14 Pies are drawn using DrawPie or FillPie in the System.Drawing.Graphics object.

A Painting to Remember

So far, everything we have done would be destroyed if anything covered it at runtime. For instance, if I switched to another application and then switched back to my form, all the graphics would be gone. The Paint event for the current form can be used to "remember" graphics (actually, redraw them) when they become "dirty." To help understand the problem, test any of the previous GDI code by minimizing and maximizing the form containing the graphics to see how the graphics are destroyed and not repainted. The term *dirty* is often used to refer to graphics that need to be repainted for whatever reason.

Each event has an argument e that contains arguments specific for that event. One of the arguments for e in the Form Load event is Graphics. The following code draws a polygon from inside a Paint event handler for the current form and uses e.Graphics as a drawing client. This polygon will persist through the events that caused our earlier graphics to disappear.

```
Private Sub Form1_Paint(ByVal sender As Object, _
ByVal e As System.Windows.Forms.PaintEventArgs) _
Handles MyBase.Paint
   Dim G As System.Drawing.Graphics = e.Graphics
   Dim points(3) As System.Drawing.Point
   points(0) = New Point(120, 60) 'Top Left of Trapezoid
   points(1) = New Point(180, 60) 'Top Right of Trapezoid
   points(2) = New Point(240, 120) 'Bottom Right of Trapezoid
   points(3) = New Point(60, 120) 'Bottom Left of Trapezoid
   G.DrawPolygon(New Pen(Color.Blue), points)
End Sub
```

To understand when the Paint event occurs, it may be quite useful to place a MessageBox.Show("Paint occurred") statement inside the Paint event handler. The Paint event occurs whenever the form is minimized, resized, maximized, covered, uncovered, or stretched. There are certainly other triggers for this event, but these are the most common. Sometimes I want to refresh my graphics programmatically. To accomplish this, we can use the Invalidate method. Invalidate has a few overloads but in general, we use Invalidate with no parameters to redraw everything on the form and Invalidate with a region or rectangle to redraw specific regions of the form's client area.

There is no concept of the Visual Basic 6 AutoRedraw Form property in .NET.

Lab 5.3: A Lesson in Objectivity

This lab demonstrates how an understanding of both the GDI objects and certain object-oriented behaviors can be of crucial benefit to developers in .NET. This lab is meant to be more experimental than functional but explains some very interesting things about the development environment in .NET. The purpose of introducing GDI+ was to familiarize you with some of the more common objects used throughout .NET. Keeping that in mind, this lab helps extend that understanding while providing insight into the nature of objects. We'll end the lab by creating a form shaped like a trapezoid.

Perform the following steps:

1. Start a new Visual Basic .NET Windows application.
2. Add a ListBox control (ListBox1) to Form1.
3. Using the Properties window, add three items (any three strings) in the Items collection property for ListBox1.
4. Beneath the list box, place a new Button control (Button1).
5. To the right of Button1, add a new TextBox control (TextBox1).
6. Double-click ListBox1 to open the Code Editor window.
7. Using the drop-down scroll boxes at the top of the Code Editor window, add an event handler for ListBox1, using the following code:

```
Private Sub ListBox1_MouseMove(ByVal sender As Object, _
ByVal e As System.Windows.Forms.MouseEventArgs) _
Handles ListBox1.MouseMove
    Dim item As String
    item = ListBox1.IndexFromPoint(New Point(e.X, e.Y))
    TextBox1.Text = "Hittest Index:" & item
End Sub
```

The ListBox MouseMove event occurs whenever the mouse is moved over any portion of the list box, even if there is no list item at that location. The MouseMove event handler we have written performs a hit test by passing the current X and Y coordinates, expressed as a System.Drawing.Point, to the IndexFromPoint method of the ListBox control.

8. Add a Click event handler for Button1 using the following code:

```
Private Sub Button1_Click(ByVal sender As System.Object, _
ByVal e As System.EventArgs) Handles Button1.Click
   ListBox1.Items.Clear()
   ListBox1.Items.Add("Rectangle1")
   Dim Rectangle2 As New Rectangle(0, 0, 10, 10)
   ListBox1.Items.Add(Rectangle2)
End Sub
```

Whatever we add to a ListBox control, it ends up being cast as System.Object. In our Button1_Click event handler, we added a String object ("Rectangle1") and a Rectangle object (Rectangle2). If we store a Rectangle in a list box, it continues being a Rectangle, despite the cast to System.Object. If you checked the type of these items in ListBox1, you would find that Rectangle1 is a System.String and Rectangle2 is a System.Drawing.Rectangle.

9. Modify the ListBox1 MouseMove event handler to reveal the underlying types of objects stored in the list box, using the following code:

```
Private Sub ListBox1_MouseMove(ByVal sender As Object, _
    ByVal e As System.Windows.Forms.MouseEventArgs) _
    Handles ListBox1.MouseMove
        Dim item As String
        item = ListBox1.IndexFromPoint(New Point(e.X, e.Y))
        If item >= 0 Then 'mouse is over an item
            TextBox1.Text = "Hittest Index:" & item & _
            " is a " & ListBox1.Items(item).GetType.ToString()
        End If
    End Sub
```

10. Test the application by clicking the button to populate the list box with the String and the Rectangle. Move your mouse pointer over each of the two items to cause their underlying types to be displayed in TextBox1.

    It is the use of this information that is important. We can literally render a rectangle by using a list box item as long as the underlying item is a Rectangle and we cast the item accordingly.

11. Modify the ListBox1 MouseMove event handler one last time to appear as follows:

```
Private Sub ListBox1_MouseMove(ByVal sender As Object, _
ByVal e As System.Windows.Forms.MouseEventArgs) _
Handles ListBox1.MouseMove
   Dim G As System.Drawing.Graphics = _
   Graphics.FromHwnd(Me.Handle)
   Dim item As String
   item = ListBox1.IndexFromPoint(New Point(e.X, e.Y))
   If item >= 0 Then 'mouse is over an item
   TextBox1.Text = "Hittest Index:" & item & " is a " & _
      ListBox1.Items(item).GetType.ToString()
      If ListBox1.Items(item).GetType.ToString() = _
      "System.Drawing.Rectangle" Then
         G.DrawRectangle(New Pen(Color.Blue), _
         CType(ListBox1.Items(item), Rectangle))
      End If
   End If
End Sub
```

12. Run the application. Click Button1 and move your mouse pointer over the second item in the list to cause Rectangle2 to be drawn to the form and to obtain the results shown in Figure 5.15.

    Have you ever wanted a form that wasn't a rectangle? The following steps walk you through this process in Visual Basic .NET.

13. Add a new Windows form (frmPolygon) to the application and make it the startup object.
14. Set the FormBorderStyle for frmPolygon to None.
15. Set the TransparencyKey property to Silver. The TransparencyKey color causes any objects with that color to be transparent. Because the form itself is Silver, the entire form's surface will be transparent.

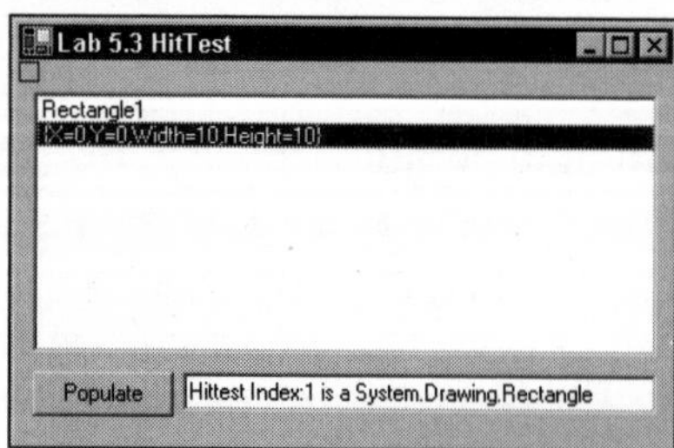

Figure 5.15 Lab 5.3 Results for a list box hit test.

16. Add the following code to handle the Paint event for frmPolygon:

```
Private Sub frmPolygon_Paint(ByVal sender As Object, _
ByVal e As System.Windows.Forms.PaintEventArgs) _
Handles MyBase.Paint
Me.WindowState = FormWindowState.Maximized
Dim G As System.Drawing.Graphics = e.Graphics
Dim points(3) As System.Drawing.Point
Dim bbrush As New SolidBrush(Color.GhostWhite)
   points(0) = New Point(160, 160)
   points(1) = New Point(580, 160)
   points(2) = New Point(640, 520)
   points(3) = New Point(100, 520)
   G.FillPolygon(bbrush, points) 'Fill the Trapezoid
   G.DrawPolygon(New Pen(Color.Black, 2), points) 'Draw Border
End Sub
```

17. Add a few controls just to make it look like a form. Add the controls to a location on the form that will be inside the region occupied by the polygon.
18. Run the application. The results should be similar to Figure 5.16.

This lab reinforces the understanding of object casting while demonstrating that some methods, such as ListBox.IndexFromPoint, can be used in unique ways. Although rendering a rectangle from a list box item may not be practical in a real application, this lab opens up some interesting possibilities. Thinking of controls and features in .NET as being related to similar controls in Visual Basic 6 is almost harmful. For example, it took me quite a while to realize that a list box in .NET could hold anything but a string. Considering that a list box can hold virtually any creatable object in .NET, I would call it more than an improvement over a Visual Basic 6 list box, which can only contain strings. Making forms out of polygons is pretty cool, too.

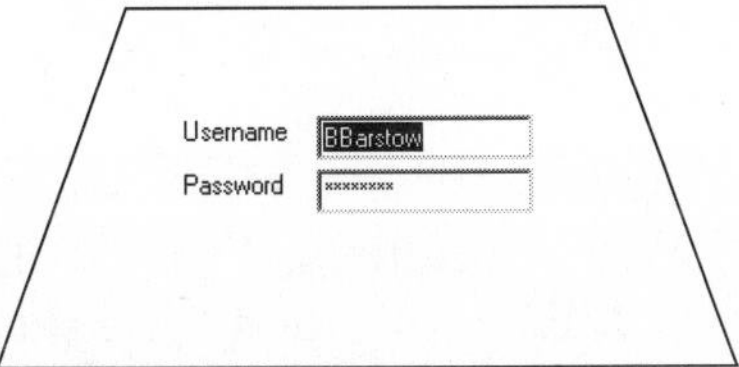

Figure 5.16 The TransparencyKey property for a form can be used to create forms out of any polygon.

Classroom Q & A

Q: Is it possible to create a list box that contains only a certain type of element, such as a list box of type Image?

A: Technically, anything is possible, but you'd have to create your own control specifically for a particular type. The performance for this type of object binding in controls is acceptable because of the flexibility, but you won't see me casting too many things to objects in my class libraries.

Q: Isn't it bad to cast things as objects?

A: Not inherently; as with all things, it has a time and a place. It has been helpful to us that all of these collections and list-based controls do it. In controls and client-side code, performance is certainly important but not nearly the issue it can be for server-side components. Having said that, let me make the exception that certain client applications such as the typical Autodesk products are extremely optimized for client-side performance because they are so math and graphics intensive. If, at compile time, we know and state exactly what object type we'll be working with (early binding), our runtime code will execute faster. If a conversion has to be made from System.Object to the appropriate type at runtime (known as late binding), it executes less efficiently.

Q: Are there any alternatives when we want to use different types of objects and hold them in a container with a generic type?

A: Yes. We could create an interface that defines the common members of the disparate classes and create a container with that interface as its data type.

Summary

With so much we could possibly do in Windows applications, it's difficult to choose what to place in such a pivotal chapter. MDI applications and multipanel applications represent the bulk of the applications we might build in a Windows .NET application. While building these applications, we've added quite a few new controls, classes, and namespaces to our .NET repertoire. As we begin to create and test our class libraries and XML Web services, we will implement even more of the rich collection of features and objects in .NET.

Review Questions

1. Which of the following causes frmDocument to become a child of frmContainer?
    a. frmContainer.Children.Add(frmDocument)
    b. frmDocument.MDIParent = frmContainer
    c. frmContainer.MdiChildren.Add(frmDocument)
    d. frmContainer.MdiChildren.AddMdiChild(frmDocument)
2. How do you create an MDI parent form?
    a. By adding an MDIForm from the Project menu.
    b. By setting a normal Form's MDIContainer property to True
    c. By setting a normal Form's IsMdiContainer property to True
    d. Setting the parent form property to a particular form automatically causes that form to become an MDI Container.
3. How can you add a list of open MDI child forms to the bottom of the Window menu?
    a. Set the WindowState property for the Window menu.
    b. Set the WindowList property to True for the Window menu.
    c. The list of MDI children is automatically maintained under the Window menu if it exists.
    d. Set the MdiList property to True for the Window menu.
4. Which of the following can be used to arrange children?
    a. The LayoutMDI method
    b. The MDILayout method
    c. The Arrange method
    d. The MDIArrange method
5. How can you change a ListView control to display a detailed view?
    a. ListView1.View = View.Details
    b. ListView1.View = Details
    c. ListView1.ViewDetails
    d. ListView1.View = ViewDetails

6. Which of the following will cause the entire contents of a TreeView control to expand?
   a. TreeView1.Nodes(0).Expand()
   b. TreeView1.Expand()
   c. TreeView1.Nodes(0).ExpandAll()
   d. TreeView1.ExpandAll()
7. Which of the following are acceptable Rectangle constructions?

```
Dim r1 as New Rectangle(10, 10, new Size(10,10)
Dim r2 As New Rectangle(New Point(10, 10), New Size(10, 10))
Dim r3 As New Rectangle(10, 10, 10, 10)
Dim r4 As New Rectangle()
```

   a. r1, r2, r3, and r4.
   b. r2 only.
   c. r2 and r4.
   d. r2, r3, and r4.

Answers to Review Questions

1. **b.** Setting a form's MDIParent to a valid MDI container establishes a parent/child relationship. The MDIChildren collection does not have an Add method. MDI Containers do not have a Children collection.
2. **c.** An MDI Parent form is created by setting the IsMdiContainer property to True for a normal Form. Answer **a** is correct only in Visual Basic 6. MDIContainer is not a valid property for a Form.
3. **d.** To add a list of all open MDI children to a menu, set the menu's MdiList property to True. WindowList is specific to Visual Basic 6. The WindowState property for a Form can be used to change the form to a minimized or maximized state.
4. **a.** and **b.** The LayoutMdi method of an MDI container form can be set to one of the predefined MDILayout constants. The Arrange method is specific to Visual Basic 6. MDIArrange is a fictitious property.
5. **a.** The View property for a ListView control can be set using one of the predefined View constants.
6. **d.** If the ExpandAll method is used on Nodes(0), only the first root-level node will be expanded. Expand is not a valid method.
7. **d.** Even though the Rectangle object appears to have only two constructors; r2, r3, and r4 will all be constructed as Rectangle objects.

CHAPTER

6

Building Class Libraries in .NET

We've used so many powerful and reusable objects that understanding why we create objects should be straightforward. The more classes available in a system, the less work we have to do. As the template for an object, if a class is created with the foresight of future use and extensibility, it becomes a valuable asset for future development. This chapter focuses on the object-oriented principles related to developing classes and the techniques related to building libraries of classes in .NET. Now that Visual Basic is just as object oriented as its C-like counterpart C#, you gain quite a bit of flexibility and power. Let's start learning to wield that power.

Class Libraries

Classes are most often created as members of a DLL, which are created in Visual Basic .NET as a class library project. The terms *library*, *class library*, and *DLL* are interchangeable, except when referring to a library of functions (a concept no longer employed). It is impossible to declare a method (sub or function) in .NET unless that method is a member of a Structure or Class definition. Although classes can be added directly to a Windows application, you should place them in a class library project so that they may be easily used by other projects.

Referencing Local Class Libraries

For a Windows application to use objects declared in a class library assembly, the Windows application must have a reference to that assembly. To add a reference to a local assembly (an assembly on the same machine as the client) use Project, Add References, or right-click on the References folder in the Solution Explorer and select Add Reference.

Referencing Remote Class Libraries

The intended remote communication model for .NET components places an object called an XML Web service between the class library and its clients. After an XML Web service has wrapped functionality in a class library, virtually any programmer using any language on any operating system can consume the services and the underlying objects (after logging in, of course). XML Web services are covered in Chapter 15, "XML Web Services."

Object Oriented Programming

Although no system is perfect, the consistency provided through common interfaces and the usability we've found in classes so far have provided a lot of capabilities. With well-overloaded methods, the .NET class libraries make great examples for how object-oriented systems should be designed. To this point I've tried to point out reasons why things work, always with explanations in the underlying object-oriented design. Before we leap into designing classes, we'll look at the core OOP principles that allow objects a high degree of reusability and flexibility.

Abstraction

Abstraction is something Visual Basic 6 programmers might be more than familiar with in concept than in practice. Visual Basic 6 represented an environment where every underlying detail of an object was abstracted (hidden away). Programmers used hundreds of forms but cared little about how the forms were implemented. What you needed to know to use a form in Visual Basic 6 was what properties, methods, and events the Form object had. That's the point of abstraction. By designing public property procedures that encapsulate private variables and collections that encapsulate nonabstract concepts such as arrays, you can greatly simplify the use of classes. Visual Basic 6 was easy to use because of this abstraction.

Encapsulation

The class as a construct represents the encapsulation of an entity. *Encapsulation* is closely related to abstraction but is not limited to classes. Whenever you encapsulate an object, enable the abstraction of the internal details by implementing a public interface at the level of encapsulation. By doing this, you gain the capability to change the underlying implementation as long as the interface to the encapsulated object remains the same.

To explain, if you wanted to create a Name property for a class, you could create a public variable called Name. The problems with giving a user of a class direct access to the variable include an inability to change the implementation, the inability to separate the getting and setting of property values, and the inability to raise an event as a property is changed. Property procedures such as the following encapsulation of a private variable in a Visual Basic .NET class are no strangers to the Visual Basic language:

```
Public Class Person
Private m_name As String
'Declare a Property Procedure To Encapsulate m_name:
   Public Property Name() As String
      Get
         Return m_name
      End Get
      Set(ByVal newValue As String)
         m_name = newValue
      End Set
   End Property
End Class
```

Users of the Person class (other programmers) won't know how you are storing the value for the Name property. Figure 6.1 shows how the property appears to users of the Person class.

```
Private Sub Button1_Click(...
    Dim c As New Person()
    c.Name = "Jody"
    [GetType]    x.Show(c.Name)
    [Name]
End Sub
```

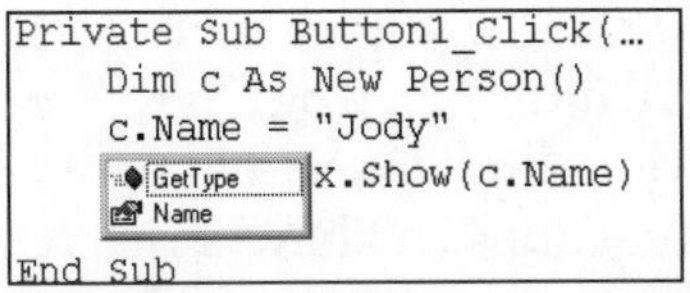

Figure 6.1 Property procedures hide the implementation of data in a class and appear to the user of a class to be no different than public variables.

Composition/Aggregation

Composition (also called *aggregation*) is something you have seen while working with Visual Basic .NET. Remember how a toolbar has a Buttons collection and a list box has an Items collection? Well, these are examples of composite classes—classes of one type acting as members of another type. In the case of a list box, the Items collection is a class member that holds any number of another object type.

When a car is assembled, it is assembled from premade parts that are slapped together (well, maybe with a little welding) to form a final product. In coding, when we indicate that a prebuilt class will be part of a larger object, we just instantiate it as a member of a class we are building.

Let's pretend that we have a Date class and a Person class and we want to create a class called EventClass that contains information about a seminar. The following code represents a simplified view of the composition used to create such a class:

```
Public Class Person
   '...
End Class
Public Class Date
   Public day As Integer = 0
   Public month As Integer = 0
   Public year As Integer = 0
End Class
Public Class Event
   Public EventDate As New Date()
   Public Coordinator As New Person()
   Public Attendees() As Person
   Public Function AddAttendee()
      '...
   End Function
End Class
```

Of course, this is just an example, but for the record, you cannot create classes named Date and Event because they are keywords. You wouldn't recreate a class named Date because it's already nicely done and you would encapsulate Attendees into an ICollection. The point is that after you have a rich set of types (classes and structures), you can build objects very quickly without a lot of redesigning.

Inheritance

Composition embeds one type into another. Inheritance is much different but also involves reusing objects. What if you have an object that represents a great deal of functionality but don't like the way in which some of the members were implemented? Maybe we want to inherit 90 percent of what a class does because it would take weeks to rewrite and test, but we want to refine what the other 10 percent does for our inheriting class. These problems are solved by implementation inheritance, which is often useful for extending what a class does for a particular use. A Windows form is a good example. Every time you create a form, you inherit from System.Windows.Forms.Form, so you don't have to recreate any of the code that builds the form in memory, maps the event handlers, or works with mouse events.

Because all objects inherit from System.Object, we can place our classes in an ICollection. The question I had early on in .NET was, "When does that inheritance take place?" On one hand, I'm being told that everything is out in the open and not hidden away from me as in Visual Basic 6, but there is certainly no indication in code that our class inherits from System.Object.

Lab 6.1: Inheriting System.Object

Our objective is merely to discover how objects become System.Objects. This lab is a demonstration of inheritance. Chapter 8, "Implementation Inheritance," goes deeper into this subject.

Perform the following steps:

1. Start a new Visual Basic .NET class library application. For future explanations and figures, I named my project InheritingSystem-Object, but you can name yours whatever you want.

Class libraries become DLLs when they are compiled, typically contain a collection of related classes, and cannot be executed.

2. Open the Object Browser by selecting View, Other Windows, Object Browser.
3. The top item displayed within the Object Browser should be your class library. Expand your class library in the Object Browser as far as you can and what you will *not* find is an inheritance from System .Object. You can try saving the application or even try selecting Build from the Build menu, but the inheritance will not appear.

   We know that something happens when the assembly is compiled that causes the class to be a System.Object, but let's force this relationship to appear in the Object Browser at design time.
4. Return to the Code Editor view of Class1 in your class library project.

5. Modify Class1 to implicitly inherit from System.Object as shown in the following code:

   ```
   Public Class Class1
       Inherits System.Object
   End Class
   ```

6. Repeat Steps 2 and 3 to view the relationship between System .Object and Class1 in the Object Browser as shown in Figure 6.2.

Although we'll discuss Inheritance later, it's important to remember that everything we have used so far in .NET inherits from at least System.Object and for some classes, from a multitude of other classes. If all types didn't inherit from System.Object, we wouldn't be able to use the ICollections such as a list box's Items collection or an ArrayList. It is the inheritance from System.Object that gives us the method ToString() that we've used so much in MessageBox.Show statements. This and other methods in System.Object can be seen in Figure 6.2. That the following statement compiles and executes without a problem proves that at runtime, all things inherit from System.Object:

```
MessageBox.Show(10.ToString())
```

The preceding statement, when compiled, creates the following object hierarchy in memory:

```
System.Object
     System.ValueType Inherits System.Object
             System.Int32 Inherits System.ValueType
```

System.ValueType is referred to as the base type for System.Int32, and System.Object would be System.Int32's ultimate base type.

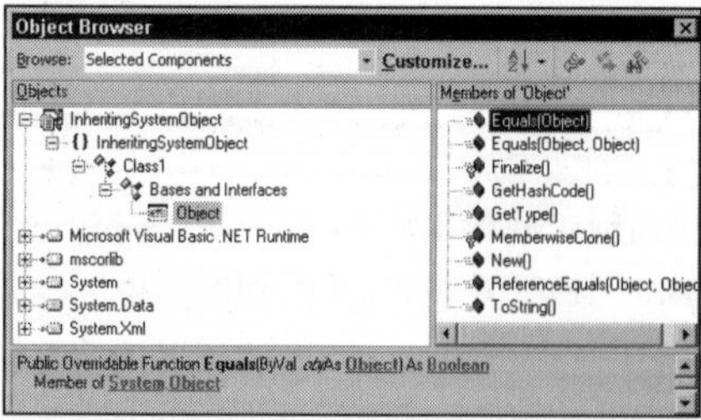

Figure 6.2 The inheritance of System.Object in a custom class will appear in the Object Browser only if you explicitly inherit from System.Object in the class declaration.

State

State refers to data stored in an instance of a class. For a Person class, the state might be the person's date of birth, name, and so on. For a user session in a Web application, state might include the session ID and the login name. State is most often declared as private variables in classes, exposed via public property procedures.

Messages

Messages is one of those college OOP book phrases that refers to the fact that some objects need to communicate to and receive communications from other objects. Typically, these messages come by way of event handlers. It is the need to send or receive messages that very often determines whether we will build a type using a class or a structure. Structures are for building types such as Integers that don't need messages and are said to be *state oriented.* Classes are for building objects that are *behavior oriented* and can, unlike Structures, contain events.

Behaviors

First of all, a *behavior* is another abstract OOP term that is used to describe something a class does. Whether this behavior is in response to an explicit invocation or in response to an event, we usually refer to these behaviors as methods of a class. In Visual Basic .NET, we can implement methods using the Sub or Function keywords.

Polymorphism

Polymorphism is, in my opinion, the most "you have to see it to understand it" topic in all of programming. The beauty of polymorphic code is that it provides an elegant simplicity that is only ugly and complicated when it is missing from an application.

To explain what polymorphism will do for you, I'll use what we already know to be true. If I had a circle, a rectangle, and a square (each with a Draw method) and I stored them inside some ICollection, we know they would be cast to System.Object. We also know that if we tried OurCollection(0).Draw, it would complain that System.Object doesn't have a Draw method. Furthermore, we know that to call the Draw method on members of a collection of System.Object, we have to first cast the individual collection member to its actual underlying type (whatever GetType says it is).

Now, let's say that I want to create a function that accepts any shape and calls the Draw method on the shape that was passed to it. Without polymorphism, this function would never be complete and would grow larger as we added more shapes to our library of shape classes. The following code demonstrates a tedious, nonpolymorphic solution to the DrawAnyShape problem:

```
Private Sub DrawAnyShape(ByVal someshape As Object)
        Select Case someshape.GetType.ToString()
            Case "Rectangle"
                CType(someshape, aRectangle).Draw()
            Case "Circle"
                CType(someshape, aCircle).Draw()
            Case "Square"
                CType(someshape, aSquare).Draw()
            Case "Dodecahedron"
                CType(someshape, aDodecahedron).Draw()
            Case "GooglePlex"
                CType(someshape, aGoogleplex).Draw()
            Case "Torus"
                CType(someshape, aTorus).Draw()
            Case Else
                'Endless other possibilities
        End Select
    End Sub
```

This is not a function I would personally want to maintain. Now, if this function worked polymorphically, we could pass any shape and have a single line of code that simply called the Draw method, and each object would draw itself using its own unique draw method. That would mean that we could add any shape we wanted to the system, and we wouldn't have to change the DrawAnyShape function to use that shape.

Well, that tells us what the benefits of polymorphism are but doesn't really describe it, does it? *Polymorphism* is the ability to send the same message to two different objects and get two different results. In this case, the message was the invocation of the Draw method. To accomplish polymorphism, we must create a class or interface that all shapes derive (inherit) from that contains a Draw method. Each shape in turn would then redefine (override) what the Draw method does for its particular needs. In Chapter 8 you will use polymorphism through implementation inheritance and virtual functions.

Classroom Q & A

Q: A book on OOP used the terms *concrete* and *abstract inheritance*. Could you explain what these terms mean and how we can relate them to the terms discussed here?

A: No other programming topic has more terms that mean the same thing. To avoid stepping too much on later chapters, the short answer is that an abstract method has no code in it and is just a declaration (pure interface), and a concrete method does have code in it (implementation). The terms *concrete* and *abstract* in relation to inheritance refer to the inheritance of these two types of base class members. This becomes clearer when we discuss inheritance.

Q: What exactly is a member?
A: Anything we can put in a class is referred to as a member of that class. Any public variable in a class becomes a property member, and public subs or functions in a class become method members. Other members include events, enumerated lists, and other objects.

Q: Encapsulation isn't limited to classes. Can you expand on that and give an example?
A: Many people use encapsulation to refer to the concept that everything that represents a member of a class is contained in the class, meaning that the class totally encapsulates an entity type. When I design enterprise systems, I try very hard to build entire components as if they were black boxes, so if my business needs change, I can remove and replace any aspect of the system without breaking clients. I can pull this off only if I encapsulate groups of objects or components of a subsystem and only expose an abstracted interface to users of my components.

Q: Why is discussing OOP so important?
A: Everything you use, see, or do in .NET is an example of multiple OOP principles. Not understanding the concept of polymorphism can cripple an application's maintainability and performance. Conversely, the understanding of a concept such as polymorphism requires understanding of several, more basic OOP principles.

Class Basics

Classes are one of two templates used to create objects in .NET. Objects created from classes become reference types, created on the heap in memory, and are copied by reference. Objects created using a Structure become value types, are created on the stack in memory, and are copied by value. Every form, button, list box, or image you have used was created using a class. A class becomes a blueprint for an object type. As an architect builds a house from a blueprint, the architect can *inherit* the basic design of the house while adding a balcony or a turret (okay, well maybe not a turret). After the house has been built, the color scheme, family, latitude and longitude, and city location will be different for each house. When we create objects from a Person class, each person object in memory will have its own Name property value.

Classes can also have members that are shared among all instances (copies in memory) of a class. Maybe as each object is created, it increments some count variable so that the next instance will be created with an ID different from the others. In the house analogy, a water or electrical supply feeding a block of houses might be seen as a shared member.

Declaring Classes

Every form we have looked at in the Code Editor window is an example of a class declaration. Classes are declared using the Class keyword as in the following:

```
Public Class Person
    '...
End Class
```

Instantiating an Object from a Class

Instantiation refers to the creation of a separate object in memory based on some type. The following code creates an instance of type Person:

```
Dim someone as new Person()
```

Class Member Access Modifiers

Each member of a class is a modifier that determines its scope and visibility in an assembly. Private and Public work much the same as they do in Visual Basic 6.

Private Members

A member declared as private is only known and usable within the class that declared the member, but all other members of that class can see and use other private members of the same class.

Public Members

Any piece of code in any application, even a script written in Notepad, can access public members of a class. Because of this unlimited visibility, it's important to use a Public access modifier only when that extreme level of visibility is required.

Protected Members

Declaring a member of a class as Protected means that only code inside the class and classes derived (inheriting) from this class can see and use this member. This is useful when a method is meant only to be part of a particular inheritance hierarchy.

Friend Members

Because an assembly can contain more than one DLL, .NET needed an access modifier that allows a member in one class in a DLL to access a member of a class in another DLL within the same assembly. Declaring a member as Friend allows intra-assembly visibility. This access modifier in other .NET languages is called Internal, meaning internal to an assembly.

Protected Friend Members

In an either/or case, if a member in a class is declared as Protected Friend, any class that either inherits from or is in the same assembly as the declaring class will have access to this member.

If a class is declared as part of a Windows application, a form would have access to all Public, Friend, and Protected Friend members because they would be part of the same assembly. However, if the Windows application referenced a class library assembly containing a class, a form in the Windows application would have access only to Public members.

The following two classes were used to create Figure 6.3. The class SomeClassInAnotherAssembly represents a class in an assembly external to the assembly referencing the class. The class SomeClassInMyAssembly represents a class in the same assembly as that of referencing code.

```
Public Class SomeClassInAnotherAssembly
    Private vPrivate As Integer
    Friend vFriend As Integer
    Public vPublic As Integer
    Protected vProtected As Integer
    Protected Friend vProtectedFriend As Integer
End Class
```

```
Private Sub Button2_Click(...
    Dim obj1 As SomeClassInMyAssembly()
    Dim obj2 As ClassLibrary1.SomeClassInAnotherAssembly
    obj2.
End Sub  GetType
         vPublic

Private Sub Button2_Click(...
    Dim obj1 As SomeClassInMyAssembly()
    Dim obj2 As ClassLibrary1.SomeClassInAnotherAssembly
    obj1.
End Sub  GetType
         vFriend
         vProtectedFriend
         vPublic
```

Figure 6.3 Code from within a form in a Windows application would have access only to Public members of classes external to its assembly, but would have access to all Public, Friend, and Protected Friend members of classes in the same assembly.

```
Public Class SomeClassInMyAssembly
    Private vPrivate As Integer
    Friend vFriend As Integer
    Public vPublic As Integer
    Protected vProtected As Integer
    Protected Friend vProtectedFriend As Integer
End Class
```

Class Members

Some of theses items are abstract concepts, but class members can include properties, fields, constants, methods, enumerated lists, events, delegates, indexers, collections, constructors, destructors, and a great number of method variations that determine how they will be used in an object hierarchy.

Field and Property Members

Fields are variables declared within a class. Properties represent an accessor and mutator pair, used to access (Get) or manipulate (Set) the contents of a field. The following class demonstrates how you can create read- and write-only properties in Visual Basic .NET:

```
Public Class SomeClass
    Private m_name As String 'A Field
    Private m_data As String
    Public ReadOnly Property Name() As String 'A Property
        Get
            Return m_name
        End Get
    End Property
```

```
    Public WriteOnly Property Data() As String
        Set(ByVal Value As String)
            m_data = Value
        End Set
    End Property
End Class
```

Although Visual Basic 6 and some .NET languages allow you to omit the mutator (the Set statement) to make this a read-only property, in Visual Basic .NET you must specify ReadOnly or WriteOnly if you omit a Get or a Set statement in a property procedure.

Method Members

Public subs and functions in a class become methods of that class and are represented at runtime as MethodInfo objects for a class.

Overloading Methods

One of the most valuable things we can do in a class is to overload methods with useful variations so that programmers with different requirements can use the methods to suit their needs. Overloading a function is defined as multiple declarations of a method with the same name but with different arguments. Two methods with the same name and same arguments but with different return values are not considered overloaded and will not compile. The following code provides two overloads of a method GetDataSet. Both of these methods return a data set, but one requires a connection string and a command to be passed, whereas the other overload requires only a command to be passed and hard codes the connection string. Figure 6.4 shows how this appears in the IDE to a user of our class.

```
Dim o As New DataSvcs()
o.getDataSet(
  1 of 2  getDataSet (connection As String, command As String) As System.Data.DataSet
```

Figure 6.4 Intellisense shows two overloads for the method getDataSet. Overloads for a method have the same name but different parameter types.

```
Imports System.Data.OleDb
Imports System.Data
Public Class DataSvcs
    Public Function getDataSet(ByVal connection As String, _
ByVal command As String) _
As System.Data.DataSet
        Dim OA As New OleDbDataAdapter(command, connection)
        Dim DS As New System.Data.DataSet()
        OA.Fill(DS)
        Return DS
    End Function
    Public Function getDataSet(ByVal command As String) _
As System.Data.DataSet
        Dim OA As New OleDbDataAdapter(command, "data
source=(local)...")
        Dim DS As New System.Data.DataSet()
        OA.Fill(DS)
        Return DS
    End Function
End Class
```

Constructors

Class constructors are special method members of a class that are called when an object is created from that class. When you instantiate an object as new classtype(), you are calling a method with no arguments that has the same name as the class. Where other .NET languages might create constructors as methods with the same name as the class, Visual Basic .NET specifies a constructor for a class with a Sub New(). Many rules apply to the creation of a constructor in Visual Basic .NET, including the following:

- Declaration of a constructor is not allowed within an interface.
- Constructors cannot be declared as overrides.
- Constructors must be a sub, not a function.
- Constructors may be declared using any access modifier, including Private.

Overloading Constructors

Overloaded constructors allow you greater flexibility to create objects. In the case of our Person class, we might want to create a new Person and provide information to describe that person later, or we might want to create a new Person object and pass in the value for the Name property at the time of creation. The following class declaration provides overloaded constructors to support that:

```
Public Class Person
    Public Name As String
    Public Sub New(ByVal newName As String)
        Name = newName
    End Sub
    Public Sub New()
        Name = ""
    End Sub
End Class
```

By overloading the constructor in the Person class, you can create instances of class Person using either of the following declarations:

```
Dim object1 As New Person("Student1")
Dim object2 As New Person()
```

Shared Constructors

Normal constructors are referred to as instance constructors because each instance of the object has its own copy of any members not marked as Shared. What if each instance of a particular object needed to create its own data set object, but all objects used an identical connection string? By declaring the database connection object as a shared member and instantiating the connection object in a shared constructor, all objects of our type could share a single connection. In the case of a shared resource among objects, you have to be sure that you release the resource only when all objects are no longer in use. In the case where one of the objects might perform operations that require exclusive use of a resource, synchronization may become an issue. The following class uses a shared constructor to instantiate a shared member of type SqlConnection that is shared by all objects of that type:

```
Imports System.Data
Imports System.Data.SqlClient
Public Class DSVendor
   Shared con As SqlConnection
   Private adapter As SqlDataAdapter
   Shared Sub New()
      con = New SqlConnection("data source=(local);" & _
      "initial catalog=Northwind;integrated security=SSPI;" & _
      "persist security info=False;workstation id=BRUCE;" & _
      "packet size=4096")
   End Sub
   Public Function GetDataset(ByVal command As String) _
   As System.Data.DataSet
      adapter = New SqlDataAdapter(command, con)
      Dim DS As New DataSet()
      adapter.Fill(DS)
      Return DS
```

```
    End Function
'code should be modified to handle the
'eventual release of the connection object
End Class
```

Destructors

A destructor is similar to a Class Terminate event in Visual Basic 6. Destructors in Visual Basic .NET are implemented using a Public Sub name Finalize. The concept of object destruction is more complicated than simply declaring a destructor and placing code in the destructor to free resources. We cannot explicitly destroy objects in any .NET language. In virtually every class you ever build, you will implement an interface named IDisposable. That interface requires that you declare a single method named Dispose. It is an idiom in .NET programming that when you are done using an object, you call the Dispose method on your reference to that object and the Dispose method frees any resources that object was holding (but the object will not be removed from memory). After you have called Dispose on the object reference, you should set the reference to Nothing to decrease by 1 the underlying usage count for the object it was referencing.

A .NET subsystem known as the GC is responsible for freeing memory to the GC heap on your behalf. Because you have no way of knowing when the GC will free the objects in memory, use a Dispose method to be sure any files or database connections are freed as soon as the user of the object no longer needs the object. The GC only frees objects that do not have references to them. Remove a reference to an object by setting the reference to nothing. When the GC is about to free the object in memory, it looks to see if SuppressFinalize has been called on the object; if it has, the GC just destroys the object. Presumably, the reason SuppressFinalize would have been called is that the user of the object called Dispose when he or she was done. If SuppressFinalize has not been called for this object, the GC will invoke the Finalize method for the object. The latter is certainly not the desired scenario because the resources would be freed up potentially much later. The following code illustrates how Dispose and Finalize are used together and why there is a separate chapter for garbage collection and memory management:

```
Public Class SomeClass
    Implements IDisposable
    Public Overridable Sub Dispose() Implements IDisposable.Dispose
        'free any owned resources...
        System.GC.SuppressFinalize(Me)
    End Sub
    Protected Overrides Sub Finalize() 'Destructor
        Me.Dispose()
    End Sub
End Class
```

Programmers using this class must make a habit of calling Dispose to prevent things such as open files and open database connections from being freed only when the GC gets around to freeing unreferenced objects on the heap. The following code represents how users of this class would indicate that they are done using it:

```
Private Sub SomeClientCode(ByVal sender As System.Object, _
ByVal e As System.EventArgs) Handles Button4.Click
   Dim obj As New mychildclass()
   obj.Dispose()
   obj = Nothing 'just removes the reference, setting obj to Nothing
   '..does not have any effect on the memory pointed to by obj.
End Sub
```

Object destruction and the GC system are fully covered in Chapter 11, "Memory Management and Performance Monitoring."

Events

Whereas a method of an object is a way in which you can send messages to that object, an event is a way in which an object can send messages to a client. When an object is written to produce events, you only need to write code in the client for the events you want to capture. For a Button control, the number of events it supports is amazing, but I've never had to use 70 percent of them. Regardless of whether you write code to capture the events, the objects will raise these events anyway. Events are declared and raised in a class but can be handled (defined) differently for each client.

Adding Events to a Class

One method of adding events to a class is virtually identical to the process in Visual Basic 6. To add a new event, simply declare the event with any parameters it might take, as in the following:

```
Public Event namechanged(ByVal EmployeeID As Long)
```

When code in the class detects that this event condition has been met, the RaiseEvent statement can be used to raise the event in the client.

```
Public Class Employee
    Private m_Name As String
    Private m_ID As String
    Public Property Name()
        Get
            Return m_Name
        End Get
        Set(ByVal Value)
```

```
            m_Name = Value
            RaiseEvent NameChanged(m_ID)
        End Set
    End Property
    Public ReadOnly Property ID()
        Get
            Return m_ID
        End Get
    End Property
    Public Event namechanged(ByVal EmployeeID As Long)
End Class
```

Capturing Events in the Client

To capture events in the client that are raised in objects the client is using, declare the object reference using the WithEvents keyword in the client. In Visual Basic 6 you could declare object references with the WithEvents keyword inside a procedure, but it would have no effect. In Visual Basic .NET, the compiler complains if a WithEvents statement is used inside a procedure. After you declare a reference with the WithEvents keyword, that object appears in the Class Name drop-down list box in the upper left of the Code Editor window. The following example shows how you can cause and capture the NameChanged event for the Employee class:

```
Private WithEvents emp1 As New Employee()
Private Sub cmdTestClassEvent_Click(ByVal sender As System.Object, _
ByVal e As System.EventArgs) Handles cmdClassEvent.Click
   emp1.Name = strName 'causes event to occur in object
End Sub
'Employee NameChanged Event Handler:
Private Sub emp1_NameChanged(ByVal EmployeeID As Long) _
Handles emp1.NameChanged
   MessageBox.Show("event occurred")
End Sub
```

There are a few rules and notes of interest for Event declarations. Events can be declared using any access modifier, cannot have return values, cannot use optional arguments, and cannot specify ParamArray arguments.

Handling Events with Dynamic Delegates

WithEvents is one way of handling events, but it is unique to Visual Basic .NET in the .NET world. Another, more powerful method for event handling uses a concept known as delegation. Delegation is a process by which one method in the class handles an event notification on our behalf. Delegates work by using the AddHandler statement to indicate that a particular local method should be invoked when a particular event in an external component occurs.

Classroom Q & A

Q: In the previous example, shouldn't the reference emp1 be set to Nothing when you're done with it?

A: In the example that code was taken from, I set emp1 to Nothing in the Closing event for the Form in which I made the instantiation.

Q: Why would I want to dynamically unhandle an event?

A: Let's answer that by describing a set of objects I recently worked with and why I found the ability useful then. The customer used server-side components that provided critical situation data to listener stations via events. Each of these objects was creating roughly 10 events and each client workstation was responsible for monitoring exactly one object type. The first design approach was in Visual Basic 6, which had 10 separate windows logging events as they occurred—it was doggedly slow and not very useful. The customer did try building the event handlers so that when an event occurred, it wrote to the window only if the window was already open. But the events were still occurring on the client side because the object variable producing the event was declared in the MDI parent form and was executing a check to see if the form was open almost every second. I rebuilt the client rather quickly in Visual Basic .NET using dynamic handlers that severed the receipt of events when a particular message portal (event window) was closed so that no needless processing was occurring.

Q: Could you show us how that might be implemented?

A: Lab 4.2 walks you through a process that simulates the customer's event-noisy classes and writes an interface similar to what I built for the customer.

Lab 4.2: Understanding Dynamic Delegates

This lab helps you feel comfortable with the implementation and use of delegates and dynamic event handling. It starts off by implementing a class with three separate events that are triggered by a programmatic Timer to simulate real-time events. After you have created the class, you'll build delegates associated with simple message portals for each event type.

This lab incorrectly makes a direct reference to a class library that presumably resides on the server. In reality, clients make a Web Reference to an XML Web service that contains or wraps server-side functionality for consumption by remote clients. Web services have not been introduced yet.

Perform the following steps:

1. Start a new Visual Basic class library Application named EventSource.
2. Add a client application to the same solution by selecting File, Add Project, New Project, Windows Application and name it EventPortals.

   If you look at the projects in the Solution Explorer, you will see that the class library project is in boldface, indicating that it is the startup project. The Windows application EventPortals should be the startup application.
3. Right-click on the Project EventPortals in the Solution Explorer and select Set As Startup Project to make it the startup project.
4. Rename Class1.vb to mission.vb in the Solution Explorer Window by right-clicking Class1.vb and selecting Rename.

   Your Solution Explorer window should be similar to Figure 6.5.
5. Double-click Mission.vb in the Solution Explorer window to open your class in the Code Editor window.
6. In the Code Editor window, change the name of the class to Mission and add the three events as shown here:

```
Public Class Mission
   Event MissionDataType1(ByVal data As String)
   Event MissionDataType2(ByVal data As String)
   Event MissionDataType3(ByVal data As String)
End Class
```

Figure 6.5 Your Solution Explorer window should contain a Windows application, EventPortals, and a class library named EventSource, which contains a single class mission.

7. Next, add a simulator to cause these events to continually fire in the class. Do this with a Timer object. Add the following code to create a Timer that raises events in the client:

```
Public Class Mission
    Event MissionDataType1(ByVal data As String)
    Event MissionDataType2(ByVal data As String)
    Event MissionDataType3(ByVal data As String)
    Private t As New Timers.Timer()
    Public Sub New()
        t.Interval = 1000 ' one second
        'Make The Function TimerEventHandler The Event Handler
        'Event Handler for the Timer's Elapsed event.
        AddHandler t.Elapsed, AddressOf TimerEventHandler
        t.Enabled = True
    End Sub
    Private Sub TimerEventHandler(ByVal sender As Object, _
    ByVal e As System.Timers.ElapsedEventArgs)
        RaiseEvent MissionDataType1(Now.ToString() & "type1")
        RaiseEvent MissionDataType2(Now.ToString() & "type2")
        RaiseEvent MissionDataType3(Now.ToString() & "type3")
    End Sub
End Class
```

8. Right-click the EventSource project in the Solution Explorer window and select Properties to open the EventSource Property Pages.
9. In the EventSource Property Pages, verify that Common Properties, General, Root Namespace is set to EventSource as shown in Figure 6.6.

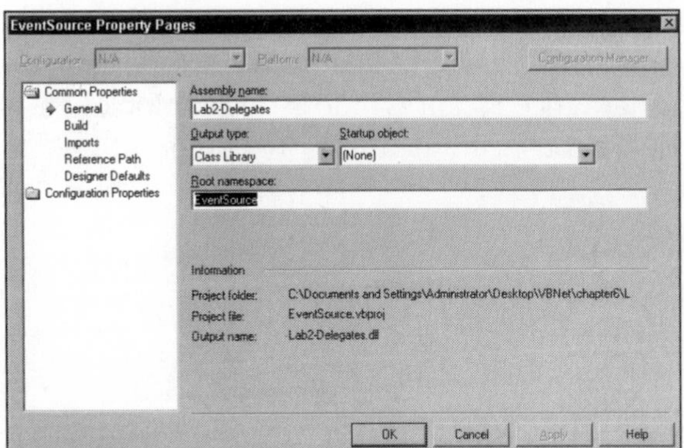

Figure 6.6 The Root namespace determines how classes in the DLL can be referenced from client applications. The default for this name is the name of the current solution in Visual Studio.

10. In the Windows application EventPortals, rename Form1 to frmMain in the Solution Explorer window.
11. In the Properties window, change frmMain's Name property to frmMain.
12. Make frmMain a MDI parent by setting its IsMdiContainer property and WindowState properties to True.
13. Add a new Form named frmPortalTemplate.
14. Add a ListBox control lstMissionData to frmPortalTemplate.
15. Change lstMissionData's Dock property to All to cause it to fill the entire design area of the Form.
16. Select Build from the Build menu. Be sure there are no errors before continuing.
17. To access the Mission class in the class library, you need to set a reference to the class library from the Windows application. To set a reference, select Project, Add Reference, Projects tab; double-click EventSource; and click OK. To verify that the reference has been made, expand References in the Solution Explorer window for your Windows application. Figure 6.7 shows the addition of the new reference to the class library.

Step 18 adds a form using a concept known as Visual Inheritance. Be careful to select Add Inherited Form when adding additional forms in the following step.

18. Select Project, Add Inherited Form and add a new form named frmMD1Portal and choose frmPortalTemplate from the Inheritance Picker window. If the Inheritance Picker window doesn't look like Figure 6.8, select Build from the Build menu before reattempting this step.

Figure 6.7 References to external assemblies are listed in the References folder in the Solution Explorer. References can be added via the Project menu or by right-clicking on the References folder.

19. Repeat the previous step for frmMD2Portal and frmMD3Portal.

    The next step is to add a subroutine that acts as an event handler and use the Load and Closing events to assign and unassign that event handler to capture incoming event data.

20. Add the following code to frmMD1Portal:

```
Dim objMission As New EventSource.Mission()
Private Sub Handler(ByVal msg As String)
   lstMissionData.Items.Add(msg)
End Sub
Private Sub frmMD1Portal_Load(ByVal sender As Object,
ByVal e As System.EventArgs) Handles MyBase.Load
   Me.Text = "Portal: Mission Data Type 1"
   AddHandler objMission.MissionDataType1, AddressOf Handler
End Sub
Private Sub frmMD1Portal_Closing(ByVal sender As Object, _
ByVal e As System.ComponentModel.CancelEventArgs) Handles
MyBase.Closing
   RemoveHandler objMission.MissionDataType1, AddressOf Handler
   objMission = Nothing
End Sub
```

21. Add the following code to frmMD2Portal:

```
Dim objMission As New EventSource.Mission()
Private Sub Handler(ByVal msg As String)
   lstMissionData.Items.Add(msg)
End Sub
Private Sub frmMD2Portal_Load(ByVal sender As Object, _ _
ByVal e As System.EventArgs) Handles MyBase.Load
   Me.Text = "Portal: Mission Data Type 2"
   AddHandler objMission.MissionDataType2, AddressOf Handler
End Sub
Private Sub frmMD2Portal_Closing(ByVal sender As Object, _
ByVal e As System.ComponentModel.CancelEventArgs) Handles
MyBase.Closing
   RemoveHandler objMission.MissionDataType2, AddressOf Handler
   objMission=nothing
End Sub
```

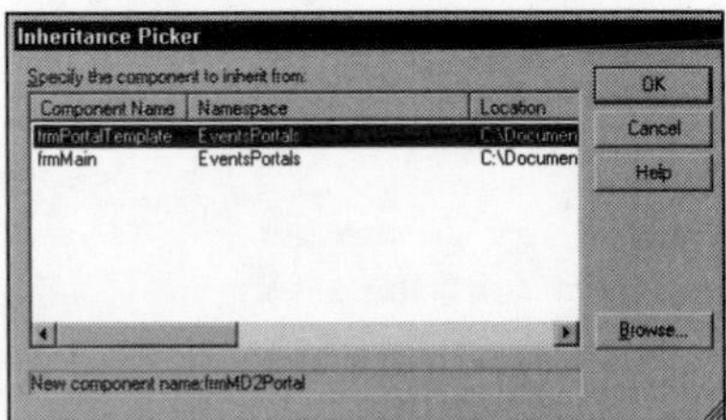

Figure 6.8 The Inheritance Picker window is used to determine from which forms visual inheritance will be derived.

22. Add the following code to frmMD3Portal:

```
Dim objMission As New EventSource.Mission()
Private Sub Handler(ByVal msg As String)
   lstMissionData.Items.Add(msg)
End Sub
Private Sub frmMD3Portal_Load(ByVal sender As Object, _ _
ByVal e As System.EventArgs) Handles MyBase.Load
   Me.Text = "Portal: Mission Data Type 3"
   AddHandler objMission.MissionDataType3, AddressOf Handler
End Sub
Private Sub frmMD3Portal_Closing(ByVal sender As Object, _ _
ByVal e As System.ComponentModel.CancelEventArgs) Handles
MyBase.Closing
   RemoveHandler objMission.MissionDataType3, AddressOf Handler
   objMission=nothing
End Sub
```

23. Double-click frmMain in the Solution Explorer window to enter Designer mode for frmMain.
24. Change the Text property for frmMain to Portal Viewer.
25. Add a MainMenu control to frmMain and create the following menus:

MENU TEXT	MENU NAME
&File	mnuFile
&Open	mnuFileOpen
MD1Portal	mnuFileOpenMD1Portal
MD2Portal	mnuFileOpenMD2Portal
MD3Portal	mnuFileOpenMD3Portal
E&xit	mnuFileExit

26. Add the following code for the open portal menu items:

```
Private Sub mnuFileOpenMD1Portal_Click(ByVal sender As
System.Object, _
ByVal e As System.EventArgs) Handles mnuFileOpenMD1Portal.Click
   Dim myform As New frmMD1Portal()
   myform.MdiParent = Me
   myform.Show()
End Sub
Private Sub mnuFileOpenMD2Portal_Click(ByVal sender As
System.Object, _  ByVal e As System.EventArgs) Handles
mnuFileOpenMD2Portal.Click
   Dim myform As New frmMD2Portal()
   myform.MdiParent = Me
   myform.Show()
```

```
End Sub
Private Sub mnuFileOpenMD3Portal_Click(ByVal sender As
System.Object, _
ByVal e As System.EventArgs) Handles mnuFileOpenMD3Portal.Click
   Dim myform As New frmMD3Portal()
   myform.MdiParent = Me
   myform.Show()
End Sub
```

Although you could literally leave this particular implementation running for a long time, it is inappropriate to continually fill a list box without occasionally clearing it to a file. It is also inappropriate to continually write to a file, for performance reasons.

27. Test the application by running it and using the File, Open menus to open each of the three windows. Your application should be similar to Figure 6.9.

    You could change quite a few things to improve on this, but let's finish the optimization of removing the need for three separate objMission variables. Because you are already inheriting implementation from frmPortalTemplate in each of the three child forms, you could just add the declaration there. Without the background of several of the later chapters in this book, you'll find that making that work is more difficult than it seems. For now, the easiest implementation is to declare the variable objMission as Friend in frmMain.

28. Remove the declaration of objMission from all three child forms.

    You may recall from our discussion of access modifiers that Friend allowed objects in the same assembly access to members.

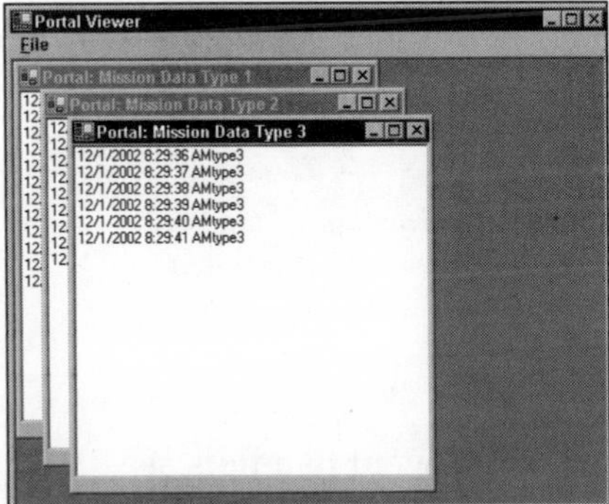

Figure 6.9 The event handlers in each form continually respond to events from a Mission object and report the event data to the inherited lstMissionData list box.

29. Add the following line of code to frmMain. This code must appear as a member of the frmMain class and not be placed inside any method or event.

```
Friend objMission As New EventSource.Mission()
```

You have another issue now, however. Now that objMission is in a centralized location, you shouldn't be setting it to Nothing as each form closes because other forms may still be using the variable.

30. Remove the statement from the Closing event for each of the child forms that sets objMission to Nothing and add a statement that sets it to Nothing in the Closing event for frmMain, as shown here:

```
Private Sub frmMain_Closing(ByVal sender As Object, _
ByVal e As System.ComponentModel.CancelEventArgs) Handles
MyBase.Closing
   objMission = Nothing
End Sub
```

The next step may seem strange but should certainly be something the previous chapters have prepared you to do. You need to adjust each of the forms to refer to the objMission reference variable that is declared in frmMain. There are different ways to accomplish this, but the following solution uses a reference to Me.MdiParent to refer to frmMain. The problem is that objMission is a variable on frmMain, but MdiParent is not an object of type frmMain, so some casting is required.

31. Modify frmMD1Portal's Load and Closing event handlers as follows:

```
Private Sub frmMD1Portal_Load(ByVal sender As Object, _
ByVal e As System.EventArgs) Handles MyBase.Load
   Me.Text = "Portal: Mission Data Type 1"
   AddHandler
CType(Me.MdiParent,frmMain).objMission.MissionDataType1, _
   AddressOf Handler
End Sub
Private Sub frmMD1Portal_Closing(ByVal sender As Object, _
ByVal e As System.ComponentModel.CancelEventArgs) Handles _
MyBase.Closing RemoveHandler CType(Me.MdiParent,frmMain)._
objMission.MissionDataType1, _
   AddressOf Handler
End Sub
```

32. Modify frmMD2Portal's Load and Closing event handlers as follows:

```
Private Sub frmMD2Portal_Load(ByVal sender As Object, _
ByVal e As System.EventArgs) Handles MyBase.Load
   Me.Text = "Portal: Mission Data Type 2"
```

```
    AddHandler
CType(Me.MdiParent,frmMain).objMission.MissionDataType2, _
    AddressOf Handler
End Sub
Private Sub frmMD2Portal_Closing(ByVal sender As Object, _
ByVal e As System.ComponentModel.CancelEventArgs) Handles
MyBase.Closing
    RemoveHandler
CType(Me.MdiParent,frmMain).objMission.MissionDataType2, _
    AddressOf Handler
End Sub
```

33. Modify frmMD3Portal's Load and Closing event handlers as follows:

```
Private Sub frmMD3Portal_Load(ByVal sender As Object, _
ByVal e As System.EventArgs) Handles MyBase.Load
    Me.Text = "Portal: Mission Data Type 3"
    AddHandler
CType(Me.MdiParent,frmMain).objMission.MissionDataType3, _
    AddressOf Handler
End Sub
Private Sub frmMD3Portal_Closing(ByVal sender As Object, _
ByVal e As System.ComponentModel.CancelEventArgs) Handles
MyBase.Closing
    RemoveHandler
CType(Me.MdiParent,frmMain).objMission.MissionDataType3, _
    AddressOf Handler
End Sub
```

34. Test the application again to be sure everything is working accordingly. You should be able to open and close as many of these forms as you want without having any errors associated with an uninstantiated objMission variable. If errors occur, ensure that no piece of code other than the frmMain Closing event handler is setting objMission to Nothing.

This lab tied together most of the chapter by adding several server-side events, dynamic event handlers in the client, and the capability to "turn off" events. By inheriting some rather simple UI from frmPortalTemplate, we used a .NET feature known as Visual Inheritance, which is a form of implementation inheritance. Although it's nice to see the implementation of a programmatic Timer implemented, please keep in mind that it was used to simulate my customer's server-side event messaging disseminator. There is actually another type of Timer available to Windows forms, called Timer, that uses a Tick event instead on an Elapsed event.

Classroom Q & A

Q: In the Lab 4.2, to set objMission to Nothing, couldn't we have just added code to each of the Closing event handlers in the child forms but check Me.MdiParent.MdiChildren.Length, and only set the variable to Nothing if Length was 1, indicating that the child we are destroying is the last child?

A: If you tried that and opened all three forms, closed all three forms, and then tried to open another form, that form would crash. There are two notes of interest that help explain why. First, each time a child form inherits from frmPortalTemplate, it creates a new frmPortalTemplate in memory that is unique to that child form. The problem is that objMission is a static member and persists separately from each of the instances of frmPortalTemplate. So if the last remaining MDI form set the objMission object to Nothing, the next child opened would cause the creation of its own frmPortalTemplate, which would expect to find a static (*shared* in Visual Basic .NET) variable objMission. But that would not be the case. We'd get an exception for use of an uninstantiated variable.

Q: In the code in the portal forms that refer to frmMain by casting Me.MdiParent to frmMain, why couldn't we just reference frmMain directly?

A: It does look like that would work, but frmMain is a type, not an instance of a type. It would be like referencing TextBox.Text and trying to get the data out of txtUserName.Text.

Summary

This chapter introduced the class as a template for an object. We successfully used a class library and dynamically handled events from an object in an external assembly. With a solid understanding of the basics of classes in .NET we can now begin to add complex support to our objects. As we progress through the remaining chapters, we will continually add features and support for numerous interfaces in the .NET framework and extend our understanding of .NET enterprise architecture.

Review Questions

1. How do Windows applications consume remote objects in .NET?
   a. By referencing the remote assembly using Add Reference
   b. By using Add Web Reference to reference an XML Web service that provides Web-callable versions of objects in class library
   c. By using Add Reference to reference an XML Web service that provides Web-callable versions of objects in class library
   d. By using Add Web Reference to reference a remote class library containing the objects
2. Which of the following are acceptable ways to create a read-only property in Visual Basic .NET?
   a. Declaring the property procedure without a Get statement
   b. Declaring the property procedure without a Set statement
   c. Declaring the property procedure without a Let statement
   d. Declaring the property procedure without a Set statement and marking the property ReadOnly
3. Which of these are benefits of classes that have a high level of abstraction? Select all the correct answers.
   a. Simplified class interface.
   b. Details can be changed without breaking the client.
   c. Client doesn't need to know about implementation details.
   d. Decrease in development time for developers using those classes.
4. How do you call a destructor for a class?
   a. The destructor is called automatically when you set an object to Nothing.
   b. By using the Delete keyword.
   c. By calling Dispose on the object reference.
   d. You can't.
5. Which of the following correctly associates myHandler as an event handler for myObj.Event1?
   a. AddHandler myHandler, AddressOf myObj.Event1
   b. AddHandler myObj.Event1, AddressOf myHandler
   c. AddHandler AddressOf myHandler, myObj.Event1
   d. AddHandler AddressOf myObj1.Event1, myHandler

6. True or False: Just like in Visual Basic 6, declaring an object variable WithEvents inside a sub will compile but will not allow access to events.

7. Which of the following are true? Select all correct answers.
   a. Class events are declared, defined, and raised inside the class.
   b. Class events are declared and raised inside the class, but each client must provide a method definition for handling a class event.
   c. Class events are declared and defined external to the class, but events are raised from the class using the RaiseEvent keyword.
   d. Class events are defined inside and raised inside the class but declared in client code.

8. What is the expected procedure for indicating that your client code has finished using a particular object?
   a. Call Dispose on the object; then set the object to Nothing.
   b. Set the object to Nothing; then call Dispose.
   c. Set the object to Nothing; then call IDisposable.
   d. Set the object to Nothing.

9. When are objects destroyed?
   a. When the GC is executed and when there are no references to the object.
   b. The GC runs at regular intervals to clean up objects that have no valid references.
   c. When the GC is executed and when Dispose has been called on the object.
   b. The GC runs at regular intervals to clean up objects that have been disposed.

10. A developer started a new solution in Visual Studio .NET, adding a new class library and a new Windows application. After writing client and server code, she set a reference to the class library from the Windows application and pressed F5. A warning message popped up and would not allow her to execute the project. How can this be resolved?

Answers to Review Questions

1. **b.** Windows applications consume remote objects in .NET by using Add Web Reference to reference an XML Web service that provides Web-callable versions of objects in class library.
2. **d.** Declaring the property procedure without a Set statement and marking the property ReadOnly will make the property read-only. Let statements are no longer used in Visual Basic, and simply removing the Set statement will produce a compiler error stating that the omission of the Set statement requires a ReadOnly modifier.
3. **a**, **b**, **c**, and **d.** All these are benefits of classes that have a high level of abstraction.
4. **d.** You can't explicitly call a destructor or explicitly destroy objects in any .NET language. The destructor for an object is called only when the GC is about to destroy an object for which SuppressFinalize has not been called. The Delete keyword is used in C++ to destroy objects instantiated with New but has no place in a GC environment.
5. **b.** The other choices are simply bad form and will not compile.
6. False. In Visual Basic 6, declaring an object variable WithEvents inside a sub will not allow access to events, but in .NET it also won't compile.
7. **b.** The term *defined* is reserved for the actual implementation of code, whereas a class simply declares the event and raises it as needed.
8. **a.** To indicate that your client code has finished using a particular object, call Dispose on the object and then set the object to Nothing.
9. **a.** An object is destroyed when the GC is executed and there are no references to the object. In addition, although we haven't fully discussed the GC yet, it may still not free certain objects if it frees up what it sees as significant memory before getting to a particular object's generation.
10. Right-click on the name of the Windows application in the Solution Explorer and make it the startup project.

CHAPTER

7

Extending Visual Basic .NET Classes

Simply creating classes for the sake of having objects won't provide us with the types of class libraries that actually get reused. Beyond the syntax of declaring a class and discussing members and such, we must look at alternative development and design options for classes such as collection classes and classes that support high reusability. In this chapter we discuss the implementation of collection-related interfaces and other methods for adding value to our classes. With the power provided by the myriad of classes and interfaces in Visual Basic .NET we not only create applications quickly as we did in Visual Basic 6, but we can add a certain elegance and sophistication that quickly becomes intoxicating for developers unfamiliar with OOP languages such as C++. C++ developers who migrate to C#, on the other hand, gain a development system for building applications that makes Windows application development much easier. The primary focus of this chapter is to show you how classes must be built with requirements in mind and how to apply various design features to meet those requirements. Even in such a common collection as a deck of cards, because of the tremendous variation of games played with cards, the implementation can become surprisingly complex.

Building Collection Classes

Let's start the process of extending a class to support a collection by looking briefly at an incorrect approach and moving gradually toward the implementation of the IList, IEnumerable, and ICollection interfaces. Ultimately, we will use the CollectionBase class to help us toward that goal.

The Card Class

Let's see what would be involved in creating the concept of a deck of cards and the types of operations associated with that deck. This particular example is one of my favorites because it's a collection of things we all know and conceptually understand, and it represents a perfect set of requirements to implement all the features we need to focus on at the moment.

We create a collection by creating a class to act as a collection. In Microsoft Excel, for example, all WorkSheet objects are contained in and managed by a collection object named WorkSheets. To create a library to deal with cards, we need objects of type Card, Cards, Deck, and Hand. The collection class, of course, is Cards, and when created as an object, it will contain Card objects. By separating Cards and Deck into two separate objects, we can have Decks of various sizes for games that do or do not require jokers, or games such as pinochle that don't require a full deck. To begin our library, we'll build a Card class.

The examples related to cards are to elicit understanding of extended class library development concerns and do not make any attempt to render associated graphics for card faces.

Building a Card Class

The basic class to represent a playing card should have at least a suit property and a property for its face value. Let's start with that. The following class represents the basic Card class:

```
Public Class Card
    Public Suit As ?
    Public FaceValue As ?
    Public Sub New(ByVal suit, ByVal value)
        Me.Suit = suit
        Me.FaceValue = value
    End Sub
End Class
```

Adding Enumerated Lists

The Suit and FaceValue properties need to be some type that makes sense, but it would also be nice to somehow limit the suits to hearts, clubs, spades, and diamonds and to limit the face value of the card to ace through king or, possibly, joker. Another problem is that if we use something like an Integer to control the face card values, what a value of 13 might be may become ambiguous.

One solution is to create an enumerated list for both properties, as shown in the following modified version of class Card:

```
Public Class Card
   Public Enum SuitType
      Hearts = 1
      Clubs = 2
      Diamonds = 3
      Spades = 4
      None = 5 'reserved for Jokers
   End Enum
   Public Enum FaceType
      Ace  = 1  : Two = 2  : Three = 3 : Four = 4
      Five = 5  : Six = 6  : Seven = 7 : Eight = 8
      Nine = 9  : Ten = 10 : Jack = 11 : Queen = 12
      King = 13 : Joker = 14
   End Enum
   Public suit As SuitType
   Public value As FaceType
End Class
```

To use these enumerated lists, anyone implementing this class can create a card by using this syntax:

```
Dim c As New Card()
c.Suit = Card.SuitType.Clubs
c.FaceValue = Card.FaceType.Ace
```

Using three lines of code to create a new object and make it usable is certainly something we can improve upon.

Controlling Construction

The problem with this class now is that it requires knowledge of the class members even to create a useful Card object. Although it wouldn't take much for someone to figure out what two properties need to be set to make a valid card, remember that this example is something we all already understand conceptually. Not every class you use is based on such an easily grasped foundation, and we shouldn't rely on a consumer of our class to set additional properties for an object after its construction just to create a valid object. In the case of a card, we have to ask ourselves if we really need to make the Suit and FaceValue properties both public and write-able. It is probably best, in this class, to prevent the creation of a Card object that has no suit or face value and to make both properties read-only. Our class could be rewritten like this:

```
Public Class Card
   Private m_suit As SuitType
   Private m_facevalue As FaceType
   Public Enum SuitType
      Hearts = 1
      Clubs = 2
      Diamonds = 3
      Spades = 4
      None = 5
   End Enum
   Public Enum FaceType
      Ace = 1 : Two = 2 : Three = 3 : Four = 4
      Five = 5 : Six = 6 : Seven = 7 : Eight = 8
      Nine = 9 : Ten = 10 : Jack = 11 : Queen = 12
      King = 13 : Joker = 14
   End Enum
   Public ReadOnly Property Suit() As SuitType
      Get
         Return Me.m_suit
      End Get
   End Property
   Public ReadOnly Property FaceValue() As FaceType
      Get
         Return Me.m_facevalue
      End Get
   End Property
'constructor
   Public Sub New(ByVal value As FaceType, _
      ByVal suit As SuitType)
      Me.m_suit = suit
      Me.m_facevalue = value
   End Sub
End Class
```

These modifications are most clearly seen as improvements to the user of our class. Figure 7.1 shows how easy it is to use the new constructor because of the enumerations.

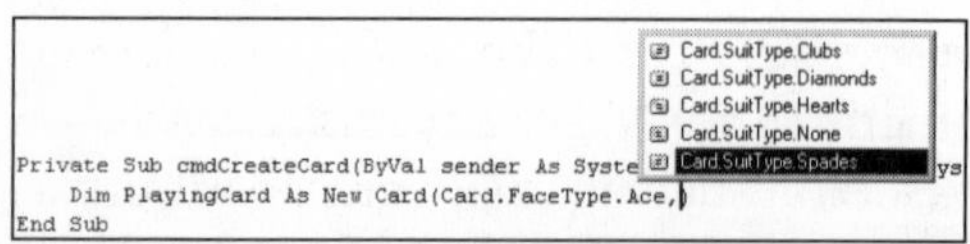

Figure 7.1 The Card class abstracts the underlying details and is easy to use.

Obtaining the Card Value

Obtaining a Card value by separately accessing the card's face value and suit is terse. We still need some method of obtaining the card's face and suit that is intuitive and doesn't require the class consumer to call the individual properties. The ToString method inherited from System.Object is most certainly something a developer will try when experimenting with a new class. ToString is declared as an overridable function in System.Object. The Overridable keyword and inheritance are covered in Chapter 8, "Implementation Inheritance." Declaring a method in a base class (like system.Object) as overridable allows classes that inherit from that base class to redefine what that method does for a derived class (like Card). The following code overrides the ToString method in our class to retrieve the card value:

```
Public Overrides Function ToString() As String
   'This code is not yet optimized:
   If Me.m_facevalue <> FaceType.Joker Then
      Return Me.m_facevalue.ToString() & " of " & _
      Me.m_suit.ToString()
   Else
      Return "Joker"
   End If
End Function
```

The purpose of this particular modification isn't to talk about overriding method but rather, the enhancement of a class in an expected way. For a Person class, the ToString method is expected to return the person's name. .NET programmers intuitively attempt to use ToString on almost every class they use, hoping it has a useful override.

Requirements and Class Design

Although we've all built traditional client-side applications without first gathering a detailed set of requirements, object-oriented systems don't lend themselves to that type of development. Well-defined objects and object relations can be described and built only after we identify the requirements on those objects.

We could go a very long way with such a class as Card before someone mentioned to us that in many variations of the game Spades, there aren't just two jokers; there is actually a big and a little joker, of which the big joker is the superior. Such a requirement in a system might be missed until late in development, requiring hours of rewrites on our classes because of supporting code and logic. This won't be too painful because we haven't progressed too far, but the following changes to the SuitType enum and the ToString() override are necessary to differentiate between the two types of jokers. Additionally, both the SuitType and FaceType enums must be changed to support value comparisons for our cards, requiring Joker to be a SuitType. This does, however, allow us to also simplify our ToString override, also shown in the following code:

```
Public Enum SuitType
  Hearts = 1
  Clubs = 2
  Diamonds = 3
  Spades = 4
  Joker = 5 'must move here since Big and Little are values
End Enum
Public Enum FaceType
  Ace = 1 : Two = 2 : Three = 3 : Four = 4
  Five = 5 : Six = 6 : Seven = 7 : Eight = 8
  Nine = 9 : Ten = 10 : Jack = 11 : Queen = 12
  King = 13 : Little = 14 : Big = 15
End Enum
Public Overrides Function ToString() As String 'works more
                                               'intuitively now
  Return Me.m_suit.ToString() & " " & Me.m_facevalue.ToString()
End Function
```

Our Experience Can Limit Our Design

After having changed the implementation of our Card class to support big and little jokers, you may find that Pinochle values a 10 over a king and values a 9 of trump (a deece) at 10 points. My point is that there is an infinite number of variations for card games and our class only has to support, not implement, them. Our Card class should represent a card, our Deck class should represent a deck, and neither should implicitly take into account a game variation.

In the Navy, I found that most people from the East Coast prefer to play Spades with joker, ace, and deuce as the three highest cards. Because of this problem with value, we need to add a property to enable the implementers of our Card class to assign a value to each card that makes sense to the game they happen to be supporting. The addition of such a field member class warrants something describing the intended usage, so I add a description attribute in the following code:

```
Imports System.ComponentModel
Public Class Card
   ...
   <Description("Game-Specific Value")>
 Public AssignedValue As Integer
   ...
End class
```

If the designer of a class omitted such a flexible way of handling value, the consumer of the class can inherit from Card and add a new value in the derived class.

The Deck Class

We'll produce our Deck in stages. First, we create a simple implementation that works well enough but will need some changes to better protect the class. To construct a deck of cards, we need some sort of collection to hold the cards.

Using a Simple Array

This first attempt uses an array to hold a full deck, including jokers. It's important to see what the limitations of this version are, and whether any changes are warranted, to understand why some improvements might be needed for this class.

```
Public Class Deck
   'This code is not yet optimized:
   Public cards(53) As Card '54 cards
   Public Sub New() 'constructor
      createdeck()
   End Sub
   Public Sub createdeck()
      Dim TheSuit As Integer
      Dim TheFace As Integer
      Dim currentcard as Integer = 0
      For TheSuit = 1 To 4
         For TheFace = 1 To 13
            Cards(currentcard) = New Card(CType(TheFace,
Card.FaceType), _
            CType(TheSuit, Card.SuitType))
            currentcard += 1
         Next
      Next
         Cards(52) = New Card(Card.FaceType.Big,
Card.SuitType.Joker)
         Cards(53) = New Card(Card.FaceType.little,
Card.SuitType.Joker)
   End Sub
End Class
```

This class creates an array of Card objects, using our enumerated lists to make the process simple. Also, note how readable the code is when consuming our Card class with just what we've implemented so far.

Using a Deck

Consuming the Deck class is pretty straightforward because the work is done during its construction. The Deck class doesn't support a shuffle method yet, but the following code can at least be used to prove we're playing with a full deck before we start extending this class:

```
Dim D As New Deck()
Dim C As Card
For Each C In D.Cards
   MessageBox.Show(C.ToString())
Next
```

Problems with the Lack of Abstraction

It may seem that this approach looks and acts correctly, but a user of this class can do several things that are, at best, disturbing even for an object hierarchy that only uses decks of cards.

Consumers of the Deck class can actually clear the entire contents of the deck, leaving it in a state where almost any operation causes an error:

```
Dim D As New Deck()
D.Cards.Clear(D.Cards, 0, D.Cards.Length)
MessageBox.Show(D.Cards(1).FaceValue.ToString()) 'ERROR, no
                                                  'object at index
```

If that isn't enough, it is also possible for Deck class consumers to violate array bounds because the underlying array isn't abstracted from public view. The following code causes an out-of-bounds error on an attempt to access an array position past the end of our cards collection:

```
Dim D As New Deck()
MessageBox.Show(D.Cards(54).FaceValue.ToString()) 'ERROR,
                                                   'bounds violation
```

For each class we implement, we must determine what capabilities and limitations users of our classes should have. It's safe to assume that the Deck object on a poker machine that pays the winner doesn't have the ability to change individual cards as a public-exposed method. Each class you create has different needs.

Creating a Proper Collection Class (Cards)

We have several options for creating a collection, but they come in varying degrees of complexity. Most collections are implementations of the IList, ICollection, and IEnumerable interfaces. Manually supporting these interfaces was the first thing I tried in .NET, not having the experience to know better, and it took a great deal of code for each class. What I learned is that most collections can be implemented well enough with the CollectionBase class, which provides much of the internal plumbing for collection interfaces.

CollectionBase

CollectionBase provides prebuilt implementations of a Clear method, a Count property, and a List property. To include the built-in support for a collection in our collection class, we start by inheriting from the CollectionBase class:

```
Public Class Cards
    Inherits System.Collections.CollectionBase
End Class
```

Implementing CollectionBase Members

To provide the required functionality for our Cards collection, we must implement an Add method, Remove method, and an Item property to refer to individual items in the underlying collection (List). The following implementations of Add and Item ensure that only Card objects can be added to a CardCollection object:

```
Public Class CardCollection
   Inherits System.Collections.CollectionBase
   Public Sub Add(ByVal c As Card)
      List.Add(c)
   End Sub
   Public Sub Remove(ByVal index As Integer)
      If index < Count And index >= 0 Then
         List.RemoveAt(index)
      Else 'invalid index
      End If
   End Sub
   Public ReadOnly Property Item(ByVal index As Integer) _
   As Card
      Get
         Return CType(List.Item(index), Card)
      End Get
   End Property
End Class
```

When implementing CollectionBase in C#, Item must be a method instead of a property because C# methods can't take parameters.

Using Our Custom Collection Class

Now that we have effectively replaced the embedded array in the Deck class with a custom collection, we need to integrate the use of CardCollection. The following Deck class modification implements the new CardCollection class functionality:

```
Public Class Deck
    Public Cards As New CardCollection()
     Public Sub New() 'constructor
        CreateDeck()
     End Sub
     Public Sub CreateDeck()
        Cards.Clear()
        Dim TheSuit As Integer : Dim TheFace As Integer
        For TheSuit = 1 To 4
           For TheFace = 1 To 13
              Cards.Add(New Card(CType(TheFace, _
              Card.FaceType), CType(TheSuit, Card.SuitType)))
           Next
        Next
        Cards.Add(New Card(Card.FaceType.Big, _
        Card.SuitType.Joker))
        Cards.Add(New Card(Card.FaceType.Little, _
        Card.SuitType.Joker))
        Me.Shuffle()
     End Sub
End Class
```

The client code, however, reveals that even though certain issues are resolved, several remain. For example, although classes using a CardCollection need access to members to aid in the manipulation and creation of collections, client-side applications should not have this level of access. Figure 7.2 shows that client code in a Windows application still has full access to both the CreateDeck method and the Cards collection.

Appropriate Member Access

Windows applications that are consuming the Deck object should only be able to draw cards and shuffle the deck. Games that recycle cards might need to place a card back into the deck. The point is that when implementing such a class, we need to take a hard look at members such as Cards and CreateDeck to see if a client application should have access to them.

```
Private Sub btnTest(ByVal sender As System.Object,
    Dim D As New Deck()
    D.|
End  Cards
     CreateDeck
     GetType
```

Figure 7.2 Client-side applications should not have this level of access.

Public as a member access modifier is certainly too broad, and Protected won't work because Deck doesn't inherit from CardCollection, so we are left with Friend. The following shows a more proper declaration for a method that should be callable from inheriting classes (protected) and code in the same assembly (Friend) but not callable from outside the assembly. Keep in mind that for each class type, the needs change. Limitations on classes in this particular class library may severely limit its adaptability for different games.

```
Protected Friend Sub CreateDeck()
   ...
End Sub
```

Classroom Q & A

Q: Why wouldn't CreateDeck be Private?

A: Suppose we wanted to allow a developer to extend the functionality of Deck with inheritance. That developer wouldn't be able to call Private CreateDeck even using the base reference keywords myclass and mybase. In many class libraries we hide members, prevent derivation, and prevent overriding to avoid misuse and to enhance the security in our class libraries, but with this model, flexibility and adaptability are key concerns.

Q: Shouldn't CreateDeck then also be overridable?

A: Yes, it should. By making CreateDeck overridable, we give developers the capability to create specific decks for their own needs.

Completeness: Extending Functionality

Classes must initially have enough functionality to support a wide range of uses, sometimes going beyond anything the initial implementation of the class might perform. We make classes more complete by overloading constructors and methods and by providing any functionality that would reasonably be requested of an object. If we don't create flexible classes, implementers of our classes can inherit from them and extend their methods in the derived classes.

One certain candidate for a complete Deck class would be a shuffle method. Because the intention for this chapter is to provide some insight into what choices might affect your class design, we won't actually implement every possible member of these classes, but the Draw and Shuffle methods are more of a necessity.

The Shuffle Method

One prime candidate for a complete Card library would certainly be the capability to shuffle the deck. Besides providing a mechanism for shuffling cards, the following Shuffle method demonstrates how our CardCollection can be cast as an ICollection and used to fill an ArrayList:

```
Private r as System.Random(Now.Millisecond)
Public Sub Shuffle()
   Dim startdeck As New ArrayList() 'unsorted deck
   startdeck.AddRange(CType(Cards, ICollection))
   'Create a new, shuffled deck
Dim shuffleddeck As New ArrayList(startdeck.Capacity)
Dim draw As Object = 0 'used to
   Dim i As Integer
   Cards.Clear() 'erase the deck before shuffling
   For i = 0 To startdeck.Count - 1
      Dim pos As Integer
      Do
         pos = r.Next(0, startdeck.Count) 'get random card
         draw = startdeck(pos)
      Loop Until draw.ToString <> 0.ToString()
      startdeck(pos) = 0 'mark card position as already used
      'Add randomly selected card to Cards:
      Cards.Add(CType(draw, Card))
   Next
   End Function
```

Figure 7.3 shows the result of shuffling the cards using the shuffle method. The ToString method determines what is actually displayed in the list box.

The Draw Method

The combination of a public CardCollection class and a versatile Draw method go a long way in making the classes reusable. Understanding that the various implementations of our classes require hands of different sizes, the following overloads support either drawing a single card or obtaining an entire hand of any given size:

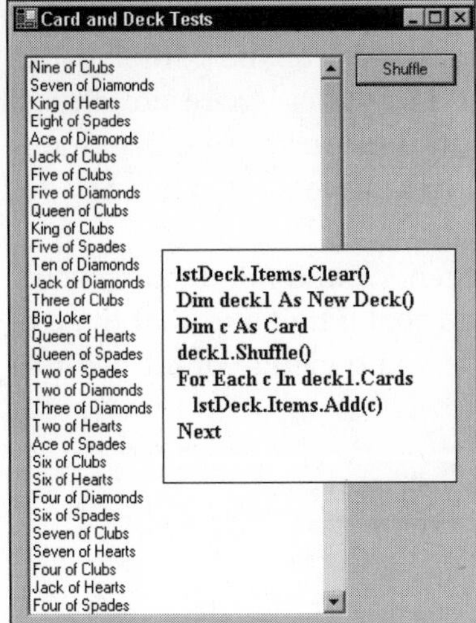

Figure 7.3 An object's ToString() value determines how it displays in the list box.

```
Public Function Draw() As CardCollection
    Dim drawcard As New CardCollection()
    drawcard.Add(Cards.Item(0))
    Cards.Remove(0)
    Return drawcard
End Function
Public Function Draw(ByVal howmany As Integer) As
 CardCollection
    If Cards.Count < howmany Then
        Throw New System.Exception("Not enough cards")
    End If
    Dim drawcards As New CardCollection()
    Dim i As Integer
    For i = 0 To howmany - 1
        drawcards.Add(Cards.Item(0))
    Cards.Remove(0)
    Next
    Return drawcards
End Function
```

Although these two overloads work well enough, there are several points of interest surrounding the Draw overload, which takes no arguments and returns one Card inside a CardCollection. That overload could be written without the overhead of being a CardCollection by returning a single Card, if you don't mind overloaded methods with differing return types. Another option is to leave the second version by itself and force the user of this class to always pass a value when drawing cards. One benefit of not having different return values is that the code to use the returned cards doesn't change. The following code uses the draw method to deal four hands for the game Spades and produces the output shown in Figure 7.4. In Spades, there are almost always four players, and the red two's are not used. Specific logic like that is not appropriate inside the class library and is better implemented in a Spades game that implements our Card library.

Two primary benefits of keeping base classes generic and not detail-specific are that derived classes can then more easily add that detail and that the creator of the base class doesn't need to have expert knowledge of all possible variations.

```
Private Sub btnDeal_Click(ByVal sender As System.Object, _
'Deal Spades to 4 Players 1 at a time (the correct way)
   Dim ctrl As Control
   Dim cards As Integer
   Dim newcard As Card
   For cards = 1 To 13
      For Each ctrl In Me.Controls
         If TypeOf ctrl Is ListBox Then
            Do
               MsgBox(deck1.Cards.Count.ToString())
               newcard = deck1.Draw().Item(0)
            Loop Until newcard.ToString() <> "Two of Hearts" _
            And newcard.ToString() <> "Two of Diamonds"
            CType(ctrl, ListBox).Items.Add(newcard)
         End If
      Next
   Next
End Sub
```

Replacing Overloaded Methods

The concept may sound strange, but the Optional keyword used on a function parameter is a form of overloading. If the only reason for the first Draw overload is to give the user of our class the ability to call Draw with no parameters, we may as well just modify the second overload and remove the first entirely.

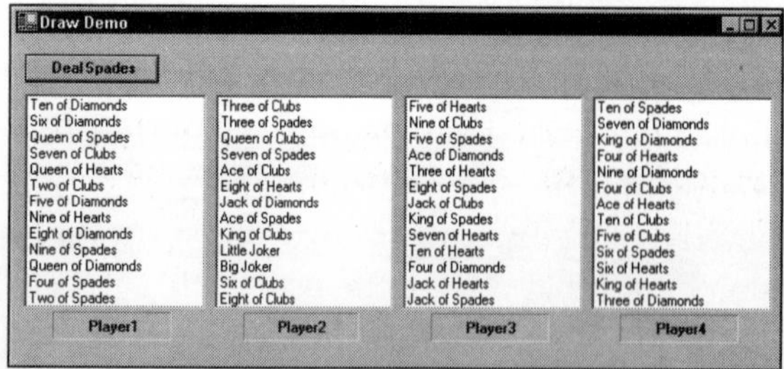

Figure 7.4 The Draw mechanism can be used to support virtually any card game, but game-specific logic must be provided by the Card library consumer.

The Optional keyword in Visual Basic .NET requires that a default value be provided in the event that the user does not pass in an acceptable value.

The following code not only provides a single method that performs the tasks of both Draw overloads but does so without forcing us to change our client code or the Draw method code:

```
Public Function Draw(Optional ByVal howmany As Integer = 1) _
As CardCollection
    If Cards.Count < howmany Then
        Throw New System.Exception("Not enough cards")
    End If
    Dim drawcards As New CardCollection()
    Dim i As Integer
    For i = 0 To howmany - 1
        drawcards.Add(Cards.Item(0))
        Cards.Remove(0)
    Next
    Return drawcards
End Function
```

Indirect Support Means More Support

Sometimes providing support for every conceivable use of our class libraries doesn't seem possible. So far in this ever-expanding Card library, there really isn't much of a way to create a deck that doesn't contain jokers or that supports variations of games like Euchre. Providing a GameType enum wouldn't be appropriate because it would be enormous, too implementation-specific, and invalidated with the introduction of any new game or variation. By providing a base class constructor that accepts an object of its collection type, we can provide a much greater level of support for such cases.

Classroom Q & A

Q: We made quite a few changes to our classes. Can we modify a class and keep old versions of methods without having them be available?

A: Aside from commenting them out, we could use an Obsolete attribute on the methods we don't want people to use anymore, and developers will see a message stating that the method has been marked obsolete. We'll look at attributes near the end of this chapter.

Q: Would you ever combine optional parameters and overloaded methods?

A: I don't like to combine the two in the same method, but sometimes it makes sense. The rule is to avoid confusion. In Lab 7.1, you will use an overload of the Deck constructor that has an optional parameter, and it works well both logically and functionally. Earlier we removed an overload of Draw and replaced it simply by adding an optional parameter to a second Draw overload. Each method in each class has different uses and should be considered separately. Whether it's right or wrong depends chiefly upon how intuitive it is to users of your class and how your decision affects derivation or use of the class.

When Is a Class Library Complete?

I suppose a class library is only complete when it can reasonably support anyone's needs for such a library, but remember that as long as we build the Card, CardCollection, and Deck classes adequately, other developers can easily build Hand, DiscardPile, and other such objects that are just implementations of CardCollection. Before embarking on a lab to further optimize the Card library, take a look at the following source code, which represents the total contents of all classes in the Card library thus far:

```
Option Strict On
Public Class Card
   Private m_suit As SuitType
   Private m_facevalue As FaceType
   Public AssignedValue As Integer
   Public Enum SuitType
      Hearts = 1
      Clubs = 2
      Diamonds = 3
      Spades = 4
      Joker = 5
   End Enum
   Public Enum FaceType
      Ace = 1 : Two = 2 : Three = 3 : Four = 4
      Five = 5 : Six = 6 : Seven = 7 : Eight = 8
      Nine = 9 : Ten = 10 : Jack = 11 : Queen = 12
      King = 13 : Little = 14 : Big = 15
   End Enum
   Public ReadOnly Property Suit() As SuitType
      Get
         Return Me.m_suit
      End Get
   End Property
```

```
    Public ReadOnly Property FaceValue() As FaceType
        Get
            Return Me.m_facevalue
        End Get
    End Property
    Public Sub New(ByVal value As FaceType, _
        ByVal suit As SuitType)
        Me.m_suit = suit
        Me.m_facevalue = value
    End Sub
    Public Overrides Function ToString() As String
        If Me.m_facevalue < 14 Then
            Return Me.m_facevalue.ToString() & " of " & _
            Me.m_suit.ToString()
        Else
            Return Me.m_facevalue.ToString() & " " & _
            Me.m_suit.ToString()
        End If
    End Function
End Class
Public Class CardCollection
    Inherits System.Collections.CollectionBase
    Public Sub Add(ByVal c As Card)
        List.Add(c)
    End Sub
    Public Sub Remove(ByVal index As Integer)
        If index < Count And index >= 0 Then
            List.RemoveAt(index)
        Else 'invalid index
        End If
    End Sub
    Public ReadOnly Property Item(ByVal index As Integer) _
    As Card
        Get
            Return CType(List.Item(index), Card)
        End Get
    End Property
End Class
Public Class Deck
    Public Cards As New CardCollection()
    Public Sub New()
        CreateDeck()
    End Sub
    Dim r As New System.Random(Now.Millisecond)
    Public Sub Shuffle()
        Dim startdeck As New ArrayList()
        startdeck.AddRange(CType(Cards, ICollection))
        Dim shuffleddeck As New ArrayList(startdeck.Capacity)
        Dim draw As Object = 0
        Dim i As Integer
        Cards.Clear()
```

```
            For i = 0 To startdeck.Count - 1
                Dim pos As Integer
                Do
                    pos = r.Next(0, startdeck.Count)
                    draw = startdeck(pos)
                Loop Until draw.ToString <> 0.ToString()
                startdeck(pos) = 0
                Cards.Add(CType(draw, Card))
            Next
        End Sub
        Public Function Draw(Optional _
        ByVal howmany As Integer = 1) As CardCollection
            If Cards.Count < howmany Then
                Throw New System.Exception("Not enough cards")
            End If
            Dim drawcards As New CardCollection()
            Dim i As Integer
            For i = 0 To howmany - 1
                drawcards.Add(Cards.Item(0))
                Cards.Remove(0)
            Next
            Return drawcards
        End Function
        Protected Friend Sub CreateDeck()
            Cards.Clear()
            Dim TheSuit As Integer : Dim TheFace As Integer
            For TheSuit = 1 To 4
                For TheFace = 1 To 13
                    Cards.Add(New Card(CType(TheFace, Card.FaceType), _
                    CType(TheSuit, Card.SuitType)))
                Next
            Next
            Cards.Add(New Card(Card.FaceType.Big, _
            Card.SuitType.Joker))
            Cards.Add(New Card(Card.FaceType.Little, _
            Card.SuitType.Joker))
            Me.Shuffle()
        End Sub
    End Class
```

Lab 7.1: Card Library Optimization

The objective of this lab is to provide some useful additions to the Card library of classes that test what you've learned about class development and to help prepare you for future chapters. This lab presents several challenges for modifying the Card, Deck, and CardCollection classes. Solutions are provided.

Perform the following steps:

1. Build an interface similar to Figure 7.5 to test the modifications you will make to the class library. Make this the startup form. The controls I used in my solution were named btnTest1, btnTest2, btnTest3, btnTest4, and lstCards.
2. Create a Deck constructor that takes a CardCollection object. Test this from a Visual Basic .NET Windows application by manually creating a CardCollection that contains only face cards.
3. Create a Deck constructor that takes an array of cards. Test the new constructor by passing all four aces.
4. Modify the default constructor for Deck to allow a developer to indicate that jokers should not be created. Test and verify that both 52- and 54-card decks can be created. Modify the CreateDeck method to take the same parameter. Pass this parameter from the Deck constructor to the CreateDeck function. Modify the CreateDeck function to handle the change, and add the Overridable keyword to the declaration of CreateDeck.
5. Remove the ability to create the erroneous cards shown in Figure 7.6. Test this modification by trying to create a joker of hearts.

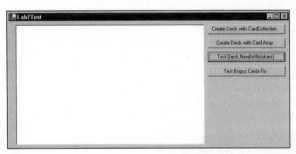

Figure 7.5 Build an interface to help test changes to the class library.

Figure 7.6 Enumerated lists, when used together, need to create meaningful and valid combinations or be disallowed.

6. Review the following code and compare with your solution for creating a Deck constructor that takes a CardCollection object (step 2). If your solution worked satisfactorily, skip this step. Figure 7.7 shows the result.

```
'The Solution Code
Public Sub New(ByVal CustomDeck As CardCollection)
   Me.Cards.Clear()
   Me.Cards = CustomDeck
End Sub

'The TestClient Code
Private Sub btnTest1_Click(ByVal sender As System.Object, _
ByVal e As System.EventArgs) Handles Button3.Click
'create deck using only facecards
   lstCards.Items.Clear()
   lstCards.Items.Add( _
   "Passed CardCollection - FaceCards Only:")
   Dim TheSuit As Integer
   Dim TheFace As Integer
   Dim cards As New CardCollection()
   For TheSuit = 1 To 4
      For TheFace = 10 To 13
         cards.Add(New Card(CType(TheFace, Card.FaceType), _
         CType(TheSuit, Card.SuitType)))
      Next
   Next
   Dim deck1 As New Deck(cards)
   Dim crd As Card
   For Each crd In deck1.Cards
      lstCards.Items.Add(crd)
   Next
End Sub
```

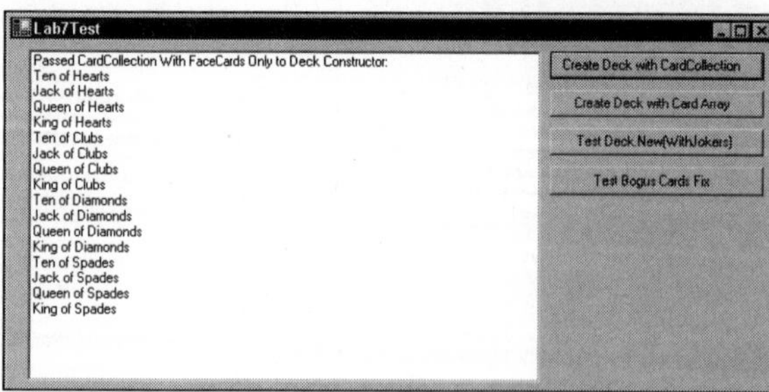

Figure 7.7 Results of passing a CardCollection containing only face cards when calling a Deck constructor.

7. Review the following code and compare with your solution for creating a Deck constructor that takes an array of Card objects (step 3). If your solution worked satisfactorily, skip this step. Figure 7.8 shows the results.

```
'The Solution Code
Public Sub New(ByVal CustomDeck As Card())
   Me.Cards.Clear()
   Dim i As Integer
   'cards are manually added to the CardCollection
   'because no conversion exists for Card() to CardCollection
   For i = 0 To CustomDeck.Length - 1
      Cards.Add(CustomDeck(i))
   Next
End Sub

'The TestClient Code
Private Sub btnTest2(ByVal sender As System.Object, _
ByVal e As System.EventArgs) Handles Button4.Click
   'Create deck with aces only using array of Card objects
   lstCards.Items.Clear()
   lstCards.Items.Add("Passed Card Array - Aces Only:")
   Dim cards(3) As Card
   cards(0) = New Card(Card.FaceType.Ace, _
   Card.SuitType.Spades)
   cards(1) = New Card(Card.FaceType.Ace, _
   Card.SuitType.Diamonds)
   cards(2) = New Card(Card.FaceType.Ace, _
   Card.SuitType.Hearts)
   cards(3) = New Card(Card.FaceType.Ace, _
   Card.SuitType.Clubs)
   Dim deck1 As New Deck(cards)
   Dim crd As Card
   For Each crd In deck1.Cards
      lstCards.Items.Add(crd)
   Next
End Sub
```

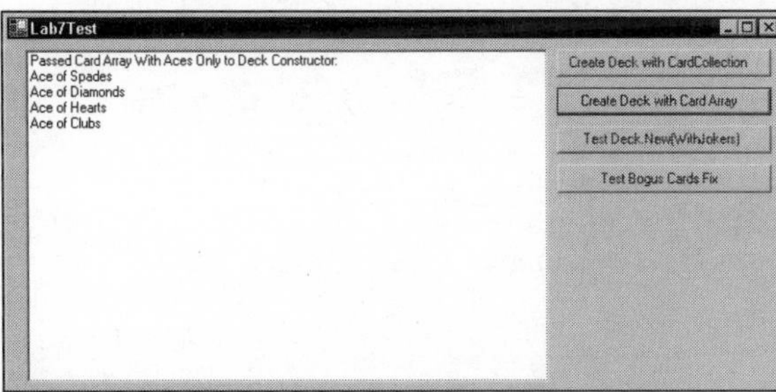

Figure 7.8 Results of passing a Card array containing four aces when calling a Deck constructor.

8. Review the following code and compare with your solution for implementing optional jokers (step 4). If your solution worked satisfactorily, skip this step. Figure 7.9 shows the result. Note that a single constructor handles all three cases and works as it did before when no parameter is supplied.

```
'The Solution Code
Public Sub New(Optional ByVal WithJokers As Boolean = True)
   CreateDeck(WithJokers)
End Sub
Protected Friend Overridable Sub CreateDeck(Optional _
ByVal WithJokers As Boolean = True)
   Cards.Clear()
   Dim TheSuit As Integer
   Dim TheFace As Integer
   For TheSuit = 1 To 4
      For TheFace = 1 To 13
        Cards.Add(New Card(CType(TheFace, Card.FaceType), _
        CType(TheSuit, Card.SuitType)))
      Next
   Next
   If WithJokers Then
      Cards.Add(New Card(Card.FaceType.Big, _
      Card.SuitType.Joker))
      Cards.Add(New Card(Card.FaceType.Little, _
      Card.SuitType.Joker))
   End If
   Me.Shuffle()
End Sub

'The TestClient Code
Private Sub btnTest3_Click(ByVal sender As System.Object, _
ByVal e As System.EventArgs) Handles Button1.Click
   lstCards.Items.Clear()
   lstCards.Items.Add("Passed 'False' to Deck Constructor:")
   Dim deck1 As New Deck(False)
   lstCards.Items.Add(" ...Returned " & deck1.Cards.Count & _
   " cards.")
   lstCards.Items.Add("Passed 'True' to Deck Constructor:")
   Dim deck2 As New Deck(True)
   lstCards.Items.Add(" ...Returned " & deck2.Cards.Count & _
   " cards.")
   lstCards.Items.Add("Passed Nothing to Deck Constructor:")
   Dim deck3 As New Deck()
   lstCards.Items.Add(" ...Returned " & deck3.Cards.Count & _
   " cards.")
End Sub
```

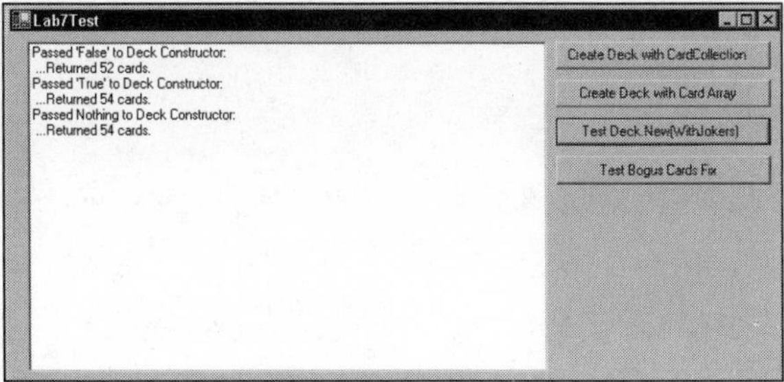

Figure 7.9 Results of passing True, False, and Nothing to a Deck constructor.

9. Review the following code and compare it with your solution for preventing bogus cards from being created (step 5). If your solution worked satisfactorily, skip this step. Figure 7.10 shows the result.

```
'The Solution Code
Public Sub New(ByVal value As FaceType, ByVal suit As SuitType)
   If value = FaceType.Big Or value = FaceType.Little Then
   'SuitType must then be a Joker
      If suit <> SuitType.Joker Then
         Throw New System.Exception("Big and Little can " & _
         "only be used with the Joker SuitType")
      End If
   Else 'FaceType is not Big or Little
      If suit = SuitType.Joker Then
         Throw New System.Exception("Joker can only " & _
         "be used with Big and Little FaceTypes")
      End If
   End If
   Me.m_suit = suit
   Me.m_facevalue = value
End Sub

'The TestClient Code
Private Sub btnTest4(ByVal sender As System.Object, _
ByVal e As System.EventArgs) Handles Button2.Click
   Try 'try to add bogus cards
      lstCards.Items.Add(New Card(Card.FaceType.Big, _
      Card.SuitType.Diamonds))
      lstCards.Items.Add(New Card(Card.FaceType.Ace, _
      Card.SuitType.Joker))
      lstCards.Items.Add(New Card(Card.FaceType.Little, _
      Card.SuitType.Hearts))
      lstCards.Items.Add(New Card(Card.FaceType.King, _
      Card.SuitType.Joker))
      Catch ex As Exception
      MessageBox.Show(ex.Message, _
      "Illegal FaceType-SuitType Combination", _
      MessageBoxButtons.OK, MessageBoxIcon.Error)
   End Try
End Sub
```

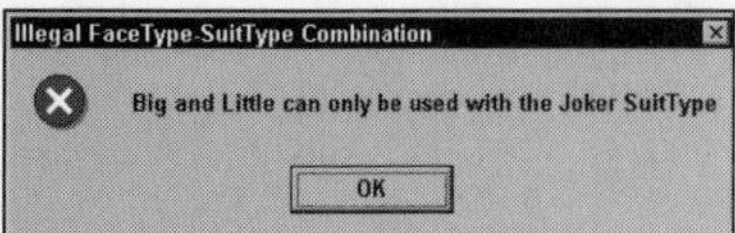

Figure 7.10 Result of attempting to create a bogus card by combining illogical FaceType and SuitType values.

There will always be a developer who needs to derive from Deck. We've added a reasonable bit of capability and flexibility to the classes, but you might have noticed that it would take a bit of code every time someone wanted to create a specific deck type, regardless of our efforts. Because of this, most developers will likely opt for creating a game-specific class that derives from Deck and hard-code the game-specific deck details.

Extending Design Time Support with Attributes

We know that Assemblies are described with attributes that are collectively known as metadata, but these attributes don't just exist at the Assembly level; examples are the attributes in the AssemblyInfo.vb file in our projects. Each element in .NET can be described with attributes that make development using those elements more intuitive and controllable.

Common Attributes

All attributes are actually declared in .NET with the suffix, attribute. For instance, the Obsolete attribute is actually declared as ObsoleteAttribute. There are an extreme number of attributes in .NET. The purpose of these attributes ranges from marking class members as obsolete to making a class serializable through SOAP. Following are some of the more commonly used attributes:

Attribute. Description.

Category. Used to help a Visual Studio .NET designer organize properties into categories for things such as property pages and property groupings. Examples are Appearance, Layout, and Format.

ComClass. Greatly simplifies the process of making an object visible to COM. This attribute is specific to Visual Basic .NET.

Description. Provides a descriptive element for properties and events.

DefaultEvent. Marks an event as the default event for a class.

DefaultProperty. Marks a property as the default property for a class.

DllImport. An attribute for a method to indicate that the method being called is in unmanaged code, such as the Win32API.

```
d.Deal()
    'Public Function Deal() As Integer' is obsolete: 'Deal() Has Been Replaced with Draw()'
```

Figure 7.11 Trying to use obsolete functions produces compile errors and displays the message parameter used inside the ObsoleteAttribute declaration.

Obsolete. Marks a class member as obsolete and provides developers with a description string when they attempt to use an obsolete method.

VBFixedArray. Visual Basic .NET-specific attribute that allows the creation of a fixed-size array.

VBFixedString. Visual Basic .NET-specific attribute that allows the creation of a fixed string.

WebMethod. Marks a method in a Web service as available through SOAP. Web methods can be invoked over the Web.

For a more complete list of attributes and their respective hierarchy and namespace, search for "attribute hierarchy" (in quotes) using Search from the Help menu in Visual Studio .NET.

Using Attributes

Attributes are always enclosed in brackets and directly proceed the elements they describe. To mark a method as obsolete we could use the following code:

```
<Obsolete("Deal() Was Replaced with Draw()")> Function
 Deal() As Integer
End Function
```

Any attempt by a developer to use this function produces the results shown in Figure 7.11.

Summary

We've progressed through quite a few changes to the Card library, ranging from providing intuitive class interface to support for collections. You've seen from the changes we made that the design needs and choices for each class vary greatly. In one case you used an optional parameter to remove the need for an overloaded method, and in another case you created both in one method. The reusability so often mentioned in OOP is a product of the developer's experience and understanding of the possible uses of a given class and is not a by-product of simply using classes. As you learn more about inheritance in the next chapter, you may want to try deriving from Deck (such as SpadesDeck) and make a deck that overloads CreateDeck for a specific game.

Review Questions

1. What is a primary benefit of using enumerated lists in a class?
   a. Efficiency
   b. Reliability
   c. Readability
   d. Adaptability
2. Which of these are benefits of overloaded methods?
   a. They help limit the size of member lists presented to developers using our classes.
   b. They provide a higher level of adaptability for our classes.
   c. They simplify the developer interface to our classes.
   d. They prevent the need for derivation of our classes.
3. What are the benefits of keeping the base classes generic?
   a. Generic base classes, if properly designed, aid in the support for derivation.
   b. Base class authors don't need to know the details of every derivation of the base classes.
   c. Future developers can add details to base classes at a later time.
   d. Future developers can inherit from the base classes and extend them for each specific need.
4. The Friend access modifier provides access to which of the following?
   a. Anything that can obtain a reference to the object containing the Friend member.
   b. Any code in the assembly.
   c. Any code in inheriting classes.
   d. Any code in the assembly or in an inheriting class.
5. Which of the following is implemented by CollectionBase?
   a. Add
   b. Remove
   c. Item
   d. List
6. What's wrong with the following declaration?

   ```
   Public Function Greet(Optional ByVal Name as String)
   ```

7. What is the benefit of inheriting from CollectionBase instead of implementing ICollection, IList, and IEnumerator?

Answers to Review Questions

1. **c.** Enumerated lists make code more readable and classes more intuitive to use.
2. **a**, **b**, and **c.** Overloaded methods provide a greater level of adaptability and flexibility. By not having a separate method name for each variation of functionality, overloads decrease the number of members presented to developers, thereby simplifying the use of our classes.
3. **a**, **b**, and **d.** By not placing implementation details in base classes, we provide greater support for derived classes where the implementation-specific details are appropriate. No future developers should be modifying the base classes for source control reasons. If they need to extend the base class functionality, they should use inheritance.
4. **b.** Anything that can obtain a reference to the object containing the Friend member can access the Friend member.
5. **d.** CollectionBase provides implementations for List, Clear, RemoveAt, and Count but does not provide implementations for Add, Remove, and Item.
6. The following declaration uses an optional parameter, but the Optional keyword requires a default value to be assigned to the argument:

   ```
   Public Function Greet(Optional ByVal Name as String="User")
   ```
7. The benefit of inheriting from CollectionBase is that we gain almost all of the control and flexibility of having a collection but don't have to do very much work.

CHAPTER

8

Implementation Inheritance

By now the word *inheritance* should be a familiar one. You've seen how forms inherit from System.Windows.Forms.Form and have implemented an example of visual inheritance. One thing we have not done is explore the variations of what can be done with class hierarchies to customize and control this inheritance. In this chapter, we examine abstract classes, polymorphism, sealed classes, and class hierarchies.

Understanding Implementation Inheritance

Implementation refers to code, and *implementation inheritance* means inheriting code. So far the implementation inheritance we have experienced is that in which we inherit everything, as is, from some base class and extend that functionality. But what if we want to create a class from which no one can inherit or a class that can't be instantiated but only inherited from. What if we only want half the members as they are written in the base class and want to redefine the other half in the derived classes? All these things can be resolved by using various keywords related to inheritance.

If this reuse of code is so important, why not just give all of the developers on the team a copy of the original class as source code and let them rewrite the class to suit their needs? I feel like an idiot even typing that hypothetical question. Can you imagine trying to maintain and keep track of all the various versions of the class? If we establish a strong set of base classes and inherit from those classes in our applications, we can build applications much faster than "fixing" classes every time we build a new application.

Single Versus Multiple Implementation Inheritance

What is available to a derived class when we inherit from another class depends on how the inherited members are declared. Access members such as Private, Public, Friend, and Protected are not the only factors that govern how we can see and use inherited members. The Inherits keyword is used to establish a relationship between a base class and a derived class. The Inherits keyword must be the first line of code in a class declaration and can be used only to inherit from a single class. The limitation of inheriting from one class is referred to as *single implementation inheritance.* Multiple implementation inheritance exists in C++ but is omitted entirely in all .NET languages. The following example uses a base class, Person, and a derived class, Student, which inherits from class Person:

```
Public Class Person
    Public Name As String
    Public DOB As Date
End Class
Public Class Student
    Inherits Person 'must be first line. There can be only one
    Public Sub New(ByVal StudentName As String, _
        ByVal BirthDate As Date)
        MyBase.Name = StudentName
        MyBase.DOB = BirthDate
    End Sub
    Public StudentID
End Class
```

Keep in mind that this is an example to elicit understanding of a basic concept and is not a pair of solidly built classes.

When a Student object is created in memory, a Person object is created for each Student object. It can be said that class Student extends class Person. The base class is guaranteed to be created by the time we enter the constructor of the derived class. Using an object reference of type Student, we would have access to Name, DOB, and StudentID members, as shown in Figure 8.1.

I said that for every Student object that gets created, there is a corresponding Person object in memory because Person is the base class for Student. That is to say that creating an instance of a derived class automatically creates an instance of its base class. This automatically created instance can be referred to with the MyBase keyword. In the constructor of my Student class I use MyBase to refer to that instance's base object. When we want to refer to the actual instance of an object (and not a member in its base type), we can use either the Me or MyClass keywords. Just as the Me keyword in Visual Basic 6 refers to the current form, the Me keyword in Visual Basic .NET refers to the current instance of the class in which it is used. The difference between using Me and MyClass is that calls to methods using MyClass act as if the methods were NotOverridable.

To understand what we might do with the Me keyword, let's think about the previous example. Looking at the list of members in Figure 8.1, would it surprise you to know that I could invoke ToString on a reference to a Student object? Of course, that doesn't come as a surprise because all objects are ultimately derived from System.Object, and System.Object has a ToString method.

ToString is declared in System.Object as Overridable, a keyword that means classes on down the hierarchy can redefine what ToString() returns for them as long as it returns a String. Technically, the class Person inherits from System.Object, and the class Student inherits from the class Person. Either or both classes may redefine ToString().

The following modification of the Student class overrides (redefines for local use) what ToString means for objects of type Student. Inside the definition of a class, the Me keyword ensures that any code always refers to the current instance of a class.

```
Public Class Student
    Inherits Person 'must be first line. There can be only one
    Public Sub New(ByVal StudentName As String, _
    ByVal BirthDate As Date)
        MyBase.Name = StudentName
        MyBase.DOB = BirthDate
    End Sub
    Public StudentID
    Public Overrides Function ToString() As String
        Return (Me.Name)
    End Function
End Class
```

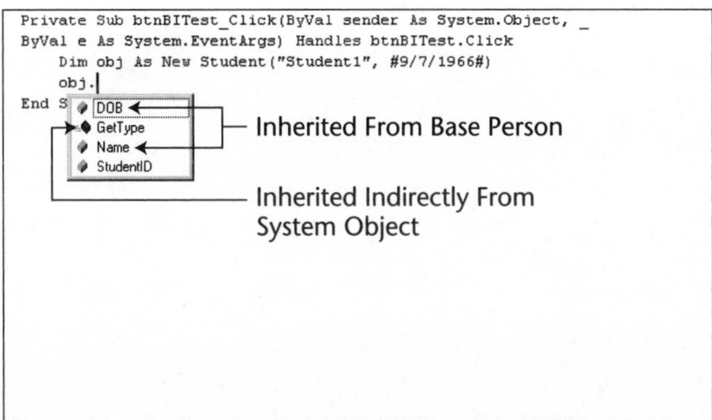

Figure 8.1 The class Student extends the list of inherited members to its own declared members to build objects that are a combination of the Person and Student classes.

Either Me or MyClass works in this simple example, but be careful because although MyClass appears to be a synonym for the Me keyword, all method calls used against MyClass act as if the methods were NotOverridable.

Prohibiting Instantiation of a Class

What if we had a base class that was such an abstract type that it didn't make sense to instantiate objects of that type? The declaration of such a class would require the MustInherit keyword. This keyword indicates that the only way to create this object in memory is through inheritance by becoming some other object's MyBase reference. The following class declaration cannot be instantiated but can be derived (inherited) from.

```
Public MustInherit Class Shape
   public MustOverride Sub DrawMe()
End Class
```

Forcing Implementation of a Member

In the preceding example of a Shape class, the single member, DrawMe, was declared as MustOverride. Any inheriting class has two options: It can declare itself with the MustInherit keyword or redeclare all MustOverride methods from all inherited classes using the Overrides keyword. The following three-class hierarchy creates a situation where Class3 cannot even compile unless it overrides all MustOveride methods defined in *both* classes in its inheritance hierarchy:

```
Public MustInherit Class Class1
    Public MustOverride Function greet1() As String
End Class
Public MustInherit Class Class2
    Inherits Class1
    Public MustOverride Function greet2() As String
End Class
Public Class Class3
    Inherits Class2
    Public Overrides Function greet1() As String
    End Function
    Public Overrides Function greet2() As String
    End Function
End Class
```

If I declare an object of type Class3, a Class1 object and a Class2 object will be created during its instantiation. Declaring Class1 and Class2 as MustInherit is the only way these classes will be loaded into memory. All MustOverride members must be implemented in any derived class that is not marked as MustInherit. Any class containing MustOverride members must be marked as MustInherit. A method marked as MustOverride is referred to as a virtual method in most languages.

Prohibiting Inheritance of a Class

As we discussed in Chapter 3, "Examining Visual Basic .NET," one of the differences between value types and reference types in .NET is that value types are sealed. *Sealed* refers to a class that cannot be further derived from (cannot be inherited). Visual Basic .NET uses the NotInheritable keyword to seal a class where other .NET languages might use a Sealed keyword. An Int32 is a value type and is therefore sealed, so if I try to inherit from Int32 to "build a better Int," the resulting warning will look like Figure 8.2.

The declaration of System.Int32 would be similar to the following:

```
Public NotInheritable Structure Int32
```

Sometimes we create classes as NotInheritable because we just don't want people extending our classes for various reasons, or we don't want to spend a lot of time making sure certain methods aren't overridden.

Because NotInheritable prohibits any form of inheritance, no member of a class marked as such can contain members with Overridable, NotOverridable, or MustOverride modifiers.

Preparing for Polymorphism

Before we continue down the road to polymorphism, we need to revisit some matters related to memory and object assignments. We have seen many times how ICollections are collections of objects and how adding items to an ICollection casts the added object to a System.Object. But what really happens in memory depends on the item being added. If the item being added is a value type, the item is copied by value. If the item being added is a reference type, it is copied by reference. Copying by reference simply creates another reference variable that points to the same object in memory. Figure 8.3 shows what happens in memory as items are added to an ArrayList.

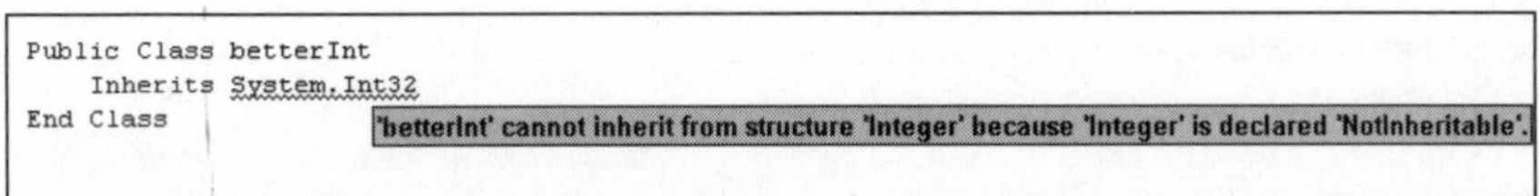
Public Class betterInt
Inherits System.Int32
End Class
'betterInt' cannot inherit from structure 'Integer' because 'Integer' is declared 'NotInheritable'.

Figure 8.2 System.Int32 is a value type, which is sealed and cannot be further derived.

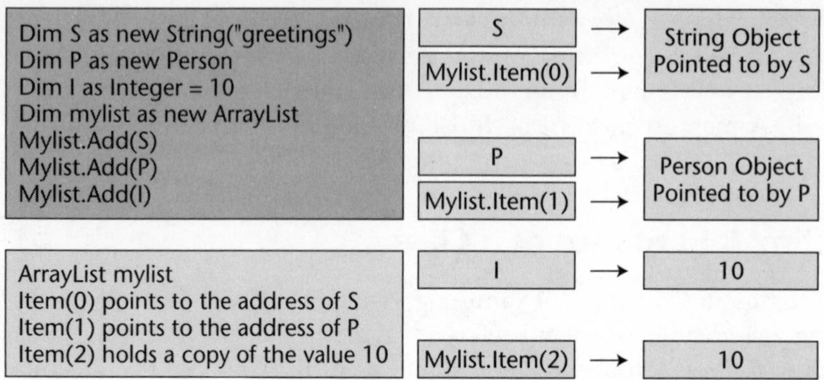

Figure 8.3 An assignment of one reference variable to another causes both reference variables to point to the same object in memory.

The following code proves the example in Figure 8.3 by assigning a reference type to an ArrayList, modifying the reference type "stored" in the ArrayList, and discovering that the original variable sees the change:

```
Dim P As New Person() 'Create a new reference type
P.Name = "Samson"
'ArrayList is a collection of System.Object:
Dim a As New ArrayList()'Only makes a.Item(0) reference
                        'the Person referenced by P:
a.Add(P) 'Actually replaces "Samson":
CType(a.Item(0), Person).Name = "Delilah"
'The following prints Delilah because any change
'to a.Item(0) or P affect the same object in memory:
MsgBox(P.Name)
```

This was a slight tangent but a necessity for our next topics, which deal quite a bit with object assignments and behaviors associated with casting objects to their base type.

Overriding Versus Hiding

There are actually two methods that allow you to redeclare a base class member in a derived class: Overrides and Shadows. The difference between the two may seem indistinct at first, but as we progress, it will become clearer. First, let's see how they compare syntactically:

```
Public Class ClassA
    Public Function greet1() As String
        Return "Hello from ClassA, Greet1 (no modifiers)"
    End Function
```

```
    Public Overridable Function greet2() As String
        Return "Hello from ClassA, Greet2 (Overridable)"
    End Function
End Class
Public Class ClassB
    Inherits ClassA
    Public Shadows Function greet1() As String 'Hides
        Return "Hello from ClassB, Greet1 (shadows)"
    End Function
    Public Overrides Function greet2() As String 'Overrides
        Return "Hello from ClassB, Greet2 (overrides)"
    End Function
End Class
```

The syntactical difference is that when redeclaring a method in a derived class that was not declared as Overridable in the base class, that redeclaration must use the Shadows keyword. If the base class member being overridden in the derived class was marked as Overridable, the redeclaration must use the Overrides keyword.

The functional difference between the two types of member redeclaration is one of Polymorphism. To help understand polymorphism, let's use a language analogy. Take, for example, the word *executes*. I could say that code executes or that the President executes his duties, or I could even say that a person, filling the job of executioner, executes a criminal. As far as the English language goes, executes is polymorphic because the same word has different meanings depending on the context in which it is used. The word *run* is another example, in the contexts of code, people, and cars, but that should be enough for you to see where I'm going.

When I redeclare a method in a derived class using Shadows, an object reference of a base type, referencing a derived object makes no attempt to use the shadowed method in the context of the derived object. In this case the method is not acting polymorphically.

When I redeclare an Overridable method using Overrides, an object reference of a base type, referencing a derived object uses the method in the context of the derived class. In this case, the method is acting polymorphically.

The difference between hiding (Shadows) and overriding (Overrides) is a difference of virtual versus nonvirtual behavior. Greet1 in ClassA is a nonvirtual method, whereas Greet2 in ClassA is a virtual method. I could tell you that virtual methods provide polymorphic behavior, or I could say that polymorphic functions, when invoked on a reference object of a base type that has been cast from a derived type, exhibit the behavior of the derived type, but seeing is much more helpful. Using the previous classes, the following code shows that the second method, because it was virtual, exhibits polymorphic behavior by invoking a derived member even when cast as a base type.

```
Private Sub btnVirtualvsNonVirtual_Click( _
ByVal sender As System.Object, _
ByVal e As System.EventArgs) _
Handles btnVirtualvsNonVirtual.Click
    Dim B As New ClassB()
    Dim A As ClassA
    A = B 'A is now a reference pointing to the same memory
          'address as B. A is a base type for B.
    MsgBox(A.greet1()) 'Class A, Greet1 - What we have always
                       'seen when a derived object is cast to
                       'its base...the method invocation used
                       'the version in the base type
    MsgBox(A.greet2()) 'Class B, Greet2 - Something new! even
                       'though he was cast as his base type, the
                       'method invocation used the version of
                       'the method in the most derived type.
                       'That is, he works polymorphically!
End Sub
```

When I use the statement A = B, I'm doing more than causing A to reference the same thing as B. Stating A = B is just like saying, "Let A reference B but see it as an A." Just as any form of casting, the cast doesn't affect the original value; it simply puts a mask on the value on the left of the assignment that makes it see one type as another. In this example, the second method call to greet2 is made in the context of derivedclass.method.

Lab 8.1: The Proof Is in the Polymorphism

This lab will help you appreciate the importance of, realize the need for, and develop the desire for polymorphism in solutions. To accomplish this, we'll build a solution twice, once with and once without polymorphism. When you're finished, you will have solved a problem polymorphically to resolve a number of design flaws in the nonpolymorphic version. Although the class library used in this lab represents a library of shapes, we won't implement the many methods and properties for the shapes involved; instead, we focus on how polymorphism can be used to solve a common problem.

Perform the following steps:

1. Start Visual Studio .NET and create a new blank solution by selecting File, New, Blank Solution and naming it Lab 8.1. This method of starting a project enables you to create an initial solution where the name of the solution doesn't have to be the same name as one of the projects.

2. Add a new Visual Basic .NET Windows application by selecting File, Add Project, New Project, Windows Application. Name it Lab 8.1 Test Client.
3. Add a new Visual Basic .NET Class Library by selecting File, Add Project, New Project, Class Library. Name it Shapes.
4. Rename Class1.vb to Shape.vb in the Solution Explorer window.
5. Double-click Shape.vb to open the file in the Code Editor window.
6. Rename class1 in the Code Editor window to Shape. Add the following code to the new Shape class:

```
Public Class Shape
'non polymorphic version
   Public Function DrawMe() As String
      Return "DrawMe in Shape base class"
   End Function
End Class
```

7. Add a new class by selecting Project, Add Class, Class. Name it Rectangle.
8. Add the following code to the Rectangle class:

```
Public Class Rectangle
    Inherits Shape
    Public Shadows Function DrawMe() As String
        Return "Drawing Rectangle..."
    End Function
End Class
```

9. Add a new class named Oval and add the following code to it:

```
Public Class Oval
    Inherits Shape
    Public Shadows Function DrawMe() As String
        Return "Drawing Oval..."
    End Function
End Class
```

10. Add additional classes that implement the DrawMe method for three additional shapes. In future examples, I use Cone, Cylinder, and Cube.
11. Select Build from the Build menu to build the class library.
12. In the Windows application, add a reference to the Shapes class library: Select Project, Add Reference, Projects tab; double-click Shapes; and click OK.

13. The following code can be used to test the application at this point but is not a required step:

```
Dim child As New Shapes.Rectangle()
Dim base As Shapes.Shape
base = child
MsgBox(base.DrawMe()) 'Calls DrawMe in Shape.
```

14. Now let's build a function in the client that attempts to draw any shape sent to it. Because all shapes in our class library are derived from Shapes.Shape, we make that the input parameter for the function. Add the following function to Form1 in the test client:

```
Private Function DrawShape(ByVal s As Shapes.Shape) As String
   Return s.DrawMe()
End Function
```

15. Add a new button (btnTestDrawShape) to Form1. Add the following code to the button:

```
Private Sub btnTestDrawShape_Click( _
ByVal sender As System.Object, _
ByVal e As System.EventArgs) Handles btnTestDrawShape.Click
   Dim ShapeArray As New ArrayList()
   ShapeArray.Add(New Shapes.Cone())
   ShapeArray.Add(New Shapes.Cube())
   ShapeArray.Add(New Shapes.Cylinder())
   ShapeArray.Add(New Shapes.Rectangle())
   Dim shape As Shapes.Shape
   For Each shape In ShapeArray
      MsgBox(DrawShape(shape))
   Next
End Sub
```

16. Run the application and test by clicking btnTestDrawShape.

    Well, now that wasn't very useful. Every time I pass it a shape and call DrawMe, it calls base.DrawMe, as you can see in Figure 8.4. Without using polymorphism, let's "fix" the code.

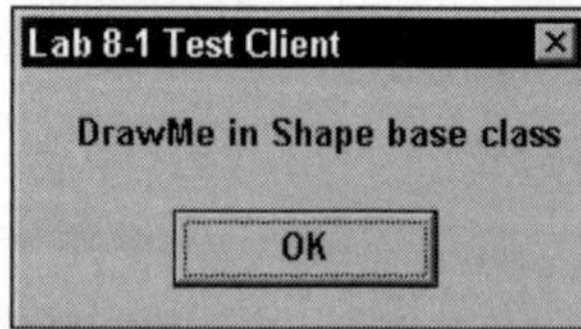

Figure 8.4 Passing a Cone as a Shape and calling Shape.DrawMe invokes the base member, not the derived member.

17. Modify the DrawShape function to detect the underlying type of each shape passed in, cast to that type, and call DrawMe on the cast. The following code provides the new version of DrawShape:

```
Private Function DrawShape(ByVal s As Shapes.Shape) As String
   Select Case s.GetType().ToString()
      Case "Shapes.Cone"
         Return CType(s, Shapes.Cone).DrawMe()
      Case "Shapes.Cylinder"
         Return CType(s, Shapes.Cylinder).DrawMe()
      Case "Shapes.Oval"
         Return CType(s, Shapes.Oval).DrawMe()
      Case "Shapes.Rectangle"
         Return CType(s, Shapes.Rectangle).DrawMe()
      Case "Shapes.Cube"
         Return CType(s, Shapes.Cube).DrawMe()
      Case Else
         MsgBox(s.GetType().ToString() & " not handled.")
         Return s.DrawMe()
   End Select
End Function
```

18. Run the application again and test the new DrawShape function. Passing a Cone to the new version of this function should produce the results shown in Figure 8.5.

    Success? Hardly. What we have done is create a brute-force approach that requires an enormous function to handle every possible shape. That's not the only problem with the solution. If I ever add another shape to the class library, I have to recompile any client before anything can pass a shape of that new type. But wait! There's more. There is absolutely nothing that forces each shape to implement DrawMe. It's time to stop playing around and really fix these problems.

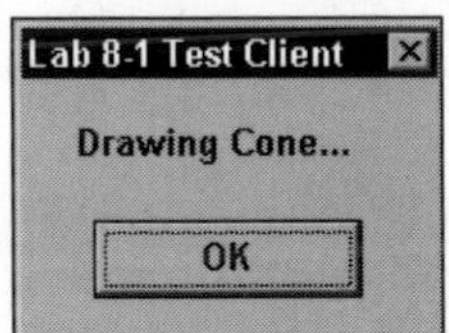

Figure 8.5 To call the nonvirtual DrawMe method on the derived type, we have to cast to the derived type before calling DrawMe.

19. Return to the class library project, Shapes, and modify your Shape class to elicit polymorphic behavior of its members as the following code indicates. This new version of class Shape cannot be instantiated, can only be inherited from, and contains a new MustOverride version of DrawMe that any inheriting class must implement if it is to claim inheritance from Shapes.Shape.

```
Public MustInherit Class Shape
    'Polymorphic version
    Public MustOverride Function DrawMe() As String
End Class
```

20. To modify all shapes to adjust to the change in the declaration of class Shape, select Edit, Find And Replace, Replace. In the Find What text box, enter the word *Shadows*. In the Replace With textbox, enter the word *Overrides*. Select the All Open Documents option button and click Replace All. That was painless, right?

I don't recommend using Replace All in production code. Consider what would happen to the comment "FunctionX used to be called FunctionY" if you did a Replace All from FunctionX to FunctionY after inserting the comment. The comment would now read "FunctionY used to be called FunctionY."

21. Do you think it will take a lot of work to rewrite the DrawShape function? I hope not; remember, polymorphic behavior saves us from writing a lot of bulky code, and moving to polymorphism is a snap. Modify the DrawShape function as follows:

```
Private Function DrawShape(ByVal s As Shapes.Shape) As String
    Return s.DrawMe()
End Function
```

Now run the application and test it again to receive your reward for not doing any work.

I sincerely hope that by now you not only appreciate polymorphism but that you are asking the question, "Why would anyone *not* do it that way?" I know I made you add all that code to the first version of our DrawShape function, but I'm sure you can see now that polymorphism is only difficult and ugly when it's missing.

Classroom Q & A

Q: Could we have done this in Visual Basic 6?

A: Not with implementation inheritance because that isn't available in Visual Basic 6; but we could implement polymorphic behavior in Visual Basic 6 with interfaces, using the Implements keyword.

Q: There are interfaces in Visual Basic 6?

A: We have pure abstract classes that we refer to as Interfaces. Although the keyword Interface is a *thing* in .NET and COM, neither C++ nor Visual Basic as defined languages has anything more than the concept of an interface. *Interface*, in the English dictionary sense of the word, means what we need to use (interface with) something. The interface for a computer is a keyboard, mouse, or whatever else we have as a peripheral. In programming terms, an interface to an object is its public members. Having said that, technically our Shape class is *pure interface*, meaning that it cannot be instantiated and has only declarations and no definitions. In Visual Basic 6 we use the Implements keyword to inherit the interface of an abstract class just like we do in Visual Basic when we use an interface like IDisposable.

Q: What is a pure abstract class?

A: A pure abstract class is any class that has only declarations and no definitions. Our Shape class is a pure abstract class. We could also say that it is pure interface if we mean it in the nonkeyword, programming concept sense.

Q: So what's the difference between a pure abstract class and an interface?

A: There really isn't a difference in the way they work, but using interfaces is a lot easier because we don't use any keywords to make polymorphism happen or to enforce implementation of methods. Those things just happen with interfaces. If a class is still pure abstract when you're ready to go to production, you should have made it an interface. We can implement any number of interfaces in a class, but we can only inherit from a single class.

Prohibiting Redefinition of a Member

We've seen a base class with members marked as MustOverride that forces a derived class to locally redefine the inherited method and with members marked with Overridable that simply states that derived classes *may* override the method locally if they choose.

If you want to prohibit a derived class from locally redefining what an inherited method does, you might be led to believe from its name that you can use the NotOverridable modifier in the method declaration in the base class. It doesn't quite work that way.

First of all, by default, if I do not mark the method as Overridable, I am ensured than whenever I use a reference variable of type base, regardless of how derived an object is that it references, I get the base functionality. Unless I declare my base class to allow for polymorphism, there is nothing a derived class can do to make that happen.

What NotOverridable Cannot Do

Before we see what the NotOverridable keyword can do, let's see what it cannot do. The following code is illegal and will not compile:

```
Public Class baseclass
    'COMPILE ERROR:
    Public NotOverridable Function greet() As String
        Return "baseclass greet"
    End Function
End Class
```

Figure 8.6 shows the compiler's complaint about an apparently intuitive use of a keyword. It is the lack of the Overridable keyword that makes a method act in the way this attempted code might suggest. If my intention is to disallow a virtual override of a method in a derived class for method greet, that is already the default behavior for a method. If the method is marked as Overridable, it can be overridden virtually (provides polymorphic behavior) in a derived class. Without the Overridable keyword, the method can only be shadowed in a derived class (nonpolymorphic behavior).

```
Public Class baseclass
    Public NotOverridable Function greet() As String
        Return "b'NotOverridable' cannot be specified for methods that do not override another method.
    End Function
End Class
```

Figure 8.6 NotOverridable cannot be used to prevent overriding a method that is not already being overridden in this class.

What NotOverridable Can Do

NotOverridable is intended for use in the middle of an inheritance hierarchy when you no longer want further derived classes to override a method. The following code demonstrates the use of the NotOverridable keyword:

```
Public Class top
   Public Overridable Function greet() As String
      Return "Greeting from the top!"
   End Function
End Class
Public Class secondtier
   Inherits top
   Public Overrides Function greet() As String
      Return "Greetings from 2nd Tier" 'an acceptable override
   End Function
End Class
Public Class thirdtier
   Inherits secondtier
   Public NotOverridable Overrides Function greet() As String
      Return "Greetings from 1st Tier" 'an acceptable override
      'that prohibits any further derived classes from deriving
      'this method
   End Function
End Class
'The following class will not compile:
Public Class bottom
    Inherits thirdtier
    'ERROR CANNOT OVERRIDE
    Public Overrides Function greet() As String
       Return "Greetings from the bottom"
    End Function
End Class
```

Once a class in an inheritance hierarchy specifies that a method is NotOverridable, no further derived classes may override that method. It is also a requirement that any method using the NotOverridable keyword on a method must also override that method using the Overrides keyword.

Inheriting for Less?

Remember in all this discussion of inheritance and hiding members via Shadows and such that we have access modifiers to help us. In some languages, hiding an inherited member and then making that inherited member private effectively hides the inherited member from users of the derived type. That is not the case in Visual Basic .NET or any .NET language. Allowing this would essentially be enabling a class to inherit less than what is in the base class (the opposite of extending). In the following Visual Basic .NET and C# examples, attempts to invoke the member in the derived class actually invoke the base class version:

```
'Visual Basic .NET Version:
Public Class Class1
   Public Function greet() As String
      Return "Class1 greet"
   End Function
End Class
Public Class Class2
   Inherits Class1
   Private Shadows Function greet() As String
   End Function
End Class

'C# Version:
public class Class1
{
   public string greet()
   {
   return "class1 greet";
   }
}
public class class2 : Class1 'The colon means inherits in C#
{
   new private string greet() 'new is the same as Shadows
   {
      return "class1 greet";
   }
}
```

Testing either of these reveals that they might as well not exist because any attempt to invoke a greet on the derived class still invokes greet as it exists in the base class. Figure 8.7 clearly shows that for the previous Visual Basic .NET example, an object of type Class2 certainly still has access to the member we attempted to hide with a Private keyword. That is to say, we can still see and invoke the greet method() on an object of type Class2!

Transitive Inheritance

Inheritance is a transitive thing. If ClassC is derived from ClassB and ClassA is derived from ClassB, it is true that ClassC can be cast to either a ClassA or a ClassB. This also means ClassC will be a collection of all things from all members. Let's use the following example to test this:

```
Public Class ClassA
   Public Overridable Function greet() As String
      Return "Greetings from ClassA"
   End Function
End Class
Public Class ClassB
   Inherits ClassA
   Public Overrides Function greet() As String
      Return "Greetings from ClassB"
   End Function
End Class
Public Class ClassC
   Inherits ClassB
End Class
```

Given that example, the fact that the following code compiles and executes proves that ClassC is both a ClassA and a ClassB because objects of type ClassC can be cast to ClassA and ClassB.

```
Dim objC As New Class_C()
Dim objA As Class_A
Dim objB As Class_B
objA = objC
objA.greet()
objB = objC
objB.greet()
objC.greet()
```

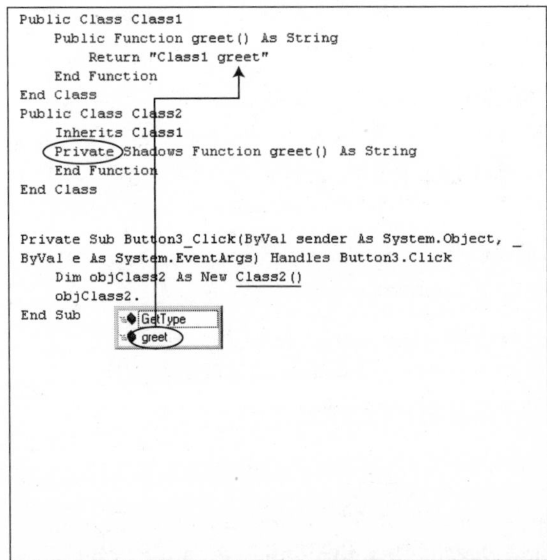

Figure 8.7 Attempting to locally hide a public inherited member by creating a Private Shadows version has absolutely no effect on the base member's visibility in derived objects.

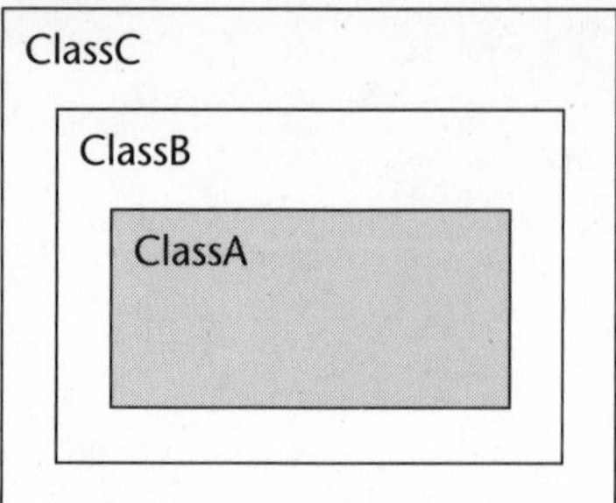

Figure 8.8 It's clear that ClassC is more than either a ClassA or a ClassB.

Given that C derives from B and B derives from A, we know that anything down the inheritance hierarchy is also an A, but A is only an A. Figure 8.8 illustrates the unionlike nature of class inheritance.

Lab 8.2: Polymorphism Challenge

This lab tests what you've learned from our discussion of inheritance and such. It is a descriptive problem with enough complexity for you to show some mastery of the subject but not so much that it takes you half a day to complete.

Perform the following steps:

1. Create a class hierarchy of classes of varying types of people (Manager, Customer, Student, and so forth; create whatever you want as long as you include at least two subtypes and a base type).
2. Make sure that the base type cannot be instantiated directly and is a pure abstract base class even after completing the remaining steps.
3. Include at least a Name member as a Public property in the base type.
4. Override ToString as appropriate in your object hierarchy to return Name or whatever you want for each subtype.
5. Create your object hierarchy so that the following function always acts polymorphically and returns the Name in the derived type:

```
Public Function GetName(ByVal p As Person) As String
   Return p.Name
End Function
```

Please attempt to implement the simple polymorphic example before continuing. The solution is the next step.

6. Check your solution against the following code:

```
Public MustInherit Class Person
   Public MustOverride Property Name() As String
End Class
Public Class Employee
   Inherits Person
   Private m_Name
   Public Overrides Property Name() As String
      Get
         Return m_Name
      End Get
      Set(ByVal Value As String)
         m_Name = Value
      End Set
   End Property
   Public Overrides Function ToString() As String
      Return Name
   End Function
End Class
Public Class Customer
   Inherits Person
   Private m_Name
   Public Overrides Property Name() As String
      Get
         Return m_Name
      End Get
      Set(ByVal Value As String)
         m_Name = Value
      End Set
   End Property
   Public Overrides Function ToString() As String
      Return Name
   End Function
End Class
```

7. Test your application with something similar to the following code. This code assumes a class library named People, so adjust that if you need to.

```
Private Sub Button1_Click(ByVal sender As System.Object, _
ByVal e As System.EventArgs) Handles Button1.Click
   Dim Emp1 As New People.Employee() 'People is the namespace
                                     'in my library
   Emp1.Name = "Brian"
   MsgBox(GetName(Emp1))
   Dim Cus1 As New People.Customer()
   Cus1.Name = "Tamra"
   MsgBox(GetName(Cus1))
End Sub
Public Function GetName(ByVal p As People.Person) As String
```

```
        Return p.Name 'Should always return Name for the
                      'derived type
    End Function
```

The class hierarchies you build will often be based on a description of objects in a system and their relationships with other objects. You might have noticed that by forcing the derived classes to inherit a property instead of a variable, we also forced abstraction.

Classroom Q & A

Q: Wouldn't it be better to create Person as an Interface?

A: Certainly, if that was the only member it was going to have in it. If there is no base class-specific implementation (no code, only declarations), making Person an interface would actually save us the trouble of having to declare the methods Overridable. Often we have a class that has some members we always want to be abstract and some members we don't. I tend to remove the abstract portion of classes and make both a class and an interface, which usually makes things cleaner in the process.

Q: Why don't interfaces need to declare members using the Overrides keyword?

A: Because with implementation inheritance between classes, both the base and the derived types have implementation, and there can be ambiguity about which version of a method to use. With interfaces, there is no implementation, so there can be no ambiguity, and polymorphism just happens.

Q: What happens if I inherit the same method from two different classes?

A: Although that is possible in C++ and a handful of other languages, multiple implementation inheritance is not allowed in any .NET language.

Summary

Implementation inheritance offers much in the way of code reuse as indicated by the myriad of classes that we have been reusing in the .NET arena. So many classes and interfaces have been defined for us that I opted not to translate many of my class libraries to .NET. We've looked at several variations and options for implementation and interfaces inheritance through abstraction, from forcing member inheritance to forcing an entire class to be noninheritable. A solid set of classes and interfaces isn't just about code reuse for rapid application development (RAD); it's also about clarity and control. Inheritance is only a tool with which you relate classes. If those classes are poor, it won't do you any good to use inheritance. When you build class hierarchies, keep in mind everything you have ever admired about classes that you've used in .NET: well-overloaded constructors, well-overloaded members, use of English-like member names, and implementation of well-known interfaces in lieu of reinventing an implementation. Build class hierarchies with the intention of future use, and later you can inherit from them proudly. The first time you build a lousy class and a programmer asks for the source code so it can be "fixed," say No and make that programmer extend its functionality through inheritance. I have met countless programmers more than able to fix my classes but have regretted every time I handed source code to the masses when 12 versions of the same class made their way into the same application

Review Questions

1. The Inherits statement can appear after a comment at the beginning of a Class definition. True or False?
2. What is wrong with the following code?

```
Public Class Class1
   Public NotOverridable Function GetRecords() _
   As System.Data.DataSet
   End Function
End Class
```

3. What is wrong with the following code?

```
Public Class Class1
   Public Function GetRecords() As DataSet
   End Function
End Class
Public Class Class2
   Inherits Class1
   Public Function GetRecords() As DataSet
   End Function
End Class
```

4. What is the difference between MyClass and Me?
   a. Nothing; they are synonymous and both refer to the current instance of an object.
   b. Me and MyClass can refer to the same instance of an object, but any method calls made against MyClass act as if methods were not overridable.
   c. Me and MyClass can refer to the same instance of an object, but any method calls made against Me act as if methods were not overridable.
   d. Me refers to the current instance of an object, and MyClass refers to the base class.
5. How do you make a method nonoverridable in a class that contains the original declaration of that method but is still inheritable as a public member in the derived class?
   a. Do nothing.
   b. Make it Protected.
   c. Make it NotOverridable.
   d. Make it Private.
6. Earlier, we wrote an Overrides version of ToString(). Name the members that are declared as Overridable in System.Object. Use the Object Browser to help you answer the question.

7. Which of the following accurately describes the inheritance hierarchy for a String class?
    a. System.Object, System.ValueType, System.String.
    b. System.Object, System.Values, System.String.
    c. System.Object, System.ReferenceType, System.String.
    d. System.Object, System.String.
8. In the inheritance hierarchy for a Form, which class actually inherits directly from System.Object?
    a. Component
    b. MarshalByRefObject
    c. Windows.Form
    d. ContainerControl
9. Why doesn't a System.Int64 have any overridable members?
    a. The designer of the Int64 class was lazy.
    b. The designer of the Int64 class didn't want any derivations to modify the way in which the members of an Int64 worked.
    c. Int64 is based on a Structure.
    d. Int64 is declared as Private.
10. The String class can be extended. True or False?

Answers to Review Questions

1. True. The Inherits statement can appear after a comment in the beginning of a Class definition, but it must be the first line of actual code and can specify only a single class.
2. The code sample attempts to use the NotOverridable keyword without the Overrides keyword. NotOverridable can be used only for a method that is being overridden. The following code is correct:

```
Public Class Class1
   Inherits SomeOtherClass
   Public NotOverridable Overrides Function GetRecords() _
   As System.Data.DataSet
   End Function
End Class
```

3. Class2's redeclaration of GetRecords attempts to hide the base implementation but failed to include the Shadows keyword. The following code is correct:

```
Public Class Class1
    Public Function GetRecords() As DataSet
    End Function
End Class
Public Class Class2
    Public Shadows Function GetRecords() As DataSet
    End Function
End Class
```

4. **b.** Me and MyClass can refer to the same instance of an object, but any method calls made against MyClass act as if methods are not overridable. MyBase refers to the base class portion of an object.
5. **a.** By default, members are not overridable unless they are declared with the Overridable keyword in the declaring class. Protected is a member access modifier that ensures that any inherited class will have access to a member. Marking the original declaration of a class member as Private limits that member's visibility to the class in which it was declared.
6. To find the members of System.Object that are declared as Overridable, we locate System.Object in the Object Browser, click on System.Object, click on a member of System.Object, and note the method declaration at the bottom of the Object Browser, below the Objects pane. Figure 8.9 shows that the Equals method of System.Object is overridable. Equals, Finalize, GetHashCode, and ToString are all declared as Overridable in System.Object.
7. **d.** Because String is a reference type, it wouldn't inherit from ValueType. The String class happens to directly inherit System.Object and directly implement the ICloneable, IComparable, IConvertable, and IEnumerable interfaces.

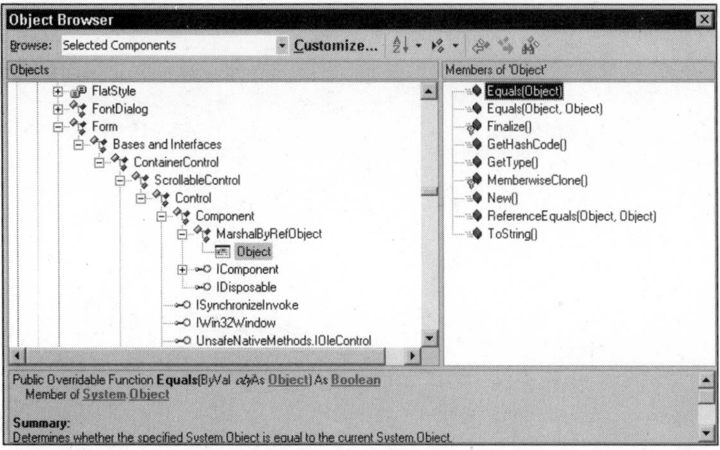

Figure 8.9 The bottom left of the Object Browser indicates that Equals is declared as Overridable.

8. **b.** As shown in Figure 8.9, in the inheritance hierarchy for a Form, the MarshalBy-RefObject class inherits directly from System.Object.

9. **c.** System.Int64 has no overridable members because it is declared as a Structure, which forces it to be a value type, which forces it to inherit from System.ValueType, which forces it to be a sealed class marked with NotOverridable. Figure 8.10 shows that Int64 inherits from System.ValueType but makes no reference to being Sealed or NotInheritable. As a matter of fact it *does* have overridable members! Well, if you attempt to inherit from System.Int64, you get a message stating that Long is declared as NotInheritable, but when you right-click on the Long keyword and select Go To Definition, it takes you to the definition of Int64. Regardless of the absence of proof, it's a Structure, so we know for sure that it will not be inheritable.

10. True. The String class is a reference type and is not marked NotInheritable.

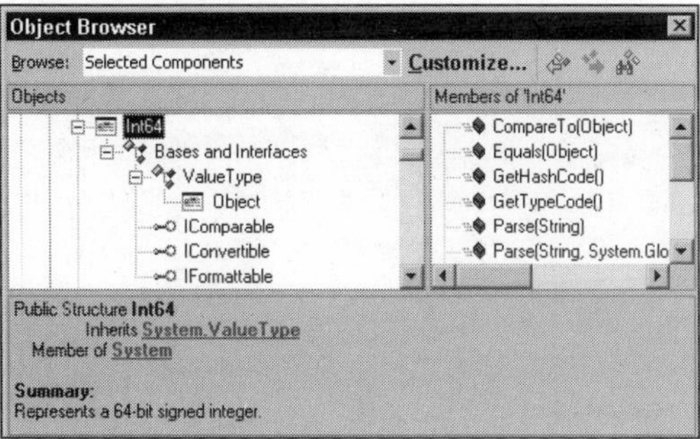

Figure 8.10 System.Int64 (Long to a Visual Basic .NET programmer) inherits from System .ValueType because it is a Structure.

CHAPTER

9

Interfaces and Polymorphism

It would have been impossible to have gotten this far and not used several interfaces. We have certainly become familiar with the collection-based interfaces, but this chapter demonstrates how interfaces are declared, used, and implemented for polymorphic results and to aid in building robust, reusable classes. This chapter also introduces and demonstrates the use of the IComparable, IComparer, ICloneable interfaces.

Interfaces

Interfaces are a contract. If a class implements an interface, it guarantees to users of that class that all members in that interface will be supported by the class.

When we say *interface*, sometimes it means the programming construct, and sometimes it refers to that portion of a thing with which users interact. The two uses are not at odds with each other; in fact, use of the Interface keyword guarantees that a specific set of methods will be there on an object for the user to interact with. An expected interface goes a long way to object reusability. If you take a car as an object example, you can see quickly how a standard interface allows you to quickly use new objects supporting an expected interface. What if a car manufacturer decided that the gas pedal should be on the left and the brake on the right? As a user, you would press firmly on the right pedal and start the car, resulting in a remodeled garage. This is a critical concept because a car interface might only demand that you *have* a brake pedal.

When interfaces become expected, they make development much easier and more productive. When Microsoft first bundled Word, PowerPoint, and Excel and provided the common menu interface, it was much easier to learn one tool, having used another. Today, all Windows users can close their eyes and say aloud half of the menu items shared by applications. Where would Exit be if not at the bottom of a File menu?

Conceptually, a pure abstract class (one with only abstract methods and no code) and an interface are the same thing. Interfaces aren't that new to Visual Basic. In Visual Basic 6, we could declare an abstract class and implement using the Implements keyword.

Declaring an Interface

Interfaces are declared using Interface...End Interface blocks and implemented in classes using the Implements keyword as shown here:

```
Public Interface Shape
    Sub Draw()
End Interface
Public Class Rectangle
    Implements Shape
    Public Sub Draw() Implements Shape.Draw
        'implementing code doesn't actually have
        'to exist to compile
    End Sub
End Class
```

Interfaces declared external to a type (as in the preceding code) can be declared as Public or Friend. If no Interface access modifier is specified, Friend is implied. Interfaces declared within another type may be declared as Private and are thereby only implementable within the type in which they reside. The following are possibilities that I don't personally use. This avoids confusion regarding intent:

```
'Interface nested in a class
Public Class Class1
    Private Interface I1
        Function greet() As String
    End Interface
End Class
'Class nested in an Interface
Public Interface I1
    Class classA
        '...
    End Class
End Interface
```

Interface Members

Valid interface members are methods, properties, events, enums, and type declarations.

Members of an interface are public and attempts to declare members using the Public, Private, Friend, or Protected access modifiers will not compile. Enums and nested types, declared as members of an interface, do not have to be referenced in any way in implementing classes. Declaring an enum inside an interface simply creates an interface.enumtype and does not become a member of an implementing class. This is demonstrated using the following code:

```
Public Interface I1
    Enum myenum
        val = 0
    End Enum
    Function something() As I1.myenum
End Interface
Public Class classA
    Implements I1
    Public Function something() As I1.myenum Implements I1.something
    End Function
End Class
```

Implementing Interfaces

Although a class can directly inherit only from a single class, it may implement any number of interfaces. After a class states that it implements an interface, it will not compile until all required members of that interface are implemented. Implementing an interface from the sense of satisfying the compiler doesn't require that any of the methods in the implementing class actually have any code. Figure 9.1 provides the syntax error message for a class that has not yet fully implemented an interface it supports.

```
Public Interface Shape
    Sub Draw()
End Interface
Public Class Rectangle
    Implements Shape
              'InterfaceDemo.Rectangle' must implement 'Sub Draw()' for interface 'InterfaceDemo.Shape'.
End Class
```

Figure 9.1 After a class indicates that it will support an interface, it will not compile until all members are implemented for that interface.

Enums and nested types are not members that an implementing class is required to declare, nor are they truly members of the interface in which they reside.

When two interfaces supported by a class require implementation of identical method signatures, Visual Basic .NET syntax does not support the following:

```
Public Interface I1
   Sub Method1()
End Interface
Public Interface I2
   Sub Method1()
End Interface
Public Class Class1
   Implements I1, I2
   Public Sub Method1() Implements I1.Method1 '<-Error, ambiguous
signature
   End Sub
   Public Sub Method1() Implements I2.Method1
   End Sub
End Class
```

The issue isn't a bug; it's simply stopping us from trying to implement two identical methods that aren't really overloads of each other. If both methods in both interfaces actually are intended to do the same thing for the implementing class, the following code could be used to handle that:

```
Public Class Class1
    Implements I1, I2
    Public Sub Method1() Implements I1.Method1, I2.Method1
    End Sub
End Class
```

The preceding declaration allows the declaration of Method1 to satisfy the requirement of implementing both interfaces.

Classroom Q & A

Q: What exactly is the difference between a pure abstract class and an interface?

A: A pure abstract class and an interface act the same and represent the same thing—pure interface. Personally, I don't use pure abstract base classes for two reasons: First, I have an actual Interface construct that makes things clearer; second, once you inherit from one class, you can never inherit from another. What a waste that would be if the one class you inherited from didn't even provide anything beyond what an interface does.

Q: Isn't it a problem that a class can be compiled and used even it if really doesn't have any code inside the members it implements? I mean, to use your car analogy, it's like having a brake pedal but someone cut the brake line.

A: That's not an inaccurate twist on the analogy, but it is best this way because we often develop applications in an under-construction mode. It's actually not that big of a deal considering that a method that has a hundred lines of code still could not be doing what it's supposed to be doing. Just having code doesn't mean it's logically correct or appropriate for the derived class implementation. That responsibility falls on our shoulders.

Q: What happens when two interfaces require an identical method to be supported by an implementing class?

A: In all implementations in .NET, dynamic method dispatching requires that all method signatures for an object be unique. Also, any method our class implements becomes a public member for objects of that type. Look at Figure 9.2 to see the problem.

Polymorphism Through Interfaces

In Chapter 8, "Implementation Inheritance," we implemented polymorphism through abstract classes and with virtual methods using overridable and overrides keywords. With class inheritance you have a base class and a derived class where methods can be shadowed or overridden. Overridden methods provide polymorphic behavior, meaning that when a derived class is cast to the base type and an overridden method is invoked, the functionality of the derived class will be exhibited. With interfaces, you don't have any implementation in the interface and there is no base class, so the only functionality that can ever be exhibited is that of the implementing class. That is to say that polymorphism just happens with interfaces. Figure 9.3 depicts the relationship between various implementations, and they are support for polymorphism.

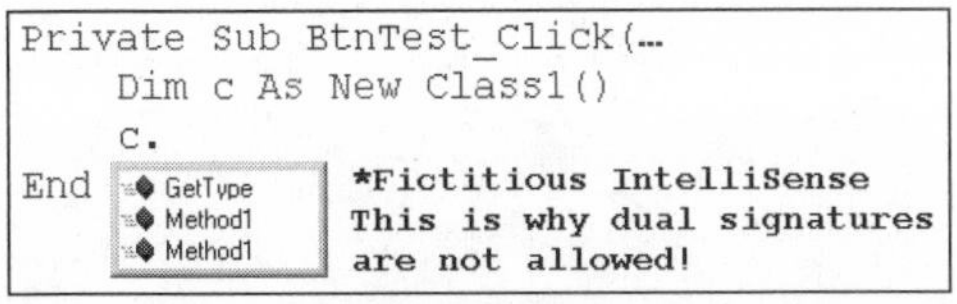

```
Private Sub BtnTest_Click(...
    Dim c As New Class1()
    c.
End  GetType      *Fictitious IntelliSense
     Method1      This is why dual signatures
     Method1      are not allowed!
```

Figure 9.2 Dual signatures are not allowed, regardless of why they are being declared. This is to avoid ambiguity when calling methods.

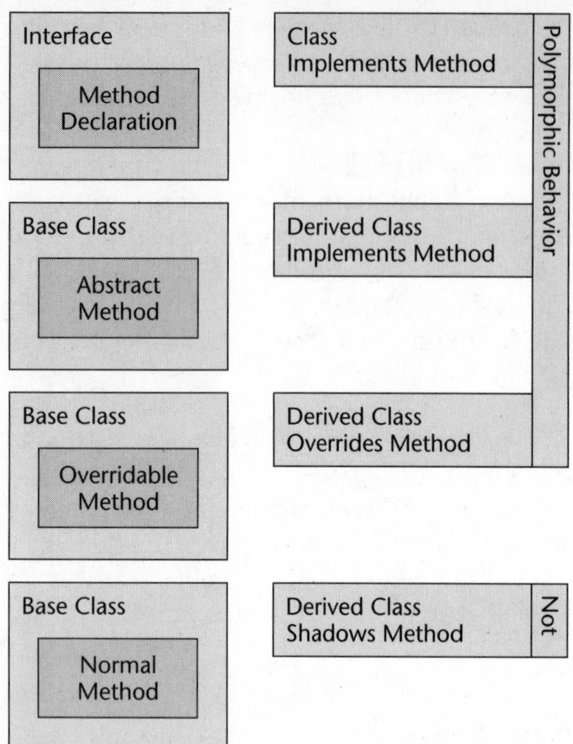

Figure 9.3 Polymorphism can be achieved in a number of ways in Visual Basic .NET, but interfaces provide polymorphic behavior as a rule.

Given the following declarations:

```
Public Interface IShape
   Function Draw() As String
End Interface
Public Class Rectangle
   Implements IShape
   Public Function Draw() As String Implements IShape.Draw
      Return "Drawing Rectangle"
   End Function
End Class
Public Class Trapezoid
   Implements IShape
   Public Function Draw() As String Implements IShape.Draw
      Return "Drawing Trapezoid"
   End Function
End Class
```

The following DrawAny() function can then be used to print any shape that is passed in without checking the passed type or doing any casting:

```
Private Sub btnTest_Click(ByVal sender As System.Object,
ByVal e As System.EventArgs) Handles Button1.Click
   Dim rect As New Rectangle()
   Dim trap As New Trapezoid()
   DrawAny(rect)
   DrawAny(trap)
End Sub
Private Sub drawany(ByVal s As IShape)
   MessageBox.Show(s.Draw())
End Sub
```

Interface Inheritance

An interface can actually inherit other interfaces. This feature allows you to extend an interface's description with a newer version of the interface, as shown here:

```
Public Interface IShape1
   Function Draw() As String
End Interface
Public Interface IShape2
   Inherits IShape1
   Property Dimensions() As Integer
End Interface
```

Any class now implementing IShape2 must implement both the Draw method and the Dimensions property, as in the following example:

```
Public Class Circle
   Implements IShape2
   Private m_dimensions As Integer
   Public Function Draw() As String Implements IShape1.Draw
      Return "Drawing circle..."
   End Function
   Public Property Dimensions() As Integer Implements IShape2.Dimensions
      Get
         Return m_dimensions
      End Get
      Set(ByVal Value As Integer)
         m_dimensions = Value
      End Set
   End Property
End Class
```

This indirect inheritance isn't new. Keep in mind that for an Int32, it doesn't directly inherit from System.Object but rather, through System.ValueType, which inherits from System.Object. An Int32 "is a" System.ValueType as well as a System.Object, meaning that these are base types that an Int32 can be cast as. To test for "is a" relationships in Visual Basic .NET, use the TypeOf method.

In the preceding code, a Circle is a System.Object, a Circle, an IShape1, and an IShape2.

Implementing Common .NET Interfaces

Beyond the interfaces we have discussed up to this point, many interfaces are so commonly used and looked for by .NET components and developers that they are much more than optional. When items are sorted using the Array.Sort method, it is the CompareTo method of the IComparable interface that is supporting the comparisons. When developers are done using an object, they call the Dispose method of the IDisposable interface.

Common Interfaces

The following list describes some of the more common interfaces implemented in .NET:

ICloneable. Allows you to make a new and separate copy of an object by performing a member-by-member copy.

ICollection. Defines size, enumerators, and synchronization methods for all collections.

IComparable. Allows objects to be compared by selecting a specific member on which to perform the comparison.

IComparer. Allows comparisons between like objects based on different members (sort by age, sort by name, and so on).

IConvertable. Allows for the conversion of an object value to some common language runtime value type.

IDictionary. Represents a collection of key and value pairs for creating dictionaries.

IDisposable. Contains only a Dispose method used to aid in the destruction of object resources.

IEnumerable. Exposes the enumerator, which supports a simple iteration over a collection.

IEvidenceFactory. Gets an object's System.Security.Policy.Evidence.

IFormattable. Provides functionality to format the value of an object into a string representation.

IList. Represents a collection of objects that can be individually accessed by index.

ISerializable. Allows an object to control its own serialization and deserialization.

Implementing IComparable

Sorting occurs differently in different places. An ArrayList is a collection of generic objects and can guarantee only that all objects have some implementation of ToString, so it performs a string comparison using that value. The Array.Sort mechanism, however, uses the CompareTo method in the object's IComparable interface to perform a sort based on the preferences of the object's author. The IComparable interface declares a single method, CompareTo, that returns the following values:

VALUE	MEANING
-1	me.comparefield < other.comparefield
0	me.comparefield = other.comparefield
1	me.comparefield > other.comparefield

For the Card class we created in Chapter 7, "Extending Visual Basic .NET Classes," we had no way of sorting the cards based on their actual value. Adding support for the IComparable interface to Cards would allow for a more natural sorting. Because most games need to compare the values of cards, this would be a sad omission. Looking at the card class, we could use several things to sort by, but for this first example, FaceValue will suffice. Instead of performing a comparison of greater than, less than, or equal to, I'll just use the fact that all enums already implement IComparable and call the CompareTo method for FaceValue enum and return its return value.

```
Public Class Card
    Implements IComparable
    Private Function CompareTo(ByVal obj As Object) _
    As Integer Implements IComparable.CompareTo
        If obj Is Nothing Then Return 1
        Dim othercard As Card = CType(obj, Card)
        Return Me.FaceValue.CompareTo(othercard.FaceValue)
    End Function
    '
    'same additional members as before
    '
End Class
```

To test the new sorting mechanism, the contents of Deck.Cards need to be transferred to an array; then the sort method for the array will perform the comparisons for us. The following code uses Array.Sort to sort a deck of cards by its FaceValue and then places the cards in a list box. This would not work if the ListBox.Sorted property was True because that would cause the items to be re-sorted by their ToString value.

```
Private Sub btnTest1_Click(...) Handles Button3.Click
   Dim d As New Deck()
   Dim c As Card
   Dim i As Integer
   Dim cardarray(d.Cards.Count - 1) As Card
   For i = 0 To d.Cards.Count - 1
      'Me.lstCards.Items.Add(c)
      cardarray(i) = d.Cards.Item(i)
   Next
   Array.Sort(cardarray)
   Me.lstCards.Items.AddRange(cardarray)
End Sub
```

As long as the Sorted property for the list box is False, the preceding code will produce the results shown in Figure 9.4.

Implementing IComparer

It's readily apparent that for the Card class there are multiple ways that cards should be sorted. As a matter of fact, they are usually sorted twice, once by suit and then by relative value within that suit. When an object needs to be sorted by more than one value, the class must support the IComparer interface.

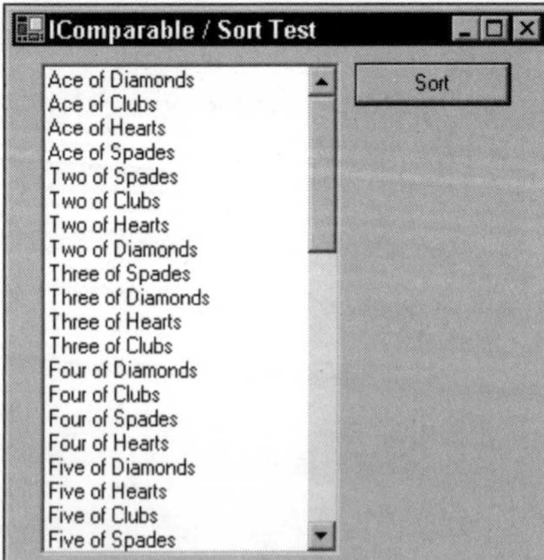

Figure 9.4 The CompareTo method return value is used to sort items when an Array.Sort is used. After items are sorted in this manner, placing them into a list box with a Sorted property of True would resort them to their ToString value.

Implementing the IComparer interface is very different than implementing Comparable. To implement the IComparable interface a nested class is created for each sort option that implements the single method, Compare. The following code shows the modifications for the Card class to support sorting by ToString, FaceValue, SuitType, or AssignedValue. In addition to Comparer classes, I added a single line to the end of the constructor in the Card class to give AssignedValue a more useful default.

```
Public Class Card
   Private m_suit As SuitType
   Private m_facevalue As FaceType
   Public AssignedValue As Integer = 0
   Public Enum SuitType
      Hearts = 1 : Clubs = 2 : Diamonds = 3
      Spades = 4 : Joker = 5
   End Enum
   Public Enum FaceType
      Ace = 1 : Two = 2 : Three = 3 : Four = 4
      Five = 5 : Six = 6 : Seven = 7 : Eight = 8
      Nine = 9 : Ten = 10 : Jack = 11 : Queen = 12
      King = 13 : Little = 14 : Big = 15
   End Enum
   Public ReadOnly Property Suit() As SuitType
      Get
         Return Me.m_suit
      End Get
   End Property
   Public ReadOnly Property FaceValue() As FaceType
      Get
         Return Me.m_facevalue
      End Get
   End Property
   Public Sub New(ByVal value As FaceType, ByVal suit As SuitType)
      If value = FaceType.Big Or value = FaceType.Little Then
         If suit <> SuitType.Joker Then
            Throw New System.Exception("Big, Little can only be used " &
_
                "with the Joker SuitType")
            End If
         Else 'FaceType is not Big or Little
            If suit = SuitType.Joker Then
               Throw New System.Exception("Joker usable only with " & _
              "Big and Little FaceTypes")
            End If
      End If
      Me.m_suit = suit
      Me.m_facevalue = value
      Me.AssignedValue = value 'Added for this example
   End Sub
```

```
    Public Overrides Function ToString() As String
        If Me.m_facevalue < 14 Then
            Return Me.m_facevalue.ToString() & " of " &
Me.m_suit.ToString()
        Else
            Return Me.m_facevalue.ToString() & " " & Me.m_suit.ToString()
        End If
    End Function
    Class ComparerByString
        Implements IComparer
        Function Compare(ByVal obj1 As Object, ByVal obj2 As Object) _
        As Integer Implements IComparer.Compare
            If (obj1 Is Nothing) And (obj2 Is Nothing) Then Return 0
            If (obj1 Is Nothing) Then Return 1 'null is < not null
            If (obj2 Is Nothing) Then Return -1
            Dim Card1 As Card = CType(obj1, Card)
            Dim Card2 As Card = CType(obj2, Card)
            Return StrComp(CType(obj1, Card).ToString(), _
            CType(obj2, Card).ToString(), CompareMethod.Text)
        End Function
    End Class
    Class ComparerByFaceValue
        Implements IComparer
        Function Compare(ByVal obj1 As Object, ByVal obj2 As Object) _
        As Integer Implements IComparer.Compare
            If (obj1 Is Nothing) And (obj2 Is Nothing) Then Return 0
            If (obj1 Is Nothing) Then Return 1
            If (obj2 Is Nothing) Then Return -1
            Dim Card1 As Card = CType(obj1, Card)
            Dim Card2 As Card = CType(obj2, Card)
            'all enums support the IComparable interface method CompareTo:
            Return Card1.FaceValue.CompareTo(Card2.FaceValue)
        End Function
    End Class
    Class ComparerBySuitType
        Implements IComparer
        Function Compare(ByVal obj1 As Object, ByVal obj2 As Object) _
        As Integer Implements IComparer.Compare
            If (obj1 Is Nothing) And (obj2 Is Nothing) Then Return 0
            If (obj1 Is Nothing) Then Return 1 'null is < not null
            If (obj2 Is Nothing) Then Return -1 'null is < not null
            Dim Card1 As Card = CType(obj1, Card)
            Dim Card2 As Card = CType(obj2, Card)
            Return Card1.Suit.CompareTo(Card2.Suit)
        End Function
    End Class
    Class ComparerByAssignedValue
        Implements IComparer
        Function Compare(ByVal obj1 As Object, ByVal obj2 As Object) _
        As Integer Implements IComparer.Compare
            If (obj1 Is Nothing) And (obj2 Is Nothing) Then Return 0
            If (obj1 Is Nothing) Then Return 1
```

```
        If (obj2 Is Nothing) Then Return -1
        Dim Card1 As Card = CType(obj1, Card)
        Dim Card2 As Card = CType(obj2, Card)
        If Card1.AssignedValue = Card2.AssignedValue Then Return 0
        If Card1.AssignedValue > Card2.AssignedValue Then Return 1
        If Card1.AssignedValue < Card2.AssignedValue Then Return -1
    End Function
End Class
```

Testing IComparer Implementations

To use a specific IComparer implementation, the comparer is passed as an argument to the Array.Sort method as in the following:

```
Array.Sort(cards, New Card.ComparerBySuitType())
```

The following code tests each of the four Comparer implementations and produces the output shown in Figure 9.5:

```
Private Sub btnTest_Click(ByVal sender As System.Object, _
ByVal e As System.EventArgs) Handles Button1.Click
   Dim deck1 As New Deck()
   Dim i As Integer
   Dim cardarray(deck1.Cards.Count - 1) As Card
   For i = 0 To deck1.Cards.Count - 1
      cardarray(i) = deck1.Cards.Item(i)
   Next
   SortBySuitType(cardarray)
   SortByFaceValue(cardarray)
   SortByAssignedValue(cardarray)
   SortByToString(cardarray)
   'SortByBoth(cardarray) 'To be implemented
End Sub
Private Sub SortBySuitType(ByRef cards As Array)
   Array.Sort(cards, New Card.ComparerBySuitType())
   Me.ListBox1.Items.AddRange(cards)
End Sub
Private Sub SortByFaceValue(ByRef cards As Array)
   Array.Sort(cards, New Card.ComparerByFaceValue())
   Me.ListBox2.Items.AddRange(cards)
End Sub
Private Sub SortByAssignedValue(ByRef cards As Array)
   Array.Sort(cards, New Card.ComparerByAssignedValue())
   Me.ListBox3.Items.AddRange(cards)
End Sub
   Private Sub SortByToString(ByRef cards As Array)
   Array.Sort(cards, New Card.ComparerByString())
   Me.ListBox4.Items.AddRange(cards)
End Sub
```

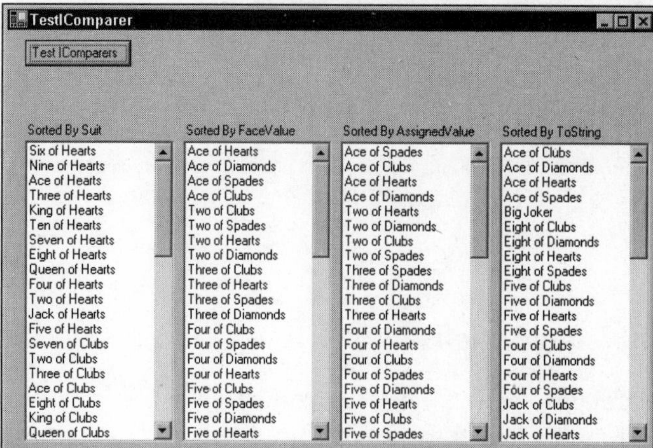

Figure 9.5 Each of the IComparer interface implementations provides a unique sorting option, although AssignedValue is up to the class consumer to modify for game-specific values.

Classroom Q & A

Q: How does a user of our class know that we have created the IComparable implementations in the class?

A: After a while as a .NET developer you will intuitively look for certain interfaces. Just as when you get into a new car, it takes time to find out how to turn on the wipers without signaling a turn. After a while, you have driven so many cars that you know what to try because you've seen virtually every implementation. Figure 9.6 provides a nice view of what lies within our class library.

Q: Why in the Object Browser and in Figure 9.6 are our IComparer implementation classes exposed at the Assembly level?

A: When you embed a class, technically it resides at the assembly level but requires a class followed by a dot to access it. You really embed the class to make your intentions clear that it is to be used only in conjunction with the class in which it was embedded.

Q: What happens if we want to sort by the suit and then by the face value in that suit? Does our class do that yet?

A: The class itself doesn't support that sorting directly, but it can be done in the client. The next code example demonstrates what you could do in the client to perform that type of sorting, if the class didn't expose a method for it.

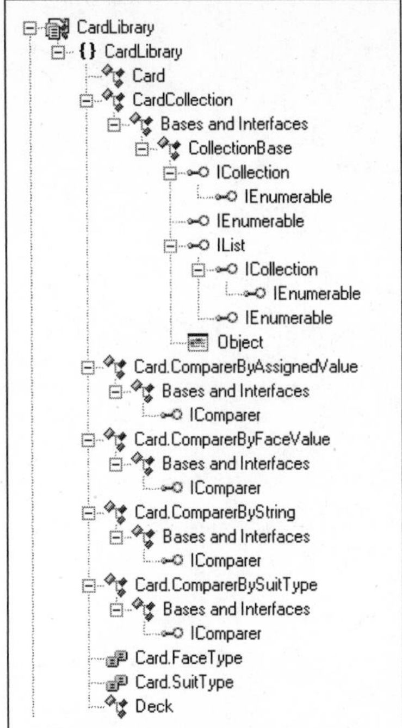

Figure 9.6 The Object Browser shows the various implementations of classes and interfaces in the card class library.

Unfortunately, implementing a dual sort for this particular class is probably too game-specific, but we have at least provided enough to indirectly support it in a class consumer, as in the following code:

```
Private Sub SortByBoth(ByRef cards As Array)
'just provide solution for full deck
   If cards.Length < 54 Then Exit Sub
   Dim hearts() As Card
   Dim clubs() As Card
   Dim spades() As Card
   Dim diamonds() As Card
   Dim Jokers() As Card
   Dim i As Integer
   For i = 0 To cards.Length - 1
      Select Case CType(cards(i), Card).Suit
         Case Card.SuitType.Clubs
            If clubs Is Nothing Then
               ReDim clubs(0)
            Else
               ReDim Preserve clubs(clubs.Length)
            End If
            clubs(clubs.Length - 1) = CType(cards(i), Card)
         Case Card.SuitType.Diamonds
```

```
            If diamonds Is Nothing Then
               ReDim diamonds(0)
            Else
               ReDim Preserve diamonds(diamonds.Length)
            End If
            diamonds(diamonds.Length - 1) = CType(cards(i), Card)
         Case Card.SuitType.Hearts
            If hearts Is Nothing Then
               ReDim hearts(0)
            Else
               ReDim Preserve hearts(hearts.Length)
            End If
            hearts(hearts.Length - 1) = CType(cards(i), Card)
         Case Card.SuitType.Spades
            If spades Is Nothing Then
               ReDim spades(0)
            Else
               ReDim Preserve spades(spades.Length)
            End If
               spades(spades.Length - 1) = CType(cards(i), Card)
         Case Card.SuitType.Joker
            If Jokers Is Nothing Then
               ReDim Jokers(0)
            Else
               ReDim Preserve Jokers(Jokers.Length)
            End If
            Jokers(Jokers.Length - 1) = CType(cards(i), Card)
      End Select
   Next
   Array.Sort(Jokers, New Card.ComparerByFaceValue())
   Array.Sort(hearts, New Card.ComparerByFaceValue())
   Array.Sort(spades, New Card.ComparerByFaceValue())
   Array.Sort(diamonds, New Card.ComparerByFaceValue())
   Array.Sort(clubs, New Card.ComparerByFaceValue())
   Dim newarray(53) As Card
   Array.Copy(Jokers, 0, newarray, 0, Jokers.Length)
   Array.Copy(hearts, 0, newarray, 2, hearts.Length)
   Array.Copy(spades, 0, newarray, 15, spades.Length)
   Array.Copy(diamonds, 0, newarray, 28, diamonds.Length)
   Array.Copy(clubs, 0, newarray, 41, clubs.Length)
   ListBox5.Items.AddRange(newarray)
End Sub
```

The results of the SortByBoth are displayed in Figure 9.7.

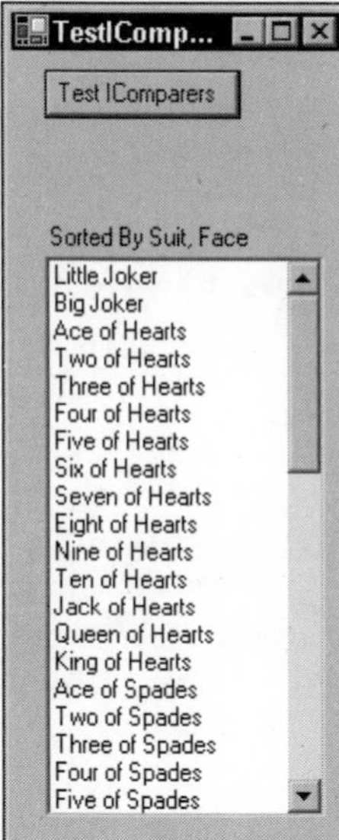

Figure 9.7 SortByBoth sorts by Suit, then by FaceValue.

Implementing ICloneable

By default, value types copy by value and reference types copy by reference. What if you wanted to copy a reference type such as Card to another memory location by value? You would have to implement the ICloneable interface in the Card class. To copy a reference type, you need to indicate what exactly you need to copy and make a member-by-member assignment of values. Like the other interfaces we've used, ICloneable has a single method. All a class has to do to be cloneable is to implement ICloneable.Clone. Typically, the clone method would go down the list of property values that you want to copy and make assignments from the currentobject.value to the newobject.value, but both major properties are ReadOnly in the Card class. Furthermore, you don't have a default constructor to create a new, empty Card. To implement ICloneable in the Card class, I had to modify the existing constructor to take a third, optional parameter of AssignedValue:

```
Public Class Card
   Implements ICloneable
   Public Function Clone() As Object Implements ICloneable.Clone
      Dim newcard As New Card(Me.FaceValue, Me.Suit, Me.AssignedValue)
      Return newcard
   End Function
   'Constructor added to support testing only:
   Public Sub New()
   End Sub
```

```
    'Constructor modified to support cloning:
    Public Sub New(ByVal value As FaceType, _
    ByVal suit As SuitType, Optional ByVal gameValue As Integer = 0)
       If value = FaceType.Big Or value = FaceType.Little Then
       'SuitType must then be a Joker
          If suit <> SuitType.Joker Then
             Throw New System.Exception("Big, Little can only be used " &
_
             "with the Joker SuitType")
             End If
         Else 'FaceType is not Big or Little
             If suit = SuitType.Joker Then
                 Throw New System.Exception("Joker only usable with " & _
                 "Big and Little FaceTypes")
             End If
         End If
         Me.m_suit = suit
         Me.m_facevalue = value
         If gameValue <> Nothing Then
             Me.AssignedValue = gameValue
         Else
             AssignedValue = value
         End If
     End Sub
 '
 'Same additional members as before
 '
 End Class
```

Testing the ICloneable Interface

Testing the Clone method is simple. All you have to do is call Clone and use the returned object to assign to a new Card object. The following code describes the difference between copying by reference and cloning and produces the output in Figure 9.8:

```
Private Sub btnTest1_Click(...)
   'copying by reference, the assignment of card2 to card1
   'causes both reference variables to modify the same memory location
   'changing card1.assignedvalue changes card2.assignedvalue
   Dim card1 As New Card()
   Dim card2 As New Card(Card.FaceType.Ace, Card.SuitType.Spades, 0)
```

```
    ListBox1.Items.Add("card2 assigned value before assignment: " & _
    card2.AssignedValue.ToString())
    card1 = card2
    card1.AssignedValue = 10 'modifies what both card1 and card2 point to
    ListBox1.Items.Add("card2 assigned value after assignment: " & _
    card2.AssignedValue.ToString())
End Sub
Private Sub btnTest2_Click(...)
    'When cloning, the assignment of card2 to card1
    'simply copies members by value from one memory location to another
and
    'card2 and card1 always reference different memory locations
    'Changing card1.assignedvalue does not change card2.assignedvalue
    Dim card1 As New Card()
    Dim card2 As New Card(Card.FaceType.Ace, Card.SuitType.Spades, 0)
    ListBox1.Items.Add("card2 assigned value before clone: " & _
    card2.AssignedValue.ToString())
    card1 = card2.Clone()
    card1.AssignedValue = 10
    ListBox1.Items.Add("card2 assigned value after clone: " & _
    card2.AssignedValue.ToString())
End Sub
```

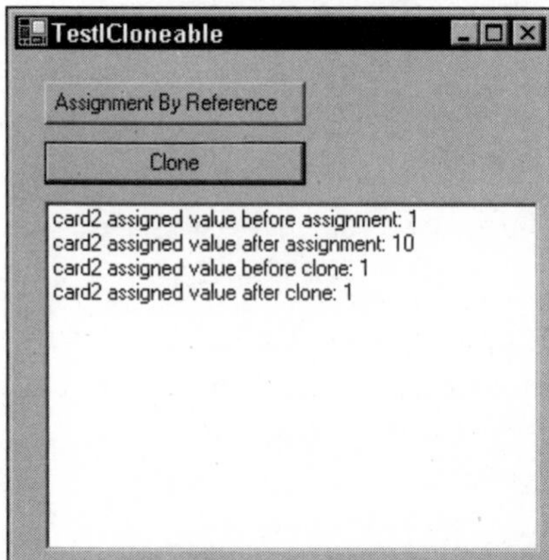

Figure 9.8 Copying by reference causes two references to a single location, whereas Clone creates a completely separate object with copies of the original object's values.

Strongly Typed Clones

Although Clone works well enough, it's annoying that Clone wants to return a generic Object. Every client that uses the Clone method goes through a boxing and unboxing operation to deal with the fact that we're assigning an Object to a Card even though we knew that would be the case going in. Fixing the issue can be done by wrapping a private implementation of Clone in a public function. As long as TypeOf object is ICloneable, it returns True. The public method is named Clone; this wrapped implementation doesn't go against the .NET grain. The following code shows the modifications necessary to make Clone strongly typed:

```
Public Class Card
    Implements ICloneable
    Private Function PrivateClone() As Object Implements ICloneable.Clone
        Dim newcard As New Card(Me.FaceValue, Me.Suit, Me.AssignedValue)
        Return newcard
    End Function
    Public Function Clone() As Card
        Return CType(PrivateClone(), Card)
    End Function
    '
    'Same additional members as before
    '
End Class
```

Lab 9.1: Creating Person

This lab tests your understanding of and ability to adapt what we have discussed so far by creating a Person class that supports a strongly typed Clone operation and is at least IComparable by LastName and FirstName.

Perform the following steps:

1. Create a Person class with FirstName and LastName properties.
2. Overload ToString to return LastName and FirstName.
3. Implement ICloneable.Clone.
4. Implement IComparable.CompareTo.
5. Test Clone by creating a copy of a Person object.
6. Test CompareTo by creating an array of Persons, sorting them, and placing the sorted results in a list box.

7. Compare your code and results to the following Person Class:

```
Public Class Person
   Implements IComparable, ICloneable
   Public Sub New(ByVal fname As String, ByVal lname As String)
      Me.FirstName = fname
      Me.LastName = lname
   End Sub
   Public Overrides Function ToString() As String
      Return Me.LastName & ", " & Me.FirstName
   End Function
   Public Function CompareTo(ByVal obj As Object) _
   As Integer Implements IComparable.CompareTo
      If Me.ToString = CType(obj, Person).ToString() Then
         Return 0
      If Me.ToString > CType(obj, Person).ToString() Then
         Return 1
      Else
         Return -1
      End If
   End Function
   Private Function PrivateClone() As Object Implements
ICloneable.Clone
      Dim p As New Person(Me.FirstName, Me.LastName)
      Return p
   End Function
   Public Function Clone() As Person
      Return PrivateClone()
   End Function
   Private m_firstname As String
   Private m_lastname As String
   Public Property FirstName() As String
      Get
         Return m_firstname
      End Get
      Set(ByVal Value As String)
         m_firstname = Value
      End Set
   End Property
   Public Property LastName() As String
      Get
         Return m_lastname
      End Get
      Set(ByVal Value As String)
         m_lastname = Value
      End Set
   End Property
End Class
```

We test the Person class (results are shown in Figure 9.9) as follows:

```
Private Sub btnTestClone_Click(ByVal sender As System.Object, _
ByVal e As System.EventArgs) Handles Button1.Click
    Dim p As New Person("Jody", "Barstow")
    Dim p2 As Person = p.Clone()
    Me.ListBox1.Items.Add("p2.FirstName after clone: " &
p2.FirstName)
End Sub
Private Sub btnTestComparable_Click(ByVal sender As System.Object,
_
ByVal e As System.EventArgs) Handles Button2.Click
    Dim People(4) As Person
    People(0) = New Person("Mary", "Jo")
    People(1) = New Person("Betty", "Bilderback")
    People(2) = New Person("Marcie", "Palzer")
    People(3) = New Person("Ray", "Ober")
    People(4) = New Person("Fred", "Wood")
    Array.Sort(People)
    Me.ListBox1.Items.AddRange(People)
End Sub
```

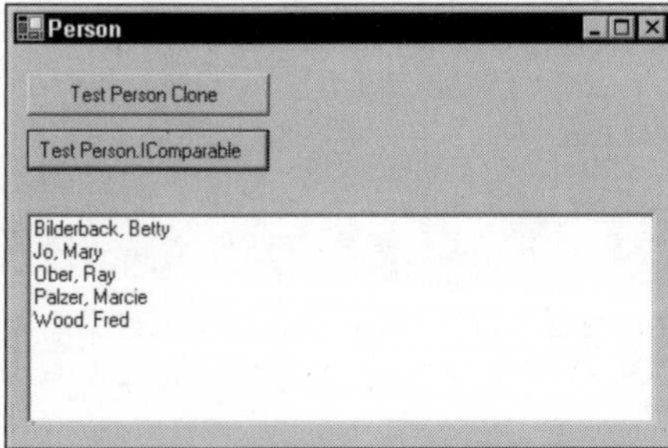

Figure 9.9 Here are the results after testing the Person class.

The capabilities to clone and sort objects are common and should be supported on any type where it makes sense. For this example, obviously Person isn't nearly as complete a class as Card, but it's clear that the need for IComparers exists for at least IComparerFirstName, IComparerLastName, and IComparerLastNameFirstName. Try implementing those interfaces to support that additional functionality.

Summary

You've reached a major turning point in .NET. After implementing classes and interfaces common throughout .NET and with a firm foothold in OOP, class design, .NET libraries, and the .NET way of life, we can now focus on specific tasks such as memory management, database access, and multithreaded applications. You will find from this point forward that although the libraries you will be using are new, they are just libraries, built on rules, classes, and interfaces to which you have been exposed. Of all the libraries in .NET, the next library, ADO.NET, seems the most foreign, so take heart and believe me anyway!

Review Questions

1. A class can inherit from any number of interfaces. True or False?
2. How would you make a new version of an interface without removing or changing the original interface?
   a. Create a second interface that implements the first
   b. Create a second interface that inherits and extends the first
   c. Embed a second interface in the first
   d. Create an abstract class that implements and extends the original interface
3. Why would you want to create an interface as opposed to a pure abstract class?
   a. Because pure abstract classes are nothing more than declarations and act exactly like interfaces. Because classes can only directly inherit from a single class but can implement any number of interfaces, inheriting from a pure abstract class is a waste.
   b. Because pure abstract classes are not creatable in .NET.
   c. Because pure abstract classes require more work.
   d. Because pure abstract classes have too much overhead.
4. How do list boxes sort items?
   a. By using the CompareTo return value
   b. By using the Compare return value
   c. By using the ToString value for comparisons
   d. By using the Item index value
5. How does Array.Sort sort items?
   a. By using the CompareTo return value
   b. By using the Compare return value
   c. By using either the Compare or CompareTo return value, depending on what was passed to the Sort method
   d. By using the ToString return value

6. What is the fundamental difference between IComparer and IComparable?

   a. IComparer can be used to allow sorting on any number of fields, but IComparable only allows for a single field sort.

   b. IComparable can be used to allow sorting on any number of fields, but IComparer only allows for a single field sort.

   c. IComparer is directly implemented on the class to be compared, whereas IComparable is not.

   d. IComparable is implemented in a nested class, and IComparer is not.

7. What is the importance of an "expected" interface (select one or more of the following)?

   a. Developers can quickly pick up new objects and use them intuitively.

   b. An expected interface helps provide standards and aids rapid application development.

   c. An expected interface allows for the resulting implementation to more easily work with objects of differing types.

   d. Whether in class construction or in user interface design, an expected interface provides a common base for understanding when using otherwise foreign objects.

8. Which of the following can be included in an interface declaration (select one or more answers)?

   a. Class definitions

   b. Structure definitions

   c. Enums

   d. Methods and properties

9. What interface should all .NET classes support to aid in garbage collection efforts?

   a. IDispose

   b. IDisposable

   c. IDisposer

   d. ICollectable

10. What interface would a class support to provide conversions from a custom type to common language runtime types?
    a. IComparable
    b. IComparer
    c. IDictionary
    d. IConvertable
11. What does Clone return?
    a. An object of the type being compared
    b. An object of the type being compared to
    c. An Object
    d. An Integer
12. How do you make a strongly typed version of Clone?
    a. By wrapping ICloneable.Clone
    b. By overloading ICloneable.Clone
    c. By overriding ICloneable.Clone
    d. By shadowing ICloneable.Clone

Answers to Review Questions

1. False. Only an interface can inherit from an interface. A class can implement any number of interfaces and directly inherit from, at most, a single class.
2. **b.** To make a new version of an interface without removing or changing the original interface, you would create a second interface that inherits and extends the first. Any class that implements the second interface must then implement all members of both interfaces. When using inherits in this manner, the second interface can actually shadow members in the original interface.
3. **a.** You would create an interface as opposed to a pure abstract class because pure abstract classes are nothing more than declarations and act exactly like interfaces. Because classes can only directly inherit from a single class, but can implement any number of interfaces, inheriting from a pure abstract class is a waste. In addition, many people prefer to take a class that has part abstract and part nonabstract members and make a separate class and interface.
4. **c.** List boxes sort items by using the value returned from ToString(). They can be sorted by setting the Sorted property for the list box to True.
5. **c.** Array.Sort sorts items by using either the Compare or CompareTo return value, depending on what was passed to the Sort method. Sort has many overloads. When Sort is passed to an IComparer, the IComparer.Compare return value is used to compare and sort items. If only the name of the array is passed to the Sort method, the IComparable.CompareTo method's return value will be used.
6. **a.** The fundamental difference between IComparer and IComparable is that IComparer can be used to allow sorting on any number of fields, but IComparable only allows for a single field sort. In addition, IComparable is directly implemented on the class to be compared, whereas IComparer is not.
7. **a**, **b**, **c**, and **d.** An expected interface allows developers to quickly pick up new objects and use them intuitively, helps provide standards, and aids rapid application development. Whether in class construction or in user interface design, an expected interface provides a common base for understanding when using otherwise foreign objects.
8. **a**, **b**, **c**, and **d.** An interface declaration can include class definitions, structure definitions, enums, methods, properties, and events.
9. **b.** All .NET classes should support IDisposable to aid in garbage collection efforts. Users of your objects will call the Dispose method on the IDisposable interface to signal that they are done using your object and that local resources should be freed. The other interfaces mentioned are fictitious.

10. **d.** A class can support the IConvertable interface to provide conversions from a custom type to common language runtime types. The IDictionary interface allows for creation of key, value pairs.

11. **c.** IConeable.Clone returns an Object regardless of what is being compared.

12. **a.** You can make a strongly typed version of Clone by wrapping a private implementation of ICloneable.Clone with a public method that converts the Object to an appropriate type.

CHAPTER

10

Data Access in .NET

In our progression toward building an enterprise application in .NET, this chapter focuses on not only ADO.NET but also on how we architect .NET systems to maximize the number and types of users who can use a given system. This chapter does not take us to a point where we have a fully architected system but leads us one step forward to that goal while exploring the new features and possibilities related to ADO.NET. By building centralized libraries to access our data, anyone in the world can connect to our system as a developer or user, using any operating system and any language via Web services. Although the class libraries provide the actual database connectivity and maintenance for our client applications, those clients will still be using quite a bit of data access technology that is new to ADO.NET. Because of this, we'll also be looking at how data-centric clients can make the most of ADO.NET features.

ADO.NET's Place in .NET Architecture

Before we begin, we need to examine the architecture typically used in .NET and also examine how this chapter fits into the big picture. However, until we add a Web service into the picture in Chapter 15, "XML Web Services," we're missing a crucial architectural step that would cripple a .NET enterprise system. Figure 10.1 illustrates what it is we will be progressing toward.

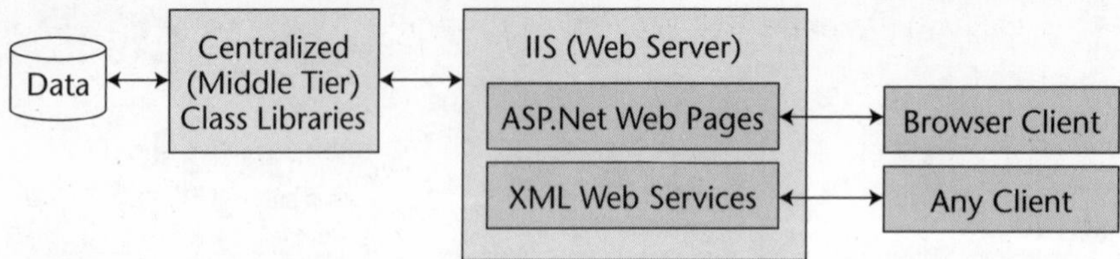

Figure 10.1 By exposing class libraries via Web services, developers using any OS and writing in any language can be class consumers.

This chapter focuses primarily on the use of ADO.NET from the aspect of utilizing centralized libraries for connection to and operations on a database. For this chapter, we will connect directly to the class libraries from Windows .NET clients and bypass the Web technologies for now. Even when we adjust our architectural approach later, we won't be changing our code or the placement of that code, only the way in which we connect from client to server.

The Benefits of ADO.NET

Unlike ADO, ADO.NET is connectionless by default. Because everything in .NET uses XML as a standard for passing data, we don't have the COM dependencies and lack of portability that plagued previous versions of ADO. With the connectionless environment coupled with the flexibility of using a universal medium such as XML, the underlying theme for .NET seems to be: Everyone can connect; now get out. Many saw the benefits of using disconnected record sets in ADO and eventually even adopted XML and Web services, so most of the major changes we see in .NET are adaptations of popular architectural decisions geared toward scalability and improvements that provide greater connectivity. Scalability is the ability of a system to function within acceptable performance baselines regardless of the number of concurrent users.

Comparison of ADO and ADO.NET

There are quite a few differences between ADO and ADO.NET. Other than comparing the high-level objects in the two libraries and methodologies, it is probably best to accept ADO.NET as an entirely new technology rather than an upgrade to ADO. Tables 10.1 and 10.2 outline some of the major differences between ADO and ADO.NET.

Table 10.1 Comparison between ADO and ADO.NET Features

FEATURE	ADO	ADO.NET
Record navigation	MoveNext.	Iteration through DataSet.DataTables .Rows.
Use of disconnected data	Uses COM Marshalling.	Uses XML DataSets.
Business to business	COM Marshalling requests don't pass through firewalls.	Data sets pass through firewalls with no problems.
Set relations	Relations between tables are limited.	Tables in a DataSet can be related even if they consist of data from very disparate data sources.

Centralized Data Access

Although we will be building data-centric clients, those clients will be accessing class libraries that establish the database connectivity and perform the actual database communication on our behalf. After we have established a relatively versatile set of methods for providing data to a client, we can explore the varied methods for consuming and managing that data.

Table 10.2 Comparison of Objects between ADO and ADO.NET

ADO OBJECT	ADO.NET	PURPOSE
Connection	Connection	Connect to database.
Command	Command	Build and send commands to database, such as SQL queries and stored procedure invocations.
RecordSet	DataSet	Where RecordSets represent a collection of records, DataSets represent a collection of tables potentially from multiple and varied data sources, making them far more flexible than RecordSets.
	Adapter	An adapter object is responsible for populating a DataSet using connection and command information.

How Data Flow Typically Works

Via Web services, applications typically request data in the form of a DataSet object, modify that DataSet object, and pass it back to the server. Any code that connects to or modifies actual data in any way should exist on the server in a class library that is consumed on the client application's behalf by a Web service. Figure 10.2 shows the typical data flow and architecture for data-centric clients in a .NET architecture.

.NET Data Providers

Data providers are the actual entities that manage the communication between ADO.NET and the database. To use these providers and their object libraries without having to type the entire object hierarchy, use the Imports statement, specifying System.Data and the appropriate provider namespace such as System.Data.OleDb or System.Data.SqlClient. Table 10.3 displays the common data providers used in .NET.

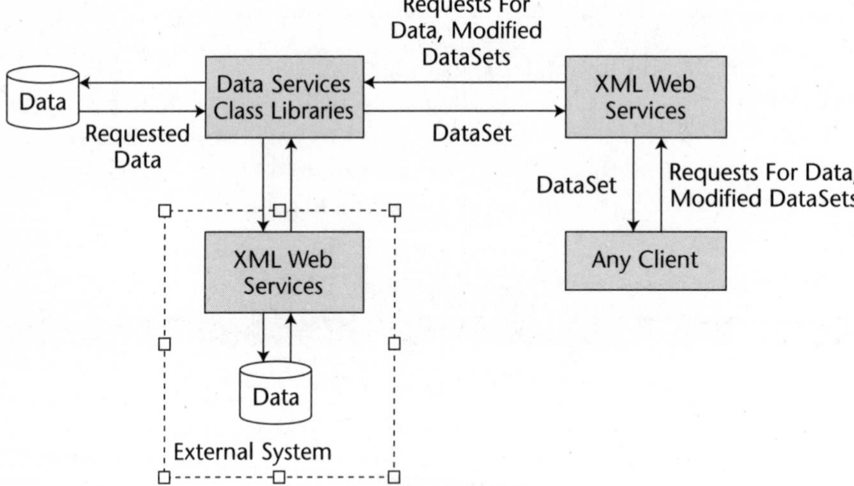

Figure 10.2 Client applications typically request data in the form of a DataSet object, modify records in that object, and pass the object back to a class library responsible for communicating those changes to the database.

Table 10.3 Data Providers

PROVIDER	DESCRIPTION
System.Data.SQLClient	Built-in provider for SQL Server 7.0 and later.
System.Data.OleDb	Built-in provider for any data source exposed using OLEDB.
ODBC.NET Data Provider	Released separately and available at the MSDN download site, this provider is intended to work with all ODBC-compliant drivers.
DataDirect Providers for .NET	With full support from Microsoft and third-party vendors, DataDirect offers data provider support for multiple vendors including Oracle and Sybase.
Additional Providers	As with all things, check Microsoft's .NET download site for additional providers.

Connection Objects

Establishing a connection to a SQL Server database should be done using objects in the System.Data.SQLClient namespace because the SQLClient provider offers a dramatic performance improvement over using the OleDb provider to access the SQL Server. Use of the Connection object in ADO.NET is similar to that of ADO, as shown here:

```
imports System.Data.SqlClient
Dim con As New SqlConnection()
con.ConnectionString = "data source=(local);" & _
"initial catalog=Northwind;integrated security=SSPI;" & _
"persist security info=False;packet size=4096;Connect Timeout=30"
con.Open()
```

Because connections to the database in a disconnected world are fleeting things, you can expect to find a much smaller set of events related to connection objects in ADO.NET. Programming for these events is identical to capturing events in Visual Basic 6. After an object variable that exposes events is declared using the WithEvents keyword, we can select the object and the exposed events using the drop-down select boxes in the Code Editor window, as shown in Figure 10.3.

Figure 10.3 By declaring a connection object using the WithEvents keyword, we can write handlers for its InfoMessage and StateChange events.

Although the InfoMessage doesn't seem to be a frequent event when no errors exist, the StateChange event occurs every time we open or close a connection. The following code provides handlers for the connection object's InfoMessage and StateChange events and produces the output shown in Figure 10.4:

```
Private WithEvents con As New Data.SqlClient.SqlConnection()
Private Sub cmdConnect1_Click(ByVal sender As System.Object, _
ByVal e As System.EventArgs) Handles cmdConnect1.Click
   con.ConnectionString = "data source=BRUCE\BRUCE2;" & _
   "initial catalog=Northwind;integrated security=SSPI;" & _
   "persist security info=False;packet size=4096"
   con.Open()
   '
   con.Close()
End Sub
Private Sub con_InfoMessage(ByVal sender As Object, _
ByVal e As System.Data.SqlClient.SqlInfoMessageEventArgs) _
Handles con.InfoMessage
   MsgBox("InfoMessage Event Message: " & ControlChars.CrLf & _
   e.Message)
End Sub
Private Sub con_StateChange(ByVal sender As Object, _
ByVal e As System.Data.StateChangeEventArgs) Handles con.StateChange
   MsgBox("StateChange Event.State: " & ControlChars.CrLf & _
   e.CurrentState.ToString())
End Sub
```

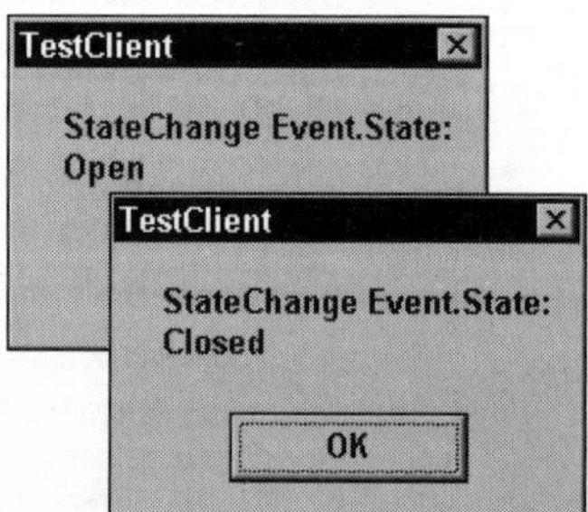

Figure 10.4 The StateChange event fires whenever the database connection is opened or closed. Additional state values exist for System.Data.ConnectionState but are not yet implemented (connecting, fetching, executing, and broken).

The state object passed to the statechange event is a system.Data.ConnectionState enum.

Command Objects

As in ADO, the Command object in ADO.NET represents the command we want to communicate to the database. Commands can be inserts, updates, select statements, stored procedure invocations, or any other valid command.

CommandType

The Command object, in ADO, has a CommandType that can be set to StoredProcedure, TableDirect, or Text. When using SQL statements, the CommandType can be left to the default, which is Text, but a CommandText value that contains the text to be passed to the database must be specified. When invoking stored procedures, use the Command object's parameters collection and set the CommandType to StoredProcedure. Regardless of the CommandType value, after we have set the appropriate values for the Command object, either manually or via its constructor, one of the methods in Table 10.3 is used to invoke some behavior in the database. Table 10.4 describes the primary methods of the ADO.NET Command Object.

The following code creates a new SQLCommand object by manually passing both the command string and the connection object to the SQLCommand's constructor and implicitly uses a CommandType of Text:

```
Dim cmd2 As New SqlClient.SqlCommand(cmdtext, con)
```

Table 10.4 Command Object Methods

COMMAND METHOD	DESCRIPTION
ExecuteNonQuery	Used to execute statements such as Inserts, Updates, and Deletes and does not return anything other than the numbers of rows affected or –1.
ExecuteScalar	Returns only the first value of the first row in a result set. Useful when performing a select on an aggregate value such as count.
ExecuteReader	Provides the equivalent of a fire hose cursor; that is, forward-only, read-only cursor for quickly reading through records. The ExecuteReader statement maintains a database connection until the reading has completed.
ExecuteXmlReader	Used with SQL Server 2000 by adding a valid For XML clause to the CommandText string.

Both the CommandType and CommandText property values can be set prior to relating the Command object to the Connection object:

```
Dim cmd As New SqlClient.SqlCommand()
cmd.CommandType = CommandType.Text
cmd.CommandText = "select firstname + ' ' + lastname as name " + _
"from employees"
cmd.Connection = con
```

Using a Command Object with a DataReader

Before considering the DataReader as an option for your architecture, it's important to understand that the DataReader requires a client to be connected to the data source until all the records have been retrieved. The following code shows how the SQLCommand object in the SQLClient namespace can be used to create a DataReader object for quickly reading through a result set:

```
Private Sub btnConnect_Click(...) ...
   'establish a connection, con
   Dim cmd As New SqlClient.SqlCommand()
   cmd.CommandType = CommandType.Text
   cmd.CommandText = "select firstname + ' ' + lastname as name " + _
   "from employees"
   cmd.Connection = con
   Dim reader As SqlClient.SqlDataReader = cmd.ExecuteReader()
   Dim i As Integer
   While reader.Read()
      For i = 0 To reader.FieldCount - 1
         ListBox1.Items.Add(reader(i))
      Next
   End While
   reader.Close()
   con.Close()
End Sub
```

The DataAdapter Object

The DataAdapter object acts as a bridge between a DataSet object and a data management system such as SQL Server. The SQLDataAdapter is specifically designed to work with Microsoft SQL Server. The DataAdapter constructor is used to relate a command and a connection. After a DataAdapter object is created, the Fill and Update commands can be used to provide data transfer between the database and the DataSet object, as indicated in Figure 10.5.

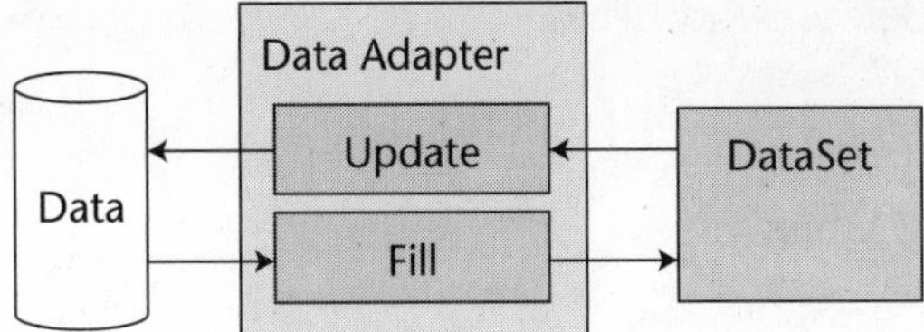

Figure 10.5 The Fill and Update commands are used to transfer data to and from a DataSet and one or more data providers.

The DataAdapter constructors seem to be missing an overload. Although there are constructor overloads for passing both a command and a connection as strings and a constructor for passing a command string with a connection object, there is no constructor that takes both a command object and a connection object.

The following code passes both arguments as strings and uses the Fill method to populate a DataSet:

```
Dim strCon As String = "data source=(local);" & _
"initial catalog=Northwind;integrated security=SSPI;" & _
"persist security info=False;packet size=4096"
Dim strCmd As String = "Select * From employees"
Dim myAdapter As New SqlClient.SqlDataAdapter(strCmd, strCon)
Dim ds As New DataSet() myAdapter.Fill(ds)
```

The DataSet Object

The DataSet object doesn't exist in a specific data provider namespace such as SqlClient, but rather in the System.Data namespace. A DataSet holds a collection of tables, which in turn contain a collection of rows. By default, if a simple Select statement is used as a command, the DataSet object will contain the result set in index 0 of its Tables collection. If multiple Select statements are used either in a stored procedure or in CommandText, the Tables collection will be populated with result sets in the order the Select statements were executed.

```
Dim strCmd As String = "Select * From orders;Select * From [Order
Details]"
Dim myAdapter As New SqlClient.SqlDataAdapter(strCmd, strCon)
Dim ds As New DataSet()
myAdapter.Fill(ds) 'ds.Tables.Count = 2
```

Basic navigation through a DataSet is done by traversing the Tables collection and then the Rows collection in each Table. The following snippets are useful in navigating through a DataSet.

The number of tables in the DataSet:

```
myDataSet.Tables.Count
```

The number of rows in the current table:

```
SomeTable.Rows.Count
```

The number of fields in the current table:

```
SomeTable.Columns.Count
```

To obtain the data for a specific field:

```
SomeTable.Rows(rowindex)(columnindex).ToString()
```

Using these together, the following code displays all field data for all rows in the first table in the DataSet:

```
Dim curTab As Integer
Dim dt As DataTable = ds.Tables(0)
Dim curRow As Integer
Dim curCol As Integer
For curRow = 0 To dt.Rows.Count - 1
   ListBox1.Items.Add("NEW ORDER:")
   For curCol = 0 To dt.Columns.Count - 1
      ListBox1.Items.Add(dt.Columns(curCol).ColumnName + ": " + _
      dt.Rows(curRow)(curCol).ToString())
   Next
Next
```

DataView Objects

A DataView object acts as a filter for a DataSet that allows us to view specific portions of a DataSet based on some criteria. This allows us to work with a large result set without having to make multiple trips to the server every time we want to view another subset of records. The DataView object has more than one constructor, but the most useful constructor takes a table, a filter, a sort field, and a viewstate. The following DataView constructor selects only those records in which OrderID is equal to the OrderID selected in the list box named lstOrders:

```
Dim detailsView As DataView = New DataView(ds.Tables(1), _
"OrderId = '" & lstOrders.SelectedItem.ToString() & "'", _
"ProductID", DataViewRowState.CurrentRows)
```

The DataRowState parameter dramatically affects which rows will be displayed in the view. Table 10.5 provides the possible DataRowState values and their descriptions.

Table 10.5 Data Row State Values

DATAROWSTATE VALUE	DESCRIPTION
Added	Displays only rows that have been added since the DataSet was retrieved.
CurrentRows	Displays all rows in the DataSet, old, new, changed, or unchanged.
Deleted	Displays rows that have been deleted.
ModifedCurrent	Displays records that were originally in the DataSet in their current modified state.
ModifiedOriginal	Displays records that were originally in the DataSet in their old unmodified state even though they have since been modified.
OriginalRows	Includes all original rows even if they were deleted or modified.
Unchanged	Displays only those rows that were original to the DataSet and have not been modified.

This section laid the groundwork by introducing the objects we'll be working with. Next, we'll create a class library to perform some of the data operations for us, and then we'll start working with some more complex applications of ADO.NET.

Classroom Q & A

Q: How does the DataSet object maintain communication with the database?

A: The DataSet is similar to the adLockBatchOptimistic cursor type we had in ADO; it's completely disconnected and can be sent back as an object by value to a client.

Q: Why can't we have a connected DataSet? Is there any way to have the equivalent to a server-side dynamic cursor with ADO.NET?

A: There is currently no way to have the equivalent to a server-side dynamic cursor with ADO.NET, and we think the disconnected approach should be the default, but entirely removing the option for maintaining a database connection might be a little drastic.

Lab 10.1: Creating Our DataServices Class

This lab creates a DataServices class that will eventually be capable of returning DataSets, XML documents, and schemas or performing database operations by passing commands and connection information from various clients. This lab requires SQL Server 7.0 or later to be installed.

Perform the following steps:

1. Create a new Visual Basic .NET Windows application named Lab1TestClient.
2. Select File, Add Project, New Project and create a new Visual Basic .NET Class Library named DataServices.

   Your Solution Explorer window should now contain two projects. Lab1TestClient should appear as bold, indicating that it will be executed when the solution is executed as an application.
3. In the DataServices project, rename the file Class1.cs to Services.cs.
4. In the Code Editor window, change the name of the class to Services.

   You need to obtain a connection to the SQL Server Northwind database. To obtain a connection string, you can use an existing string or create a new one by dragging a SQLAdapter object onto the current form.
5. In the Solution Explorer window, double-click Form1 in the Lab1TestClient project to enter Designer view for Form1.
6. Drag a SqlDataAdapter object from the ToolBox Data tab to Form1. The object appears in the control tray beneath the form and a wizard launches. Perform the following steps to finish the wizard and create a connection string:
   a. Click Next.
   b. Click New Connection.
   c. On the Provider tab, select Microsoft OLEDB Provider for SQL Server.
   d. Click Next to move to the Connection tab.
   e. Type (local), with the parentheses into the Select Or Enter a Server Name text box.
   f. Select the Use Windows NT Integrated Security option button.
   g. In the Select the Database On The Server textbox, scroll down, and select the Northwind database. The Data Link Properties page should be identical to Figure 10.6 and should indicate success when the TestConnection button is pressed.

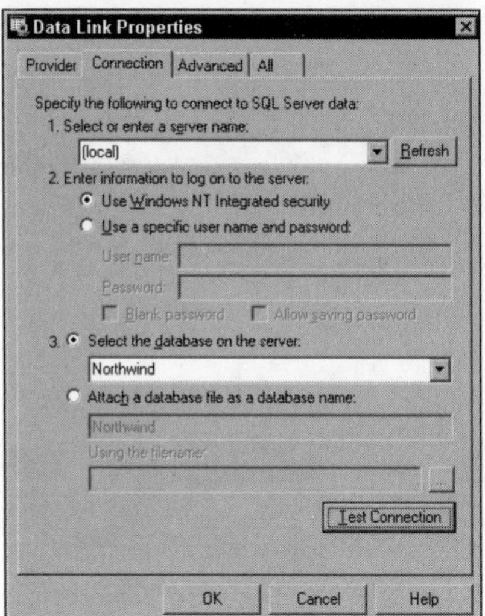

Figure 10.6 Be sure you have specified the Northwind database on the (local) server and that you have specified the Integrated Security option before continuing.

   h. Click OK.

   i. Click Next to progress to the Choose a Query Type page.

   j. On the Choose a Query Type page, leave the default option of Use SQL Statements and click Next to progress to the Generate the SQL Statements page.

   k. On the Generate the SQL Statements Page, enter the following command:

```
Select * From Employees
```

7. Click Finish to close the wizard and create a new connection object.

8. Select the new connection object (SqlConnection1) in the control tray and copy the ConnectionString property value into memory from the Properties window.

9. Put the connection string somewhere you can use it later. One method for doing so is to paste the string into the Code Editor window, highlight it, and then drag it to a tab on the Toolbox. Later, the connection string can be dragged back into the Code Editor window from the Toolbox.

10. Return to the Services class in the DataServices project.

We'll add a few simple methods to the class library to work with.

11. Using your connection string for the strcon property, modify the Services class as follows:

```
Public Class Services
   Private strcon As String = "data source=(local);" _
```

```
    & "initial catalog=Northwind;" _
    & "integrated security=SSPI;" _
    & "persist security info=False;" _
    & "packet size=4096"
    'Accept a command and a connection and return a DataSet object
    Public Function getDataSet(ByVal command As String, _
    ByVal connection As String) As System.Data.DataSet
       Dim adt As New SqlClient.SqlDataAdapter(command,
connection)
       Dim ds As New DataSet()
       adt.Fill(ds)
    End Function
    'Accept a command only and return a DataSet object
    Public Function getDataSet(ByVal command As String) _
    As System.Data.DataSet
       Dim adt As New SqlClient.SqlDataAdapter(command, strcon)
       Dim ds As New DataSet()
       adt.Fill(ds)
       Return ds
    End Function
    'Accept a command and return an XMLDataDocument object
    Public Function getXmlDocument(ByVal command As String) As _
    System.Xml.XmlDataDocument
       Dim adt As New SqlClient.SqlDataAdapter(command, strcon)
       Dim ds As New DataSet()
       adt.Fill(ds)
       Dim xdoc As New Xml.XmlDataDocument(ds)
       Return xdoc
    End Function
End Class
```

12. Add a reference to the DataServices library in the Lab1TestClient by selecting Add Reference from the Project menu and double-clicking DataServices in the Projects tab of the Add Reference dialog box.
13. Add the following controls:
    a. A button named btnConnect. Text:=Connect
    b. A list box named lstOrders
    c. A list box named lstOrderDetails
    d. Two labels, labeling the list boxes as Order Number and Order Details.
14. Add the following form level variables (fields of Form1) to the form:

```
Private oServices As New DataServices.Services()
Private ds As DataSet
```

15. Add the following click event handler for btnConnect:

```
Private Sub btnConnect_Click(ByVal sender As System.Object, _
ByVal e As System.EventArgs) Handles btnConnect.Click
```

```
    'pass in multiple select statements, and receive
    'a DataSet containing every row in both the Orders (tables(0))
    'and the Order Details (Tables(1)) tables from Northwind:
    ds = oServices.getDataSet("select * from orders;" & _
    "select * from [order details]")
    'Fill lstOrders with only the OrderID for Each Order
    Dim curRow As Integer
    lstOrders.Items.Clear()
    For curRow = 0 To ds.Tables(0).Rows.Count - 1
       lstOrders.Items.Add(ds.Tables(0).Rows(curRow)(0).ToString())
    Next
End Sub
```

16. Test the application. Running the application at this point should fill lstOrders with the OrderID of each record in the Orders table, as shown in Figure 10.7.

17. Next add a click event handler for the lstOrders list box that causes the lstOrderDetails list box to display the order detail records associated with the product ID in lstOrders. Add the following code to the lstOrders click event handler:

```
Private Sub lstOrders_SelectedIndexChanged(ByVal sender _
As System.Object, ByVal e As System.EventArgs) Handles _
lstOrders.SelectedIndexChanged
    'Remove any previous contents in the list box:
    lstOrderDetails.Items.Clear()
    'Create view based on Order Details table in ds.Tables(1)
    'containing only order detail records associated with the
OrderId
    'that was just selected in lstOrders:
    Dim detailView As DataView = New DataView(ds.Tables(1), _
    "OrderId = '" & lstOrders.SelectedItem.ToString() & "'", _
    "ProductID", DataViewRowState.CurrentRows)
    'Iterate through the new DataView and display the records in
the new
    'view:
    Dim drv As DataRowView
    Dim i As Integer
    'ds.Tables(0).Columns(0).
    For Each drv In detailView
       For i = 0 To detailView.Table.Columns.Count - 1
          lstOrderDetails.Items.Add(detailView.Table.Columns(i) _
          .ColumnName & ": " & drv(i))
       Next
    Next
End Sub
```

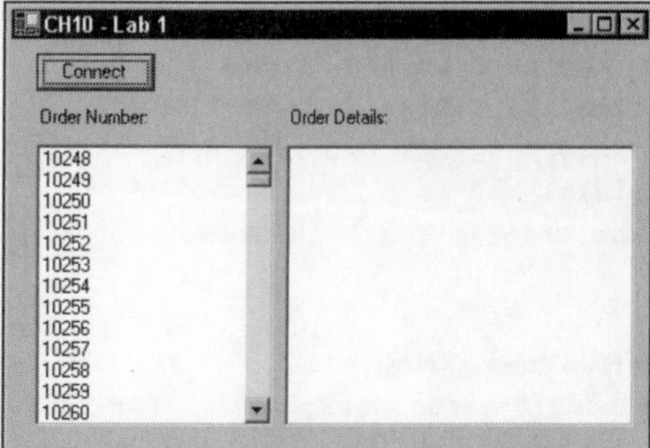

Figure 10.7 Your application should look like this.

18. Test the application by running the application and clicking the Connect button. Next, click one of the items in lstOrders to cause lstOrderDetails to populate with related data. Your application should look similar to Figure 10.8.

    Modifying the application to display the detail for each order in a grid control is actually very simple. You just have to set the Grid control's DataSource property to the DataView object.

19. Add a DataGrid control named gridDetails to the form.
20. Modify the lstOrders_SelectedIndexChanged event handler to populate the new Grid control with order details using the following code:

```
Private Sub lstOrders_SelectedIndexChanged(ByVal sender As
System.Object, ByVal e As System.EventArgs) Handles
lstOrders.SelectedIndexChanged
    lstOrderDetails.Items.Clear()
    Dim detailView As DataView = New DataView(ds.Tables(1), _
    "OrderId = '" & lstOrders.SelectedItem.ToString() & "'", _
    "ProductID", DataViewRowState.CurrentRows)
    gridDetails.DataSource = detailView
End Sub
```

21. Test the application. Your application should look similar to Figure 10.9.

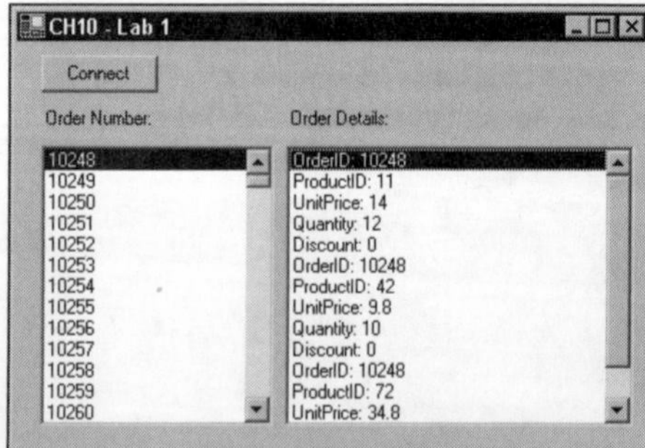

Figure 10.8 Using Views you can manipulate data any way you want to without making multiple trips to the server.

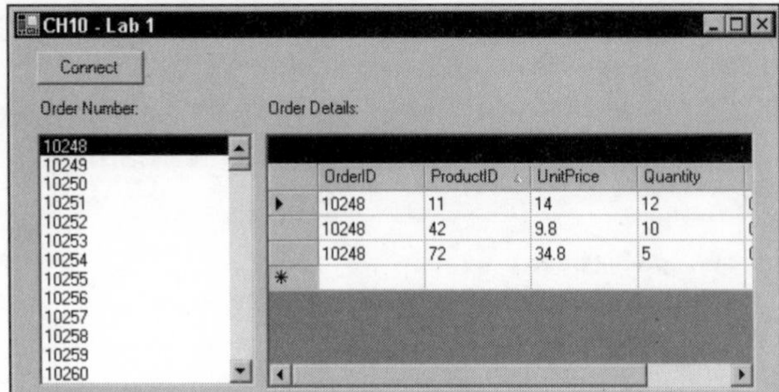

Figure 10.9 To display the contents of a given DataView in a DataGrid control, simply assign the DataView object to the DataView's DataSource property.

The last step for now is to indicate that you are done using the objects you declared as Form fields, so end this lab with a little cleanup. In Chapter 11, "Memory Management and Performance Monitoring," we will look at how to properly dispose of objects and how to create objects that lend themselves to such disposal.

22. Add code to the form's Closing event handler to indicate that we are done using our objects:

```
Private Sub Form1_Closing(ByVal sender As Object, _
ByVal e As System.ComponentModel.CancelEventArgs) Handles
MyBase.Closing
   'ds.Dispose() 'chapter 11
   ds = Nothing
   'oServices.Dispose() 'chapter 11
   oServices = Nothing
End Sub
```

By placing the actual code that manages the data connectivity in a class library, you can centralize data logic and consume those services from Web services, ASP pages, Windows services, and any remote client via .NET Remoting and Web services. In this lab, you passed a multiselect SQL statement to a class library that returned a multitable DataSet. By using a DataView object, you to changed the current view of data without making unnecessary trips to the server.

Classroom Q & A

Q: How does data access work in an ASP.NET application?

A: ASP.NET is covered in Chapter 13, "ASP.NET," but the same ADO.NET objects are used regardless of the .NET project type or language.

Q: How does all the code we have been using change when using a database that doesn't have direct .NET provider?

A: To change ADO.NET code from SQL specific to the OLEDB version you could literally do an edit/replace on the object names. This code should help:

```
Private Sub OLEDBconnect(ByVal strcon As String)
   Dim con As New OleDbConnection(strcon) con.Open()
   Dim adt As New OleDbDataAdapter("select * from authors",
con)
   Dim ds As New DataSet()
   adt.Fill(ds)
   'perform some operation
   con.Close()
End Sub
Private Sub SQLconnect(ByVal strcon As String)
   Dim con As New SqlConnection(strcon)
   con.Open()
   Dim adt As New SqlDataAdapter("select * from authors", con)
   Dim ds As New DataSet()
   adt.Fill(ds)
   'perform some operation
   con.Close()
End Sub
```

Q: Is there a way to load a client form faster if the Load event is taking too long to populate controls with data?

A: Chapter 12, "Threading," shows how multithreading can help issues like this. First, specify imports System.Threading, and then start a new thread that spawns the process performing the connection. Use this code to support that:

```
Private Sub Form2_Load(ByVal sender As System.Object, _
ByVal e As System.EventArgs) Handles MyBase.Load
   Dim t As New Thread(AddressOf GetDataSet)
   t.Start()
   'Any code following occurs immediately and doesn't wait for
   'the thread to finish executing.
End Sub
```

Persisting Changes

Performing inserts, updates, and deletes in ADO.NET is different than in ADO. ADO.NET has quite a few different methods of performing database operations related to persisting changes in the database. Criteria such as how many tables we have in our DataSet or whether we want to return records will affect the methods we might choose for performing these operations.

Updates Using CommandBuilder Objects

When an Adapter object attempts to perform updates using its Update method, somewhere an InsertCommand, UpdateCommand, or DeleteCommand must have been generated or specified. The following code seems to work well enough, but when executed, it will produce the message shown in Figure 10.10:

```
ds.Tables(0).Rows(0)("SomeFieldName") = "SomeNewValue"
Try
   adt.Update(ds.Tables(0)) 'Causes ERROR
Catch ex As System.Exception
   MessageBox.Show(ex.Message, "Errors occurred"...)
End Try
con.Close()
```

A similar update can be resolved simply by declaring a CommandBuilder object and associating it with the connection object so that it can gain the appropriate schema for the underlying data. The following code successfully updates the Phone field for a specific author:

```
Private Sub ModifyAuthor_Click(strcon as string...)...
   Dim con As New SqlConnection(strcon)
   con.Open()
   Dim adt As New SqlDataAdapter("select * from authors " & _
   "where au_id = "'724-08-9931'", con)
   Dim ds As New DataSet()
   adt.Fill(ds)
   'Change his phone number
   ds.Tables(0).Rows(0)("phone") = "555-1212"
   Dim cmdBuilder As New SqlClient.SqlCommandBuilder(adt)
   Try
      adt.Update(ds.Tables(0))
   Catch ex As System.Exception
      MessageBox.Show(ex.Message)
   End Try
   con.Close()
End Sub
```

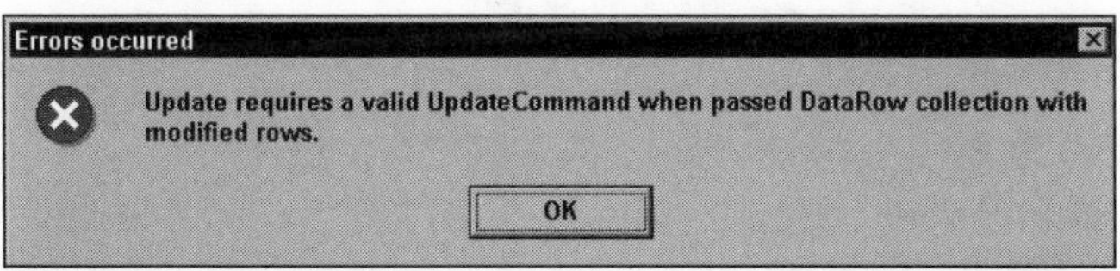

Figure 10.10 Simply attempting to perform an Update without first specifying an InsertCommand, UpdateCommand, or DeleteCommand raises an error.

By right-clicking on the Authors table in the Pubs database in Server Explorer, we can select Retrieve Data From Table or Refresh and view the changes to the database without leaving Visual Studio. Figure 10.11 shows that the underlying database was updated with the modified phone number.

Similar to modifying an existing row, we still need to have the appropriate plumbing for performing an Insert, but in this case we also need to physically add a new row to the existing DataSet. The object Type that represents a row in a DataSet's Table is a DataRow. The NewRow method of a Table object returns a blank record template that can be populated and included in the DataSet using the Add method of the Table's Rows collection. The following code uses these steps together and adds a new author to the database:

```
Private Sub AddAuthor_Click(strcon as string...)...
    Dim con As New SqlConnection(strcon)
    con.Open()
    Dim adt As New SqlDataAdapter("select * from authors", con)
    Dim ds As New DataSet()
    adt.Fill(ds)
    'add new row to dataset and populate
    Dim dRow As DataRow = ds.Tables(0).NewRow()
    dRow("au_id") = "000-99-5674"
    dRow("au_lname") = "Barstow"
    dRow("au_fname") = "Bruce"
    dRow("phone") = "555-1212"
    dRow("address") = "1 Toomany "
    dRow("city") = "Pleasanton"
    dRow("state") = "CA"
    dRow("zip") = "94566"
    dRow("contract") = False
    ds.Tables(0).Rows.Add(dRow)
    Dim cmdBuilder As New SqlClient.SqlCommandBuilder(adt)
    Try
       adt.Update(ds.Tables(0)) 'persist changes to database
    Catch ex As System.Exception
       MessageBox.Show(ex.Message)
    End Try
    con.Close()
End Sub
```

If all I was going to do was add a new author, this would not be appropriate code. Use of ExecuteNonQuery or a stored procedure would be much better. The preceding example is to illustrate concept.

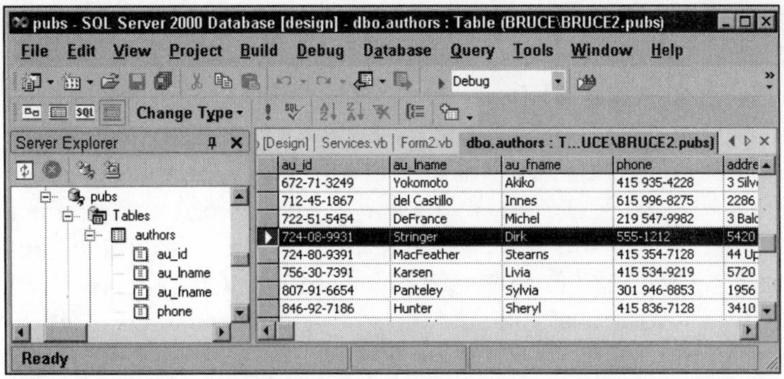

Figure 10.11 The Server Explorer can be used to view database structures, view and modify records, and modify and execute stored procedures.

Submitting Changes Instead of the Entire DataSet

When the client makes several changes to a DataSet and needs to update those changes to the server, it is not appropriate to just send back the entire DataSet, especially when only a few records were added or modified. To avoid this we can use the HasChanges method of the DataSet to detect if there were, in fact, any changes to the original records. Next, we can use the GetChanges method of the DataSet to select only those records that are different from the original records in the DataSet. GetChanges includes any rows that were changed even if those rows were given the exact same values they already had. The method is actually returning a copy of the DataSet with changes made to it since it was loaded or since the last time AcceptChanges was called on the DataSet.

Both GetChanges and HasChanges can be called with a parameter. If no parameter is specified, both methods will assume that you mean additions, changes, or deletions, although you can more specifically target these by specifying a DataRowState argument, as in the following:

```
ds.GetChanges(DataRowState.Modified)
```

The following code uses these two methods to produce the output in Figure 10.12 and persist these changes to the database:

```
ds.Tables(0).Rows(0)("phone") = "555-0001"
ds.Tables(0).Rows(1)("phone") = "555-0002"
GridBefore.DataSource = ds
Dim dsChanged As DataSet
If ds.HasChanges Then 'Returns true for deletions, additions,
modifications
   dsChanged = ds.GetChanges() dsChanged will be null if no changes
   GridAfter.DataSource = dsChanged
```

```
        Dim cmdBuilder As New SqlClient.SqlCommandBuilder(adt)
        adt.Update(dsChanged.Tables(0))
    End If
    con.Close()
```

This code lacks some obvious error-handling to save space here, but it should be stated that if no changes are present, any attempt to reference dsChanged will fail because it will still be null (Nothing). In addition, always pass the same parameter value to both HasChanges and GetChanges to avoid update errors. This is because HasChanges may be true because of an addition, but you might have used a value of Modified for the GetChanges method, resulting in an empty result set. Attempting to update a null result set will cause an error.

Performing DataSet Merging

Often, with multiple client architectures we have many individuals modifying different portions of the same database, table, or possibly even the same record. Merging records from multiple DataSets can be done through the use of the Merge method on a DataSet object.

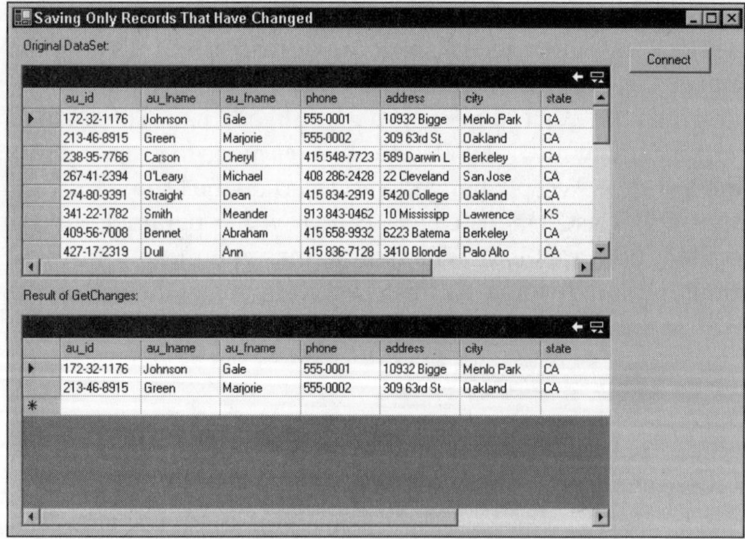

Figure 10.12 The GetChanges method creates a new DataSet, including only modified records from the original DataSet, helping to ease traffic for updates.

The Merge method also compares data types and schemas between the two DataSets being merged and will generate errors if it detects a perceived conflict between the two. For example, an author's record, generated as an XML file, cannot be merged back into the same DataSet that created it unless the XML file was created with a schema that defined the data types for each field. An author with a Contract field value of 1 would have a value of True when written as XML using the WriteXML method of the dataset. Without a schema associated with the XML file, this inconsistency would translate as a data type mismatch. To see what a valid XML representation (with schema) of your DataSet might look like, you can use the following code:

```
ds1.WriteXml("c:\authors.xml", XmlWriteMode.WriteSchema)
```

For the following merge example, I created an authors.xml file containing two authors using an appropriate schema and the following XML:

```
<Table>
  <au_id>222-22-2222</au_id>
  <au_lname>Farhead</au_lname>
  <au_fname>Lukintu</au_fname>
  <phone>555-1212</phone>
  <address>1 SomeStreet</address>
  <city>SomeCity</city>
  <state>CA</state>
  <zip>94000</zip>
  <contract>true</contract>
</Table>
<Table>
  <au_id>333-33-3333</au_id>
  <au_lname>Mucsh</au_lname>
  <au_fname>Thinktu</au_fname>
  <phone>555-0002</phone>
  <address>1 SomeStreet</address>
  <city>Oakland</city>
  <state>CA</state>
  <zip>94000</zip>
  <contract>true</contract>
</Table>
```

When DataSets are returned from a database in ADO.NET, they include a complete schema that describes every property and aspect of the data in that result set.

To demonstrate the merge, I created the interface shown in Figure 10.13, using Grid controls to show the original DataSet, the records read from the XML file, and finally, the results of merging the two. These records could then be persisted to the database in the same manner as before, using the Adapter's update method. The following code produces the output in Figure 10.13:

```
con.Open()
Dim adt As New SqlDataAdapter("select * from authors", con)
Dim ds1 As New DataSet()
Dim ds2 As New DataSet()
'Fill the first Grid with data from Authors:
adt.Fill(ds1) 'Fill ds1 from the authors table
Grid1.DataSource = ds1.Tables(0)
'Fill the second Grid with data from an XML file:
ds2.ReadXml("c:\authors.xml") 'Fill Ds2 from authors.xml
Grid2.DataSource = ds2
'Merge the two DataSets:
ds1.Merge(ds2, False, MissingSchemaAction.Add) 'Merge ds1 and ds2 into
ds1
'Display the merged set in Grid3:
Grid3.DataSource = ds1.Tables(0)
con.Close()
```

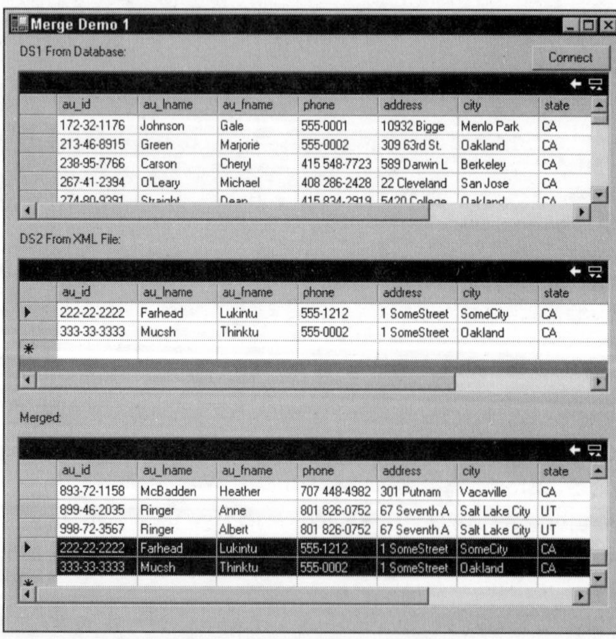

Figure 10.13 The DataSet Merge method combines the contents of two DataSet objects.

The MissingSchemaAction parameter being passed to the Merge method determines what action should take place if a merge is attempted and no schema is present. The default value is Add, which attempts to add missing columns to complete the schema. AddWithKey extends that functionality by also adding primary key information. The value of Error just generates an error when a schema is missing. The remaining value of Ignore can be used to merge rows that have extra columns and will strip off any columns that do not exist in the target schema.

For an informative reference about handling merge (concurrency) conflicts, see the built-in walkthrough entitled *Walkthrough: Handling a Concurrency Exception* in Visual Studio .NET.

Classroom Q & A

Q: What is placed in the middle tier?

A: We do things exactly as we did in ADO when we used disconnected record sets: request a result set, modify that result set, and send either the entire result set or the changes back to the server. To do this, the client uses two methods in a class library that return and accept these DataSets. By client I mean Windows applications, other objects, and Web services, not just a client-side application.

Q: Will the expected architecture place a Web service between the class library and the client application?

A: Yes.

Q: How does this process work with a Web service?

A: In most scenarios, the Web service is just a collection of Web-visible wrappers for those methods in the class library that you want exposed to remote clients. The real logic remains in the class library. There are only two ways to connect any of the pieces: either with a reference or a Web reference in the case of a Web service, both of which are quite simple. Web services are covered in Chapter 15, "XML Web Services."

Q: What about the loosely coupled, connect-the-world buzzword sitting between me and my middle tier?

A: You are not limited to Web services for remoting. XML Web services are so easy to create that you can leave them in place for those clients that need them to connect and then create more tightly coupled solutions for clients with different needs. An entire range of technologies in .NET falls under the umbrella of .NET remoting to extend the options for remote operations.

Lab 10.2: Moving Logic to the Server

This lab implements what we've talked about but moves all direct communication with the database to a class library. Client-side code requests a DataSet from a method in our library, makes modifications and additions to that DataSet, and returns to the server only the changes to the DataSet .

Perform the following steps:

1. Start a new solution, but keep the code in your class library from Lab 10.1 handy. The new solution should include the following:
   a. Windows application named Lab2TestClient
   b. A Class Library named DataServices2
2. Add a reference to the class library from the Windows application. Later this will be a Web reference to a Web service that makes a reference to a class library.
3. Add an imports statements to the top of both projects for System.Data and System.Data.SqlClient to avoid having to type the namespaces when you refer to ADO.NET objects.
4. Build a class in the class library project with the following features:
   a. Form level, private variables for an adapter, connection, data-set connection string, and a command string.
   b. A public method, getauthors() that takes no parameters and returns the entire Authors table as a DataSet object.
   c. A public method, updateAuthors that takes a DataSet and updates that DataSet to the database.
5. Build client code in the Windows application (don't worry about an interface; it's just to test the methods) that performs the following:
   a. Calls the getAuthors method to obtain a DataSet.
   b. Modifies at least one record.
   c. Adds at least one additional record.
   d. Sends only the changes to the DataSet to the updateAuthors method.
6. Verify that the changes made their way to the database using the Server Explorer or by viewing the data in SQL Enterprise Manager.

If everything went well, congratulations. If it didn't or if you're just curious, the following code provides a class and a client that meet the criteria. The class is:

```
Imports System.Data
Imports System.Data.OleDb
Imports System.Data.SqlClient
Imports System.Windows.Forms
Public Class Services
   Private strcon As String = "data source=(local)" _
   & "initial catalog=Pubs;" _
   & "integrated security=SSPI;" _
   & "persist security info=False;" _
   & "packet size=4096"
   Private strcmd = "select * from authors"
   Private adt As New SqlDataAdapter()
   Private ds As New DataSet()
   Private con As SqlConnection
   Public Function getAuthors() As System.Data.DataSet
      con = New SqlConnection(strcon)
      con.Open()
      adt = New SqlDataAdapter(strcmd, con)
      adt.Fill(ds)
      con.Close()
      Return ds
   End Function
   Public Sub updateAuthors(ByVal modifiedDS As DataSet)
      If modifiedDS Is Nothing Then MessageBox.Show("yes")
      con = New SqlConnection(strcon)
      con.Open()
      adt = New SqlClient.SqlDataAdapter(strcmd, con)
      Try
         Dim cmdBuilder As New SqlClient.SqlCommandBuilder(adt)
            adt.Update(modifiedDS.Tables(0))
         Catch ex As Exception
            Throw New System.Exception(ex.Message)
         Finally
            If con.State <> ConnectionState.Closed Then
               con.Close()
            End If
      End Try
   End Sub
End Class
```

The client is:

```
Dim ds As New DataSet()
Dim obj As New DataServices2.Services()
Private Sub btnConnect_Click(ByVal sender As System.Object, _
ByVal e As System.EventArgs) Handles btnConnect.Click
   ds = obj.getAuthors()
```

```
    Me.DataGrid1.DataSource = ds
    AddAuthor()
    ModifyAuthor()
    SendChanges()
    ds.AcceptChanges()
End Sub
Private Sub SendChanges()
    If ds.HasChanges Then
        obj.updateAuthors(ds.GetChanges())
    Else
        MessageBox.Show("no changes to submit")
    End If
End Sub
Private Sub Modifyauthor()
    ds.Tables(0).Rows(0)("phone") = "555-0000"
End Sub
Private Sub AddAuthor()
'simulate data from interface
    Dim dRow As DataRow = ds.Tables(0).NewRow()
    dRow("au_id") = "000-00-0002"
    dRow("au_lname") = "body"
    dRow("au_fname") = "some"
    dRow("phone") = "555-1212"
    dRow("address") = "1 street "
    dRow("city") = "mycity"
    dRow("state") = "ms"
    dRow("zip") = "90210"
    dRow("contract") = False
    ds.Tables(0).Rows.Add(dRow)
End Sub
```

There are many benefits from doing the actual database operations centrally. One is the ability to change everything, including the database without affecting any type of client as long as the interface to the client remains intact. Another important benefit is that you're not reproducing code in different client types that can be centralized and written once. Furthermore, security is tighter and much easier to maintain in this scenario. One certain optimization for this data access component you have created would be to add constructors that accept connection or command information or to allow the constructor to initialize the appropriate variables. What you have done is to move any direct communication with the database to the server and off the client, which is sound, but lacking in a realistic support for stored procedures.

Working with Stored Procedures

There's no mystery behind why stored procedures are valuable replacements to passing SQL statements to the database. Stored procedures are SQL procedures that are literally part of the database, preverified and precompiled. Because statements sent to the database still have to be verified and compiled, they have obvious performance issues when compared to stored procedures. I like to build stored procedures for anything and everything if possible, but to handle a diverse range of needs, they need to be generic. That is, they often need to accept parameters that define exactly what operation should be performed and on what data. For example, if a Sales Total By Year stored procedure was invoked, you can expect to pass it the year and have it return only the sales total for that year.

This small section doesn't go into much detail on the actual creation of stored procedures in SQL server because that hasn't changed and really has nothing to do with ADO.NET. Calling these stored procedures from ADO.NET, on the other hand, is certainly of prime concern.

Calling Stored Procedures in ADO.NET

Stored procedures are physically part of the database in which they reside. Just as we used the CommandType default of Text to pass a SQL statement, we can use the Command Object's CommandType property with a value of StoredProcedure to invoke stored procedures. The Authors database has a stored procedure named byroyalty. Figure 10.14 shows the byroyalty stored procedure in Pubs.Authors in the Server Explorer (left), the properties for its one input parameter, @percentage (right), and the actual stored procedure (bottom).

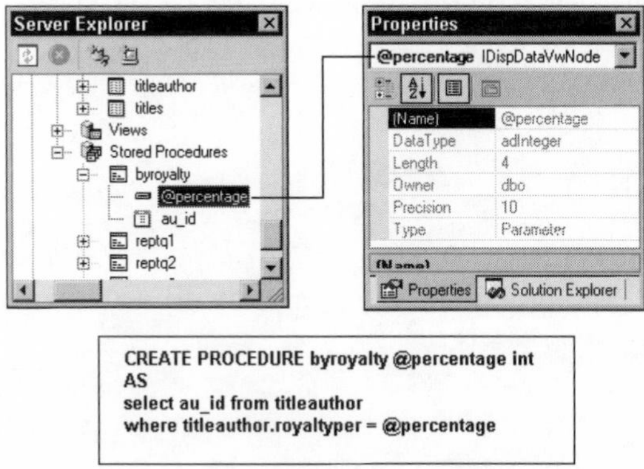

Figure 10.14 The byroyalty stored procedure accepts a single input parameter (@percentage) as an integer and selects only the author IDs for all authors whose royalty percentage matches @percentage.

When we need to pass a parameter to a stored procedure, we create a SqlParameter object for each parameter and add it to a Command Object's Parameters collection. To use a parameter, we have to specify the name of the parameter, its type, the direction, and value. To add a function to our data services class that exposes this stored procedure we could use the following:

```
Public Function getAuIDsByRoyalty(ByVal percent As Integer) As DataSet
   con = New SqlConnection(strcon)
   con.Open()
   'Create a new command object, specifying the name of the stored
   'procedure and associating the connection object:
   Dim cmd As New SqlCommand("ByRoyalty", con)
   cmd.CommandType = CommandType.StoredProcedure
   'Create a parameter object for passing the percentage value:
   Dim pRoyalty As New SqlParameter()
   pRoyalty = cmd.Parameters.Add("@percentage", SqlDbType.Int)
   pRoyalty.Direction = ParameterDirection.Input
   pRoyalty.Value = percent 'passed into function
   adt = New SqlDataAdapter(cmd)
   adt.Fill(ds) 'invokes the stored procedure, returns author ID's only
   con.Close()
   Return ds
End Function
```

The client code to consume the stored procedure doesn't need to know anything other than how to call a method that needs an integer and returns a DataSet. The following code calls the previous wrapper, passing in a percent value in a text box, and produces results shown in Figure 10.15. For the record, the percent values in that table aren't realistic.

```
Private Sub BtnTest(ByVal sender As System.Object, _
ByVal e As System.EventArgs) Handles Button1.Click
   Grid1.DataSource = obj.getAuIDsByRoyalty(CType(TextBox1.Text, _
Integer))
End Sub
```

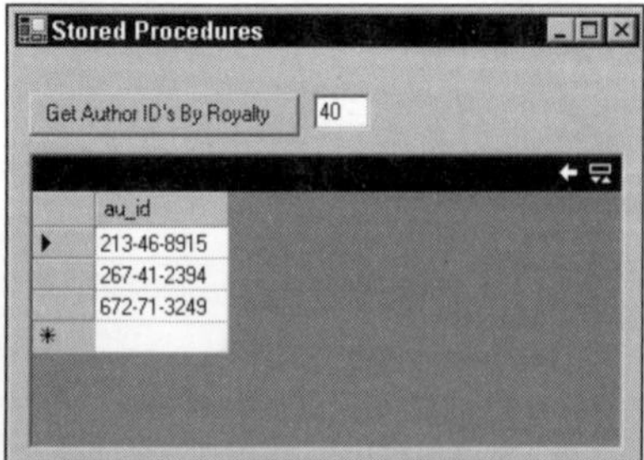

Figure 10.15 Grid contents show the result of passing 40 to the byroyalty stored procedure via the wrapper function.

Summary

There is so much to talk about in ADO.NET that no single chapter can do it justice. As we progress through the following chapter, we will explore more possibilities for ADO.NET in ASP.NET, Web services, and other areas of .NET programming. We've seen how the ADO.NET objects work together to provide a more scalable, open, and resource-friendly solution than its predecessor. As we learn to add Web services to the architecture, we've seen so far the fact that ADO.NET works so well that XML persistable data will quickly become something to appreciate. Working with libraries such as ADO.NET and resources such as database connections, Chapter 11, "Memory Management and Performance Monitoring," is overdue.

Review Questions

1. How is navigation accomplished in a DataSet?
   a. Using move methods.
   b. Using manipulations of the Tables, Rows, and Columns collections in the DataSet.
   c. Using a DataReader object.
   d. Using a Command object.
2. Why are ADO.NET DataSets better than ADO record sets for business-to-business and remote connectivity?
   a. Because ADO.NET is more tightly coupled than ADO.
   b. Because DataSets are persistable as XML and pass through firewalls.
   c. Because DataSets are designed using a universal object specification.
   d. Because DataSets are persistable as HTML and pass through firewalls.
3. Which of the following are accurate differences between ADO and ADO.NET?
   a. ADO.NET provides disconnected result sets, whereas ADO did not.
   b. ADO.NET result sets are collections of tables with enhanced relationship support, whereas ADO record sets were collections of rows with hierarchical support.
   c. ADO.NET is connectionless, whereas ADO is connection-oriented by default.
   d. ADO is completely XML-focused, whereas ADO.NET barely supports the standard.
4. What namespace contains a DataSet object for use by the SQL provider?
   a. System.Data
   b. System.Data.DataSet
   c. System.Data.OleDb
   d. System.Data.SqlDb
5. What events are available for the Connection object in ADO.NET?
   a. InfoMessage
   b. StateChanging
   c. ConnectInfo
   d. StateChange

6. What command object method is used to execute statements such as Inserts, Updates, and Deletes and does not return anything other than the numbers of rows affected or a –1?
   a. ExecuteNonquery
   b. ExecuteScalar
   c. ExecuteReader
   d. ExecuteXMLReader
7. What is the benefit of a DataReader?
   a. For a situation where you can establish a direct connection to a database, the DataReader object selects the entire result set into a navigable object.
   b. For a situation where you do not have a direct connection to a database, you can return a DataReader object to the client for a forward-only, read-only stream of data.
   c. For a situation where you cannot establish a direct connection to a database, the DataReader object selects the entire result set into a navigable object.
   d. For a situation where you can establish a direct connection to a database, the DataReader object provides a forward-only, read-only stream, similar to a fire-hose cursor.
8. What object acts as a bridge between a result set and a data management system such as SQL Server?
   a. The Connection object
   b. The DataSet object
   c. The Data Adapter object
   e. The Command object
9. Which Adapter methods transfer data to and from the database?
   a. Refresh and Fill
   b. Refresh and Update
   c. Update and Fill
   d. Fill and Refresh
10. How do you create a DataSet with multiple tables?
   a. By using a command or stored procedure that has multiple Select statements in it.
   b. By issuing an ExecuteNonQuery statement that returns a multitable result set.
   c. By using an InvokeCommand on a Command object.
   d. You can't.

11. How can you change what records the user is viewing without modifying the DataSet or making an additional trip to the server?
    a. By using a multitable DataSet containing a separate table for each representation of data
    b. By making different SQL Select statements during a form's Load event for all possible representations of data
    c. By requesting a new view from a data services class
    d. By using a DataView object
12. How can you make an XMLDataDocument object from a DataSet?
    a. By using the GetXml method of the DataSet
    b. By using the WriteXml method of the DataSet
    c. By passing the DataSet to the XMLDataDocument's constructor
    d. By casting a DataSet to an XMLDataDocument using CType
13. What must exist before the Update command will actually persist changes to a database?
    a. An Update query.
    b. A CommandBuilder object or appropriate InsertCommand, UpdateCommand, or DeleteCommand.
    c. Just an Update method call on the Adapter while passing the DataSet is sufficient.
    d. The DataSet must be opened for Update access.
14. What is the most likely way in which a client application will persist updates to a DataSet to a remote database?
    a. The client will call Update on the Adapter object.
    b. The client will pass an entire DataSet to method in a class library that calls update on an Adapter object.
    c. The client will pass a DataSet with changes only to a method in a class library that calls update on an Adapter object.
    d. The client will pass a DataSet with changes only to a method in a class library, via a Web service, and that method will call update on an Adapter object.

Answers to Review Questions

1. **b.** Navigation is accomplished in a DataSet using manipulations of the Tables, Rows, and Columns collections in the DataSet. The DataReader is not a navigable object. The Command object can produce a result set but does not represent or have the capability to manipulate one.

2. **b.** Unlike tightly coupled ADO, ADO.NET DataSets are persistable as XML and pass through firewalls. XML is a universal data specification.

3. **b**, **c**, and **d.** ADO.NET result sets are collections of tables with enhanced relationship support, whereas ADO record sets are collections of rows with hierarchical support. ADO.NET is connectionless, whereas ADO is connection-oriented by default. ADO is completely XML-focused, whereas ADO.NET barely supports the standard.

4. **a.** Regardless of the provider, the DataSet object resides in the System.Data namespace. System.Data.DataSet is not a valid namespace.

5. **a** and **d.** InfoMessage and StateChange are the only events in the Connection object.

6. **a.** The ExecuteNonQuery method is used to execute statements such as Inserts, Updates, and Deletes and does not return anything other than the numbers of rows affected or a –1.

7. **d.** The DataReader object is used in a situation where you can establish a direct connection to a database to provide a forward-only stream of data. The DataReader object creates the equivalent of a fire-hose cursor.

8. **c.** The DataAdapter object acts as a bridge between a result set and a data management system such as SQL Server.

9. **c.** The Adapter uses the Fill and Update methods to transfer data to and from the database.

10. **a.** You can create a DataSet with multiple tables by using a command or stored procedure that has multiple Select statements in it.

11. **d.** You can change what records the user is viewing without modifying the DataSet or making an additional trip to the server by using a DataView object.

12. **c.** You can make an XMLDataDocument object from a DataSet by passing the DataSet to the XMLDataDocument's constructor.

13. **b.** Before the Update command will actually persist changes to a database, you must have a CommandBuilder object or appropriate InsertCommand, UpdateCommand, or DeleteCommand.

14. **d.** The client will pass a DataSet with changes only to a method in a class library, via a Web service, and that method will call update on an Adapter object.

CHAPTER

11

Memory Management and Performance Monitoring

This chapter guides you through the way in which classes are designed and consumed with memory management in mind. You will see what the GC system will and won't do for you, how to work within a memory-managed environment, and how to optimize the benefits of such as environment. After becoming familiar with the GC process, we move on to working with performance-monitoring tools and techniques to gain a better understanding of how memory management can be validated.

Garbage Collection

All code managed by the common language runtime is managed code. That is, it is automatically collected by the GC system. The process of automatic garbage collection resolves many of the problems with memory leakage, but it is restricted to reclaiming memory on the managed heaps. It does not perform tasks, such as closing database connections, files, or sockets. The GC has no control over unmanaged resources. As in all GC systems, our primary concern is learning how to construct and work with classes that support such collection while properly freeing any resources our objects might have acquired.

First, when we create objects in .NET, memory is allocated on the *managed heap*. The common language runtime manages this heap by manipulating a pointer to the address in memory where the next object is to be allocated. As each object is allocated on the heap, common language runtime moves the pointer to the next allocatable address. The size of this so-called managed heap isn't infinite. Eventually some New operation causes this pointer to advance past the allocatable memory in the managed heap and triggers garbage collection, which occurs when this pointer needs to move past the end of the heap. Figure 11.1 shows how this allocation pointer is associated with the managed heap and a collection due to resource needs.

Inside the GC

Although the internal workings of the GC system are more complicated than I'll let on at first, the basic process of garbage collection starts when an application requests memory allocation exceeding what is available on the heap.

One responsibility of the GC system is to visit all objects in the heap and determine which objects do and do not have references. These references are referred to as roots. All objects that have valid references are marked and not available for collection, leaving only objects that are unreachable and ready to be reclaimed.

After objects are returned to the heap, the GC system compacts the remaining objects on the heap to provide the largest possible contiguous block of memory for future heap allocation. Figure 11.2 depicts the compacted, reorganized objects in the managed heap.

In essence, an object is collected some time after the last reference to that object was set to Nothing. By setting an object reference to Nothing, we are removing one of its traceable roots and no more.

When an object is about to be collected, the GC calls the Finalize event (destructor in C#), if one exists, prior to performing any reclamation as long as the SuppressFinalize was not called. The process of calling the finalizer and executing the code in such a method is referred to as *finalization.*

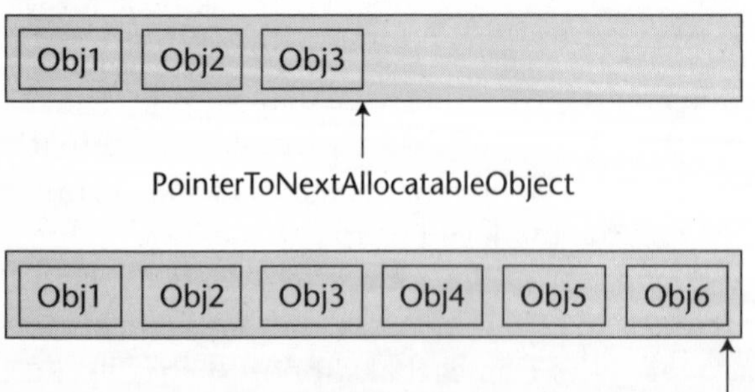

Figure 11.1 A GC is triggered when there are no more allocatable units in a heap.

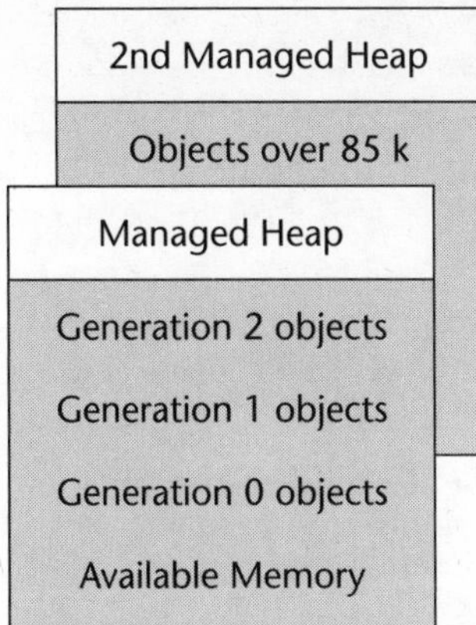

Figure 11.2 The GC reorganizes objects on the managed heap according to generation.

Because the compacting role of the GC requires it to move objects to different memory addresses in the managed heap, it would be inefficient for very large objects. Because of this, large objects are maintained on a separate heap that is never compacted.

Nondeterministic Finalization

Finalization refers to the process involving the call to an object's Finalize method (or destructor, in C#) and the release of unmanaged resources in that method. The GC in .NET uses nondeterministic finalization, which simply means that although the GC may eventually call the object's finalizer, as a .NET programmer, you really have no idea when the finalization code will be called. Because it's not known when an object will be reclaimed, we must design objects in such a way that when we are done using the objects, we can force the release of any resources our objects have acquired.

Visual Basic 6 Automatic Memory Management

In Visual Basic 6 we can set an object reference to Nothing and the destructor for that object would fire, which is to say that the Terminate event would occur. Visual Basic 6 also has automatic memory management, but it has deterministic finalization. If you set an object to Nothing, the object's destructor is called and the object is destroyed. Following are four examples in Visual Basic 6:

- Object declared with class scope and never set to Nothing:

```
Dim c As Class1
Private Sub Command1_Click()
```

```
    Set c = New Class1 'constructor called here
End Sub
'destructor called when form is closed because it has form scope
```

- Object declared with class scope and set to Nothing in event:

```
Dim c As Class1
Private Sub Command1_Click()
    Set c = New Class1 'constructor called here
    Set c = Nothing 'destructor manually called here (deterministic)
End Sub
```

- Object declared with method scope and never set to Nothing:

```
Private Sub Command1_Click()
    Dim c As Class1 'constructor called here
    Set c = New Class1
End Sub 'destructor called here because of its local scope
```

- Object declared As New but never used:

```
Private Sub Command1_Click()
    Dim c As New Class1
    Set c = Nothing
End Sub 'neither the constructor or destructor ever fires, but if you
assigned a property value between the two lines, both would fire.
```

Visual Basic .NET Automatic Memory Management

Memory management in .NET is a little different. There is no way we can cause the destructor for an object to be called at a specific time. All we can do is set the object to null (Nothing in Visual Basic .NET) to indicate that the object has one less reference. When there are no references (unless they are Weak References) to an object, the GC system is able to reclaim memory for that object. The problem is that you can't predict when garbage collection will occur for an object. Most of the objects we create don't need any special support, and the GC system can reclaim them when it needs to do so. But for objects that utilize unmanaged resources, such as file handles, we must provide a more proactive approach. The GC can follow root references to managed objects to determine when a managed object should be released. In the process of destroying the object, however, the GC won't know that it's supposed to also end a network session, close a file, or release other unmanaged resources. The problem is that this lack of knowledge won't stop the GC from destroying the object.

Because finalization is nondeterministic and the GC is ignorant of unmanaged resources, we must, as architects of classes, provide support for a Dispose method that frees up unmanaged resources. As users of classes we must get in the habit of calling Dispose on an object we are done using even if we don't think it has any such resources.

For object types for which it would be more intuitive for a class consumer to call a Close method, we simply expose a public Close and call Dispose from the Close method for consistency.

To compare similar scenarios for automatic memory management in Visual Basic .NET to the Visual Basic 6 scenarios I outlined before, we need to know the following:

- When the sole reference to an object goes out of scope, it doesn't matter if it was set to Nothing; it will be collected because it has no valid roots (get into the habit of setting them to Nothing anyway).
- Declaring an object using the As New syntax is perfectly fine in Visual Basic .NET.
- When the application ends, objects on its managed heap are reclaimed regardless of original scope due to a final GC process.

Classroom Q & A

Q: How are circular references handled for abandoned objects?

A: First let me restate the question in case that term is not familiar to some. What if two objects exist that have no references except to each other? Technically, they are unreachable. The good news is that the GC system is smart enough to reclaim them both because a reference from an unreachable object is not enough to keep an object from being destroyed.

Q: Doesn't a GC system use nearly twice as much memory?

A: That might have been true when GC systems were still in their infancy. However, this GC is highly optimized, and there are really only benefits in having it.

Q: If we can't tell when our objects will be destroyed, why don't we just set all the references to Nothing and call Collect?

A: It's important to understand that the GC has a proprietary algorithm that determines how and when garbage collection will occur while optimizing a great number of things, including the impact on a system. If you have intimate knowledge of the exact state of a system at a current time and you just finished using a rather large number of objects, you might feel free to use the Collect method.

Q: In the past my company has designed custom memory management systems for our applications that I'm willing to bet against the speed of the GC in the same scenario. Any comments on the speed of the GC in comparison to a customized collection system?

A: I also have worked with custom collection systems. In almost every case, these systems were being customized for each application, didn't follow one idiom for usage, and usually required so much code to implement that I heartily welcomed built-in garbage collectors. You are correct that when it is eventually customized and in place, any technology specifically fitted for an implementation provides greater optimization over a generic solution.

Q: Does the system come to a complete halt while garbage collection occurs?

A: The common language runtime has to freeze all threads except for that thread on which the GC system runs. This is expected and necessary behavior for a GC.

Designing Objects for Collection

I've mentioned both a Dispose method and a Finalize method as I described some of the inner workings of the GC in .NET. To build objects that truly consume unmanaged resources, implementing a Finalize method is crucial, but it is also crucial that not all objects should have a Finalize method. Before we get into the impact of having a Finalize method, let's look at the pattern for using Dispose and Finalize together:

```
'Used to demonstrate Dispose and Finalize Patterns Only
Public Class Person
   Implements IDisposable
   Private Disposed As Boolean = False
   Public Overloads Sub Dispose() Implements IDisposable.Dispose
      'If Disposed Then Exit Sub
      Dispose(True)
      System.GC.SuppressFinalize(Me)
   End Sub
   Protected Overloads Sub Dispose(ByVal disposing As Boolean)
      If Not (Me.Disposed) Then
         If (disposing) Then
            'free managed resources
         End If
         'free unmanaged resources
      End If
      Me.Disposed = True
   End Sub
   Protected Overrides Sub Finalize()
```

```
        Me.Dispose(False)
    End Sub
End Class
```

To ensure that finalization code only appears in one place we use two versions of the Dispose method together, as shown in Figure 11.3.

The Dispose method is an implementation of the only method in the IDisposable interface, and Finalize is an override of an empty method inherited from System.Object.

Here are some garbage tips and interesting facts:

- Don't use Finalize unless you really need to. Unless you actually have unmanaged resources not controlled by the common language runtime, implementing a Finalize method can cause significant overhead because objects with Finalize methods are destroyed twice.
- Always call MyBase.Finalize in your Finalize. Even if your object inherits directly from System.Object, which has an empty Finalize method, it doesn't hurt anything because the compiler ignores empty method calls. Not calling MyBase.Finalize eventually results in loss of resources.

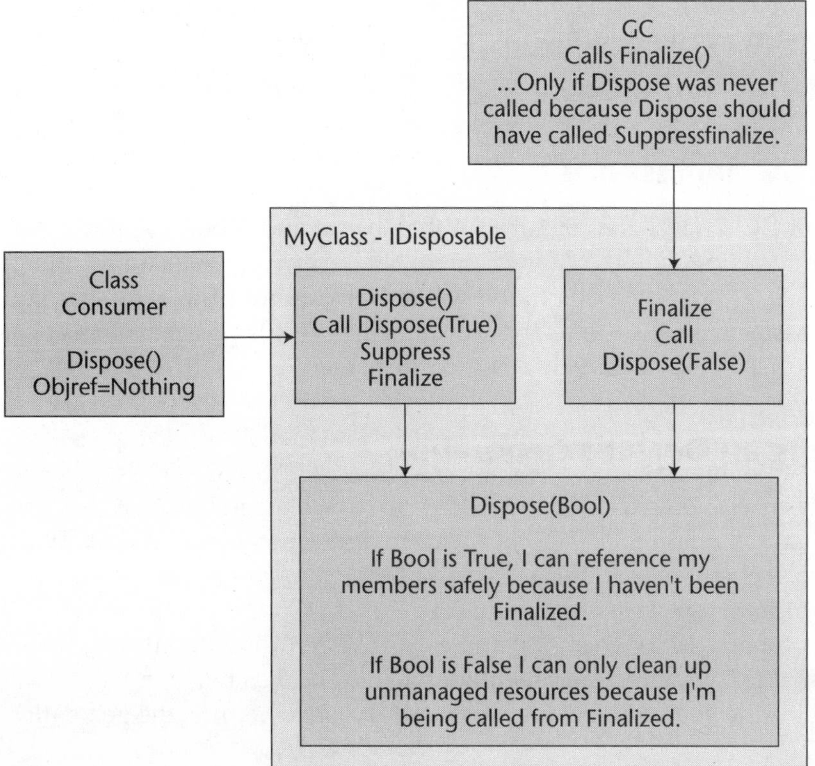

Figure 11.3 There are two very different times in which Dispose may be called, and we want to use Finalize only once.

- Wrap the call to MyBase.Finalize in a Try and place that call in the Finally block to make sure it gets called.
- If an error occurs in a Finalize method, the GC ignores it and continues with the rest of the object finalizers for objects in the finalization queue.
- You can't access other managed objects from within a finalizer because you can't predict the order in which objects are destroyed. Objects you reference might be gone already. A failed attempt to access destroyed objects would cause an error that would terminate the finalize code prematurely and cause resource leak.
- Don't make Dispose() Overridable.
- You can't assume that members of your object are even initialized. Our Finalize method might have been called because of something that happened during its creation.
- When you are done using an object, call Dispose and set the reference to Nothing:

```
If TypeOf myobj Is IDisposable Then
   myobj.Dispose()
End If
myobj = Nothing
```

- In the Finalize method, only the Debug object and MyBase are guaranteed to exist.

System.GC Namespace

The System.GC namespace contains all the objects and members at our disposal for interacting with the GC system in .NET. Although a few of the members in this namespace are commonly used, it is important to state that you should just trust the GC system. The only activities you can perform that affect collection are likely to negatively affect performance.

Obtaining an Object's Generation

An object's generation refers to how many garbage collection passes it has survived. When the object is created in memory, it has a generation of 0. Every time that object still exists after a garbage collection, its generation is incremented by 1 until it reaches the maximum generation of 2 (for verification, the read-only property, MaxGeneration, in System.GC returns a 2). The GetGeneration method for obtaining the generation of an object has two overloads. One overload gets the generation of an object and the other returns the generation for a weak reference. Weak references are covered later in the chapter. Although calling Collect() manually is inherently bad, the following code demonstrates how objects generations are elevated in relation to a collection:

```
Private Sub DemoCollect_Click(ByVal sender As System.Object, _
ByVal e As System.EventArgs) Handles DemoCollect.Click
    Dim myobj As New Class1()
    MessageBox.Show(System.GC.GetGeneration(myobj)) 'GENERATION is 0
    System.GC.Collect()
    System.GC.WaitForPendingFinalizers()
    MessageBox.Show(System.GC.GetGeneration(myobj)) 'GENERATION is 1
    myobj = Nothing
    System.GC.Collect()
    System.GC.WaitForPendingFinalizers()
    'myobj is reclaimed
End Sub
```

Because objects are reclaimed by the GC when it makes a pass and finds no valid references to the object, the second call to Collect here would destroy the object.

Although the example helps to explain an object's generation, it is not recommended that you call Collect unless you are positive that it will provide some benefit over the built-in collection algorithms.

The WaitForPendingFinalizers method is necessary because Finalize methods run in separate threads of execution. Calling this method waits until the GC has successfully called Finalize for all objects being destroyed.

Forcing a Manual Collection

Except in rare circumstances on the client side, forcing a manual collection is not recommended. Manually forcing a collection can be done using System.GC.Collect. A manual call to the Collect method is referred to as an *Induced GC*. The Collect method has two overloads. If no parameters are passed to the Collect method, it will attempt to clean up objects in all generations. If a parameter is specified, the collection will occur in generations 0 through the generation specified. The following are examples for using the Collect method:

```
System.GC.Collect( ) 'Collect generation 0 through 2
System.GC.Collect(0) 'Collect from generation 0 only
System.GC.Collect(2) 'Same results as Collect()
```

Remember that as long as there is a direct or indirect strong reference to an object, that object is not eligible for garbage collection. In addition every time the object survives a collection, its generation is incremented until it equals 2. The following code helps demonstrate this:

```
//Class Person:
Public Class Person
    '
    '
    '
    Protected Overrides Sub finalize()
        Debug.WriteLine("In Person Finalize")
        'Debug and MyBase are the only object safe to call from here
    End Sub
End Class
//Client Code:
Dim myobj1 As New Person()
Private Sub Button4_Click(ByVal sender As System.Object, _
ByVal e As System.EventArgs) Handles Button4.Click
    Dim myobj2 As Person = myobj1 'creates a second reference to object
    Debug.WriteLine("calling 1st collect...")
    System.GC.Collect(0) 'nothing is collected because myobj2 is a valid
ref
    myobj2 = Nothing 'There are no more valid references
    Debug.WriteLine("calling 2nd collect...")
    System.GC.Collect(0) 'Still nothing collected because obj was
generation
    'one because of the first collection but now it is generation 2.
    Debug.WriteLine("calling 3rd collect...")
    System.GC.Collect() 'object is freed because collect() with no
parameter
    'passed to it collects all generations of objects that have no valid
    'references'
    System.GC.WaitForPendingFinalizers()
End Sub
```

This code produces the results shown in Figure 11.4. The Debug object is one of a very small number of objects available from within a Finalize method.

Preventing Garbage Collection for Objects

When an object is passed to unmanaged code and there are no references to that object in managed code, the object is at risk of being destroyed because the GC system doesn't see the reference in unmanaged code. To prevent garbage collection from reclaiming this object, we use the KeepAlive method. System .GC.KeepAlive ensures that an object is kept alive from the start of a routine to the point where the method is invoked. Because of this, KeepAlive should be used near the end of a method, not the beginning.

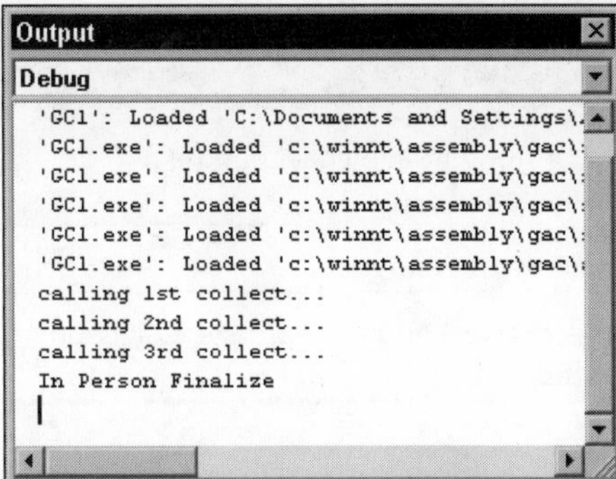

Figure 11.4 Debug.Write statements are perfect for determining when Finalize methods are actually called.

Determining Allocated Memory

The GetTotalMemory method can be used to obtain all memory allocated in bytes. The GetTotalMemory method takes a single boolean argument, ForceFullCollection, which causes the method to wait while garbage collection and finalization occur. Exactly how long it will wait isn't determinable, but it is always a relatively short time and specified internally. The time it will wait before returning depends on the number of garbage collection cycles completed and the relative amount of reclaimed memory between those cycles. The following example returns a value representing all allocated memory after forcing a full collection:

```
System.GC.GetTotalMemory(True)
```

Weak References

Normally, holding onto a reference of an object prevents the object from being destroyed. A reference to a reachable object in memory is referred to as a strong reference. A weak reference to an object can actually point to an object in memory after all valid references to the object were removed. When the object a weak reference points to is destroyed, the weak reference will point to Null. Table 11.1 describes the three commonly used members of the Weak Reference class.

Although a strong reference can be set to the target object of the weak reference, doing so after garbage collection occurs for that target and it's been finalized produces very unpredictable results.

TABLE 11.1 Weak Reference Object Members

MEMBER	DESCRIPTION
IsAlive	Determines whether or not garbage collection has occurred for the referenced object.
Target	Gets or Sets the object being referenced.
TrackResurrection	Determines if an object is tracked after garbage collection occurs and it is finalized.

If TrackResurrection is True, the object referenced (the target) will be tracked even after garbage collection occurs and it is finalized, creating what is referred to as a *long weak reference*. If TrackResurrection is False, the weak reference is referred to as a *short weak reference*. The reason something might be trackable after its supposed destruction is clearer when we understand that finalized objects (objects that have destructors or finalizers) are actually destroyed twice.

Avoiding Finalizers

This destruction of finalized objects removes objects from one internal structure (Finalization queue), uses a resurrection to place the object on a second queue (Freachable queue), and then eventually destroys the object from the second queue. Because of this, it is important to design objects with Finalize methods only if they absolutely need it. Of equal importance, we must design our Dispose methods to call SuppressFinalize to make sure the object is removed from the Finalization queue and can be destroyed in a single collection. Figure 11.5 describes the process by which objects with finalizers are destroyed twice.

Classroom Q & A

Q: Does the GC guarantee that all unreachable objects are freed during a collection?

A: Actually, it doesn't. Different internal optimizations revolving around reclaiming an acceptable amount of memory and causing minimal system impact will prematurely end a collection. This is evident from watching collections take place through a performance monitor.

Obj1 and Obj2 were allocated and have Finalized methods:

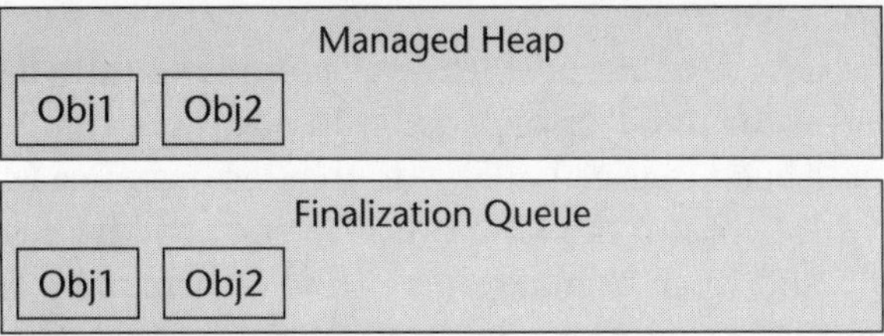

Obj1.Dispose was called, but Obj2.Dispose was not (assuming SupressFinalize).

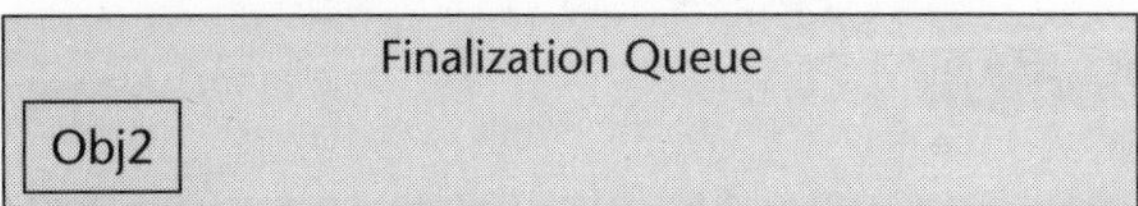

A collection destroys Obj1 because it's not on the Finalization Queue, but Obj2 is destroyed only to be resurrected to the FReachable Queue.

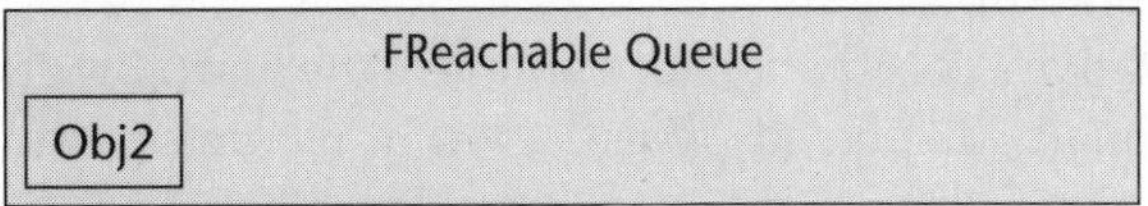

A second collection destroys Obj2.

Figure 11.5 Objects with finalizers that are not removed from the finalization queue must be destroyed twice.

Q: What is the internal difference between Finalize in .NET and Terminate in Visual Basic 6?

A: In Visual Basic 6, the Terminate event occurs right *before* an object is made unreachable; but in .NET, the Finalize event occurs *after* the object is made unreachable.

Q: If I understand correctly, every time I open a file within a class, I need to implement a Finalize method or the file won't be closed. Is that true?

A: Actually, if you never did anything at all, and if the file was opened using a .NET object such as System.IO.FileStream, it would be closed when the application terminated. You can test this easily enough: open a file with new FileStream("fullpath" mode) and try to modify the file from Notepad. You won't be able to save the file from Notepad until the FileStream object is manually closed or the application ends.

Performance Monitoring

.NET has built-in support for using performance counters in the IDE to aid in performance monitoring for .NET applications. In addition, many .NET performance counters have been made available to the Performance Monitor that has long shipped with Microsoft applications. We start by discovering what counters are available and how to make use of them, primarily focusing on memory objects. Eventually, we write an application in .NET that uses programmatic counters to monitor memory allocation and reclamation in .NET.

Performance Monitor

Performance Monitor is a standard part of most Microsoft operating systems and is part of the Administrative Tools menu in Windows. As its name suggests, the Performance Monitor utility (perfmon.exe) allows developers and administrators to monitor different aspects of an environment for performance. If Administrative Tools do not appear under the Start, Programs menu, they need to be manually displayed. To cause Administrative Tools to appear under Start, Windows, select Start, Settings, Task Bar and Start Menu, Advanced tab and check the Display Administrative Tools check box. Now Start, Programs, Administrative Tools, Performance should open the Performance Monitor shown in Figure 11.6.

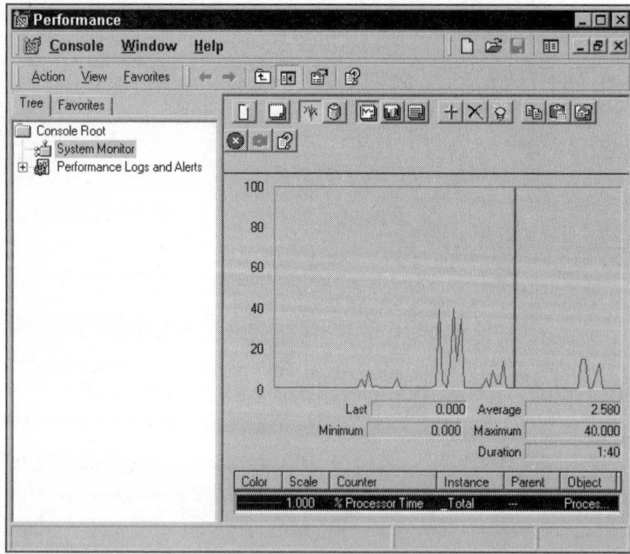

Figure 11.6 The Performance Monitor monitors objects such as CPU, memory, networking, and security.

Counters and Objects

The Performance Monitor watches primary and secondary units it refers to as Counters and Objects. An *Object* is a high-level thing we can monitor, such as Processor, whereas an individual unit, or *Counter*, for the Processor could be %Processor Time, as shown in Figure 11.6. Table 11.2 describes the objects that are added to the list of available performance objects when .NET is installed for monitoring .NET application performance. Any object added for monitoring appears in both a data view and a graph view.

TABLE 11.2 .NET-Related Performance Objects

OBJECT	DESCRIPTION
.NET CLR Data	This object is used to aid in monitoring ADO.NET interaction with SQL Server. The counters for .NET CLR Data can be used to monitor SQLClient connection pooling and to detect failed commands and connections.
.NET CLR Exceptions	The CLR Exceptions counters can be used to detect code that is throwing excessive exceptions either by our doing or by the environment. The total number of exceptions thrown, the number of exceptions per second, and the number of Finally's per second are examples of useful counters for this object. Because exceptions are expensive, these are commonly used exceptions to help determine problem areas.
.NET CLR Interop	This object is used to aid in monitoring Interop between managed and unmanaged code. The total number of COM Callable wrappers (CCWs), total number of times arguments and return values have been marshaled between managed to unmanaged code, and the number of marshalling stubs can all be determined via this objects counters.
.NET CLR JIT	This object is used to monitor the Just In Time (JIT) compilation activity in a .NET application. The common language runtime JIT counters track the total bytes JITted, the number of methods JITted, the amount of time spent performing JIT, and to track JIT failures.
.NET CLR Loading	The CLR Loading object can be used to monitor the loading, unloading and failure to load Classes, Assemblies, and AppDomains in .NET. Additional counters for this object monitor the number of app domains, assemblies, and classes and the amount of memory currently in the Loader heap.

(continued)

TABLE 11.2 *(continued)*

OBJECT	DESCRIPTION
.NET CLR LocksAndThreads	As its name suggests, this object is used to manage things such as the number of threads waiting for locks, the total number of failed attempts to acquire managed locks, and the number of threads created per second that are recognized by the common language runtime.
.NET CLR Memory	The CLR Memory object is used to monitor the common language runtime GC system. Counters for this object monitor everything from collections by generation to which objects survived finalization. Specific counters for this object are discussed later in this chapter.
.NET CLR Networking	The Networking object is used to track all bytes and datagrams sent or received over all sockets as well as to track established connections for a process.
.NET CLR Remoting	The Remoting counters monitor remoting contexts, context bound classes, and Remote Procedure Call (RPC) activity for .NET remoting.
.NET CLR Security	The CLR Security counters monitor Code Access Security (CAS) check activity in .NET applications.
ASP.NET	Multiple objects and counters are available for monitoring Application and Session activity in ASP.NET applications to monitor everything from the number of requests per second to the number of active sessions.

Common Language Runtime Memory Counters

Because we've just been discussing common language runtime memory, next we focus on the counters associated with the garbage collector in .NET. The common language runtime Memory Object is actually the largest set of counters for all of the .NET objects. Table 11.3 provides a complete list of common language runtime Memory counters and their descriptions.

TABLE 11.3 Common Language Runtime Memory Counters

COUNTER	DESCRIPTION
# Bytes in all Heaps	The counters monitor each generation of objects (0, 1, and 2) as separate heaps. This counter displays the bytes for all objects allocated, in all generations, including those objects that have been allocated on the large object heap.
# GC Handles	First of all, a GC Handle is a handle to an unmanaged resource. The handles themselves take up only a small space, but they indicate resources over which the GC has no control. These are the types of resources for which Finalize methods are created in our classes.
# Gen 0 Collections	Generation 0 objects represent objects that have recently been allocated and have never experienced a garbage collection. This counter monitors all generation 0 garbage collections. Technically, *any* garbage collection causes a generation 0 garbage collection.
# Gen 1 Collections	Generation 1 objects have survived a single garbage collection. A generation 1 collection also occurs whenever any generation 2 collection occurs.
# Gen 2 Collections	Generation 2 objects represent those objects that are the least likely to need to be collected. Because generation 0 objects are the most likely objects to need collection, often only a generation 0 collection is necessary or performed. Monitoring generation 2 collections with this counter on real application will prove that there are far more generation 0 collections than generation 2 collections.
# Induced GC	This counter is incremented whenever we use the System.GC.Collect method to perform a manual (induced) collection.
# of Pinned Objects	You may remember that the compacting operation performed by the GC system moves objects around on the managed heap. If the client holding the reference to those moved objects is a .NET client, it's okay because the address it references is adjusted to point to the new location. If the consumer is in unmanaged code, the change of address that it points to could cause some unfriendly results. A Pinned object is one whose address is fixed in memory (pinned) so that the unmanaged client won't ever be working with a bogus address. This counter, of course, provides the total number of such objects.

(continued)

TABLE 11.3 *(continued)*

COUNTER	DESCRIPTION
# of Sink Blocks in use	This counter aids in locating performance issues related to heavy use of synchronization primitives. A Sink Block is a data structure (associated with an object) used to store synchronization information or COM interop metadata.
# Total committed Bytes # Total reserved Bytes	These counters simply display the amount of virtual memory currently reserved by the GC.
% Time in GC	This isn't really an average but rather a computation to determine the relative time spent for subsequent collections.
Allocated Bytes/sec	Another misleading counter. This counter is neither an average of bytes allocated per second nor is it even updated until a collection has occurred. It is still useful in comparing allocated bytes per second across a duration spanning two or more collections.
Finalization Survivors	This counter has nothing to do with tracking all objects that survived a collection but rather those objects that survived the collection because they were awaiting finalization. This counter is useful in tracking the overhead involved in object finalization.
Gen 0 Heap Size	Often mistaken for the bytes allocated on the generation heap, this counter is actually the maximum bytes that can be allocated before a generation 0 garbage collection will occur. This counter is one of many that is only updated following a garbage collection.
Gen 0 Promoted Bytes/sec	This counter tracks the total bytes that were promoted from generation 0 to generation 1 averaged over at least the last two collections and is only updated following a collection. Be aware that pending finalizers are not represented in this byte total.
Gen 1 Heap Size	Unlike generation 0, nothing can be allocated for generation 1, and this counter is confusing when compared to Gen 0 Heap Size. Gen 0 Heap Size is what *can* be allocated, and Gen 1 Heap Size is a byte total that *is* allocated for generation 1 objects.

TABLE 11.3 *(continued)*

COUNTER	DESCRIPTION
Gen 1 Promoted Bytes/sec	The bytes per second promoted from generation 1 to generation 2, which is the highest attainable generation (just in case this changes, use GC.MaxGeneration to verify). This number is an average over the last two or more collections and is updated only following a collection.
Gen 2 Heap Size	The total allocated bytes in generation 2.
Large Object Heap Size	I've seen the actual size of this heap described as a wide range of values ranging from 20 to 85K in different sources, but suffice it to say that "large" objects are maintained on a separate heap that is not compacted. Objects on this special heap are not affected by generations, so pay attention to this heap in addition to the generation heaps when determining how much memory is being allocated. This counter is also updated only following a collection.
Promoted Finalization Memory from Gen 0	This value is only a representation for the last collection and indicates the number of bytes promoted from generation 0 to generation 1 because objects were awaiting finalization.
Promoted Finalization Memory from Gen 1	This value is only a representation for the last collection and indicates the number of bytes promoted from generation 1 to generation 2 because objects were awaiting finalization.
Promoted Memory from Gen 0	A noncumulative count of the bytes surviving the last collection that were promoted to generation 1, excluding those objects that survived because they were awaiting finalization.
Promoted Memory from Gen 1	A noncumulative count of the bytes surviving the last collection that were promoted to generation 2, excluding those objects that survived because they were awaiting finalization.

Adding Counters in Performance Monitor

If you look back to Figure 11.6, you'll notice a Toolbar button with a plus sign on it. This button is used to add counters to the display in Performance Monitor. With the appropriate Administrative privileges, the Add Counters window allows you to select Performance objects from any machine you have access to.

Certain counters are instanced-specific, as you will see in the upcoming lab, so the instance you actually want to monitor also should be selected in the Add Counters window.

Lab 11.1: Using Performance Counters and Objects in System.Diagnostics

The objective of this lab is to gain familiarity with using objects, counters, and instances by manipulating objects in the System.Diagnostics namespace. Some objects apply to the system at large, whereas other objects are specific to an instance. The CLR Memory object is a perfect example of an object whose counters are meant to target a specific instance. When using such an object, we need to provide the instance we want to monitor when we request the object's counters.

Let's perform the following steps:

1. Start a new .NET Windows application name Performance1.
2. On Form1, add the controls listed in Table 11.4 so that your starting form appears similar to Figure 11.7.
3. Before we begin writing code to obtain all the objects, instances, and counters, add the following statements to the top of Form1:

```
Option Strict On
Option Explicit On
Imports System.Collections
Imports System.Diagnostics 'contains objects for working with
Performance 'objects, counters and instance objects.
```

Table 11.4 Controls with Indicated Properties

CONTROL TYPE	NAME	TEXT
ListBox	ObjectListBox	
ListBox	InstanceListBox	
ListBox	CounterListBox	
Label		Performance Objects
Label		Instance Objects
Label		Performance Counters
TextBox	CounterValueTextBox	
Label		Raw Value

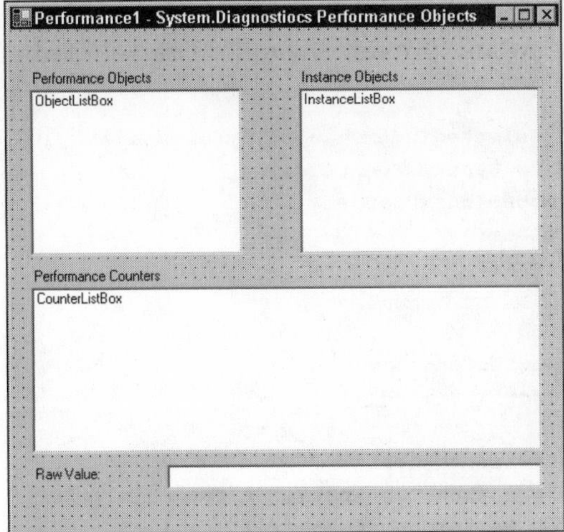

Figure 11.7 This is what your starting form for Lab11.1 should look like.

4. Add the following form fields to Form1:

```
Private counters As New ArrayList()
Private counter As New PerformanceCounter()
Private cat As New PerformanceCounterCategory()
```

5. The objects for monitoring are available as PerformanceCounter-Category objects in the System.Diagnostics namespace. Cause the Form1 Load event handler to automatically populate the ObjectList-Box with all performance objects available, using the following code:

```
Private Sub Form1_Load(ByVal sender As System.Object, _
ByVal e As System.EventArgs) Handles MyBase.Load
   Dim categories As PerformanceCounterCategory()
   ObjectListBox.Sorted = True
   ObjectListBox.Items.Clear()
   categories = PerformanceCounterCategory.GetCategories
   Dim i As Integer
   For i = 0 To categories.Length - 1
      ObjectListBox.Items.Add(categories(i).CategoryName)
   Next
End Sub
```

6. Some of the objects listed now in ObjectListBox provide counters that apply to the entire system, but others are specific to a running instance. The following code occurs when an item is selected in the ObjectListBox. For a selected object, if it is instance-specific, the available instances are placed inside InstanceListBox so that users can specify Instance for which they want to produce counters. If the selected object in ObjectListBox is not instance-specific, its counters

are displayed in CountersListBox. Double-click ObjectListBox to enter the Code Editor Window and provide the following Selected-IndexChanged event:

```
Private Sub ObjectListBox_SelectedIndexChanged(ByVal sender _
As System.Object, ByVal e As System.EventArgs) _
Handles ObjectListBox.SelectedIndexChanged
   InstanceListBox.Items.Clear()
   CounterListBox.Items.Clear()
   Dim i As Integer
   Dim instances() As String
   cat = New PerformanceCounterCategory( _
   ObjectListBox.SelectedItem.ToString())
   Try
      instances = cat.GetInstanceNames()
      If instances.Length = 0 Then 'no instances for this object
         Dim counter As New PerformanceCounter()
         For Each counter In cat.GetCounters()
            CounterListBox.Items.Add(counter.CounterName)
         Next
      Else
      'There ARE instances for this object so fill
instanceListBox
         For i = 0 To instances.Length - 1
            InstanceListBox.Items.Add(instances(i).ToString())
         Next
      End If
   Catch ex As Exception
      MessageBox.Show(ex.Message)
   End Try
End Sub
```

7. If an object is selected in ObjectListBox that is instance-specific, the possible instances to choose from should be displayed in InstanceListBox. If the user selects an instance from InstanceListBox, a PerformanceCounterCategory object based on the object in ObjectListBox should call GetCounters, passing in the instance selected in InstanceListBox. The resulting collection of Performance-Counter objects should then be displayed in CounterListBox. Allow the user to select a specific instance to monitor and populate the CounterListBox with instance-specific counters using the following code:

```
Private Sub InstanceListBox_SelectedIndexChanged( _
ByVal sender As System.Object, ByVal e As System.EventArgs) _ _
Handles InstanceListBox.SelectedIndexChanged
   CounterListBox.Items.Clear()
   cat = New PerformanceCounterCategory( _
   ObjectListBox.SelectedItem.ToString())
   CounterListBox.Items.Clear()
```

```
    Dim i As Integer
    counters.AddRange(cat.GetCounters( _
    InstanceListBox.SelectedItem.ToString()))
    For Each counter In counters
       CounterListBox.Items.Add(counter.CounterName)
    Next
End Sub
```

8. To display the raw value for any counter selected in CounterListBox, add the following code to Form1:

```
Private Sub CounterListBox_SelectedIndexChanged(ByVal sender _
As System.Object, ByVal e As System.EventArgs) _ _
Handles CounterListBox.SelectedIndexChanged
   Me.CounterValueTextBox.Text = _
   CType(counters(CounterListBox.SelectedIndex), _
   PerformanceCounter).RawValue.ToString()
End Sub
```

To test the application, follow these steps:

1. Verify that all performance objects are loaded into ObjectListBox.
2. Click .NetClrData. The counters for this non-instance-specific object should now be displayed in CounterListBox as shown in Figure 11.8.
3. Click .NET CLR Memory in ObjectListBox. CounterListBox should clear, and InstanceListBox should display all available instance objects.

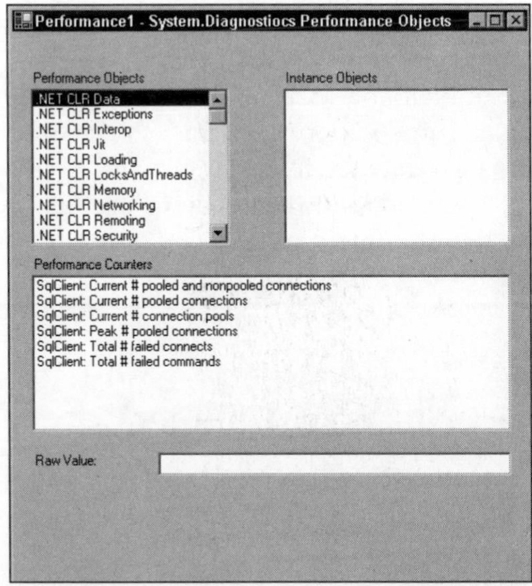

Figure 11.8 Clicking any non-instance-specific performance category should just display its counters.

4. From InstanceListBox, select the instance that represents your application to fill CounterListBox with the appropriate counters.
5. Select a counter in CounterListBox. The appropriate raw value should be displayed in CounterValueTextBox, as shown in Figure 11.9.

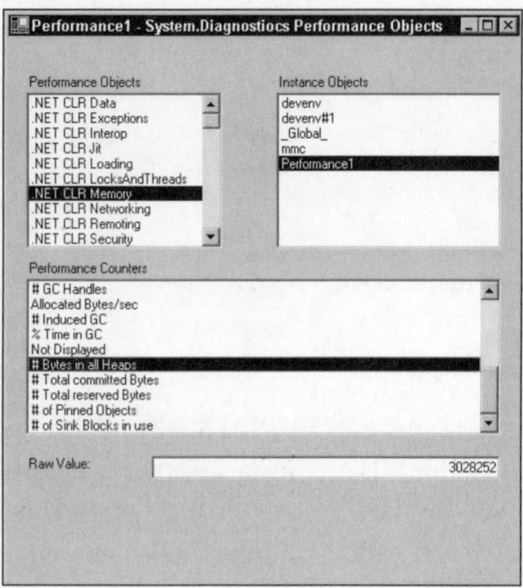

Figure 11.9 Counter.RawValue displays the raw, uncalculated value for the # Bytes In All Heaps counter.

When working with performance objects in the System.Diagnostics namespace or with the counter objects from the Server Explorer window, we can use CounterSample and CounterSampleCalculator to help calculate samples of counter data over a sampling period. In this lab, we used the relationship between Performance Categories, Instances, and Counters to extract raw counter data. When adapting the code in this lab to your applications, remember that these counters are updated only after a collection occurs.

Performance Counter Objects in Server Explorer

Server Explorer has counters that can actually be dragged to a form. To view the list of performance counters, open Server Explorer and keep expanding things until you see something similar to Figure 11.10.

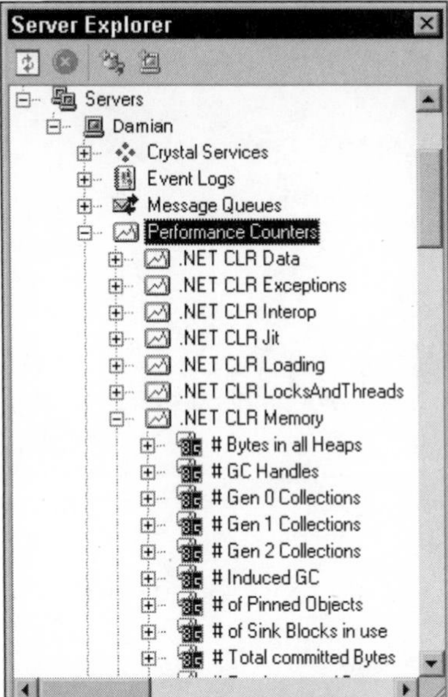

Figure 11.10 Performance counters can actually be dragged directly from the Server Explorer to a form for development.

After a performance counter has been dragged from the Server Explorer, it appears in the control tray beneath the form. One thing you will notice after completing the lab is that using the objects in System.Diagnostics at runtime provides more flexibility over instance counters than the counters in Server Explorer. At runtime we can programmatically extract data from each counter object we dragged onto the form.

```
ListBox1.Items.Add("Category: " & PerformanceCounter2.CategoryName)
ListBox1.Items.Add("Counter: " & PerformanceCounter2.CounterName)
ListBox1.Items.Add("Instance: " & PerformanceCounter2.InstanceName)
ListBox1.Items.Add("Machine: " & PerformanceCounter2.MachineName)
ListBox1.Items.Add("RawValue: " & PerformanceCounter2.RawValue)
```

These extracted values are shown in Figure 11.11.

Visual Basic .NET Performance Tips

Although not an exhaustive list, the following tips certainly aid in maximizing performance in Visual Basic .NET:

- Use With statements where possible.
- Send parameters in bulk to a method if possible instead of sending individual parameters in subsequent method calls.

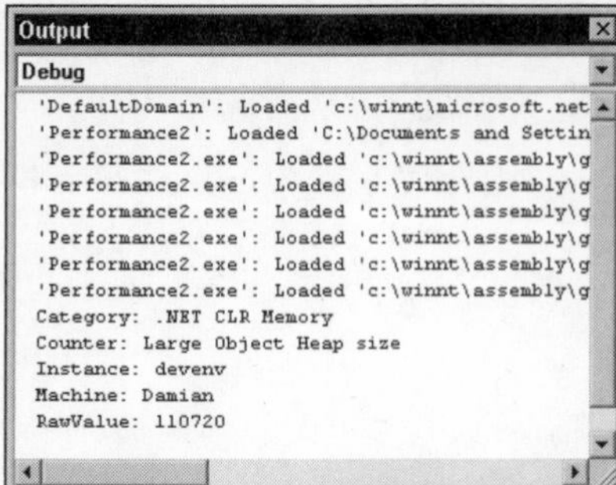

Figure 11.11 PerformanceCounter objects have quite a few useful properties for displaying the raw data and the scope of the counter.

- Use stored procedures for anything you can.
- In a garbage-collected system such as .NET, don't fool around with Collect. Live with it.
- Forget the Visual Basic 6-style error handling statements; they add useless garbage in IL and don't follow the .NET idiom.
- Always program with Option Strict On to avoid costly late-binding and poor code.
- Don't do a debug build when you no longer need one.
- Remember that loading any portion of an assembly loads the entire assembly.
- Contrary to popular belief, ngen only provides an initial boost in performance as the application is loaded. Much of the time, I find that my applications seem to execute faster if I use JIT compilation. I recommend that you try it out and compare it to using ngen.
- For collections, if AddRange can be used to do a bulk copy, use it instead of individual Adds to trim the overhead involved.
- Contrary to popular belief, the performance difference between For and For Each (at least from my own comparisons) isn't enough to make me want to stop using For Each loops, which are more readable and flexible than a For loop.
- The Return statement produces more optimized code than the Visual Basic 6 way of returning function values.
- Exceptions are not playthings. They should represent true exceptions to the normal flow of logic and not be used as a means to convey status. Use Events or Functions return values for status instead. Exceptions have more overhead that normal conditional or branching type statements.

- For objects that have an inheritence relationship, DirectCast can be used instead of CType for a slight performance improvement.
- Treating anything, especially a ValueType, as an Object type should be avoided for a number of reasons, chiefly because it doesn't promote polymorphic code. Another reason is because the so-called boxing and unboxing involved has rather noticeable overhead.
- ValueTypes has much less overhead than Reference Types. Simply using Chars instead of Strings is a difference of Stack (Char) versus Heap (String) based memory because of the nature of ValueTypes and Reference Types.

Summary

Many things define what is acceptable for different counters. The best advice I can give you for monitoring system performance is to monitor these counters before things go wrong to establish solid system baselines. Keep these baselines in an easy-to-read format so that they can be compared to current system values. As systems vary in the number of concurrent users or other factors, these counters can provide a meaningful indication of relative system performance only when they are compared to prior values. When establishing baselines for system performance, be as harsh and demanding on the system as possible to find out what will cause problems. Don't just watch counters; keep track of the conditions occurring at the time a sampling was made and store this data together to build a performance baseline. A common misconception is that performance monitoring will help you figure out what terrible thing has happened to a system, but if it is used correctly to create reasonable performance baselines, you can detect potential problems before they get out of hand.

Review Questions

1. How is memory acquired in .NET?
   a. A pointer to allocable memory in the generation 0 managed heap is moved passed a newly allocated object. The next object will be allocated at that pointer position.
   b. Objects are allocated as generation 2 objects and decremented by one generation as references are removed.
   c. Managed and unmanaged objects are allocated on the managed heap by incrementing an object pointer.
   d. A pointer to allocable memory at the end of the managed heap is moved before a newly allocated object. The next object will be allocated at that pointer position.
2. When does a garbage collection occur for generation 0 objects?
   a. When any generation 2 collection occurs
   b. When any collection occurs
   c. When an induced collection occurs
   d. When the allocation pointer for the managed heap would move past the end of the managed heap
3. Which of these is not a function of the GC system?
   a. Compacting all managed heaps
   b. Placing large objects on a large object heap
   c. Tracing object roots and marking objects with valid references
   d. Performing collections
4. Why is it important to call SuppressFinalize at the bottom of the Dispose method?
   a. Because it is required
   b. Because otherwise the object won't be finalized
   c. Because objects that are collected when they are still waiting to be finalized have to be destroyed twice and have far more overhead than objects without finalizers
   d. Because if we don't use SuppressFinalize, our object won't receive a notification when they are about to be collected
5. When a .NET application terminates, a final collection occurs and all managed objects, regardless of scope, are collected. True or False?

6. If we forget to set the last reference to an object to Nothing before that object reference goes out of scope, the object's collection will be delayed. True or False?
7. When the GC performs a collection, the common language runtime freezes all threads except the thread on which the GC runs. True or False?
8. Which of the following will stop ObjectX from being permanently destroyed during a garbage collection?
   a. Another object with no valid root reference holds a reference to ObjectX that has other references to it.
   b. Another object with a valid reference to it has a reference to ObjectX.
   c. ObjectX has no references of any kind and a Finalize method. Dispose was never called.
   d. ObjectX has only one weak reference and a Finalize method. Dispose was called, which in turn called Suppressfinalize.
9. You just allocated several sizable objects and several rather small objects in memory, but when you look at the counters in Performance Monitor, the values for the generation 0, 1, and 2 heaps don't look like they were affected at all. What is the probable cause?
   a. The objects were probably placed on the large-object heap.
   b. A collection hasn't occurred.
   c. A collection occurred.
   d. The # Bytes in all Heaps counter should have been used.

Answers to Review Questions

1. **a.** Objects are allocated by incrementing a pointer on the generation 0 managed heap.
2. **a**, **b**, **c**, and **d.** Garbage collection occurs for generation 0 objects when any collection occurs or when the allocation pointer for the managed heap would move past the end of the managed heap.
3. **a.** Compacting the normal managed heap where generation 0, 1, and 2 objects reside is a function of the GC system, but it does not compact the large-object heap.
4. **c.** Objects that are collected when they are still waiting to be finalized have to be destroyed twice and have far more overhead than objects without finalizers. Objects with Finalize methods that have no valid references and were never disposed are notified prior to destruction by a call to the Finalize method.
5. True. When a .NET application terminates, a final collection occurs, and all managed objects, regardless of scope, are collected.
6. False. If we forget to set the last reference to an object to Nothing before that object reference goes out of scope, the object's collection will occur anyway because there are no valid roots.
7. True. When the GC performs a collection, the common language runtime freezes all threads except the thread on which the GC runs.
8. **b** and **c.** If a strongly referenced object holds the only reference to ObjectX, that is enough to prevent ObjectX from being collected. If an object has no references but still has to wait to be finalized, it will survive a collection and be destroyed on the next collection (from the Freachable queue). Weak references are not enough to stop an object from being collected.
9. **b.** A collection needs to occur for the .NET common language runtime counters to get a new raw value. It also is true that the # Bytes in all Heaps counter should have been used to view the overall impact of memory, but it is not the reason for the inconsistent data.

CHAPTER

12

Threading

If you have ever waited for data to populate an interface during a Form_Load event or patiently watched an hourglass while a task was performed, you have seen what *not* having multithreaded applications is like. Threads are individual units of execution that comprise a process. Threads can be started, stopped, and made to run separately to perform tasks asynchronously. Performing asynchronous tasks has been made quite easy in Visual Basic .NET. For instance, even a simple ListBox control has BeginUpdate and EndUpdate methods for performing asynchronous operations on the ListBox contents. This chapter guides you through a myriad of options for creating multithreaded applications as you move from the Visual Basic 6 apartment-model threading to the free-threading model in Visual Basic .NET.

Threading Basics

Although Windows applications may appear to be executing at the same time, that is not the case. First, processor time is allocated to threads within an application. A running application is referred to as a *process* and a process contains at least a single thread. All running threads are given a time slice in which they can run for a moment, for a period appropriate for a given thread's priority. Modern versions of the Windows operating system use preemptive multitasking, which refers to the capability to pause one thread and give processor time to another thread. Nearly everything in .NET associated with threads, and multithreaded applications can be found in the System.Threading namespace. Unlike objects in Visual Basic 6, objects in Visual Basic .NET are not tied to the thread on which they are created. This is referred to as the absence of *thread affinity*.

What Is a Thread?

Threads represent singular, sequential flows of control within an application. That is to say, a thread is a unit of execution that has a beginning, a series of instructions, and an end, just like a traditional application. A thread, however, is not an application and cannot exist without being part of one. A part of the operating system, the thread scheduler, is responsible for scheduling and preemptively suspending threads. Threads must be scheduled because the CPU can only recognize a single thread at any given time. For machines that actually have multiple processors, threads can be scheduled across those processors for a much greater impact. The term *lightweight process* is sometimes used to describe a thread. Figure 12.1 depicts the relationship between the thread scheduler and running threads.

A thread contains information pertinent to itself within a *thread context*. Operating systems separate running applications into processes. Threads maintain exception handlers, a priority, and a set of structures. These structures are used by the system to store the thread context until it is scheduled. The thread context includes the thread's CPU registers, stack values, and any other information the thread needs to resume execution.

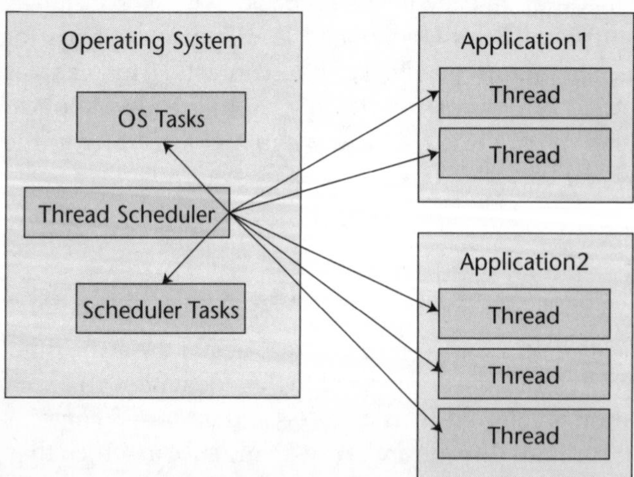

Figure 12.1 The thread scheduler is the portion of the operating system responsible for scheduling threads for execution.

Thread with Care

Using threads for the sake of using threads will cause more harm than good. As Figure 12.1 suggests, the thread scheduler needs a portion of the CPU's attention for its own scheduling activity. If there are too many threads being actively scheduled, this scheduling activity can ultimately degrade performance. Threads should only be created when necessary. The System.Threading namespace also provides a ThreadPool from which threads can be used. ThreadPool usage will be covered later in this chapter.

The Thread Object

In .NET, a thread is represented by the Thread object within the System .Threading namespace. Thread objects are instantiated by passing the name of a method the thread will execute as a parameter to its constructor. The Thread object has several notable members, listed in Table 12.1.

Table 12.1 System.Threading.Thread Members: Partial List

THREAD MEMBER	DESCRIPTION
Abort Method	Starts the termination of a thread by raising a ThreadAbortException in a thread. Changes the thread's state to AbortRequested.
ApartmentState property	A thread's apartment state can be unknown, MTA (multithreaded apartment), or STA (single threaded apartment). The default value is STA.
CurrentCulture Property	Returns the localization culture applied to the thread such as en-US.
CurrentPrincipal	Used with role-based security. Examples of use include the ability to determine the current principal identity, what roles that identity has, the authentication mode, and whether that identity has been authenticated.
CurrentThread	Frequently used as a generic way of referring to the current executing thread.
Interrupt	Interrupts a thread with a thread state of WaitSleepJoin.
IsAlive	Used to determine if a particular thread is executing.
IsBackground	Can be used to get or set a thread's background state.

(continued)

Table 12.1 *(continued)*

THREAD MEMBER	DESCRIPTION
IsThreadPoolThread	Determines if a given thread was taken from the thread pool (ThreadPool).
Join	Blocks the calling thread until a thread terminates.
Name	Used to get or set a thread's name.
Priority	Used to get or set a thread's priority. The ThreadPriority enumeration defines these thread priorities from lowest to highest: Lowest, BelowNormal, Normal, AboveNormal, and Highest.
ResetAbort	Cancels an Abort operation.
Reset	Resumes a thread that has been suspended.
Resume	Reactivates a suspended thread.
Sleep	Suspends a thread either for a period in milliseconds or for the duration of a TimeSpan object.
Start	Executes a thread. The Start method changes a thread's ThreadState to Running.
Suspend	Suspends a thread if it's not already suspended. Changes the thread's state to SuspendRequested.
ThreadState	ThreadState can be Aborted, AbortRequested, Background Running, Stopped, StopRequested, Suspended, SuspendRequested, Unstarted, or WaitSleepJoin. Setting a thread's ThreadState to Highest should be done with great caution because it could starve system processes.

Passing zero to Sleep causes a thread to give up the remainder of its time slice.

Advantages of Using Threads

Multithreaded applications have several advantages over single-threaded applications. The most prominent of these advantages are:

- No blocking
- Improved UI performance
- No limitation related to thread affinity

- The ability to asynchronously accomplish remote tasks
- The ability to distinguish between tasks of varying priorities and to assign those priorities

In a multitiered application, clients may be blocked from consuming server-based resources if those resources only provide a single thread. As you might imagine, this affects scalability. User interfaces can be made more responsive by running intensive operations, such as reformatting, searching, and data population in separate threads. This is often a far better approach than displaying an hourglass to the user, who must sit and wait. Without thread affinity, you are free to create an object on one thread and pass it to another. This capability has great significance in an object-pooled system such as Component Services.

Disadvantages of Using Multiple Threads

Although multiple threads can be used to solve an array of problems, you should use as few threads as possible to improve performance. Multithreaded applications have many considerations that must be taken into account, including some drawbacks to thread usage. The following list describes some of the issues and disadvantages to using threads:

- Managing an application with several threads can become excessively complex. Bugs related to threading logic errors can be nightmarish to track down and resolve.
- Destruction of threads requires quite a bit of knowledge concerning the ramifications of such an action.
- With or without multithreaded applications, providing shared access to resources can create conflicts. Access to shared resources must be synchronized.
- Be aware of the affect on system performance. The operating system uses memory for all threads, AppDomains, and processes, thereby limiting the maximum number of all three to available RAM. Furthermore, when scheduling threads, if too many threads exist, the mere amount of time spent scheduling can become quite noticeable. If a majority of the current threads exists in a single process, threads belonging to other processes will not receive equal shares of processor attention. Processes can be broken down into AppDomains in .NET.

Creating Threads

Threads are created using a declaration of a Thread object. A Thread constructor requires the address of a method that will be invoked when the thread starts running. The following example demonstrates the declaration of a Thread object and its association to a method:

```
Dim thread1 As New System.Threading.Thread(AddressOf method1)
```

Any method passed to the Thread constructor must be parameterless. The compiler will complain if a parameterized procedure is used.

Starting Thread Execution

After a declaration has been made, the Start method of the Thread object, thread1, can be used to execute method1 in a separate thread. The following demonstrates how a thread can be used to execute a method within that thread context:

```
thread1.Start() 'target method is invoked, under the context of thread1
```

Lab 12.1: Simple Threading

This lab demonstrates the use of running methods in separate threads. It ensures that you understand the basic concepts presented so far and provides a starting point for future discussions.

Perform the following steps:

1. Start a new Visual Basic .NET Windows application.
2. Add two Button controls to the form with the following properties:

   ```
   Name: btnStart1, Text: "Start without threads"
   Name: btnStart2, Text: "Start with threads"
   ```

3. Add an Imports statement for System.Threading to the top of Form1.
4. Add an Imports statement for System.Diagnostics to the top of Form1.
5. Add the following two methods to Form1:

   ```
   Private Sub method1()
      Dim i As Integer
      For i = 1 To 4
         Debug.WriteLine("Method1: " & i)
      Next
   End Sub
   Private Sub method2()
   ```

```
    Dim i As Integer
       For i = 1 To 4
        Debug.WriteLine("Method2: " & i)
       Next
End Sub
```

6. Add the following code for btnStart1 to call these methods without the use of threads:

```
Private Sub btnStart1_Click_1(ByVal sender As System.Object, _
ByVal e As System.EventArgs) Handles btnStart1.Click
   'synchronous, no threads:
   Debug.WriteLine("RESULTS WITHOUT THREADS: ")
   method1()
   method2()      'will not run until method1 has completed
End Sub
```

7. Run the application and test the code by clicking btnStart1 and viewing the contents of the Output window. The Output window can be viewed at runtime by selecting View, Other Windows, Output. The result of executing this code, shown in Figure 12.2, is just as we would expect from sequentially executed methods. Stop the application.

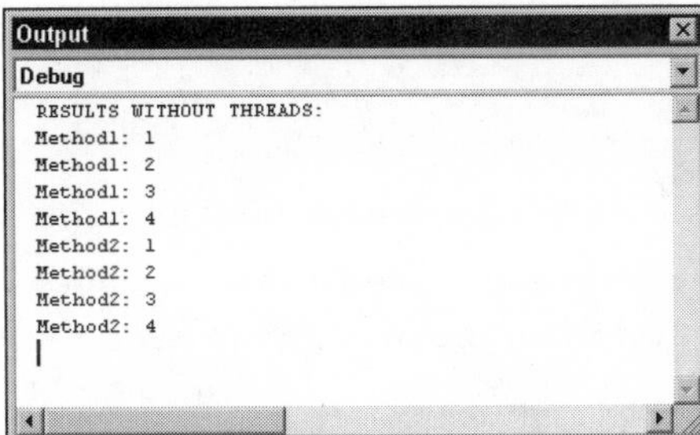

Figure 12.2 Output created by testing the application so far, without threads.

8. Now, to call the same methods via threads, add the following code for the second button, btnStart2:

```
Private Sub btnStart2_Click(ByVal sender As System.Object,
ByVal e As System.EventArgs) Handles btnStart2.Click
   'methods run asynchronously in separate threads:
   Debug.WriteLine("RESULTS WITH THREADS: ")
   Dim thread1 As New Thread(AddressOf method1)
   Dim thread2 As New Thread(AddressOf method2)
   thread1.Start()
   thread2.Start() 'method2 runs immediately and doesn't wait for
method1
End Sub
```

Before you test this code, remember that a thread is given a time slice in which to execute. It may be possible for that thread to execute in its entirety within a single time slice. Executing the code at this point with such a small enumeration will most likely produce the same results we encountered without threads.

9. To force the execution of the two methods to produce results indicative of concurrently executing threads, add the following line of code beneath the WriteLine() statement in *both* method1 and method2:

```
Thread.CurrentThread.Sleep(250)
```

10. Run the application and test the code by clicking btnStart2 and viewing the contents of the Output window. The result of executing this code, shown in Figure 12.3, proves that these two methods are running concurrently. Stop the application.

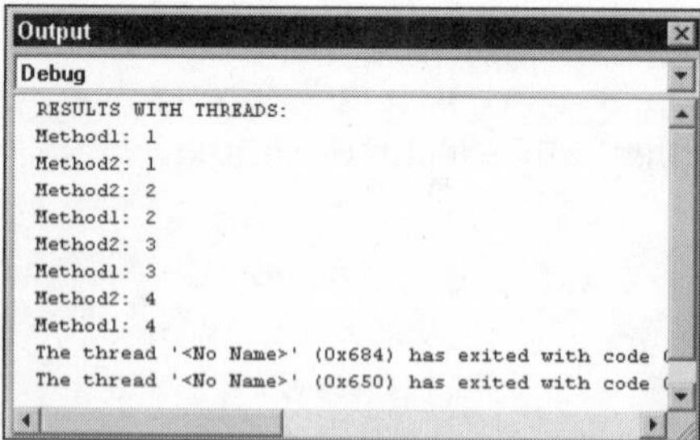

Figure 12.3 Two threads running concurrently.

11. Optionally, by placing breakpoints within the two For loops, stepping through the code causes control to jump between the two methods.

In this lab, you saw that traditionally sequential operations can be made to run concurrently. Oftentimes, a lengthy operation in a form's Load event can significantly delay the loading of the form. From what we have seen already of threads, we could avoid such issues. Use of multiple threads, however, requires understanding of a great number of related topics, not the least of which is synchronization of threads.

Debugging Threads

Besides placing breakpoints in the code to see when and where things are happening, we have several tools at our disposal for determining the state of threads in our application and for the system.

The Debug Location Toolbar

The Debug Location Toolbar can be viewed by selecting View, Toolbars, Debug Location. Use the Debug Location toolbar to view the current executable threads (see Figure 12.4).

The Threads Window

The Threads window can be viewed during break mode to view the status, ID, name, location, and priority of executing threads. Figure 12.4 displays the contents of the Threads window during execution of the application in Lab 12.1. The Threads window can be opened by selecting Debug, Windows, Threads during break mode.

Suspending and resuming a thread are referred to as *freezing* and *thawing* threads, respectively. By right-clicking a thread listed in the Threads window, you can switch to that thread (select Switch To Thread), suspend a thread (select Freeze), or resume a suspended thread (select Thaw.)

Performance Monitor

In Chapter 11, "Memory Management and Performance Monitoring," we looked at the Performance Monitor utility in Windows but focused almost entirely on the .NET CLR Memory object. As you can see in Figure 12.5, .NET also exposes a .NetCLRLocksAndThreads object for monitoring thread activity in .NET. Table 12.2 explains the counters available for the .NetLocksAndThreads object.

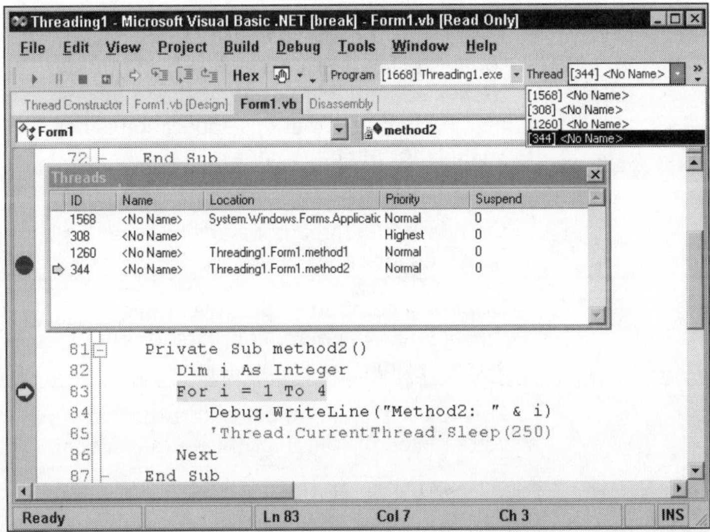

Figure 12.4 The Threads window in Visual Studio.NET displays information about current threads.

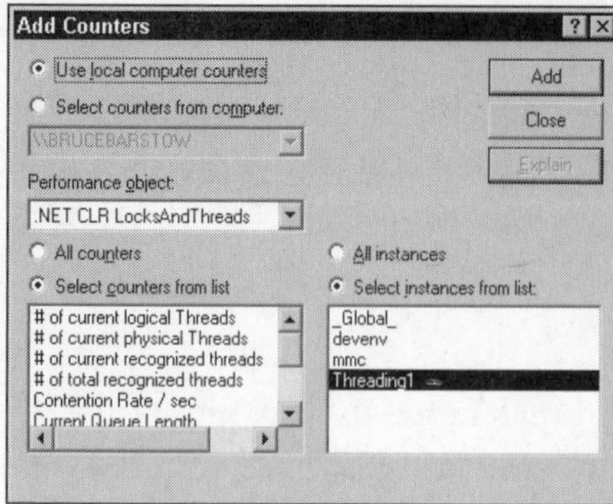

Figure 12.5 The Performance Monitor exposes a .NetCLRLocksAndThreads object for monitoring thread activity.

Table 12.2 .NetCLRLocksAndThreads Counters

COUNTER	DESCRIPTION
# Of Current Logical Threads	Displays the last observed value for all managed threads regardless of thread state.
# Of Current Physical Threads	Displays just the native OS threads owned by the common language runtime.
# Of Current Recognized Threads # Of Total Recognized Threads	Tracks threads that were not created by the common language runtime (either the current number of such threads or the total since the start of the application). Recognized threads may be threads created from P/Invoke or COM interop calls.
Contention Rate / Sec	Represents the rate at which our managed threads fail to acquire a lock. A high number for this counter can be very bad and may be a grand indicator that this application is not suitable for multithreading.
Current Queue Length	Displays the last observed value representing the number of threads waiting to acquire a managed lock.
Queue Length / Sec	Displays a computed value over time, representing the number of threads per second waiting to acquire a lock.
Queue Length Peak	Records the total number of threads that were forced to wait to acquire a managed lock.

Table 12.2 *(continued)*

COUNTER	DESCRIPTION
Rate of Recognized Threads / Sec	Displays the number of threads per second that have been recognized by the common language runtime that were not created by the common language runtime.
Total # Of Contentions	Displays the total number of times common language runtime managed threads have been unable to acquire a managed lock.

Threads Don't Work for Everything

Some objects are naturally protected from multithreaded operations. Controls, for instance, can be accessed only by the thread that created them. Because a control created on one thread cannot be used by another thread, the following code fails. When thread t1 creates a new Button control and then attempts to add that control to the current form, a runtime error occurs. This attempt fails because the thread controlling the form is not t1. The second, direct call to makecontrol() succeeds because a direct call to the method uses the same thread that controls the current form.

```
Private Sub Button1_Click(ByVal sender As System.Object, _
ByVal e As System.EventArgs) Handles Button1.Click
'Assumes: Imports System.Threading
Dim t1 As New Thread(AddressOf makecontrol)
   t1.Start()           'cannot successfully call makecontrol
   makecontrol()     'can successfully call makecontrol
End Sub
Private Sub makecontrol()
   Dim x As New Button()
   x.Name = "btnNew"
   x.Location = New Point(0, 0)
   x.Visible = True
   Try
      Me.Controls.Add(x) 'Will fail unless the main thread is current
   Catch Ex As System.ArgumentException
   MessageBox.Show(Ex.Message)
   End Try
End Sub
```

Classroom Q & A

Q: If I don't manually create any threads, do methods still execute within a thread?

A: Yes, although the application uses only one thread at a time. You can verify this by using the System.Thread.CurrentThread object inside a method that is not running from an explicitly created thread. Thread.CurrentThread.ThreadState.ToString() returns Running if you use it in a Form load event. Multithreaded applications take a lot of experience to manage and control.

Q: What if two threads try to modify a field in an object at the same time?

A: That is why threads must be synchronized. You also must synchronize access to that field. There are several ways to accomplish this, but for now, I'll just say that one thread obtains a lock on the field, writes to it, and releases the lock. Otherwise, you have pandemonium. We'll cover synchronization later in this chapter. Synchronization of nonstatic variables declared within a procedure is not necessary because these cannot be shared even by two threads declared in that procedure.

Q: How are the lifetime of a thread and the lifetime of a process related?

A: When all threads have terminated, the process will terminate. The exception is that background threads don't stop an application from terminating. A thread will terminate programmatically or will terminate naturally when the End Sub or End Function of its target procedure is reached.

Q: What if an application terminates while a background thread is running?

A: Background threads are destroyed when the application ends. You should be careful to determine if a thread with an IsBackground property value of True also has an IsAlive property value of True before exiting the application. As an alternative, you can simply use the Thread.Priority property to set the thread to a lower priority than the default of Normal.

Synchronization

When multiple threads access the same data, access to that data must be synchronized to ensure consistent results. Lack of synchronization in conjunction with multithreaded applications can produce errors that are very difficult to track down.

Using SyncLock for Synchronized Access to Fields

One method of providing synchronized access to shared fields is the SyncLock statement, which guarantees that multiple threads don't modify data on an object at the same time. When a thread encounters a SyncLock statement, it waits until it has a lock on the object that is returned by the expression in the SyncLock block. The single required parameter for the SyncLock statement must be a reference type. That reference type must not be null (Nothing) and must represent a shared variable. Locks acquired using SyncLock block are released when the SyncLock block ends.

When a SyncLock...End SyncLock statement is entered, the shared method System.Monitor.Enter is called on the object instance provided in the SyncLock statement. System.Monitor.Enter blocks execution of code until the thread has an exclusive lock on the object. Using a SyncLock block is an easier-to-use implementation of the Monitor class, but it offers less flexibility than manually working with Monitor.

Avoiding Collisions by Using ThreadStatic

Synchronization of threads isn't the only way to avoid collisions resulting in inconsistent data. Suppose you wanted to create a variable in a class but wanted each thread to store its own, unshared value for that variable when referencing the same instance of that class. The ThreadStatic attribute can be applied to such a variable. In the following example, MyClass1 has two members. The first member is declared using the ThreadStatic attribute, causing each thread that accesses objects of this type to store its own value for this field. The second field, SharedData, is a normal field and is shared by all threads on a particular instance of MyClass1.

```
Public Class MyClass1
   <ThreadStatic()> Public threadUniqueID As Integer
   Public SharedData As Integer = 0
End Class
```

When the following method is executed, the current thread will write to both fields in an instance of MyClass1. Because the first field is declared using the ThreadStatic attribute, only the current thread's copy is affected. Because all threads share access to the SharedData field (as long as those threads are using the same instance of MyClass1), they all see changes to that field.

```
Private Sub doSomething()
   Dim i As Integer
   For i = 1 To 3
      obj.threadUniqueID = AppDomain.GetCurrentThreadId()
      obj.SharedData = I 'not thread safe
      Debug.WriteLine("ID: " & obj.threadUniqueID & ", I:=" & _
      i & ", SharedData: " & obj.SharedData.ToString())
      Thread.CurrentThread.Sleep(250) 'pause
   Next
End Sub
```

Using the following code to test doSomething() produces the results shown in Figure 12.6. The figure shows clearly that each thread is using a unique value for threadUniqueID, but they share values given to the variable, SharedData. In this example, access to SharedData is not thread-safe. It just happens that the threads are not providing conflicting data for that value.

ThreadStatic cannot be used on local, static variables.

```
Dim obj As New MyClass1()
Private Sub btnStart_Click(ByVal sender As System.Object, ByVal e As
System.EventArgs) Handles btnStart.Click
   Dim thread1 As New Thread(AddressOf doSomething)
   Dim thread2 As New Thread(AddressOf doSomething)
   Dim thread3 As New Thread(AddressOf doSomething)
   thread1.Start()
   thread2.Start()
   thread3.Start()
End Sub
```

```
Output
Debug
'Threading3.exe': Loaded 'c:\winnt\assembly\gac\system.window
'Threading3.exe': Loaded 'c:\winnt\assembly\gac\system\1.0.33
'Threading3.exe': Loaded 'c:\winnt\assembly\gac\system.drawin
'Threading3.exe': Loaded 'c:\winnt\assembly\gac\accessibility
'Threading3.exe': Loaded 'c:\winnt\assembly\gac\microsoft.vis
'Threading3.exe': Loaded 'c:\winnt\assembly\gac\system.xml\1.
ID: 1404, I:=1, SharedData: 1
ID: 1816, I:=1, SharedData: 1
ID: 1616, I:=1, SharedData: 1
ID: 1404, I:=2, SharedData: 2
ID: 1816, I:=2, SharedData: 2
ID: 1616, I:=2, SharedData: 2
ID: 1404, I:=3, SharedData: 3
ID: 1816, I:=3, SharedData: 3
ID: 1616, I:=3, SharedData: 3
The thread '<No Name>' (0x57c) has exited with code 0 (0x0).
The thread '<No Name>' (0x718) has exited with code 0 (0x0).
The thread '<No Name>' (0x650) has exited with code 0 (0x0).
```

Figure 12.6 Each executing thread has a unique ID, obtainable by AppDomain .GetCurrentThreadId().

Synchronizing Entire Objects

For rare cases when it might be required, synchronized access to entire objects can be provided easily by adding the Synchronization attribute to the class declaration. The one requirement for such a class is that it must inherit from ContextBoundObject. Marking a class with the Synchronized attribute provides synchronized access only to all instance members. The following is an example of how a class can support this type of synchronization:

```
<System.Runtime.Remoting.Contexts.Synchronization()> _
Class MyClass1
    Inherits ContextBoundObject
    Public data as String 'I am thread safe
    Public Sub someTask1()
        'I am thread safe
    End Sub
    Public Shared Sub someTask2()
        'I am NOT thread safe
    End Sub
End Class
```

Marking a class with the Synchronization attribute does not provide synchronized access to shared members.

Marking Individual Methods for Synchronized Access

So far, we have seen SyncLock, which put the onus of synchronized access to a single method on the caller, and the Synchronization attribute, which marks an entire class so that only one thread can access instance members at a time. Individual methods within a class that should always be synchronized can be marked with the System.Runtime.CompilerServices.MethodImpl attribute. There are several options for using the MethodImpl attribute, specified by setting the attributes MethodImplOptions parameter. Setting MethodImplOptions.Synchronized in the following example ensures that only one thread at a time may execute the method *someTask1*. Figure 12.7 shows how the corresponding code is marked as IL.

```
Imports System.Runtime.CompilerServices
Public Class MyClass1
    <MethodImpl(MethodImplOptions.Synchronized)> _
    Public Sub someTask1()
        Debug.WriteLine("Task1...")
    End Sub
End Class
```

Using the Monitor Class for Synchronization

Although SyncLock is a syntactical wrapper for the basic functionality of Monitor, direct use of the Monitor Class is often required. We can use the Monitor class to control access to objects by granting a thread an exclusive lock for the object. Using the SyncLock block, it is impossible for a thread to test a SyncLock block and avoid becoming blocked. The TryEnter shared method of the Monitor class will attempt to acquire a lock and will not become blocked if an object is already locked. Control of objects using the Monitor class is maintained by using the shared methods of the Monitor class, as shown in Table 12.3.

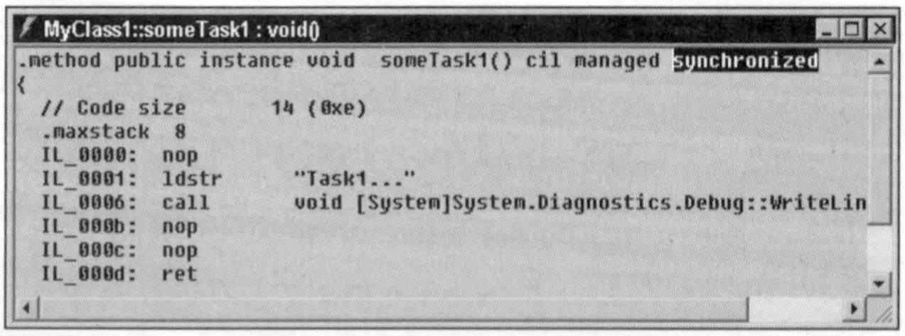

```
MyClass1::someTask1 : void()
.method public instance void  someTask1() cil managed synchronized
{
  // Code size       14 (0xe)
  .maxstack  8
  IL_0000:  nop
  IL_0001:  ldstr      "Task1..."
  IL_0006:  call       void [System]System.Diagnostics.Debug::WriteLin
  IL_000b:  nop
  IL_000c:  nop
  IL_000d:  ret
```

Figure 12.7 Methods marked with MethodImplOption.Synchronized simply acquire a Synchronized tag in IL.

Table 12.3 Monitor Class Members

MEMBER	DESCRIPTION
Enter, TryEnter	Acquires the object lock and represents the start of the critical section of code.
Wait	Temporarily releases the locked object so that another thread can obtain a lock.
Pulse, PulseAll	Sends a message to one or more waiting threads, indicating that the state of the locked object has changed and that the owner of the lock is ready to release the lock.
Exit	Releases the lock on an object and represents the end of a critical section of code.

Synchronized Access to Managed Objects

Many objects in .NET aren't naturally thread-safe and provide a shared method, Synchronized, that produces a thread-safe version of an object. An example of such objects is the member of System.Collections and System.IO. The following code demonstrates how a System.Collections.Stack object can be made thread-safe. Objects that expose a Synchronized method also have an IsSynchronized property to determine if an instance is synchronized. This example produces the results shown in Figure 12.8.

```
Private Sub btnStart_Click(ByVal sender As System.Object, _
ByVal e As System.EventArgs) Handles btnStart.Click
'Imports System.Collections
   Dim S1 As New Stack()
   Dim SyncS1 As Stack = Stack.Synchronized(S1)
   MessageBox.Show("SyncS1: " & _
   SyncS1.IsSynchronized.ToString() & _
   ControlChars.NewLine & "S1: " & _
   S1.IsSynchronized.ToString(), _
   "Synchronized?...", MessageBoxButtons.OK, _
   MessageBoxIcon.Information)
End Sub
```

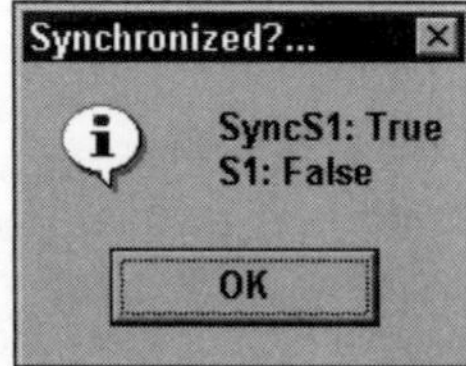

Figure 12.8 The IsSynchronized attribute of an object should return True when using a version of that object returned from its Synchronized method.

Lab 12.2: Using SyncLock for Synchronization

This lab demonstrates the need for synchronization of access to data in a multithreaded application. In addition, it illustrates how to enforce such synchronization using a SyncLock statement.

Perform the following steps:

1. Start a new Visual Basic .NET Windows application.
2. Add an Imports Statement to the top of Form1 for the System.Threading namespace.
3. Create a simple class with a shared field. For the purposes of this lab, place the declaration above the declaration for Form1, although I prefer to place classes in separate files, if not in class libraries. The following class is all that is necessary for this lab:

   ```
   Public Class someClass
      Public someData As Integer
   End Class
   ```

4. Provide the following declaration/instantiation as a member of Form1.

   ```
   Dim obj As New someClass()
   ```

5. Add two TextBox controls to Form1. No properties need to be changed for these controls.
6. Add a Button control named btnStart to Form1.
7. Create two methods named method1 and method2 using the following code that will contend for access to the field, someData on the same instance of the class, someClass:

   ```
   Private Sub method1()
      Dim i As Integer
      For i = 0 To 20
         obj.someData += i
         TextBox1.Text = obj.someData
      Next
   End Sub
   Private Sub method2()
      Dim i As Integer
      For i = 0 To 20
         obj.someData += i
         TextBox2.Text = obj.someData
      Next
   End Sub
   ```

8. Add the following code to the btnStart_Click event handler:

```
Private Sub btnStart_Click(...)...
   method1()
   method2()
End Sub
```

Running the application right now should display the value of 210 in TextBox1 and 420 in TextBox2. They are the expected, verifiable results. In the next step, you will spawn the two methods from threads and let them access the variable, someData, without synchronization. This unsynchronization will not only produce inconsistent results, but it may very well produce results that vary from one execution to another. For now, just modify the code to use threads.

9. Run the application to verify that textBox1 and textBox2 always end up with 210 and 420, respectively.

10. Modify the btnStart_Click event handler to use threads for calling method1 and method2 using the following code:

```
Private Sub btnStart_Click(...) ...
   'Imports System.Threading
   Dim thread1 As New Thread(AddressOf method1)
   Dim thread2 As New Thread(AddressOf method2)
   thread1.Start()
   thread2.Start()
End Sub
```

11. Run, test, and stop the application several times. Each time you click btnStart, note the values displayed in the text boxes. Be sure you stop the application between subsequent tests. The results can be highly confusing at best and certainly nowhere close to consistent. Figure 12.9 shows how inconsistent subsequent tests results were for this unsynchronized access to the variable, someData.

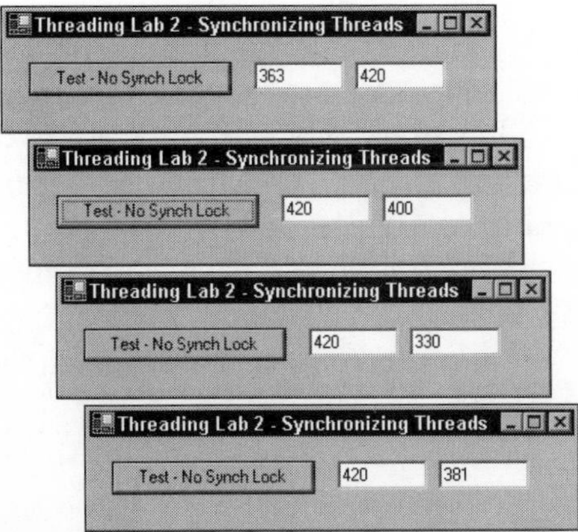

Figure 12.9 Unsynchronized threads can play havoc on shared data and can produce very unpredictable results.

12. Wow, that was ugly! Let's synchronize the variable's access from these two methods, using SyncLock. Wrap the entire contents of method1 and method2 in SyncLock blocks as shown here:

```
Private Sub method1()
    SyncLock (obj)
      '...same code as before
    End SyncLock
    End Sub
Private Sub method2()
    SyncLock (obj)
      '...same code as before
    End SyncLock
End Sub
```

13. Run the application. Testing now should provide consistent results.

Although the example is simple, the need for synchronization should be clear now. Also, you should feel comfortable using the SyncLock block to provide synchronized access to data. The examples will become increasingly more involved as we explore more issues related to multithreaded applications.

Advanced Threading

A large number of classes have been added to .NET to provide a wide array of application and flexibility. Understanding the purpose and unique features of these classes is crucial to efficiently architecting multithreaded applications in an enterprise environment.

The ThreadPool Class

The System.Threading.ThreadPool class provides a collection (a pool) of threads that can be used to perform tasks. The .NET Framework uses thread pools for many tasks such as socket connections, asynchronous I/O, and timers. Having too many threads can seriously degrade performance. Because threads spend much of their time sleeping or simply polling for resources, using threads from the thread pool can be more efficient. Each thread in the thread pool uses the default priority and stack size.

As you might expect, the Thread Pool is not a class you can instantiate. ThreadPool follows a Singleton design pattern, implementing a private constructor and nothing but shared members. Table 12.4 describes the members of the ThreadPool class.

Table 12.4 ThreadPool Members

MEMBER	DESCRIPTION
BindHandle	Takes an IntPtr argument, represents an operating system handle to be bound to the thread pool.
GetAvailableThreads	Takes two integer arguments that are given values inside this method to represent the number of available worker threads and the number of available asynchronous I/O threads.
GetMaxThreads	Takes two integer arguments that are given values inside this method to represent the maximum number of available worker threads and the number of available asynchronous I/O threads. The maximum value for either of these is currently 25.
QueueUserWorkItem	Two overloads. Allows you to use a thread from the thread pool. QueueUserWorkItem queues a user work item to the thread pool, invokes a delegate (supplied in the call), and specifies an object to be passed to the delegate.
RegisterWaitForSingleObject	Four overloads. Registers a delegate that is waiting for a WaitHandle. A WaitHandle wraps OS-specific objects that wait for exclusive access to shared resources.
UnsafeQueueUserWorkItem	An unsafe version of QueueUserWorkItem. Both methods queue a work item to the thread pool, but this version doesn't propagate the calling stack onto the worker thread as does the safe version. Using this version allows code to lose the calling stack, resulting in elevated security privileges.
UnsafeRegisterWaitForSingleObject	Five overloads. Queues a delegate to the thread pool. This is an unsafe version of RegisterWaitForSingleObject.

Borrowing Threads from the Thread Pool

You can obtain a thread from the thread pool by using the QueueUserWorkItem method. To call this method you must pass in a WaitCallBack delegate that points to a procedure that accepts a single Object argument. For quick tasks that don't run the risk of blocking other tasks, obtaining a thread from the thread pool is usually the way to go (see the section *Threading Tips* in this chapter).

The following class contains a method used as a WaitCallBack delegate. For the sake of simplification and space constraints, Option Strict is off.

```
Imports System.Threading
Imports System.Diagnostics
Public Class SomeJob
   Dim availWorker As Integer = 0 : Dim maxWorker As Integer = 0
   Dim availCPT As Integer = 0 : Dim maxCPT As Integer = 0
   Public Sub someTask(ByVal ThreadStateData As Object)
      Debug.WriteLine("Performing Task. Data Passed: " & _
ThreadStateData)
      ThreadPool.GetAvailableThreads(availWorker, availCPT)
      ThreadPool.GetMaxThreads(maxWorker, maxCPT)
      Debug.WriteLine("--Available Worker Threads: " & availWorker)
      Debug.WriteLine("--Maximum Worker Threads: " & maxWorker)
      Debug.WriteLine("--Available Completion Port Threads: " & _
availCPT)
      Debug.WriteLine("--Maximum Completion Port Threads: " & maxCPT)
   End Sub
End Class
```

Now, the next step is to borrow a thread from the thread pool and pass the someTask method as the delegate.

```
Private Sub btnStart_Click(ByVal sender As System.Object, _
ByVal e As System.EventArgs) Handles btnStart.Click
   Dim msg As String : Dim i As Integer
   Dim job As New SomeJob()
   For i = 1 To 5
      'Obtain a thread from the thread pool:
     ThreadPool.QueueUserWorkItem(New WaitCallback(AddressOf _
        job.someTask), i)
   Next
   Thread.Sleep(1000)  'making sure threads complete before exiting
End Sub
```

Because this task is so simple, the threads start and complete almost immediately, as you can see from the output produced by this code (see Figure 12.10).

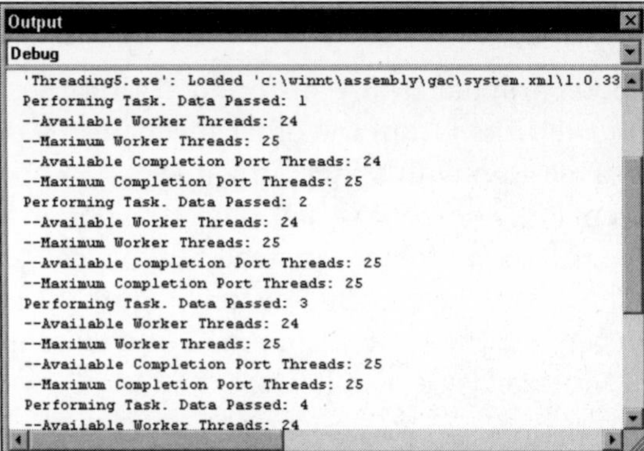

Figure 12.10. The ThreadPool object contains a pool of 25 threads that can be used via the QueueUserWorkItem method.

The Interlocked Class

The Interlocked class is used to provide atomic operations for variables that are shared by multiple threads. Errors can occur when the scheduler switches context while a thread is updating a variable. The methods of the Interlocked class prevent such errors. As with SyncLock and Monitor, the Interlocked members allow you to syntactically surround critical sections of code. One major difference with the Interlocked class is that it can allow more than one thread access to the critical section. The Increment and Decrement members can be used to keep track of the number of locks on a critical section of code, as shown in the following example:

```
Const maxLocks = 1
Private Sub Button1_Click(ByVal sender As System.Object, _
ByVal e As System.EventArgs) Handles Button1.Click
Dim locks As Integer
   If System.Threading.Interlocked.Increment(locks) <= maxLocks  Then
   'only enter if there were no locks (as long as maxLocks is 1
   '
   'Critical Section
   '
   '
End If
System.Threading.Interlocked.Decrement(locks)
End Sub
```

The Mutex Class

The Mutex class also provides methods to syntactically surround a critical section of code for synchronization, but it differs from the other mechanisms in that it can attempt to enter the critical section with a timeout value.

The WaitOne method, which accepts this timeout value, is used to obtain a lock and enter a critical section. The call to WaitOne is matched with a call to ReleaseMutex to release the lock and exit the critical section. Figure 12.11 depicts the operation associated with using the WaitOne method of obtaining a lock. The basic syntax for using a Mutex class is as follows:

```
Dim mutex1 As New Mutex()
Private Sub btnDoWork(ByVal sender As System.Object, _
ByVal e As System.EventArgs) Handles Button1.Click
   'Passing in False causes the method
   'return when a lock is acquired or when
   'the specified number of milliseconds
   'has elapsed
   If (mutex1.WaitOne(200, False)) Then
   '
   'Critical section
   '
    mutex1.ReleaseMutex()
   End If
End Sub
```

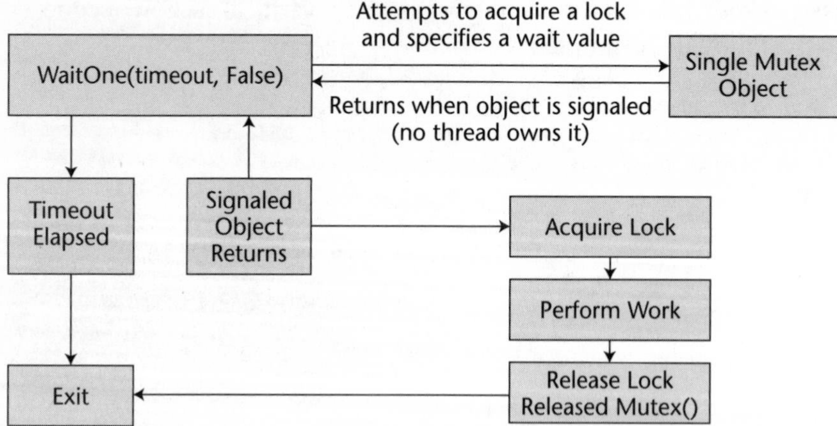

Figure 12.11 The WaitOne method of the Mutex object will return when a lock or the timeout value has elapsed and no lock was acquired.

Additional methods of WaitAll and WaitAny exist for the Mutex object to provide much broader application. The WaitAll method accepts an array of Mutex objects and returns when they have all signaled. A thread is in a *signaled* state when no thread owns it. WaitAll is perfect for situations when you need ensure that all threads have completed their tasks before proceeding.

WaitAny is very useful, but for completely different scenarios. Suppose you have a pool of limited resources that are heavily used and you want to reuse one of those resources the moment it becomes available. The WaitAny method is perfect for handling that type of situation. Like the WaitAll method, WaitAny accepts an array of Mutex objects, but its return value is the array index of a signaled (available) Mutex object. Once WaitAny returns, the newly freed object can be reused.

Threading Tips

Threading is the poster child for the statement, "A little knowledge can do a lot of damage." No single chapter on threading can prepare you for everything you might face when applying threading to client-server applications. The following list should guide you toward a solution in most cases:

- Avoid locks whenever possible.
- Never provide static methods that alter static state.
- Know when and when not to use ThreadPool. The ThreadPool class is a simple way to handle multiple threads for relatively short tasks that won't block other threads. You should not use a thread pool when any of the following are true:
  - You need to create a thread in an STA and all threads from the thread pool are in an MTA.
  - If you need to assign a thread priority.
  - If a thread will run long enough to risk blocking other tasks.
  - If you require a thread to have a static identity (threads in the thread pool don't have a stable identity).
- Static state must be made thread-safe.
- Look for ways to avoid the need for synchronization before simply using it.
- Asynchronous delegates are a preferred method for threading.
- Be aware of the differences between using SyncLock and the Interlocked class.

- By default, classes in .NET are not thread-safe. If you need a thread-safe version of a class, use GetSynchronized to obtain a synchronized version of the class.
- Avoid method calls within locked sections of code to prevent the possibility of deadlocks.
- Remember that SyncLock is only one way of providing locks and that the Monitor, Interlocked, and Mutex classes offer varying degrees of flexibility that will help you prevent starvation of threads.

Summary

In this chapter, we covered many topics related to multithreaded applications. As you build multithreaded applications in Visual Basic .NET, the many classes, objects, and attributes related to threading can seem to be a rather daunting collection. Remember, multithreaded applications only provide solutions when you create only as many threads as you need and maintain a careful watch over the tasks those threads are performing. The overuse of threads can have a dramatically negative effect on performance and unsynchronized threads can produce frightening logic errors. The Visual Basic .NET built in the walkthroughs, "Walkthrough: Multithreading" and "Walkthrough: Authoring a Simple Multithreaded Component in Visual Basic," are useful to extend and reinforce your understanding of multithreaded applications.

Review Questions

1. Which one of the following is true?
   a. Running applications are referred to as threads.
   b. Threads can be broken down into AppDomains.
   c. Running applications are referred to as processes and can contain one or more threads.
   d. Processor time is allocated for threads.
2. What is thread affinity?
3. You can tell that a Thread object is active by using which one of the following properties?
   a. IsActive
   b. IsAlive
   c. IsCurrent
   d. IsExecuting
4. What are the assignable priorities for threads?
   a. 1, 2, 3, and 4
   b. Lowest, BelowNormal, Normal, AboveNormal, and Highest
   c. Low, Normal, and High
   d. Lowest, Normal, and Highest
5. How can you pause a thread for 2 seconds?
   a. Thread.Sleep(2)
   b. Thread.Pause(2000)
   c. Thread.Pause(2)
   d. Thread.Sleep(2000)
6. How can you obtain the ID of a thread (select one or more of the following)?
   a. The Thread.ID property
   b. AppDomain.GetCurrentThreadID
   c. Use the Threads window
   d. You can't

7. Using the CLRLocksAndThreads object, what does a high Contention Rate/Sec probably indicate?
   a. You should hire a consultant.
   b. Threads are interacting normally.
   c. The application probably isn't suitable for multiple applications.
   d. You should implement more locking.
8. When should you use a thread from the ThreadPool Class?
   a. When you need a thread in a single-threaded apartment.
   b. When the thread's task is very short.
   c. When you need to acquire a thread's identity.
   d. When you need to assign a thread a priority.
9. What does the ThreadStatic attribute do?
   a. Marks a class field in such a way that each thread will have its own value for that field.
   b. Marks a class field in such a way that each thread will share values for that field.
   c. Marks a class constructor in such a way that each thread will have its own version.
   d. Marks an entire class for exclusive use by a single thread.
10. What does the Synchronization attribute do?
    a. Marks a method as single-threaded.
    b. Marks a class field for exclusive use by a single thread.
    c. Marks a class in such a way that all of its members are usable by only one thread at a time.
    d. Marks a class in such a way that all of its instance members are usable by only one thread at a time.
11. When would you use WaitAll with a Mutex object?
    a. When you need to monitor a single thread's access to an object.
    b. When you must wait until multiple threads complete their tasks before continuing.
    c. When you want to immediately reuse an object as it enters a signaled state.
    d. WaitAll is not a valid method of the Mutex class.
12. When would you use WaitAny with a Mutex object?
    a. When you need to monitor a single thread's access to an object.
    b. When you must wait until multiple threads complete their tasks before continuing.
    c. When you want to immediately reuse an object as it enters a signaled state.
    d. WaitAny is not a valid method of the Mutex class.

Answers to Review Questions

1. **d.** Running applications are referred to as processes. Processes are broken down into AppDomains. Threads are the individual units of execution that are allocated time from the operating system. All processes have at least one thread.
2. Thread Affinity is a restriction where an object is usable only by the thread that created that object. Although that is not the case with normal objects in .NET, controls created by one thread cannot be passed to another thread. For a dynamic control to be added to the current form, the control must be created by the same thread in which Me (the current form) is running.
3. **b.** The IsAlive property for a thread can be used to determine if a thread is active. The other choices are fictitious.
4. **b.** The assignable priorities for threads are Lowest, BelowNormal, Normal, AboveNormal, and Highest.
5. **d.** Thread.Sleep(2000) pauses a thread for 2 seconds.
6. **b** and **c.** Although the Thread object doesn't expose an ID property, the ID for a thread can be obtained by using Appdomain.GetCurrentThreadID or by viewing the thread in the Threads window.
7. **c.** A high Contention Rate/Sec means that threads are constantly contending for the same resources.
8. **b.** You should use a thread from the ThreadPool Class only when the thread is expected to perform a short task, you don't need a STA thread, you don't require a stable thread identity, and the default thread stack size and priority are acceptable. Threads from a thread pool do not have stable IDs, are always MTA threads, and can have only the default priority and stack size.
9. **a.** The ThreadStatic attribute can be used to mark a class field so that each thread has its own value for that field.
10. **d.** The Synchronization attribute marks a class so that all its instance members are usable by only one thread at a time.
11. **b.** You should use Mutex.WaitAll when you must wait until multiple threads complete their tasks before continuing.
12. **c.** You should use WaitAny with a Mutex object when you want to immediately reuse an object as it enters a signaled state.

Web Technologies in .NET

CHAPTER 13

ASP.NET

As part of the .NET initiative, Microsoft has glued ".NET" onto the end of many of its technologies, such as Visual Studio .NET, Visual Basic .NET, and ADO.NET. ASP is no exception, and now it also sports the new suffix. Is it more than just a name change? Are the decimal point and three letters more than just a marketing scheme?

ASP, in acquiring its .NET badge, has undergone one of the most striking and beneficial changes of the Microsoft technologies. Productivity, performance, and capability have all been vastly improved. Even the programming model is significantly different. In this chapter and those that follow, we'll take a look at what's changed and how ASP.NET can make your Web development dreams come true.

What's the Big Deal?

When ASP arrived on the scene, it was rather revolutionary. It allowed you to build server-side Web functionality much more easily than current alternatives, such as CGI scripting. However, it had some drawbacks, most notably that it used Visual Basic Script as a programming language. It was interpreted at runtime instead of being compiled, so it ran fairly slowly. It was also a limited subset of the Visual Basic language, and Visual Basic programmers frequently ran into walls thrown up by the language's shortcomings.

So how has the playing field improved with ASP.NET? There are numerous benefits and changes, such as the following:

ASP.NET is compiled. Unlike ASP, the Visual Basic code you write is compiled ahead of time and placed on the server. It runs at least 4 times faster than Visual Basic Script code. Compiled code is also stored on the server in a memory cache after it's been loaded, improving performance.

ASP.NET is true Visual Basic. Although Visual Basic Script is a subset of the Visual Basic language, ASP.NET provides access to almost the entire Visual Basic language.

ASP.NET separates code from content. All your server-side code is compiled into class modules that are referenced by your ASP.NET page. This allows you to modify and recompile the code without affecting the page itself.

ASP.NET supports multiple browsers. ASP.NET renders code for your client based on the actual browser in use by the client. This saves time by eliminating large chunks of code you have to write that distinguishes between browsers and executes differently depending on which browser is in use.

ASP.NET has an event model. The older ASP really had no event model, and you had no control over when events would fire or in what order. ASP.NET provides a consistent event model that fires specific events in a specific order that you can rely on.

ASP.NET events run on the server. Events that fire on your page, such as a button click, get propagated to the server. Your compiled code can then respond to events, sending results back to the client.

ASP.NET deployment is simple. Setting up or redeploying your Web application is simple. XCOPY all your new files to the server and you're done, even while your site is live. IIS will finish up what it's doing, handle all pending requests, and then incorporate your new code.

These are huge advances in the world of Visual Basic and Web programming. Taken together, they yield fundamental changes in the way you build Web applications with Visual Basic.

Building ASP.NET Applications

If you are primarily a Visual Basic programmer and have not used ASP much, building ASP.NET applications should be fairly easy for you. This is because building Web applications with ASP.NET is now more like building Visual Basic applications than not. You'll follow familiar development patterns, such as dropping controls on forms (pages), wiring up event code, and writing classes that contain supporting functionality.

The process for building ASP.NET applications looks something like this:

1. Lay out your page content using the HTML Editor or Page Designer.
2. Add controls to the page, setting properties as required.
3. Add event-handling code in the associated class module.
4. Add supporting code into the associated class module or additional class modules.
5. Compile, run, and debug your application just like you would a Visual Basic application.
6. Marvel at how much easier this is compared to ASP.

Sound familiar? Sometimes the only visible difference is that your application is fired up in a browser window instead of its own window.

When building ASP.NET applications, the editing environment in Visual Studio is mostly the same as it is for normal Visual Basic applications. However, there are some differences.

When you start a new Web application, you normally begin by creating a new project. The project type, however, is ASP.NET Web Application. When you enter a location, it refers to a directory on your Web server.

The editing environment is a little different, too. The form (or page) design and layout area starts out like a large grid. By default, it starts in Grid Layout mode. This means that when you drop controls on a page, they stay exactly where you put them. Your control positions will be translated to HTML-absolute coordinates. This results in a layout exactly like working with WinForms. You can, however, switch to Flow Layout mode. This is more like traditional HTML, where control and content positioning are controlled by the browser, using tables and HTML rules. Select whichever works best for you. Figure 13.1 illustrates what the editor looks like in Grid Layout mode.

There's one other change that's important if you are using the Design tab. Take a look at the list of controls in the Toolbox. They look very similar to those you're used to when building regular Windows applications; however, these are WebForms controls. They mirror many of the standard controls, but provide Web-based versions of them. You'll become familiar with them later.

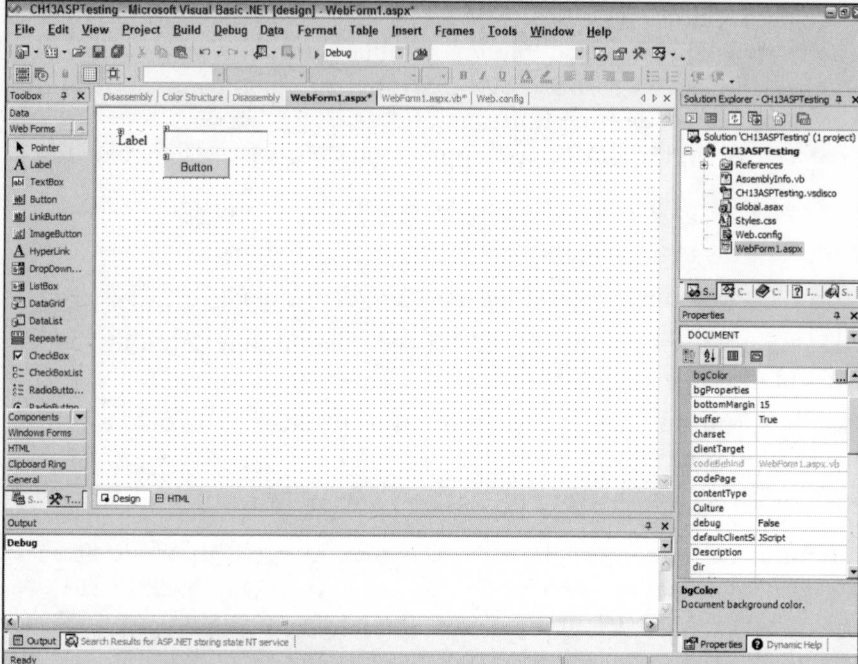

Figure 13.1 Grid Layout mode.

Note the two tabs at the bottom of the editing window, labeled Design and HTML. The design page is what we've been talking about. It allows you to drag and drop controls and other content. The HTML tab provides a view of the same page, but in its corresponding HTML format. The HTML tab will be more familiar to ASP programmers who have worked with Visual InterDev.

The Design tab is useful for fast layout or when you're still getting the hang of the new ASP.NET tags and capabilities. However, most of the programmers I've worked with have switched fairly quickly to exclusive use of the HTML tab. They prefer the code-oriented work environment and their own code formatting. If you use the designer, even after you've entered all your own code in the HTML tab, the environment will reformat your code to its own liking. Figure 13.2 shows the HTML editor.

If you accidentally switch to the Design tab after entering and formatting your own HTML code, the editor will reformat it for you in its own image. If this is not what you want, you still have one chance to get your own style back. As soon as you switch back to the HTML tab, select Edit, Undo (or press Ctrl-Z). If you haven't done any edits since you switched back from the design tab, it will undo the reformatting it thought you might like.

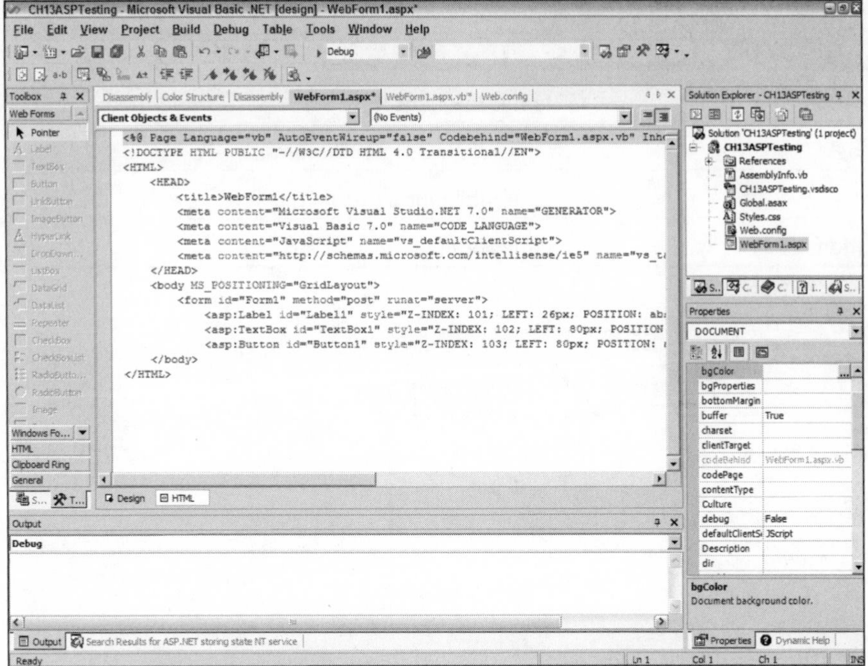

Figure 13.2 The HTML editor.

Lab 13.1: Our First ASP.NET Application

This lab jumps right in to get a sense of what it's like to write an ASP.NET application by building a sample, single-page application that calculates the volume of a sphere.

Perform the following steps to get started:

1. Start a new ASP.NET Web application by selecting File, New, Project from the Visual Studio .NET menu and name it whatever you like.
2. Drag four labels, one text box, and a button onto the page. Create and set up the controls for this form as shown in Table 13.1. The general layout of the controls is illustrated in Figure 13.3.

Table 13.1 Controls and Their Settings

CONTROLS	SETTINGS
Label	Name=Label1, Font=Arial Black 16 pt (or similar), Text="Sphere Volume"
Label	Name=Label2, Text="Radius:"

(continued)

Table 13.1 *(continued)*

CONTROLS	SETTINGS
TextBox	Name=tbRadius
Label	Name=Label3, Text="Volume:"
Label	Name=lblVolume, Text="0.0"
Button	Name=btnCalc, Text="Calculate"

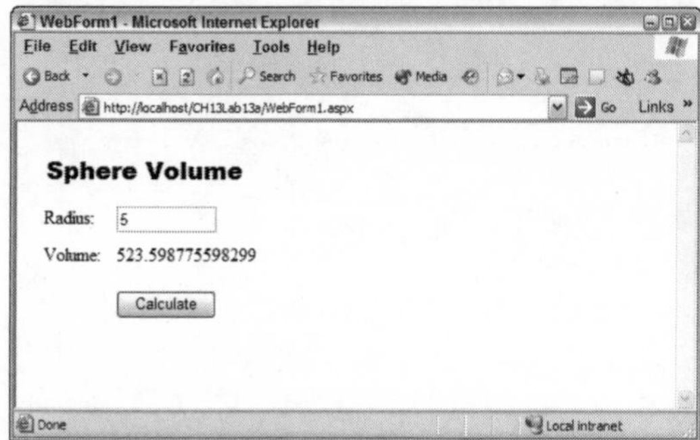

Figure 13.3 Lab 13.1 running in the browser.

3. Double-click the Calculate button to bring up the code window. Enter the following code:

```
Private Const PI As Double = 3.1415926535897931
Private Sub btnCalc_Click(ByVal sender As System.Object, _
     ByVal e As System.EventArgs) Handles btnCalc.Click
     Dim r As Double
     Try
          r = CDbl(tbRadius.Text)
          If r <= 0.0 Then
               lblVolume.Text = "0.0"
          Else
               lblVolume.Text = _
                    CStr((4.0 / 3.0) * PI * (r ^ 3))
          End If
     Catch ex As Exception
          lblVolume.Text = "Error"
     End Try
End Sub
```

4. Run the application. A browser should fire up with your application. Enter the number *5* for a radius and click the Calculate button. You should get a value in the neighborhood of 523.598. Refer to Figure 13.3 to see the program running with the correct result.

You just successfully built a Web application. Here are some of the things that happen when you execute the program:

1. The server processes our request for the page and renders a version of it that executes in our specific browser.
2. When we enter a value in the radius field and click the Calculate button, an event fires that is processed on the server.
3. The server matches up the event with its associated event handler, in this case, btnCalc_Click. This is located in a class module associated with the ASP.NET page.
4. The page is rendered again with the result and sent back to the client.

Server-Side HTML Generation and Execution

In Lab 13.1, you saw a small sample ASP.NET application running and behaving much like a standard Visual Basic program; however, the server played a major part in this activity. It completely handled the generation of the page that was sent to the user. It created the page using server-side HTML generation and server-based Web controls.

Code Generation

It really doesn't matter from the perspective of the server and the Web controls you use which browser a client is running. The ASP.NET renderer figures out which browser your client is using and generates code that will run correctly in that browser. If you've ever done any straight HTML or DHTML coding, you know that each browser has many differences that can drive you mad. These differences are known to the renderer and it accounts for them. It knows about more than just Internet Explorer and Netscape, too. With the addition of the Mobile Internet Toolkit, you can even target cell phones and personal digital assistants (PDAs).

Client-side code is still up to you. Any script code or manually created HTML (such as your own tables) still requires you to account for which browser is in use and create your code so that it works in any browsers you want to support. This alone may be a good reason to use the Web controls for as much of your content as you can.

Controls

The Web controls are at the heart of the server-side HTML generation. For IIS and ASP.NET to generate browser-independent code as well as code that can change at runtime, you need to use the Web controls for your content. This is because each server-based Web control is responsible for generating its own HTML-based representation.

Consider the following example: If you drop a calendar Web control on your form, it is rendered on the spot in a specific way (see Figure 13.4). However, its visual representation may change based on the browser in use. In fact, there are still text-based browsers out there, and the calendar would generate a textual representation of itself on that platform.

There's another good reason to use these controls. They are simple to reference in your code, like you would any Visual Basic control. If you use standard client-side elements in your page, they are more difficult to access and don't provide the same flexibility.

Using the Controls

Controls drop onto a page. But how do you get these controls onto your page if you're working in HTML mode? What does the syntax look like?

You'll find that once you learn the basic syntax for the controls you use most often, the HTML editor is faster than the designer. You won't need to learn all the syntax because the editor's IntelliSense is very good.

At the root of all server-side controls is one attribute, the runat=server tag. Each control has this attribute, indicating that it should execute on the server instead of in the browser. Consider Lab 13.1. Switch to the HTML tab and look at the code. Here's the HTML representation of one of the controls from that page:

```
<asp:TextBox id="tbRadius" style="Z-INDEX: 104; LEFT: 79px;
     POSITION: absolute; TOP: 52px" runat="server" Width="64px"
     Font-Names="Verdana" Font-Size="10pt"></asp:TextBox>
```

The first important item to note here is the runat=server attribute. This tells the server that the control should be run on the server and render HTML. The second important item is the beginning of the TextBox tag. All controls start with the ASP prefix, as in <ASP:TextBox>. Be sure both are in your tags.

There are several categories of Web controls. Each is slightly different and serves its own purpose. Let's explore each one.

Figure 13.4 The calendar Web control in design mode.

HTML Controls

HTML Web controls match up with standard HTML elements you are familiar with, such as <img>, <table>, and <button>. HTML Web controls generate single HTML elements and are fairly simple. A sample as it would look in your HTML goes something like this:

```
<asp:Image id="Image1" runat="server" Width="175px"
     Height="17px"></asp:Image>
```

You can also use standard HTML controls that are client-based instead of the server-side Web controls. They are located on a different tab in the Toolbox, under HTML instead of Web Forms. They generate standard HTML tags from the designer. Within the designer, you can set properties for these controls in the properties window, which will add standard HTML attributes to the tags.

Server Controls

The server controls are the meat and potatoes (or just potatoes for you vegetarians out there) of ASP.NET applications. They typically look just like standard Visual Basic controls when rendered on the page. You also get quite a variety of controls, including hyperlink buttons, a calendar control, radio buttons, check boxes, combo boxes, panels, labels, and an ad rotator, which automates the process of changing banner ads on a Web page. You even get a suite of server-side data bound controls, which we'll cover in Chapter 14, "Data Control and XML in Web Applications."

All these controls generate HTML on the server to be rendered on the client. They take into account all the properties you've laid out. When entering code for these controls manually, you may have many attributes and options available. Consider the Calendar control. Here is a listing of the HTML used to define a Calendar control on a page after specifying a few choice options and properties for it. Figure 13.5 illustrates the Calendar control that this code creates.

```
<asp:Calendar id="Calendar1" style="Z-INDEX: 101; LEFT: 27px; POSITION:
 absolute; TOP: 31px" runat="server" Width="200px" Height="180px"
 BackColor="White" DayNameFormat="FirstLetter" ForeColor="Black"
 Font-Size="8pt" Font-Names="Verdana" BorderColor="#999999"
 CellPadding="4">
     <TodayDayStyle ForeColor="Black"
          BackColor="#CCCCCC"></TodayDayStyle>
     <SelectorStyle BackColor="#CCCCCC"></SelectorStyle>
     <NextPrevStyle VerticalAlign="Bottom"></NextPrevStyle>
     <DayHeaderStyle Font-Size="7pt" Font-Bold="True"
          BackColor="#CCCCCC"></DayHeaderStyle>
     <SelectedDayStyle Font-Bold="True" ForeColor="White"
          BackColor="#666666"></SelectedDayStyle>
     <TitleStyle Font-Bold="True" BorderColor="Black"
          BackColor="#999999"></TitleStyle>
     <WeekendDayStyle BackColor="#FFFFCC"></WeekendDayStyle>
     <OtherMonthDayStyle ForeColor="#808080"></OtherMonthDayStyle>
</asp:Calendar>
```

Be sure you explore all the options for the Web controls. For example, if you right-click the Calendar control in the designer, there is an option called Auto Format, much like Microsoft Word's table AutoFormat feature. It will make your calendar look professional and clean with just a couple clicks. Other controls have similar features and many more properties than you might be used to. Get to know them to gain unparalleled flexibility.

Figure 13.5 The look of the Calendar control after specifying some formatting options.

User Controls

Have you ever used Visual Basic 6's user controls feature? It allows you to build composite controls. These are controls made up of other controls, with your own code and property settings. For example, you might need a control that accepts a user's address and validates it. You could build a user control with several labels, text fields, and properties to set or access the name and address data and your own code to validate the zip code. Once complete, you can use that control anywhere on your forms, as many times as you like.

You can build similar user controls in ASP.NET made of other Web controls, HTML elements, and your own code. This is a fabulous reuse mechanism and helps to encapsulate your UI functionality that needs to appear in multiple locations. You can even build your own server-side controls that render HTML on the client.

Keep these controls in mind. When you need UI reuse, you'll find it really fits the bill.

Validator Controls

Handling data validation in an ASP page is a pain in the chops, especially when the validation happens on the server. You have to pack all the user-entered data, ship it to the server with a form Post operation, and validate it there. The worst part is sending back results. If there is bad data, you have to indicate it on the page and send the page back with all the fields repopulated.

To your rescue come the new validator controls. They are designed to handle the most common types of validation, without the need to repopulate the page with previous values.

These controls work in conjunction with another control that contains the value you want to validate, such as a text box. You drop a validator control on the form. For this example, let's use the RequiredFieldValidator control, which ensures that a field has a value in it. There are two main properties for the validator control that need to be set. The ControlToValidate property gets set to the name of the control you want to validate. The ErrorMessage property gets set to the actual text of the message to display when the field is in error, and in our case, when it has no value. The controls are invisible when the page executes until an error is found.

When the form is submitted, such as an OK button being clicked, the validator controls on the page kick in. They perform their validations, and if a control is found to be in error, the validator control is made visible and displays itself as a label containing the text of the error message you set. The fields in the page retain their values (if any), and the user has a chance to make changes and click the OK button again. See Figure 13.6 for a simple example of the Required Field Validator in action.

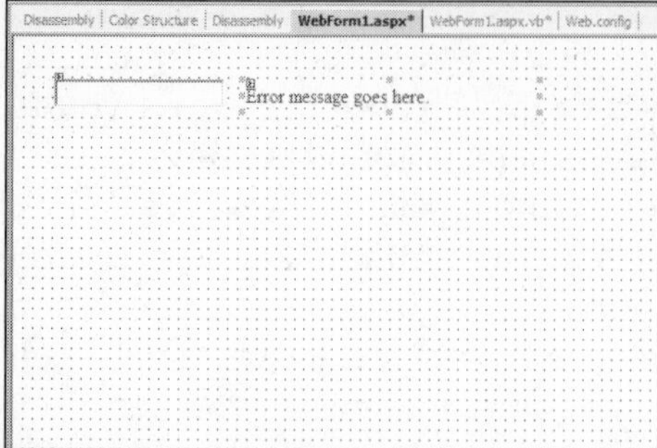

Figure 13.6 The Required Field validator control in action.

There are several types of validator controls, including the following:

Required Field. Makes sure a field has a value in it but makes no claims about the actual contents.

Compare. Validates the contents of one control against either the contents of another control or a constant value. You can perform several types of comparisons, such as equal to, less than, or less than or equal to. It can even perform a data type check.

Range. Makes sure that the value in an associated control falls within a preset range of valid values. The valid range is determined by setting the MaximumValue and MinimumValue properties. It works on multiple data types, including string and date.

Regular Expression. Checks the value of an associated control to see if it matches a pattern specified by a preset regular expression. You'll need to know about regular expression syntax to use this one.

Custom. Allows you to specify your own validation code for a control. You write code to handle the ServerValidate event for the validator control. This gives you great flexibility.

Events and Event Handling

If you've worked with ASP before, you're probably used to a system that handles all the work within a page on the client and then sends the entire page to the server. For example, if you have a form that accepts data from the user, you had a couple of options for validating it. If you required real-time validation as the user enters data in a field, you would probably perform that validation in client code to make it happen quickly. If you needed access to server functionality to perform your validations, you'd send it all at once to the server with a form post. And when it came to handling events on individual controls, you pretty much had to deal with those events on the client. There are exceptions, of course, but they require custom solutions and lots of work.

Enter the ASP.NET event system. It provides a mechanism to handle all kinds of events. The interesting part is that they are all handled on the server. Once there, the event is handled by the class associated with the page. So, if your user makes a selection in a combo box, the event is propagated to the server where your compiled code handles it, sending any results back to the client.

Sequence of Events

ASP pages handled events to some degree, but you could never be assured of the sequence or order of events. ASP.NET provides a specific sequence of events that always occur in the same order. This, combined with the fact that all events are handled on the server in compiled code, creates a robust event model that allows you to write Web applications that are consistent and reliable.

Every time a page is loaded, either initially or each time an event on the page is fired, the following sequence of events takes place on the server:

1. Client requests a particular ASPX page. This could be either through an initial request or through an event being fired.
2. The initial page image is created from the ASPX page on the server, or if available, it is loaded from the cache.
3. The page_load event is executed if one exists on the page.
4. Events that are included with the request are executed. This includes button click handlers, combo box selection change handlers, and any other event handlers connected to controls on the page.
5. Any data-binding events are executed. If you have any data binding on the page, code associated with it executes here.
6. The page_unload event is executed if you have defined it.
7. The final page for the client is rendered. This stage takes into account the client browser in use.
8. Return the final HTML to the client.

There are a couple of important points to take away from this list. There are page_load and page_unload events. The page_load event allows you to execute any initialization code for your page before it is rendered, including defaulting values into controls, setting up the page based on user preferences, retrieving information from a database that has to go onto the page, or any other useful activity. The page_unload event can do the opposite. Use it for any cleanup you might need to do.

The All-Important Postback

The most important thing we can see from the sequence of events is that every time an event is fired, the page is reloaded. This is a key point to keep in mind as you build your pages. You need to be able to detect the difference between an initial page load and a reload based on an event. Here's an example that illustrates why this is important.

You've built a page that allows the user to enter data of some sort. When the page loads, you initialize the fields on the page with values from a database that the user can modify. This is done in your page_load event handler. The user makes changes to the data, finally clicking the Submit button to save the changes. The click event on the button is handled on the server in your code. However, part of the sequence of events is the page_load event, which executes *before* the click event and events included with the page request. In your page_load event handler, of course, you have code to initialize all the fields to values from a database. Therefore, all the edits that the user made and sent back to you to be saved have just been overwritten again by the defaulting code, just before your event handler for the button click is executed. So default values are then written right back to the database.

What we need is a way to tell the difference between the first time the page is loaded and subsequent loads based on events. Subsequent loading of a page after the initial load is called a *postback*, and there is a way to tell the difference. In your page_load event, you can use a method called IsPostBack() to determine how a page is being loaded. Consider the following simple example:

```
Private Sub Page_Load(ByVal sender As System.Object, _
     ByVal e As System.EventArgs) Handles MyBase.Load
     If Not IsPostBack() Then
          ' Do your initialization code here.
     Else
          ' If you have any noninitialization code,
          ' do it here.
     End If
End Sub
```

The IsPostBack method (which belongs to the Page object) returns True if the page is being loaded as part of an event. It returns False if the page is undergoing its initial load. In our example, the code to load initial values into form fields would go into the following clause:

```
     If Not IsPostBack() Then
```

This prevents your edited values from being overwritten by the initialization code.

It is important to get into the habit of using the IsPostBack technique in all your applications. If you forget to use it, tracking down the problems it causes can be difficult.

Writing Event Handlers

Event handlers can be written much like those for standard Visual Basic applications. From the page designer, you can double-click any control and get its default event handler in the class module. More useful, however, is the ability to select the control and event from the code editor. This not only lets you choose the event you want to work with, but it also allows you to skip the use of the page designer.

The real trick with event handlers is getting them to connect with the controls they are associated with. Although we can select a control and event from the code editor, the editor itself needs to know about the control. If you add the control using the page designer, it's taken care of for you. If you are creating your page code from the HTML editor, you assign the control an ID attribute to assign it a name that the code editor can reference, like this:

```
<asp:Button ID="btnOK" Text="OK" Runat="server"></asp:Button>
```

The ID should be able to be referenced in the code editor, and when you pull down the control list, btnOK should be available. This normally works. However, there are times when it does not, and the control will not show up or be able to be referenced in the code editor.

To correct this problem, you need to tell the environment to refresh everything. You can use the designer to do this. Here is the procedure:

1. From your HTML editor pane, switch to the Designer pane using the tabs at the bottom of the window. This creates a visual representation of your page and, consequently, reformats all your code.
2. Click the HTML tab to switch back to the editor. Your code formatting will be changed, so select Edit, Undo from the menu to undo all the changes it did for you.
3. Press F7 to switch back to the code editor. At this point, any controls you created in the HTML editor should be known to the code editor.

Classroom Q & A

Q: Why should we even mess with HTML user controls? Do ASP server-side includes still exist? Aren't they good enough?

A: ASP server-side includes still exist and work like they used to; however, an ASP page can have only a single server-side include.

You can place as many HTML user controls on a page as you like, even multiple instances of the same control. They are a more flexible reuse mechanism than server-side includes.

Q: Can I still use client-side script code? You know, Dynamic HTML? Are JavaScript and VBScript still supported?

A: Absolutely. Most of ASP.NET's changes are on the server side. Client-side code can still be used for real-time processing that does not require the use of any resources on the server. All that code is still handled by the browser, so the same scripting languages and syntax are available. However, all the event handling is up to you.

Q: Aren't all these trips to the server to handle events expensive? We always try to avoid round-trips to maximize performance.

A: It's a matter of balance and environment. Use the server-side event handling when you need it. In addition, if your application will be hosted in a high-speed environment, more event round-trips will not hurt. Slower Internet speeds may demand fewer event-handling trips. We have not noticed any significant problems with turnaround time from events, even with 56K connections. Still, it pays to be frugal with round-trips.

Building Your Classes and Pages

We've already mentioned that the code you write to handle ASP.NET events is compiled and located on the server. However, the page runs in a browser on the client. How are they associated with each other? Take a look at the top of the main ASPX page when you create a new project. It looks something like this:

```
<%@ Page Language="vb" AutoEventWireup="false"
Codebehind="WebForm1.aspx.vb" Inherits="Project.WebForm1"%>
```

The Codebehind attribute indicates the code module that is linked to the page. This is set up by the Visual Studio environment when the project is created. The name used here is based on the default WebForm1. However, you should rename your main page when you first create the project to something more meaningful. The derivative names, such as Project.WebForm1 and WebForm1.aspx.vb, will also be renamed.

After your ASP.NET project is created, you get a default class that has only some basic generated code and an empty page_load event. To this class you can add whatever code you like, including event handlers or other methods that you need to support the functionality you are building. Treat this just like any other class you've worked with, with one exception.

Many times classes maintain information about the objects they represent, stored in private data members and accessed through properties. Doing this assumes that the object is still in memory and continues to maintain that information until it is disposed of. However, ASP.NET classes are not maintained in memory between calls from the client. You cannot rely on them to maintain information from call to call. You have to use other mechanisms to do this. They are covered later when we discuss maintaining state. However, for now, it is important to note that you should not use your class to hold information on a long-term basis. Instead, think of your classes as more service-oriented than data-oriented.

Class References

You can add references to other classes in the main class associated with your page. In fact, this is common practice when building multitiered applications that need to scale to a large number of users. We'll talk more about that later. You might want to do this to make use of classes written by others or to compartmentalize your functionality.

If you need to reference another class in your code, do it just like you would in a standard Visual Basic WinForms application. Use the project menu or the context menu on the project explorer to add a reference, and then navigate to and select the appropriate DLL. You'll then have access to all its functionality in the ASP.NET project you are building.

Old and New ASP Objects

ASP-proficient programmers are familiar with the following standard ASP object set:

- Request
- Response
- Session
- Server
- Application

Are these objects still around? Can we still use them? Yes, they're still there, but use them with caution. They have been changed to some degree. You'll want to investigate before you rely on them too much. The Visual Studio .NET help system has excellent information about the changes to these objects.

There are also a few new objects in the ASP.NET system available for your use. They are all part of the Page object and include:

The Cache object. Allows you to store or retrieve objects or information in memory.

The Controls collection. Returns a ControlsCollection object, giving you access to all the controls of the page.

The Trace object. Helps with application debugging and instrumentation.

The ValidatorControls collection. Returns a list of all the validator controls on the page.

Storing State

State maintenance has always been a little tricky, but also critical, with Web applications. Knowing what has happened from request to request is important to making a Web site work like an application. From storing user selections when moving to a new page to keeping track of the score in a trivia game, state maintenance is part the everyday life of the Web developer.

There are several mechanisms available to ASP developers, including the Session object, cookies, and user data on the client, as well as writing your own code to save and load state from a database. Each has its own problems, however. Session object storage is not a good choice when you have an environment with multiple Web servers, such as a Web farm. The Session object resides in the memory space on one server, and multiple servers cannot handle requests from the same session. The solution might seem like a database server to store and save state information. This option requires lots of manual handling of the data and code to make it work. User data or cookies are not a reliable option because the user can shut these off at the browser level. In fact, some organizations require that cookies and user data options be turned off as a security measure.

So what has ASP.NET done for us in this area? Although the old options, including the Session object, are still around and work like they used to, there are three new options available that help by providing more scalable options. They are Application State, the Session Service, and the built-in SQL Server state feature.

Application State

The Application object works much like the Session object for maintaining state. However, whereas the session object stores information at the Session level for a single user, the Application object stores information across an application for multiple users. Several users can access the same storage area. For example, your application may want a count of users in the system. When a user attaches to the application, it could increment a known variable name in the Application object, such as UserCount. It would look like this:

```
Application("UserCount") += 1
```

And when the user is done, the code could execute:

```
Application("UserCount") -= 1
```

Any time the application needed to know how many users were in the system, it could simply reference Application("UserCount"). Although this is a powerful feature, it has some issues that are important to understand:

Application data is stored in Web server memory. As more data is used in the Application object, server performance will start to suffer.

Application data is global. Anyone in the application has access to it, for good or ill. Mistakes are easy to make and hard to track down.

Application data has concurrency issues. More than one person may try to access the same memory space at once. This could cause inaccuracies in your data. You need to use the Lock and Unlock features of the Application object to be sure that users and threads don't mess up your information.

Having said that, the Application object is a nice addition to the Session object.

The NT Service

The NT service option creates a single NT service on one server in a Web farm. All sessions can access the service to store state. In this way, servers can come and go in the Web farm, and session state is still maintained. This option is worth looking into if you work in a highly scalable Web farm environment.

The SQL Server Feature

Although the option to store state information in a database has always been available, it was completely up to you to implement it. Now, ASP.NET provides you with built-in SQL Server access to save state. You have to provide a server and connection string so that it knows where to go. Although there are more complex coding and hardware setup issues, this option is good when you have to store large amounts of session information or need better security for your session information, such as for e-commerce applications.

Images and StyleSheets

Although not typically an integral part of the code and applications you create with ASP.NET, images and stylesheets are an important component of most Web applications and functionality-rich Web sites. You need to be able to accommodate them in your ASP.NET projects.

This is simple to do. Images can be added to your application by adding an existing item to the project. Right-click the project name and select Add Existing Item from the context menu. This allows you to browse to the images you need to add. It is best to create an Images directory in the project to house them all before you add them. Keeping them organized will be extremely helpful as your application gets larger and has more images.

Stylesheets, which help you control the look and form of your pages, can be added the same way, by adding an existing item if you already have one defined. You can also create a new one for your application by right-clicking the project in the project explorer pane and selecting Add New Item and selecting Style Sheet from the dialog that appears.

Visual Studio .NET also has a new style editor that makes creating style sheets easier. Take a look at Figure 13.7 to see what it looks like.

The Web.Config File and Security

An important part of any Web-based application or Web site is security. Most programmers really have no interest in security, and see it as something that the next person will take care of. I don't like security work either. However, I have discovered that Web security in ASP.NET applications is much easier to deal with than before. Although there are still many complex and advanced aspects to it, you can get security working on a Web application fairly quickly by understanding a few basic concepts.

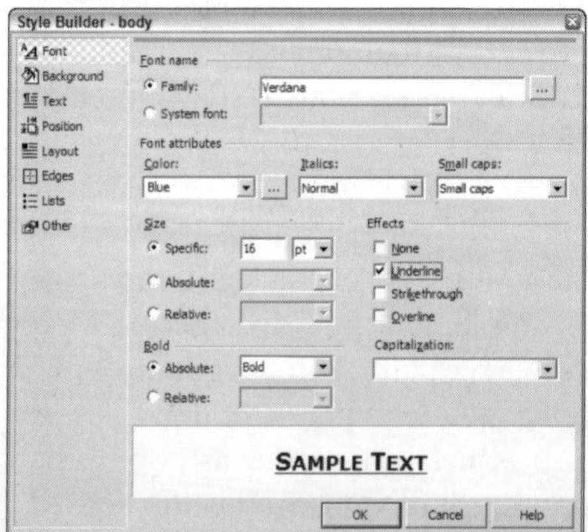

Figure 13.7 The new stylesheet editor.

The Web.Config File

Each Web application, and potentially each directory in a Web application, will have a file in it called web.config. This is a text file, or more exactly, an XML file (as are most things in .NET), that defines options for the application or directory in the application. Mostly, it contains security information. It uses XML syntax and can be edited directly by any text editor. When you create an ASP.NET application project, the Visual Studio .NET environment automatically creates a default web.config file for you.

The SessionState Option

One of the options you can specify in your web.config file that is not related to security is how your Session state will be maintained. You simply change the option and the server will take care of most of it. The options available to you are:

InProc. This option uses standard in-memory storage, including Session and Application storage. This is the default when the web.config is created for you. The option looks like this:

```
<sessionState mode="InProc" />
```

StateServer. This option tells the server to use the NT Service version of session state management. It is great for Web farms but not used too often. It look like this:

```
<sessionState mode="StateServer" />
```

SQLServer. The server will use the SQL Server database to store session state information. If you use this, you'll need to provide additional parameters, such as the server and connection string. The options look like this:

```
<sessionState mode="SqlServer"
     sqlConnectionString="data source=127.0.0.1;user
id=sa;password="/>
```

Security Options

Setting up security is pretty easy using the web.config file. The first thing you have to deal with is which security mechanism you want to control access to your Web application. The available choices are:

Forms. Allows you to handle security using your own Web forms and code. This is the best option for open Web sites where you want complete control over how security is handled.

Windows. Allows you to let Windows security handle access to your application, requiring the user to be defined in your domain at some level. This is the default value in a generated web.config file.

Passport. Uses Microsoft Passport security. This is a financially expensive option indeed, and you can safely ignore it unless you really need it.

None. Does not implement security. This is a dangerous but necessary option for implementing completely open applications or Web sites.

After deciding at a design level which mechanism to use, you can look at the implementation details. Assuming that you have chosen either the Forms or Windows option, you can proceed with setting these options in the web.config file. The two components of security, Authentication and Authorization, are defined in the file.

Authentication

Authentication, the first part of security, determines what method will be used to validate a user's credentials and decides whether to allow that person into the system at all. These were just discussed and consist of Forms, Windows, or Passport authentication. To set up the authentication method you have decided on, simply specify it in the authentication section of the web.config file. It looks like this:

```
<authentication mode="Windows" />
```

The Windows option is often useful for intranet-based applications where the only people accessing the site are those who are part of a domain. Users must be defined in the domain to gain access.

Forms authentication, on the other hand, is more flexible, but it requires more work. It is up to you to provide the interface, usually an ASPX page, that allows the user to log in. Using your page to log in, the server uses the web.config file and its redirection mechanism to present your login page to users who have not yet been authenticated on the application site.

Forms authentication requires an extra parameter: your login page. The syntax for forms authentication looks like this:

```
<authentication mode="Forms"
     <forms loginURL="myLogin.aspx"
</authentication>
```

Once authenticated, authorization can take place.

Authorization

Authorization is the process of allowing authenticated users access to specific resources. For example, you may allow Mary access to everything on your Web site, including sensitive information, whereas Otto is only allowed access to the Joke of the Day page in your application. Both are *authenticated* users in your application, but only Mary is *authorized* to view sensitive information.

Authorization is specified in the web.config file. Inside the web.config file, you define authorization at the user and role level using allow and deny attributes. The user level allows you to grant or deny access to secured pages to specific users by listing them. Wildcards are also supported. For example, the following authorization section allows access to everyone except Mary and Otto:

```
<authorization>
     <allow users="*" />
     <deny users="Mary, Otto" />
</authorization>
```

This example lets everyone in the Manager role have access to the secured pages:

```
<authorization>
     <deny roles="*" />
     <allow roles="Manager" />
</authorization>
```

You can set up authorization at the directory level. This means that you can have only one set of rules for everything in a directory. It also means that you have to plan your directory structure around the different levels of authorization that you want to implement. For example, assume that you need three levels of authorization in your application:

- Employee level (read-only access to basic information)
- Accountant level (access to Employee-level information and company financial information)
- Manager (access to Employee level-information, Accounting information, and subordinate payroll information)

Given this setup, you could arrange your directories either by authorization or information type. Our structure might have three directories called Employee, Accounting, and Manager. Each would have its own web.config file, with different settings in the authorization setting. Their settings might look something like this:

- Employee:

```
<authorization>
     <!-- Let everyone in here -->
     <allow roles="*"/>
</authorization>
```

- Accounting:

```
<authorization>
     <!--  everyone except Employees in here -->
     <allow roles="*" />
     <deny roles="Employees" />
</authorization>
```

- Manager:

```
<authorization>
     <!-- Let managers in here -->
     <deny roles="*" /<
     <allow roles="Managers" />
</authorization>
```

Using some judicious directory organization and the options provided in the web.config file allows you to provide different levels of security and access to the various parts of your Web application.

Using Forms-Based Authentication and Authorization

After your directories and web.config files are defined, Forms authentication follows a sequence of events that's fairly easy once you understand it. The process goes something like this:

1. The user requests a secure resource from the server. Depending on your web.config file setup, this could be your main page or a page at a lower level in the application. At this point, it is the user's first access to the secure page; the user has not yet been authenticated, so the server redirects the person automatically to your login page.
2. The user enters login information on your login page, usually a user name and password and is sent to the server when a Submit button is clicked.
3. The login credentials are validated on the server. This validation is done by your code. This could be as simple as checking against a hard-coded list of names in your class or by looking it all up in a database and matching it up. If the user passes based on your own criteria, you can allow that user access to the secure page.
4. A user who passes your inspection is sent to the originally requested page. This is done automatically; you don't have to know what the specific page was. The user will now be authenticated on the application, and the authentication information will be passed from page to page.

5. At this point authorization is checked. If the user is not allowed access to a requested resource, he or she will be informed of this. A user who is authorized will be passed on to the secured page normally.
6. If users do not pass authentication, you can leave them on the current URL and display an error message for them. They are not authenticated in the application, and if they try to access it again, they will be presented with the login page.

Here's what the code would look like. Assume you have created your own login page with a user ID textbox, a password textbox, and a Submit button and named it myLogin.aspx. The next step would be to create an event handler for the Submit button. Our example that follows validates the user ID and password using a simple string comparison allowing only Mary to log in. You could replace the validation with anything, including validation against a user list in a database or even a separate component to validate everything for you.

```
Private Sub btnLogin_ServerClick(ByVal sender As System.Object, _
     ByVal e As System.EventArgs) Handles btnLogin.ServerClick
     If tbUserID.Text = "MARY" Then
          If tbPassword.Text = "doh!" Then
               ' Everything is valid, so go on to requested page
               FormsAuthentication.RedirectFromLoginPage( _
                    tbUserID.Text, False)
          Else
               ' Code to tell user that password was not right.
          End If
     Else
          ' Code to tell user that User ID was not found
     End If
End Sub
```

The call to FormsAuthentication.RedirectFromLoginPage sends the user on to the originally requested secured page. The system knows what that page was; you don't need to worry about it.

Enterprise Development Considerations

So far we've seen all the nice, new benefits that ASP.NET provides over the more pedestrian ASP technology. Most of our examples, for the sake of brevity, show code placed directly into the classes associated with the ASPX page. This is fine for small functions or those that don't get called often. However, large or often-called methods will not scale well if placed into these classes. We cannot expect the Web server to handle all the functionality load if we need to provide access to lots of users.

A better solution would be to let the Web server get on with its job of serving up pages and handling requests and let another server handle business functionality. This is standard multitier development practice, and it allows you to transplant your business functionality elsewhere. Additionally, this practice makes it easier to develop your business functionality separately from the Web portions. More than one programmer can develop it, and maintaining the system is much easier.

Take, for example, an application that allows a user to pay bills online. The Web server should handle the display of the user interface and collection of user-entered information. Code in your ASP.NET pages would put information about your account into fields on the page; collect bill payment information such as payee, amount, and date, and send the information to the payment service. However, a separate component or components could easily handle all the data-retrieval tasks and handle all the data-validation tasks, such as making sure that the customer has enough money in the account to pay the bill, that the date is valid, and that the payment is submitted to the payment service.

The process is simple. Design your code to segregate the functionality based on UI and server-side business functionality. When the business components are complete, you can reference them in your ASP.NET application by adding a reference to the component in your ASP.NET project. After the reference is in place, you can use the functionality normally. The benefits of separate development and better scalability manifest themselves for all but the smallest applications.

We'll see an example of this sort of separation of functionality in Chapter 15, "XML Web Services."

Lab 13.2: Defect Reporting Page

In this lab we'll get a feel for what it's like to build a simple ASP.NET Web application that allows users to enter information about a defect in a product and have it saved to a database. You'll see how the events are wired to the page, how to interact with the database, and how the validator controls work.

First, be sure you understand the database and that it's in a place you can access. Our database design is illustrated in Figure 13.8. There are three tables. Defect is the primary table that stores the defect information entered by the user. The Severity table holds the possible values for the Defect Severity field, and the Category table stores possible values for the Defect Category field. Values from these two tables will be loaded into the drop-down lists on the page. They are related to the Defect table by the SeverityID and CatID columns.

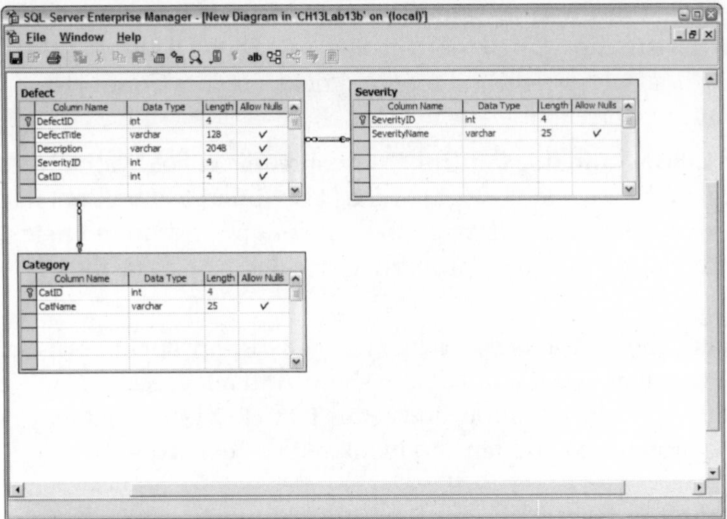

Figure 13.8 The database used in this lab.

So, let's get rolling by laying out the UI on the page. You need controls to allow the user to enter information about a defect in a product.

1. Start a new ASP.NET Web application by selecting File, New, Project from the menu. Name it whatever you like, such as CH13Lab13b.
2. On the main page, add a few controls. The following lists what you need on the page. Figure 13.9 shows what it should look like when complete.
   - **Title Label.** This controls titles on the application page. Give it a large, bold font and set the text property to Report a Defect.
   - **Control Labels.** Add four more labels and position them along the left side. They will be labels for each of the controls. Their text properties should be set to Title, Category, Severity, and Description.
   - **Title Textbox.** Add a text box that will allow the user to enter a title for the defect. Change its ID to tbTitle.
   - **DropDown Lists.** Add two drop-down list controls under the Title text box. Set the IDs of the first cbCat and the second cbSeverity.
   - **Description Textbox.** Add one more text box at the bottom that will hold the longer description of the defect. Set its ID to tbDesc. Set its TextMode property to Multiline.
   - **Save Button.** Add a button at the bottom to use to save the defect. Set its ID to btnSave and its Text property to Save.

- **Title Validator Control.** Add a required field validator control to the page to the right of the Title text box. Set its ID to rfvTitle, its ErrorMessage to Title is a required field., and its ControlTo-Validate property to the title textbox, tbTitle.
- **Description Validator Control.** Add a required field validator control to the page to the right of the Description text box. Set its ID to rfvDesc, its ErrorMessage to Description is a required field., and its ControlToValidate property to the description textbox, tbDesc.
- **Results Label.** You need a label that will display any messages to the user that you might want to show. Add a label control to the right of the Save button, and set its ID to lblResults. Set its Visible property to Hidden and blank out its Text property.

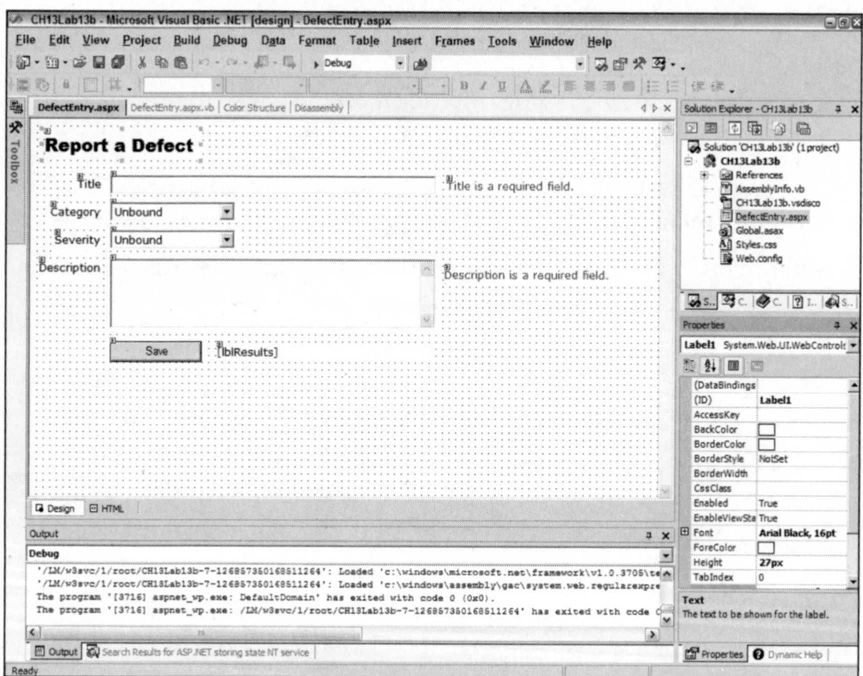

Figure 13.9 The lab page layout in Design mode.

3. There are a couple of supporting lines of code you need to add. First, add a line to import the SQLClient namespace at the top of the code module:

```
Imports System.Data.SqlClient
```

Next, add a constant to the class that contains the database connection string. Change yours to match your database needs:

```
Private Const CONNSTR As String = "SERVER=(local);
DATABASE=CH13Lab13b; UID=sa; PWD=;"
```

4. There are two main sections of code you need to write. The first populates the two lists on the page, Category and Severity. The values will be retrieved from the database and loaded into the lists on the page. We'll do this in the page_load event handler. Enter the following code into the class module:

```
Private Sub Page_Load(ByVal sender As System.Object, _
    ByVal e As System.EventArgs) Handles MyBase.Load
    ' For the initial page, load the dropdown lists with data.
    If Not IsPostBack() Then
        Dim conn As New SqlConnection(CONNSTR)
        Dim da As New SqlDataAdapter( _
            "Select * From Severity", conn)
        Dim ds As New DataSet()
        ' Get the list data from the db
        Try
            conn.Open()
            da.Fill(ds, "Severity")
            da.SelectCommand.CommandText = _
                "Select * From Category"
            da.Fill(ds, "Category")
            conn.Close()
        Catch ex As SqlException
            lblResults.Text = ex.Message()
            lblResults.ForeColor = Color.Red
            lblResults.Visible = True
            conn.Close()
            Exit Sub
        End Try
        ' Load the data into the lists
        Dim aRow As DataRow
        For Each aRow In ds.Tables("Severity").Rows
            cbSeverity.Items.Insert( _
                CInt(aRow("SeverityID")) - 1, _
                Row("SeverityName"))
        Next
        For Each aRow In ds.Tables("Category").Rows
            cbCat.Items.Insert( _
                CInt(aRow("CatID")) - 1, aRow("CatName"))
        Next
    Else
        ' Reset the results label to hidden
        lblResults.Visible = False
    End If
End Sub
```

You are loading list values from the database using two queries and a single DataSet that holds both result sets. All the values, once loaded, are inserted into the drop-down list controls. Notice that you can reference the controls on the page just like a Visual Basic WinForms application. Also, note the use of the IsPostBack property. You only want to load the lists if this is the first time the page is loaded. In this case, it would not hurt to reload the lists every time, but why waste the processing time if you don't have to?

5. Next, add the code to save the information to the database. In the code editor, select the btnSave control and the Click event. Then enter the following code into the event handler:

```
Private Sub btnSave_Click(ByVal sender As System.Object, _
     ByVal e As System.EventArgs) Handles btnSave.Click
     ' Save the data to the database
     Dim conn As New SqlConnection(CONNSTR)
     Dim sSQL As String
     Dim cmd As New SqlCommand("", conn)
     ' Build the INSERT SQL using values from the UI
     sSQL = "INSERT INTO Defect (DefectTitle, Description, _
          SeverityID, CatID) " & _
          "VALUES ('" & tbTitle.Text & "', '" & _
               tbDesc.Text & "', " & _
          CStr(cbSeverity.SelectedIndex + 1) & ", " & _
          CStr(cbCat.SelectedIndex + 1) & ")"
     ' Execute the insert statement
     Try
          cmd.CommandText = sSQL
          conn.Open()
          cmd.ExecuteNonQuery()
          conn.Close()
     Catch ex As SqlException
          ' Report error in the lblResults control.
          lblResults.Text = ex.Message
          lblResults.ForeColor = Color.Red
          lblResults.Visible = True
          conn.Close()
          Exit Sub
     End Try
     ' Tell the user everything went well.
     lblResults.Text = "Defect successfully saved."
     lblResults.ForeColor = Color.Black
     lblResults.Visible = True
End Sub
```

The code collects the values from the controls on the page and uses them to construct a SQL Insert statement. Once built, the statement is executed. If there were any errors, our lblResults control displays them to the user.

Now run the program. There are a few things you can test that are quite interesting. First, run the program and leave out a value for either the Title or Description, and then click the Save button. Your validator controls should kick in and display a message for the user. Figure 13.10 shows this message.

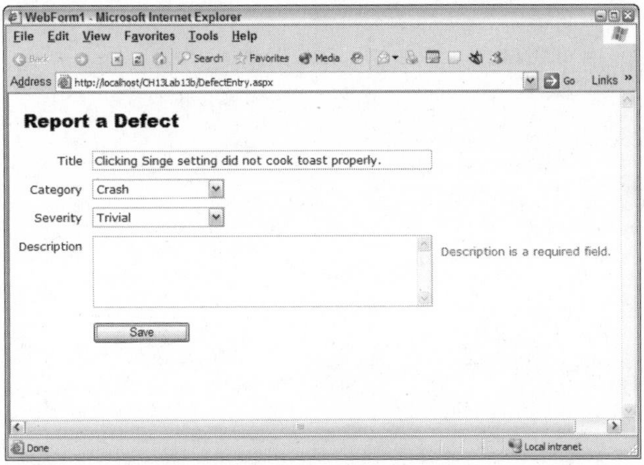

Figure 13.10 The validator controls in action.

Now run the application by turning off your database server or removing the database. This simulates a database error and illustrates the use of the results label. After you click the Save button, the label should display the contents of the database error, as shown in Figure 13.11.

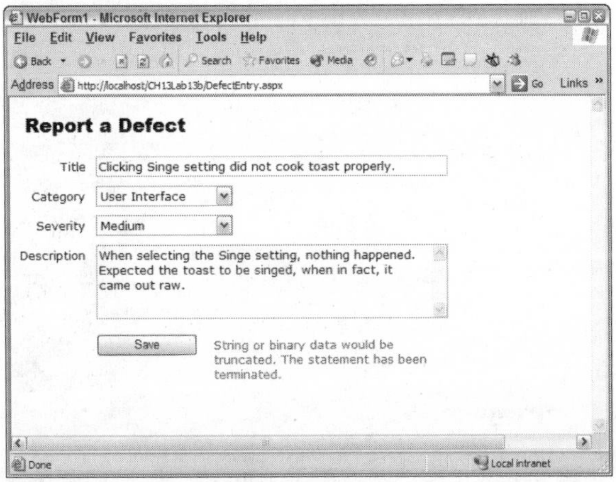

Figure 13.11 Handling the database error.

If you run the program with everything working correctly and fill in all the fields, the program will also give you a message. Figure 13.12 shows a success message.

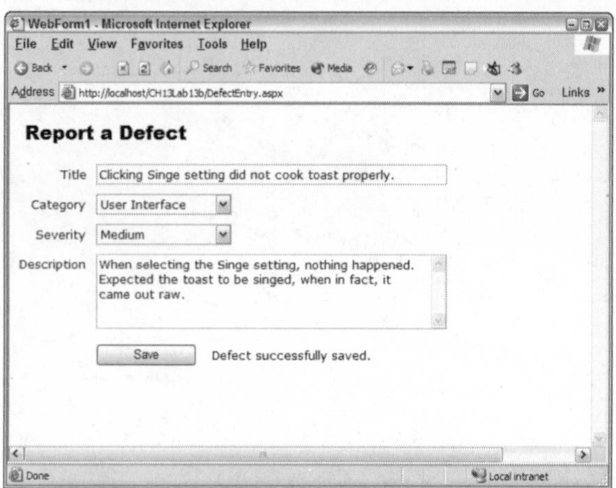

Figure 13.12 Defect report saved successfully.

Figure 13.13 shows the data successfully inserted into the database.

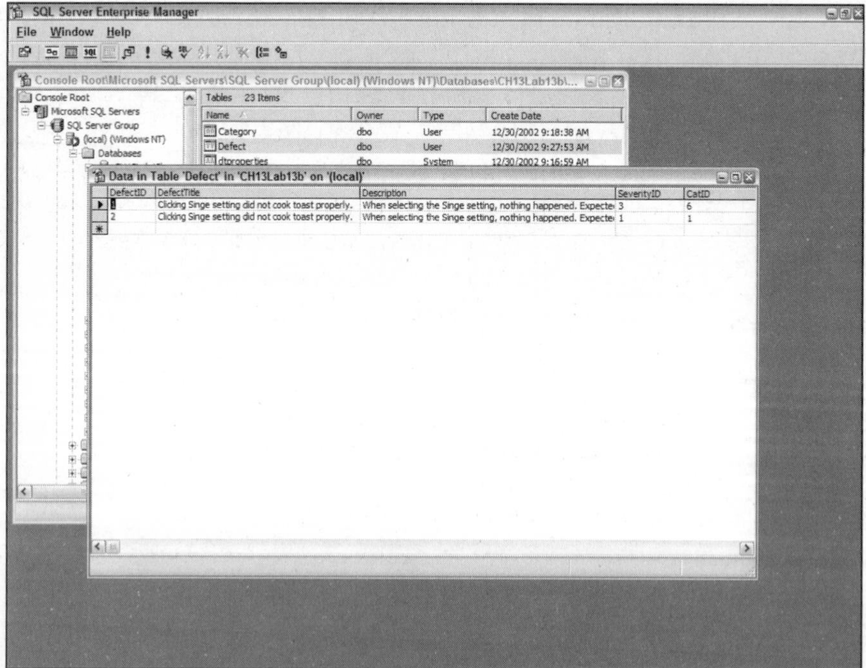

Figure 13.13 Defect data saved in the database.

This lab showed you how to pull together many of the aspects of ASP.NET development to get useful work done. This page could be used to report defects in your own applications. Just host it and put a link to it in your application. Note that if it were used in a live environment, it would probably be beneficial to move most of the functionality we've seen into a separate component and simply reference it from the class associated with the Web page.

Summary

ASP.NET clearly has many benefits and advancements over ASP, including better speed, ease of development, and better scalability. The development environment is vastly improved over Visual InterDev, being more like standard Visual Basic form creation. Server-side HTML generation helps us support multiple browsers with ease.

There are many types of controls, including new server-side, code-generating controls and the time-saving validator controls. Events are handled on the server, allowing you to respond to them with compiled code and still provide client-side browser and platform independence. Some new and improved options maintain state, which makes Web-based applications easier to build. ASP.NET also makes building security into your Web applications much easier and more flexible.

To learn more about ASP.NET, check out another book in this series, *ASP.NET in 60 Minutes a Day*.

Given all these tools, improvements, and use of the entire Visual Basic language, there are no more excuses to avoid building Web-based applications. Besides, they're fun.

Review Questions

1. Name four of the seven listed advantages of ASP.NET over ASP.
2. What are the two layout modes in the ASP.NET form designer?
3. What are HTML user controls?
4. What are the two elements of the server control tag that distinguish it as a server control?
5. What are validator controls? Name three of the five.
6. Which occurs first in the sequence of events that fire when a server-side event handler executes: data-binding events, the page_load event, or the event included with the request?
7. What is the purpose of the IsPostBack method? Which object is it part of?
8. What is the purpose of the Codebehind attribute?
9. Should you store information in your Web page class? If so, why?
10. What are the three options for the SessionState parameter in the web.config file?
11. Explain the difference between authorization and authentication.
12. What are the four options for security authentication?
13. Create an authorization section of a web.config file that will allow access for users Mary and Otto, as well as the roles Manager and CEO. All others should be locked out.

Answers to Review Questions

1. The seven benefits listed are: ASP.NET is compiled (yielding faster execution), ASP.NET is true Visual Basic (yielding access to the whole language), it separates code from content (making development and maintenance easier), it supports multiple browsers (reducing your coding load), it has an event model (providing consistency), its events execute on the server (providing faster execution and more capability), and its deployment is simple (just copy it to the server).
2. Flow Layout and Grid Layout. Flow layout builds pages like traditional HTML pages, whereas Grid layout uses absolute positioning to function more like standard Visual Basic WinForms.
3. HTML user controls are composite controls similar to Visual Basic user controls. You can build them from any number of ASP.NET controls, HTML elements, and other content. They can have their own methods and properties accessible through code. They are more useful than server-side includes because they can be included more than once on a page.
4. First, each control tag starts with asp: followed by the name of the tag. Second, each control must have the runat=server attribute.
5. Validator controls perform some standard types of validation with little or no code, also providing a mechanism for informing the user of the error. They are typically invisible until an error occurs, at which time they display themselves and their error messages. There are five validator controls: RequiredField, Compare, Range, the regular expression validator, and Custom.
6. Of the three events listed, the page_load comes first, then the event that was included with the request (such as the button click event), and then the data-binding events. Other events occur, of course.
7. The IsPostBack function returns True if the page is loading based on an event. If the page is loading for the first time, IsPostBack returns False. This allows you to execute any page initialization you might need only when the page is initially loading (IsPostPack=False). It prevents you from performing initializations when they are not appropriate.
8. The Codebehind attribute is located in the HTML part of the page and tells the server which component contains the code associated with the page.
9. No. The class will go away between events and postbacks, taking all its private data with it. You can't rely on private data to be maintained in the class. Use one of the session state mechanisms instead.

10. InProc, SessionService, and SQLServer. InProc tells the server to use standard in-memory mechanisms, such as the Session and Application objects. The SessionService option tells the server to use the NT Service-based session mechanism, essentially creating a session server. The SQLServer option, along with a few extra parameters, uses SQL Server for session storage.
11. Authentication refers to the validation of a user's credentials, usually a user ID and password. This allows or denies the user access to the application. Authorization defines what parts of the application the authenticated user is allowed to access. An authenticated user may have access to the application but not be authorized to use certain parts.
12. The four options for authentication are Forms, Windows, Passport, and None. Forms authentication allows you to provide your own authentication mechanism. Windows authentication validates users based on their user credentials in the domain. Passport security uses Microsoft's Passport authentication scheme. None creates a completely open site or application.
13. The code for the authorization section is:

```
<authorization>
     <deny users="*" />
     <allow users="Mary, Otto" />
     <deny roles="*" />
     <allow roles="Manager, CEO" />
</authorization>
```

CHAPTER

14

Data Control and XML in Web Applications

In previous chapters you've seen ASP.NET in action, and you've seen ADO.NET perform fabulous tricks with databases. You've even seen them working together to some degree. Now it is time to see them work together more intimately. ADO.NET data controls bridge the gap for us, bringing data binding to the Web world. The use of data controls is familiar to most WinForms developers but is a fairly new feature to Web application developers. These controls are a marvelous boon to those who must present data in a Web browser.

Basics of ASP.NET Data Binding

Data binding is the process by which data is retrieved and then displayed automatically by controls on a user interface. This doesn't seem new. It's been done before. However, proper real-time data binding has not been part of ASP Web pages until now. Data binding of a sort was possible, but it was mostly a manual process and had to be handled on a page post. The real-time part was a myth.

With ASP.NET, there is not only a robust data-binding model, but many Web controls that are capable of data binding. Individual controls such as the text box can be data bound, containing a single field of data. There are also more complex controls, such as the data grid and the data list, that automate large chunks of functionality that used to be the responsibility of the programmer. In fact, it is the data controls that are at the heart of data binding.

The Simple Data Controls

Simple data controls are those that display data from only a single column in the database. They can be minimal, like the label control, which does nothing more than display a single value from a single row of a single column in the database, or they can be more useful, such as the list box that shows many values from a single column in the database.

The basic process of using these controls is fairly easy and is similar for most data-bound ASP.NET Web controls. Load the data from the database, attach the DataSet to the bound control, and bind it. Let's take a quick look at an example that puts values from two tables into two separate list boxes on an ASP.NET Web page. Figure 14.1 shows the simple Web form we have laid out.

Without data binding, we'd have to load the data into the controls in a loop. We'd also have to load the primary keys for the data and track them, returning the matching key values when the user made a selection from the list. We're going to take care of most of that automatically. All we need to do is retrieve the data.

The two main items on the page are the list boxes we want to fill. These will contain the names of customers and suppliers from the Northwind database (which comes with Microsoft Access and SQL Server). A label under each list will display the related primary key when the user makes a selection. The event we want to watch for on the lists, SelectedIndexChanged, fires only when a postback occurs, so we added a button on the page to simulate submission of the form.

The controls are in place, but how do we link them to data? Let's take a look at the code for the page_load event. In this event handler, we load the data, populate the lists with display values as well as their associated primary key values, and bind the data. Here's the code:

```
Private Sub Page_Load(ByVal sender As System.Object, _
    ByVal e As System.EventArgs) Handles MyBase.Load
    'Put user code to initialize the page here
    If Not IsPostBack Then
        Dim conn As New SqlConnection( _
            "database=Northwind; server=(local); uid=sa; pwd=;")
        Dim da As New SqlDataAdapter("select * from Customers", conn)
        Dim ds As New DataSet()
        Try
            ' 1. Get the data for the lists
            conn.Open()
            da.Fill(ds, "Customers")
            da.SelectCommand.CommandText = "Select * from Suppliers"
            da.Fill(ds, "Suppliers")
            conn.Close()
```

```
                    ' 2. Fill listbox1 with Customers
                    ListBox1.DataSource = ds.Tables("Customers")
                    ListBox1.DataTextField = "CompanyName"
                    ListBox1.DataValueField = "CustomerID"
                    ' 3. Fill listbox2 with Suppliers
                    ListBox2.DataSource = ds.Tables("Suppliers")
                    ListBox2.DataTextField = "CompanyName"
                    ListBox2.DataValueField = "SupplierID"
                    ' 4. Bind everything
                    Page.DataBind()
                Catch ex As SqlException
                    Label1.Text = ex.Message()
                End Try
            End If
        End Sub
```

After creating our standard collection of ADO.NET objects, we connect up to the database and load a DataSet with two result sets: a list of customers and a list of suppliers. Once we have the data, we would normally be sitting in loops filling data into the list boxes. Instead, we just set a few parameters and let the data-binding engine take care of it.

The DataSource property defines where the data comes from. In this case, we set the DataSource property on each of our list boxes to a table in our data set. To specify the field we want, we set the DataTextField property on each control, giving it the name of the appropriate column name from the DataSource. This is what displays in the list. We identify the value we want returned, the primary key for each value, by setting the DataValueField property to the appropriate column name in the DataSource.

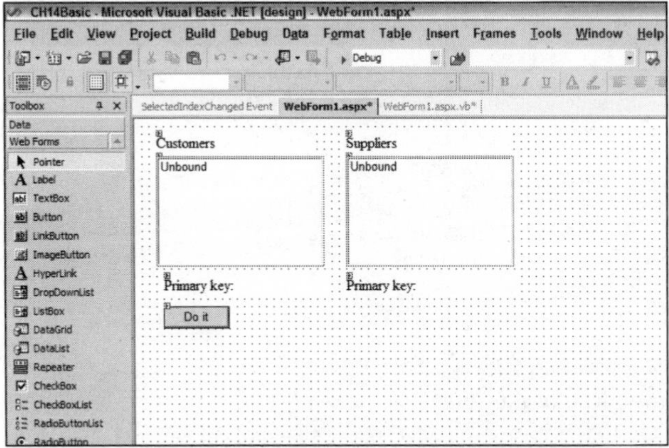

Figure 14.1 List boxes and other controls to show values from a database.

Most of this is probably familiar to you, although the syntax is slightly different. Once all these are set, we need a single call to make all the controls on the page bind to the data: Page.DataBind(). This forces all the controls on the ASP.NET page and the data-binding engine to render themselves for the resulting trip to the client. The data-binding engine combines the controls with the data you've sent it, generating HTML that can be displayed in the user's browser.

Run the Web application, select an item from each list, and click the Do It button; the primary keys for the items selected are returned. This is clearly a useful technique for many applications. How often do you need the primary key for a selected text item? All the time. Figure 14.2 shows the result.

The Page.DataBind() method forces all the controls on the page to bind all at once. However, most data-bound controls can be bound individually. For example, the ListBox has its own DataBind method that forces it to data bind without other controls on the page doing the same. This can be useful for making your pages more efficient. Say you have a control that allows users to select a supplier from a list. When they do, you want to display a list of all that supplier's products. You can tell just the products list to data bind, loading the list of products and taking less time to execute than binding the entire page.

There are other simple data-bound controls, all of which can be found in the ASP.NET Page Designer if you want to investigate them. Yet, there are more interesting controls that do a lot more work for you.

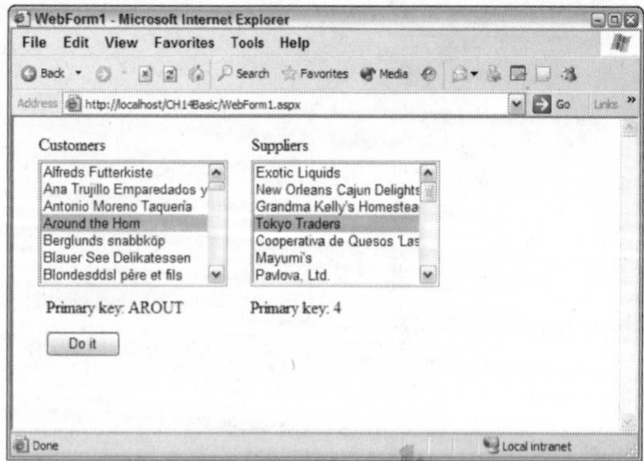

Figure 14.2 Primary keys returned from data-bound list boxes.

The DataGrid Control

The DataGrid control is very similar to those you may have used in the past. Bind a grid to the database and display data in it. This is pretty straightforward; however, this data grid takes data from a data source and then renders an HTML table to display it for you. It has some nice functionality, such as the capability to edit data and then post the changes back to the data source, as well as an autoformat feature that makes your grids look good with minimal work.

You can get a basic data grid up and running with just a few lines of code. After you drop a data grid on the page, add the following code to connect it up. This example displays all the data in the suppliers table:

```
Private Sub Page_Load(ByVal sender As System.Object, _
     ByVal e As System.EventArgs) Handles MyBase.Load
     'Put user code to initialize the page here
     If Not IsPostBack Then
          Dim conn As New SqlConnection( _
               "server=(local); database=northwind; uid=sa; pwd=;")
          Dim da As New SqlDataAdapter("select * from suppliers", conn)
          Dim ds As New DataSet()
          Try
               conn.Open()
               da.Fill(ds, "Suppliers")
               conn.Close()
               DataGrid1.DataSource = ds.Tables("Suppliers")
               DataGrid1.DataBind()
          Catch ex As SqlException
               lblError.Text = ex.Message()
          End Try
     End If
End Sub
```

Figure 14.3 shows an example of a data grid in action.

The data grid has other excellent capabilities. For example, if you want some near-automatic data paging, the data grid is your only choice. Other data controls won't do it for you.

There is at least one other data control that is outstanding, the data list, and we'll cover it in detail.

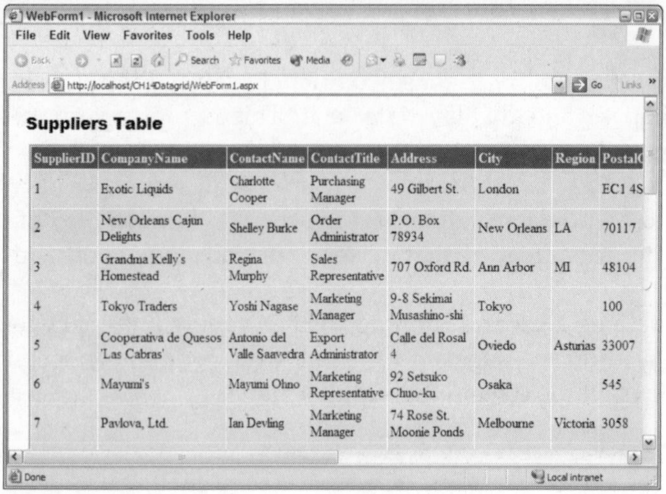

Suppliers Table

SupplierID	CompanyName	ContactName	ContactTitle	Address	City	Region	PostalC
1	Exotic Liquids	Charlotte Cooper	Purchasing Manager	49 Gilbert St.	London		EC1 4S
2	New Orleans Cajun Delights	Shelley Burke	Order Administrator	P.O. Box 78934	New Orleans	LA	70117
3	Grandma Kelly's Homestead	Regina Murphy	Sales Representative	707 Oxford Rd.	Ann Arbor	MI	48104
4	Tokyo Traders	Yoshi Nagase	Marketing Manager	9-8 Sekimai Musashino-shi	Tokyo		100
5	Cooperativa de Quesos 'Las Cabras'	Antonio del Valle Saavedra	Export Administrator	Calle del Rosal 4	Oviedo	Asturias	33007
6	Mayumi's	Mayumi Ohno	Marketing Representative	92 Setsuko Chuo-ku	Osaka		545
7	Pavlova, Ltd.	Ian Devling	Marketing Manager	74 Rose St. Moonie Ponds	Melbourne	Victoria	3058

Figure 14.3 The ASP.NET data grid bound to the Northwind suppliers table.

The DataList Control

The Data Grid is a great option when you want to display data directly from a data source in table form or you want to edit the data. If you want to display data in your own format and don't mind a read-only presentation, the control you want is the DataList. It enables you to define an HTML template with markers for the data fields and then binds the data to the template. The template is then repeated for each record in the data source.

For example, assume you have a list of aircraft models you're selling on a Web site. You want to present a photo gallery of all your offerings, along with some information about each one. You can define a single template for one record, say in an HTML table, and let the data list repeat it for each row in the database. Let's take a look at how it works.

For this example, we want to show some photos of aircraft models along with associated information, and we don't want to enter everything manually in HTML. We put information about the models in a database and place photographs of them in a subdirectory called images. There is a large photo of each aircraft and a thumbnail to display on the catalog page.

You start by dropping a DataList control on the page. Then switch to the page_load event of the page and add the code to load the data and bind it to the data-list control. The code, which follows, looks very much like the code we've already used to perform data binding:

```
Private Sub Page_Load(ByVal sender As System.Object, _
     ByVal e As System.EventArgs) Handles MyBase.Load
     If Not IsPostBack Then
          Dim conn As New SqlConnection( _
               "server=(local); database=Airplanes; uid=sa; pwd=;")
```

```
            Dim da As New SqlDataAdapter( _
                  "select * from models order by aircraftname", conn)
            Dim ds As New DataSet()
            Try
                  conn.Open()
                  da.Fill(ds, "models")
                  conn.Close()
                  DataList1.DataSource = ds.Tables("models")
                  DataList1.DataBind()
            Catch ex As SqlException
                  lblError.Text = ex.Message()
            End Try
      End If
End Sub
```

After the control is data bound, we tell it how to display the data. In the HTML editor, the initial code that creates the data list is pretty simple and looks like this:

```
<asp:DataList id="DataList1"
      style="Z-INDEX: 102; LEFT: 24px; POSITION: absolute; TOP: 56px"
      runat="server" Width="496" Height="248">
</asp:DataList>
```

The interesting part is the template, which is added between the beginning and ending tags of the data control. We create a template that will show our data with the small thumbnail photo on the left and information about the aircraft on the right. Each row from the database will be displayed like this, contained in its own HTML table. Here's what the code for the data list looks like with the template added:

```
<asp:DataList id="DataList1"
      style="Z-INDEX: 102; LEFT: 24px; POSITION: absolute; TOP: 56px"
      runat="server" Width="496" Height="248">
      <ItemTemplate>
            <table cellpadding=4 cellspacing=0 border=0 width=500>
                  <tr>
                  <td align=right valign=top width=170
                        style="background-color: #DDDDDD;">
                       <a href="images/<%# Container.DataItem("PhotoBaseName")
                             %>_small.jpg">
                        <img border=0 src="images/
                             <%# Container.DataItem( "PhotoBaseName")
                             %>_thumb.jpg">
                        </a>
                  </td>
                  <td align=left valign=middle style=
                        "background-color: #DDDDDD; font-family:
                             Verdana; font-size: 10pt;">
                       Aircraft name: <%# Container.DataItem("AircraftName")
```

```
                                  %><br>
                              Scale: <%# Container.DataItem("Scale") %><br>
                              Builder: <%# Container.DataItem("Builder") %><br>
                              Price: <%# Container.DataItem("Price") %>
                         </td>
                         </tr>
                    </table>
          </ItemTemplate>
</asp:DataList>
```

Take a look at the template. There are places in the code that look like the familiar ASP replaceable tags, the <%...%> markers, but they are slightly different. They have a number sign in there, so they look like <%#...%>. The extra symbol tells the data-binding engine that this is a replaceable database field, not just a normal ASP field. Between the markers, you place code like the following:

```
Container.DataItem("Price")
```

This tells the data-binding engine that data from the Price column in the data source should be placed here. There are other fields in the template, such as the base image filename, called PhotoBaseName, that we use to construct a filename for the image tag. These can be used just like ASP replaceable fields. The only difference is that they are filled automatically with data. We define the template once, and it is repeated for every row in the data source. Take a look at Figure 14.4 to see what it looks like when we run it.

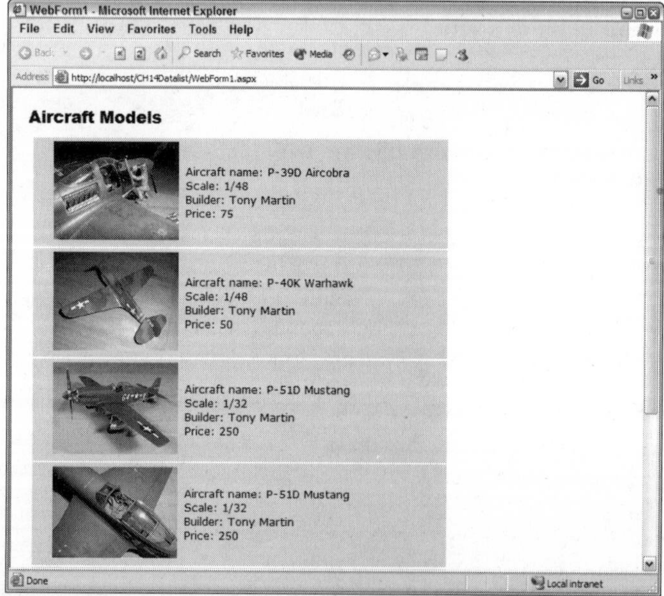

Figure 14.4 The DataList control after defining a template and binding it to a data source.

Building Data Access Applications

When building a data access Web application, it is best to make sure that it will scale well when more than one user is connected and using it. The normal tenets of enterprise *n*-tier development apply. Specifically, we need to make sure that as much functionality as possible is built into separate components. This has many benefits, not the least of which is that it is easier to build and maintain.

To make this happen, we usually build business logic and database access code into class modules and let the Web code handle as little actual work as possible. How do we logically divide this functionality? There are a couple guidelines. If you have functionality that deals with user interface manipulation or data binding, it goes into the Web code. This code needs direct access to the controls and other elements on the form, so it works best in the class associated with the Web page.

Other functionality, such as database access code and other business logic, should go into separate components. For example, if your program performs some physics calculations, why burden the Web server with them? You could put them into a component that can reside on another server or in another process. They could also be developed and maintained separately. Database access code in a disconnected environment, such as the one ADO.NET supports, can return DataSets to the calling Web page, which can then be data bound to controls by relatively small amounts of code in the Web code.

We do this shortly in our first lab. All data access is built into a separate component that we reference in the Web application. In practice, this allows one engineer to develop the data access code while another builds the Web interface. We follow this practice for the rest of the ASP.NET labs.

Talking Securely to the Database

Many of us need to provide Web-based interfaces to data in a secure environment. It's a scenario that is becoming more common each day. The question is, "How do we grant access to authorized users without requiring them to log in again or building our security system, yet still keep the deadbeats out of the system?" Ideally, we want to make use of the user's existing NT domain login, without requiring an additional login.

The answer is to use Internet Explorer, IIS, ASP.NET, and SQL Server. The solution is even pretty easy once you see it, easier than building your own security system with something like Forms-based security. There's one little key that holds the entire process together.

When a user with a Web browser hits a Web site, a connection with the server and IIS is made. Any functionality that the Web server then executes, including accessing a database, is done as an anonymous user, as IIS itself. The IIS process acts as the user. This isn't terribly secure and just about anything can be executed. What we need is the capability to execute processes and data as the user making the request. How does this happen across the HTTP wire? By using impersonation.

Impersonation is a process whereby IIS acts on behalf of the user, making the request using the user's Windows login credentials. Instead of accessing the database, for example, as IIS, it accesses it as the user. Anything the user has access to, the IIS process has access to. Anything denied to the user is denied to the process. The best part is that once it's set up, all the authentications and security checks are handled automatically.

Setting up your Web application and database to use impersonation isn't hard, but it involves several steps, described next. Then we'll do a lab that puts it all into practice. Configuring your application goes like this:

1. Disable anonymous access in IIS. This prevents IIS from allowing just anybody through the gates and enables it to use Windows NT security.
2. Set SQL Server to use Windows security. The database must be able to define and authenticate access using the Windows security system.
3. Add users to the database. Once Windows security is enabled, add domain users to SQL Server and then grant them access to the databases they need.
4. Enable impersonation in your Web application by setting a switch that tells IIS to impersonate the authenticated user.
5. Connect to the database as a trusted user. This is pretty easy and is done through the connection string you use in your application.

There is one important thing to note when using impersonation. Because the application is acting on behalf of the user and has the same access permissions as the user, your application may not end up with the correct permissions. For example, if the users have more permissions than you expect, they may have access to information or functionality you don't want them to have. Conversely, if your users don't have enough permissions, your application may not be able to function correctly because it doesn't have the permissions it needs. Make sure you carefully consider the repercussions of the settings you choose when defining permissions for your application.

Lab 14.1: Building a Secure Web Database Application

In this lab we configure SQL Server to accept only authenticated users and create a data access Web application that talks to it as the authenticated user. You can use the same techniques when securing your own applications.

Let's start by securing SQL Server.

1. Start the SQL Server Enterprise Manager. Right-click the database server in the Console Manager window. From the context menu, select Properties. When the Properties window appears, select the Security tab. Change the authentication option to Windows Only. Click the OK button to finish it up. Figure 14.5 shows the dialog and the correct setting.

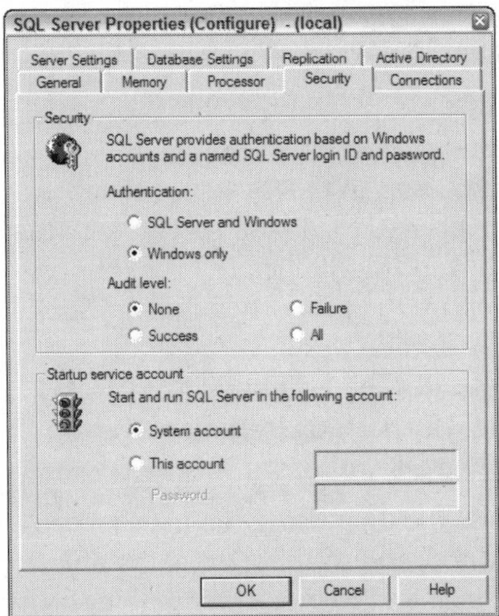

Figure 14.5 The correct authentication setting for SQL Server.

2. Now we grant users access to the database. We're using the Northwind database for this example. Click the New Login button on the toolbar to open the New Login dialog, shown in Figure 14.6. Click the ellipsis (...) button to the right of the Name field to open the user selection dialog.

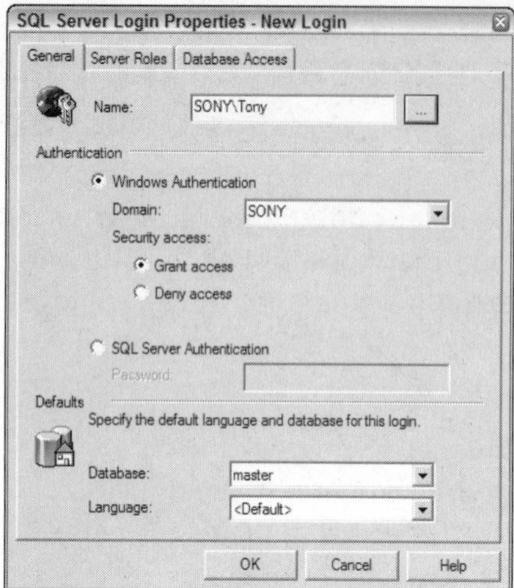

Figure 14.6 The New Login dialog.

3. Select the user to whom you want to grant access to the database, and click the OK button to accept your changes and close the dialog. Then click the OK button on the Database Properties dialog to close it out. Your user should now have access to the database.

4. Now we have to disable anonymous access so that only authenticated people have access to our resources, in this case, our database. Open up the Internet Information Services manager. Navigate to the Default Web Site in the directory list and right-click it. From the context menu, select Properties to bring up the Properties dialog. Click on the Directory Security tab. In the section titled Anonymous Access and Authentication Control, click the Edit button to display the Authentication Methods dialog. Uncheck the setting at the top labeled Anonymous Access. Click the OK button.

5. We need a Web application to access the data using the user's Windows login credentials. We'll build a simple Web form that enables you to view the Northwind Territories and Regions from tables of the same name. These tables are related through a RegionID key. The page allows the user to select a region and view all the territories in it or to view all the territories and regions in a data grid. First, create a new class library project in Visual Studio .NET. This will handle all our data access for us. Name the library CH14Lab14aClass and click OK.

6. Rename the source file to CH14Lab14aClass.vb by right-clicking it in the Solution Explorer and changing the name. Rename the class to Ch14DataAccess by changing it in the Code editor.

7. We need three main functions. The first simply returns a list of all the available regions and their IDs. The second returns a list of territories that are in the selected region, identified by the RegionID sent to the function. The last function returns a list of all territories and their regions, collected using an inner join. Create the first method by adding the following line of code to the top of the source file. The Imports statement is standard and gives us access to the SQL Server data library namespace.

```
Imports System.Data.SqlClient
```

8. Add the following constant definition to the class. The connection string is a little different. It has no user ID and no password. Instead, there's a new attribute called trusted_connection, which is set to a value of True. This parameter tells the database that it should use the Windows login credentials from the user that IIS will pass down to it. This is an important step in the path to using NT security.

```
Private Const CONNSTR As String = _
    "SERVER=(local); DATABASE=Northwind; TRUSTED_CONNECTION=true"
```

9. Now add the following code to the class for our first function. The function itself is also straightforward. It loads data into the data set and returns it to the caller. If there is an error, it throws it to the caller.

```
Public Function GetRegions() As DataSet
    Dim conn As New SqlConnection(CONNSTR)
    Dim da As New SqlDataAdapter("SELECT * from Region", conn)
    Dim ds As New DataSet()
    Try
        conn.Open()
        da.Fill(ds, "Region")
        conn.Close()
    Catch ex As SqlException
        Throw ex
    End Try
    Return ds
End Function
```

10. Here's the code for the function that takes a RegionID and returns a list of territories that match it. Add the code to the class.

```
Public Function GetTerritories(ByVal iRegionID As Integer) As
DataSet
    Dim conn As New SqlConnection(CONNSTR)
    Dim da As New SqlDataAdapter("", conn)
    Dim ds As New DataSet()
    Dim sSQL As String
    ' Build the SQL statement
    sSQL = "SELECT * FROM Territories " & _
```

```
            "WHERE RegionID = " & iRegionID.ToString
        da.SelectCommand.CommandText = sSQL
        ' Load the data
        Try
            conn.Open()
            da.Fill(ds, "Region")
            conn.Close()
        Catch ex As SqlException
            Throw ex
        End Try
        Return ds
    End Function
```

11. The final function, which returns data from both the Region and Territories tables, uses an inner join to relate the tables. Here's the code to add to the class:

```
    Public Function GetEverything() As DataSet
        Dim conn As New SqlConnection(CONNSTR)
        Dim da As New SqlDataAdapter("", conn)
        Dim ds As New DataSet()
        Dim sSQL As String
        ' Build the SQL statement
        sSQL = "SELECT Territories.TerritoryID, " & _
               "Territories.TerritoryDescription, " & _
               "Region.RegionDescription " & _
               "FROM Territories INNER JOIN " & _
               "Region ON Territories.RegionID = Region.RegionID" & _
               "ORDER BY Territories.RegionID"
        da.SelectCommand.CommandText = sSQL
        ' Load the data
        Try
            conn.Open()
             da.Fill(ds, "TerritoriesByRegion")
             conn.Close()
        Catch ex As SqlException
             Throw ex
        End Try
        Return ds
    End Function
```

12. Compile the class library.

13. Begin the Web application by creating a new one in Visual Studio .NET. Select File, New, Project from the menu and name it CH14Lab14a (or something more interesting).

14. Add a reference to the component we created earlier. Right-click the project name in the Solution Explorer and select Add Reference to bring up the Add Reference dialog. Browse to the compiled component DLL we built (Ch14Lab14aClass.dll), select it, and click the OK button.

15. Now we build the interface (see Figure 14.7). In the default Web page, add the following controls with the listed attributes:

    Title label. Add a large label at the top to title the page. Change the text property to read Northwind Territories and Regions.

    Region label and territories label. Add two labels so that the user knows what the controls are. Change their text properties to Region and Territories.

    Region drop-down list. Add a drop-down list to contain our list of Regions from the database. Change its ID to ddlRegions.

    Territories list box. Add a list box to contain the territories associated with the selected region. Change its ID to lbTerritories.

    Lookup button. Add a button to the right of the Region list box to activate the region lookup. Change its ID to btnLookup and its text property to Lookup.

    Data grid. Add a data grid below the other controls. We will hide it now, and show it when the View All button is clicked. Change its ID to dgData. Right-click the grid and select Auto Format from the context menu. Choose a format you like for the data grid. Lastly, set its visible property to False.

    Error label. Add one last label to display any runtime errors we might find. Set its ID to lblError. Change its text property to an empty string. Set the text color to red.

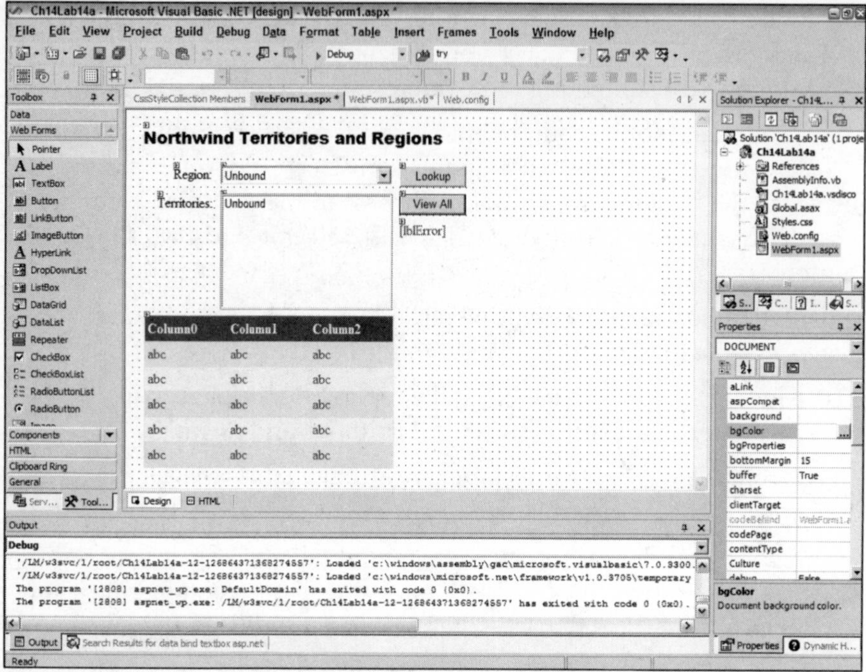

Figure 14.7 The Web UI in the Visual Studio .NET designer.

16. When the page first loads, we'll need values in the list of regions so that the user can select one. The following code creates an instance of our class library and then calls the GetRegions method in that library to retrieve a list of all available regions. We data bind the regions' drop-down list to the DataSet returned from the class library. Notice that we set the DataValueField property of the data grid so that it stores the ID of the region. This enables us to easily return the primary key ID of the selected item back to the class library when we need to get matching territories. Add the code to page_load, which uses our data-access class to get the data we need.

```
Private Sub Page_Load(ByVal sender As System.Object, _
    ByVal e As System.EventArgs) Handles MyBase.Load
    If Not IsPostBack Then
        ' Create an instance of our data access class.
        Dim ds As DataSet
        Dim obj As New CH14Lab14aClass.Ch14DataAccess()
        Try
            ' Get a list of regions to fill into the drop down.
            ds = obj.GetRegions()
            ' Set up and data bind the field.
            ddlRegions.DataSource = ds
            ddlRegions.DataTextField = "RegionDescription"
```

```
                ddlRegions.DataValueField = "RegionID"
                ddlRegions.DataBind()
        Catch ex As Exception
                lblError.Text = ex.Message
        End Try
    End If
End Sub
```

17. Now that we have a populated list, we need to do something when the user selects a region and clicks the Lookup button. The following code loads territory data that matches the selected region from the database. It works very much like the page_load code. It gets data using our data access class and binds it to the list box. The only difference is the SQL statement. We get territory data based on the ID of the region selected in the region drop-down list. Add the code to the button click event handler for the Lookup button.

```
Private Sub btnLookup_Click(ByVal sender As System.Object, _
    ByVal e As System.EventArgs) Handles btnLookup.Click
    ' Create an instance of our data access class.
    Dim ds As DataSet
    Dim obj As New CH14Lab14aClass.Ch14DataAccess()
    Try
        ' Get the list of territories that match the
        ' region in the region drop-down list.
        ds = obj.GetTerritories(ddlRegions.SelectedItem.Value())
        ' Bind the results to the territories list box.
        lbTerritories.DataSource = ds
        lbTerritories.DataTextField = "TerritoryDescription"
        lbTerritories.DataValueField = "TerritoryID"
        lbTerritories.DataBind()
    Catch ex As Exception
        lblError.Text = ex.Message
    End Try
End Sub
```

18. Our final feature is the ability to display a listing of all territories and their associated regions in a grid. The grid is sitting on the UI but is hidden. When the View All button is clicked, the grid is data bound to the data and made visible. In addition, the View All button acts as a toggle; if the grid is visible, you can click the button to hide it. Here's the code that takes care of it for us:

```
Private Sub btnAll_Click(ByVal sender As System.Object, _
    ByVal e As System.EventArgs) Handles btnAll.Click
    ' If the grid is visible, turn it off and get
    ' out of here. It acts as a toggle.
    If dgData.Visible Then
        dgData.Visible = False
        Exit Sub
    End If
```

```
        ' Create an instance of our data access class.
        Dim ds As DataSet
        Dim obj As New CH14Lab14aClass.Ch14DataAccess()
        Try
            ' Get all the data using our class.
            ds = obj.GetEverything()
            ' Bind the grid to the data.
            dgData.DataSource = ds
            dgData.DataBind()
        Catch ex As Exception
            lblError.Text = ex.Message
        End Try
        ' Turn the data grid on.
        dgData.Visible = True
    End Sub
```

19. We now have all the code in place. The business and data logic is in our class library, and the UI and data binding are in the code associated with our Web page. The database is configured to allow only certain authorized users in, and IIS is set to reject anonymous users. There is one last little piece in the puzzle. We need to tell our Web application to use impersonation. We do this in the web.config file. Open it up by double-clicking it in the Solution Explorer. Add the following line of code after the authentication section, and save it:

```
<identity impersonation="true" />
```

We're ready to run. Execute the program. If everything is configured correctly, and you are an authenticated user in the domain or workgroup, you have access and everything runs properly. The application running in the browser is shown in Figure 14.8.

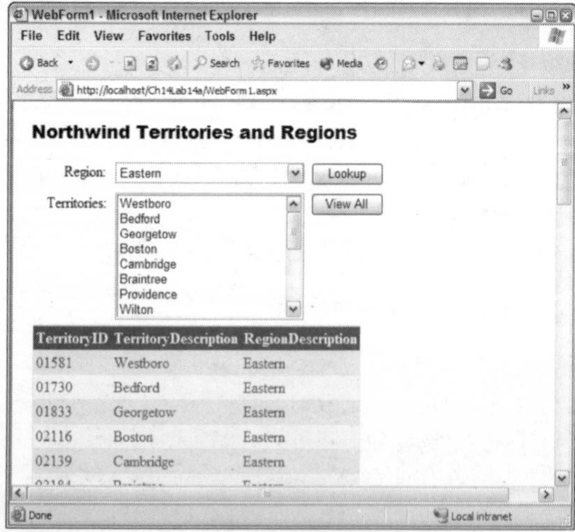

Figure 14.8 The lab application executing in the browser with a successful login.

This lab demonstrated that integrated Windows security works beautifully when going through ASP.NET Web pages. In our lab, the user's login credentials were passed automatically from the browser to IIS, to our Web application, to our data access component, and finally to SQL server. Authentication was taken care of by the applications and resources involved rather than our having to handle it.

As a bonus exercise, verify that everything works by popping back into the SQL Server Enterprise Manager and denying access to the user you previously granted access. Do this by expanding the server tree on the left until you can select your server. Expand your server, open the Security item on the tree, and click on Logins. In the right-hand pane, you should see a list of valid users, including the one to which you granted access. Right-click the user and select Properties. In the dialog, change the security access option from Grant to Deny. Click the OK button to close it. Now switch back to Visual Studio .NET and run the application again. Because you've denied access, that user should be rejected by SQL server. And because we propagate any errors in the class where it would manifest up to the caller, our application knows about the error and displays it.

XML and Visual Studio .NET

Use of XML has been on the rise in the last couple of years. Microsoft has certainly embraced it with Visual Studio .NET and has provided all sorts of tools to help you out with XML in your own projects. Microsoft even uses it in its own tools. For example, the web.config file is in XML format, and the forms you design are stored in XML format.

A complete discussion of XML could easily fill several books, but we're going to concentrate on the basic structure and syntax of XML and XML schemas, what they're good for, and what XML tools Microsoft has provided.

XML Overview

XML is a format that is used to represent and describe data in a standard, nonbinary format. It's based on Standard Generalized Markup Language (SGML), the same standard on which HTML is based.

There are several reasons for using this format to represent data. One of the best is for the interchange of data between disparate systems. You can't easily import Microsoft Access data directly into your 20-year-old IBM mainframe. With XML, you can send the data as text, using the structure to define how the data looks. In addition, because XML is text-based, you can easily send it over an HTTP wire to a Web page or back to a server. You can also use XML to store other information than just classical data. It's been used to store information about files on a server and the content and structure of application menu systems and has even been used as a Registry substitute.

A fine complement to XML is XML Schema Definition language (XSD). It looks just like XML, but it is used to define the structure of the data instead of the data itself. You could actually send the XSD file describing the layout of your data to someone else, who could use it to create data that would be compatible with your database system. In fact, in Lab 14.2 later in this chapter, we do just that, validating the external data against the schema to make sure it conforms.

Another advantage of XML is that it is an accepted standard, and there are plenty of parsers out there for it. Many platforms and browsers have code already built to read and navigate XML data, so you won't have to do it yourself.

XML Structure and Syntax

Although XML is text-based, it follows a very specific format and syntax that must be adhered to. If you've used HTML to any degree, you know it can be somewhat forgiving, allowing you to leave off trailing tags, mix tags in a odd order, or change capitalization as you desire.

Not so with XML. It is rigid in syntax and format. First, XML is case sensitive. It is very important to pay attention to this. Neither Visual Basic or HTML are case sensitive, so it takes some getting used to. Errors in case are also hard to track down. Second, unlike HTML, XML always requires closing tags; otherwise, errors are raised. Third, it is rigidly hierarchical; nested tags must be nested correctly.

So given these rules, what does XML look like? Here's a simple example of some XML data representing a little information about cars.

```
<Cars>
     <Car>
          <CarID>1</CarID>
          <EngineSize units="liters">2.0</EngineSize>
          <Brakes>Front-disc</Brakes>
          <Transmission>Automatic</Transmission>
          <BodyType>Sedan</BodyType>
     </Car>
     <Car>
          <CarID>2</CarID>
          <EngineSize units="liters">2.2</EngineSize>
          <Brakes>Anti-Lock</Brakes>
          <Transmission>5-speed Manual</Transmission>
          <BodyType>Hatchback</BodyType>
     </Car>
</Cars>
```

The outer tag, <Cars>, encapsulates the whole data set. Each record in the data set is represented by the <Car> tag. Note that each has an end tag like HTML, with a slash and the name repeated. Between the <Car> and </Car> tags are actual rows of data. We have two rows here representing two cars. There are five parts to each car in our data, each representing a column in a database table: CarID, EngineSize, Brakes, Transmission, and BodyType. All these tags are part of XML items called elements. An element is the basic unit of data in XML.

Within elements, there are any number of attributes you can define. There are many predefined attributes, and you can make up your own as well. In our example, we used an attribute on the EngineSize called units, which defines the units in which the EngineSize is measured. Here are the rules you have to follow when defining or generating your own attributes.

Quotations around attribute values are not optional. Unlike HTML, you have to use the quotes around the attribute values. You can use single or double quotes, but you must be consistent within a single value. (It's a best practice to pick one or the other to use consistently across the entire chunk of XML.)

Attributes are name-value pairs. You can't put in an attribute without an associated value. Make sure that every named attribute has a quoted value.

Attribute values can only contain text. You're not allowed to put additional markup code inside an attribute value. Values can contain numbers, dates, or currency values, but all are treated as quoted string values.

Attributes within an element must have unique names. Duplicate names are not permitted.

Attribute names must begin with a letter or an underscore. After that, the names may contain letters, digits, periods, underscores, or dashes.

You can nest elements to about any level you like, defining all sorts of data hierarchies. If you are simply representing information that does not come from a database, such as saved options for your application, you're probably fine with simple XML data standing on its own. However, if you have real application data from a database that's relational or needs to be validated, your data will need help from XML Schemas.

XML Schemas

Any database that has a table in it uses a schema to define its layout and relationships. XML is no exception, and the designers of XML created a format that enables us to define the schema of XML data and associate a schema with our data.

The schema serves two purposes. First, it is used like an interface to publish the format of your data. If you need to transmit or share your data with others, you use the schema to tell them about the format of your data. Second, schemas are used to validate external XML data. For example, if you receive XML data from an external source, you can validate the data against your schema. These are both fabulous uses for a schema, and make them worth having around.

Let's take a look at what an XML schema looks like. The following code defines the schema for our car data example:

```
<?xml version="1.0" encoding="utf-8" ?>
<xsd:schema id="CarsData"
     targetnamespace="http://www.mycardata.com">
     <xsd:complexType>
          <xsd:sequence>
               <xsd:element name="CarID" type="xsd:unsignedInt" />
               <xsd:element name="EngineSize" type="xsd:decimal" />
               <xsd:element name="Brakes" type="xsd:string" />
               <xsd:element name="Transmission" type="xsd:string" />
               <xsd:element name="BodyType" type="xsd:string" />
          </xsd:sequence>
     </xsd:complexType>
</xsd:schema>
```

This schema has a complex type in it, which is very much like a Visual Basic user-defined type. It defines the five columns we've already seen. When you dissect it a little, here's what's there.

The first line of the schema is standard, and we don't have to worry about it unless you want to generate it entirely yourself. The second line gives the schema an ID that we'll need later and a target namespace. A namespace is simply a unique name given to any chunk of code, or in this case, schema code. It enables us to refer to the schema by a unique name and differentiate it from other schemas. We'll see the namespace in use later when we link the schema to some XML data.

The next two lines are required to start a complex type. Beyond that are the lines that define our data columns and the terminating tags. Look at one of the column definitions:

```
<xsd:element name="CarID" type="xsd:unsignedInt" />
```

We've given the element a name, which corresponds to the name of the column. There's also a data type, in this case, unsigned integer. There are plenty of data types available in the XSD world, which you can find in the Visual Studio Help system.

There are far more complex things you can do with XML schemas, including defining your own simple types and creating table relationships and primary keys. For example, the following code defines a data type based on an integer that has minimum and maximum values, establishing a range:

```
<xsd:simpleType name="UpTo100">
     <xsd:restriction base="integer">
          <xsd:minInclusive value="0" fixed="true">
          <xsd:maxInclusive value="100" fixed="true">
     </xsd:restriction>
</xsd:simpleType>
```

We used two facets, or attributes, that define constraints on data types, to place minimum and maximum values on the type. We can now create elements in our schema using this type. Refer to the Visual Studio .NET Help for more information on the various facets available, as well as other capabilities such as defining relationships.

Visual Studio .NET XML Tools

You sometimes need to experiment with schemas or create them yourself and more often to create your own XML data. Microsoft provides you with a couple of editors to help out with these tasks. You can use them to create your own schemas or XML data with the added benefit of IntelliSense and visual editing. Let's take a look at schemas first because they help us create valid data.

Creating a Schema

To construct a schema, first create a new WinForms application in Visual Studio .NET. Name it whatever you like. Then add a schema to your project by right-clicking the project in the Solution Explorer and choosing Add New Item from the context menu. From the list, select XML schema. Give it a name and click OK, and it should open up to a blank screen in the editor. From the Toolbox on the left, you can drag any of the XML schema items to the work area. Drag a complex type and drop it in the work area.

Once there, the complex type looks like a little data grid, which you use to define its elements. Click in the little column on the left, and select what you want to add to the complex type from the drop-down list that appears. Select Element. It has a default name of element1, which isn't useful. Change it to the name of the first element in our car type, CarID. Then move to the last column and select a data type, in this case, unsignedInt. You can also take a look at the drop-down list of data types to see what's available to you. Add four more elements to match the Car type we made earlier. Your screen should look something like Figure 14.9.

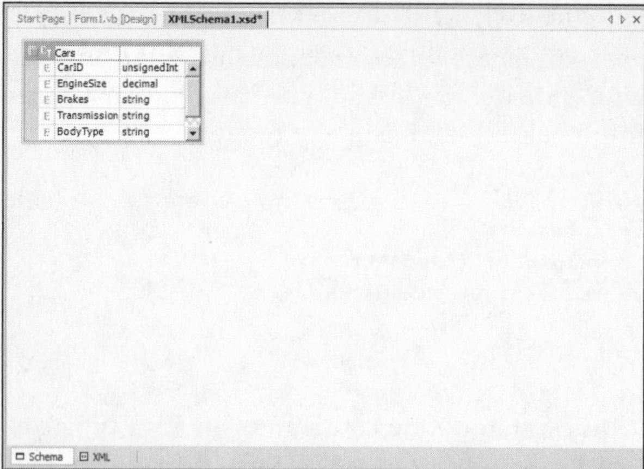

Figure 14.9 Our car data type as rendered in the Visual Studio .NET XSD Schema editor.

Notice the two tabs at the bottom of the editor, Schema and XML. The Schema tab is what we've been using to visually define our schema. Switch to the XML tab to see the coded XML representation of the schema. It looks like the following, very much resembling what we defined manually:

```
<?xml version="1.0" encoding="utf-8" ?>
<xs:schema id="XMLSchema1"
     targetNamespace="http://tempuri.org/XMLSchema1.xsd"
     elementFormDefault="qualified"
     xmlns="http://tempuri.org/XMLSchema1.xsd"
     xmlns:mstns="http://tempuri.org/XMLSchema1.xsd"
     xmlns:xs="http://www.w3.org/2001/XMLSchema">
     <xs:complexType name="Cars">
          <xs:sequence>
               <xs:element name="CarID" type="xs:unsignedInt" />
               <xs:element name="EngineSize" type="xs:decimal" />
               <xs:element name="Brakes" type="xs:string" />
               <xs:element name="Transmission" type="xs:string" />
               <xs:element name="BodyType" type="xs:string" />
          </xs:sequence>
     </xs:complexType>
</xs:schema>
```

The information in the heading is more verbose and includes additional namespace references for standard XSD definitions. The XSD prefix for the elements is abbreviated to XS. It still works well. The rest looks just like the schema we created.

If you already have an external XML schema and need to use it, you can load it right into your project as an existing item. You can then use the Schema tab to view a nice diagram of it, instead of having to pour over the code. The diagram is automatically created for you once the schema is loaded.

With a basic knowledge of schemas and one defined in the studio, we can use it to enter XML data.

Creating XML Data

Just like we added a schema to the project, we can add XML data. Right-click on the project in the Solution Explorer and select Add New Item; then select XML File. The data we create will be stored in this file. The studio opens the empty file in source mode on the XML tab. If we try to switch to the Data tab, a much better place to enter data, we'll get an error at this point because Visual Studio .NET has no idea what type of data we want to enter. To make it understand what data we will be entering, we have to associate a schema with the XML file.

In the Properties window of the studio, which we haven't seen much of in this chapter, we need to set the TargetSchema property of the XML file. Select the schema we just created from the list. Then switch to the Data tab at the bottom of the screen, and enter data based on the schema. Give it a try. It actually represents the owner and address as top-level fields and the car information as hierarchical. Figure 14.10 shows what it looks like.

Now switch to the XML tab to see the generated XML, which looks something like this:

```
<?xml version="1.0" encoding="utf-8" ?>
<schema xmlns="http://tempuri.org/XMLSchema1.xsd">
      <CarAndOwner>
            <Owner>Tony Martin</Owner>
            <Address>1234 Middle of Nowhere</Address>
            <Car>
                  <CarID>1</CarID>
                  <EngineSize>1.9</EngineSize>
                  <Brakes>Front Disc</Brakes>
                  <Transmission>5-speed manual</Transmission>
                  <BodyType>Sedan</BodyType>
            </Car>
      </CarAndOwner>
</schema>
```

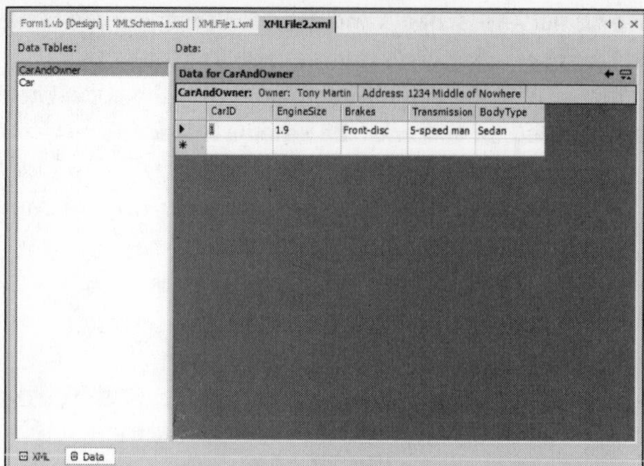

Figure 14.10 XML data in the editor, with a hierarchical relationship.

Pretty impressive. Notice at the top of the XML that our own schema is associated with the XML data. This is how they are linked together. The tempuri.org is a placeholder and should be changed to a meaningful namespace before you do anything public with the data.

Classroom Q & A

Q: All our data binding has been in code. Can I data bind ASP.NET data controls in the designer using properties, like I can with normal Windows applications?

A: Absolutely. Notice that controls such as the DataGrid have DataSource properties exposed in the studio's Properties window. Each data control has the data binding properties relevant to it. However, you have less control over the data-binding code, which will now be generated for you. And your data adapter and data sets will have to appear in the designer.

Q: How fast is data binding? Are there any performance issues I should be aware of?

A: ASP.NET data binding only requires a trip to the server when new data is needed on the client. When the binding occurs, it all happens on the server and in compiled code. It is then rendered as HTML and sent to the client. So although it has a small amount of overhead required by the fact that it has to be rendered and sent back to the client, it's still pretty quick. Treat it like you do ASP.NET events. Use it when you need it, but design so that you keep round-trips to a minimum.

Q: How often are the XML Designer tools in the studio actually useful? They seem kind of pointless for real development. How often do I need to manually create a schema or XML data?

A: Although you probably won't use them all the time, they have some specific uses that are quite beneficial. First, the Schema designer lets you design a schema visually. You can use it to play around and experiment. Also, it makes a great viewer for XML schemas. Second, the XML editor is handy for creating data that only exists as XML and not in a database. If you are storing, say, user-preference information in your application using XML, you could create default data or model the data using the XML editor. Other possibilities are up to your imagination.

Lab 14.2: XML in Code

We've looked at the basics of XML, what it can do, what it looks like, and what Visual Studio tools are available to create and edit it. However, we've yet to actually use it in an application or see it put to use. This lab shows how to load external XML data from a file, load a schema into our program, and then validate it against a schema. Once loaded and validated, we'll populate a DataSet with it and data bind it to a data grid on a Web page.

We'll create some data and a schema first to use in the project. However, instead of entering a schema and data using the Visual Studio .NET tools, we'll generate our data and schema from a database and use some code tools to create what we need. We'll then build a data generator utility to create the files. Let's get started.

Perform the following steps:

1. Create a database in SQL Server as we've done in previous chapters. Name it Ch14Lab14b. Add one table called Computer and put the following columns in the table:

   ComputerID. Data type is int; set the Identity value to True. It is our primary key.

   CPU. Data type is int and contains the CPU speed in megahertz.

   CPUBrand. Data type is char and contains the brand name of the CPU maker.

   RAM. Data type is int and contains the number of megabytes of RAM in the machine.

   HDDSize. Data type is int and stores the number of megabytes in the hard disk.

CDROM. Data type is int and contains a 1 if a CD-ROM is present, or 0 if not.

DVDROM. Data type is int and contains a 1 if a DVD-ROM is present, or 0 if not.

VideoRAM. Data type is int and contains the number of megabytes of video RAM in the machine.

2. Now we need a simple utility to generate the files we need. Create a new WinForms project in Visual Studio .NET. Ours is called Ch14Lab14bGenerator.

3. Add the following controls to the form, setting their properties as stated. When you're done, it should look like Figure 14.11.

Title label. Create a label at the top and set its text to Data Generator. (Feel free to adjust the font to make it look better.)

Data grid. Set its ID to dgData. The control should fill most of the form.

Save button. Drop a button on the bottom left. Change its ID to btnSave and its text property to Save.

Exit button. Drop a button on the bottom right. Change its ID to btnExit and its text property to Exit.

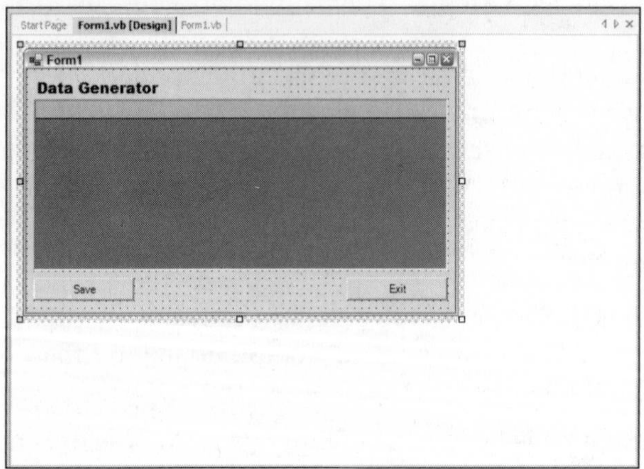

Figure 14.11 Layout of the data generator utility controls.

4. Add the following code to the form_load event. It will load all the data from the Computer table we build in the Ch14Lab14b database and bind it to the data grid.

```
Private Sub Form1_Load(ByVal sender As System.Object, _
    ByVal e As System.EventArgs) Handles MyBase.Load
    Dim conn As New SqlConnection(CONNSTR)
```

```
        Dim da As New SqlDataAdapter("select * from computer", conn)
        Try
            conn.Open()
            da.Fill(ds, "Computers")
            conn.Close()
            dgData.SetDataBinding(ds, "Computers")
        Catch ex As SqlException
            MsgBox(ex.Message)
            conn.Close()
        End Try
    End Sub
```

5. Add the event handlers for the buttons. The Exit button is simple. The few lines of code for the Save button are far more interesting: The first two lines in the Try clause make use of our preloaded data set's built-in capabilities for writing our XML and XSD files. Simply provide them with a filename and it takes care of the rest. Pretty slick.

```
    Private Sub btnExit_Click(ByVal sender As System.Object, _
        ByVal e As System.EventArgs) Handles btnExit.Click
        Me.Close()
    End Sub
    Private Sub btnSave_Click(ByVal sender As System.Object, ByVal e
    As System.EventArgs) Handles btnSave.Click
        Try
            ds.WriteXml("Ch14XML.xml")
            ds.WriteXmlSchema("Ch14Schema.xsd")
            MsgBox("Schema and XML created successfully.")
        Catch ex As Exception
            MsgBox(ex.Message)
        End Try
    End Sub
```

6. Run the program. If all goes well, the program runs, loads with whatever data you've put into the database, and displays it in the grid. Click the Save button; you should get a successful save message, and two files are written to wherever your project was created, in the BIN directory. Remember this because we'll use these files shortly.

The utility we wrote to generate XML data and schema files can be modified, with just a little work, to be a generic generator that could create these files for any database, server, and SQL select statement. You'd have a fast, easy-to-use program to create XML and schema whenever you need it.

7. Now it's time to create the ASP.NET project and lay out our page. Create a new Web project in Visual Studio.NET and name it Ch14Lab14b.

8. Create the controls on the Web page. It's pretty simple. Add the following items to the page:

   Title label. Add a label for the title of the page and change its text property to Computer XML Data.

   Data grid. Add a data grid to the page. We'll use this to display all the data for review once it's validated against the schema.

   Errors textbox. Add a large text box underneath the data grid. Set its TextMode property to Multiline, and its Visible property to False. We'll turn it on only if there were validation errors.

9. Copy the XML and XSD files we created with our utility to the Web application project directory. If you use the default directories for the Web projects, you'll place them in c:\inetpub\wwwroot\Ch14Lab14b.

10. We need to add a few imports to our code, so enter these three lines at the top of the source file, outside the class:

```
Imports System.Data.SqlClient
Imports System.XML
Imports System.XML.Schema
```

11. Now it's time to add some functional code. In the page_load event, we will load the XML file into a DataSet, validate it against our schema, and then data bind it to the grid. Here's the code:

```
Private Sub Page_Load(ByVal sender As System.Object, _
    ByVal e As System.EventArgs) Handles MyBase.Load
    If Not IsPostBack Then
        ' Declare a bunch of objects.
        Dim doc As New XmlDocument()
        Dim tr As New XmlTextReader( _
           Server.MapPath("Ch14XML3.xml"))
        Dim vr As New XmlValidatingReader(tr)
        Dim xsc As New XmlSchemaCollection()
        Dim ds As New DataSet("computers")
        Try
            ' Add the schema from the file to our list
            ' of schemas (only one).
            xsc.Add("http://tempuri.org/Ch14Schema.xsd", _
                Server.MapPath("Ch14Schema.xsd"))
            vr.Schemas.Add(xsc)
            ' Add a handler routine for validation errors.
            AddHandler vr.ValidationEventHandler, _
                AddressOf ValidCallback
```

```
            vr.ValidationType = ValidationType.Schema
            ' Load and validate the XML.
            doc.Load(vr)
        Catch ex As Exception
            tbErrors.Text = ex.Message
        End Try
        ' If there were no errors, load the data
        ' into the grid.
        If Len(sErrs) = 0 Then
            Try
                ' Read the data from the XML file.
                ds.ReadXml(Server.MapPath("Ch14XML.xml"))
                ' Bind it to the grid.
                dgData.DataSource = ds
                dgData.DataBind()
            Catch ex As Exception
                tbErrors.Text = ex.Message
            End Try
        Else
            ' Display the errors that were found.
            tbErrors.Text = sErrs
            tbErrors.Visible = True
        End If
    End If
End Sub
```

Let's take some time here to go over this code, and then we'll continue our project. First, there are a few objects we haven't seen before, all related to dealing with XML data and schemas:

XMLDocument. Stores the parsed contents of an XML document.

XMLTextReader. A fast, forward-only reader for XML data; good for simple loading.

XMLValidatingReader. A reader that provides validation services for XML data.

XMLSchemaCollection. Contains a collection of XML schemas.

We add the schema to the XMLSchemaCollection, which loads it from the file, using the collection's Add method. Then we add the schema collection to the XMLValidatingReader, which uses it to validate as it reads. The validating reader uses an error-handling function that you define. If it encounters errors, it traps them and hands them off to your function for you to do as you see fit with them. At this point, you have to give the address of your error-handling function to the validating reader. You do this with the AddHandler statement. Pass it the validating reader and the address of the handler function called ValidCallback, which we will be creating. For now, just enter the reference; we'll add the function in a moment. All our error-handling callback function does is collect the errors, appending each one to a string variable defined as class data.

Next we set the validation type of the reader to Schema and call the Load method on the XMLDocument object, passing it the validating reader to do the work. This is the call that does all the validation. When it runs, it uses the address of the validation function we gave it, calling our function when an error occurs.

Once that's done, we check to see if there are any errors. If not, use the data set to read the XML data using its ReadXML method. We pass it the name of the XML file we want to read. Note the use of the Server.MapPath() method. This finds the root path to our Web application, which is where we put the files we created. Once the data set is populated with the XML data, we simply bind it to the data grid on the page. If there were errors in the data validation process, we assign the error string, which contains all the errors that occurred during validation, to the text property of our error text control, tbErrors.

We have created an error handler in our lab that traps all the XML validation errors so that we can display them to the user. However, you may not need all the details of each error. You may only need to know if it is error-free. If this is all you need, don't provide an error-handling callback function. If you don't, the validating reader will stop on the first error it encounters, which can be trapped through normal error handling. This will make your validation faster and less complex.

Normally you wouldn't put all this processing in the page_load event handler. You'd place it in a separate method or even a separate class library to make the code more maintainable. We placed it here to illustrate XML validation as simply as possible.

12. Now we need to add the error-handling callback function that will collect our validation errors, if any. Add the following method to the code. The parameters for the method are specific and should be the same as those listed here, regardless of what you do in the method. Note that you can get the error messages from the args parameter.

```
Public Sub ValidCallback(ByVal sender As Object, _
    ByVal args As ValidationEventArgs)
    ' Collect the error messages as they occur.
    sErrs &= args.Message() & vbCrLf
End Sub
```

13. Run the program. If all goes well, you should see the data in the data grid, as shown in Figure 14.12.

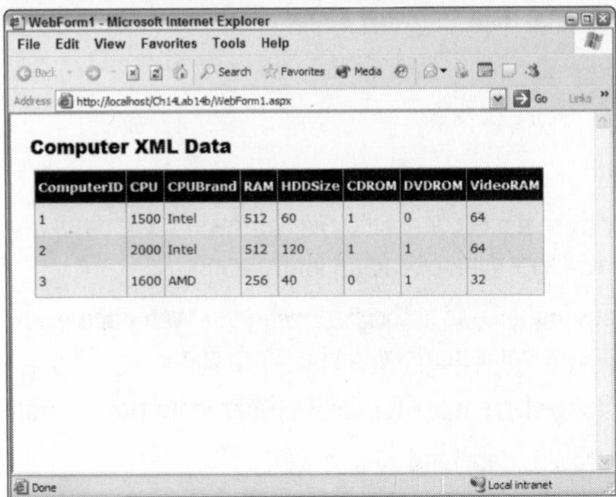

Figure 14.12 A successful run of our lab Web application, displaying XML data in a data grid.

You can simulate errors by making a few edits to the XML. For example, if you change the name of the Computer type to Computer1, you'll get all kinds of errors about all the elements that follow it. The code turns off the data grid and turns on the errors text box, displaying the errors.

This lab illustrated the process of loading external XML data, validating it against an external schema, and displaying it in a Web page. You can use the same techniques in your own programs.

Summary

This chapter covered the details of data binding in a Web environment, as well as the essentials of XML and using it in code. The Web-based data-bound controls were covered, and we talked to a database from a Web page through the IIS server, into a class library, and on to the database. The XML tools inside the Visual Studio .NET environment were demonstrated. We saw how to use XML data and validate it against an XML schema.

These data tools are fabulous items to have in your Web development repertoire. Experiment further to find out what else they are capable of, and you'll be writing killer data-driven Web applications in no time.

Review Questions

1. How do you create an XML file from a data set? How about creating an XML schema?
2. Which data control provides you with near-automatic data paging?
3. What is impersonation?
4. How is impersonation enabled for a Web application?
5. Write a database connection string that will connect to the Northwind database, on the server called EAGLEDB, using the user's Windows login information.
6. What sort of functionality belongs in the code associated with your Web page, and what sort belongs in separate classes you reference in your Web code?
7. When does the SelectedIndexChanged event fire for the Web-based list box control?
8. How do you cause multiple controls to data bind all at once?
9. Write a segment of code that will connect to the database, retrieve two columns from a table called MainCourses (MainCourseDesc and MainCourseID), and data bind both the description and ID into a list box. This enables you to get the associated ID when the user selects a text item.

Answers to Review Questions

1. Once the DataSet is populated with data, you can use its built-in methods to create XML data. The schema is created using the WriteXMLSchema method, and the actual data is created using the WriteXML method. Simply supply a filename for each, and call the methods.
2. The DataGrid is the only data-bound Web control that has paging built in. You have to supply the function that tells it what to display on each page, but it provides the paging controls that you can customize to your own needs.
3. Impersonation is the ability of IIS to act on behalf of, and be authenticated as, a Windows user. If your Web application needs to authenticate users based on their membership in a domain or workgroup, this is your best option.
4. You enable impersonation in a Web application by adding a single clause to the application's Web.config file:

```
<identity impersonate="true" />
```

5. To connect to a SQL Server database using Windows authentication and the user's credentials, you need to make use of a trusted connection. The database connection string looks like this:

```
Dim CONNSTR As String = "Database=Northwind; Server=EAGLEDB; " & _
     "Trusted_Connection=true;"
```

6. When building enterprise applications, you want to keep as much functionality as possible in separate components, so keep only what you need to in the code associated with your Web page. This means that you should limit your Web code to user interface handling and data binding. Any other functionality, such as database access and business functionality, should go into class libraries.
7. The SelectedIndexChanged event in normal WinForms applications usually fires right away, as soon as the user makes a change. However, in ASP.NET, the event only fires its event handler when the page is posted. The model is that users make changes to their selection, then post the form, and you can read the change. The event is not superfluous; you can use it when the page is posted to distinguish whether a change is being made to that list box or not.
8. Individual data-bound controls each have their own DataBind methods that cause them to be bound then and there. However, when you have many controls, it's much easier and more efficient to bind them all at once. You do this with the DataBind method on the page object, or Page.DataBind().

9. The key to using both a data-bound text value and a data-bound key value is to bind them both using two different properties of the list box, DataTextField and DataValue-Field. The code looks like this:

```
Dim conn As New SqlConnection( _
    "database=Food; server=(local); uid=sa; pwd=;")
Dim da As New SqlDataAdapter("select MainCourseDesc, " & _
    "MainCourseID from MainCourses", conn)
Dim ds As New DataSet()
Try
    conn.Open()
    da.Fill(ds, "MainCourses")
    conn.Close()
    ListBox1.DataSource = ds.Tables("MainCourses")
    ListBox1.DataTextField = "MainCourseDesc"
    ListBox1.DataValueField = "MainCourseID"
Catch ex As SqlException
End Try
```

CHAPTER

15

XML Web Services

Access to distributed functionality has been an important aspect of programming ever since the term *client server* first became popular in the early 1990s. However, it has always been full of complications involving security, protocols, performance, compatibility, and other elements of using functionality located on another machine. There are still plenty of issues to deal with, but the advent of Web services has alleviated many of the problems to the point that it's actually pleasant to build distributed components. This chapter explores Web services and shows how to build services and use them in an enterprise environment.

Introduction to Web Services

There have been many attempts to deal with remote functionality in the programming world. The most famous Microsoft attempt was Distributed COM (DCOM). It had some problems, including the fact that it required specific communication lines over a network. DCOM only was binary compatible with Intel architectures, and building applications to work with these architectures was difficult; to deploy them and have them work the first time was another story.

Lots of technologies have come together to bring about the advent of Web services: XML, the Internet, the World Wide Web, as well as the problems with other alternatives. Which brings us to the question, "What exactly is a Web service?"

A Web service is a component containing functionality, much like a class library or COM component. It is a compiled DLL just like any other component. The big difference between Web services and other components is that Web services work over an HTTP wire as well as normal network lines. There are other characteristics of Web services, including the following:

- Web services only have to be binary compatible with the system on which they reside. All communications with the service, including functionality requests and returned results, are text-based.
- Because Web services do not need to be binary compatible with other computers, they are great for functionality in heterogeneous systems. Mainframes can call services located on Linux machines or can be accessed from Intel clients. Web services can be used with any operating system, on any platform, under any component model.
- All messaging, as mentioned, is text-based and, in particular, XML-based. It uses a standard for communication that has been embraced by many people and organizations.
- Functionality can be published on the Web. You can build your components and publish them for the world. You also can use the functionality published by others.

Just about anyone or anything can use Web services, including Web pages and Web applications, Win32 applications, WinForms applications, other components, components on other servers, and even other Web services. Essentially, anything that has access to an HTTP line can consume Web services. Interestingly enough, with a little extra work, you can even access Web services from Visual Basic 6 applications.

There are several technologies that come together to make XML Web services work. We'll discuss them shortly, but for now, let's take an introductory look at what Web services are like.

Lab 15.1: A First Web Service

This lab demonstrates the basics of building a Web service, gives you a picture of what it's like to get one running, and debugs it. We'll create a simple Web service that handles a few math routines. Nothing too complex to distract from the service mechanics, but enough to see how a Web service works and dissect one.

Perform these steps:

1. Start by creating a new project in Visual Studio .NET by selecting File, New, Project from the File menu. Select the ASP.NET Web Service project type on the New Project dialog. Because Web services are Web-based, they are created in the Web server directory structure, much like ASP.NET projects. Change the default name Service1 to Math. The dialog should look like Figure 15.1.

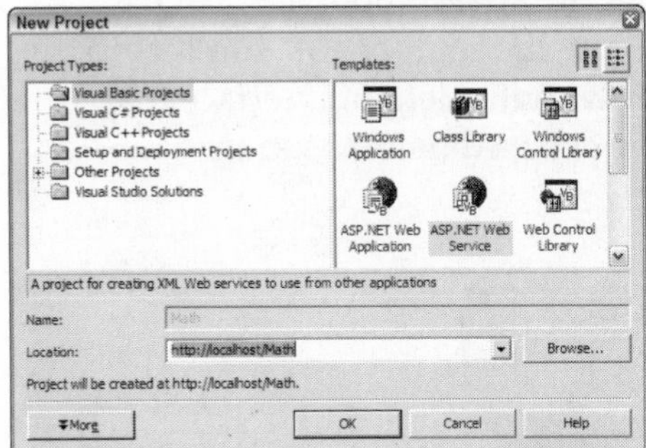

Figure 15.1 Setting up a new Web service project in Visual Studio .NET.

2. The starting page you get when you create a Web service is an empty design field. This is not terribly useful for Web services, so click the code view button at the top of the Solution Explorer. The view changes to a code editor. You'll see the normal generated section with component-initialization code, as well as a commented-out HelloWorld method. Delete the sample code and replace it with the following real code:

```
<WebMethod()> Public Function Cube(ByVal lNum As Long) As Long
    Return lNum * lNum * lNum
End Function
<WebMethod()> Public Function RandomNum(ByVal iLow As Integer, _
    ByVal iHigh As Integer) As Integer
    Return CInt(Rnd(1) * (iHigh - iLow)) + iLow
End Function
```

The code looks pretty standard. There's a method to calculate the cube of any number and another that calculates a random number in a specified range. However, there is one piece of this code that is not normal: <WebMethod()>.

The WebMethod attribute does two things. First, it tells the code generator in Visual Studio .NET to expose the method as part of the Web service interface. It becomes a method that you can call from a client that uses the Web service. Second, it allows you to specify some additional parameters between the parentheses. For example, you could put a description of the Web service in there or define its namespace. There are other options to explore later. For now, the important part is that it makes the method part of the interface. The rest of the code works as normal methods.

3. Build and run the Web service. Didn't know you could do that, did you? This type of component has a Web-based entry point, its asmx file, and can be executed in a browser. The asmx file provides a default interface to let you run and test the component. Click the Run button on the toolbar to execute the component. You'll get a new instance of the Web browser with the default interface that starts by providing a list of all the exposed methods in the Web service. It looks like Figure 15.2.

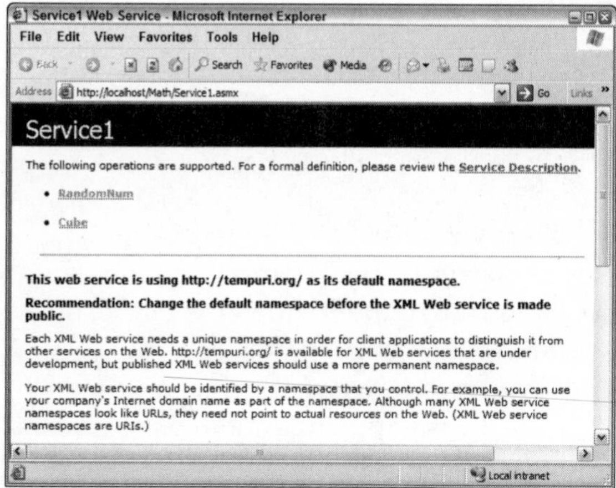

Figure 15.2 The default user interface that is created when you run a Web service from the studio.

4. Click one of the methods. In this case, we clicked the RandomNum method. This presents you with an intermediate page that allows you to enter any parameters that the selected method might take. If there are no parameters, you get only an Invoke button. Enter a minimum and maximum value for the two parameters. The page looks like Figure 15.3.

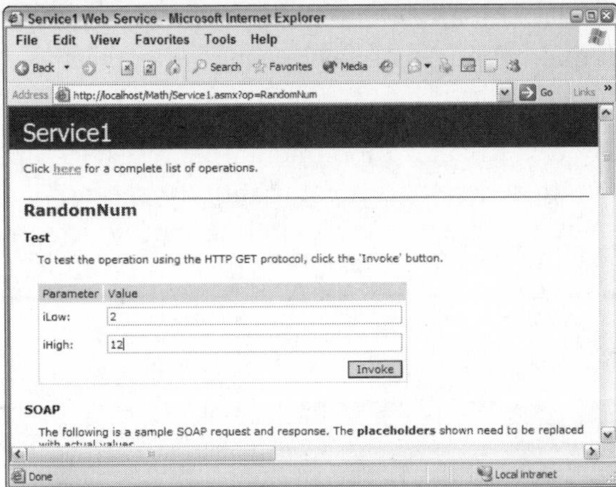

Figure 15.3 The parameter entry page for a Web service.

5. Click the Invoke button. This executes the service method selected with the parameter values supplied. A new browser instance opens with the results. As mentioned, all the inputs, outputs, and requests for a Web service are text-based. They are not based on just any text, but on XML text. Therefore, the results from the method call are returned in XML format. Figure 15.4 shows the results in the browser window.

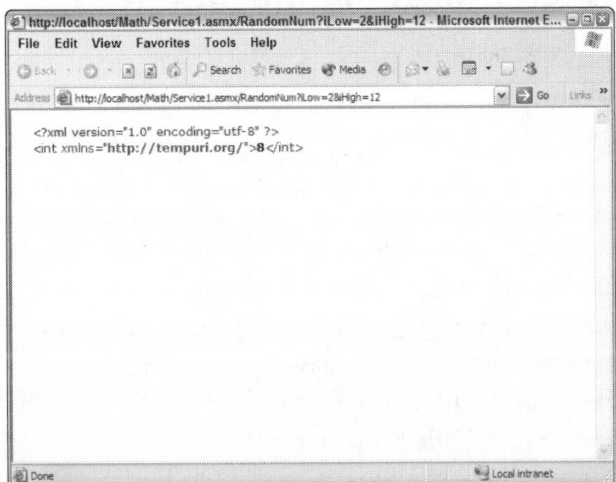

Figure 15.4 The results returned by the Web service in XML format.

6. Try one last step. Set a breakpoint anywhere in the code and run it again. You'll see that normal debugging mechanisms are in place and working properly for you.

This lab showed how easy it is to get a fundamental Web service up and running. You don't have to worry about compatibility settings or generating interfaces for use by the client. You can debug your Web services without creating test drivers, which saves lots of time and coding.

Associated Technologies

Web services at their heart are just components with text-based interfaces, inputs, and outputs; however, to make them work and be practical for use by others, several steps are required. For example, what defines the standard text interfaces for Web services? How does your own code communicate with them? And how do you find out what Web services are out there for your own use? All these questions are answered by the technologies that cooperate to solve the Web service problem. We discuss the various technologies, and then bring them together.

Universal Discovery, Description, and Integration

A tangent technology that helps with Web services is UDDI. It's more of a technique than a technology and is really just a Web services directory. You can use UDDI to find out what's out there for your own use—the services others have made available for the public.

The directories are hosted on servers run by a few large companies, including IBM, Microsoft, and Ariba. You can go to their Web sites and view the directories of services and even their WSDL contracts. Often there are descriptions of the services to go with the other information. You can also list your own services there, making them available to the rest of the world.

Understand, though, that these are simply directories, not hosting services. If you want to make your service available to others, you can list it on the UDDI servers. However, hosting your service is up to you. The directories point prospective users to your URL. Although UDDI isn't critical to using your own Web services, it is important if you want to publish them for the world.

Namespaces

We spoke briefly in the previous chapter about namespaces and what they were. Essentially, a namespace is a unique string that gives a name to a region of code or XML to help make it unique. Namespaces are used along with the names of your Web services to create a unique name combination across the Web. For example, suppose we decided to publish our Math service for the rest of the world to use (presumably, after we added some useful functionality to it). The default namespace for a Web service is a URL string that reads:

```
http://tempuri.org
```

The name Math is not terribly unique. The combination of the tempuri URL and Math is also not unique because tempuri is the default. However, if we create a new namespace name and attach it to our Web service, we could make it unique. Typically, namespaces look like URLs because they are unique to a company. If we made our namespace http://www.noeticart.com, that plus the name Math would be unique. Of course, your namespace doesn't have to be a URL. You could use the name of your dog, your favorite Monty Python quote, or the chemical formula for benzene (C_6H_6).

If a URL is used as a namespace, it really doesn't mean anything. You don't have to go to that URL for access unless the service is hosted there as well. It simply serves to distinguish your service from others.

In the end, the important thing to take away from this is that you should always change the namespace of your Web service to something other than the default. This prevents confusion should you publish it.

Simple Object Access Protocol

SOAP is a standard format for calling functionality and sending and receiving parameters and results. It is based on XML. It is also anything but simple.

SOAP is a standard, much like COM, that tells us how to remotely access functionality in a standard fashion in a heterogeneous environment. It is essentially a specification for the formatting of messages used to transfer information and make requests. Because it is text- and XML-based, any sort of functionality in any kind of binary format that understands SOAP can use any other sort of functionality that supports SOAP. As long as you follow the standard, you can communicate with any other SOAP-based component over HTTP lines.

SOAP, handled manually, can take quite a bit of work. You have to know the standard, and there are lots of details to work with. However, there are easier ways to deal with SOAP than writing the code yourself. There is a nice utility, not to mention the Visual Studio .NET environment, that will help you by creating the SOAP interface.

Web Service Description Language

WSDL is used by Web services and Visual Basic .NET. Remember when we spoke about making your Web service available to others? This is the first part of that job. WSDL uses XML to describe the interface of your Web service. The XML document that describes your interface is called the Web service contract.

Take, for example, the code we wrote in the first lab of this chapter. It was fairly simple and had only two methods. Listed here is the WSDL contract for that service. This is just a fragment of the complete contract because it's too long to list all of it here. Examine it and you'll see the definition of one of our methods:

```
<s:element name="RandomNum">
  <s:complexType>
    <s:sequence>
      <s:element minOccurs="1" maxOccurs="1" name="iLow" type="s:int" />
      <s:element minOccurs="1" maxOccurs="1" name="iHigh" type="s:int" />
    </s:sequence>
  </s:complexType>
</s:element>
<s:element name="RandomNumResponse">
  <s:complexType>
    <s:sequence>
      <s:element minOccurs="1" maxOccurs="1"
       name="RandomNumResult" type="s:int" />
    </s:sequence>
  </s:complexType>
</s:element>
<s:element name="long" type="s:long" />
<s:element name="int" type="s:int" />
```

There is an element with the name of our method. It has a complexType defined for it that details our two input parameters, using XML attributes to fill in the details. There is another element defined, RandomNumResponse, that details the return result for the method. You can see how the XML here defines an interface for this method.

How did I get access to this code, and where does it fit into the construction of a Web service? First, you can manually create the WSDL for a Web service using a utility called disco.exe (disco being short for discovery). It's a command line utility that comes with Visual Studio .NET. Here's how we execute it for the Math service we just built:

```
disco http://localhost/math/service1.asmx?wsdl
```

This creates a file called Service1.wsdl. You provide it with a URL to the service entry point, the asmx file, and add the "?wsdl" on the end. The previous listing is an excerpt from that file. The results are used by other programs to find out what your service can do, sort of like the information that the COM call QueryInterface returns.

Who uses the WSDL contract? You could use it manually if you want to load it and tear it apart in your code and then generate your own SOAP calls for it. This would work and would give you very fine control over your interface and its use. However, it's quite an effort, and most of the time you don't need this level of control. Visual Basic is famous for hiding most of the ugly details and letting you get on with real work. We can automate most of the effort using another command line utility, Visual Basic, and a little gem called the proxy.

The Proxy

So here's what we have so far. There's SOAP, which defines how messages, requests, and data are sent to and from Web services. WSDL defines the interface of a Web service so that we know what methods are available. The hole in the picture is actually putting them together and making the calls available to our own code. To do this with what we know, we'd have to formulate our own SOAP calls to get the interface information and call the functionality. That's a mess, so we'll use the concept of a proxy instead.

The proxy is a chunk of code that you can put into your own project that takes care of making the correct SOAP requests. The code in the proxy isn't too pretty. It handles the details you don't want to deal with. When you talk to the proxy, it stands in for the Web service, and you can call it just as if the Web service were on your own machine, as if it were a standard library you had access to. Let's take a quick look at some proxy code. Here is a listing that shows all the code that enables us to access the math service we built earlier:

```
<System.Diagnostics.DebuggerStepThroughAttribute(), _
    System.ComponentModel.DesignerCategoryAttribute("code"), _
    System.Web.Services.WebServiceBindingAttribute(Name:="Service1Soap", _
    [Namespace]:="http://tempuri.org/")> _
Public Class Service1
    Inherits System.Web.Services.Protocols.SoapHttpClientProtocol
```

```
        Public Sub New()
            MyBase.New
            Me.Url = "http://localhost/math/Service1.asmx"
        End Sub
        <System.Web.Services.Protocols.SoapDocumentMethodAttribute(
            "http://tempuri.org/Cube", _
            RequestNamespace:="http://tempuri.org/", _
            ResponseNamespace:="http://tempuri.org/", _
            Use:=System.Web.Services.Description.SoapBindingUse.Literal, _
            ParameterStyle:=_
            System.Web.Services.Protocols.SoapParameterStyle.Wrapped)>
        Public Function Cube(ByVal lNum As Long) As Long
            Dim results() As Object = Me.Invoke("Cube", New Object() {lNum})
            Return CType(results(0),Long)
        End Function
        Public Function BeginCube(ByVal lNum As Long, _
            ByVal callback As System.AsyncCallback, _
            ByVal asyncState As Object) As System.IAsyncResult
            Return Me.BeginInvoke("Cube", New Object() {lNum}, callback, _
                asyncState)
        End Function
        Public Function EndCube(ByVal asyncResult As System.IAsyncResult) _
            As Long
            Dim results() As Object = Me.EndInvoke(asyncResult)
            Return CType(results(0),Long)
        End Function
        <System.Web.Services.Protocols.SoapDocumentMethodAttribute( _
            "http://tempuri.org/RandomNum", _
            RequestNamespace:="http://tempuri.org/", _
            ResponseNamespace:="http://tempuri.org/", _
            Use:=System.Web.Services.Description.SoapBindingUse.Literal, _
            ParameterStyle:= _
            System.Web.Services.Protocols.SoapParameterStyle.Wrapped)>  _
        Public Function RandomNum(ByVal iLow As Integer, _
            ByVal iHigh As Integer) As Integer
            Dim results() As Object = Me.Invoke("RandomNum", _
                New Object() {iLow, iHigh})
            Return CType(results(0),Integer)
        End Function
        Public Function BeginRandomNum(ByVal iLow As Integer, _
            ByVal iHigh As Integer, ByVal callback As System.AsyncCallback, _
            ByVal asyncState As Object) As System.IAsyncResult
            Return Me.BeginInvoke("RandomNum", New Object() {iLow, iHigh}, _
                callback, asyncState)
        End Function
        Public Function EndRandomNum( _
            ByVal asyncResult As System.IAsyncResult) As Integer
            Dim results() As Object = Me.EndInvoke(asyncResult)
            Return CType(results(0),Integer)
        End Function
    End Class
```

For each method in our service, there is a stand-in method and a Begin and End method for it. The only one we have to worry about is the actual stand-in. When we use a Web service, instead of calling it directly, we make a call to its proxy stand-in, which then calls the service. The question remains, however, where does the proxy code come from?

We can generate it using another command-line utility. Strangely enough, the utility we saw earlier to generate WSDL is called disco.exe, and the utility to generate proxy code is called wsdl.exe. Sounds a little backward, but there's not much we can do about it. We'll just use it. To generate the preceding proxy code, use the following command:

```
Wsdl /language:vb http://localhost/math/service1.asmx?wsdl
```

Now our process for using an existing Web service looks like this:

- Create the proxy using the wsdl.exe utility.
- Add the proxy code module to your project.
- Create an instance of the proxy and use it to call the service methods.

That closes all the holes, but believe it or not, it gets even easier. A second precious stone in our treasure chest of Web service programming wonders is Web references.

Web References

When you build a Visual Basic .NET WinForms application, you typically add references to other components that you need to use, such as a class library that you wrote last month. The reference allows your own program to talk to another component.

When talking with Web services, we've seen how the proxy takes care of communicating with the Web service component; however, it was a bit of a pain to manually generate the proxy code. Visual Studio .NET has made our lives easier yet again by adding the Web reference. It is much like a regular reference, except that when you add a Web reference to your project, the studio actually generates a proxy for you and places it in your project. This eliminates the step where you used the wsdl.exe utility to generate the proxy and add it to the project yourself.

Here's how to make it work, using a simple walkthrough. First, create a new client project that make uses of the Web service created in the first lab. To keep this easy, make it a regular WinForms project. After it comes up with the default form, right-click the References item in the Solution Explorer. From the context menu, select Add Web Reference. This brings up the Add Web Reference dialog, seen in Figure 15.5.

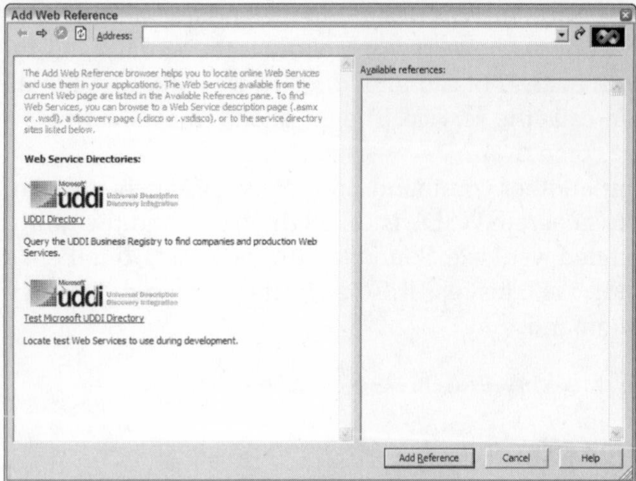

Figure 15.5 Adding a Web reference to a client project.

Adding a Web reference is a little different from adding a normal reference. When adding a standard component reference, you browse to the DLL you want. When adding a Web reference, you effectively browse to the location of the WSDL Web service contract.

If you know the location of the WSDL contract, such as when it is on your own server, you can enter the address directly into the address text box at the top of the dialog. Use the following syntax:

```
http://localhost/math/service1.asmx?wsdl
```

After you press Enter, the dialog navigates to the location and attempts to find the contract. If it is successful, it will display the contract XML in the left pane and enable the Add Reference button (see Figure 15.6).

Once added, you can see the reference in the Solution Explorer under Web References; however, it lists the reference by the name of the server. In this case, the reference is called localhost. It is important to change the name of the reference to something meaningful because this is the name that we use to refer to it in our own code. To rename the reference, right-click the reference name and select Rename from the menu (or click the reference name and press F2). Enter a new name and press Enter. We named ours MathSvc. Figure 15.7 shows what it should look like when done.

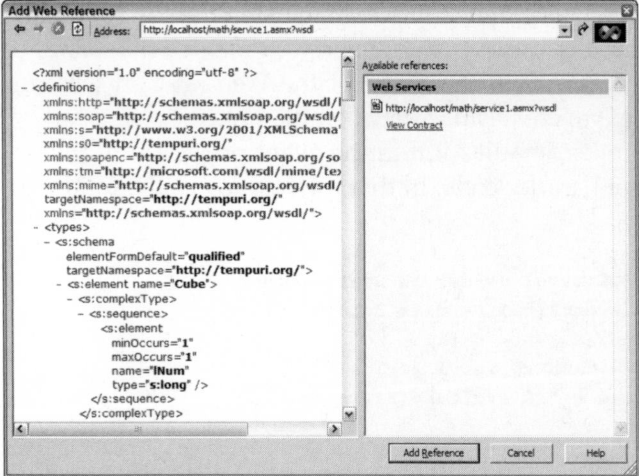

Figure 15.6 The Add Web Reference dialog has successfully found a contract.

I told you that the studio takes care of adding the proxy code, didn't I? If so, where is it? First, click the Show All Files button at the top of the Solution Explorer. The proxy code is normally hidden until you do this. Once done, you'll see that you can expand the Web reference using the plus sign that appears next to it. Click the plus sign, expanding any further plus signs you see. A couple levels down you'll see a file called reference.vb. This is the proxy code. Double-click the file to open it, and you'll see our proxy code, looking very much like the code we manually generated earlier.

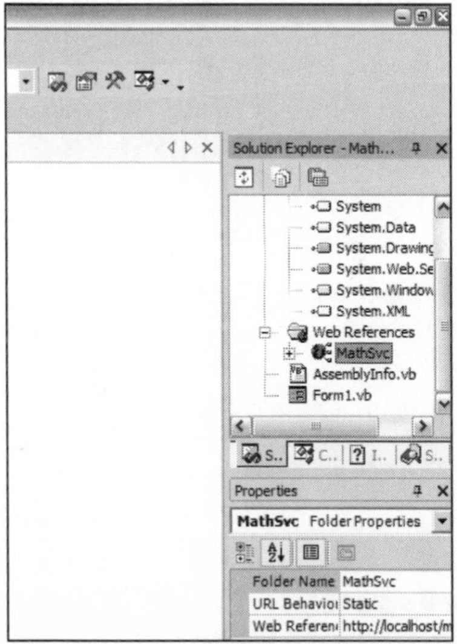

Figure 15.7 The Web reference is renamed to be more meaningful.

So we have a proxy, and it was easier to create than using the command line utility. Now we need to put it to use. A moment ago we renamed the reference to something more meaningful than the name of the Web host on which it resided. We'll use that name to create an instance of the proxy.

Drop a single button on the default form in the client project, and double-click it to bring up its event handler code. In that method, place the following code:

```
Private Sub Button1_Click(ByVal sender As System.Object, _
      ByVal e As System.EventArgs) Handles Button1.Click
      Try
            Dim svc As New MathSvc.Service1()
            MsgBox("5 cubed = " & svc.Cube(5).ToString)
      Catch ex As Exception
            MsgBox(ex.Message)
      End Try
End Sub
```

First, we create an instance of the service proxy. It looks just like we're creating an instance of the Web service itself. The proxy lets us do that. IntelliSense even works. If you enter the name of the service proxy, MathSvc, and press the period (.) key, the studio will pop up a list of all the available classes in the service. In our case, there is only one, Service1. This is the default name given to the class when you create a Web service, and we'll see how to change it later.

Second, we make a call to one of the methods in the class we picked from the service; in this case, it is the Cube method. After our instance of the service proxy has been created, we can use it just like any other component. How convenient! Run the program and see how it works. The result should look something like Figure 15.8.

Now that you know the mechanics of Web services and their use, it is time to learn a little more detail about building your own Web services.

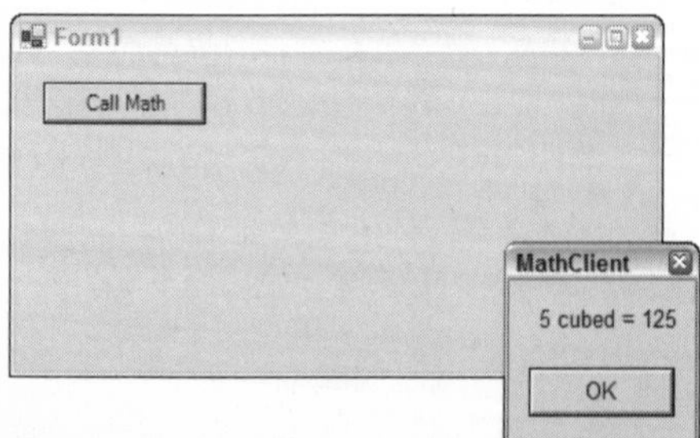

Figure 15.8 A simple client makes use of our Math Web service.

When the Web service is referenced for the first time in a session, it has to load the service and start it up. This takes time. Subsequent calls during the session come from the cached service and are much faster. Therefore, it can be beneficial to preload the service at a time when the user expects to wait anyway. For example, when the program starts up, the user is waiting for things to get rolling. You could make a call to a simple method in your Web service to get it loaded. After that, performance should not be a problem, as long as the session doesn't time out.

Building Your Own Web Services

You can build Web services that are as simple or as elaborate as you like. You can place a single class or multiple classes into your service. Your Web services can be complete class libraries that provide all kinds of functionality. However, there are some details you need to work with, as well as some limitations you need to be aware of.

Building Class Libraries

Web services can be used much like normal class libraries. You can build any functionality you like into them. However, there is an important aspect of class libraries that, when used with Web services, needs special handling. When you have built polymorphic classes, or those that have overloaded methods, Web services need help.

When the .NET runtime calls an overloaded method, it can distinguish between the overloaded methods using the parameters and return type as part of the method's signature. SOAP messages are assumed to be unique. When referencing a Web service method, it simply sends the name of the method it needs to call. It does not use the parameters or return type of the method to distinguish overloaded method names when making a request.

Of course, there is a way to account for this. You wouldn't want to be prevented from using overloaded methods. The trick is in the use of a Web method attribute called MessageName. It goes into the <WebMethod()> attribute of the method declaration. You use it to give each method that has an overloaded name a unique name that will be used when making requests. Consider the following example:

```
<WebMethod()> Public Overloaded Function Cube(ByVal lNum As Long) As
Long
     Return lNum * lNum * lNum
End Function
```

```
<WebMethod()> Public Overloaded Function Cube(ByVal iNum As Integer) _
     As Integer
     Return iNum ^ 3
End Function
```

Although a regular class library would be able to distinguish between these two, a SOAP message cannot. In the IDE, it will not generate an error, either in the editor or during a build. It will only cause a problem when you try to add a Web reference to the service in your own code.

The modified version using the MessageName attribute follows. We gave the second method a new name, a name used by the communication mechanism only, to allow it to tell the two apart.

```
<WebMethod()> Public Overloaded Function Cube(ByVal lNum As Long) As
Long
     Return lNum * lNum * lNum
End Function
<WebMethod(MessageName := "CubeInt")> Public Overloaded Function Cube( _
     ByVal iNum As Integer) As Integer
     Return iNum ^ 3
End Function
```

Now go to the client program that we created previously. Delete the Web reference and then add it back in, renaming it again to MathSvc. Next, navigate to the proxy code, reference.vb, and open it up. Take a look at the proxy methods that refer to our two Cube methods. It looks like this:

```
<System.Web.Services.Protocols.SoapDocumentMethodAttribute( _
     "http://tempuri.org/Cube", RequestNamespace:=
     "http://tempuri.org/",
     ResponseNamespace:="http://tempuri.org/", _
     Use:=System.Web.Services.Description.SoapBindingUse.Literal, _
     ParameterStyle:= _
     System.Web.Services.Protocols.SoapParameterStyle.Wrapped)> _
Public Overloads Function Cube(ByVal lNum As Long) As Long
    Dim results() As Object = Me.Invoke("Cube", New Object() {lNum})
    Return CType(results(0),Long)
End Function
<System.Web.Services.WebMethodAttribute(MessageName:="Cube1"),  _
     System.Web.Services.Protocols.SoapDocumentMethodAttribute( _
     "http://tempuri.org/CubeInt", RequestElementName:="CubeInt", _
     RequestNamespace:="http://tempuri.org/", _
     ResponseElementName:="CubeIntResponse", _
     ResponseNamespace:="http://tempuri.org/", _
     Use:=System.Web.Services.Description.SoapBindingUse.Literal, _
     ParameterStyle:= _
     System.Web.Services.Protocols.SoapParameterStyle.Wrapped)>  _
Public Overloads Function Cube(ByVal iNum As Integer) _
```

```
        As <System.Xml.Serialization.XmlElementAttribute(
            "CubeIntResult")>
        Integer
        Dim results() As Object = Me.Invoke("Cube1", New Object() {iNum})
        Return CType(results(0),Integer)
    End Function
```

Notice that we have two Visual Basic methods, both called Cube, that take the proper parameters, one Long and the other Integer, both defined as Overloads for our own use. Internally, these methods make Invoke calls to Cube (for the Long version) and Cube1 (for the Integer version). The proxy generator renamed each one so that SOAP can differentiate them. If you look in the XML header for each method, you can see that the RequestElementName attributes match the names we gave each method in the Web service using the MessageName attribute.

So, there is a nice mechanism in place that handles overloaded methods for us. This makes all the class library mechanisms available and allows us more freedom when building Web services. But this brings us to another question. Should we really put this much functionality into something that runs on a Web server?

You've run Web services in the Visual Studio .NET environment and seen how it displays a list of the methods available in the Web service. However, if you publish this Web service, or come back to it months later, how will you know what each method does? You can use the description Web method attribute to tell others what each method does. The syntax allows you to enter a description, and when the Web service is run stand-alone, the description is displayed. A typical example might look like this: <WebMethod(Description:="This method generates random numbers.")>. Use this attribute to help your Web services be more self-documenting. There are plenty of additional attributes that you can look up in the Visual Studio .NET help system.

Using the Web Service as an Interface

When building *n*-tier applications, it is important to keep functionality on servers that can properly handle it. When we built ASP.NET applications in previous chapters, we noted that it was important to keep your database and business functionality in separate components, not running inside IIS. This bogs down IIS by using up all its memory and slowing it down. The same is true for Web services.

When building Web services, the same principles of *n*-tier Web development apply. The more functionality you put into them, the more IIS memory they take up and the slower IIS runs. In this case, you should use your Web service to grant access to your functionality to the world and then put the guts into other class libraries. Reference and call those libraries from your Web service.

What we're advocating here is that you use Web services primarily as a Web-based interface to whatever functionality you want to provide. This is not only a great idea, but it is easy to do. Consider the following example. We create a Web service for the math routines we built earlier. However, we move the math routines themselves to a normal class library and reference them from a math Web service. The following code shows the math code moved to regular class; it is followed by a modified math Web service that is simply an interface to the math library. Although this is a simple example, we'll see a much better specimen in Lab 15.2.

```
Public Class MathClass
     Public Overloads Function Cube(ByVal lNum As Long) As Long
          Return lNum * lNum * lNum
     End Function
     Public Overloads Function Cube(ByVal iNum As Integer) As Integer
          Return iNum ^ 3
     End Function
     Public Function RandomNum(ByVal iLow As Integer, _
     ByVal iHigh As Integer) As Integer
          Return CInt(Rnd(1) * (iHigh - iLow)) + iLow
     End Function
End Class

Imports System.Web.Services
<WebService(Namespace := "http://tempuri.org/")> _
     Public Class Service1
     Inherits System.Web.Services.WebService
#Region " Web Services Designer Generated Code "
     <WebMethod(MessageName:="CubeLong")> _
     Public Overloads Function Cube(ByVal lNum As Long) As Long
          Dim objMath As New MathClass.MathClass()
          Return objMath.Cube(lNum)
     End Function
     <WebMethod(MessageName:="CubeInt")> _
     Public Overloads Function Cube(ByVal iNum As Integer) As Long
          Dim objMath As New MathClass.MathClass()
          Return objMath.Cube(iNum)
     End Function
     <WebMethod()> Public Function RandomNum( _
     ByVal iLow As Integer, ByVal iHigh As Integer) As Integer
          Dim objMath As New MathClass.MathClass()
          Return objMath.RandomNum(iLow, iHigh)
     End Function
End Class
```

Granted, this is more code than it took to implement the math functionality purely as Web service. However, if our volume of math functionality was much larger, it would be very beneficial. Our Web service, acting as an interface, would be small and efficient, making calls to more complex functionality in the math class library. If we ever found errors in our complex math functions, we could correct them without the need to change the Web service, which everyone else references. Updates and replacement are simple.

Classroom Q & A

Q: You've stressed the importance of keeping as little functionality in the Web service as possible and hosting most of it in separate class libraries. Where can we draw the line, and how much can you really put in a Web service?

A: You probably want a straight, clear-cut answer, but it isn't quite that simple. The answer is governed by several factors. First, how resource-intensive is your functionality? If you talk to the database a lot, perform lots of disk activity, or require large amounts of memory, you should consider using a separate class library. These things will slow down IIS and reduce your scalability. Second, what are the resources like on your hosting server? If you have tons of memory, disk space, and CPU power, you can host more in your service. Third, how scalable does your application need to be? Will there be 5 users or 5,000? At the lower end, scalability is less important, and you can put more functionality into the Web service itself. If you have to service thousands of users, every cycle is important, and you should keep as much out of the Web service as possible. In the end, it's a balancing act, and you'll have to decide how high your tightrope is. Build and test if you are unsure.

Q: Can you give us an example of how a Web service might be used in a practical application?

A: Sure. Consider that you are an application developer building programs for others to use, either commercially or as internal applications for your company. These applications that you create, despite the fact that you are a superstar programmer, occasionally have a defect or two. Testing finds a fair number of these, but inevitably, some sneak into the application. You can use a Web service to let your users report defects to you. The Web service would sit on a server waiting for calls to log new defects. You build a simple interface into your application that allows the user to enter some defect information and then click a Send button. Your application then calls a method on the Web server that accepts the information, validates it, and then saves it to a database. In half an hour, you have a system that allows your users to help you debug your applications.

Q: What kinds of Web services have others built and published, and how do I find about them or use them?

A: There are some out there, but the market is far from inundated with them. I think most people are still trying to figure out what Web services are, if they are practical, and how to put them to use. However, you can see what's out there simply by opening the Add Web Reference dialog in Visual Studio .NET. When the dialog opens, the left pane has two links available to you. Click on the one that says UDDI directory, and you'll get a search page. You can also browse by clicking the links below the search fields. For example, if you click on the ntis-gov link, you'll see some categories of Web services, including agriculture, construction, mining, manufacturing, retail trade, and others. Just browsing around I found some weather services, credit card authorization services, stock price services, math libraries, and others. You can use them by simply clicking the Add Reference button when it is enabled. Visual Studio .NET will read the Web service's WSDL contract and generate a proxy for you, automatically pointing to the correct hosted location for it. Of course, some of these require licensing fees and won't work until you get a license key.

Web Service Security

As with most of the technologies we've seen surrounding ASP.NET and Web-related functionality, Web services have a role to play when securing your applications. Every aspect of your application must be secured, or not only will the program be unsecured, but it probably won't work, denying access to your users.

There are two parts to securing a Web service using integrated Windows security. First, like an ASP.NET Web application, you must make sure that it is set up to use impersonation, which was discussed in the previous chapter. Your Web service also has a Web.config file that must be edited. To enable impersonation, add the following line of code just after the authentication section of the file:

```
<identity impersonate="true" />
```

After this is in place, the Web service, which runs in IIS just like an ASP.NET application, passes on any credentials received to other components it calls or databases that it accesses.

The second part involves the client. If your client is a Web application, you don't need to do this next step. Instead, simply set it to use impersonation as well. However, if you are building a WinForms client, it is definitely required.

A WinForms client that calls the facilities of a Web service must manually pass on the user's login credentials. It's very easy and involves only a few lines of code. First, add the following two Imports statements to the top of your source file that calls the Web service:

```
Imports System.Web.Services.Protocols
Imports System.Net
```

These give you access to the credentials properties needed. Next, after you create an instance of the Web service proxy in your code, and before you make any calls to the service, add the following line of code:

```
svc.Credentials = CredentialCache.DefaultCredentials
```

The DefaultCredentials property in the credential cache contains the user's integrated Windows security login credentials. Attaching them to the service proxy takes care of our obligation to pass them along to any Web service functionality we need. If the Web service is properly set up to use impersonation, these credentials represent the user that the Web service will impersonate. You can now make any secure Web service calls you need to.

Lab 15.2: A Secure Class Library with Web Service Interface

It's time to bring together everything we've learned in the chapter, as well as other things from previous chapters. We've discussed many technologies, such as Web services, ASP.NET, and Web-based secure database access, all of which work together to help create secure applications that are efficient, scalable, and maintainable. This lab illustrates exactly that.

Our customer wants an application that displays inventory data about computer parts. The application could be used by a computer manufacturer or perhaps a parts outlet. The user will be able to select a part type and then see what parts in that category are available, some information about each part, and how many of each part are in stock. The customer would like to be able to access the data from various sites, either stores or different buildings at their facility. They also want access restricted only to those users from the Windows domain that they define. Finally, they would like to use the Web network or HTTP lines to access the data. This will facilitate the client program running from just about anywhere: laptops, store locations, or heterogeneous networks.

Given what we need to build, here's how we are going to build it. The client will be a WinForms application. The customer did not specify what type of client it wanted, and for the purposes of this lab, we will show that Web services work just as well from a WinForms client as they do from a Web client. In fact, we could very easily replace the client we're building here with an ASP.NET Web client. Feel free to do so if you would like to extend the project. It should take you about 10 minutes.

The client accesses all the data through a Web service. This Web service acts strictly as an interface between the client and the data access functionality. All data access is handled by a separate class library. The class library talks to the database, retrieving the requested inventory data. All this is done securely using Windows integrated security.

We'll be building the project in four parts:

The database. We need to lay out our database and populate it with information. We'll show you the schema and the columns available.

The data access class library. Retrieval of data for the client will be done through this class using specific methods that limit access to just what we want.

The Web service interface. After the class is built, we can create a Web service interface that the client will use, isolating the class library for easy scalability and maintenance.

The client program. The final step will be to create a client that references the Web service, using it to get the data the user requests.

The Database

1. For the purposes of this exercise, we have created a fairly simple database. There is a primary table called Parts, which contains the essential information about a computer part, including its description, type of part, cost, number in inventory, and other items. There is a second table that stores the part type descriptions. The tables are related by the PartTypeID column. The database schema diagram is shown in Figure 15.9.
2. If you don't want to create the database yourself, you can import it from the companion Web site of the book. There is a Microsoft Access version of the database on the Web site called Ch15data.mdb, complete with sample data.

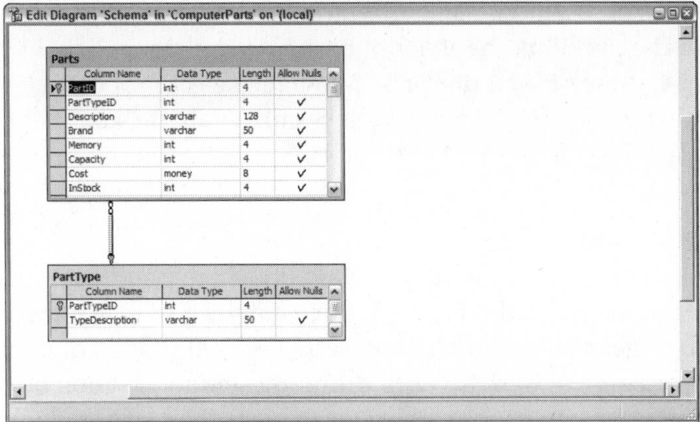

Figure 15.9 The database schema containing two tables and one relationship.

3. After the data is in place, you need to be sure that your users have access to it. You can do this in the SQL Server Enterprise Manager. If the user exists in the database system already, you can add this database to his or her access list. In Enterprise Manager, navigate the tree in the left pane to your server. Under your server, open the Security branch and then highlight the Logins branch. The users for that server appear in the right pane. Select the user you want to grant access to and right-click it. From the context menu, select Properties. When the dialog appears, select the Database Access tab, as shown in Figure 15.10. Find our new database and click the check box for it. Click OK and your user has access. Repeat for any additional users.

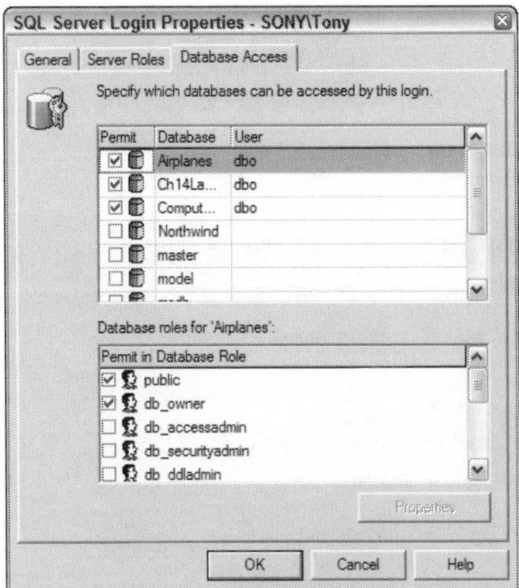

Figure 15.10 Be sure your users have access to your database.

4. Be sure your database server is using Windows-only authentication. We did this in the previous chapter, but basically you right-click the server in the left pane of the Enterprise Manager, select properties from the context menu, and then click the Security tab. Be sure the Windows Only option is selected and click OK.

The Data Access Class Library

It is time to get at some data. We'll build a class library to handle all the data access. We'll build four methods into it, three of which will be public. They will be used to get two different result sets. The first is a list of part types, essentially categories of parts. We'll dump these into a combo box on the client so that users can choose what sort of parts they want to look at. The second result set will contain the actual data the user requested.

1. Begin by creating a new class library project in Visual Studio .NET. Name it ComputerParts. You will be presented with a new and empty class library project.
2. Add the Imports statement you'll need to access SQL Server. Enter the following code at the top of the source module, outside the class:

   ```
   Imports System.Data.SqlClient
   ```

3. Rename the class to something meaningful, in this case, Parts. Change the code at the top of the class so it's properly named.
4. Add a constant to the class to hold the connection string. Be sure that you use the trusted_connection parameter in the connection string so that the class plays its part in the Windows security loop. Set the server and database to the names pertaining to your own system:

   ```
   Private Const CONNSTR As String = _
   "server=(local); database=ComputerParts;
   trusted_connection=true;"
   ```

5. Now the real code. Add the method that handles the retrieval of the part types for use in the user interface. Here's the code:

   ```
   ' Get a list of all the computer part types and
   ' send it back to the caller.
   Public Function PartTypes() As DataSet
        Dim conn As New SqlConnection(CONNSTR)
        Dim da As New SqlDataAdapter("", conn)
        Dim ds As New DataSet()
        ' Try to retrieve all the data.
        Try
             da.SelectCommand.CommandText = "SELECT * FROM PartType"
   ```

```
            conn.Open()
            da.Fill(ds, "PartTypes")
            conn.Close()
        Catch ex As SqlException
            conn.Close()
            Throw ex
        End Try
        Return ds
    End Function
```

The code uses standard ADO.NET objects and techniques to access the database and request information from it. You retrieve all the information available in the PartType table. If everything works, the data set is sent back. If an error occurs, you simply propagate it back to the caller.

6. Next add the code to retrieve actual inventory data from the Parts table. You will be building two of these methods, one that retrieves information based on a PartTypeID and another that does the same but is based on a string PartType value. Because the methods will be almost identical, with the exception of the SQL statement, we chose to put the core functionality into a private method and then create two small public methods that create the SQL and call the private method. The code for the private method looks like this:

```
Private Function GetPartsListing(ByVal sSQL As String) As DataSet
    Dim conn As New SqlConnection(CONNSTR)
    Dim da As New SqlDataAdapter("", conn)
    Dim ds As New DataSet()
    ' Try to retrieve all the data.
    Try
        da.SelectCommand.CommandText = sSQL
        conn.Open()
        da.Fill(ds, "Parts")
        conn.Close()
    Catch ex As SqlException
        conn.Close()
        Throw ex
    End Try
    Return ds
End Function
```

This method accepts a SQL statement string and feeds it into a standard set of ADO.NET data retrieval calls.

7. Next, add the two methods that call the private GetPartsListing method. They build the SQL statement that they require based on the selection criterion passed to them. One accepts an integer that is

a PartTypeID from the database and retrieves matching data. The second does the same thing, but based on a string that represents a PartType. Here they are:

```
' Get a list of parts that match a part type id.
Public Overloads Function GetParts(ByVal iPartType As Integer)
    As DataSet
    Dim ds As DataSet
    Dim sSQL As String
    ' Try to retrieve all the data.
    Try
        sSQL = _
            "SELECT * FROM Parts, PartType " & _
            "WHERE Parts.PartTypeID=" & _
                iPartType.ToString & " " & _
            "AND Parts.PartTypeID = PartType.PartTypeID"
        ds = GetPartsListing(sSQL)
    Catch ex As SqlException
        Throw ex
    End Try
    Return ds
End Function

' Get a list of parts that match a part type id.
Public Overloads Function GetParts(ByVal sPartType As String) As
DataSet
    Dim ds As DataSet
    Dim sSQL As String
    ' Try to retrieve all the data.
    Try
        sSQL = _
            "SELECT Parts.PartID, Parts.PartTypeID, " & _
            "Parts.Description, Parts.Brand, Parts.Cost, " & _
            "Parts.InStock, PartType.PartTypeID, " & _
            "PartType.TypeDescription " & _
            "FROM PartType " & _
            "INNER JOIN Parts " & _
            "ON PartType.PartTypeID = Parts.PartTypeID " & _
            "WHERE PartType.TypeDescription='" & sPartType & "'"
        ds = GetPartsListing(sSQL)
    Catch ex As Exception
        Throw ex
    End Try
    Return ds
End Function
```

Each of these methods creates a SQL statement and passes it to the GetPartsListing method. The SQL for the first one is fairly easy because it already has a PartTypeID. The second one, however, has only a string from the related table. We'll have to pull a match using an inner join. You can examine the SQL in more detail if you like.

The other important detail is that these functions overload the GetParts method name. Both make use of the Overloads keyword. The runtime system will distinguish them by their parameter types. Polymorphism is lots of fun!

That finishes up our class library. Compile it and remember where it went because you'll need it when you build the Web service.

The Web Service Interface

Normally we could use the class library directly with any application. However, we need to use this thing remotely over HTTP lines. DCOM is dead as far as .NET is concerned, and we need an alternative. How about if we put a Web service around our class module and then have our client talk to that?

1. Start a new project in Visual Studio .NET. Name it IComputerParts. Use this name because it acts as an interface to the ComputerParts component.
2. Add a standard Imports statement to the top of the source code that gives you access to SQL Server:

   ```
   Imports System.Data.SqlClient
   ```

3. Rename the class to ComputerPartsSvc where it is declared at the top of the code. This is the name that you'll refer to in the client code.
4. Next you need access to the data access class library you just wrote. Add a reference to it in the Web service by right-clicking the References item in the Solution Explorer. From the context menu, select Add Reference. When the dialog appears, browse to the location of your compiled ComputerParts component. Select it, click OK, and you're done with that.
5. Add the method that wraps a call to the PartTypes call in your class library. Here's what it looks like:

   ```
   <WebMethod()> Public Function PartTypes() As DataSet
         Dim ds As DataSet
         Try
               Dim svc As New ComputerParts.Parts()
               ds = svc.PartTypes()
         Catch ex As Exception
               Throw ex
         End Try
         Return ds
   End Function
   ```

The method creates a data-set variable to hold the returned data set. Now create an instance of the data access class library component ComputerParts.Parts. Use it to call the PartTypes method, thus returning a list from the database. The class library handles all the data access. You only have to worry about calling the component and handing the data back to the client, which is the last thing you do. Any errors that propagate from the class library, or that you create, are passed on to the caller.

6. Now you need to add the methods that wrap the calls to the GetParts methods in the class library. These methods need special handling because they wrap an overloaded method. As you've seen earlier in this chapter, this won't cause any compile or runtime problems until you try to add a reference to the Web service later. However, you'll still have to take care of it now. First, here's the code for both methods:

```
<WebMethod(MessageName:="GetPartsInt")> _
    Public Overloads Function GetParts(ByVal iPartType As Integer) _
    As DataSet
    Dim ds As DataSet
    Try
        Dim svc As New ComputerParts.Parts()
        ds = svc.GetParts(iPartType)
    Catch ex As Exception
        Throw ex
    End Try
    Return ds
End Function

<WebMethod(MessageName:="GetPartsStr")> _
    Public Overloads Function GetParts(ByVal sPartType As String) _
    As DataSet
    Dim ds As DataSet
    Try
        Dim svc As New ComputerParts.Parts()
        Return svc.GetParts(sPartType)
    Catch ex As Exception
        Throw ex
    End Try
    Return ds
End Function
```

The majority of the code looks just like our first method. It creates an instance of the class library, calls the appropriate method, and returns the result to the caller. The only real difference is the use of the MessageName parameter. This helps SOAP distinguish between the two overloaded methods that have the same name. You simply append a type specifier on the end of the name to create a new name. You never have to refer to it yourself, but meaningful names are always good.

7. That's all the code you have to write for the service, but you're not done yet. As you've seen with other secure applications in this book, every piece has a part to play in the security chain of events. Our class library had to use a trusted connection to talk to the database. This Web service is no exception. As we saw with ASP.NET applications, our Web service must use impersonation to pass on the user's login credentials. To enable impersonation, edit the Web.config file for the Web service project. Double-click it in the Solution Explorer to open it. Underneath the authentication section, add the following line:

   ```
   <identity impersonate="true" />
   ```

   This line turns on impersonation for your Web service. Once activated, you'll have to be sure that the credentials for the user are passed on when the Web service is called, or you'll get an access-denied error.

If you want to test your Web service before you write the client, you can do so. Run it like you would a normal Web service. If everything has been done correctly thus far, it will run in a Web browser, allowing you to choose which method you want to test. Try it, and select the PartTypes method. It returns a data set, which as you know, is really XML underneath. Figure 15.11 shows what some of the returned results look like.

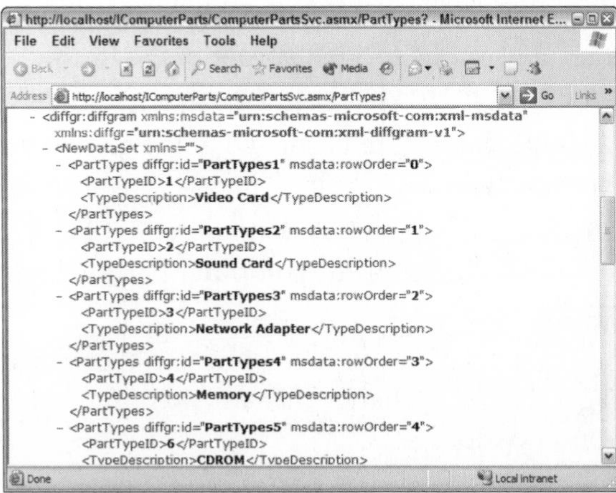

Figure 15.11 Results returned from the execution of our Web service.

The Client Program

It is time for the final stage of our solution, the client program with which our users will interact. We chose to make a WinForms application, but a Web-based client would work just as well. When we're done, we'll have a pretty slick, albeit simple, system to play with.

1. Start by creating another project in Visual Studio .NET. Make it a WinForms project this time, and name it Ch15Lab15bClient. Click the OK button to move on.
2. Be sure you have access to your Web service. Right-click the references item in the Solution Explorer, and from the context menu, select Add Web Reference. Enter the following URL in the address text box to enable the Add Reference button. Change it to match any other name you may have given your Web service. Click the Add Reference button to complete the transaction.

   ```
   http://localhost/IComputerParts/ComputerPartsSvc.asmx?wsdl
   ```

3. Now that you have a reference to your Web service, you need to rename it to something sensible. The name of the server isn't too helpful. Be sure you are viewing all files in the Solution Explorer and expand the Web references item so you can see the localhost item (unless you're using another server). Right-click the localhost and select Rename from the menu. Enter the new name ComputerPartsInterface.
4. It is time to build the user interface. Stretch the default form and get it ready for a few controls. Change the text property of the form to read Computer Parts Inventory.
5. Next, put all the controls on the form. The following list details each control and the relevant properties of each that need to be set:

   Title label. Drop a large label on the top-left corner of the form. Change the font to something more visible and bold.

   Part type label. Add a simple label to tell users what the combo box is for. Change its text property to Part Type:.

   Part type combo box. This is the combo box that you will fill with part types, which act like categories for the computer parts. Change the name to cbPartTypes and clear the text field.

   Lookup button. The user selects a part type to view and then clicks the Lookup button to get the data. Change its name to btnLookup and the text property to Lookup.

Lookup text button. This button does the same parts lookup but uses the text-based method instead of the ID-based one. Change its name to btnLookupText and its text to Lookup (text).

Data grid. Drop a data grid on the form and size it to take up most of the form. Set its name to dgData, and its caption text to Parts Data. Change its anchor property so that it is attached to all sides. If you right-click the grid, you can set its appearance by clicking Auto-Format and selecting a style you like. We chose Professional 4.

Done button. Slap the button onto the bottom-right corner of the form. Name it btnDone, and change its text property to Done.

When you're finished, your form should look similar to the one in Figure 15.12. It shows the controls laid out in Design view.

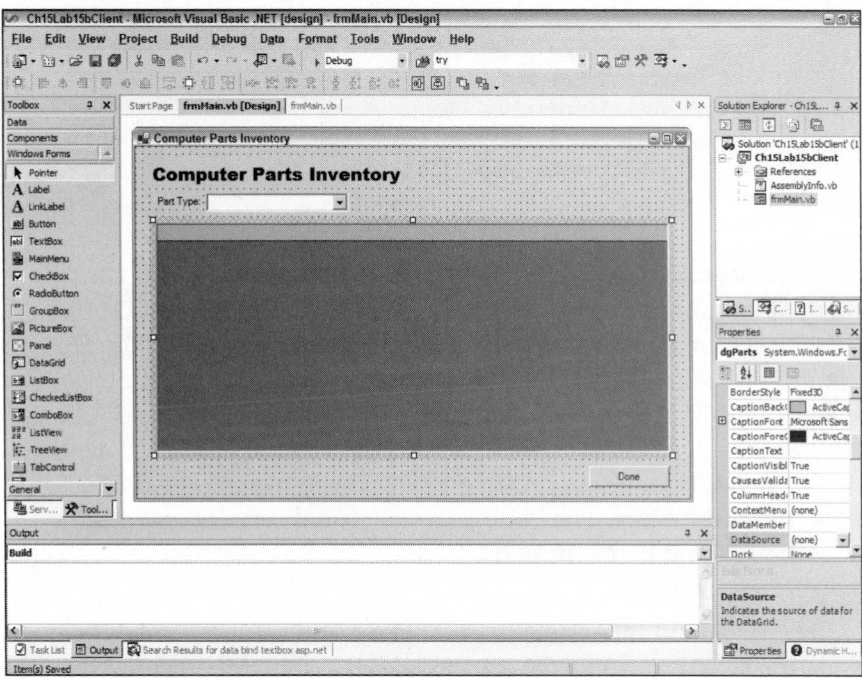

Figure 15.12 All the controls of the lab client in Design view.

6. You need some Imports in your code that give you access to the database and the security calls for your Web service. Add the following code to the top of the source file:

```
Imports System.Data.SqlClient
Imports System.Web.Services.Protocols
Imports System.Net
```

7. This program has to do something other than sit there looking pretty. The first bit of code populates the list of part types when the program loads. Double-click a blank spot on the form to open the code editor in the form load event. Add the following code:

```
Private Sub frmMain_Load(ByVal sender As System.Object, _
     ByVal e As System.EventArgs) Handles MyBase.Load
     Try
          ' Create a dataset variable and an instance of our Web
          ' service.
          Dim ds As DataSet
          Dim svc As New ComputerPartsInterface.ComputerPartsSvc()
          ' Make sure the login credentials are set.
          svc.Credentials = CredentialCache.DefaultCredentials
          ' Get the data from the service.
          ds = svc.PartTypes()
          ' Bind the data to the combo box.
          cbPartTypes.DataSource = ds.Tables("PartTypes")
          cbPartTypes.DisplayMember = "TypeDescription"
          cbPartTypes.ValueMember = "PartTypeID"
     Catch ex As Exception
          ' Report any errors.
          MsgBox(ex.Message)
     End Try
End Sub
```

The code starts by creating an instance of the Web service. Once done, you need to pass along the user's login credentials. Do this with the credentials property of the service object you made. This property is available only with the Imports statements you have included. This is also the step that closes the security loop. It passes the security credentials along to the Web service. Because you set the Web service to use impersonation, it will pass the credentials on to the class library. The library uses a trusted connection with the database, and that's the end.

After that, simply call the service, get the data set back from it, and then data bind the results to the list box. You set the DisplayMember to the actual part type description and the ValueMember to the part type ID. This way you can easily get the ID to send back to the service and get some matching data. Any errors that occur along the way are displayed to the user.

8. Now the user has access to the list of part types. After selecting one, the user will click the Lookup button and expect some data. Add the code to do this by double-clicking the Lookup button to open the code editor to the click event. Add the following code to the event handler:

```
Private Sub btnLookup_Click(ByVal sender As System.Object, _
    ByVal e As System.EventArgs) Handles btnLookup.Click
    Try
        ' Create a data-set variable and an instance of our Web
        ' service.
        Dim ds As DataSet
        Dim svc As New ComputerPartsInterface.ComputerPartsSvc()
        ' Make sure the login credentials are set.
        svc.Credentials = CredentialCache.DefaultCredentials
        ' Get the data from the service.
        ds = svc.GetParts(cbPartTypes.SelectedValue)
        ' Bind the data to the grid.
        dgParts.DataSource = ds.Tables("Parts")
    Catch ex As Exception
        ' Report any errors.
        MsgBox(ex.Message)
    End Try
End Sub
```

This method is similar to the previous one. It creates an instance of the Web service proxy, sets up the credentials, and makes the call, in this case, to the GetParts method. You use the integer version of the GetParts method and pass it the ID of the selected item. Once returned, the data is bound to the grid and you're done.

9. One last bit of code. You need to add the functionality that handles the other Lookup button. It's just the same but use the string version of the GetParts method instead of the integer version, passing it the string contents of the combo box.

```
Private Sub btnLookupText_Click(ByVal sender As System.Object, _
    ByVal e As System.EventArgs) Handles btnLookupText.Click
    Try
        ' Create a data-set variable and an instance of our Web
        ' service.
        Dim ds As DataSet
        Dim svc As New ComputerPartsInterface.ComputerPartsSvc()
        ' Make sure the login credentials are set.
        svc.Credentials = CredentialCache.DefaultCredentials
        ' Get the data from the service.
        ds = svc.GetParts(cbPartTypes.Text)
        ' Bind the data to the grid.
        dgParts.DataSource = ds.Tables("Parts")
    Catch ex As Exception
        ' Report any errors.
        MsgBox(ex.Message)
    End Try
End Sub
```

Additionally, feel free to add a handler for the Done button that closes the application.

Now run this bad boy, and see all your hard work come to fruition. Select a few different items from the list and see how the data looks. Figure 15.13 displays an example run.

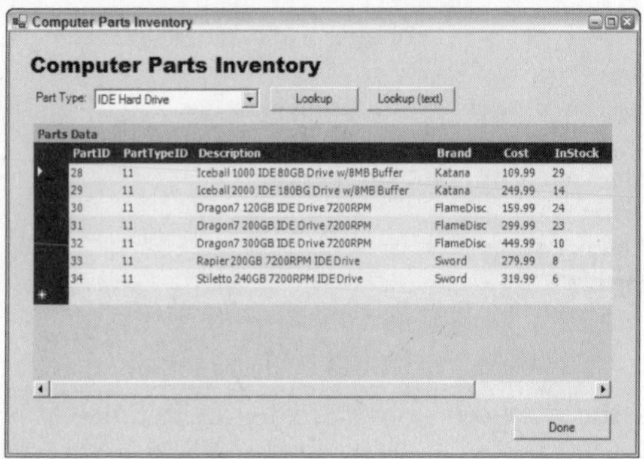

Figure 15.13 The final results of our lab running in the browser.

If you should find yourself with time on your hands, or just have a keen interest, there are a couple different things you could do to this project to enhance it. First, you could replace the WinForms client with an ASP.NET client. Building a new Web-based interface should be quick and easy. You could also modify it so that editing the data was possible or allow the user to change the data, send it back to a new method in the Web service and class library, and allow it to be posted back to the database. There are other possibilities as well, but we'll leave those up to you.

Summary

This chapter provided you with an overview of Web services, including what they are, what their benefits are, and how to put them to use. We built a sample Web service to see just how easy it is to get one up and running. We saw that there are many technologies that come together to make Web services work and examined some of those technologies more closely, including UDDI, WSDL, SOAP, and namespaces. The proxy was exposed as a key player in Web service access, making our programming lives much easier. The importance of performance and the use of Web services as class interfaces was discussed and illustrated.

Finally, we went though a fairly large lab that built a complete multitier application from client to Web service interface to class library to database. It had good performance, probably scaled well, and most interestingly, was secured using integrated Windows security.

We've seen most of the ASP.NET picture now, as well as a complete cycle of secured *n*-tier application development. I haven't had this much fun programming in years. I hope that you found it equally fun and useful.

Review Questions

1. Name two advantages of using Web services to host your remote functionality.
2. UDDI servers host your Web service for you, allowing you to provide access to it for any user worldwide. True or False?
3. What is the purpose of the <WebMethod()> attribute?
4. What purpose do namespaces serve when used with Web services?
5. What part does SOAP play in the Web services game?
6. What is the proxy, and why do you need it? How do you create one?
7. How does a Web service make known the functionality it offers?
8. How do you allow a Web service to use polymorphic, or overloaded, methods?
9. Why would you use a Web service solely as an interface to another class?
10. How are Web and WinForms clients different when it comes to accessing secured Web services?

Answers to Review Questions

1. Two of the following will answer the question. Web services do not require binary compatibility between themselves and their calling systems. They are excellent for providing functionality in heterogeneous computing environments. Communication is text- and XML-based, providing compatibility across many platforms and easier interoperation. Web services use HTTP as a communication mechanism, making them easy to access worldwide.
2. False. Although UDDI servers tell others around the world how to access your Web service and what functionality it provides, it is only a directory. Hosting the service is up to you.
3. The <WebMethod()> attribute serves two purposes. It allows you to further define your Web service method by adding other attributes to it, such as a description or alternate name. Second, <WebMethod()> exposes the method it is attached to as part of the public Web service interface. In effect, it makes the method available to callers of the service.
4. A namespace, defined as a unique string, serves along with the name of your service to keep it separate from others on the Web. If you create a Web service library called math, 15 others might do the same. The namespace helps keep those math libraries separate and unique.
5. SOAP is the specification that Web services use to call Web-service functionality and send and receive data. It defines a message format that allows calls to be made between clients and the service using text instead of proprietary binary data. As long as the SOAP standard is adhered to, heterogeneous systems can use Web services.
6. The proxy is a code module in your client that stands in for the Web service. It allows you to make calls to the Web service as if it were on your local machine. It also handles the process of using SOAP to make the calls to the Web service. You can create a proxy the hard way, by using the WSDL command line utility, or the easy way, by adding a Web reference to your project in Visual Studio .NET.
7. Web service uses an XML description of its interface, called a Web service contract, to advertise its wares. The XML follows a standard format called WSDL so that others know how to read it. Visual Studio .NET reads the WSDL when it creates a proxy for you.
8. SOAP cannot distinguish between overloaded method names because it uses only the method name for its request message. We use a <WebMethod()> attribute called MessageName to provide an alternate name for the overloaded methods. Assuming your overloaded method was called GetParts, the declaration would look like this:

```
<WebMethod(MessageName:="GetPartsInt")> _
    Public Overloads Function GetParts(ByVal iPartType As Integer) _
    As DataSet
```

9. As with ASP.NET Web applications, Web services run in IIS memory. The more IIS memory that gets used up, the more slowly IIS runs. To maximize IIS performance, keep the Web services as small and efficient as possible. In addition, separating the functionality from the interface makes it much easier to update the core code, as long as the interface doesn't change.
10. Both types of clients need to pass on the user's login credentials to the Web service they are calling. However, a Web application uses impersonation to do this. WinForms clients use a different approach; they pass the credentials along using the Credentials property of the Web service proxy instance.

Distribution and Interoperability in .NET

CHAPTER

16

Interoperability

Interoperability refers to the effective communication between two disparate entities. This chapter focuses primarily on .NET's interoperability with COM and the Win32API and explains the process by which assemblies are signed and made public, and their type libraries exposed to COM. COM and .NET components are different and exist in two different worlds known as the registry and the GAC. Two types of interoperability exist for .NET components: the ability to call unmanaged code and the ability to interop with COM components. For interoperability with unmanaged code, this is a one-way interop (barring callbacks). For COM and .NET, the common language runtime provides for two-way communication.

Consuming COM Components from .NET

All .NET assemblies expose information about themselves, including type information, via the assembly's metadata. Assemblies have no dependency on or relationship with the Windows registry. Using COM components in .NET is so easy that I was quite pleasantly surprised the first time I attempted to consume a class from one of my COM libraries. Internally, for a .NET assembly to consume a COM class, a wrapper known as a Runtime Callable Wrapper (RCW) must exist between the client assembly and the COM class as depicted in Figure 16.1.

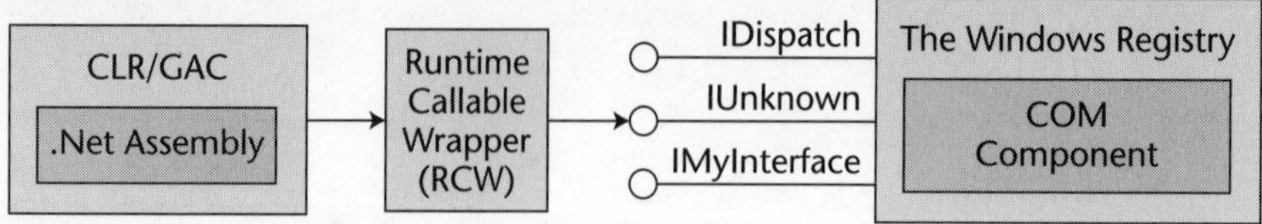

Figure 16.1 The RCW for a .NET assembly works in identical fashion to a normal COM component from the COM consumer's point of view.

An RCW can be created in Visual Studio using a simple reference or by using the Type Library Importer (tlbimp) utility in the .NET SDK, or you could even write code to do it using the System.Runtime.InteropServices.TypeLibConverter class.

The RCW makes internal calls to COM's CoCreateInstance to create the COM objects that it wraps.

Using COM DLLs in .NET

By far the easier of the two ventures, using a DLL in .NET is quite simple. By setting a reference to a COM DLL from .NET, we can use its members as we would any other .NET component. Looking at an imported version of the COM DLL For ADO (see Figure 16.2), we can see that the conversion has produced objects based on the .NET framework.

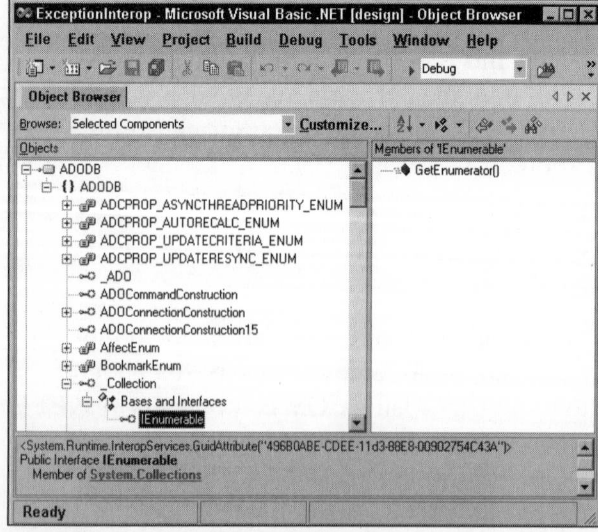

Figure 16.2 Here we can see that the COM ADO library inherits .NET classes and interfaces as a result of its import to .NET.

The .NET Framework SDK also provides a tlbimp.exe tool to manually import COM type libraries for .NET consumption.

Classroom Q & A

Q: What about the differences between data types in Visual Basic 6 and Visual Basic .NET? What if a Visual Basic 6 function asks for a byte and we send it a Unicode-compliant .NET byte?

A: The RCW created for the Visual Basic 6 component automatically recreates methods on the .NET side with compatible parameters for the Visual Basic 6 side.

Q: Do exceptions that Visual Basic 6 code throws cause problems on the .NET side?

A: Visual Basic 6 throws its errors, and .NET simply catches them as System.Exceptions.

Q: My company made an entire library of controls that had complex container relationships, and we couldn't even come close to migrating these to .NET. Is that to be expected?

A: It was most likely an issue with conflicting members in what exists in the OCX control and what the controls need to have to exist as .NET controls. Sometimes .NET needs to modify a controls interface so that it may inherit properly from the System.Windows.Forms.Control class.

Q: What is a RCW created for? Does it wrap a class, a method, or a DLL?

A: The common language runtime creates a RCW for every object.

Q: How is referencing of a COM object affected when it's created from a RCW?

A: The self-destroying manner of COM components doesn't change. The RCW still causes the same calls to Addref and Release that we would expect from any usage of COM components.

Using OCX Controls in .NET

As with COM DLLs, OCX controls also can be consumed effortlessly in .NET. There are, however, some issues that can arise when an OCX control is used that has properties that conflict with the properties belonging to all .NET controls. There are quite a number of properties that will be subjugated in favor of the .NET version should a conflict arise. For example, take the following ActiveX control in Visual Basic 6, which I compiled to CH16_OCX.ocx:

```
Public Location As String
Private Sub Timer1_Timer()
    Text1.ForeColor = QBColor(CInt(Rnd * 15))
End Sub
Private Sub UserControl_Resize()
   'resize text box as control is resized
   Text1.Width = UserControl.Width
   Text1.Height = UserControl.Height
End Sub
```

Right-clicking the Toolbox and selecting Customize ToolBox opens a dialog from which I can add a reference to this ActiveX control and automatically create an RCW. Any control selected in this manner will be displayed in the Toolbox. After an OCX is added to .NET, the RCW version is very different than the OCX from which it came.

First, let me explain what happened to my Location as String property placed in the original version. When a control is used in .NET, it must inherit from System.Windows.Forms.Control and must expose certain members because of that inheritance. Because the Control class already has a Location property that is of type Point, the derivation of my ActiveX class from the Control class would not be allowed to override that property with a completely different Type. The following code shows what happened to the imported ActiveX control:

```
Private Sub btnTest_Click(ByVal sender As System.Object, _
ByVal e As System.EventArgs) Handles Button2.Click
   'The original property Location has been changed to CtlLocation
   AxUserControl11.CtlLocation = "MyOldProperty"
   'And replaced with the required Location property
   AxUserControl11.Location = New Point(1, 1)
End Sub
```

You can imagine how this might affect an application that is moving over to .NET with several custom controls. I haven't found many controls that have conflicting members, but you should be familiar with the members in System.Windows.Forms.Control to know what you might be up against.

OCX controls imported into .NET appear with an Ax prefix to avoid any confusion with the original OCX control.

Handling COM Exceptions in .NET

As you'll experience in the upcoming lab, all necessary data types and exception conversions are handled automatically by marshalling through the RCW. Methods in COM produce errors by returning an HRESULT. Regardless of what language the COM component is written in, any exceptions thrown from those COM components are translated by the RCW, so they appear to the .NET consumer to be nothing more than a System.Exception. For each HRESULT type, there is a matching .NET derivation of System.Exception. For example, an HRESULT of type COR_E_APPLICATION maps to an application exception in .NET. For those HRESULTS that don't have a specific match, they are mapped to COMException.

Lab 16.1: Consuming COM Components in .NET

This lab demonstrates the process by which COM components can be consumed in .NET. A portion of this lab requires Visual Basic 6 to be installed, but it provides a second option that suffices for the example. This lab consumes a Visual Basic 6 COM DLL, the ActiveX ADO 2.x DLL, and an ActiveX Control and tests a wide range of functionality while explaining the roles of the RCW.

Perform the following steps:

1. Open Visual Basic 6 and create a new ActiveX DLL project. For future reference, the library used in my examples will be named CH16_VB6DLL to ensure that it is unique in my system Registry.
2. Enter the following two methods into Class1 in the ActiveX DLL:

```
'CH16_VB6DLL_Class1
Public Sub Boom()
   'Used only to test how exceptions are handled through the RCW
   Err.Raise 11 'simulates a divide by zero error
End Sub
Public Function Test(L As Long) As Long
   'Used to test how disparate data types are handled through the
RCW
   Test = L 'pass it back and make sure it works both directions.
End Function
```

3. Select Project, Properties, Component tab and check the Remote Server Files checkbox as shown in Figure 16.3. This check box forces Visual Basic to extract type information from the class library into a separate type library (appears as a .tlb file). Close the Project Properties dialog box.

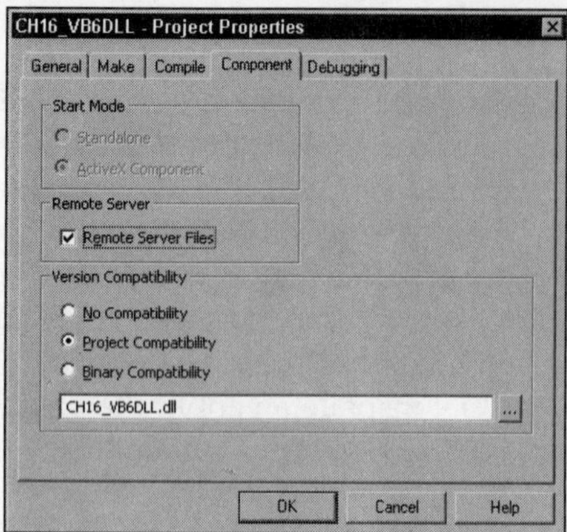

Figure 16.3 If Remote Server Files is not checked for a Visual Basic 6 DLL, its type library will remain embedded in the DLL. Checking this option creates a separate .tlb file.

4. Save the project.
5. Create a DLL by selecting File, Make CH16_VB6.DLL. This also performs the equivalent of running regsvr32 by registering the DLL in the Windows registry.
6. Close Visual Basic 6.
7. In Visual Studio 7.0, start a new .NET Windows application.
8. In the new .NET Windows application, set a reference to CH16_VB6.DLL (or whatever you named this DLL).

   Now, let's discuss the function named Test in the Visual Basic 6 DLL. The function accepts a Visual Basic 6 Long and returns a Visual Basic 6 Long. That data type in Visual Basic 6 is only 4 bytes, but in .NET a Long is much larger. What if we created a Visual Basic .NET Long, filled it to its capacity, and sent it to Visual Basic 6? Wouldn't it overflow the 4-byte Visual Basic 6 version? I did say that these types were converted nicely for us, but let's see how nicely.
9. Set a reference to the Visual Basic 6 DLL by selecting Add Reference from the Project menu, selecting the COM tab, and double-clicking the name of the COM DLL you just created, as shown in Figure 16.4.

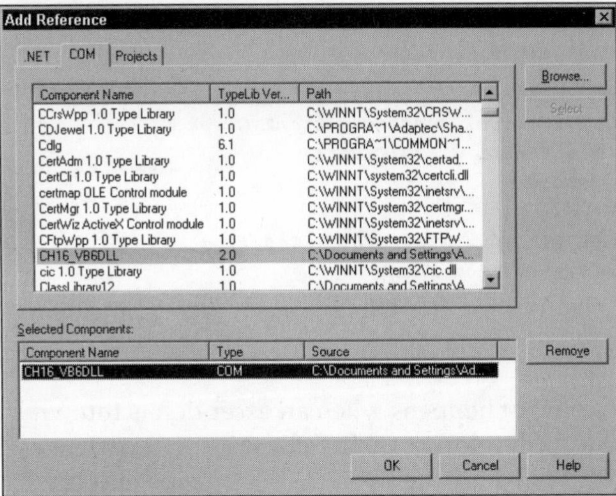

Figure 16.4 Setting a reference to the Visual Basic 6 DLL from a .NET client actually sets a reference to its RCW assembly.

10. Add a Button control to the form.
11. Open the Code Editor window and, as always, add Option Strict On and Option Explicit On to Form1.
12. In the Click event handler, declare a new CH16_VB6.Class1 object, and look at the resulting function signature for Test, which is shown in Figure 16.5.

```
Dim c As New CH16_VB6DLL.Class1Class()
```

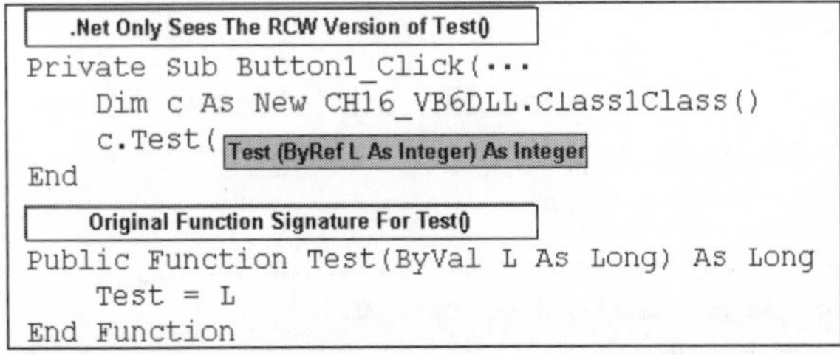

Figure 16.5 Clearly, the RCW sees that a Visual Basic 6 Long needs to be translated to an Integer in .NET and modifies the function signature accordingly.

As far as the .NET programmer is concerned, Test takes an Integer and returns an Integer. The RCW not only handles disparities in the data types between .NET and COM, but it actually abstracts these disparities from either system.

13. Modify the Click event handler for your button and test to be sure the data was sent and returned without issue.

```
Private Sub Button1_Click(ByVal sender As System.Object, _
ByVal e As System.EventArgs) Handles Button1.Click
    Dim c As New CH16_VB6DLL.Class1Class()
    Dim result As Integer
    Try
        MessageBox.Show(c.Test(1234567890).ToString())
        Catch ex As System.Exception
            MessageBox.Show(ex.Message)
    End Try
End Sub
```

The next step is to see what happens when an exception is thrown from a Visual Basic 6 application to a .NET client.

14. Replace the line of code that calls the Test function with a call to the function Boom. If you look back to our declaration of Boom in the Visual Basic 6 class, it just raises a Divide by zero exception.

15. Run the application and test the button. You should see nothing more than a nicely handled exception that was, as our code proves, a System.Exception.

    Wow, the RCW is so abstracted that you could really get used to never having to worry about its existence. That was a test of a rather simplistic class, but how about an infinitely more complicated class library—the ADO Library?

16. Add a reference in your .NET Windows application to the Microsoft ActiveX Data Objects 2.0 Library (any version will do; they're all based on COM).

17. Add a second button to Form1 with the following Click event handler for testing the ADO Library, adjusting the path or database accordingly.

```
Private Sub btnTest_Click(ByVal sender As System.Object, _
ByVal e As System.EventArgs) Handles btnTest.Click
    Dim con As New ADODB.Connection()
    Dim rec As New ADODB.Recordset()
    con.ConnectionString = _
    "Provider=Microsoft.Jet.OLEDB.4.0;Data Source=" & _
    "C:\Program Files\Microsoft Visual Studio\VB98\" & _
    "NWIND.MDB;Persist Security Info=False"
    con.Open()
    rec.Open("select FirstName from employees", con)
    MsgBox(rec.Fields(0).Value.ToString())
    con.close()
End Sub
```

Even if you never used ADO, you can tell from the reference we made that this is an ActiveX library. Again, the RCW makes everything extremely simple. As a matter of fact, you could even use the ADO data control in .NET if you wanted to, but that is the next step.

Now, add an ActiveX control to test to your Toolbox in your .NET Windows application.

18. Right-click the Toolbox and select Customize Toolbox to open the Customize ToolBox dialog, as shown in Figure 16.6.

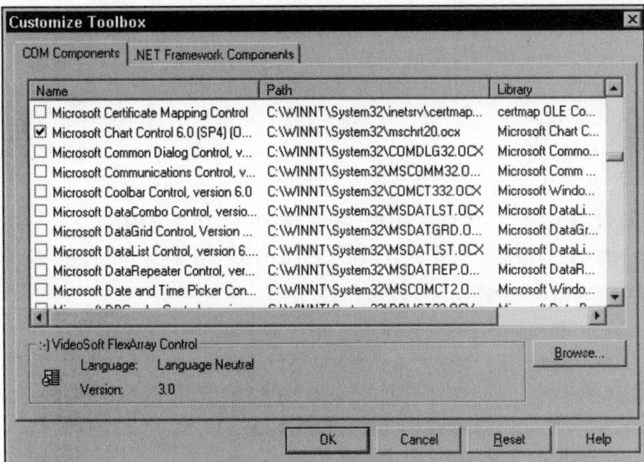

Figure 16.6 The Customize Toolbox dialog can be used to add either .NET or COM controls to the Toolbox in Visual Studio .NET.

19. Select the Microsoft Chart Control 6.0 from the COM Components tab and click OK. The Microsoft Chart control now appears at the bottom of the Toolbox.

20. Inspect the properties of this Chart control in both Visual Basic 6 and Visual Basic .NET, and you will see that there is quite a difference.

21. Inspect the files in your project folder. You should find files named Interop.MSChart20Lib.dll and ax Interop.MSChart20Lib.dll. Open Interop.MSChart20Lib.dll in ILDASM.

    ILDASM is an Intermediate Language Disassembler. Figure 16.7 shows that this file is an assembly, complete with manifest.

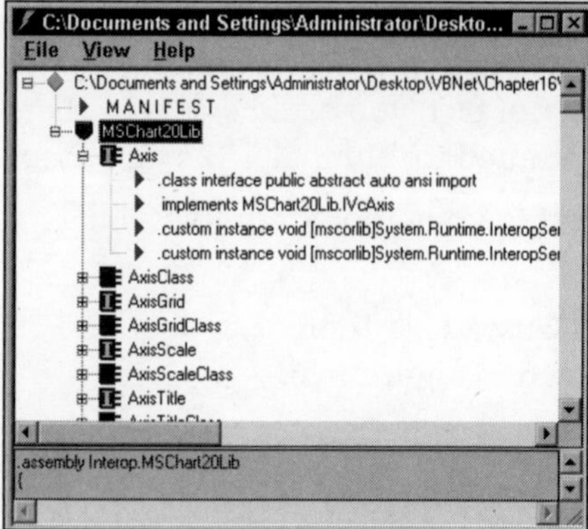

Figure 16.7 The Interop versions of COM components created by .NET are the actual RCW assemblies used for Interop between COM and .NET. This is the Interop Assembly for the COM Control, Microsoft Chart.

22. Although I have no intention of making you a master of the Microsoft Chart control, the following code should suffice in testing the control's implementation in .NET:

```
Private Sub btnTest2_Click(ByVal sender As System.Object, _
ByVal e As System.EventArgs) Handles Button2.Click
    AxMSChart1.chartType =
MSChart20Lib.VtChChartType.VtChChartType3dLine
    AxMSChart1.ShowLegend = True
    AxMSChart1.ColumnLabel = ""
    Dim r As New Random(Now.Millisecond)
    Dim i As Integer = 0, j As Integer = 0
    For i = 1 To AxMSChart1.RowCount
        AxMSChart1.Row = System.Convert.ToInt16(i)
        For j = 1 To AxMSChart1.ColumnCount
            AxMSChart1.Column = System.Convert.ToInt16(j)
            AxMSChart1.Data = r.Next(1, 20).ToString()
        Next
    Next
End Sub
```

The code for testing the Microsoft Chart assembly produces output similar to Figure 16.8.

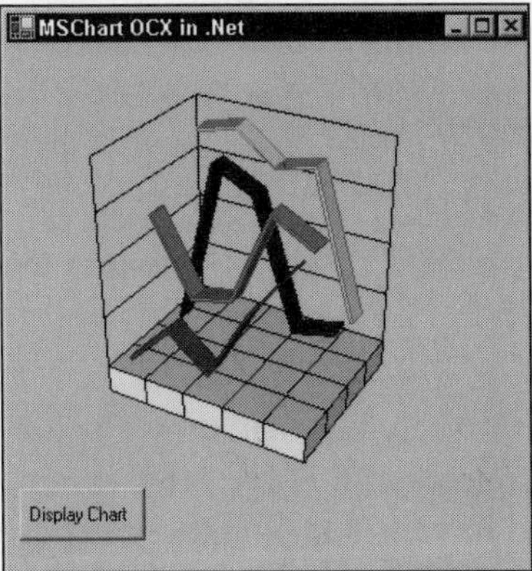

Figure 16.8 Experimentation with various properties and methods of the imported Microsoft Chart control demonstrates that this particular control migrated without problems and works as it did in Visual Basic 6.

By now you should be relatively comfortable that this direction of interoperability will cause you few problems. In this lab you imported both a COM DLL and an ActiveX control into .NET and used them as if they were a natural part of .NET. By using ILDASM and the Object Browser, you have also seen that the RCW version of these controls is an assembly and that imported controls are truly .NET controls.

Consuming .NET Components from COM

Every class library project you created in Visual Basic 6 was based on an object model known as COM, and every DLL you made in it had internal IDispatch and IUnknown interfaces with methods for performing internal object reference counting and method invocation. These types of objects are completely dependent on the existence of the Windows registry and are made "public" by a process that installs them into a section of the registry known as the HKEY_CLASSES_ROOT hive. Each COM component exposes type information via external type library files or with type information embedded in a DLL (the default in Visual Basic 6).

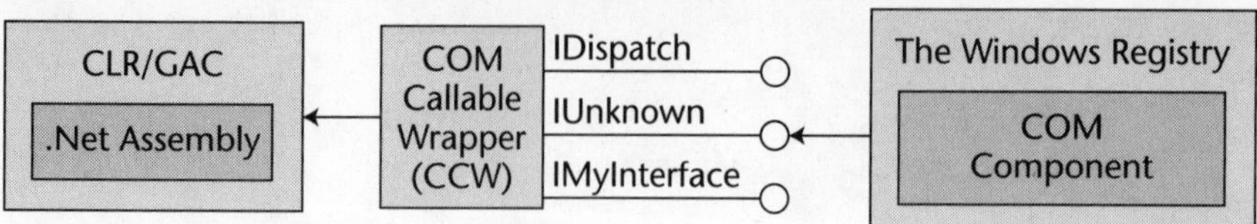

Figure 16.9 Any call to CoCreateInstance for our exported classes is redirected to the common language runtime for creation.

COM components can talk to each other intuitively because they all share a common set of interfaces that define a COM component. For a .NET assembly to masquerade as a COM component, it would have to support these expected interfaces. In reality, creating a proxy wrapper for the .NET component that exposes interfaces for COM as well as for .NET supports this communication. This proxy wrapper is referred to as a CCW, shown in Figure 16.9.

When a COM client calls CoCreateInstance to create an object from an assembly that was exported to COM, the InProcServer causes the request to be directed back to the common language runtime. The mscoree.dll file actually contains a DLLGetClassObject function that, as with all COM Servers, looks at a requested CLSID, finds the associated assembly for that CLSID, and builds a CCW dynamically for the COM client. Just as with the RCW, the wrapper handles all conversions.

Although .NET assemblies don't necessarily need to be installed in the GAC to be used by another .NET client, this is a necessity for COM interoperability. The following list provides the requirements for a .NET assembly to be consumable by a COM client:

- Assemblies must be strongly named to be visible to COM.
- COM-visible assemblies must reside in the GAC.
- Classes to be consumed by COM clients need to expose a default constructor.
- The .NET classes to be exposed must have registry entries.
- Any class you want to hide from COM needs to be marked with a ComVisible(False) attribute.

Creating Strongly Named Assemblies

A strongly named assembly is one that has been compiled with a digital signature. We sign .NET assemblies by providing the name of a strong name key pair file in the AssemblyKeyFile attribute. The AssemblyKeyFile attribute is an assembly-level attribute and should be added to the AssemblyInfo.vb file and modified similar to the following:

```
<assembly: AssemblyKeyFile("keypair.snk")>
```

Key pairs can be obtained from authorities such as VeriSign or Microsoft. For debugging and testing purposes, the sn.exe utility can be used to create temporary key pair files. The following Command Line command creates a new file named keypair.snk with which you could sign an assembly:

```
sn -k keypair.snk
```

After the key pair is created and referenced in the AssemblyKeyFile attribute, compilation of the class library will result in a strongly named assembly and meet the only requirement for GAC installation.

Installing Assemblies into the GAC

After an assembly is strongly named, it may be installed into the GAC. Assemblies installed into the GAC are available to any entity requesting that assembly. We'll skip the intricate details again for now, but the GAC acts as a storage system for installed assemblies and keeps copies of all DLLs comprising an assembly inside the assembly GAC directory structure. If your operating system resided at c:\winnt, the GAC would appear to Explorer as being at c:\winnt\assembly, but actually it resides at c:\winnt\assembly\GAC (proven well enough using the .NET Command Prompt).

Installing an Assembly into the GAC

The gacutil.exe utility is used to install assemblies into the GAC. To install an assembly, you actually target the library for your assembly that contains the manifest for that assembly. For multiple-DLL assemblies, only one of those DLLs contains the manifest. This special assembly is referred to as the Library assembly, whereas subsequent DLLs in the assembly are referred to as modules. Because the manifest in the library assembly contains a list of all other modules that belong to this assembly, the following command creates the assembly and places a copy of the library and all supporting modules into the GAC:

```
gacutil -i mylibrary.dll
```

The conceptual results of executing gacutil –i are shown in Figure 16.10.

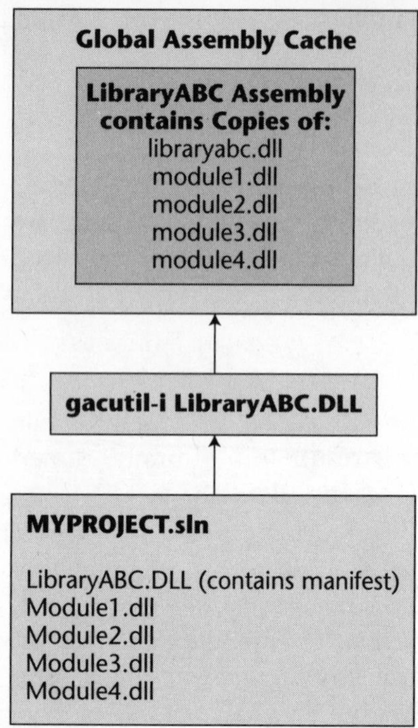

Figure 16.10 When we install a multi-DLL assembly, all modules listed in the manifest are copied to that assembly's folder in the GAC.

Registering .NET Assemblies with COM

For COM components to use a .NET assembly, besides having a CCW, there must be an entry in the registry that COM components can find that somehow leads them back to .NET. The regasm utility is used to create a type library and register our assembly types in the Windows registry. After the objects exist as types in the registry, instead of pointing to a DLL as normal COM components do, they will point back to mscoree.dll. The following command creates a type library and exports those types to the system registry for the indicated library:

```
regasm /tlb:MyLib.tlb MyLib.dll
```

The tlbexp utility also can be used to create a type library for an assembly.

Lab 16.2: Consuming .NET Components in COM

This lab demonstrates the process by which a .NET class library can be made visible to the Windows registry and consumable by COM clients. To perform this level of interoperability, you will create a DLL in .NET, strongly name it with a digital key pair, register it in the GAC, and register its types in the system registry. You will then view the installed component in the registry and use the component using COM. Because the purpose of this exercise is to stress the interoperability between COM and .NET, there is no emphasis whatsoever placed on creating a realistic class library. A small part of this lab uses Visual Basic 6, although it is not required to test the interoperability.

Perform the following steps:

1. Start a new Visual Basic .NET class library named CH16_DotNetLib.
2. Modify the name of Class1 to Person in the Solution Explorer.
3. Replace all code in class Person with the following:

```
Option Strict On
Option Explicit On
Public Class Person
   Public FirstName As String
   Public LastName As String
   'COM-Exposed classes need default constructors:
   Public Sub New()
   End Sub
   Public Sub New(ByVal fname As String, _
   ByVal lname As String)
      Me.FirstName = fname
      Me.LastName = lname
   End Sub
End Class
```

4. Add a second class and except the default name of Class1.

   Some types are necessarily appropriate for COM consumption for various reasons. To hide a type from COM add the ComVisible(False) attribute value to the declaration of the .NET class.

5. Add the following code for the new Class:

```
'Class Hidden From COM
<System.Runtime.InteropServices.ComVisible(False)> _
Public Class Class1
    Public Function foo() As Integer
        Return "foo"
    End Function
End Class
```

6. Choose Build Solution from the Build menu and ensure that there are no build errors in the Output window.
7. Open the .NET Command Prompt by selecting Start, Programs, Microsoft Visual Studio .NET, Visual Studio .NET Tools, Visual Studio .NET Command Prompt.
8. Change the current directory in the command window to that of your project's obj\debug directory.

Files and folders in a Windows Search dialog can be dragged directly to a command window to save considerable typing.

9. Typing DIR, the directory list command, should verify that CH16_DotNetLib.dll exists at this location.

   The next steps create a key pair file so you can sign your assembly.

10. At the command prompt, type the following command to create a keypair file:

```
sn -k keypair.snk
```

11. If the previous command executed successfully, leave the .NET Command window open and return to your .NET project.
12. Open the AssemblyInfo.vb file and add the following line:

```
<Assembly: AssemblyKeyFile("keypair.snk")>
```

   After this reference to a key pair gets compiled into the DLL, it will be what the GAC refers to as strongly named.

13. Select Rebuild Solution from the Build menu to compile the assembly with the key pair. Ensure that there were no build errors.
14. Return to the .NET command prompt.
15. Issue the following command to install your strongly named assembly into the GAC:

```
gacutil -i ch16_dotnetlib.dll
```

16. Verify that the results highlighted in Figure 16.11 were achieved, successfully installing the assembly.

Figure 16.11 Pay attention to command line messages. A successful gacutil attempt should produce the message: Assembly successfully added to the cache.

17. Leaving the .NET Command Window open, select Start, Run, c:\winnt\assembly, or an appropriate path on your system, to view the assembly. Your assembly should appear as shown in Figure 16.12.

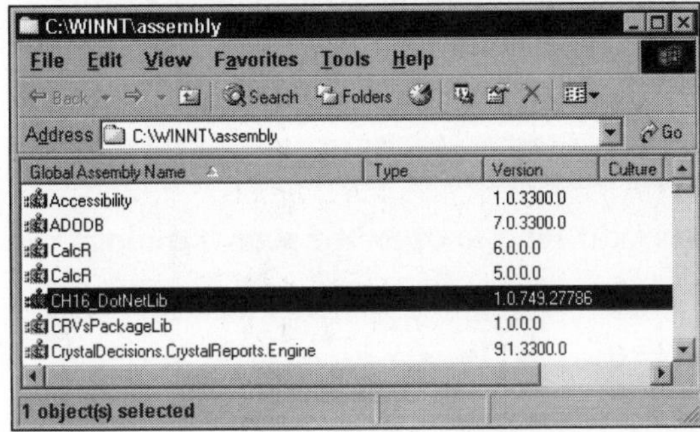

Figure 16.12 Assemblies that need to be visible to COM should be installed in the GAC. GAC-installed assemblies are referred to as public assemblies.

As with other windows, the GAC Explorer updates itself. Press F5 if your newly installed assembly does not appear.

The next step is to register the types in our assembly in the registry. I guarantee you will swear that this process is, as my child says, "wack." It is something I had to see work to believe, but let me explain before we do it. We placed our DLL in an assembly in the GAC, right? Well, we are about to register a DLL using a reference to a file location other than the one in the assembly. It's not a problem because any calls to the assembly will be routed to the GAC, and the appropriate assembly name and version will be located. Yes, I know,

I didn't trust it either, but in a few steps we'll even delete the original DLL to prove that the one in the GAC was used. The next step registers those types.

18. From the .NET command prompt, enter the following command to create a type library for our component and register its types in the registry:

```
regasm /tlb:ch16_dotnetlib.tlb ch16_dotnetlib.dll
```

The absence of a separate type library isn't a show stopper for COM interoperability, but it is required to perform early binding to types in our assembly from COM.

Congratulations! At this point you have successfully exposed a DLL to COM. Now we will prove it. Let's start by searching for our control in the registry.

Do not delete or modify entries in the system registry unless you are comfortable doing so. The registry controls virtually every aspect of how Windows behaves and does not have an Undo feature.

19. Open the registry by selecting Start, Run, Regedit.
20. In the Registry Editor, select Edit Find to open the search dialog.
21. Do not deselect any check boxes.
22. Type ch16_dotnetlib.Person in the Find What textbox and click Find Next. You should find two references to the Person class in the registry. The second reference, when expanded, will look like Figure 16.13.

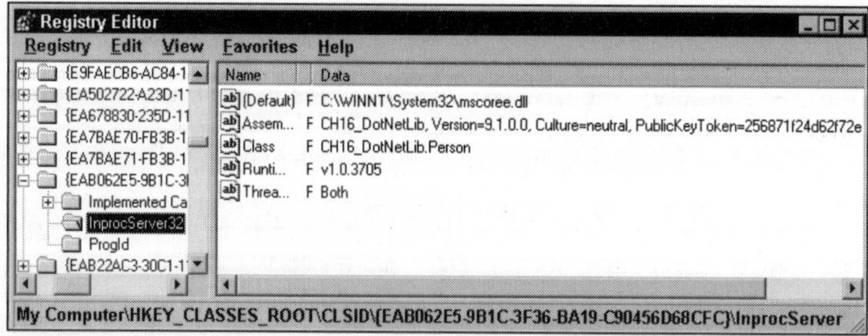

Figure 16.13 Here you can clearly see that instead of the normal COM InprocServer32 entry, which points to the containing DLL, you see a redirection to the common language runtime (mscoree.dll).

23. Close the Registry Editor.

24. Open Notepad by selecting Start, Run, Notepad and enter the following code:

```
Dim obj
Set obj = CreateObject("ch16_dotnetlib.Person")
obj.Firstname = "yourname"
MsgBox obj.Firstname
```

25. Save the file in Notepad to your desktop as Test.vbs and execute it. The CreateObject method, used to create COM objects, should have had no problem returning the data.

26. Open a standard Windows application in Visual Basic 6.

27. Set a reference to the exported assembly by selecting Project, References; checking ch16_dotnetlib; and clicking OK.

28. Add a new Command button and use the following code for its Click event handler:

```
Private Sub Command1_Click()
   Dim obj As CH16_DotNetLib.Person
   Set obj = CreateObject("ch16_dotnetlib.Person") 'forces use of
COM
   obj.Firstname = "Bruce"
   MsgBox obj.Firstname
End Sub
```

29. Run the application by pressing F5 and test the button. This should also work as if it were any other COM component being accessed. Ah, but is it using the DLL in the GAC? The next steps will prove that it is.

30. Perform a Windows search for any copy of CH16_DotNetLib.dll and rename it. (A Windows search will never reveal the copy of the DLL being used by the GAC.)

31. Run the Visual Basic 6 application again to be sure it still executes appropriately. The successful test should ease concerns that the appropriate DLL is not being used.

    Did you notice that the class we marked with ComVisible(False) didn't appear in the IntelliSense for CH16_DotNetLib? Figure 16.14 clearly indicates that we successfully hid the second class we created in our .NET class library.

```
Private Sub Command1_Click()
   Dim obj As CH16_DotNetLib.
   Set obj = CreateObject("  Person   tlib.Person")
   'Set obj = New CH16_DotNetLib.Person
   obj.Firstname = "Bruce"
   MsgBox obj.Firstname
End Sub
```

Figure 16.14 By using ComVisible(False) for Class1, we successfully hid that class from COM. In Visual Basic 6, IntelliSense sees only the Person class, which defaulted to ComVisible(True).

It took quite a few steps to make our assembly available to COM, but they weren't difficult steps. This direction of interop is less like .NET than COM and will be for a while because most of our existing code is still invested in COM. If errors arose during the lab, regasm /unregister can be used to remove registry entries, and gacutil –i assemblyname can be used to remove assemblies from the GAC.

Classroom Q & A

Q: What if we unregister and re-register the assembly? Will that break the Visual Basic 6 client?

A: As long as the assembly version remains the same, the Visual Basic 6 client does not have to be recompiled. If that happened, you would have to go in to Visual Basic 6 and deselect and re-select the reference to the library.

Q: What if we forgot to unregister the assembly when we re-registered the assembly with the new version in the registry?

A: COM developers coined the term *DLL Hell* to describe what would happen. Be careful to remove assemblies from the registry before registering a different version and be aware that by doing so, you will break existing COM clients.

Q: Why can't we use regasm against the DLL inside the GAC? Doesn't that work?

A: It's just easier to locate the version used here to create the assembly. I actually use the one located in the GAC assembly folder when I'm using automating builds and component upgrades.

Non-COM DLL Interoperability

Many DLLs aren't created using a COM interface. These traditional DLLs, such as those found in the Win32API, can be accessed using a Microsoft-specific technology known as P/Invoke or PlatForm Invoke. Platform Invoke can be used in two ways, with a Declare statement similar to Visual Basic 6 or by using the DLLImport attribute. There are differences between the two. Although DLLImport has a great number of attributes, making it more flexible than a Declare, DLLImport can be used only for static (shared in Visual Basic) methods and cannot use a MarshalAs attribute. The MarshalAs attribute allows a developer to be specific about how a value will be passed. This is useful for dealing with functions in Visual Basic 6 that contain parameters declared with the type AsAny.

P/Invoke using a Declare statement:

```
Declare Auto Function Msg Lib "user32.dll" _
Alias "MessageBox" (ByVal hWnd As Integer, ByVal text As String, _
ByVal caption As String, ByVal Type As Integer) As Integer
'
'Test the function:
Private Sub Button1_Click(ByVal sender As System.Object, _
   ByVal e As System.EventArgs) Handles Button1.Click
   Msg(0, "Greetings", "My App", 0)
End Sub
```

P/Invoke using DLLImport:

```
'Imports System.Runtime.InteropServices
<DllImport("user32.dll", EntryPoint:="MessageBox")> _
Public Shared Function Msg2(ByVal hWnd As Integer, _
ByVal text As String, ByVal caption As String, _
ByVal Type As Integer) As Integer
End Function
'
Test the function:
Private Sub Button2_Click(ByVal sender As System.Object, _
ByVal e As System.EventArgs) Handles Button2.Click
   Msg2(0, "Greetings2", "My App", 0)
End Sub
```

If you're thinking that going directly to the WINAPI is faster than using the corresponding classes in .NET, it's not. It is true that most of what is in the Win32API (and much more) is available through classes in .NET, but using these built-in classes is more efficient for a .NET programmer because they are in managed assemblies. By going directly to an unmanaged DLL, we incur a good deal of overhead. As you might imagine, the use of P/Invoke calls produces nonportable code.

The Win32API.txt file still exists for .NET and is typically located at c:\Program Files\Microsoft Visual Studio .NET\Common7\Tools\Bin.

Summary

In this chapter we saw how cleanly .NET clients can consume COM components and how adaptive the RCW (and CCW) can be. We've used COM components and Active control in .NET apps and .NET libraries in Visual Basic 6. This interoperability is important for systems that still need to bridge the gap between these systems. For most systems, the interop will be from .NET to COM, in which case, life is as simple as it gets. Either direction, we can extend what the callable wrappers do for us with relative ease with the help of System.Runtime.InteropServices.

Review Questions

1. What is responsible for creating both RCWs and CCWs?
   a. The .NET common language runtime is responsible for the RCW and COM is responsible for the CCW.
   b. The .NET common language runtime is responsible for the CCW and COM is responsible for the RCW.
   c. COM is responsible for creating both the CCW and RCW, but the common language runtime is responsible for the proper marshalling of data through these wrappers.
   d. The .NET common language runtime handles everything related to both CCWs and RCWs.
2. From a .NET client programmer's perspective, what is different between using an exported COM component and using a normal .NET assembly?
   a. Nothing, except for what tab they use in the Add reference dialog. The objects are used in the same manner.
   b. The exported COM component must be used with care because it can throw exceptions that Visual Basic .NET can't handle.
   c. The exported COM component must be called using Visual Basic 6 coding conventions.
   d. Although exported Visual Basic 6 COM DLLs work just like .NET assemblies, C++ COM DLLs will fail when called from Visual Basic .NET.
3. COM DLLs can be accessed through an RCW regardless of the language in which they were written. True or False?
4. If a specific HRESULT is thrown from a COM component through an RCW and that exception is not specifically mapped to an exception type, what type is returned to the .NET client?
   a. COMException
   b. System.Exception
   c. ApplicationException
   d. InteropException
5. If a Visual Basic 6 function asks for a Long, what type would the RCW ask for from a .NET client?
   a. Integer
   b. Int16
   c. Int32
   d. Int64

6. Why are CoCreateInstance calls (requests for object creation for a COM object) able to create objects for an exported .NET assembly?

   a. Because the registry entry for the exported types contains the location of each DLL in the assembly

   b. Because the registry entry for the exported types contains a reference to mscoree, which causes the dynamic creation of a CCW with which the COM client can interact

   c. Because the registry contains information that points to the assembly in the GAC

   d. Because the registry entry for the exported types contains a reference to mscorlib, which causes the dynamic creation of a CCW with which the COM client can interact

7. Which of the following are required for an assembly to be exported to the registry from .NET? Select all correct answers.

   a. The assembly must be strongly named.

   b. The assembly must be in the GAC.

   c. The types to be exported must be marked with COMVisible(True).

   d. The types to be exported must adhere to COM specifications.

8. Which of the following can be used to create a type library for .NET assembly? Select all correct answers.

   a. tlbexp.exe

   b. tlbimp

   c. regasm

   d. ildasm

9. Production applications should be compiled using a key pair created using the sn.exe. True or False?

Answers to Review Questions

1. **d.** The .NET common language runtime handles everything related to both CCWs and RCWs; it handles everything that has any interaction with .NET.
2. **a.** From a .NET client programmer's perspective, the only difference between using an exported COM component and using a normal .NET assembly is the tab used in the Add Reference dialog. The objects are used in the same manner.
3. True. COM DLLs can be accessed through an RCW regardless of the language in which they were written.
4. **a.** If a specific HRESULT is thrown from a COM component through an RCW and that exception is not specifically mapped to an exception type, a COMException is returned to the .NETclient.
5. **c.** If a Visual Basic 6 function asks for a Long, the RCW will ask a .NET client to provide an Int32. A Long in Visual Basic 6 is 4 bytes, whereas a Visual Basic 6 integer is only 2 bytes.
6. **b.** CoCreateInstance calls can create objects for an exported .NET assembly because the registry entry for the exported types contains a reference to mscoree, which causes the dynamic creation of a CCW with which the COM client can interact.
7. **a** and **b.** For an assembly to be exported to the registry from .NET, the assembly must be strongly named and be installed in the GAC. All .NET types are the equivalent of COMVisible(True) by default.
8. **a** and **c.** Both tlbexp and regasm can be used to create a type library for .NET assembly.
9. False. Production applications should be compiled using a key pair obtained from a signature authority such as Microsoft or VeriSign.

CHAPTER

17

Mobile Internet Toolkit

Like most technologically inclined people, I have a cell phone with a Web browser built into it. I can use it for a few things, most of which I don't ever think about: movie tickets and show times, the weather, and some news headlines. I would use it more often if there was a wider variety of content and functionality available for it. I've heard the same thing from friends who use Web-enabled cell phones and PDAs. The trick to making the mobile Web device useful and commonplace is to make it easy to develop mobile content.

The Mobile Internet Toolkit for Visual Studio .NET promises to make the development of mobile Web-based applications and sites easy. If it lives up to its promise, the world may soon have access to a greater magnitude of mobile content. The question is Does it live up to the hype? In this chapter, we examine the toolkit in detail to see what it does, and you can decide for yourself.

Background

Remote Web technology has been around for a while. Back in 1996 I bought one of the first Windows CE devices, a Philips Velo 1. It came with a version of Internet Explorer called Pocket Internet Explorer. It actually did a decent job of browsing the Web, given its platform. However, it was severely limited, and most Web sites of any functionality or size were beyond it. Microsoft put out guidelines for developing special versions of Web sites that were Pocket IE-friendly. Needless to say, this did not happen very often.

Mobile devices today, especially cell phones, take a different approach. They have built-in Web browsers, but they are not all the same. There are many different Web browsers, the various versions of which run on assorted cell phones and PDAs with different processors. Some are more advanced, offering color displays, better HTML rendering, and access to features of the device itself. When targeting your Web content for these devices, you have the option of going for the lowest common denominator and reaching more users or targeting the features of specific devices and limiting your audience. You could, of course, spend lots of development time accommodating each device, but that is a serious pain and costs lots of money.

Imagine doing just that. To build your Web application such that it could accommodate different platforms, you'd have to build a hardware isolation layer. It would need to know about the capabilities of each device you support and be able to render content for each. You'd need a device database that stored this information. Your pages would have to write their output to the isolation layer, which would parse it, interpret the content, translate it to the target device (assuming you could identify it), and send it down the wire. There probably would be some sort of translation you'd have to do for requests from the device as well.

Personally, I have no interest in building such a system. It would take huge amounts of time and resources, which few companies have. However, one of those companies that has the capital, wherewithal, and interest is Microsoft. The result is the Mobile Internet Toolkit. It allows you to build Web content intended for mobile devices without worrying about the target platform. It contains the hardware isolation capabilities we talked about and has an extensive database of supported devices.

Essentials

The Mobile Internet Toolkit is an add-on for Visual Studio .NET. It's free for the downloading from Microsoft. That's the first bit of good news. Second, it's based on ASP.NET, so if you know that, you've got a big head start. You can write your code just like ASP.NET, using the studio or even Notepad. Third, it has a complete set of server-side controls designed especially for mobile Web applications. You don't have to live without rich functionality just because your target platform is a cell phone or PDA. Fourth, all of this, on the server side, runs in good old Internet Information Server. All you need is the Mobile Internet Toolkit installed on your Web server. And fifth, as we've alluded to, you write your code once, and the toolkit and controls take care of rendering everything for the target device.

The Mobile Device

Each Web-enabled device has its own implementation of a Web browser. Although some may license a browser from the same vendor, resulting in some devices that use the same browser, there is still a large proliferation of browsers and flavors. Pocket PCs have their own version of Pocket IE. There are third-party browsers available for Palm OS devices. And cell phones have all kinds of browsers.

For the purpose of this chapter, we concentrate on cell phones for the following good reasons:

- Cell phones are cheap and prolific. There are plenty of them, and as a reader, you (and your potential customers) are more likely to have them.
- They are essentially the baseline for Web capabilities, and whatever you build will be upwardly compatible with PDAs.
- The cell phone platform dramatically illustrates the differences between the Web controls you use in the designer and how they are rendered on the target platform. We see more about this later.

There are plenty of browsers on cell phones, and each may support a different mobile flavor of HTML, such as Compact HTML (cHTML) or Wireless Markup Language (WML). Regardless of which one your device supports, the code emitted by the Mobile Internet Toolkit should work properly on it.

Designing Content for Mobile Devices

If you haven't tried the Web on a cell phone yet, you ought to, just to gauge the current mobile Web landscape. You probably will be a little underwhelmed at first. Current devices and browsers are limited by their small screen size and lack of decent input capabilities. Just try to send email using the keypad on a cell phone. There are some new developments that are improving this, but it's still no pleasure. There is no mouse cursor, usually only up and down arrows.

Because of these limitations, there are some important design considerations that must be kept in mind when building content for mobile devices.

Think small. The pages on a mobile device can scroll vertically, but the screen is small. The width is tiny. Your content has to fit here, so keep that in mind as you design your pages. For example, my cell phone's display is 96 pixels wide and four lines tall.

Stay focused. Because you can fit only a very small amount of content on a page, you have to keep your pages very focused. Concentrate on one purpose, one function. You have to rethink how you build your pages.

Don't be vain. Appearance is not of paramount importance when designing mobile Web content. Function is much more important. Graphics capabilities may be severely limited, and unless you want to target only the more advanced platforms, graphics should be small and monochrome. Don't worry too much about fancy details until the bandwidth and the browsers become more advanced.

Type less. As mentioned, it is difficult for users of cell phones to do lots of alphanumeric data entry. When you need input, use controls such as lists that allow users to make selections by scrolling. Keep the text entry to a minimum. You don't want users trying to enter the name of a movie in order to buy tickets as they drive down the road.

As you look around the mobile Web, as well as get more experience with the toolkit, you get a better feel for what's practical and desirable. You'll learn what graphics are possible, what performance is like, and how to organize your content intelligently. Of course, we give you the benefit of our experience as well.

The Tools You'll Need

Visual Studio .NET provides you with some excellent tools to design Web pages using ASP.NET and their marvelous editors. You've seen them before and will continue to use them while building mobile Web content. However, there are a few other items you'll need as well. This includes the Mobile Internet Toolkit itself, and the Microsoft Mobile Explorer.

The Mobile Internet Toolkit modifies Visual Studio .NET so that it can build mobile Web applications. It updates the designer with new editing tools so that you can build the somewhat different mobile forms and pages. It also adds a whole pile of new controls designed specifically for the mobile Web. They'll be found in a new category on the control bar. For a free download from Microsoft, go to http://msdn.microsoft.com and search for Mobile Internet Toolkit.

Lastly, you will need a way to test out your mobile Web applications. You could easily use regular Internet Explorer. It will render the controls well enough. However, it does not really change the look of the controls to show what they would look like on a cell phone. To remedy this, you use an emulator. There are plenty of emulators available from cell-phone manufacturers. However, Microsoft provides a generic one that you can use called the Microsoft Mobile Explorer (MME). It emulates the appearance and display of a cell phone and allows you to see the changes that controls undergo when they are put on a mobile device. You can download the MME from Microsoft's MSDN site, but you'll have to hunt for it. It isn't easy to find.

Getting Your Development Environment Ready

Before we can work on any labs, and before you can dive in and experiment for yourself prior to doing the labs (we know you're doing it), you'll need all the tools installed and configured. Let's go ahead and get that out of the way.

Install the Toolkit

This is pretty simple but still has to be done before you can build content. Download the toolkit and install it, making sure you already have Visual Studio .NET installed. It will add all the goodies you need, as well as some very useful documentation. It's pretty small and compact, so the download and installation will be fairly painless.

Install the Mobile Explorer

Testing your applications on a real mobile device, although important at later stages, is cumbersome and difficult to debug. Given cell phone Web access rates, it could also be expensive. So we use a cell phone emulator as a stand-in. It's quite easy to use and integrates nicely with Visual Studio .NET. Once installed, in the studio, you can select a page in the solution explorer, right-click it, and select Browse With. You can select the mobile explorer and view your page as if it were in a cell phone. Download the MME from Microsoft's MSDN Web site and install it on your machine.

If you would like to test your page on a particular device, you can download device-specific emulators from cell phone manufacturers' sites. Most have emulators for the various browsers they use and may even have different skins you can put in the emulator to make it look like a specific model. They're pretty much always free, too.

Using a Real Mobile Device

At some point, you will want to test your content on a real mobile device or two, just to make sure it works well. To do this, you'll have to publish your content on the Web, even if not publicly. Because mobile applications are Web projects, you simply need to connect your Web server to the Internet. Then set up a bookmark in your cell phone that points to your machine's IP address and the project directory. If you can't, you'll need to post your application to a Web server that has IIS 5.0 or higher installed, as well as Microsoft .NET Framework and the Mobile Internet Toolkit.

Building Mobile Web Content

Mobile Web development is a lot like building ASP.NET applications. The underlying principles are the same. However, there are lots of differences that will keep you busy, especially if you build both.

Six Steps to Mobile Web Development

After building a few mobile Web applications, we came up with a generic overview of the process that makes it easy to grasp. Once you understand the various steps, we can move on to the details. Although the steps listed next are intended to cover many situations, no doubt there will be deviations from your own projects. However, these will do for a start.

1. Create a new mobile Web application project in Visual Studio .NET. Once you install the Mobile Internet Toolkit, this new project type is available to you. Because this is really an ASP.NET application of sorts, the project is created in your Inetpub directory.
2. Create your style sheets. Style sheets are a powerful way to control the look of your content in a centralized fashion. However, it's a good idea to create them ahead of time so that they are ready when you start building your forms.
3. Build your forms. The Toolbox has been updated to include all sorts of mobile Web controls, and you can drop them onto forms much like ASP.NET applications. However, the layout works a little differently. We cover this soon.
4. Write your code. This includes server-side event handlers, business objects and functionality, database access, and client-side script code. There are a few differences from regular ASP.NET development.
5. Run your application. Debugging works just like ASP.NET, with your application running in the MME.
6. Deploy your application. Place it on an IIS server somewhere that has the toolkit installed. You should be able to copy everything over and make a virtual directory for it.

There are variations on this theme. For example, you can use a text editor to lay out your forms instead of the designer. This works faster for some people (myself included). Although the tools are a big help, the bulk of the work is up to you. One requirement, for example, is that all pages have to begin with the following header:

```
<%@ Page Language="vb" AutoEventWireup="false"
  Codebehind="MobileWebForm1.aspx.vb" Inherits="MIT_One.MobileWebForm1"
%>
<%@ Register TagPrefix="mobile" Namespace="System.Web.UI.MobileControls"
  Assembly="System.Web.Mobile, Version=1.0.3300.0, Culture=neutral,
  PublicKeyToken=b03f5f7f11d50a3a" %>
```

These lines are specific to your application and are generated by the designer if you use it. If you're typing your code, you'll have to include them yourself.

Your own code is implemented much like ASP.NET in a compiled module that works behind the scenes. If you look at the preceding code, you will see that the codebehind attribute points to your Visual Basic code module. There are other details to work with as well, so let's dive a little deeper.

Pages and Forms

Visual Basic programmers are intimately familiar with the concept of forms and work with them all the time. Web programmers are equally familiar with pages and do all their UI work there. Mobile Web application developers must be familiar with both. Building mobile content blends the concept of pages and forms and puts them both to use to improve performance on cell phones and other narrow bandwidth portable devices.

A form in the Mobile Internet Toolkit is actually a type of control, a container that holds other controls. It represents what is seen by users when they use your application. A page in the toolkit is just like a page in a Web application. It contains any number of forms. Although forms are what the user sees, one at a time, the page is what is sent to the device all at once. If your page has three forms on it, all three forms come down to client at the same time, when the page is sent. If it has 50 forms, 50 forms are sent at once.

A page can have only one active form at a time, which is the one the user sees. The page has a property called ActiveForm that takes the name of one of the forms on the page. Set the property to change the page that is viewed. For example, assume you have two forms on a page, frmMain and frmLookup. You could wire an event to a control, such as a button, on frmMain that is meant to navigate to frmLookup. The following line of code goes into the button click event handler to do this:

```
ActiveForm = frmLookup
```

As soon as this code executes, the page changes. As mentioned, you need to think about efficiency all the time when designing your pages. There are two aspects to this efficiency. First, you need to keep all your forms small and oriented around a single operation. This could mean that to implement a particular feature, you may need to break it up into several forms. For example, suppose you are presenting a mobile Web application that lists movie times. You might want to break your functionality into the following forms:

1. Form1 gets a zip code from the user in a simple text box.
2. Form2 presents a list of theaters near the zip code entered and allows the user to select one.
3. Form3 presents a list of films showing at the theater the user selected.
4. Form4 shows a list of movie times for the movie the user selected.

A mobile form represents each of these steps. All these forms relate to the same function and can be placed on the same page. This is a fairly efficient design that keeps the input focused yet does not require the downloading of a new page each time. It creates a balance between forms and pages and prevents the following problems:

- Too many forms on a single page. This would result in slow performance and make the user wait until all the pages come down the wire.
- Too many small pages with a single form on each. This results in more trips to the server and more waiting while pages come down between steps.

In addition, switching from one form to another can be done very quickly, whereas downloading new pages takes somewhat longer. Keep this in mind while designing your forms and pages. Make sure all the steps for a process are in forms on a page and that you separate features with pages.

Lab 17.1: Mobile Quotations

I don't know about you, but I'm ready for some programming. It's time to get our feet wet and see some actual code working in the emulator. We will build a two-form, single-page mobile application that allows the user to select a category and then displays a famous quotation from that category. We'll keep our data small in the interest of efficiency.

Perform the following steps:

1. Begin by creating a new Mobile Web Application project in Visual Studio .NET. Name it MobileQuotes and click OK to begin. Figure 17.1 shows the correct settings.

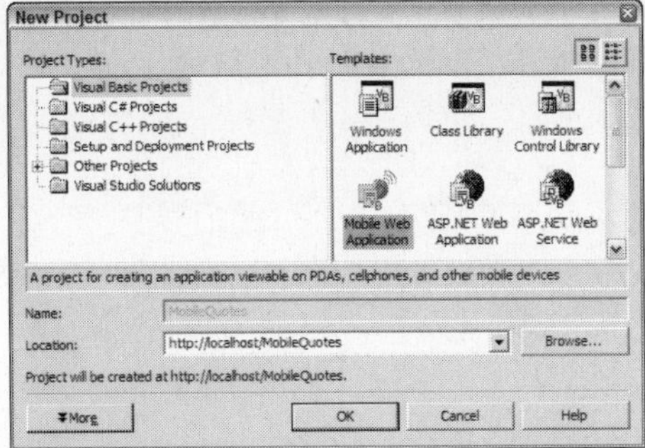

Figure 17.1 Begin a new mobile Web application project.

2. Take a look at the new landscape. The most obvious change is the way the empty form looks. It's fairly simple and is really just an area with a title. On the left is the Toolbox. It has lots of new controls that are specific to mobile Web applications. Figure 17.2 lets you take a look at the changes without starting up the studio.

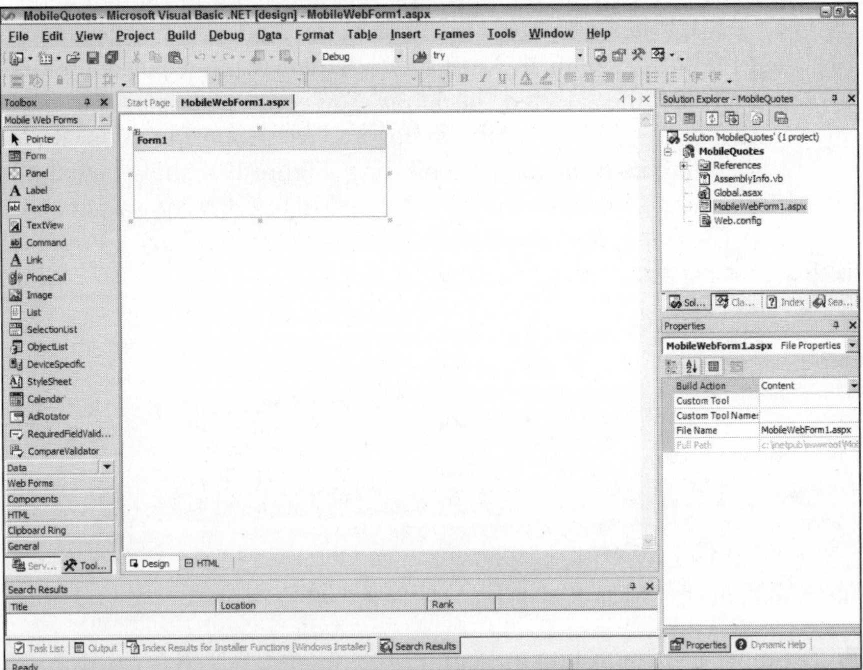

Figure 17.2 The mobile Web environment is slightly different.

3. Drag a label control onto the form. Once there, change its text property to Select a category. Notice that the control is dropped inline,

and you can't move it around once it's in place. The page is set up like a flow layout in ASP.NET. Figure 17.3 shows what it should look like.

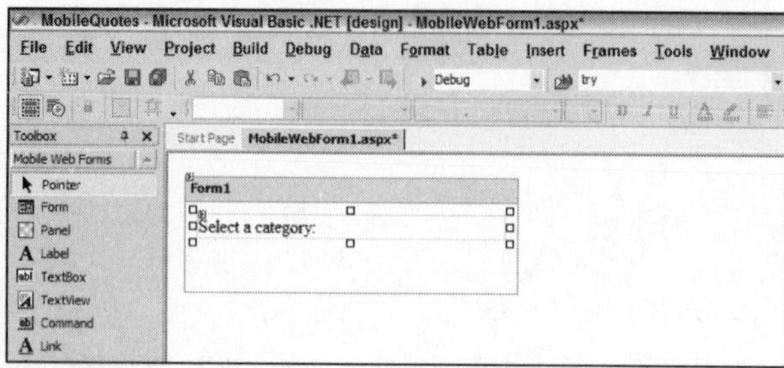

Figure 17.3 Drop a label control in your blank mobile form.

4. Drop a SelectionList onto the form underneath the label. Again, you will not be able to move it around except to switch its order. Once in place, click the Items property in the properties window of the studio. It will bring up an editor dialog that lets you add canned items to your list. Put in two items by clicking the Add Item button, one called Life After Death and another called Happiness. Select the first item and click the Selected check box. You could also select the General item on the left side of the dialog and set properties about the list, including its style and data binding. Figure 17.4 shows what the settings should look like.

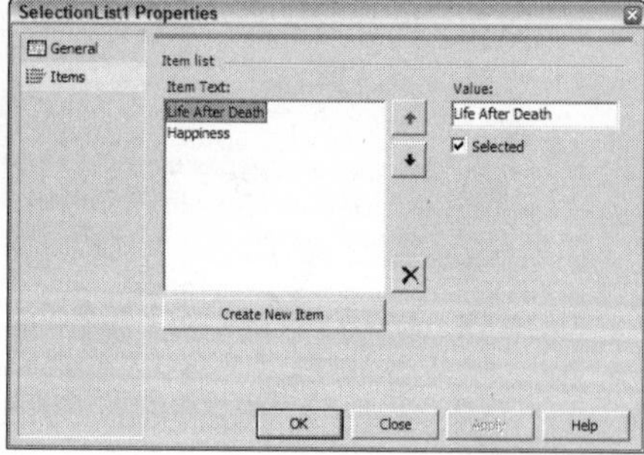

Figure 17.4 The SelectionList control can have a prebuilt list of items.

5. Drop our last control on the form, a Command, which is really a button. Put it at the bottom and change its text property to Get Quote. The form should now look like Figure 17.5.

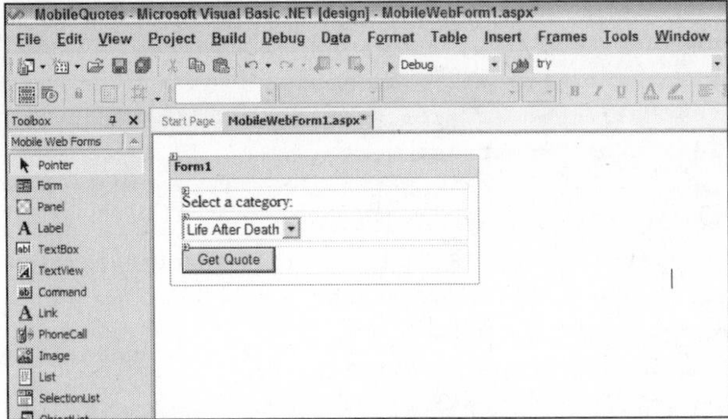

Figure 17.5 Our form is complete with three controls.

6. Drag a new form from the Toolbox onto the page and drop it below the first form. Add a single label to it and change its text property to an empty string. This form will be used to display our results to the user. It should like Figure 17.6.

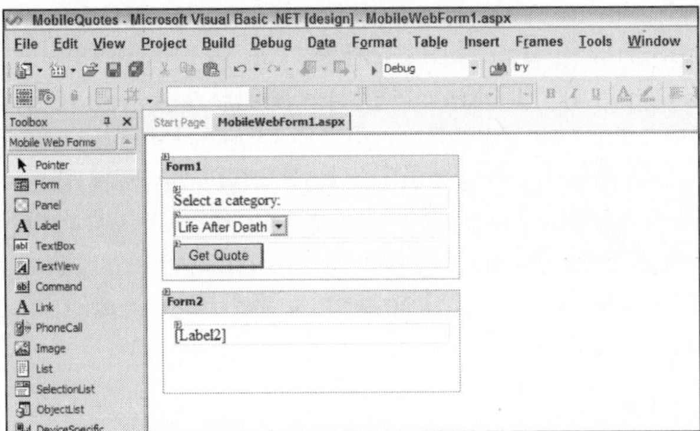

Figure 17.6 The second form will show results to the user.

Now that the page is laid out, take a look at the code that has been generated for us by the designer. It looks like this:

```
<%@ Register TagPrefix="mobile"
Namespace="System.Web.UI.MobileControls"
  Assembly="System.Web.Mobile, Version=1.0.3300.0,
Culture=neutral,
  PublicKeyToken=b03f5f7f11d50a3a" %>
<%@ Page Language="vb" AutoEventWireup="false"
  Codebehind="MobileWebForm1.aspx.vb"
  Inherits="MobileQuotes.MobileWebForm1" %>
  <meta name="GENERATOR" content="Microsoft Visual Studio .NET
7.0">
```

```
<meta name="CODE_LANGUAGE" content="Visual Basic 7.0">
<meta name="vs_targetSchema"
  content="http://schemas.microsoft.com/Mobile/Page">
<body Xmlns:mobile="http://schemas.microsoft.com/Mobile/WebForm">
     <mobile:Form id="Form1" runat="server">
          <mobile:Label id="Label1" runat="server">
               Select a category:</mobile:Label>
          <mobile:SelectionList id="SelectionList1" runat="server">
               <Item Value="Life After Death"
                Text="Life After Death"
                    Selected="True"></Item>
               <Item Value="Happiness" Text="Happiness"></Item>
          </mobile:SelectionList>
          <mobile:Command id="Command1" runat="server">
               Get Quote</mobile:Command>
     </mobile:Form>
     <mobile:Form id="Form2" runat="server">
          <mobile:Label id="Label2"
runat="server"></mobile:Label>
     </mobile:Form>
</body>
```

If you ignore all the header declarations and skip to the body tag, you can see how the forms are declared. All the controls it contains are created within the form tag, and like ASP.NET server controls, they have the runat=server attribute. Unlike ASP.NET controls, they use a prefix of mobile instead of asp. The mobile prefix is mapped to an XML namespace that defines the mobile Web forms schema. You can see this mapping in the body tag. The rest is pretty clear and declares the rest of our controls and the second form.

Note that the names for controls must be unique at the page level because the forms are really just controls themselves, containers for other controls. That's why our only label on the second form was automatically named Label2. We already had a Label1 on Form1. Keep this in mind as you name controls in your projects.

7. Double-click the command button to bring up the code editor. In the event handler for the button click, add the following code:

```
Private Sub Command1_Click(ByVal sender As System.Object, _
     ByVal e As System.EventArgs) Handles Command1.Click
     Select Case UCase(SelectionList1.Selection.Text())
          Case "LIFE AFTER DEATH"
               Label2.Text = "Death isn't something to be " & _
                   "feared. Think of it as a very effective " & _
                   "way of reducing your expenses. - Woody Allen"
          Case "HAPPINESS"
```

```
                    Label2.Text = "Most people would rather be " & _
                        "certain they are miserable, than risk " & _
                        "being happy. - Robert Anthony"
        End Select
        ' Show the form.
        ActiveForm = Form2
    End Sub
```

This code fills in a quotation for the text property of the Label2 control based on the item selected in the SelectionList. Once done, the code uses the ActiveForm property of the page to make the second form visible with the new results.

8. Right-click the aspx page in the Solution Explorer, and from the context menu, select Browse With. In the dialog that appears, select the Microsoft Mobile Explorer. Click the button labeled Set As Default, and you won't have to do this again for the duration of the chapter. Click the browse button to run the application. Note that now that you have the default browser set to the MME, you can use the standard Visual Basic Run button to kick off your mobile Web applications. Figure 17.7 shows Form1 running in the emulator on the left and the results in Form2 on the right.

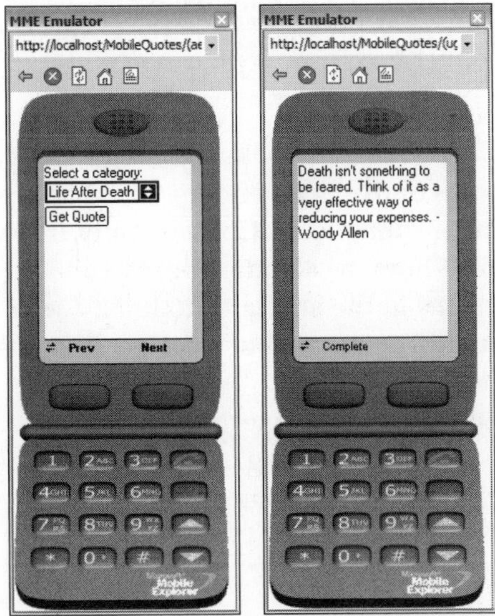

Figure 17.7 Our application pages run perfectly in the Microsoft Mobile Explorer.

This lab exposed you to the basics of building a mobile Web application. You can now create multiform pages, switch between them, and use labels, lists, buttons, and trap events. This is just scratching the surface, however. It's time to get some more detail about building mobile Web applications.

Some More Depth

Now that we've been standing in a puddle (gotten our feet wet), we're ready for the real meat of mobile Web applications. Many interesting topics await, including a survey of available controls, validating input, displaying images, and even data binding.

Surveying the Mobile Controls

As you've seen, the mobile controls are much like ASP.NET server controls. They run on the server and render themselves for the target browser. This is even more important in the mobile world. Internet Explorer, for example, can run ActiveX controls embedded in your page. Cell phones have no idea what ActiveX controls are, but they can make use of content rendered for them by mobile server controls.

One of the side effects of this is that when controls are dropped into the designer, they look as you expect. A calendar control looks like a monthly calendar. However, the calendar is a server control and renders itself for a cell phone browser that has little or no calendar capabilities. Consequently, it looks very different on a cell phone. Figure 17.8 shows a calendar control running in the emulator. Note that it takes four screens in the emulator to finally select a date. Other cell phones may do it in fewer steps, but you get the idea. Although it is not very impressive, it gets the job done.

So what controls are there? We've seen the label, a selection list, a calendar, and a button. We'll need more than that if we are going to build compelling mobile content. A tour through the available facilities is in order.

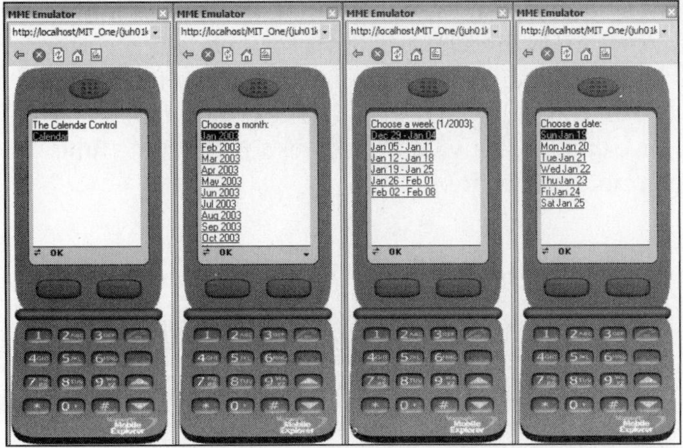

Figure 17.8 The calendar control is rendered quite differently on the target browser.

When placing controls on a form, they can be placed only above or below other controls because of the width limitations of a cell phone and the flow-oriented nature of the page. However, you may be targeting other devices that are more capable, such as PDAs or more advanced cell phones with bigger displays. You can change the way the layout works in this case. Each control has a property called BreakAfter. If you set this property to False, the control that follows it is placed on the same line if there is room. For example, you could place a label that describes a text box first, then its text box below it in the designer. If you set the BreakAfter property of the label control to False and you have the room, the controls appear side by side. If not, the label appears on top of the text box, which is still quite acceptable. This type of layout accommodates small and large displays, maximizing screen real estate in a seller's market.

The Form Control

We've already seen the Form control and had a basic description of it. It's a container for other controls and is the basic unit of content on the target browser. There is more to them, however, than just being a container. For example, just like ASP.NET forms, they can be submitted to the server using a Get or Post operation. There are also other properties that you can set to control appearance of the form, including foreground and background colors, font, alignment, visibility, and its title. There's even an action property that controls the URL to which the form is submitted.

There are two events that a form can raise that can be quite useful: Activate and Deactivate. They allow you to detect when the form is shown and when it is removed from the display. These events are fired when the form is made active using the ActiveForm property of the page. Once a form is set to active using the ActiveForm property, its Activate event fires. At the same time, the Deactivate event on the prior form is fired.

The Label Control

A simple control, the Label control simply renders text on the display. It allows you to control aspects of the text using its properties, such as its alignment, colors, font, text wrapping, style, and the very useful BreakAfter property. We've seen these, and although useful, don't need much discussion.

The Command Control

The Command control equates to a button, though how it is rendered on the target browser is up to interpretation. It shows up in the designer as a button. The user can click on it and fire an event that you can respond to. You can even adjust its appearance by using the Format property, telling it to appear as a button or a link.

The Text Control

The Text control is the mobile equivalent of the TextBox control and allows you to accept alphanumeric input. Although it does not have all the properties of the normal text box, it is perfectly adequate for mobile use. The Text control may appear on the mobile device as a regular text box or might actually fill the entire screen to allow for more input.

You can change the behavior of the Text control using its properties. It can be made to accept only numeric input using the Numeric property. You can also make it function like a password field using the Password property. However, you will want to make sure that your target devices can support these field types, because some don't.

As mentioned before, text input can be tedious and difficult on a cell phone. It's probably a good idea to limit the use of the Text control in your mobile applications if at all possible. However, if you need it, you need it.

The TextView Control

The TextView control is like a viewer for larger volumes of formatted information. It can display multiple lines of text using HTML codes to do the formatting. For example, you could use the <BR> tag to force a line break. If your target device supports it, you can also use bold and italic attributes. You can set the contents of the TextView control using its Text property.

The Link Control

The Link control represents an HTML anchor tag and shows as a Web link. The exact representation, as usual, is up to the browser. All you have to do is drop one on a form and assign it a URL and text value, and you've got it. The user can click it to activate the link.

The List Control

You might think initially that this control allows the user to select something from a list of items. However, that is relegated to another control. The List control is much simpler. It displays a list of text items, much like the HTML <UL> or <OL> tags. They are read-only controls.

There is a nice editor available at design time that allows you to add items to the list. However, you will probably want to add items at runtime as well. You can do this easily using the following code fragment:

```
Dim li As New MobileListItem()
li.Text = "Maxwell Smart"
li.Value = 1
List1.Items.Add(li)
```

It is important to note that if you create multiple items in code, you cannot reuse the single MobileListItem object once it has been added to the list. You have to create a new object for each item in the list, or you will have a lot of references in the list to the same item.

Like some other list controls, the Text property sets what is displayed on the screen, and the Value property lets you assign a secondary value that is stored with the list item but is not displayed.

The SelectionList Control

Although the List control is for display only, SelectionList allows the user to make a choice or choices from the list. We've seen this in action in our previous lab. It usually requires another control, such as a Command control, that allows users to indicate that they are done making selections.

There are several modes in which the control can operate. It can behave as a drop-down list, such as we saw in our lab. It also can be a scrolling list with a number of items in view at the same time, allowing one selection or multiple selections. Or it can be a list of radio buttons, allowing the user to make a single selection, or a list of check boxes for multiple selections. However, if you select one of these options, make sure you test it on a real mobile device. There is no other way to tell how it will render on a specific device in these other modes.

The ObjectList Control

Yet another control in our list of lists, the ObjectList, is made to store instances of objects. You can use it to store a list of your own objects, such as class instances, or perhaps rows of data from a data set. You can add items to this control much like the other lists, either manually in code or using data binding.

The Calendar Control

This is pretty obvious, plus we've seen it already. It renders, in one form or another (pun intended), a calendar control from which a specific date can be selected. It has a handful of properties that allow you to define its appearance (use with caution based on your target browser), as well as a few more that let you define a starting date and other calendar behavior.

There are various flavors of HTML that mobile devices support. A couple examples include cHTML and WML. Normally, you shouldn't have to worry about this because the Mobile Internet Toolkit runtime can determine what is in use at the time and render the correct HTML for that device. However, there is one important exception. On browsers that use WML, the Mobile Internet Toolkit cannot use a calendar control and text box controls on the same page. They conflict with each other in the toolkit version 1.0. This probably will be fixed in the next version, but it is important to keep this in mind as you design your pages.

The PhoneCall Control

PhoneCall is quite a powerful little control. It allows you to provide a visible link that the user can click and programmatically initiate a phone call from the client device. You can use the PhoneNumber property to define the number it will call. For example, you could provide a list of phone numbers of people from your office, and when the user selects one, grab the selected phone number and put it into the PhoneCall control's PhoneNumber property. When clicked, the phone will dial the number. I think the most amazing thing about this control is that someone thought of it. It is so useful and so obvious, exactly the sort of thing that takes years to develop.

And the Rest

There are quite a few other controls, including a Panel control, a bunch of validator controls that we'll cover later, and even an ad rotator. Prowl around the studio and see if you can make them dance.

Displaying Images

Mobile devices can display images just like regular Web browsers. However, they typically have to be smaller and use fewer colors. Most cell phone browsers can still only display monochrome images, although color devices are fast becoming cheap and prolific.

Designing Your Images

When planning the images in your mobile Web content, you'll have to take into account the target browsers that you want to support. If you're only interested in color PDAs, you can make larger, more colorful images. However, if you want to support the maximum number of devices, you'll need to think ahead a little. Here are a couple things to remember.

Plan for your lowest common denominator. If you need to support both cell phones and PDAs, but only care about color devices, create smaller color images. If you want to support everything, you'll have to stick to purely monochrome images or even no images at all.

Pick an image format. There are plenty of graphics formats available, but only a few are supported by Web content, including JPG, GIF, PNG, and occasionally, BMP. However, most cell phones only support GIF files. Some support JPG for more color depth (GIF is limited to 8-bit color), but this format and the browsers that support them can have problems with lower color depths, especially monochrome. BMPs are huge. GIF is usually your best bet.

There are, of course, exceptions to these design rules. If you want to go to greater lengths (and more work) to gain both maximum color possibilities and support the most devices possible, read on. The MobileCapabilities object is your new friend.

Displaying Your Images

Displaying images is fairly easy to do using the Image control and usually renders an IMG tag in the HTML. You need to add the image to your project, usually in an images directory, and set the ImageURL property for the Image control.

You also can set a link on the images in your form. The Image control has a property called NavigateURL to which you can assign a URL. Once the image is clicked, the browser will navigate to the URL.

Mobile Capabilities Object

One of the important benefits of using the Mobile Internet Toolkit, as we've mentioned several times, is that you can write code once and the system takes care of rendering your content for the target browser. The only problem with this is that you have to design for the lowest common denominator. For example you might want to show color graphics on your forms. However, because they may look bad on a monochrome display, you design monochrome graphics instead of color. You sacrifice the quality of your content for maximum compatibility.

There is an alternative. Using a globally available object called MobileCapabilities, you can determine some of the capabilities of the browser in use and act accordingly. Given our example, we want to display color graphics if the browser can handle it, but we also want to be compatible with browsers that can't handle it. The following code will take care of our dilemma:

```
Dim mc As MobileCapabilities = Ctype(Request.Browser, _
MobileCapabilities)
If mc.IsColor() Then
      ' Display color graphic
Else
      ' Display monochrome graphic
End If
```

There's even a second syntax you can use by requesting the information by name instead of using the properties syntax. It looks like this:

```
If Request.Browser("IsColor") Then
      ' Display color graphic
Else
      ' Display monochrome graphic
End If
```

There are nearly a zillion properties in the MobileCapabilities object. It's fairly easy to use and provides you with lots of information. Following is a listing of some of the more interesting properties available:

ActiveXControls. Returns True if the browser supports the use of ActiveX controls.

AOL. This one always makes me laugh. It Returns True if the client is running through America Online.

BackgroundSounds. Returns True if the device supports the playing of background sounds.

Browser. Returns a string describing the browser in use. Two possible values are IE and Microsoft Mobile Explorer.

CanInitiateVoiceCall. This is quite useful and returns True if the device can make a voice telephone call, which is important if your target clients include both cell phones and PDAs.

CanSendMail. Returns True if the browser supports the use of the mailto: method.

HasBackButton. Returns True if the browser has a back button that is used for navigation.

InputType. Returns a string that describes the input mechanism on the device. A few of the possible values (after some digging around) include virtualKeyboard, telephoneKeyboard, telephoneKeypad, and keyboard.

IsColor. One of the most useful, it returns True if the display supports color.

MobileDeviceManufacturer. Returns a string with the name of the target device maker.

NumberOfSoftKeys. Returns the number of soft keys on the device that are available for your use.

RendersBreaksAfterHtmlLists. Returns True if the browser automatically forces a line break after an HTML list.

ScreenBitDepth. Returns a number representing the color depth of the device's screen. This is very useful for the best in color support.

ScreenCharactersHeight, ScreenCharactersWidth. Returns the height and width of the screen in characters.

ScreenPixelsHeight, ScreenPixelsWidth. Returns the height and width of the screen in pixels.

SupportCSS. Also useful, this returns True if the browser supports the use of client-side style sheets.

There are more properties, of course. Use IntelliSense in the studio editor to explore them, or look it up in the online help.

Validating User Input

In Chapter 13 we saw that Web-based validation of user inputs was made fairly easy with special controls called validator controls. There were several types to handle various kinds of validations. We even used them in our labs.

The good news is that there are equivalent validator controls for the mobile platform.

The mobile versions of the validator controls are pretty much like the grown-up versions, with a few minor differences. The validator controls available include a required field validator and a compare, a range, a regular expression, and a custom validator. There's even a new item called the validation summary control that displays the results of several validation controls on a single form in one place. It works beautifully for displaying any errors on a form with more than the result. The validation summary control goes on a different form, and you tell it which other form to validate.

Let's take a brief look. Suppose you have a form with a required field validator control on it that's tied to a text box. When the Submit button is clicked, you want to check the control to see if there are any input errors. If not, you can display a prompt in a label control on a second form that says thanks. If not, you let the validator control display its error message. The code looks like this:

```
Private Sub Command1_Click(ByVal sender As System.Object, _
     ByVal e As System.EventArgs) Handles Command1.Click
     If Page.IsValid Then
          Label3.Text = "Thanks for your input!"
          ActiveForm = Form2
     End If
End Sub
```

The Page.IsValid property checks all the validator controls on a page to see if any are in error. If so, it returns False, and you know there is at least one error. It will return True if all the validator controls return False, or in other words, if there are no errors.

Note that the Page.IsValid applies to the entire page. That means that it checks all the validator controls on all the forms on that page. Make sure you only put forms on that page that you want to be validated by the check.

Content Pagination

Sometimes you will have too much content on a single form to fit on the screen. The Mobile Internet Toolkit uses a mechanism called pagination to show only partial content and allows the user to scroll through it. It can make the display of large amounts of information or UI easier and more convenient.

How Pagination Works

There are two types of pagination: automatic and manual. Automatic is far easier to use. You simply set the Paginate property of the form to True, and the system provides a mechanism to do the pagination and handles the paging for you. Suppose you have a long list of data to display, perhaps an ingredient list, that goes beyond the size of the screen. The pagination feature will automatically break the content into pages that fit on a screen, providing navigation controls that allow movement from one page to the next. This mechanism handles most of your pagination needs.

Simple content is not the only thing that can be paginated. Forms with lots of controls can also be paginated. The Paginate property will automatically break the form into pages that can be navigated by the user, making the decision on how to break the pages by itself. You can control the pagination to some degree by using the Panel control. This is a control container, much like a form, but you can put more than one on a form. The pagination system will do its best to keep all the controls in a panel together. Use them to organize your controls and make the paging decisions yourself, instead of leaving it entirely to the pagination system.

You can even modify the pagination mechanism appearance a little bit. You can control how the paging controls appear using the PagerStyle property. You also can change the text on the paging controls using the PreviousPageText and NextPageText properties.

There will be some occasions where automatic paging does not behave the way you want it to. These are opportunities to try your hand at manual paging. You have to write your own pagination code that responds to paging events and sends the next or previous page of content. The process is often called chunking. This would be beneficial if you have large amounts of data that you don't want to send over the wire to the client all at once. For example, if a user is looking for something in the data, and you have 50 pages of it, what the user is looking for might be on page 2. Why waste time with the other pages?

The Pagination Decision

Most of the time, automatic pagination will take care of most of your paging needs, and you can use it when appropriate. However, it is usually better to design your forms so that they fit on the screen all at once. It is much more user friendly. However, there are occasions where paging is appropriate. If you have to support devices that have widely varying screen sizes, you may design the forms to fit on the larger screens and allow them to paginate on the smaller ones. If you do this, try to use panels to organize the controls such that they break logically.

Mobile Data Binding

Chapters 14 and 15 covered data binding extensively. We saw how to attach data to controls in both WinForms projects and ASP.NET applications. Fortunately, data binding works much the same way in the Mobile Internet Toolkit.

You can bind data to most of the controls where it makes sense. You even can create your own array of data and bind it to controls. However, actual data from a live database is pretty powerful for a mobile Web application.

The mobile controls that support data binding have some properties and methods that allow you to bind data to them. They are as follows:

DataSource. This property is set to the ADO.NET DataSet that you presumably filled with data from the database. It also can be an ArrayList.

DataMember. This is the specific table within the DataSet that contains the data to put into the control.

DataTextField. This property should be set to the column in the DataSet that holds the values you want to display, such as in a list box.

DataValueField. This contains the name of the column from the DataSet that holds a value to be returned when the user makes a selection. Typically, it will be the unique ID from the database that matches the item selected from the control.

DataBind. This method actually tells the controls to data bind. It is called after the other properties are set.

A typical example is the need to fill a list box with data from the database, allowing the user to make a selection for further database activity. When the user makes a selection, we usually don't want the text from the list box, but its associated ID from the database. For example, assume we put a SelectionList on a mobile form and bind it to a categories table in a quotations database. The code to load the data and bind it to the control looks like this.

```
Private Sub Page_Load(ByVal sender As System.Object, _
     ByVal e As System.EventArgs) Handles MyBase.Load
     If Not IsPostBack() Then
          Dim conn As New SqlConnection( _
               "server=(local); database=Quotes; uid=sa; pwd=;")
          Dim da As New SqlDataAdapter( _
               "SELECT * FROM Category", conn)
          Dim ds As New DataSet()
          Try
               conn.Open()
               da.Fill(ds, "Categories")
               SelectionList1.DataSource = ds
               SelectionList1.DataMember = "Categories"
               SelectionList1.DataTextField = "CatDesc"
               SelectionList1.DataValueField = "CatID"
               SelectionList1.DataBind()
               conn.Close()
          Catch ex As SqlException
```

```
            End Try
        End If
    End Sub
```

This code will look familiar from Chapter 14. It follows standard data binding procedure. The only difference is that results go to a mobile device. Figure 17.9 shows it running in the emulator. Our emulator renders the SelectionList as a single scrollable value, so there are several values shown.

As you can see, the Mobile Internet Toolkit is no stranger to data binding. As long as we plan our pages and forms such that they fit and look good in a mobile screen, limiting alphanumeric input, we can build just about anything that runs on a mobile device.

Classroom Q & A

Q: I'm not sure I understand the relationship between pages and forms. How do they work together and differ from each other?

A: A page can contain multiple forms, only one of which is visible at any time. When you send a page down to the client device, all the forms on the page go with it. That's why you want to strike a balance between speed and number of trips back to the server. You don't want too many forms on a page because it will take too long to download. You don't want too few because the browser will have to go back to the server for more content too frequently, making the user wait between steps in your application.

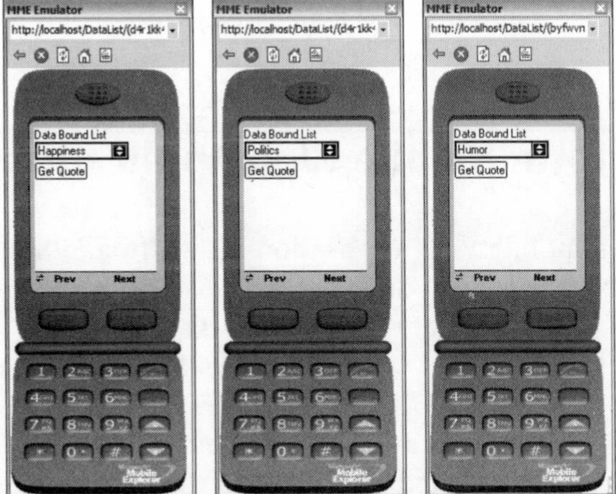

Figure 17.9 The SelectionList works in data-bound mode in the emulator.

If it helps, think of the whole page as an MDI program. The page is the MDI parent that contains all the child windows. The forms are the child windows that only run in a maximized state; thus, only one can be visible at a time. You even change child windows, or forms, the same way as an MDI application, by setting the ActiveForm property.

Q: Can I build secure mobile Web applications?

A: You can build secure applications as long as you handle security yourself, using forms-based security. This was demonstrated in Chapter 13. It would be up to you to handle the password encryption and decryption, as well as build the forms to support it. Integrated security is not supported. However, if you are part of an organization that has purchased Microsoft Passport authentication, there are some mobile devices that support it. You can make use of Passport 2.1's Single Sign In (SSI) feature to let them log in easily with limited input.

Q: Suppose I already have an ASP.NET application with lots of functionality and a Web UI. Can I create a mobile front end for it?

A: Absolutely, especially if you built your application as we have built ours here, with all your functionality in components. In prior chapters, we showed that all your database access and business logic belongs in separate components that you reference in your Web code. You can easily start a new mobile Web application and build a specialized front end that speaks to the same back-end components. We've actually done this, and once the business logic is already built, the mobile Web front end is fairly easy.

Lab17.2: A Multiform Mobile Web Application

We saw a simple example of a mobile Web application in our first lab. This lab will go a step further and actually do something useful. We're going to build a mobile Web application that retrieves and displays software development news for the user. The site, called DevNews, will allow users to select what news they want to see in two ways. First, they can see all the news that falls into a specific category that they select. Second, they can see all the news after a selected date. The news will come from SQL Server database and will be accessed using a separate component that we'll build. How scalable it will be!

The application will make use of the SelectionList control, the Calendar control, and a new one, the TextViewer control. We'll also see how to use an image in our forms.

1. Let's begin by examining the database structure. It's pretty simple and uses only two tables: one for the news stories and another for the categories of news stories. Figure 17.10 illustrates the fields and the table relationship.

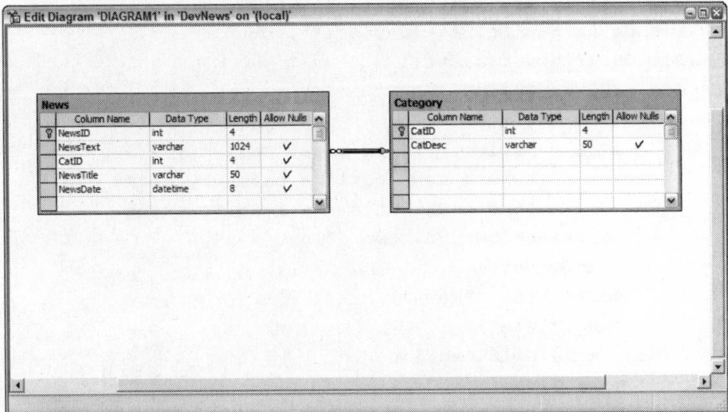

Figure 17.10 The tables and relationship of our news database.

2. Next, let's create the data access class that we'll use to get at the database. It has three public methods. The first retrieves a list of categories available so that we can display them for the user. The second gets a list of all the news items in a specified category, which is passed to it. The third selects all the news items that fall after a specified date.

   Create a new class library project in Visual Studio .NET and name it DevNewsDB. Rename the default class from Class1 to DevNewsDBAccess. Add the following code to the class to do all the work for us:

```
Imports System.Data.SqlClient
Public Class DevNewsDBAccess
    Private Const CONNSTR As String = _
        "Server=(local); Database=DevNews; UID=sa; PWD=;"
    Public Function GetCategories() As DataSet
        Dim conn As New SqlConnection(CONNSTR)
        Dim da As New SqlDataAdapter( _
            "SELECT * FROM Category", conn)
        Dim ds As New DataSet()
        Try
```

```
                conn.Open()
                da.Fill(ds, "Categories")
                conn.Close()
            Catch ex As SqlException
                conn.Close()
                Throw ex
            End Try
            Return ds
        End Function
        Public Function GetNewsByCat(ByVal iCat As Integer) As DataSet
            Dim conn As New SqlConnection(CONNSTR)
            Dim da As New SqlDataAdapter("", conn)
            Dim ds As New DataSet()
            Dim sSQL As String
            Try
                sSQL = "select * from news, category " & _
                       "where news.catid = category.catid " & _
                       "and news.catid=" & iCat.ToString
                da.SelectCommand.CommandText = sSQL
                conn.Open()
                da.Fill(ds, "News")
                conn.Close()
            Catch ex As SqlException
                conn.Close()
                Throw ex
            End Try
            Return ds
        End Function
        Public Function GetNewsByDate(ByVal dt As Date) As DataSet
            Dim conn As New SqlConnection(CONNSTR)
            Dim da As New SqlDataAdapter("", conn)
            Dim ds As New DataSet()
            Dim sSQL As String
            Try
                sSQL = "select * from news " & _
                       "where newsdate > '" & _
                       dt.ToString & "'"
                da.SelectCommand.CommandText = sSQL
                conn.Open()
                da.Fill(ds, "News")
                conn.Close()
            Catch ex As SqlException
                conn.Close()
                Throw ex
            End Try
            Return ds
        End Function
    End Class
```

Once done, compile the code and note where the completed binary is located. We'll need to add a reference to it in the mobile Web application.

3. Create a new mobile Web application just like we did in the previous lab, and name it MobileDevNews. We should be sitting in the designer, looking at a default Form1.

4. Next we'll create all four forms for this application on a single page. Figure 17.11 will serve as a reference for all of them, so when you need to see how one of the forms should look, refer to it.

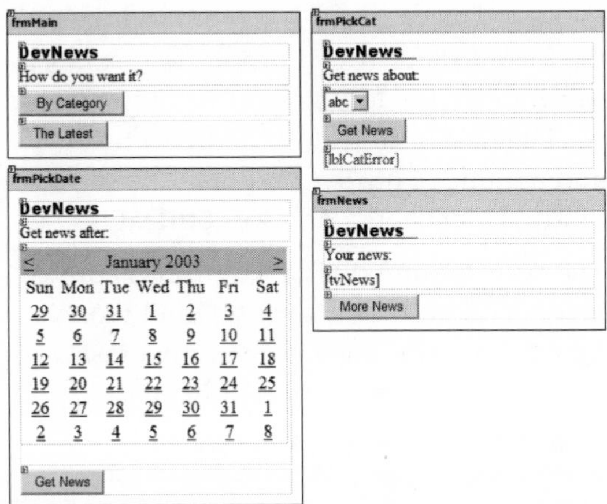

Figure 17.11 Our application uses four forms with a variety of controls.

5. The first form is our entry point and serves as the menu of options. Change its name to frmMain. We have chosen to give our application a tiny bit of personality by adding an image to it. So begin by dropping an image control at the top of the form. Before we assign an image to it, we'll need to add the image to our project. Create an images directory in the project and add your image to it. We made a simple logo for DevNews in the form of a 96-pixel-wide GIF file. Once added to your project, we can assign it to the image control. Click the button in the ImageURL property of the image control to bring up the Select Image dialog. Browse to the image in your project and click the OK button. Figure 17.12 shows what the dialog looks like.

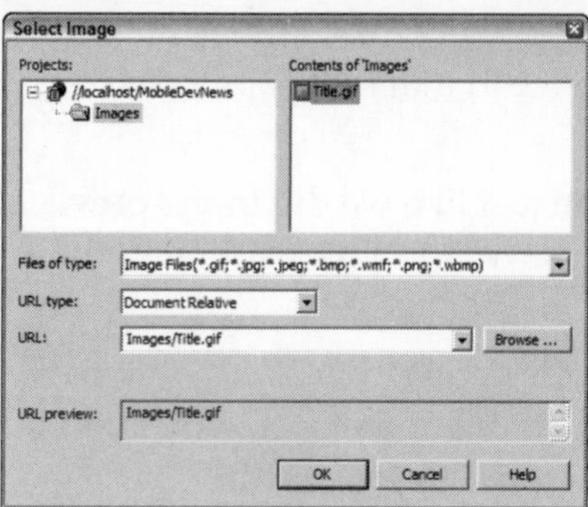

Figure 17.12 Adding an image to the image control is easy with the Select Image dialog.

6. Now we need a label on the form for our text prompt. Drop a label control on it and set its text property to How do you want it? Then add two command buttons. The first button should have a text property of By Category and a name of btnByCategory. The second should have a text value of The Latest and a name of btnDate.

   Let's add code as we go. The code behind our two buttons is pretty simple and navigates to our second and third forms. Don't worry about the new forms not being there yet. They are our next task. Add the following code to the button click event handlers:

```
Private Sub btnCategory_Click(ByVal sender As System.Object, _
     ByVal e As System.EventArgs) Handles btnCategory.Click
     ActiveForm = frmPickCat
End Sub
Private Sub btnDate_Click(ByVal sender As System.Object, _
     ByVal e As System.EventArgs) Handles btnDate.Click
     ActiveForm = frmPickDate
End Sub
```

7. Depending on what button the user clicks on the main form, we will need to activate one of two possible forms. The first allows the user to select a category of news articles, and the second allows the user to specify the oldest news article to retrieve. Lay out the date form first.

   Drop a new form onto the page under the first form by dragging it from the Toolbox, and then name it frmPickDate. Add an Image control to the top, just like we did in the first form, and select the same image we used the first time. Then add a label field and set its text property to Get news after:. Now drop a Calendar control underneath the label and name it calNewsAfter. Lastly, add a Command button at the bottom, name it btnGetNewsByDate, and set its text property to Get News.

8. We need to add some code to the activate event for the form. It defaults the date in the calendar to today's date. Add the following code:

```
Private Sub frmPickDate_Activate(ByVal sender As System.Object, _
     ByVal e As System.EventArgs) Handles frmPickDate.Activate
     calNewsAfter.SelectedDate = Today
End Sub
```

We also need some code in the click event handler for the Command button. Add the following code to the page:

```
Private Sub btnGetNewsByDate_Click(ByVal sender As System.Object, _
     ByVal e As System.EventArgs) Handles btnGetNewsByDate.Click
     Session("GetBy") = BYDATE
     ActiveForm = frmNews
End Sub
```

This code does two things for us. First, we set a value in the session object that will allow the results form to determine how it should get the news information, by date or by category (in this case, by date). The results form will look up the value in the session variable and use it to decide which method to call in our data access class. Once this is done, the code makes the final results form active. Note that we need two constants to represent the date and category options, so add the following code to the top of the class:

```
Private Const BYDATE As Integer = 1
Private Const BYCATEGORY As Integer = 2
```

9. It's time to create the other option form that allows users to specify a category of news to read. Create a third form on our page and name it frmPickCat. Put the now-familiar Image control and image at the top. Then add a Label control and set its text property to Get news about:. Next drop a SelectionList control on the form and name it slCategory. Set its SelectType property to DropDown. Now put a Command button on the form and name it btnGetNewsByCategory. Set its text property to Get News.

   Because this form will access the database to get the values for the list, there is always the possibility of errors. To display these for the user, we need to add a Label control at the bottom. Drop one in and name it lblError. Set its text property to blank (or anything you like for the moment) and its visibility property to False. It will remain hidden until an error occurs. For added emphasis, set its ForeColor property to red.

10. The form needs some code for its activate event to load the list of available categories. We'll do this using our data access component. This is our first time using it, so add a reference to the component to the project now. Once done, add the following code to the class:

```
Private Sub frmPickCat_Activate(ByVal sender As System.Object, _
     ByVal e As System.EventArgs) Handles frmPickCat.Activate
     Dim news As New DevNewsDB.DevNewsDBAccess()
     Dim ds As DataSet
     lblCatError.Visible = False
     Try
          ds = news.GetCategories()
          slCategory.DataSource = ds.Tables("Categories")
          slCategory.DataTextField = "CatDesc"
          slCategory.DataValueField = "CatID"
          slCategory.DataBind()
     Catch ex As Exception
          lblCatError.Text = ex.Message
          lblCatError.Visible = True
     End Try
End Sub
```

The code creates an instance of our DevNewsDBAccess class, as well as a DataSet to hold the results. We also make sure there are no stray error messages visible. Next, we call the GetCategories method in our class library and assign the results to our DataSet variable. Then we set up the data binding so that the SelectionList shows the category description and stores the category ID for use later when we get the news stories. If there is an error, we set the text of the error message to the text property of our error label and make it visible.

11. We need to add a handler for the Get News button on this form. Add the following code to the class:

```
Private Sub btnGetNewsByCategory_Click(ByVal sender As
System.Object, _
     ByVal e As System.EventArgs) _
          Handles btnGetNewsByCategory.Click
     Session("GetBy") = BYCATEGORY
     ActiveForm = frmNews
End Sub
```

This works just like the code for the Get News button on the calendar form, except we set the session variable to a different value so that the news results form knows what method to call.

12. Time for the final form, the one that shows the news articles chosen by the user. Create a new form at the end of the pile and name it frmNews. Put our familiar image control at the top and then a label with a text property of Your news:. Now drop a TextView control on

the form and name it tvNews. This control, as mentioned in our survey of mobile Web controls, displays longer, formatted text. Lastly, add a Command button and name it btnBack. Set its text property to More News. This button will take the user back to the main form. Enter the following code for its click event:

```
Private Sub btnBack_Click(ByVal sender As System.Object, _
     ByVal e As System.EventArgs) Handles btnBack.Click
     ActiveForm = frmMain
End Sub
```

13. The big part of the form, and indeed the application, is retrieving and displaying the news items. This happens when the form is activated, so add the following code to the activate event handler:

```
Private Sub frmNews_Activate(ByVal sender As System.Object, _
     ByVal e As System.EventArgs) Handles frmNews.Activate
     Dim ds As New DataSet()
     Dim r As DataRow
     Dim news As New DevNewsDB.DevNewsDBAccess()
     Select Case Session("GetBy")
          Case BYDATE
               ds = news.GetNewsByDate(calNewsAfter.SelectedDate)
          Case BYCATEGORY
               ds = news.GetNewsByCat(slCategory.Selection.Value)
          Case Else
     End Select
     If ds.Tables("News").Rows.Count < 1 Then
          tvNews.Text = "No matching news found."
     Else
          tvNews.Text = ""
          For Each r In ds.Tables("News").Rows
               tvNews.Text &= "<B>" & r("NewsTitle") & "</B><BR>"
               tvNews.Text &= r("NewsText") & "<BR><BR>"
          Next
     End If
End Sub
```

The code starts out by defining a DataSet, a DataRow, and an instance of our data access class. We'll use these momentarily. Back when we wrote the date and category selection forms, we set a session variable that indicated what type of selection was being made, by date or by category. It's time to make use of that variable. We define a select case statement that chooses which method in the class library to call based on the setting in the session variable. If we need to call the GetNewsByDate method, we pass it the date set in the calendar control. If we need to call GetNewsByCat, we pass it the value of the selected item in the category SelectionList control.

We now have data. If no records were returned, we set the contents of the TextView control to indicate this to the user. If records were returned, we need to process them. Because we have a news headline and a news story, and may have more than one of each, we need to concatenate them all together for display in the TextView control. We set up a For..Each loop to process each row in the DataSet. For each row, we append the current NewsTitle and NewsText columns with line breaks in between. And because the TextView control can process simple HTML formatting, we added a bold attribute to the headline and used the <BR> command for the line breaks.

14. I think we finished! Build this puppy and then right-click the page in the Solution Explorer to browse with the MME. Try out the various options and see how it works. Figure 17.13 illustrates the three steps in using the news story selection by category.

Figure 17.13 This actually looks decent and runs nicely, even on a tiny little cell phone.

Try running it again, only this time, use the calendar selection mode. Figure 17.14 shows what these steps in the process look like. Although we did not use it in these illustrations, try using the calendar by entering a date rather than selecting one. The UI is a little different.

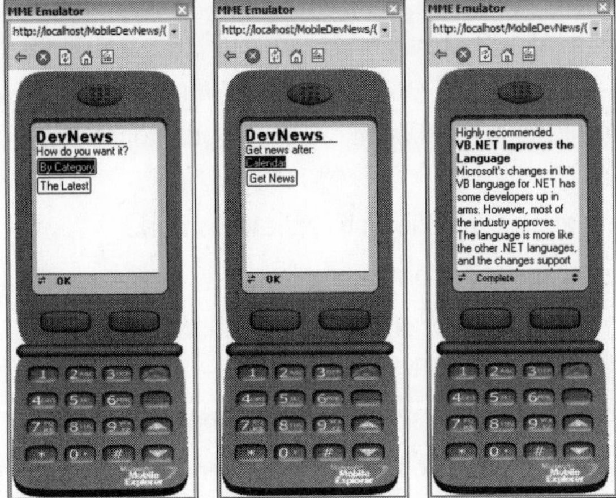

Figure 17.14 This query returned multiple news stories, which have been scrolled a page or two in the browser.

This lab showed us that we can build relatively complicated applications for a mobile device as long as user input is fairly limited. We got to use a variety of controls as well as mobile data binding. You now should have a fairly good grasp of what the Mobile Internet Toolkit can do.

Summary

The Mobile Internet Toolkit is a great tool for building Web applications that run on portable devices. Despite the often severe limitations of the target platforms, we can build rich and useful functionality. There are plenty of controls at our disposal, and building the content is very much like building ASP.NET applications. We can build in data binding, automatic input validation, and display images. And although we need to be cognizant of the limitations of the target devices, we don't have to worry about their widely varied capabilities. The system takes care of rendering code that will work on the target platform.

If you are planning to build mobile content, the Mobile Internet Toolkit and Visual Studio .NET can make it efficient and fun. If you're not, maybe you've come away with some good ideas and reasons to go for it.

Review Questions

1. Name four principles you should keep in mind when designing your mobile Web content.
2. What do you need on the server to make mobile Web applications work?
3. What is the difference between a page and a form?
4. How would you determine at runtime whether or not the target browser in use supports color?
5. What's the difference between a List control and a SelectionList control?
6. What can you do if your content on a form is too big for your intended mobile device?
7. How is data binding for mobile content different for mobile devices?
8. How do you format text contained in a TextView control?
9. What would you think if you saw mobile content built with a text label, a text box, and a calendar on the same form?

Answers to Review Questions

1. **Think small.** The screens are small to tiny, so your content has to fit.
   Stay focused. You can't fit much on a screen, so keep the concept small and focused.
   Don't be vain. Many mobile devices can't display color or graphics, so keep this in mind.
   Type less. Alphanumeric input is tough on a cell phone, so opt for selection lists and other input mechanisms that don't require typing.
2. To get your server ready for mobile Web content, you need three things: Internet Information Server, the Microsoft .NET Framework, and the Mobile Internet Toolkit. Once these are installed, you're ready to go.
3. A form is really a control that is a container for other controls. The form represents what can be shown on the device screen. Only one form can be visible at any time. A mobile page is just like an ASP.NET page and can contain as many forms as you like. Once the page is loaded, you can set which form is active and visible by the user.
4. To determine at runtime if the target browser in use can display color, you would use the MobileCapabilities object. Using properties, it returns all kinds of information about the browser, including whether or not it supports color. The property IsColor returns True if color is supported.
5. A List control displays static text in list form, much like the HTML <UL> tag. It is for display purposes only. The SelectionList control displays a list of items from which the user can make one or more selections. It has several display modes and handles just about any selection-list needs you might have.
6. If your content is too long for the target device's display, you can use pagination to allow the user to scroll through it. The content is rendered automatically to handle scrolling, and the server decides how to break up the content. If you want more control over how the controls are split between pages, use the panel control to contain content.
7. Data binding for mobile devices is no different from normal ASP.NET data binding. Although you do have to account for the fact that the display is smaller and can't hold as much data, the mechanisms are the same.
8. The TextView control allows you to format text using HTML formatting tags, including line breaks, bold, italic, and so on. Of course, the mobile device in use has to support the display of the formatting you use. The <BR> tag is pretty safe, but some devices can't display bold or italic text. Try it on any required device before you assume it will work.

9. If a single form has both a text box and a calendar on a single form, you should be concerned, especially if you are the project manager or team leader for the construction of that application. In version 1.0 of the Mobile Internet Toolkit, text boxes and calendars conflict with each other on browsers that use WML. In fact, they conflict if they are on the same page, not just the same form. (The label control was just a red herring.)

CHAPTER 18

Localization and Globalization

Localization starts with globalization. The ability to localize an application to a particular culture after it has been written is easy only if the application was written with that goal in mind. This chapter introduces the concepts of globalization to create language- and culture-neutral applications so that the final application can be localized for multiple, specific cultures. This chapter adopts Microsoft's viewpoints on localization as it applies to .NET and what Microsoft refers to as world-ready applications. We'll start by looking at the goal and process of localization. Applications written with localization in mind should be void of all slang, colloquialisms, and culture-specific nuances. This chapter is process-focused. By the end of it you should feel comfortable with the process of creating and using resources files in .NET Windows applications.

Localization Fundamentals

The goal for a world-ready application is that the application can be used in as efficient and natural a fashion in the target culture as it is in the culture in which it was designed. This process of making an application adapt to a target culture is referred to as localization.

From my experience, trying to make an application localizable after it has been built can be either impossible or, if you're lucky, only a nightmare. The term *localizable* refers to the ability of an application to be localized. An application's level of localizability is always a function of how early in the development phase localization was addressed. An application must be specifically designed to support being localized. The process of designing an application to be culture- and language-neutral enough to be eventually localized is called *globalization.*

Leave Translation to Translators

During TechEd 1996 in Korea, a speaker presented himself as being from Denmark, but everyone laughed during that introduction. We weren't sure why they laughed, so afterward we asked one of the local Microsoft employees what the reason was. She said, "He said he is like a, you know, a doughnut." Danish...A Danish...A...Doh! We laughed too until it hit us that everything we were presenting was probably being translated just the same.

You might notice that politicians have a simple hand gesture they all use when speaking. It is a closed hand, careful not to point or extend any particular finger. The reason is that literally any other gesture is an offense to at least one country or culture. The hand gesture I was taught as a diver to mean "OK" (a circle made from the pointer finger and the thumb) is an incredibly vulgar gesture in some European countries and is certainly not okay!

Many colloquialisms used in written English have some strange meanings. The saying "general rule of thumb" is used in almost every text I have seen, but has a very off-color origin. The term "rule of thumb" was derived from an old English law that stated that you can't beat your wife with anything wider than your thumb! Within the United States, there are diverse cultures that use slang and jargon to define the world around them. When I refer to a computer, I almost always mistakenly call it a "machine," a "box," or a !@#@#$! (if it's not working). If you don't always think about the phrases you use, you will be in a localized mode of speech.

Experienced translators (professional does not equal experienced) know these things and most likely have already translated everything you will have as general text in your application. One rule of thumb I can give you (sorry, I couldn't resist that) is if you have never used a translator before, talk to him or her before you design a world-ready application. Although I close this chapter with some things to look for in testing applications for localizability, experienced resource translators always have a handy guide to the most common globalization mistakes. Knowing these common mistakes before you make them is the only difficult task associated with localization. Also, don't just hand a translator a list of supposedly neutral phrases for translation. Context can make a big difference. Where you might say "Welcome!" on the introductory page of your Web site, it might translate to "Please enter my home." When you use one word in two different contexts, a translator can help you change one of the words to a more translatable synonym that fits the context. This level of communication with a third party is often where many people fail.

Set Up Your Local Machine for Multiple Cultures

To get started, follow these steps:

1. Open Regional Settings from the Control Panel.
2. Depending on your operating system and version, you may see a Language Settings for the System box on the General tab. If you do, select all available languages as shown in Figure 18.1, and click Apply. If you don't, or just don't feel like installing all the languages, it will have a minimal or no effect on your progression through the chapter.
3. Explore the various tabs in Regional Settings but be sure not to change any of the values associated with the current culture. Depending on the installed culture, these tabs portray how all data is formatted and displayed on this system for that culture.
4. Reboot your system.

CultureInfo

System.Globalization is the primary namespace for dealing with localization and globalization in .NET. The CultureInfo object represents the programmatic embodiment of a culture. Because different standards exist for cultural designators, the CultureInfo object has several properties that portray cultures in different manners. Table 18.1 provides a description and example for each CultureInfo object property.

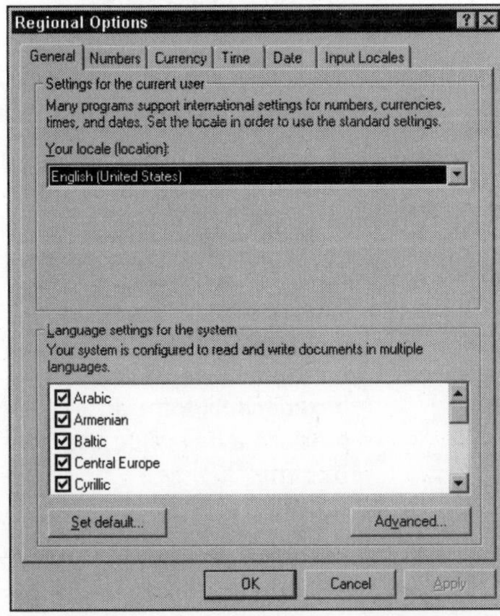

Figure 18.1 The capability to read and write in different languages can be added via the Control Panel.

Table 18.1 CultureInfo Properties

PROPERTY	DESCRIPTION	EXAMPLE
Calendar	Returns the calendar associated with the current culture.	Although most cultures use GregorianCalendar, others include HijriCalendar and ThaiBuddhistCalendar.
CompareInfo	CompareInfo is an object whose members determine how strings are compared for a culture.	N/A
CurrentCulture	This is the culture used by the current thread.	N/A
CurrentUICulture	The current user interface culture. The resource manager uses this culture to look up culture-specific resources.	N/A
DateTimeFormat	An object whose members determine how dates and times should be formatted for a specific culture.	N/A
DisplayName, EnglishName	These always return the language name followed by a region or country name.	A Name value of pa-IN would have a DisplayName of Punjabi (India) Examples : English (United States) Spanish (Argentina)
InstalledUICulture	Returns the installed culture in Windows.	InstalledUICulture is a CultureInfo object, so any of the properties in this table can be displayed for it.
LCID	An LCID is a localized culture identifier.	Although a ToString prints this number in decimal, this value is most often referred to in text in hexadecimal form. To produce a hex value use ToString("X").

Table 18.1 *(continued)*

PROPERTY	DESCRIPTION	EXAMPLE
Name	The recognized name (en-US) given to a culture.	Although most cultures have a Name in the five-character format such as en-GB, some countries such as Serbia and Uzbekistan have longer versions to differentiate between use of Cyrillic and Latin character sets (uz-UZ-Latn).
NativeName	This property returns the native representation of the country or region name.	Russia would display русский (Россия) for NativeName.
NumberFormat	An object property that has members used to define how numbers are formatted for a specific culture.	See NumberFormatInfo members in online help.
Parent	Some CultureInfo objects act as "parents" to others.	The parent to en-US is en.
TextInfo	An object property that has members that define how strings are formatted for a specific culture.	TextInfo contains members for obtaining the ANSI, MAC, EBCDIC, and OEM code pages. TextInfo.ListSeparator is also present.
ThreeLetter-ISOLanguageName	Returns the current culture, expressed as an ISO 639-2 three-letter code.	This would return eng for a Name value of en-US.
TwoLetterISO-LanguageName	Returns the current culture, expressed as an ISO 639-1 two-letter code.	This would return en for a Name value of en-US.

Culture Types

Throughout the chapter and in various texts concerning cultures you will see references to invariant, specific, and neutral cultures. The following call to Get-Cultures returns a collection of CultureInfo objects but requires a parameter of type CultureType. The possible culture types are shown in Figure 18.2.

```
CultureInfo.GetCultures(CultureTypes.SpecificCultures)
```

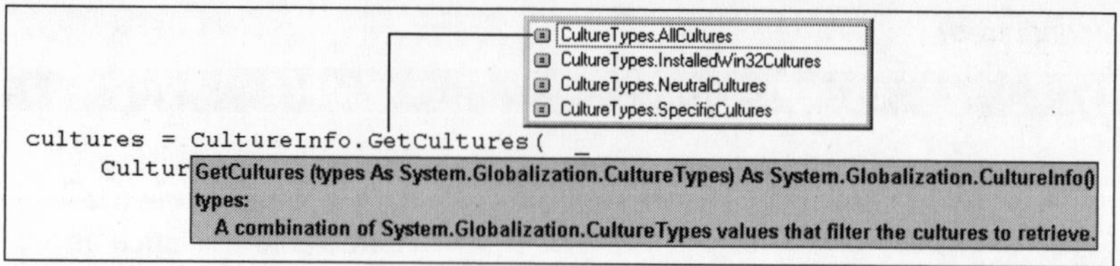

Figure 18.2 The Culture types are provided by the CultureTypes enumeration in .NET.

The invariant culture, sometimes represented as object of type InvariantCulture, is culture-insensitive. The purpose of the invariant culture is to be able to provide a culture to processes that require culture-independent results. When specifying a culture name to use, an empty string indicates the invariant culture.

Neutral cultures are simply the two-letter code associated with a culture and represent a culture with the lack of a specific country or region modifier. Where en-US would be my specific culture, en would be the associated neutral culture.

TextInfo, DateTimeFormatInfo, and NumberFormatInfo Objects

TextInfo, DateTimeFormat, and NumberFormat are all object properties associated with a CultureInfo object. TextInfo provides language-specific methods for dealing with strings and provides several properties for displaying various code pages for a given language. Figure 18.3 displays the various code page options provided by the TextInfo class members.

The DateTimeFormat class defines how all calendar, date, and time values for a culture are to be formatted or displayed. The following code uses the DayNames collection to produce the output shown in Figure 18.4, which compares the week days in Egypt, Russia, and the United States:

```
Dim c1 As New CultureInfo("en-US")
Dim c2 As New CultureInfo("ru-RU")
Dim c3 As New CultureInfo("ar-EG")
Dim EnglishWeek() As String = _
c1.DateTimeFormat.DayNames
Dim RussianWeek() As String = _
c2.DateTimeFormat.DayNames
Dim EgyptianWeek() As String = _
c3.DateTimeFormat.DayNames
Dim i As Integer = 0
For i = 0 To 6
   lstEng.Items.Add(EnglishWeek(i))
   lstRus.Items.Add(RussianWeek(i))
   lstEgy.Items.Add(EgyptianWeek(i))
Next
```

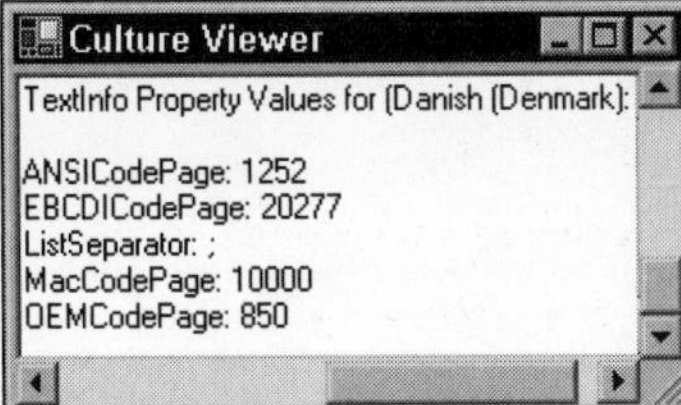

Figure 18.3 The TextInfo object member for a culture can be used to retrieve various code pages.

The NumberFormat property of a CultureInfo object is an instance of the NumberFormatInfo class. NumberFormatInfo is a rather extensive class. Its members can be used for or deal with everything from how many decimal places currency should be displayed in to what symbol denotes a positive number for a given culture. The following line of code retrieves the string designating currency for the current culture:

```
strCurrency = CurrentCulture.NumberFormat.CurrencySymbol.ToString()
```

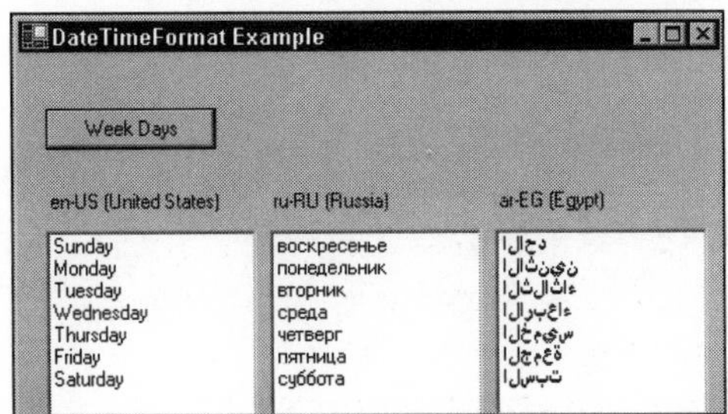

Figure 18.4 All culture-specific date and time formatting is contained within the DateTimeFormat object member of a CultureInfo object.

Lab 18.1: Culture Viewer

This lab demonstrates how the CultureInfo object can be used while producing a simple tool for discovery of culture-related information.

Perform the following steps:

1. Start a new Visual Basic .NET Windows application.
2. Change Form1.Text to Culture Viewer.
3. Add 11 Label controls, 10 TextBox controls, and 1 ListBox control to Form1 in an arrangement similar to Figure 18.5. You won't need to rename the Label, Form, or ListBox controls.

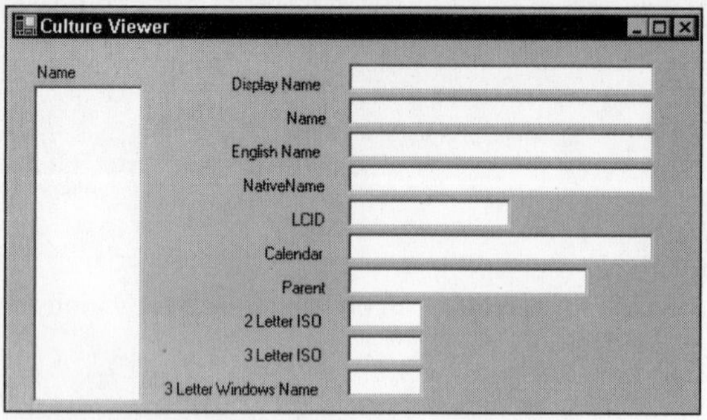

Figure 18.5 Culture Viewer Design layout.

4. Change the names of the TextBox controls to match the labels, using the following names:
   a. txtDisplayName
   b. txtNames
   c. txtEnglishName
   d. txtNativeName
   e. txtLCID
   f. txtCalendar
   g. txtParent
   h. txtISO2
   i. txtISO3
   j. txtWindows
5. Add an Imports statement for System.Globalization to the top of Form1. Globalization is the namespace that defines the CultureInfo object.

```
Imports System.Globalization
```

6. Cause the Form1_Load event handler to load the list box with all available cultures using the following code:

```
Private Sub Form1_Load(ByVal sender As System.Object,
ByVal e As System.EventArgs) Handles MyBase.Load
    Dim cultures() As CultureInfo
    Dim culture As CultureInfo
    cultures = System.Globalization.CultureInfo.GetCultures( _
    CultureTypes.SpecificCultures)
    For Each culture In cultures
        ListBox1.Items.Add(culture.ToString())
    Next
    ListBox1.SelectedIndex = 0
End Sub
```

7. Cause the selection of a specific item in the list box to populate the related text box values with information related to the selected culture. To accomplish this, add the following SelectedIndexChanged event handler to Form1:

```
Private Sub ListBox1_SelectedIndexChanged(ByVal sender As
System.Object, _
ByVal e As System.EventArgs) Handles
ListBox1.SelectedIndexChanged
   Dim c As New CultureInfo(ListBox1.SelectedItem.ToString())
   txtCalendar.Text = c.Calendar.ToString()
   txtDisplayName.Text = c.DisplayName
   txtLCID.Text = "Dec: " & c.LCID & ", Hex: " &
c.LCID.ToString("X")
   txtISO2.Text = c.TwoLetterISOLanguageName.ToString()
   txtISO3.Text = c.ThreeLetterISOLanguageName.ToString()
   txtWindows.Text = c.ThreeLetterWindowsLanguageName.ToString()
   txtName.Text = c.Name.ToString()
   txtParent.Text = c.Parent.ToString()
   txtEnglishName.Text = c.EnglishName
   txtNativeName.Text = c.NativeName
  'MsgBox(c.InstalledUICulture.DisplayName)
End Sub
```

8. Set ListBox1.Sorted to True.
9. Run the application. The results should be similar to those displayed in Figure 18.6.

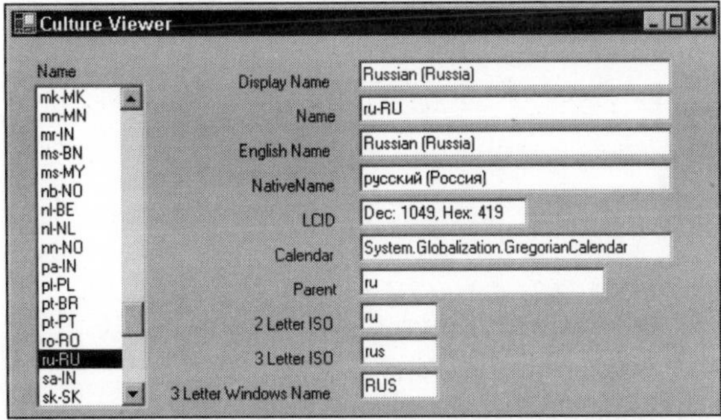

Figure 18.6 The Finished Culture Viewer application.

10. Stop the application and add a new form named frmDateTime by selecting Add Windows Form from the Project menu.
11. Add 11 Label Controls, 9 TextBox controls, 2 ListBox controls, and 1 Button control to frmDateTime and adjust all Text properties for these controls in accordance with Figure 18.7.

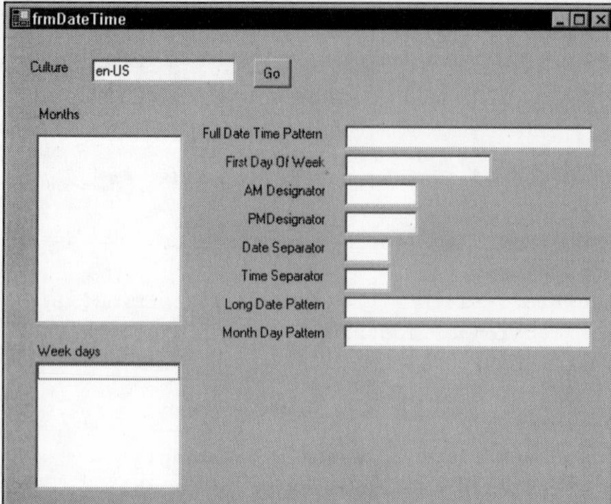

Figure 18.7 DateTimeFormat Viewer form layout.

12. Name the TextBox and ListBox controls using the following names. Make sure, of course, to match them with the appropriate labels.
    a. txtDateTimePattern
    b. txtFirstDayOfWeek
    c. txtAMDesignator
    d. txtPMDesignator
    e. txtDateSeparator
    f. txtTimeSeparator
    g. txtLongDatePattern
    h. txtMonthDayPattern
    i. lstWeekDays
    j. lstMonths
13. Declare a class-level field in frmDateTime named culture as a CultureInfo object:

```
Dim culture As CultureInfo
```

14. Add the following code for the Button1 click event handler:

```
Private Sub Button1_Click(ByVal sender As System.Object, _
ByVal e As System.EventArgs) Handles Button1.Click
   Try
      culture = New CultureInfo(txtCulture.Text)
```

```
    Catch ex As Exception
        MessageBox.Show("Check spelling and try again", "Invalid
Culture", _
        MessageBoxButtons.OK, MessageBoxIcon.Error)
        Exit Sub
    End Try
    lstWeekDays.Items.Clear()
    lstMonths.Items.Clear()
    Dim week() As String = culture.DateTimeFormat.DayNames
    Dim i As Integer = 0
    For i = 0 To 6
        lstWeekDays.Items.Add(week(i))
    Next
    For i = 0 To culture.DateTimeFormat.MonthNames.Length - 1

lstMonths.Items.Add(culture.DateTimeFormat.MonthNames(i).ToString
())
    Next
    txtDateTimePattern.Text =
culture.DateTimeFormat.FullDateTimePattern
    'if FirstDayOfWeek isn't ToString, Sunday will display a zero:
    txtFirstDayOfWeek.Text
=culture.DateTimeFormat.FirstDayOfWeek.ToString()
    txtAMDesignator.Text = culture.DateTimeFormat.AMDesignator
    txtPMDesignator.Text = culture.DateTimeFormat.PMDesignator
    txtDateSeparator.Text = culture.DateTimeFormat.DateSeparator
    txtTimeSeparator.Text = culture.DateTimeFormat.TimeSeparator
    txtLongDatePattern.Text =
culture.DateTimeFormat.LongDatePattern
    txtMonthDayPattern.Text =
culture.DateTimeFormat.MonthDayPattern
End Sub
```

15. In the Properties window, set the AcceptButton property for frm-DateTime to Button1 so that it will click when the Enter key is pressed.

16. Use the following frmDateTime_Load event handler to load the form with the default culture specified in txtCulture.Text:

```
Private Sub frmDateTime_Load(ByVal sender As System.Object, _
ByVal e As System.EventArgs) Handles MyBase.Load
    Button1_Click(sender, e)
End Sub
```

17. Run the application to produce output similar to Figure 18.8 and complete this lab.

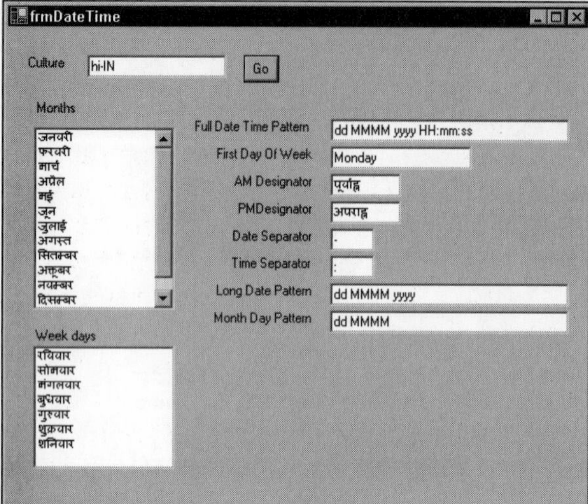

Figure 18.8 The completed DateTimeFormat Viewer.

This lab demonstrated two of the most useful objects for programmatically dealing with culture-specific information. Often, when worrying about localization to a specific culture, it is crucial to understand not only the language differences but also the myriad of differences ranging from how a culture separates lists to whether it reads from left to right or in some other manner. A simple tool provides a cross-reference between LCID, English Name, Windows Name, and two ISO standards for culture designators can come in handy. A more complete version, which identifies CompareInfo and NumberFormat variations, is certainly worth the time you might invest in adding to this lab.

Classroom Q & A

Q: What is the significance of a list separator? I noticed that it changes quite a lot from culture to culture.

A: In my culture, en-US, lists are separated with a comma, and a period is used for the decimal point. If I were to use the Control Panel in Windows to modify the list separator from a comma to a period, none of my dollar figures in Microsoft Excel would work. The value 4.5 would be a string, and 4,5 would be a numerical value equal to 4 1/2. Modifying just a single localization feature via the Control Panel can be quite confusing, but it might help to keep your accountant from being bored on April Fool's day.

Q: What exactly is a colloquialism?

A: A colloquialism is a figure of speech that is only recognized in a specific region. It also can mean a term that simply doesn't translate to any other language. If I said "Bob didn't show up today," most Americans would know what that meant, but it just doesn't translate. A good friend of mine swears that kadiwampus (confirmed as Midwestern U.S. colloquialism) is a well-known synonym for askew, but no one else I've ever known has heard of it, and my language translator just stares at the word unknowingly.

Q: If people in a different culture read from, say, right to left, do we place the controls from right to left?

A: If that is how applications are generally presented in that culture, yes. Some cultures may actually be more comfortable speaking English and seeing everything in en-US because they live in a region where English is the only common language.

Adding Resources to .NET Assemblies

The term *resources* generally refers to anything we add to an assembly that wasn't created with code. Examples of resources might include pictures, icons, sound files, and culture-mapped resource files. For each specific culture we want our application to localize to, we need culture-specific information in the form of a resource file.

There are a number of ways in which resource information can be added to an assembly. Before introducing the methods of working with resources, there are trade-offs to keep in mind. Where one method of incorporating resources into an application might be easy, it may not be easy for a nonprogrammer to maintain. The things to look for in such a mechanism are ease-of-use, maintainability, and usability by nonprogrammers (such as language translators). Resource files can be created in .NET by using resgen.exe, the ResourceWriter class, or automatically by Visual Studio .NET. The winres.exe utility is also available in the Visual Studio .NET SDK for editing resource files.

The Resource Generator Utility (resgen.exe)

Resgen is one of the tools described in starttools.htm that ships with the .NET SDK. Although resgen doesn't allow you to create resource files out of pictures, it does have a command line option for creating them out of text. Each line in the source file used with resgen.exe must have a name-value pair separated by the equal (=) sign, as in the following:

```
Moon = IO
Rotational Period = 1.769138 Days
Mean Surface Temperature = -143 C
Mass: = 1.4960e-02 Earths
Date of Discovery = 1610
```

An execution error will occur if the resgen compiler doesn't find an equal sign before it encounters a newline character. To create a resource file out of a file named io.txt, you would use the following command to create a resource output file named proj1.resources that contained a resource for each line in io.txt:

```
resgen io.txt proj1.resources
```

The reverse also is possible, as long as the contents of the resource file can be expressed as strings. To create a text file from a resource file, simply call resgen by passing the resource file, followed by the .txt output file:

```
resgen proj1.resources io.txt
```

The resgen utility also can convert to and from resx files that can be created by ResourceWrite and ResourceReader, which we'll see later in the chapter. The following command can be used to create an io.resx file from the io.resources file. The contents of io.resx using the previous entries in io.txt are shown in Figure 18.9.

```
resgen app1.resources app1.resx
```

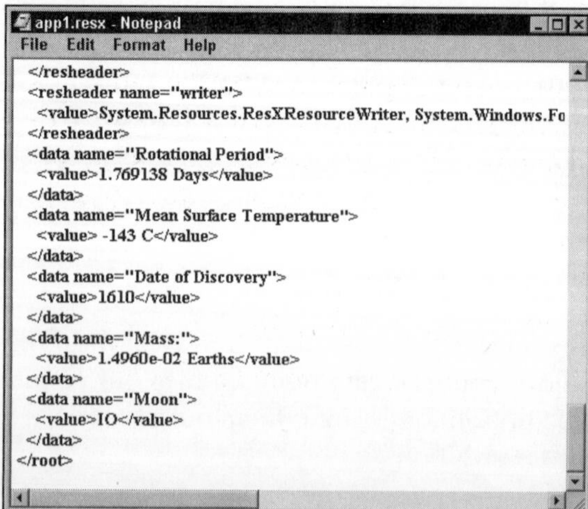

Figure 18.9 The resgen utility creates resx files from .resources files.

The resgen utility can perform batch conversions but creates separate resource files. The following command creates separate .resources files for io.xt, deimos.txt and phobos.txt:

```
resgen /compile io.txt deimos.txt phobos.txt
```

The Windows Resource Localization Editor (winres.exe)

The winres utility may seem somewhat limited in that it is capable only of opening resource and .resx files that were created in Visual Studio .NET. Attempting to open either of the files mentioned in the discussion of the resgen utility results in an error because the winres utility displays the actual form representation for each culture used for localization in your application. The winres editor is used in Lab 18.3 to produce resx files that we will link into out assemblies.

Creating Resource Files with ResourceWriter

.NET provides ResourceWriter and ResourceReader classes in the System .Resources namespace for creating and working with resource files. Unlike the resgen utility, you can create resources files out of any resource type using ResourceWriter. After you instantiate an object of type ResourceWriter, you can use the AddResource method to add resources to the file specified in the ResourceWriter constructor. Lab 18.2 demonstrates the use of the ResourceWriter and Resource Reader classes.

Lab 18.2: Using ResourceWriter and ResourceReader

This lab guides you through the process of programmatically creating a resource file using the ResourceWriter class, adding that resource file to an assembly, and reading the file using the ResourceReader class. In this exercise you won't create an application; it is only to gain familiarity with using key classes in the System.Resources namespace.

Perform the following steps:

1. Start a new Visual Basic .NET Windows application.
2. Add the following Imports statements to the top of Form1:

```
Imports System.Resources
Imports System.Drawing
Imports System.Reflection
```

3. Add the following controls to Form1:

```
Type: Button, Name: btnReader, Text: "ResourceReader"
Type: Button, Name: btnWriter, Text: "ResourceWriter"
```

4. Add the following code to handle the btnWriter_Click event:

```
Private Sub btnWriter_Click(ByVal sender As System.Object, _
ByVal e As System.EventArgs) Handles Button1.Click
   Dim rw1 As New ResourceWriter("..\app1.resources")
   rw1.AddResource("Moon", "Io")
   rw1.AddResource("Rotational Period", "1.769138 Days")
   rw1.AddResource("Mean Surface Temperature", "-143 C")
   rw1.AddResource("Mass", "1.4960e-02 earths")
   rw1.AddResource("Date of Discovery", "1610")
   Dim imgIO As Image = Image.FromFile("C:\io.jpg") 'use local
picture
   rw1.AddResource("Image", imgIO)
   rw1.Close()
End Sub
```

5. In the preceding code, change the image reference to a graphics file on your local machine.
6. Run the application and click btnWriter to create a new resource file. The file app1.resources should now be in your project directory.
7. Select Add Existing Item from the Project menu and double-click app1.resources.
8. Select the Show All Files button in the Solution Explorer. The app1.resources file, along with an image file, should now appear in the Solution Explorer.
9. Add the following controls to Form1:

```
Type: TextBox, Name: txtMoon, Text: ""
Type: TextBox, Name: txtMass, Text: ""
Type: TextBox, Name: txtDate, Text: ""
Type: PictureBox, Name: imgMoon
```

10. To read the resource file and populate fields based on that data, add the following code for the btnReader_Click event handler:

```
Private Sub btnReader_Click(ByVal sender As System.Object, _
ByVal e As System.EventArgs) Handles btnReader.Click
   'fully qualify the following, despite the imports statement
   Dim assy1 As System.Reflection.Assembly
   assy1 = System.Reflection.Assembly.GetExecutingAssembly()
   'Use your project name followed by the resource file name
(no extension)
   Dim rm1 As New ResourceManager("ClassWriterDemo.app1", assy1)
   Me.txtDate.Text = rm1.GetString("Date of Discovery")
   Me.txtMass.Text = rm1.GetString("Mass")
```

```
        Me.txtMoon.Text = rm1.GetString("Moon")
        Me.imgMoon.Image = CType(rm1.GetObject("Image"), Image)
    End Sub
```

Be sure to follow the instructions in the comments for the btnReader_Click event handler or the code will not execute properly.

11. Run the application and click btnReader to display results similar to Figure 18.10.

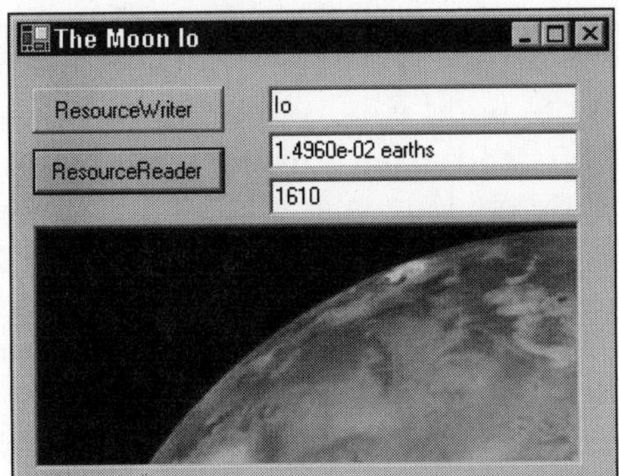

Figure 18.10 ResourceReaderWriter project final results.

The classes in the System.Resources namespace have enough power to allow you to create your own full-blown resource editor. As I mentioned, such tools already exist and many are more than satisfactory. As for programmatic control over our resources, these classes are first-class citizens in .NET, and you should continue to experiment with their capabilities and nuances. For now, let's take a look at how to let our applications build their own resource files.

Localizing Windows Forms

Lab 18.2 used the example with data from Jupiter's moon IO. We could just as easily have read in a culture-specific set of data based on a detected culture setting. Resources aren't always just culture-specific, but this chapter is. Having said that, let's look at how easy Microsoft made form localization in .NET.

The .NET built-in localization features make creating and editing resource files rather easy, but there is a decision to make: Will the developer be doing the localization or will it be done by a third-party organization or tool? If the developer will be doing all the localization (unlikely for large applications), the IDE may be the way to go. For large-scale applications that will be localized by a third party, we don't want the applications to be dependent on a .NET IDE-specific resource file (users would have to have .NET installed). They can either use winres.exe (provided by Microsoft) or a third-party tool. Many large organizations currently use tools separate from the development environment for localization and then link the resulting localized resource files back into .NET assemblies. The .resx and .resources files created in winres.exe and .NET are not directly compatible. To use the files created in winres.exe as part of an assembly, the files must be converted and linked back into the assembly. This process is described Figure 18.11.

A form in .NET has two properties associated with the process of localization: Language and Localizable. Setting a Form's Localizable property to True allows us to use the Language property to build culture-specific versions of the same form. I know that's hard to understand so far, but every time I change the Language property for a form to a different language, all design changes I make only apply if that's the language/culture used when the application is running. All the time I'm designing the form, changing it for each language I want to support, the IDE is continually tracking these changes and storing them in resources files corresponding to each culture I used. This is just one of those things you have to see, so let's start Lab 18.3 and localize a Windows Form.

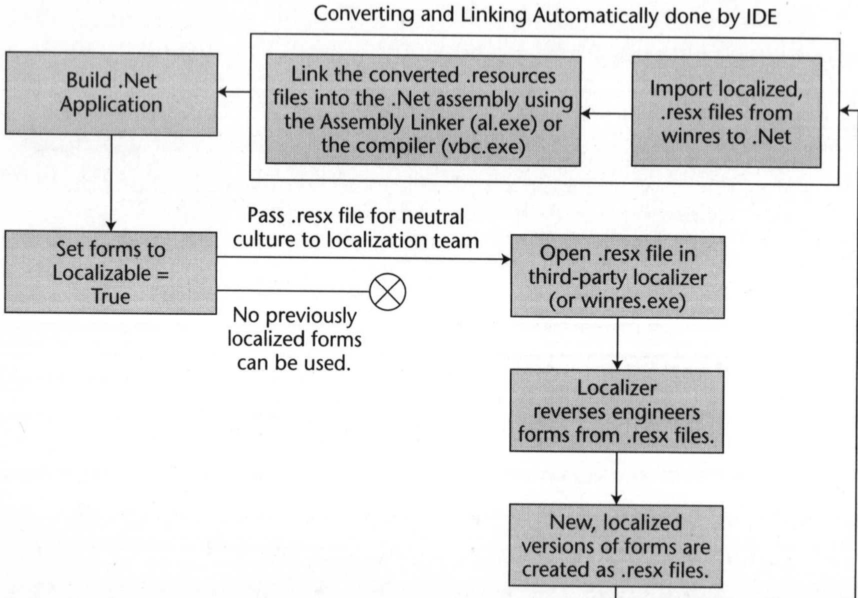

Figure 18.11 Localized forms can be created outside of the IDE using the Windows Resource Localization Editor and linked back into the original assembly.

Lab 18.3: Localizing Windows Forms

This two-part lab demonstrates the process of localizing a Windows form. The first localization uses the built-in features of the IDE to localize the form. The second part follows the process outlined in Figure 18.11 by exporting a neutral resource file and creating localized resources in winres.exe. To complete the second portion of the lab you will import and link the localized files back into your primary assembly. Neither lab makes a grand attempt at building a realistic form; even a simple form takes quite a while to localize for multiple languages. Instead, we will focus on the complete process and, ultimately, complete localization of a simple form using both common methods.

Perform the following steps:

1. Start a new Visual Basic .NET Windows application named Lab 18-3.
2. Add the following Imports statements to the top of Form1.

   ```
   Imports System.Threading
   Imports System.Resources
   Imports System.Globalization
   ```

3. Add a single button to Form1 name btnWelcome.

   The procedures you are about to follow are a combination of localization and globalization. In a real application, localization is done after you have created the culture-neutral version of your forms. That process is called globalization and is something you perform throughout development. After you have a culture-neutral version of an application, culture-specific versions of the interface can be dealt with (localization). As we go, I will identify each step as Localization, Localization Error, Globalization, or Globalization Error.

4. Set the Localizable property for Form1 to True to indicate that this form can be localized (Localization).

   Your current Language setting for Form1 should be "(Default)." That means that any changes you make to the design of the form while Localized is True will apply to the default (neutral) version of this form.

5. Set btnWelcome.Text = "Welcome!" (Localization).
6. Set Form1.Text = "Welcome." (Globalization Error).

7. Add the following code for the btnWelcome_Click event handler (Globalization Error):

```
Private Sub Button1_Click(ByVal sender As System.Object, _
ByVal e As System.EventArgs) Handles btnWelcome.Click
    MessageBox.Show("Welcome!") 'Cannot be localized,
globalization error
End Sub
```

8. Now prepare to make culture-specific changes by changing the Language property of Form1 to "German(Germany)."
9. Making sure the language is currently German(Germany), change btnWelcome.Text to "Wilkommen!"
10. Change the Language property back to "(Default)" (that choice is at the top of the list) and notice that btnWelcome.Text appears as "Welcome!"
11. Repeat Step 9 and change the Language property for Form1 and set btnWelcome.Text for each culture listed in Table 18.2.

Table 18.2 Translation Table for "Welcome"

LANGUAGE	TRANSLATION
German(Germany)	Wilkommen
Polish(Poland)	Witam
Spanish(Mexico)	Bienvenido
Portuguese(Brazil)	Bem-vindo!

Remember that many translations of common English words don't always translate to the correct context. The Armenian word for welcome, *Hamestsek*, translates into English as Good Entrance or Good Coming. In Lesotho, *Kena ka khosto* translates back into English as Enter in Peace.

If you try to change the text in Form1.Text or in the MessageBox and expect it to change, it won't. These are examples of what not to do. All displayed text should come from a resource file when building a globalized application.

12. In the constructor of Form1 (Sub New) enter the following lines before the call to InitializeComponent. Be sure all but one of the first of these new lines is commented.

```
Public Sub New()
    MyBase.New()
    Thread.CurrentThread.CurrentUICulture = New CultureInfo("de-DE")
    'Thread.CurrentThread.CurrentUICulture = New CultureInfo("pl-PL")
```

```
    'Thread.CurrentThread.CurrentUICulture = New CultureInfo("es-MX")
    'Thread.CurrentThread.CurrentUICulture = New CultureInfo("pt-BR")
    'This call is required by the Windows Form Designer.
    InitializeComponent()
End Sub
```

13. Run the application and click btnWelcome. A couple of issues are apparent, as you can see from Figure 18.12. Neither the Text for Form1 nor the MessageBox is localized. We'll fix that now.

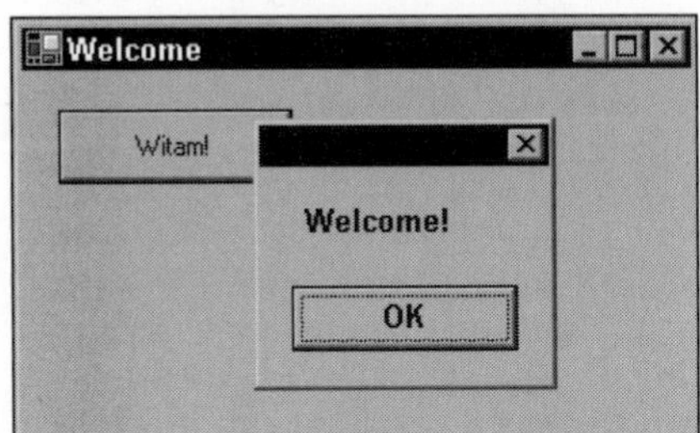

Figure 18.12 Embedded strings cannot be localized.

14. Stop the application.

    In the following instructions you will create five separate resource files, one for each culture besides the default culture. Each file will have only a single row. Each row will have values for Name and Value only.

15. Select Add New Item from the Project menu. Create a new Assembly resource File named Strings.resx.

16. In the first data row, enter strWelcome in the Name field and enter Welcome in the value field. See Figure 18.13.

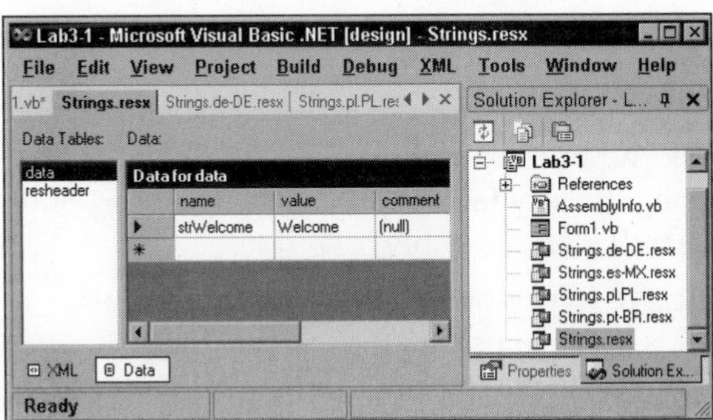

Figure 18.13 The Visual Studio .NET development environment provides a built-in resource editor.

17. Repeat Steps 15 and 16 using the following values for the file and name value pairs:

```
File: Strings.de-DE.resx, Name: strWelcome, Value: Wilkommen.
File: Strings.pl-PL.resx, Name: strWelcome, Value: Witam.
File: Strings.es-MX.resx, Name: strWelcome, Value: Bienvenido.
File: Strings.pt-BR.resx, Name: strWelcome, Value: Bem-vindo.
```

We named our application with a hyphen. If you look at the project properties, you will see that the default namespace changed Lab18-3 to Lab 18_3. This change must be reflected when referring to embedded resource files, or they will mysteriously fail.

18. Declare a ResourceManager object as a Form1 field. Most references in regard to the Resource Manager are case sensitive, so be mindful of that as you continue.

```
Dim rm As New ResourceManager("Lab18_3.Strings",
GetType(Form1).Assembly)
```

19. In the constructor for Form1, be sure that only the German reference (de-DE) is uncommented. This simulates loading the application on a system where German is the locally installed culture.
20. Add the following code to handle btnWelcome_Click:

```
Private Sub Button1_Click(ByVal sender As System.Object, _
ByVal e As System.EventArgs) Handles btnWelcome.Click
   MessageBox.Show(rm.GetString("strWelcome"))
End Sub
```

21. Now, to do the same for Me.Text, modify the Form1_Load event handler as shown here:

```
Private Sub Form1_Load(ByVal sender As System.Object, _
ByVal e As System.EventArgs) Handles MyBase.Load
   Me.Text = rm.GetString("strWelcome")
End Sub
```

22. Run the application and click btnWelcome.

    You have now successfully used the built-in resource development features in .NET. The second portion of this lab walks you through the process of outsourcing the localization process and reincorporating those localized files into your assembly.
23. Start a new Visual Basic .NET Windows application named Lab18_4. Notice that I changed this name to use an underscore. The first application name was chosen to make a point. You shouldn't use hyphens in application names in .NET.
24. Add a button to Form1.
25. Set Form1's Text property to Welcome.

26. Set Button1's Text property to Welcome.
27. Set Button1's control's Name property to btnWelcome.
28. Change the Localizable property for Form1 to True. If this isn't done, you won't be able to export anything to winres.exe.
29. Repeat Step 2 for Form1 (Add Imports statements).
30. Add the following statement in Form1's constructor, but place it before the call to InitializeComponent:

```
Thread.CurrentThread.CurrentUICulture = New CultureInfo("de-DE")
```

31. Build the application (Select Build, Build Solution.) This creates a Form1.resx file in your project folder.
32. Using the Start button in Windows, open the Visual Studio .NET Command Prompt. On my system the menu path is Start, Programs, Microsoft Visual Studio .NET, Visual Studio .NET Tools, Visual Studio .NET Command Prompt.
33. At the Visual Studio .NET Command Prompt, enter the command *winres* to open the Windows Resource Editor.
34. Select File, Open and locate your project directory, Lab 18-4, and open that folder.
35. To see the files you need to work with, change the File Name value in winres to *.*.
36. Select Form1.resx and click Open.

If the previous step failed, be sure Form1's Localizable property is set to True in the original project. If it is not, change it, rebuild the project, and reload it in winres.

37. After the form has been opened in winres, select btnWelcome and change its Text property to Wilkommen.
38. Change Form1's text property to Wilkommen.
39. Select FileSaveAs and select German(Germany) from the Select Culture dialog. This creates the file Form1.de-DE.resx in your application folder.

    The file that winres created still needs to be linked into your assembly. The easiest way to do this is to simply add the resource to the .NET application and rebuild it.
40. Back in Visual Studio .NET, select Project, Add Existing Item, Form1.de-DE.resx and click Open.

41. Select the Show All Files button in Solution Explorer and expand Form1 to verify that both Form1.resx and Form1.de-De.resx are there.
42. Rebuild the project.
43. Run the application. The Form that loads should be localized to German(Germany) and be similar to Figure 18.14.

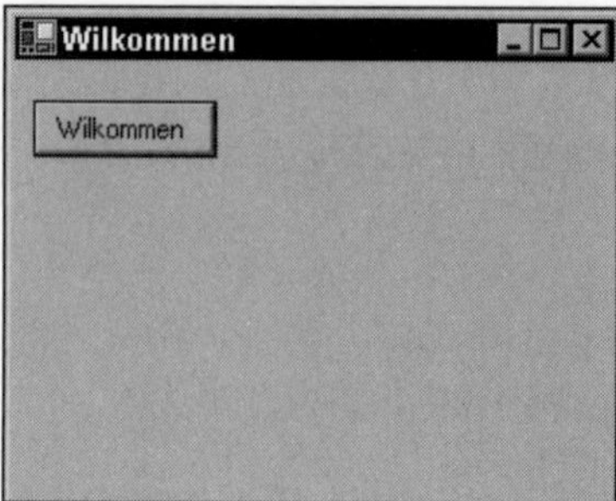

Figure 18.14 Lab18.3, Part 2 produces result localized to Germany using the imported resource file.

You should now be familiar and comfortable with both processes for localization. Although there are many detail-specific issues for globalizing a form, the process for localization can be difficult for a different reason: It can take quite a bit of time. Part of the reason for the second portion of this lab was to make you comfortable in knowing that if you send a form to be localized, the localizer can view the form without the IDE and what is created can be readily integrated into your assembly.

Testing for Localizability

There are quite a few things that can be done to better enable an application to be localized. The following nonexhaustive list summarizes these steps in no particular order:

- Don't build strings through concatenation.
- Don't embed strings.
- Be sure anything displaying text will be large enough to display the translated versions.
- Be sure to test any XML implementations to ensure that they can be localized as well.

- Be sure the test you use for the default culture is generic and free of jargon, slang, or colloquialisms.
- Don't use dynamic control creation and placement.
- Ensure that images are also localized. For instance, an advertisement for Drink MyFizzlypop would be Trink MyFizzlypop in Germany.
- Don't assume a specific file and folder structure in code references. Use the common language runtime libraries to derive paths.
- The following localizability references should be used and understood:
  - Xerox's global design site is an excellent resource for globalization and international business:

    `http://www.xerox-emea.com/globaldesign`
  - See "Localizability Testing" in Visual Studio .NET help.
  - See "Testing for Globalization and Localization" in Visual Studio .NET help.

Summary

This chapter introduced you to the concepts of localization and globalization while exposing you to several tools and procedures for creating and manipulating localized resource files. Take heed in my caution that the most seemingly harmless word or gesture can be offensive to others when you design applications. Seek the help of an expert in globalization and ensure that he or she is an integral part of the design efforts. When you decide which strategy to use for localization, remember that any localization you do in the .NET development environment doesn't translate to winres, so if you decide to move to winres late in the process, it could be painful. In addition, I avoided using a third-party tool for resource creation in this chapter, but many third-party solutions are also available.

I would like to leave the chapter with one thought: Could anyone ever have imagined that a man throwing food to starving people while dangling his legs from the bay of a helicopter was committing a terrible offense to those same people by showing them the soles of his shoes? Be aware of a country's culture, not just the way it formats numbers.

Review Questions

1. Which of the following describe globalization? Select all the correct answers.
   a. It is process of building applications in a culture-specific form.
   b. It is process by which applications can be built to support localization.
   c. It is process by which resource files are created.
   d. It is process by which applications are designed in a culture- and language-neutral form.
2. Where can localization settings be overridden in Windows?
3. What object in .NET encapsulates a culture?
4. What can be used to obtain culture-specific date and time formatting for a culture?
   a. The DateTime object
   b. The DataTimeFormat object
   c. The DateTimeFormat member of a CultureInfo object
   d. The DateAndTimeFormat object
5. For the English (United States) culture, which property of the CultureInfo object returns en-US?
   a. Name
   b. EnglishName
   c. DisplayName
   d. LCID
6. How can you display an LCID in hexidecimal format?
   a. Retrieve myculture.LCID.ToString.
   b. Retrieve myculture.LCID.
   c. Retrieve myculture LCID.ToString("X").
   d. Retrieve myculture System.Convert.ToHex(myculture.LCID).
7. What does al.exe do?
   a. Builds resource files
   b. Converts resource files
   c. Links resource files
   d. Reads resource files

8. Which can be used to create resource files programmatically?
   a. winres.exe
   b. resgen.exe
   c. The ResourceCreator Class
   d. The ResourceWriter Class
9. You created an application and exported the language-neutral version of Form1.resx to winres.exe. Winres.exe produces an unintelligible message saying there was an error. What is the most likely cause?
   a. You have a hyphen in the Form name.
   b. You forgot to set the Language property for Form1.
   c. You forgot to set the Localization property for Form1.
   d. You forgot to set the Localizable property for Form1.
10. You opened Form1.resx using winres and created a new, localized version of Form1, saved as Spanish (Mexico). What will the name of that resource file be?

Answers to Review Questions

1. **b** and **d.** Globalization is the process by which applications can be built to support localization by ensuring applications are designed in a culture- and language-neutral form.
2. Localization settings can be overridden in Windows by using the Regional Settings icon in Control Panel.
3. The CultureInfo object encapsulates a culture.
4. **c.** The DateTimeFormat member of a CultureInfo object can be used to obtain culture-specific date and time formatting.
5. **a.** For the English (United States) culture, the Name property of the CultureInfo object will return en-US.
6. **c.** To display an LCID in hexidecimal format you pass X to LCID.ToString().
7. **c.** The Assembly Linker (al.exe) can be used to link resources to an assembly.
8. **d.** The ResourceWriter class can be used to create resource files programmatically. Resgen.exe is a command line utility that creates and translates resource files, winres is a GUI used to localize .NET Windows forms, and ResourceCreator is fictitious.
9. **d.** If winres.exe produces an unintelligible message saying there was an error when opening a form.resx file that was created in .NET, the most likely cause is that you forgot to set the Localizable property for Form1 to True.
10. The name of that resource file would be Form1.es-MX.resx.

CHAPTER

19

Visual Basic 6 to Visual Basic .NET Migration

Traditionally, when faced with a language migration, I found challenges mapping features and ideologies between languages. To truly migrate from Visual Basic 6 to Visual Basic .NET, we must dramatically change the way our code works and interacts in the world around it. As wonderfully productive as Visual Basic 6 is, it is not without certain anomalies and common practices that migrate with some ambiguity of function. To say that one could possibly run an application through a migration tool and produce highly efficient, trustworthy .NET code is ludicrous. Given that Visual Basic 6 applications did not have function overloading, operator overloading, free threading, or multiple inheritance and were not typically prone to avid use of interfaces, one could argue that migrated Visual Basic 6 code is still not migrated. Depending on the type and scope of the application, we may actually be faced with a decision to rewrite the component or interop to Visual Basic 6 from Visual Basic .NET. If a component is written in either C++ or Visual Basic 6, interoperability with that component is always an option until the efficiency of such interoperability can be determined or until the component can be migrated to a managed assembly.

I have found that a programmer's first programming language drives much of his or her behavior when adopting future languages. I have also found that the easier a migration from one language to the next, the more likely I am to write code in the new language using old idioms.

Migration from one language to another should be done only with knowledge of both languages and practices. This chapter discusses what will and will not migrate from Visual Basic 6 to Visual Basic .NET, what should and shouldn't migrate, what preparations you can make to Visual Basic 6 code, and postmigration recommendations and useful techniques for such an endeavor.

Migrating Mindset

Invariably, the first question people ask me after seeing .NET is "Why do Visual Basic 6 and Visual Basic .NET need to be so different?" The answer is because the .NET framework was designed first and the languages were built on top of that framework. The syntactical similarities between many languages and their seeming .NET counterparts are to draw existing developers with the hopes that their experience will prepare them for the "new version." Without a doubt, Visual Basic .NET and .NET in general are amazing accomplishments, but are so very different. As a whole, .NET draws from many languages, offering the flexibility and OOP introduced in C++, many features strikingly similar to Java and the RAD development environment features found in Visual Basic and Visual Interdev.

You have probably either heard about or attempted a Visual Basic 6 to Visual Basic .NET migration. If so, you are likely to have come away from the experience with a negative viewpoint. It *is* hard during such a migration to maintain a focus, a plan, and an attitude that see you through the process. To that end, accept that what you are upgrading to is .NET (not Visual Basic .NET) and that any similarities of syntax are a bonus. You are migrating to the most productive development system I have ever seen, and it will be far more time-consuming than moving from Visual Basic 5 to Visual Basic 6. For now, it's time to put the hype and rumor away and face the harsh music we call migration.

The following points should help your migration process, as well as help with the reality behind a Visual Basic migration:

- The Migration Wizard provides much of the migration effort but is by no means a total solution.
- Train your developers in Visual Basic .NET *before* attempting a migration of code. Before they can truly make use of Visual Basic .NET, concepts such as polymorphism and overloading should be well understood.
- You should practice using the Migration Wizard to be aware of what you will face during a migration. Lab 19.1 provides a fair example.
- As your developers are training in Visual Basic .NET, encourage them to use the Migration Wizard as a way of discovering how something might be done in Visual Basic .NET and not just as a migration tool. If you see a feature migrated as Visual Basic 6.Compatibility something-or-other, there is probably a better way of doing whatever it is.

- Migration for an enterprise scale system should be tackled at first as a combination of migration and interoperability. This greatly simplifies the process.
- Leaving Option Strict off may allow code to migrate easier, but that code's performance will suffer because of the flagrant use of late binding in most Visual Basic 6 code. I recommend a second pass following migration, using Option Strict, after you deal with major migration issues. You should be aware of what types of issues will be raised by Option Strict On prior to making any changes in the migrated code with it turned off so that you don't write any code you will need to change later.
- Migration from Visual Basic 6 to Visual Basic .NET is easier if the Visual Basic 6 code was well written. Some guidelines I have used for Visual Basic 6 development in the past five years that happen to make my migrations easier include the following:
  - Don't use variants.
  - Don't use late binding if possible.
  - Never use implied defaults—for anything.
  - Never let the compiler do anything for you, especially casting (herein lie a hundred rules).
  - Always write Visual Basic 6 code with Option Explicit on.
  - Declare variables on separate lines.
  - Make all collections and arrays zero-based and never change Option Base from zero (yes, I know it's a default).
  - Use named constants instead of hard-coded values.

The examples in this chapter that violate these rules are to intentionally produce migration issues.

Migrating Code

Migration of code from Visual Basic 6 to Visual Basic .NET is performed first by a Migration Wizard that is automatically invoked when Visual Basic 6 code is loaded in Visual Basic .NET. Following the execution of the Migration Wizard, we typically address issues found in the Task List that must be handled in order to compile. Next, we need to address design issues in the Upgrade Report the Migration Wizard created in the Solution Explorer. Testing at this point must be stringent, and we must keep track of every change we make for the benefit of other team members and future migrations. After we have accomplished all that, we gradually work through our code to implement structured exception handling and other features .NET provides that were lacking in Visual Basic 6.

Introducing the Upgrade Wizard

The Upgrade Wizard automatically upgrades Visual Basic 6 code to Visual Basic .NET when an attempt is made to open such code in Visual Studio .NET. The wizard itself offers very little interaction, but during its execution, it translates updateable code to the appropriate Visual Basic .NET equivalent, flags suspect code, comments many migration issues, and produces a detailed report about migration failures and incompatibilities. Following the migration, the Task List in Visual Basic .NET lists all the issues that need to be resolved as a result of the migration.

Understanding exactly what will migrate is essential to using this wizard. Prior to using the wizard for an actual migration, you will find yourself in a cycle of changing the existing Visual Basic 6 code, testing migration, and repeating this cycle until a successful migration can be accomplished. Remember that migration is a multistep process.

Migrating Visual Basic 6 Project Types

With integrated Web development in .NET and major changes in development strategies, several Visual Basic 6 project and document types either have notable migration issues or no migration path at all (see Table 19.1).

Table 19.1 Visual Basic 6 Migration Issues

VISUAL BASIC 6 DOCUMENT TYPE	MIGRATION NOTES
ActiveX documents	No migration path.
DHTML applications don't migrate	No migration path.
WebClasses	Migrate to ASP WebForms, which are implementations of System.Web.UI.Page.
Forms	Forms migrate as System.Windows.Forms.Form.

Form Migration

Not much about the internal workings of forms has remained the same. Forms are classes now, with constructors that control their initialization. MDI children forms are now associated at runtime by setting the MDIParent property instead of using a MDIChild property. See Table 19.2 for the changes in Forms properties and methods in Visual Basic .NET.

Table 19.2 Changes in Forms Properties and Methods

VISUAL BASIC 6 FORM MEMBER	VISUAL BASIC .NET FORM EQUIVALENT
Appearance	Use the FormBorderStyle property in Visual Basic .NET for 3D borders and such.
AutoRedraw	Use the Form's Paint event or the Refresh method to handle repainting of dirty graphics.
BackColor	Still BackColor but set using a System.Drawing.Color.
BorderStyle	See *Appearance.*
Caption	Text (all controls that had a Caption property now have a Text property instead).
ClipControls	No equivalent. Clipboard operations are handled using the Clipboard object.
Controls	There is still a Controls collection, but because it inherits from standard interface, it works a little differently.
Font-related members	Font and FontFamily replace all Font capabilities in .NET.
Graphics members: CurrentX, CurrentY, DrawMode, DrawStyle, DrawWidth, FillColor, FillStyle, Palette, PaletteMode, HasDc, HDC, Height, Image, Width, Scale-related properties and methods, Circle, Cls, Line, Point, Pset, PaintPicture, TextHeight, TextWidth	No direct equivalent to any of these. The System.Drawing namespace replaces all this functionality.
Hwnd	Handle.

(continued)

Table 19.2 *(continued)*

VISUAL BASIC 6 FORM MEMBER	VISUAL BASIC .NET FORM EQUIVALENT
MaxButton	MinimizeBox.
Moveable	No equivalent in .NET.
Picture	BackgroundImage.
RightToLeft	Migrates to RightToLeft, but True and False are replaced with RightToLeft.Yes and RightToLeft.No.
ZOrder	Use SendToBack or BringToFront methods. The form inherits these methods from the Control class.

Migrating Form Events

Just as with the control events (a Form is actually a control in Visual Basic .NET), events such as the Resize event could be called during the call to InitializeComponent in the Form's constructor. This could crash if any controls are referenced in that code, because they may not be initialized.

Instead of using the Resize event in a form to resize controls to fill a form or dock to edges of a form, we use the Dock and Anchor properties of the .NET controls.

Several events, such as the Click event, work exactly the same for controls as they did in Visual Basic 6 but don't fire for MDI Parent forms. This does not include the arguments being passed in (Sender and e). You can write code for the Click event handler on a form with IsMdiContainer set to True, but it won't respond to the Click event. As expected, the Click event can be called programmatically (for what good that does).

Use the Upgrade Report links following a migration to find extremely useful migration information.

Loading, Instantiating, and Showing Forms

In Visual Basic 6 a Form could be loaded without being shown but in Visual Basic .NET the Load statement is not supported and will produce the following migration error when encountering an attempt to load a form using the Load method:

```
'UPGRADE_ISSUE: Load statement is not supported.
Load(fMainForm)
```

When displaying a form in Visual Basic 6, we could use a direct reference to the form or create a new instance of that form. When referring directly to a form instead of creating an instance of that form in Visual Basic 6, the following Visual Basic .NET code translation occurs. Visual Basic 6 code looks like this:

```
frmSplash.Show()
```

Visual Basic .NET translation from Migration Wizard looks like this:

```
frmSplash.DefInstance.Show()
```

It should be manually changed to instantiate a form and display the instance as follows:

```
Dim myform as new frmSplash()
myform.Show()
```

Data Type Migration

As we have already seen in .NET, data types in .NET are mapped back to common language runtime types that are consistent with other .NET languages (see Table 19.3).

Table 19.3 Comparing Data Types in Visual Basic 6 and Visual Basic .NET

VISUAL BASIC 6 TYPE	VISUAL BASIC .NET TYPE	COMMENTS
Boolean	Boolean	In Visual Basic 6, any nonzero value was True, but in Visual Basic .NET only True is True and only False is False. Trying to test an Integer as in If(myint) Then...won't even compile. Only Booleans can be used in that way. I'm also always assuming that Option Strict is on.
Byte	Byte	
Currency	Decimal	

(continued)

Table 19.3 *(continued)*

VISUAL BASIC 6 TYPE	VISUAL BASIC .NET TYPE	COMMENTS
Date	Date	ToOADate and FromOADate conversion functions are part of the DateTime type in .NET. Any use of doubles to represent dates will cause migration issues because Dates aren't stored as Doubles. Change variables in Visual Basic 6 from Doubles to Dates as appropriate prior to migration.
DefTypes	Does not migrate	None of the DefTypes, such as DefInt and DefVar, are supported in .NET.
Double	Double	
Integer	Short	Both are 16 bit.
Long	Integer	These are both 32 bit. A Long in Visual Basic .NET is actually 64 bits.
Object	Object	
Single	Single	
String * 25 (fixed size)	VB6.FixedLengthString(25)	Fixed length strings aren't directly supported and are migrated using a Visual Basic 6 compatibility type.
String (variant size)	String	
Variant	Object	All Variant and Object types from Visual Basic 6 are converted to Object in .NET.

MDI Code Migration

Several changes related to MDI forms and the way they were used in Visual Basic 6 cause migration issues. Regardless of the subject, oftentimes Visual Basic 6 developers worked directly with a form and made direct references to its members, but in Visual Basic .NET, they would create an instance of a form and then manipulate members. In Visual Basic .NET you can have any number of parent or child forms, and child forms are automatically displayed after they are associated with the parent.

ActiveMDIChild

Any time we refer to the ActiveMDIChild object in Visual Basic 6 and access members that are unique to a specific form, that code will not resolve without a cast in Visual Basic .NET. The following code demonstrates the problem and a resolution. The original Visual Basic 6 code looks like the following (assuming all active forms have a label named lblStatus):

```
strActive = frmMDI.ActiveForm.lblStatus.Caption
```

The following Visual Basic .Net migrated code has the same issue and will not compile:

```
strActive = frmMDI.DefInstance.ActiveMDIChild.lblStatus.Caption
```

To correct the problem, the ActiveMDIChild must be cast to the form type that actually contains a Label named lblStatus, as follows:

```
strActive = CType(frmMDI.DefInstance.ActiveMDIChild, _
Form1).lblStatus.Text
```

Search through all Visual Basic 6 code for use of ActiveMDIChild and be sure that it isn't using late binding to resolve member calls. This causes a migration error for every use if the Application Wizard created any code for you in Visual Basic 6. In addition, referring to a form on a parent form from a child form may require casting the reference of "parent" to the actual type of the parent form. As with most things, half the battle is casting.

frmMDI.DefInstance should be a flag to you that the original code referred directly to a form by name instead of creating an instance of the form.

Standard Control Migration

Many of the standard controls in the Visual Basic 6 Toolbox migrate effectively enough, but several either don't migrate at all or have issues. Table 19.4 summarizes migration effects on the standard controls.

Table 19.4 Visual Basic 6 Controls and Migration

VISUAL BASIC 6 CONTROL	MIGRATES TO:
CheckBox	System.Windows.Forms.CheckBox.
ComboBox	System.Windows.Forms.ComboBox.
CommandButton	System.Windows.Forms.Button.
FileListBox	Will migrate to these: Microsoft.VisualBasic.Compatability.VB6.DirListBox Microsoft.VisualBasic.Compatability.VB6.DriveListBox Microsoft.VisualBasic.Compatability.VB6.FileListBox but are technically replaced with the OpenFileDialog control in .NET.
Frame	System.Windows.Forms.GroupBox.
HScrollBar	System.Windows.Forms.HscrollBar.
Image	System.Windows.Forms.PictureBox.
ImageList	System.Windows.Forms.ImageList.
ListBox	System.Windows.Forms.ListBox.
Menu	Menus are created using a MainMenu control in the Visual Basic .NET Toolbox.
OLE	Does not migrate.
OptionButton	System.Windows.Forms.RadioButton.
PictureBox	System.Windows.Forms.PictureBox.
Shape (rectangles and squares)	System.Windows.Forms.Label. Obviously, a label doesn't do much for us, especially when a square gets migrated to a label that isn't even square. All graphics are done using the System.Graphics namespace, affectionately referred to as GDI+.
Shape (circles and ovals)	Does not migrate. *See previous reference to Shape.*
Timer	Migrates to System.Windows.Forms.Timer.
VScrollBar	System.Windows.Forms.VscrollBar.

Visual Basic 6 Control Properties Removed or Changed in .NET

Several control properties have been removed in .NET or modified to have different behaviors. All properties for a control related to OLE, linking, mouse pointer control, control arrays, or dragging have been removed. In addition, any custom control you might have created with a property that is also a standard property and defined in System.Windows.Forms.Control will be renamed in favor of the standard property. All Size and Location properties for Visual Basic 6 controls are now expressed at a Point object (Location) and a Size object (Size). Width and Height still exist as properties, although they don't appear in the Properties window.

Control Event Migration

One of the biggest changes to the controls is the change in the default event name, usage, and event behavior. All the values previously passed to Visual Basic 6 events are now passed to either a sender object or a collection of parameters named e. The default events for the Visual Basic .NET controls now also fire during the initialization of forms because of the call to InitializeComponent in the Form's constructor. Because of this change in the default event behavior, any code in the default event for a component that refers to another component could crash when it's called during Form initialization. It's best to declare a boolean variable to determine if a form is loading and adjust these events accordingly after migration. Everything from the Form Resize event to a list box's Click event will migrate with warnings related to this behavior.

Migrating Control Arrays and Bound Objects

Let me start by saying a few things to avoid immediate criticism. First, we have seen that Visual Basic .NET uses delegates and the AddHandler statement to support one event for many controls. The problem is that many Visual Basic 6 applications use controls, and they don't migrate to using delegates; they migrate to using a compatibility class. One of the primary points of this chapter is to point out this issue: Simply migrating and getting code to execute is a first step, not an ultimate goal.

Control arrays were a major feature in Visual Basic 6 Windows applications. Almost every front-end I ever built in Visual Basic 6 had some implementation of an array of controls that shared the same name, shared event handlers, and differed only by their indexes. Although it would appear that these controls don't exist in Visual Basic 6, they are available via the Customize Toolbox window and exist in .NET in classes such as the following:

```
Microsoft.VisualBasic.Compatibility.VB6.TextBoxArray
Microsoft.VisualBasic.Compatibility.VB6.LabelArray
```

In .NET, these Array controls are placed in the control tray beneath the form and are essentially key-to-data mappings for any controls created in the array. When migrating code from Visual Basic 6 that uses control arrays, everything will transfer well, as long as the Visual Basic 6 code doesn't use late binding or default properties.

In a much more complicated example of dynamic control creation, some of the first things I migrated were forms that dynamically created text boxes that were bound to data on creation. At the touch of a button, a TextBox control and Label were created for every field in a given record set. The following Visual Basic 6 code is an example of such a dynamic creation of controls (simplified for this example) using a control array. In a moment, we'll see how it migrates and what issues were involved. In the following Visual Basic 6 code, Option Explicit was turned off to make a later point. This code produces the output shown in Figure 19.1.

```
Private Sub cmdBuildControlArray_Click()
   Dim con As New ADODB.Connection
   Dim rec As New ADODB.Recordset
   con.ConnectionString = "Provider=SQLOLEDB.1; _
   Integrated Security=SSPI;Persist Security Info=False; _
   Initial Catalog=Northwind;Data Source=Marauder"
   con.Open
   rec.Open "select * from employees", con
   For i = 0 To rec.Fields.Count - 1
      If i > 0 Then
         Load txtNames(i)
         Load lblNames(i)
         txtNames(i).Move txtNames(i - 1).Left, _
    txtNames(i - 1).Top + txtNames(i - 1).Height + 20
         If rec.Fields(i).Type = 203 Then
            txtNames(i).Height = txtNames(i).Height + 600
         End If
            lblNames(i).Move lblNames(i - 1).Left, txtNames(i).Top
      End If
      If rec.Fields(i).Type <> 205 Then
         Set txtNames(i).DataSource = rec
         txtNames(i).DataField = rec.Fields(i).Name
      Else
         txtNames(i).Text = "Image Not Displayed"
         txtNames(i).ForeColor = 7
         txtNames(i).Locked = True
      End If
      lblNames(i).Caption = rec.Fields(i).Name & " _
      (Type: " &  rec.Fields(i).Type & ")"
      txtNames(i).Visible = True
      lblNames(i).Visible = True
   Next
End Sub
```

Hard-coded values are used here to show that although they are inherently bad for migration, *most* uses are caught correctly during migration. It is recommended that you use named constants instead of these values.

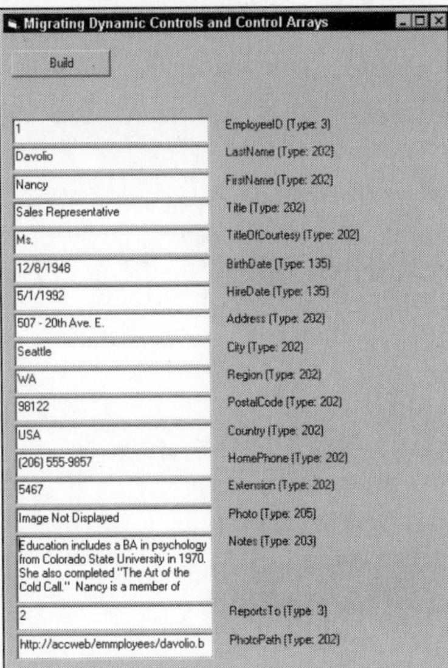

Figure 19.1 The focus for the migration example uses a dynamic control array to create TextBox and Label controls for each field in an ADO Recordset.Fields collection.

The migrated version of this code has surprisingly few problems and none of them is actually related to the control arrays. Because of the migration of i to a Short and the migration of rec.Fields.Count to a .NET Integer, several Integer casts are eventually necessary to use i, as I have done in the example (with Option Strict On). Although the syntax is slightly different for using the array compatibility controls, it is easy to follow. The following code represents the result of migrating the previous code into Visual Basic .NET. The migration tasks for Option Explicit On are shown in Figure 19.2.

```
Private Sub cmdBuildControlArray_Click(ByVal eventSender As _
System.Object, ByVal eventArgs As System.EventArgs) _
Handles cmdBuildControlArray.Click
   Dim con As New ADODB.Connection
   Dim rec As New ADODB.Recordset
   con.ConnectionString = "Provider=SQLOLEDB.1; _
   Integrated Security=SSPI;Persist Security Info=False;Initial _
   Catalog=Northwind;Data Source=Bruce\bruce2"
   con.Open()
   rec.Open("select * from employees", con)
   Dim i As Short
   For i = 0 To rec.Fields.Count - 1
      If i > 0 Then
         txtNames.Load(i)
         lblNames.Load(i)
         txtNames(i).SetBounds(VB6.TwipsToPixelsX( _
VB6.PixelsToTwipsX(txtNames(i - 1).Left)), _
```

```
VB6.TwipsToPixelsY(VB6.PixelsToTwipsY( _
         txtNames(i - 1).Top) + VB6.PixelsToTwipsY( _
         txtNames(i - 1).Height) + 20), 0, 0, _
         Windows.Forms.BoundsSpecified.X Or _
         Windows.Forms.BoundsSpecified.Y)
         If rec.Fields(i).Type = 203 Then
txtNames(i).Height =    VB6.TwipsToPixelsY(VB6.PixelsToTwipsY(_
            txtNames(i).Height) + 600)
         End If
         lblNames(i).SetBounds(VB6.TwipsToPixelsX( _
    VB6.PixelsToTwipsX(lblNames(i - 1).Left)),
    VB6.TwipsToPixelsY(VB6.PixelsToTwipsY( _
         txtNames(i).Top)), 0, 0, Windows.Forms.BoundsSpecified.X _
         Or Windows.Forms.BoundsSpecified.Y)
       End If
         If rec.Fields(i).Type <> 205 Then 'picture
    'UPGRADE_ISSUE: TextBox property txtNames.DataSource not
    'upgraded.
         txtNames(i).DataSource = rec
         'UPGRADE_ISSUE: TextBox property txtNames.DataField was not
         'upgraded.
         txtNames(i).DataField = rec.Fields(i).Name
      Else
         txtNames(i).Text = "Image Not Displayed"
         txtNames(i).ForeColor = _
         System.Drawing.ColorTranslator.FromOle(7)
         txtNames(i).ReadOnly = True
        End If
      lblNames(i).Text = rec.Fields(i).Name & _
      " (Type: " & rec.Fields(i).Type & ")"
      txtNames(i).Visible = True
      lblNames(i).Visible = True
   Next
End Sub
```

From the amount of code used to transform twips to pixels, you might want to adjust forms to use pixels in Visual Basic 6 prior to migration. In this example, the number 20 was added to Height as a twip separator between controls. That would be too large a spacer value when represented in pixels and would have to be modified as well. The first thing Visual Basic .NET complains about (with Option Strict Off) is the methods being used for binding. The syntax for performing binding is very different in .NET, requiring the binding code to be fixed before the code will run. The following changes would allow the migrated code to execute with Option Strict turned off. Under the declarations for Con and Rec, add support for .NET binding:

```
Dim ADOBind As New VB6.MBindingCollection()
ADOBind.DataSource = CType(rec, msdatasrc.DataSource)
```

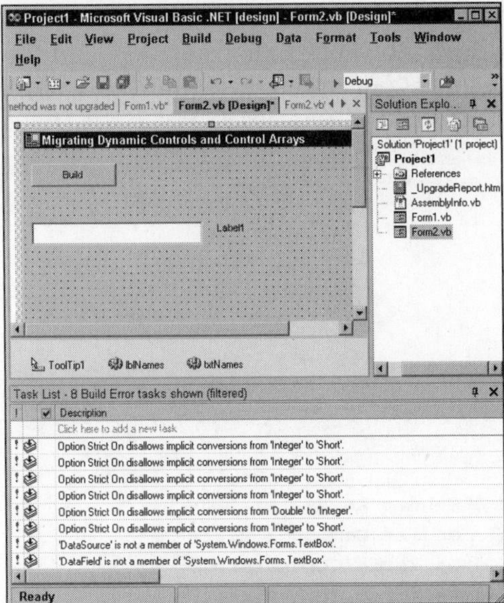

Figure 19.2 Following the migration, the Task List displays code elements that must be resolved before the application can compile. An upgrade report is also created in the Solution Explorer window for additional upgrade issues.

Next, I just replaced the previous lines for binding with a statement that uses the Add method of the BindingCollection:

```
'txtNames(i).DataSource = rec
'txtNames(i).DataField = rec.Fields(i).Name
ADOBind.Add(txtNames(i), "Text", rec.Fields(i).Name, Nothing, i)
```

With the exception of a slight font change, the form had no other migration issues. Looking back at Figure 19.2, you can see the control array controls added to the control tray for txtNames and lblNames.

Upgrading the ADO code shown here to ADO.NET would require dramatic changes to fit a disconnected model and would use yet another method of binding.

Migrating Numbers Instead of Named Constants

I mentioned that although *most* constants migrate well enough, there are certainly some inconsistencies. A good example of this inconsistency can be seen when comparing migrated code for the OptionButton and CheckBox controls.

Check boxes don't seem to have any serious migration issues. Any numbers used to set the CheckBox value will migrate as CheckState constants, and the Visual Basic 6 Value property becomes CheckState. The following code shows equivalent Visual Basic 6 and Visual Basic .NET code and produces no migration warnings:

```
'Visual Basic 6
Private Sub Command1_Click()
    Me.Check1.Value = 0
    Me.Check1.Value = vbUnchecked
    Me.Check1.Value = 1
    Me.Check1.Value = vbChecked
    Me.Check1.Value = vbGrayed
End Sub
'Migrated to Visual Basic .Net:
Private Sub Command1_Click(ByVal eventSender As System.Object, _
ByVal eventArgs As System.EventArgs) Handles Command1.Click
   Me.Check1.CheckState = System.Windows.Forms.CheckState.Unchecked
   Me.Check1.CheckState = System.Windows.Forms.CheckState.Unchecked
   Me.Check1.CheckState = System.Windows.Forms.CheckState.Checked
   Me.Check1.CheckState = System.Windows.Forms.CheckState.Checked
   Me.Check1.CheckState = _
      System.Windows.Forms.CheckState.Indeterminate
End Sub
```

Strangely, similar code from Option Button usage in Visual Basic 6 produces very different code. When hard-coded values are used with Visual Basic 6 option buttons, they migrate as hard-coded values, unlike what happens with the CheckBox control. Other than this apparent inconsistency shown in the following code, there are no control-specific issues:

```
'Visual Basic 6
Private Sub Command2_Click()
   Me.Option1.Value = 0
   Me.Option1.Value = 1
   Me.Option1.Value = vbChecked
   Me.Option1.Value = vbUnchecked
   Me.Option1.Value = vbGrayed
End Sub
'Migrated to Visual Basic .Net:
Private Sub Command2_Click(ByVal eventSender As System.Object, _
ByVal eventArgs As System.EventArgs) Handles Command2.Click
   Me.Option1.Checked = 0
   Me.Option1.Checked = 1
   Me.Option1.Checked = System.Windows.Forms.CheckState.Checked
   Me.Option1.Checked = System.Windows.Forms.CheckState.Unchecked
   Me.Option1.Checked = System.Windows.Forms.CheckState.Indeterminate
End Sub
```

Clipboard Object Changes

Clipboard operations in .NET, including the ClipControls property for standard controls, are implemented using methods of the System.Windows.Forms. ClipBoard object. The members of this object are demonstrated in Lab 19.1.

Screen Object Changes

The Screen object doesn't exist in Visual Basic .NET, and the members of the Visual Basic 6 Screen object don't exist either or have been moved to several different namespaces. Table 19.5 maps the members of the Visual Basic 6 Screen object to the Visual Basic .NET equivalent namespaces.

Table 19.5 Visual Basic 6 Screen Objects and Their Visual Basic .NET Equivalents

VISUAL BASIC 6 SCREEN OBJECT MEMBER	.NET EQUIVALENT
ActiveControl	System.Windows.Forms.Application. _ ActiveForm.ActiveControl.
ActiveForm	System.Windows.Forms.Application.ActiveForm.
FontCount	The only equivalent would be obtained with System.Drawing.FontFamily.GetFamilies, which returns an array of FontFamily objects representing installed fonts.
Height, Width	The Screen Height and Width can be obtained using System.Windows.Forms.Screen. _ PrimaryScreen.Bounds.Height (and .Width).
MouseIcon	Does not migrate. Custom mouse pointers references do not migrate. To set cursors in .NET, use the System.Windows.Forms.Cursors enumeration.
MousePointer	The MousePoint equivalent in Visual Basic .NET is System.Drawing.Cursor.Current.
TwipsPerPixelX, TwipsPerPixelY	Twips aren't supported in .NET. Visual Basic 6 compatibility converters provide migration from twips to pixels, but these properties are not supported.

App Object Changes

The members of the App object were quite useful and rather prevalent in my code as a Visual Basic 6 developer, but they don't map very well to Visual Basic .NET and will not be migrated. Table 19.6 shows the corresponding Visual Basic .NET entities for the frequently used App members in Visual Basic 6.

Table 19.6 App Members and Their Visual Basic 6 Equivalents

APP MEMBER	EQUIVALENT VISUAL BASIC .NET OBJECT
Comments	AssemblyDescription attribute.
CompanyName	AssemblyCompany.
ExeName	System.Reflection.Assembly. GetExecutingAssembly.Location.
FileDescription, LegalCopyright, LegalTrademarks, Major, Minor, ProductName, Revision	Most of the equivalents to these members can be found in the System.Diagnostics. FileVersionInfo.GetVersionInfo namespace; however, not all of them will migrate. App. Revision causes a specific migration failure.
HelpFile	Any reference to App.Helpfile causes a migration issue. Help is provided in Visual Basic .NET by adding a HelpProvider control to a form. After this control has been added, all other controls will dynamically gain methods related to providing help.
LogEvent, LogMode, LogPath, PrevInstance, RetainedProject, StartLogging, StartMode,	EventLog objects in Visual Basic .NET handle logging, and references to log-related objects will not migrate to Visual Basic .NET.
ThreadID	Almost everything related to threading is located in the System.Threading namespace. Threading references in Visual Basic 6 do not migrate.
UnattendedApp	The only real equivalent is a Console Application.
OLE members	OLE is not supported in .NET.

Migrating Size and Scale Related Code

For my forms that had a ScaleMode of Pixel, I had fewer issues when working with migrated values for positioning code. The code for migrating from a Visual Basic-specific type such as TWIP to the .NET default of Pixel can be quite ugly and rather verbose. Changing the Visual Basic 6 code to pixels before a migration really isn't much of a difference in time spent to make the Visual Basic .NET code less ugly.

Win32API Call Migration

Most of the issues related to migrating Win32API calls are that the common language runtime base classes already do almost everything we would have done using the Win32API from Visual Basic. Many API calls in Visual Basic 6 were used with As Any to make data type transformations easier for the Visual Basic 6 programmer. As Any is not supported in .NET. If all calls to a particular function in which you are using As Any always expect the same data type, change As Any to that type. If that is not the case, provide overloads for each expected type.

Calls to the Windows API should be gradually upgraded with direct calls to the common language runtime libraries even if the calls migrated successfully.

Migrating Anomalies

Without sounding overly negative, let me say that Visual Basic 6 has the potential for some rather interesting code. I'll call the most interesting of these examples anomalies and continue from there with how a couple look in Visual Basic 6 and what happens when they migrate to Visual Basic .NET. I wanted to include these two because they represent logic errors that frequently find their way into Visual Basic 6 code.

Declaration Anomaly

The first line of the following code does not create three integers. The first two variables are actually Variants and the third (z) is created as an Integer. If they were all Integers, the code would cause an overflow because 40000 is too large for Visual Basic 6's 2-byte Integer. Declaring variables on separate lines is a generally accepted element of good coding practices and would have resolved this issue.

```
Dim x, y, z As Integer 'Common mistake in Visual Basic 6 - x and y are
                       'not ints
y = 20000
z = 20
x = y * z
MsgBox (x) 'prints 40000...if they were all Integers it would overflow!
```

The migration of this sloppy code to Visual Basic .NET identifies the problem and looks like the following:

```
Dim x, y As Object
Dim z As Short
'UPGRADE_WARNING: Couldn't resolve default property of object y.
y = 20000
z = 20
'UPGRADE_WARNING: Couldn't resolve default property of object y.
'UPGRADE_WARNING: Couldn't resolve default property of object x.
x = y * z
MsgBox(x) 'prints 40000
```

This code still executes and produces 40000. Note that x and y are declared on the same line in the modified version (disappointed sigh), but this type of declaration has no side effects in Visual Basic .NET.

ByRef Procedure Call Anomaly

We all know that values are passed to procedures by reference by default in Visual Basic 6. If we pass a variable to a function and that function modifies the variable, it's actually modifying the value of the variable that was passed. Well, in Visual Basic 6 there is a specific anomaly that occurs when the following are true:

- No Call statement is used.
- Parens are used.
- Only a single parameter is passed.

Although I have yet to see this one documented, a ByVal call is forced even if the parameter is marked as ByRef! The following Visual Basic 6 code will not modify the original value of num1 in any way even though it is specifically passed to the function ByRef:

```
'Visual Basic 6:
Private Sub Command2_Click()
   Dim num1 As Integer
   AnomalySub (num1)
   MsgBox (num1) 'prints 0
End Sub
Private Sub AnomalySub(ByRef x As Integer)
   x = 10
End Sub
```

Amazingly, this bug migrates to Visual Basic .NET. Take a look at the following code. This migrated version also prints zero, which means that the resulting code forces a ByVal call in .NET even though no warning or flag is raised during the migration process.

```
Private Sub Command2_Click(ByVal eventSender As System.Object, _
ByVal eventArgs As System.EventArgs) Handles Command2.Click
   Dim num1 As Short
   AnomalySub((num1))
   MsgBox(num1) 'Amazingly, this prints zero, indicating that even
                'after migration the code forces a ByVal call.
End Sub
Private Sub AnomalySub(ByRef x As Short)
   x = 10
End Sub
```

To fix the migrated code, remove the extra parens the Migration Wizard placed around the argument being passed in the calling code. The existence of these extra parens forces a ByVal call in Visual Basic .NET.

Migrating Data Access Methodologies

As we've seen, ADO.NET is the new mainstay for data access in Visual Basic .NET. Many people still use traditional ADO in client-side applications where scalability isn't an issue. Almost everything in ADO will migrate fairly well, but there are some issues with binding to objects when trying to migrate anything older than DAO and RDO. I was able to migrate RDO to a large extent, but there seemed to be no mechanism for binding RDO to controls. Microsoft confirmed this, and I have since only attempted to migrate ADO clients to .NET. Even with ADO, binding is very different. See *Migrating Control Arrays and Bound Objects* later in this chapter. ADO migrates so well because no attempt is made to migrate it to ADO.NET. In the .NET realm, using ADO (not ADO.NET) for remote data access isn't recommended.

Migrating Use of Default Properties

Properties have a slightly different syntax in Visual Basic .NET than in Visual Basic 6. Instead of separate accessors and mutators (Gets and Sets), a single property procedure is used. Furthermore, the Let procedure does not exist in Visual Basic .NET because everything is an object.

```
Private m_dob As Date
Public Property Get DateOfBirth() As Date
   DateOfBirth = m_dob
End Property
Public Property Let DateOfBirth(ByVal newDOB As Date)
    m_dob = newDOB
End Property
```

Migrated to Visual Basic .NET we see a more encapsulated version:

```
Private m_dob As Date
Public Property DateOfBirth() As Date
   Get
      DateOfBirth = m_dob
   End Get
   Set(ByVal Value As Date)
      m_dob = Value
   End Set
End Property
```

One interesting difference between C# and Visual Basic .NET is that C# does not support parameterized properties. In C# although *Value* doesn't get passed to the mutator, it can be referenced as if it was.

Migrating Late Bound Code

All code that uses late binding in Visual Basic 6 should be modified to use early binding prior to migration. Any use of Variant or Object types in Visual Basic 6 produces generic object variables in Visual Basic .NET. The following Visual Basic 6 code late-binds an object variable to Form1 and then sets the caption on this late-bound object. This code works properly in Visual Basic 6:

```
Dim o1 As Object 'Late bound because type is unknown at compile
Dim o2       'migrates as object
Set o1 = New Form1
o2 = "Greetings"
o1.Caption = o2
o1.Show
```

The migrated code has multiple issues related to the late binding of objects. The following Visual Basic .NET is the migrated equivalent of the preceding code. This code will run only if Option Strict is turned off and will crash either way when the Caption property is referenced.

```
Dim o1 As Object
Dim o2 As Object
o1 = New Form1
'UPGRADE_WARNING: Couldn't resolve default property of object o2.
o2 = "Greetings"
'UPGRADE_WARNING: Couldn't resolve default property of object
'UPGRADE_WARNING: Couldn't resolve default property of object
o2.o1.Caption = o2
'UPGRADE_WARNING: Couldn't resolve default property of object
o1.Show()
```

When migrating late-bound code, you can either change to early-bound code in Visual Basic 6 prior to migration or cast the object types to proper types in Visual Basic .NET prior to invoking members.

Variant Issues

Because Variant types resolve to objects on migration, they also represent issues with late binding and type ambiguity. The following Visual Basic 6 code was written without Option Explicit turned on to demonstrate what happens to variables that were used but never declared (variant3). Because the + operator is used on two variants and placed into a variant, Visual Basic 6 sees an Integer and an IsNumeric string, converts the string to an Integer, and performs the addition. Here is the Visual Basic 6 code prior to migration:

```
Dim variant1
Dim variant2
variant1 = "100"
variant2 = 200
variant3 = variant2 + variant1
MsgBox (variant3) 'prints 300
```

Here is the Visual Basic .Net code following migration:

```
Dim variant3 As Object
Dim variant1 As Object
Dim variant2 As Object
'UPGRADE_WARNING: Couldn't resolve default property of object variant1.
variant1 = "100"
'UPGRADE_WARNING: Couldn't resolve default property of object variant2.
variant2 = 200
'UPGRADE_WARNING: Couldn't resolve default property of object variant1.
'UPGRADE_WARNING: Couldn't resolve default property of object variant2.
'UPGRADE_WARNING: Couldn't resolve default property of object variant3.
variant3 = variant2 + variant1
MsgBox(variant3) 'prints 300
```

The before- and after-code for this example admittedly doesn't represent realistic code (no one is *that* bad in Visual Basic 6). The point here is that any undeclared variables become Object and that only by turning off Option Strict will this code run. With Option Strict Off, this code executes and produces the same value of 300. Again, remove as many uses of Variant and Object from your Visual Basic 6 code as possible prior to migrating.

Postmigration Optimization and Advice

After a migration, the code that migrated won't necessarily be written in the most efficient manner available in .NET. The following is a list of things that you must carefully consider the value of in relation to your products and eventually incorporate these features where necessary:

- Migrate ADO to ADO.NET for distributed data systems to make use of the embedded support for XML, disconnected data, relational sets of data, and improved overall efficiency.
- Modify calls to the Win32API to use common language runtime Libraries.
- Implement threading and synchronization for improved performance where appropriate.

- Enhance classes with overloaded, parameterized constructors, overloaded methods, support for polymorphism, and support for common interfaces such as ICloneable, IDisposable, and IComparable. Many enhancements such as anchoring/docking, structured exception handling, built-in graphics support, and visual inheritance should also be considered for postmigration code improvements.
- Get the migrated code to execute with Option Strict Off, and then turn Option Strict On and fix those related errors. Carefully test the application for accuracy with a comparable test plan for the original. Make no assumptions about the accuracy of migrated code. Anywhere you see a hard-coded number instead of a type or a constant, question the value.
- Pay attention to the ToDo list and the migration report. The migration report and the upgrade comments provide links to additional resources concerning migration.
- Look for upgrades to the Migration Wizard, as well as upgrades to the .NET IDE.

Classroom Q & A

Q: Wow, that's a lot of work. Why don't we just write it all over in .NET?

A: Many companies have millions of lines of code in thousands of files. They compete with other companies that force them to be lean and quick and produce products that hit the market working and at a time when they meet the performance needs of current systems. As difficult as migration can be, it's almost always a faster route than a complete rewrite.

Q: I think the Migration Wizard is garbage. I spent almost as much time fixing the code as I did writing the code.

A: The Migration Wizard will be improved over time as we provide more feedback, so I would check the Microsoft .NET downloads frequently for updates. There are also many enhancements planned for the .NET IDE. I felt much the same way at first, but like most things, I got much better at doing the migrations. These downloads are already linked from the page that displays when you start .NET; just click Downloads or Headlines.

Q: What about migrating ASP applications?

A: I wouldn't hesitate in rewriting them all. I don't see a migration path between what I did in ASP and what I can do in ASP.NET. Luckily, I kept my server-side logic out of the ASP pages and in class libraries. Other people have differing opinions, but I just don't see the migration path personally. ASP.NET is much faster than ASP, and I wanted to treat it as a new technology to maximize its benefits.

Q: What about drag-drop type operations? How do you do that stuff in Visual Basic .NET?

A: For any topic you can imagine there are migration notes in the .NET Help system. The easiest way to get to this help might be links from the Upgrade Report following a migration. I can't even tell you how many times I have created a small snippet of code in Visual Basic 6 and migrated it to see how it might be done in Visual Basic .NET or what issues I might face.

Lab 19.1: Performing a Migration

This lab uses the pre- and postmigration techniques in conjunction with the Migration Wizard to migrate applications from Visual Basic 6 to Visual Basic .NET. The lab starts in Visual Basic 6, using the Application Wizard, and then walks through the migration process to Visual Basic .NET.

This lab requires installation of both Visual Basic 6 and Visual Basic .NET. There is no problem with (that I have ever experienced) having both installed on the same machine because they don't share components and Visual Basic .NET doesn't use the registry (for much).

Perform the following steps:

1. Open Visual Basic 6.
2. Select File, New Project, Visual Basic Application Wizard.
3. Click Next to leave the Introduction page of the Application Wizard.
4. On the Interface Type page of the Application Wizard, leave the defaults of a MDI application named Project1 and click Next.
5. On the Menus page of the Application Wizard, select &Tools and click Next.
6. Click Next to accept the defaults on the Customize ToolBar page of the Application Wizard.
7. Click Next on the Resources page to avoid creating a resource file.
8. On the Internet Connectivity page, select Yes and change the default Web page, if desired, before clicking Next.
9. On the Standard Forms page, select the CheckBoxes Options Dialog and an About Box. Click Next to move to the next page.
10. On the Data Access Forms page, click the Create New Form button.

11. Click Next on the Introduction page of the Data Form Wizard.
12. Click Next to accept Access and the default on the Database Type page.
13. On the Database page of the Data Form Wizard, click the Browse button and locate the NWIND.MDB database, typically installed as C:\Program Files\Microsoft Visual Studio\VB98\NWIND.MDB.
14. On the Form page of the Data Form Wizard, Select Grid(Datasheet) for the Layout and ADO Code as the binding type. Click Next.
15. On the Record Source page, Select Employees for the Record Source and click the double right-facing arrow button to move all fields from the available fields list to the selected fields list.
16. On the Control Selection page, click Finish to close the data form Wizard and return to the Application Wizard. Respond by clicking the No button when asked to create another form.
17. Click Finish to close the Application Wizard.
18. Run the application to test it. The only issue I have ever encountered with that wizard is when it fails to set a reference to the ADODB library. After you are done, save the application.

    Now for the migration:
19. Open Visual Studio .NET. It doesn't matter if Visual Basic 6 is opened or closed.
20. In Visual Studio .NET, select Open Project and select the project1.vbp project file you just created in Visual Basic 6. This launches the Migration Wizard.
21. On Page 1 of 5 of the Migration Wizard, click Next.
22. On Page 2 of 5 of the Migration Wizard (Choose a Project Type), you should have only an option of .EXE, as shown in Figure 19.3, so click Next.

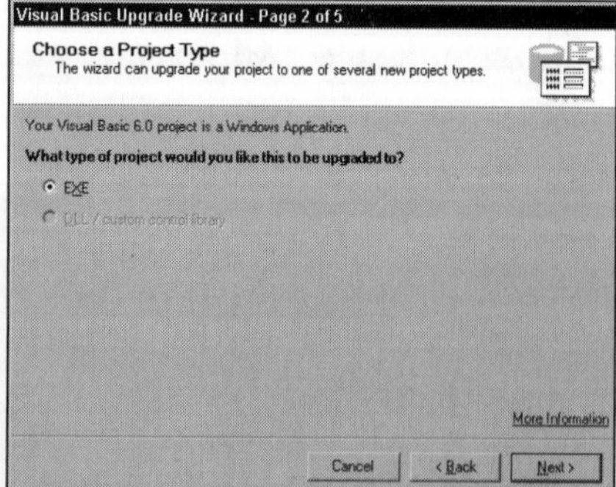

Figure 19.3 The Migration Wizard automatically provides possible project types based on the project type in Visual Basic 6.

23. For migration projects I recommend keeping the migration project close to the original code (in a source control system if possible). Page 3 of 5 of the Migration Wizard suggests a subdirectory beneath the original project directory as shown in Figure 19.4. Leave the default directory and click Next.

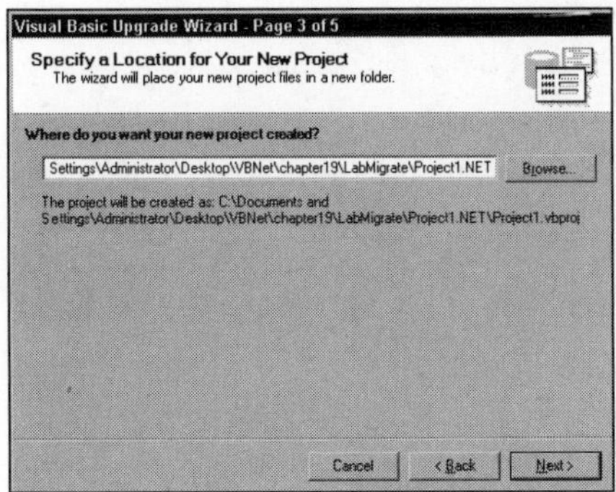

Figure 19.4 By default, the Migration Wizard suggests a migration project folder subordinate to the original project folder.

24. Click Yes when asked to create the new directory for the migration project. Later, when we migrate an additional time, it will warn about overwriting the contents of this directory. Click Next until the wizard starts migrating the project.

25. After the Migration Wizard has finished, double-click the Upgrade Report in the Solution Explorer Window and expand it. You should see a report similar to the report shown in Figure 19.5.

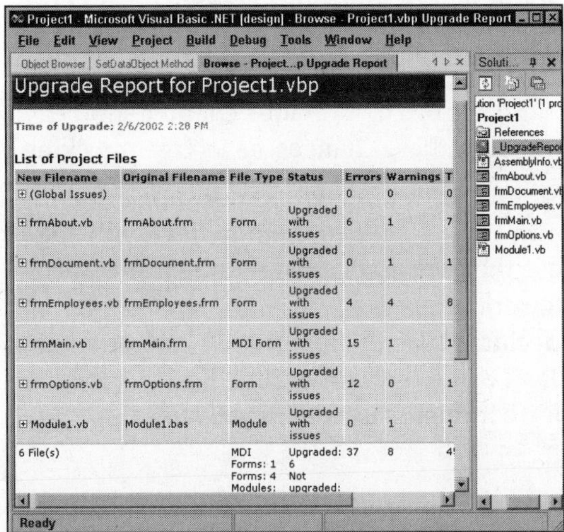

Figure 19.5 The Upgrade Report, created by the Migration Wizard, contains the most complete record regarding the success of the migration.

The Upgrade Report will be of most use for us for the items marked as Design Errors because these are almost always properties or controls that were completely removed from the migrated components and may represent serious changes in logic or form design.

26. For now, we'll deal with the code issues. Select View, Other Windows, Task List to display the current code changes necessary to get this application to execute. The list of tasks should appear as in Figure 19.6.

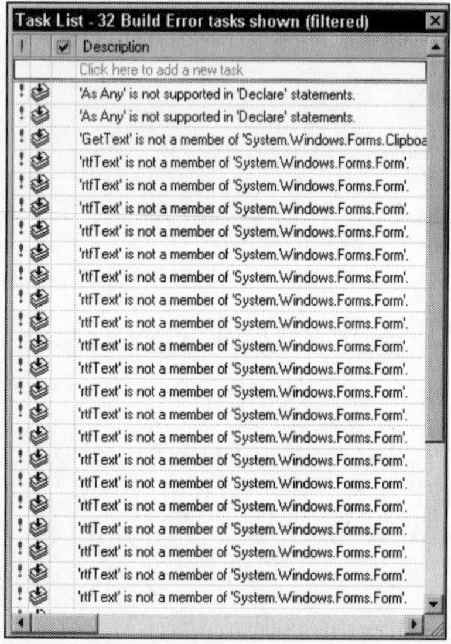

Figure 19.6 The Task List shows only those issues that need to be addressed prior to code compilation.

That's quite a few tasks (about half of mine are showing), but you will see that we can fix them fairly quickly. Please understand that statement would be bordering on ridiculous if I didn't know Visual Basic .NET as well as Visual Basic 6. The previous chapter should have prepared us well enough for these changes, so let's get cracking.

27. To start, we have two tasks stating that As Any is not supported in Visual Basic .NET. Normally, I would adjust them to deal with specific data types, but because they are associated with features such as the Help system that doesn't migrate anyway, we're going to completely remove both declare statements. Double-click the first As Any statement in the Task List to enter the Code Editor. Now, remove both Upgrade Issue comments as well as the Declare statements.

28. Now we'll deal with the GetText and SetText upgrade issues. To fix these issues we must also fix the myriad of issues related to the use of ActiveMDIChild. Double-click the GetText upgrade issue in the Task List to reach the following code:

```
Public Sub mnuEditPaste_Click(ByVal eventSender As System.Object,
_
ByVal eventArgs As System.EventArgs) Handles mnuEditPaste.Click
   On Error Resume Next
   'UPGRADE_ISSUE: Control rtfText could not be resolved ...
   'UPGRADE_ISSUE: Clipboard method Clipboard.GetText ...
   ActiveMdiChild.rtfText.SelRTF = Clipboard.GetText
End Sub
```

29. Remove the Upgrade Issue comments from mnuEditPaste.

The Clipboard object still exists, but its members are different, so we need to adjust that. We can't do anything to a reference to ActiveMDIChild until we cast the child to its proper Form type.

30. To correctly paste the contents from the Clipboard to the RTFText box, replace the entire contents of this event handler with the following code:

```
Dim strClip As IDataObject = Clipboard.GetDataObject()
If strClip.GetDataPresent(DataFormats.Text) Then
   CType(ActiveMdiChild, frmDocument).rtfText.SelRTF() _
   = CType(strClip.GetData(DataFormats.Text), String)
Else
   MessageBox.Show("Clipboard is empty or does not contain text")
End If
```

Notice how I had to cast ActiveMdiChild to its proper Form type. We have to make this same change everywhere we see a reference to that object. Also, the silly On Error Resume Next statement was replaced with a simple check to be sure that the Clipboard contained text.

You should either write code to handle or disable the Shift+Insert mechanism because this does not have the desired results of a normal paste in a .NET application.

31. Change every reference to ActiveMdiChild to use a cast to frmDocument. Do this until there are no more issues in the Task List mentioning rtfText. Use the following examples as guides:

```
CType(ActiveMdiChild, frmDocument).rtfText.SelPrint(.hDC)
CType(ActiveMdiChild, frmDocument).rtfText.SaveFile(sFile)
If CType(ActiveMdiChild, frmDocument).rtfText.SelLength = 0
Then...
```

By my account, that leaves nine items in the Task List—two related to SetText, five related to the App object, and two related to OSWinHelp. Fixing SetText is simple as long as we know to look at the members of the Clipboard object in .NET and press F1. The resulting example in Help was all I needed to migrate my first Clipboard code.

32. In the mnuEditCopy_Click and event handler, replace the SetText statement with the following line of code to perform a Clipboard copy:

```
Clipboard.SetDataObject(CType(ActiveMdiChild,
frmDocument).rtfText.SelRTF, True)
```

33. Repeat the previous step using identical code in the mnuEditCut_Click event handler to replace the call to SetText.

    Now we'll take up the references to the App object. These aren't really that big of an issue as long as we remember that the Application object in .NET holds much of the information we found in Visual Basic's App object. The major difference is that our application is now an assembly and that versioning information is not at the component level.

    The About dialog box (frmAbout) has some issues in its Load event. The only real upgrade issue is the use of App.Revision; the other information can be gained in a simpler way. The best way to fix these issues is to look at what it is trying to do and then replace it with the equivalent information in the Application object. All it is really printing is the full version and the product name, so that's what we will give it:

```
Private Sub frmAbout_Load(ByVal eventSender As System.Object, _
ByVal eventArgs As System.EventArgs) Handles MyBase.Load
    lblVersion.Text = "Version: " & Application.ProductVersion
    lblTitle.Text = "Product: " & Application.ProductName
End Sub
```

34. Remove all the code in mnuHelpContents_Click. We handle help in a different way in .NET. This removes several issues from the Task List. Replace this code with a MessageBox.Show, stating that this needs to be upgraded, or you can manually add a task to the Task List.

New tasks can be added to the Task List by right-clicking and selecting New Task.

35. Do the same for mnuHelpSearchForHelpOn_Click for the same reasons.

    Is it migrated? Hmm. I *did* say that getting it to run was only the first step, didn't I? Well then, go ahead, run it.

36. Run the application by pressing F5.

37. Test the Cut, Copy, and Paste code. If for some reason they have issues, look up GetDataObject and SetDataObject in Help.

38. Select New several times from the File menu, and you will see that there is certainly an issue in the code somewhere. Looking at Figure 19.7, we can see that for at least a moment, a frmDocument is being created with the title frmDocument.

    The code that the Migration Wizard uses to cause the creation of frmDocument makes it more efficient to create a new form with a RichTextBox than to go through all the garbage that is causing the problems evident in Figure 19.8. In addition to that, it is using a Resize event to keep the RichTextBox maximized; we'll use Dock and Anchor for that in .NET anyway. Trust me on this form; you don't want to clean that up. We'll also need to make an adjustment in frmMain.

Figure 19.7 There are some apparent issues with dirty graphics not being handled appropriately during form creation. Here we can see an image of a form before it was even given a name.

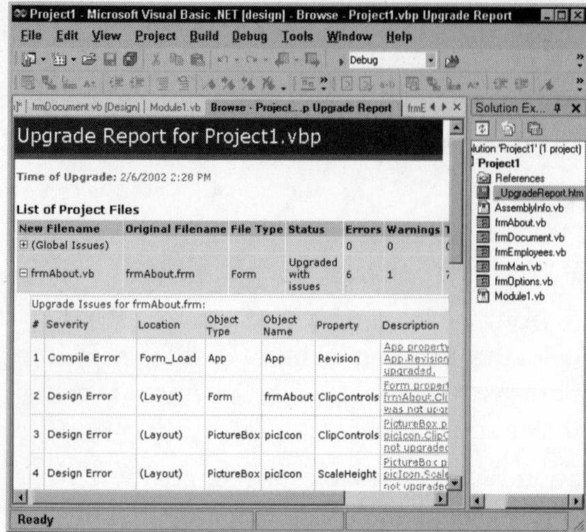

Figure 19.8 The Upgrade Report for Project1.vbp.

39. Stop the application. Right-click the RichTextBox control (the only control) on frmDocument and select copy. We will be pasting this on a new form.

40. Permanently delete frmDocument in the Solution Explorer window.

41. Add a new frmDocument by selecting Project, Add Windows Form and naming it frmDocument.

42. Right-click frmDocument and select Paste to paste the RichTextBox control on the new form.

43. Select the RichTextBox control on the new frmDocument and change its Dock property to Fill. If you kept the old form, you would still remove all the code in the Resize event handler.

44. In frmMain, remove the static variablelDocumentCount and make it a private form field (shown here) and modify the LoadNewDoc procedure as follows:

```
private lDocumentCount As Integer
Private Sub LoadNewDoc()
    Dim frmD As New frmDocument()
    lDocumentCount = lDocumentCount + 1
    frmD.Text = "Document " & lDocumentCount
    frmD.MdiParent = Me
     frmD.Show()
     Me.LayoutMdi(MdiLayout.Cascade)
     Me.Refresh() 'handles the dirty graphics issue
End Sub
```

The final line fixes the ghost image issue. The dirty graphics can be handled in a number of ways. This is the easiest way without going into a long discussion about CGI+. On that subject, learning the graphics subsystem is extremely beneficial to a .NET programmer because almost all the other libraries use elements in System.Drawing.

Are there more issues? Certainly. Test the application and you'll find some. Turn on Option Strict, and you will find a lot of code that could be made more efficient by using early binding. Look at the Upgrade Report in the Solution Explorer to see what didn't migrate. Lab 19.1 was intended to get you on track and focused on some of what you'll face during a real migration.

Summary

We've seen a wide variety of changes, omissions, and additions that affect our migration. By using the Migration tool, we can ease the migration from Visual Basic 6 to Visual Basic .NET, but for this tool to be used effectively, we have to keep in mind that bad code migrates bad code, some good code migrates badly, and not all code even migrates. These are characteristics of any code migration.

I highly recommend using the Application Wizard and then the Migration Wizard many times until you feel comfortable migrating code from simple applications. One quite useful team exercise is giving a team the same Application Wizard settings in Visual Basic 6 and having its members migrate the code separately and then discuss their solutions together. Using an overhead projector for migration training is especially useful for code walkthroughs and migration discussions.

I can't remember how long it has been since my world changed so much so quickly, but .NET is very different from Visual Basic 6 and is much more than the next version of Visual Basic. Your migrations will go much smoother if you practice using the Migration tool, just as you should be practicing using the walkthroughs in .NET Help.

Review Questions

1. The Form Resize event no longer exists in Visual Basic .NET. True or False?
2. Migrated API calls that work as designed should be left as is. True or False?
3. What .NET object contains most of the members that used to be in Visual Basic 6's App object?
4. What namespace replaces the Form methods of Circle, PSet, Line, and graphics in general?
5. Which one of the following will make a form a MDI form in .NET (parent)?
   a. Setting the form's MDIContainer property to True
   b. Setting the form's IsMdiContainer property to True
   c. Setting the form's MDIParent property to True
   d. Setting the form's MDIForm property to MDIParent
6. What is wrong with the following code?

```
mySub((myInteger))
```

7. When would DefInstance be placed in your migrated Visual Basic 6 code?
8. Which of the following steps are in the correct order?
   a. Train developers in .NET (including migration practice), prepare Visual Basic 6 Code for migration, run the Migration Wizard, address the tasks in the Task List, address the issues in the Upgrade Report, continue the migration process by adopting .NET strategies to replace less-efficient migrated code.
   b. Run the Migration Wizard, prepare Visual Basic 6 Code for migration, address the tasks in the Task List, address the issues in the Upgrade Report, continue the migration process by adopting .NET strategies to replace less-efficient migrated code.
   c. Train developers in .NET (including migration practice), prepare Visual Basic 6 Code for migration, run the Migration Wizard, address the issues in the Upgrade Report, address the tasks in the Task List, continue the migration process by adopting .NET strategies to replace less-efficient migrated code.
   d. Train developers in .NET (including migration practice), prepare Visual Basic 6 Code for migration, run the Migration Wizard, address the issues in the Upgrade Report, address the tasks in the Task List, address issues again after turning Option Explicit on, continue the migration process by adopting .NET strategies to replace less-efficient migrated code.

Answers to Review Questions

1. False. The Form Resize event still exists in Visual Basic .NET but shouldn't be used to provide control functionality already provided by Dock and Anchor properties or by the System.Drawing namespace.
2. False. Although migrated API calls might work as designed, eventually they should be rewritten to call-managed classes.
3. The Application object contains most of the members that used to be in Visual Basic 6's App object, such as the product name, path, company, and versioning.
4. Circle, PSet, Line, and graphics in general are implemented by objects in System. Drawing.
5. **b.** The IsMdiContainer value of True will make a form a MDI Container (also called an MDI parent).
6. The extra parentheses in the code force a ByVal call to method mySub even if the parameter is declared as ByRef in that method.
7. DefInstance is placed in your migrated Visual Basic 6 code whenever there is any ambiguity as to whether you are calling a form's base class or an instance of that class.
8. **d.** My recommended path is to train developers in .NET (including migration practice), prepare Visual Basic 6 Code for migration, run the Migration Wizard, address the issues in the Upgrade Report, address the tasks in the Task List, address issues again after turning Option Explicit on, and continue the migration process by adopting .NET strategies to replace less-efficient migrated code.

CHAPTER

20

Distributing .NET Projects

If you've ever built installations for your programs or components, you know what it's like to create installation scripts and deal with the myriad user options available for an installation. If you were particularly unlucky, you've also had to use the Visual Basic Package and Deployment Wizard. Dealing with different versions of COM components has been a problem. Things get so complicated that even moderate application development efforts have to budget in significant time for building the installation. Investment in a third-party installation is expensive and pretty much mandatory.

Visual Studio .NET has changed the deployment landscape. Not only is the deployment of component-based and Web systems somewhat easier, but it also has provided some excellent installation tools that make the Package and Deployment Wizard look like Notepad.

Some Background

There are a few useful concepts and technologies that we need to be conversant with to understand all that the installation tools have to offer and how to use them properly. We'll cover those and then get right into the new installation tools.

Installer Concepts

Microsoft has created a new installation engine called the Microsoft Installer. It's not a complete installation tool with a front end that runs by itself. It is actually an engine that takes as input your installation package. The nice thing about this engine is that it is now distributed with the newer operating systems, including Windows Me, Windows 2000, and Windows XP. If you need to install your application on Windows 98 or earlier, the installer provides another installer that installs the installation engine. That's a mouthful, but it works.

The installation package you create is called an MSI file, for Microsoft Installer. It is essentially a large CAB file, with supporting dialogs, graphics, and instructions included, as well as any custom code contained in executables that you have written for the installation. Once you add all your files to the MSI file, you build an installation script that tells the installer engine how to present your installation interface and custom graphics, if desired. The engine executes, loads the MSI file and instructions, and goes through the traditional installation process with the user. You can actually start an installation as simply as double-clicking the MSI file, because it is associated with the installation engine.

Uninstall

Usually considered an afterthought, the uninstall feature is a critical component of installations. Fortunately, Microsoft built one into the installer engine. But how does it work?

Windows 2000 and Windows XP both use a construct in the operating system called the Application Database to keep track of what is installed on the machine. Whenever an application is installed, information about it is entered into the application database, as well as information about any shared components. When an application that has been installed using the installation engine is uninstalled, the engine makes use of the application database to remove it from the system. It gets its information about the files to remove from the database. And the best part is that the functionality is provided free along with the installation part. The uninstall works automatically.

Another fabulous related bit of functionality is a feature called Rollback. You've certainly run an installation before and then quit before it finished, having changed your mind. Unless the installation is very well behaved, an aborted effort can leave behind incomplete Registry entries, stray files, and in the worst cases, a system that no longer works properly. To address this problem, the rollback feature takes care of undoing what has been done. When an installation is interrupted, it removes any new files, undoes Registry entries, and restores old versions of replaced files. This is a lifesaver for your users and makes it easier on you by not requiring custom installation code to remove components.

Namespaces

You've read about namespaces in several earlier chapters in this book, so you're conversant with them by now. However, there are aspects of namespaces that apply to installations that are worth covering here. You've seen how they work with Web services, as well as how to use the Imports statement to give your code access to the namespaces. You can also create your own namespaces in your classes to control scope. For the moment, trust where I'm going with this, and consider the following example.

Create a new class library project in Visual Studio .NET. Enter the following code in the editor:

```
Namespace Namespace1
    Public Class Class1
        Public Sub Fortune()
            MsgBox("You will make many friends. But shower " & _
                "often to make sure.")
        End Sub
    End Class
    Public Class Class2
        Public Sub Fortune()
            MsgBox("A simple limp will garner more sympathy than " & _
                "all the words in the kingdom.")
        End Sub
    End Class
End Namespace

Namespace Namespace2
    Public Class Class1
        Public Sub Fortune()
            MsgBox("The best defense is a fast car and a preplanned" & _
                " getaway route.")
        End Sub
    End Class
End Namespace
```

This code is all contained in a module called Namespaces and built as a single component. You can use and create the classes separately and have them work correctly, despite using the same method name and having two classes with the same name. The namespaces keep the two classes with the same name separate. So how do you use them? Like this:

```
Private Sub Button1_Click(ByVal sender As System.Object, _
     ByVal e As System.EventArgs) Handles Button1.Click
     Dim cls01 As New Namespaces.Namespace1.Class1()
     Dim cls02 As New Namespaces.Namespace1.Class2()
     Dim cls03 As New Namespaces.Namespace2.Class1()
     cls01.Fortune()
     cls02.Fortune()
     cls03.Fortune()
End Sub
```

A simple WinForms project was created to call the code. As you can see, we are able to create instances of the two classes with the same name by using the fully qualified names with the namespaces attached. However, as we learned earlier, we can shortcut the use of fully qualified names by importing the namespace. If we alter the code to do so, it looks like this:

```
Imports Namespaces.Namespace1
Imports Namespaces.Namespace2

Public Class Form1
     Inherits System.Windows.Forms.Form
     Private Sub Button1_Click(ByVal sender As System.Object, _
          ByVal e As System.EventArgs) Handles Button1.Click
          Dim cls01 As New Class1()
          Dim cls02 As New Class2()
          Dim cls03 As New Class1()
          cls01.Fortune()
          cls02.Fortune()
          cls03.Fortune()
     End Sub
End Class
```

This code will not work because the compiler cannot distinguish between the two instances of Class1 (although the instance of Class2 will work fine). You can make it work by adjusting the use of the namespaces slightly, like this:

```
Imports Namespaces

Public Class Form1
     Inherits System.Windows.Forms.Form
     Private Sub Button1_Click(ByVal sender As System.Object, _
          ByVal e As System.EventArgs) Handles Button1.Click
          Dim cls01 As New Namespace1.Class1()
          Dim cls02 As New Namespace1.Class2()
```

```
            Dim cls03 As New Namespace2.Class1()
            cls01.Fortune()
            cls02.Fortune()
            cls03.Fortune()
        End Sub
    End Class
```

We have imported just the first part of the namespace module and then used the individual namespaces within the module to distinguish the class instances. The point is to keep them all unique. You can see how the namespaces can be used to control the scope and visibility of your classes.

By now you're asking, "How does this relate to installation and deployment?" A worthwhile question, indeed. An assembly can contain multiple namespaces, each of which can be used to organize classes in the assembly. Our two implementations of Class1 can coexist peacefully because they are kept apart by their namespaces. To see the impact on installations, we need to know more about assemblies.

Assemblies

An assembly is the basic unit of distribution and deployment in the .NET world. It roughly equates to a DLL or application EXE. Although it usually contains executable code, you can put just about anything you like into an assembly DLL, including classes, namespaces, forms, resource elements such as image files, or anything else that is allowed.

An assembly also contains additional information used by the system. It contains type information about the stuff inside it. This makes the assembly more of a self-contained, self-describing component than the components of the past. An assembly and the namespaces within it help define the scope of what's available. Assemblies are also the level at which security is granted and the component is versioned. All the items you put in an assembly have the same security settings and the same version number.

In the days of traditional COM components, it was difficult to keep track of component versions and changing GUIDs as interfaces changed. This commonly resulted in a situation known affectionately as DLL Hell. It was a real pain to keep DLL versions accurate and sequential and to keep interfaces compatible with previous versions. Application installations could end up dropping incompatible versions of components on top of older versions, breaking one or more existing programs. Assemblies make it easier to version components and to keep different versions of components running safely on the same machine, using side-by-side execution. By storing their own COM activation and binding information, instead of storing it in the Registry, assemblies can have different versions running on the same computer.

The Manifest

Each assembly contains one more item called the manifest, which is essentially a list of everything the assembly contains. The manifest details the name and version of the assembly and lists all the files that make up the assembly. It also contains a list of external files upon which the assembly depends.

The list of external dependencies is called the assembly reference. It details any external DLLs you created that the assembly references, any third-party components you are using, and common runtime components such as the IL runtime engine.

If the assembly contains a manifest that describes everything in it, you can see why it does not need to be registered. Anything the runtime system needs to know about the assembly can be found in the manifest. Because of this, assemblies are much easier to deploy than earlier components. Simply put them in the same place as the application. And using them in your own applications is as simple as adding a reference to them in your project. Because assemblies don't have to be registered as COM components did, manually cleaning up the Registry after a bad component installation is a thing of the past.

You can view the contents of an assembly's manifest in a nice, easy-to-read fashion using the ILDASM utility, which is installed as part of Visual Studio .NET (you'll find it in the Framework SDK\Bin directory). Although that utility's real calling is to generate intermediate language from compiled components, it will also display the contents of an assembly. Just run the program and select an assembly that you want to explore. Figure 20.1 shows the contents of our little namespace example component being examined inside ILDASM. Notice that the assembly's version information displays in a pane at the bottom.

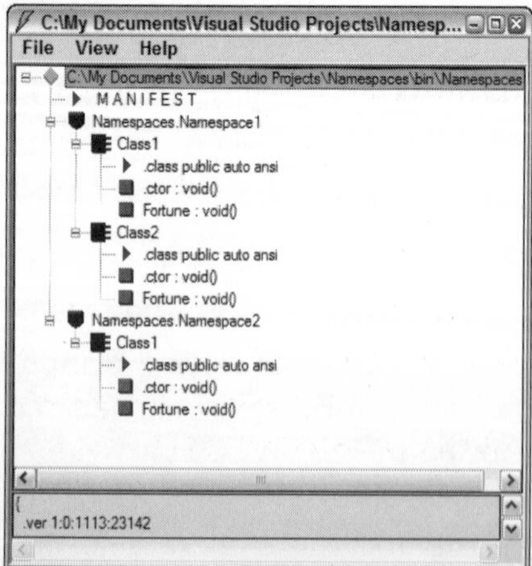

Figure 20.1 ILDASM dumps the contents of the assembly manifest in an easy-to-read fashion.

Tracking Down Assemblies

Traditional COM components, despite all the pains and difficulties that go with them, were easy to locate. The Registry knew where they were, and you knew how to get at the Registry, so locating the components wasn't difficult. Assemblies, however, are not registered, so how do you locate them in your own code when you need them?

The detailed assembly location process is fairly complicated, but as far as building your own applications is concerned, it boils down to putting your assemblies in one of two possible places: the application directory or the GAC.

The application directory seems like the obvious choice. The application will look in its own directory for assemblies it might need. This happens automatically, without any additional work on your part. The assemblies will be found at runtime.

The GAC is located in the runtime directory. In the past, common components typically went into the Windows\System32 directory, but the .NET system uses the GAC. Components that are properly created and authorized can live in the GAC and be used by more than one application, shared like traditional COM components. Components destined for the GAC must be created with strong names: a combination of the assembly name and version number, plus a security key and digital signature. Strong names are a pain to create, so deal with them only if you have to. Otherwise, stick with the application directory. You can find out more about creating strong names in the Visual Studio .NET help system or on Microsoft's MSDN Web site.

Building Installations

The new Microsoft installation tools, combined with all the new things you can do with .NET itself, yield new capabilities and options for your installations. There are several installation types, as well as new capabilities for the installer itself. All these add up to the possibility of chucking your third-party installation tool into the trash bin.

The Microsoft Installer

The Microsoft Installer and the .NET tools associated with it can build you some very professional, capable installations. However, there are more types of installations we need to deal with, thanks to .NET. Fortunately, the installation tools can handle them. There are four primary installation types we need to support:

Application installations. These are the installations with which most people are familiar. They install complete applications and drop the files where you tell them. They can set up menu items, icons, and so forth and have enough options to take care of most of your application needs.

Merge modules. These are intended to install components and are good for making sure a particular version of a component gets installed. Merge modules cannot be installed by themselves and are added to other installations. What's the point, you ask? You can create installations for your common components and then add the prebuilt installations to your application installation when you build it. The installation for that component does not have to be built again when you need to construct the installation for your new application that uses it.

CAB installations. These types of installations create standard CAB files and are used to install ActiveX components that you might need for your application. They must be created with the wizard provided with Visual Studio .NET and are primarily used for Web site deployment.

Web installations. These are used to create installations for components or applications that are to be deployed on a Web server. They are handy because they understand Web servers and virtual directories. However, don't confuse them with installations that are run from a Web page.

A fair number of items go into an installation. This is part of what makes them powerful and flexible, so it is important to understand what they all are. Fortunately, all can be created with the tools in Visual Studio .NET. Here's a list of these items, including the roles they play in an installation:

Assemblies and files. Assemblies, of course, are the components of your application. However, you might also want to include supporting files, such as images, data files, or separate utilities. The tools allow you to add whatever you like and put them wherever you want.

Folders. The installation system enables you to create folders on the target machine and then drop files into them. Later, when you start constructing your installation logic, you can use the installation system's built-in system variables to refer to standard folders, such as the Windows or Program Files folders.

Conditions. The studio provides an editor that enables you to build simple or complex conditions that you can then use to control just about anything. You could use them to control the conditional installation of a file, the creation of a directory, the display of a dialog, or even to launch the installation itself.

Custom actions. At various points in the installation process, you can create functionality called *actions*, which are just like functions you can call from the installation. The installation tools come with several common premade actions that you can use, or you can create your own with any programming language like Visual Basic.

The Registry. Quite often applications make use of the Registry to store all sorts of information. The installation tools enable you to add your own Registry keys at setup time.

File associations. Many applications associate file types with themselves. If yours need to do so, the installer tools enable you to create file associations on the target system.

Shortcuts. The installation tools enable you to create file shortcuts for your applications. You can create either desktop shortcuts or those that go in the program files menu.

The Installation Creation Process

Now that you've seen the pieces, it's time to look at how they go together. There's a process to building application installation programs that we've found to be fairly efficient. Here are the following steps:

1. Create a deployment project in Visual Studio .NET. There are several types you can create, and the studio provides you with a wizard to get you started. You can give your project a name and specify any known files you'd like to install.
2. Use the File System editor to add any other files to the installation. You can also arrange the files into target folders at this point.
3. Set the properties for the files you have added to your installation. This includes setting any files that should be made read-only and any changes to the filename once installed or perhaps to the directory into which they should be dropped.
4. Define any conditions you may need at any level in the course of your installation. Then they will be ready for use when you need them. These could be conditions for specific files, the installation itself, or the creation of Registry entries.
5. Set the properties for the deployment solution. This includes odds and ends like author, keywords, description, version, and a host of other items that you can find in the properties section of the installation project.

6. Set up and customize the user interface. The installer comes with all the standard dialogs you're used to in an installation program, as well as a few optional special-purpose dialogs. You can modify these to suit your own needs.
7. Set the build target type in the configuration manager. You can select either a debug or release option, each with its own settings.
8. If you need any file associations or shortcuts (desktop and menu), add them at this point.
9. If your installation has to support Windows 98 as one of its targets, you'll have to add the Windows installer bootstrap program files to the project. This allows the Microsoft Installer to run on that platform.
10. Build the project. The end result is an MSI file. You can double-click that file to run the installation. Test it out, and make changes as required.

That's it. Some of these steps are optional, depending on the type of installation you are building. You'll see what you have to do for each of the different installation project types when we get to the labs later in the chapter.

Starting Out

When you're ready to begin your installation project, you have yet another decision to make: There are two different ways to start it. You can begin by creating a new deployment project from scratch. This is done simply by creating a new project of the correct type, which you'll see in the labs. The second way is to add a deployment project to your existing solution.

When do you use each option? What's the difference? The first option, a completely new and separate project, is good if you do not have access to the original source code or the project for the installation's target program. It's also a good choice if you are working in an environment with multiple developers, and more than one person needs access to the original project at any time.

The second option, adding a deployment project to your existing solution, has the advantage of keeping the deployment project with the project for the program that it installs. Files that come out of an application project are called project outputs and can easily be added to your installation from the application project.

Once you've created the project, you can begin moving things around and changing them to suit your own needs, for which you will make use of the many editors included as part of the installation tool suite.

The Editors

Editors is a term used loosely when describing the deployment functionality. They are more like configuration tools. They enable you to edit and manipulate the contents of the deployment project. They comprise the installation system, and you use most if not all of them to build your deployment solutions. The editors provided include:

- File System
- File Types
- Registry
- User Interface
- Launch Conditions
- Custom Actions

Each editor deals with a different aspect of your deployment solution. In practice, you jump around the various editors all the time. Once you're familiar with them, you'll know exactly when to use each. Each editor can be started by clicking its toolbar button at the top of the Solution Explorer window.

The File System Editor

You'll spend most of your time using the File System editor (see Figure 20.2), easily the most-used editor in the suite of deployment tools. It is the default editor and is shown when you create a new deployment project. It enables you to add and remove installation files to and from your deployment project. It also enables you to organize them into folders.

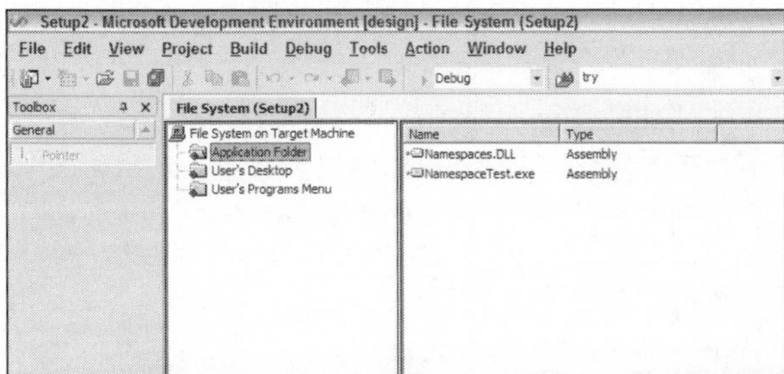

Figure 20.2 The File System editor with files in the application directory.

The editor starts with a few default directories available to you in the left pane of the window. These include the Application Folder, User's Desktop, and the User's Programs Menu. You can add anything you like to these folders, and it will be installed there. However, you have access to lots of special folders that the installation engine figures out for you automatically. Right-click the File System on Target Machine item in the folder list, and the list of these special folders is displayed, as shown in Figure 20.3. It includes cool things such as the User's Favorites, Send To menu, and Startup folders, as well as many others.

The right pane of the File System editor displays the list of files that will be installed into the folder currently selected in the left pane. You can right-click here to add new files to the selected folder. You will put assemblies and supporting files here. Note that the dependent files of any files you add are added automatically. For example, if an executable file uses a DLL, the DLL file is added automatically when the executable is dropped in.

You can even add your own folders here, although they should all be based on one of the special or default folders that the tools provide. For example, to add a directory called Data underneath the Application Folder, right-click the Application Folder in the left pane, and select Add, Folder from the context menu. The system will create a new folder for you, which you can then name. Figure 20.4 shows what it looks like with the folder added. Any new folders will be created automatically on the target machine when the installation is executed.

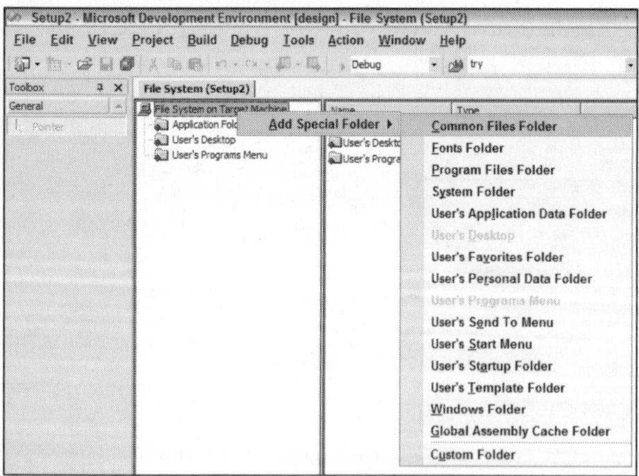

Figure 20.3 There are plenty of special folders to which you can add files.

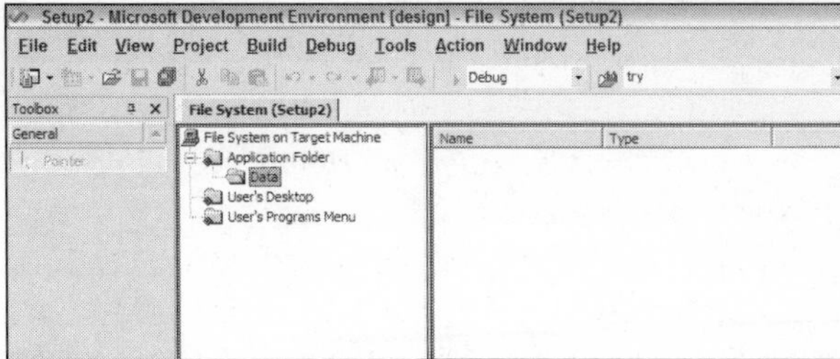

Figure 20.4 A special folder added underneath the Application Folder.

You can also set properties for each of the files in your installation. Highlight one in the File System editor and examine the Properties window (see Figure 20.5) in the studio. You will have access to such things as the file version, the assembly name, an option to include or exclude it, whether it should be made read-only, whether it is a system file, and others.

The File Types Editor

If your application has its own file types, you can create them in the File Types editor and create associations to them for your program. For example, if your program has data files with a .SAV extension, you could create an association to them with this editor. The installation program sets up the association for you automatically. Figure 20.6 shows you what the editor looks like.

Figure 20.5 You can set properties for any of the files in your installation.

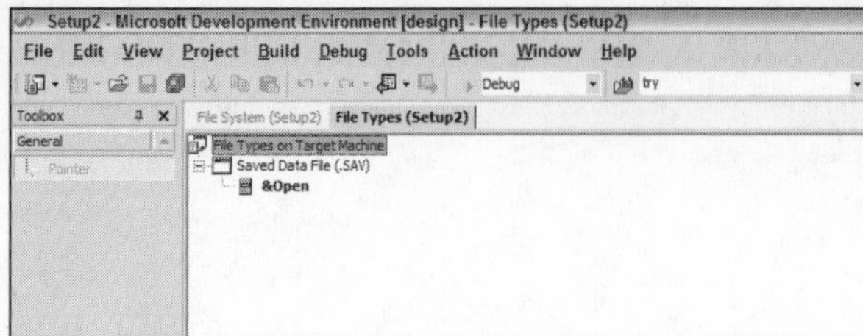

Figure 20.6 Create your own file types to set up file associations.

The editor enables you to create a named file type Saved Data File (.SAV) in the example in Figure 20.6. The real power, however, is in the Properties window. The most important part of an association is the command. For example, you associate, at a minimum, the file type with your application using an Open command. Select the file type you created, and then examine the properties window. Set the Extensions property to your own file extension, and then set the Command property to your application assembly (.exe). Once these are set (see Figure 20.7), your file association for the Open command is complete. You can select the Open command in the file type editor and see its properties as well.

The Registry Editor

Most programmers are familiar with the standard Windows Registry editor. The Registry editor in the deployment tools enables you to specify Registry settings for your application when the installation is executed. Figure 20.8 shows what this editor looks like.

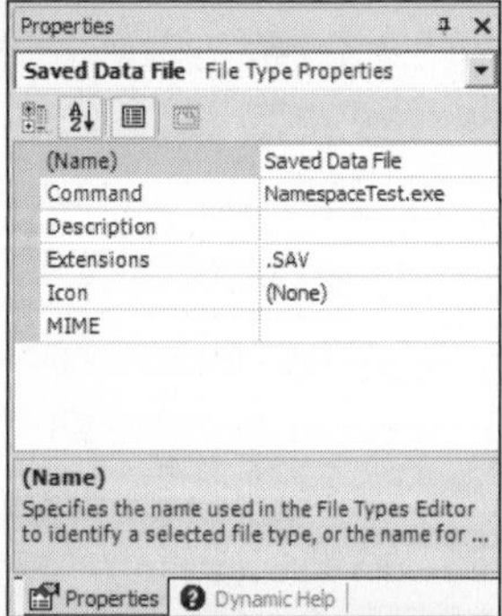

Figure 20.7 Fill in these settings and the Open command is complete.

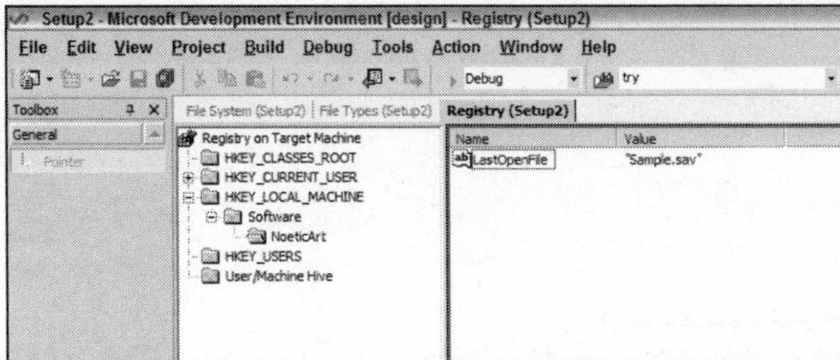

Figure 20.8 The Registry editor sets up install-time Registry changes.

The Registry editor looks much like the Windows Registry editor, with keys on the left side and values on the right. You can expand the tree on the left to find the beginning location you'd like to use and then rename it to suit your needs. Click in the right pane to add new values to the selected key. Once the item is added, such as the LastOpenFile item shown in Figure 20.8, you can set its default value in the Properties window of the studio.

As always, it is wise to be cautious when messing with the user's Registry. The tools help prevent any serious mistakes, but you still need to consider the user. For example, the Windows Registry has a limited size, and if you create lots of items, it could fill up.

The User Interface Editor

The Package And Deployment Wizard that came with Visual Basic 6 had a terrible user interface that was difficult to modify. You had to edit the twisted code that made up the tool, hoping that your changes didn't mess up anything. Small changes took time, and adding a new dialog was a big deal indeed. Now everything is different.

The UI editor in the deployment tool suite is a huge step up. You can tune the UI a little, turn dialogs on or off, and even add your own custom dialogs. Figure 20.9 shows UI editor.

The tree shows all the steps in the installation and each dialog associated with each step. Select any dialog and modify it using the Properties window. For example, in the Welcome screen, you can set the welcome text and copyright warning text.

You can add your other dialogs to the installation in addition to the default dialogs put there for you (and delete those you don't need). Right-click any step to select a new dialog to add. Figure 20.10 shows the optional dialogs, including a license agreement, a splash screen, and all kinds of control combinations. Once you add one, you can modify it through the Properties windows.

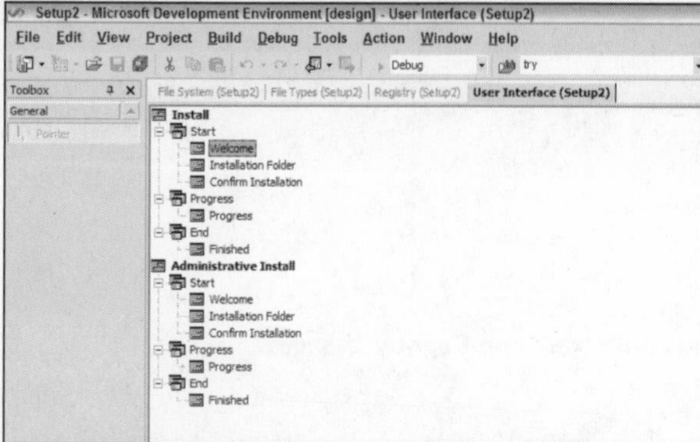

Figure 20.9 You can make all kinds of visual and functional changes with the User Interface editor.

Note that there are two separate major headings in the UI editor tree: Install and Administrative Install. The Administrative Install is a variation of the normal installation that you will need to change for the administrator. It installs an image or copy of the installation on a network somewhere so that users can then install it to their local machines. Once this install is created, the administrator can create the install image using your deployment package by starting it with a /a command line parameter. This feature can be quite useful in a multiuser environment.

The Launch Conditions Editor

There are often certain conditions that must be met before you will allow your installation to take place. Your program might have certain minimum requirements that you want to check before deploying the application, such as the amount of free disk space or the operating system version. The Launch Conditions editor takes care of this for you. Figure 20.11 shows the editor with a condition added. The tree in the editor lists all the conditions by name, and the condition parameters are shown in the Properties window.

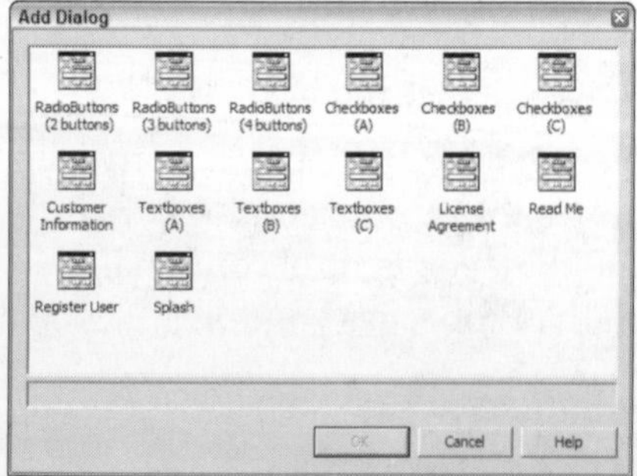

Figure 20.10 There are quite a few optional dialogs at your disposal.

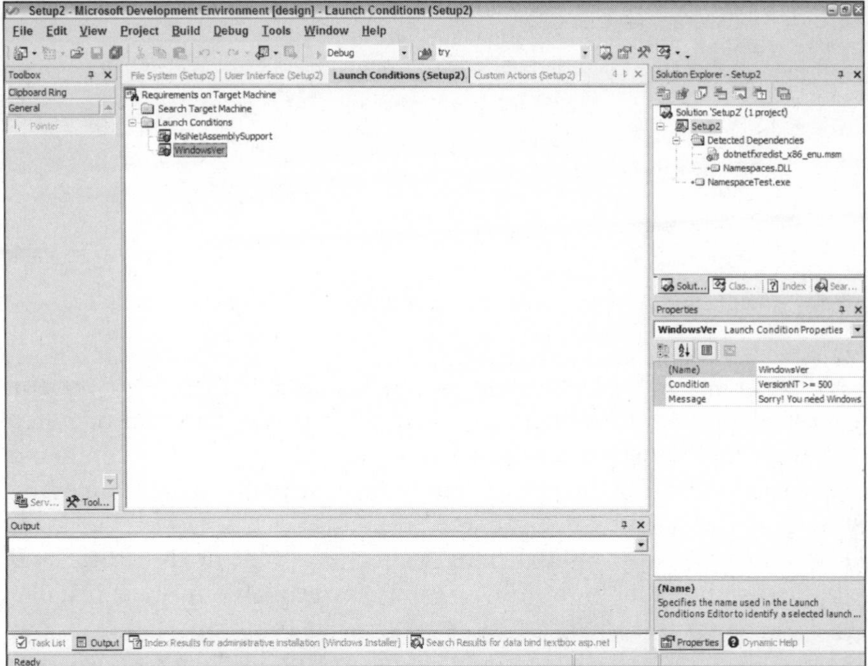

Figure 20.11 A launch condition added that requires a minimum version of the operating system.

For example, assume that you would like to make sure that the operating system is Windows 2000 or later. You can add the following condition that uses a system value called VersionNT and checks to make sure it is 500 or greater, equating to version 5.00 or later.

```
VersionNT >= 500
```

The conditions defined here are checked when the installation begins. If the conditions are met, the installation proceeds. If not, installation halts and displays the error message you set in the Properties section for the specific condition.

The Custom Actions Editor

At certain points in an installation, such as after a successful completion or when a rollback occurs, you want to launch your own functionality. This is called a custom action. It's up to you to build the functionality you want to run, but once complete, you set it up by using the Custom Actions editor, shown in Figure 20.12.

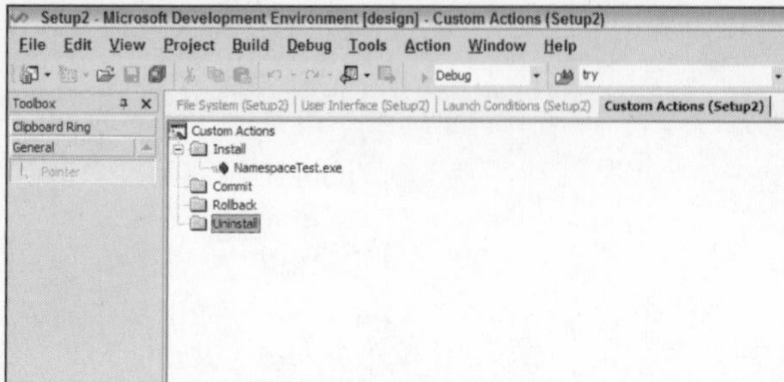

Figure 20.12 The Custom Actions editor sets up your own functionality.

The editor shows several places at which you can launch your custom actions, including after the installation itself, after it is committed or rolled back, or during the uninstallation. You might, for example, have a command line utility that runs during the uninstall to remove any stray saved game files after the user removes your game software.

You can add actions by right-clicking the action point in the editor and adding your own executable from the assemblies available in your installation. Once an action is added, set its properties in the Properties window. Using properties, you can pass arguments to the executable being launched or even set a condition that must be met before the functionality executes.

Classroom Q & A

Q: What are some of the limitations of the installation tools? I've had bad luck with things like this, starting to use them and then running into roadblocks.

A: There are some things this installer can't do. Fortunately, the custom actions capability allows you to expand its capabilities with close to no limit. The limitations I've hit are mostly in the UI area. You can customize lots of dialogs to some degree, but completely new ones are tough. If you want to put completely new functionality in the middle of your installation, that's not really possible. There are only four points at which custom actions can be launched. That's the biggest problem I've run into. However, this rarely causes difficulty, and we usually find a workaround by changing the design of our installation a little. Most of the custom functionality fits at the end, during the commit phase.

Q: Are there any other ways to customize the setup projects or set options? What you've shown is pretty flexible, but are there other ways?

A: There are, in fact, some project-level settings you can adjust to suit your own needs. The button on far right of the Solution Explorer toolbar brings up a Properties dialog, showing options you can set at the project level. It includes the name of the output MSI file. It lets you change how your files are packaged in the install, either in the MSI file, in a CAB file, or just loose and uncompressed. One of the most important is the ability to include the setup bootstrapper files. This attaches the installer engine for operating systems that don't contain it natively, such as Windows 98. If any of these operating systems are targets that you support, you should include the bootstrapper files. There are also a few other options there, such as setting different configurations for debug or release, as well as a configuration manager that lets you save your settings for later use.

Q: The ability to use your own banner graphic seems pretty cool. What size is it? Does it need to be in any specific format?

A: For best results, the graphic should be 500 pixels wide by 70 pixels high. You can use BMP or JPG formats, but of course, JPG files take up significantly less disk space. There is no problem displaying 24-bit color. One important thing to keep in mind is that the installer uses the left side of the graphic to overlay titles on. It may use up to 420 of the 500 pixels available. You'll want to account for this when you design one. Keep any company logos and such on the extreme right side.

Lab 20.1: A Merge Module

You've now seen all the tools that you need to build your own installation packages. We're going to build some of them in our labs and see how they can work together.

In Chapter 15, "XML Web Services," we built a component that provided secure access to a database of computer parts and their inventory. In this lab, we create a merge module for that component that can be included with any other application installation that might need it. It is important to note that merge modules have no user interface; they are meant to be included with other installations, letting those other installations run the show. Let's get started.

1. Create a new project in Visual Studio .NET. We'll create a deployment project using the Setup Wizard. On the left side of the new project dialog, click the Setup and Deployment Projects category. On the right side, click the Setup Wizard project option. Enter a new name for the project, PartsComponent, in this example. Click the OK button when you're ready to kick off the wizard. Figure 20.13 shows the correct settings.

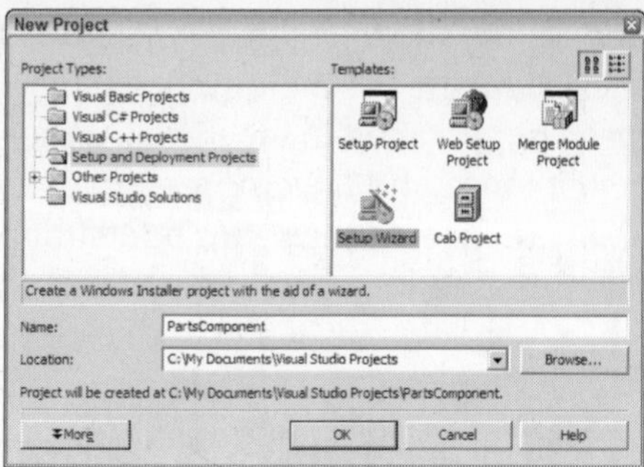

Figure 20.13 The correct settings for the New Project dialog.

2. Click Next to get past the first page of the dialog to the second, where we select a deployment type. Click the third radio button to create a merge module, and then click the Next button.
3. The third panel enables us to add any files to the installation that we want to deploy. Click the Add button to browse to the location of the DLL we built in Chapter 15 by clicking the Add button. Once found, the dialog should look like Figure 20.14.

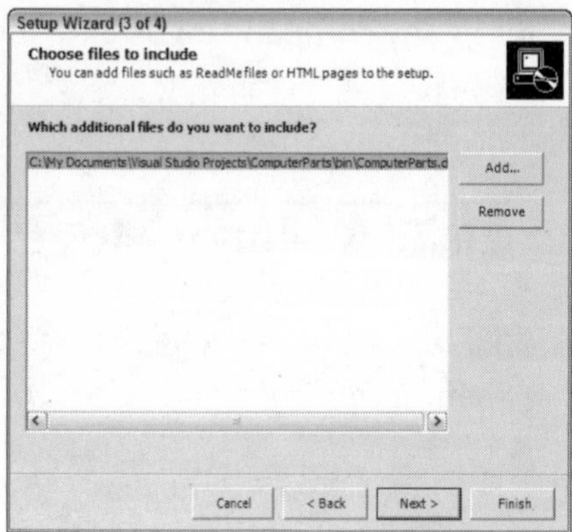

Figure 20.14 Adding installation files to the Setup Wizard.

4. Click through the rest of the wizard to complete it. This puts the studio and the project into the File System editor, as shown in Figure 20.15.

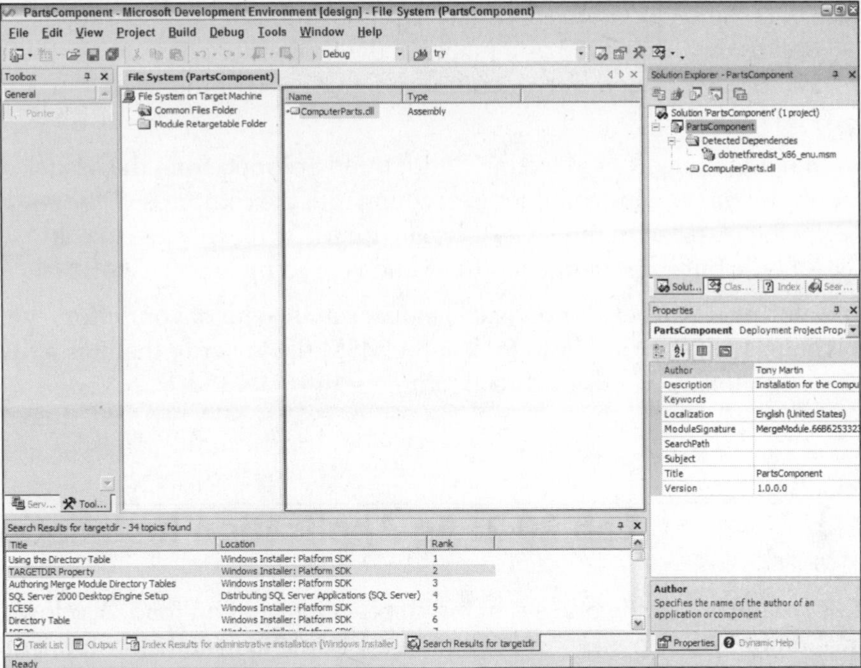

Figure 20.15 Once the wizard completes, the studio goes to the File System editor.

5. Click the Common Files Folder to see the file we added in the wizard. It will show in the right-hand pane of the File System Editor. Click on the file to adjust its properties in the Properties window of the studio. For example, you could add a condition to the file under which it will be installed or ignored. If you need to, you can also move the files added in the wizard to other directories. You can use the File System editor to add other files as well. We do not want the DLL in the Common Files folder; it must go into the application directory of the program that is installing it. Therefore, drag the file in the right-hand pane to the Module Retargetable Folder in the left-hand pane. Click on that folder to make sure the file went there. If you highlight the folder and check its DefaultLocation property, you'll see that it reads [TARGETDIR]. This is a system variable that stands in for the hosting installation's application directory, exactly what we want. So that's done.

When building application deployment projects, you have normal access to all of the editors. However, when building a merge module deployment project, some of the editors, such as the UI editor, are not available. They are not applicable, so they are turned off, in case you were wondering where they went.

6. Select the project in the Solution Explorer. You can now set properties for the installation as a whole in the Properties window. Set the author, description, version number, or any other properties you find interesting.
7. Build the project by selecting Build, Build Solution from the Visual Studio menu. This compiles everything into the compressed file used by the installer. In this case, it creates an MSM file. It's just like an MSI file but is for merge modules and is used by other installations.

Unfortunately, there is no visual feedback at the end of your efforts for this sort of project. You could look at the MSM file to verify that it is built correctly. However, it feeds directly into our next lab.

Lab 20.2: An Application Installation

This lab illustrates the process of building an installation for a Windows application. We also make use of a merge module to install a component we need.

We built a basic WinForms client that we can use as an installation target. It is similar to the client we built in Chapter 15 that provides access to computer parts data through a data access component. There are one or two additional supporting files that we need for this project; they are included on the companion Web site

1. Create the client program we want to install. Create a new WinForms project and name it PartsInventory. Lay out the controls on the main window just like they were in Chapter 15. It should look like Figure 20.16.
2. Once the controls are laid out, add a reference to the ComputerParts component. Right-click the references item in the Solution Explorer and select Add, Add Reference. Find the ComputerParts component and add it.

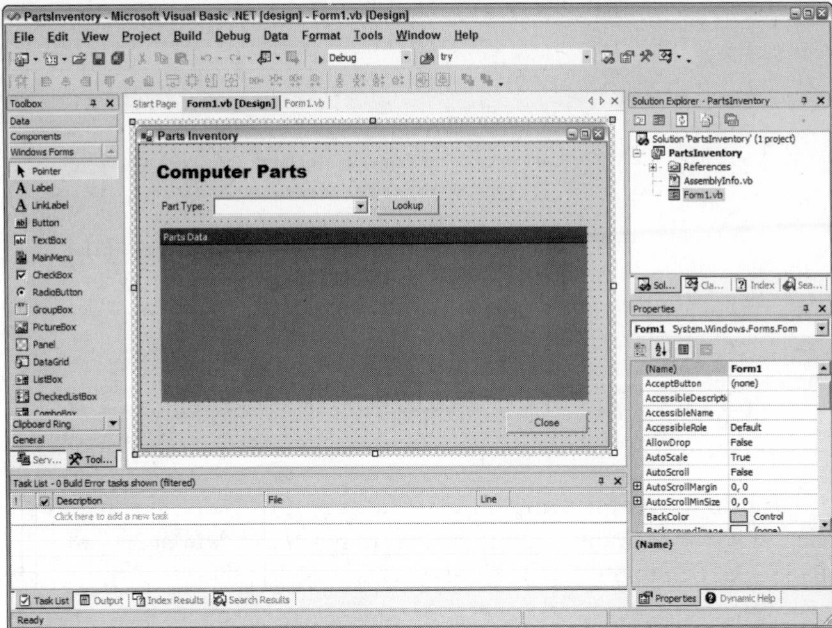

Figure 20.16 The control layout of our installation target program.

3. Add the following code to the project. It does pretty much the same thing as the code in Chapter 15 but has been edited to make direct use of the data access component instead of the Web service interface class.

```
Public Class Form1
    Inherits System.Windows.Forms.Form
    Private obj As New ComputerParts.Parts()
    Private ds As DataSet
    Private Sub Button1_Click(ByVal sender As System.Object, _
        ByVal e As System.EventArgs) Handles Button1.Click
        Me.Close()
    End Sub
    Private Sub Form1_Load(ByVal sender As System.Object, _
        ByVal e As System.EventArgs) Handles MyBase.Load
        Try
            ds = obj.PartTypes()
            cbPartTypes.DataSource = ds.Tables("parttypes")
            cbPartTypes.DisplayMember = "TypeDescription"
```

```
                cbPartTypes.ValueMember = "PartTypeID"
            Catch ex As Exception
                MsgBox(ex.Message)
            End Try
        End Sub
        Private Sub btnLookup_Click(ByVal sender As System.Object, _
            ByVal e As System.EventArgs) Handles btnLookup.Click
            Try
                ds = obj.GetParts(cbPartTypes.SelectedValue)
                ' Bind the data to the grid.
                dgParts.DataSource = ds.Tables("Parts")
            Catch ex As Exception
                MsgBox(ex.Message)
            End Try
        End Sub
    End Class
```

4. Compile and run the program to make sure it works. If it runs properly, you can click the Lookup button to get some data back that looks like what's shown in Figure 20.17.

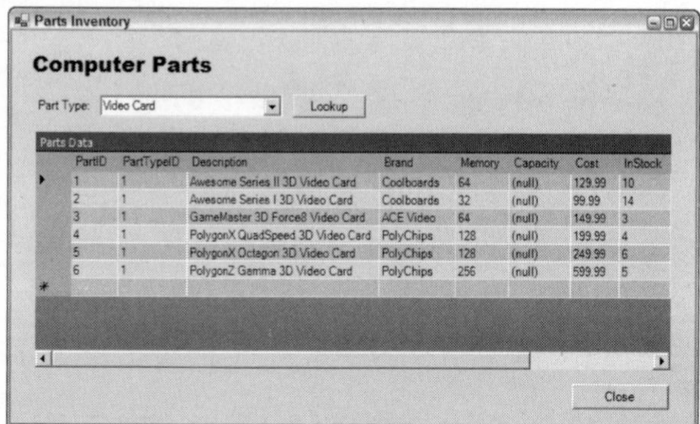

Figure 20.17 The client program should pull back data correctly.

5. Now that we have something to install, we can begin the deployment project. Create a new deployment project in Visual Studio .NET. Select the Application Wizard project type, and name it PartsInventoryInstall.

6. When the wizard starts, click through to the second panel and select the Windows Application project type. Click to the next panel.

7. On the File Selection panel of the wizard, browse to the location of the client program we just built. It will be located in the bin directory underneath the project directory. Click through the rest of the wizard to create the project.

8. You should now be in the File System editor. On the left side, click the Application Folder, and on the right side is the file we added, as well as its dependent DLL, our data access component. However, we are going to use a merge module to install the data access component. We have to get rid of the DLL that was added automatically and then add the merge module.
9. Select the DLL in the File System editor and examine the Properties window in the studio. Change its Exclude property to True, and the DLL disappears from the file list. This effectively removes it from the installation.
10. Right-click the project name in the Solution Explorer and from the context menu, select Add, Merge Module. This brings up the Add Merge Module dialog. Browse to the location of the MSM file we created in Lab 20.1 and click the OK button. You can see that PartsComponent.msm was added to the project in the Solution Explorer. It is dropped automatically when the installation is run.
11. Add a readme file to the project. Later we'll add a custom dialog asking users if they want to install it or not. For now, create a dummy readme file in WordPad or use the one on the companion Web site (it's called Readme.rtf and contains release notes for the program we are installing). Click the Application Folder in the File System editor, and right-click in the right pane. From the context menu, select Add, File. Browse to the readme file and add it to the project. Figure 20.18 shows the file added to the editor.

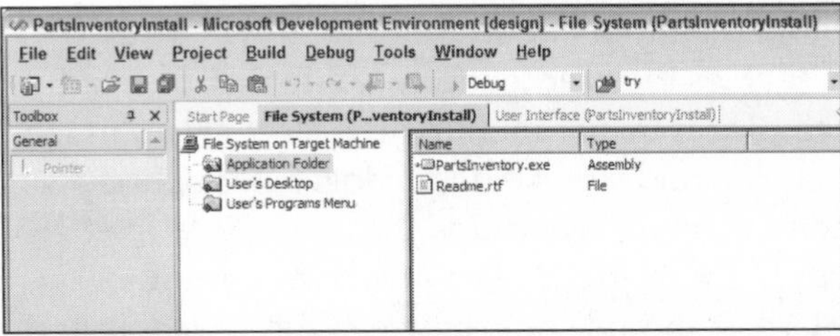

Figure 20.18 We have added our own readme file to the project.

12. We need to give our product a name, as far as the installation is concerned. In the Solution Explorer, select the project name, and then examine the Properties window. Some of these, such as the product name, can be referred to in the setup; we'll use them later. Set the following properties:

    Author. Set to your name.

    Description. Set this to anything meaningful describing the application.

Manufacturer. Set this to a mythical software development company. We chose Bronze Dove Software.

Product Name. Set this to Parts.

13. Now let's customize the installation a little for our own purposes. Switch to the UI editor by clicking its toolbar button at the top of the Solution Explorer. Once open, select the Welcome dialog in the editor. We're going to add a new banner graphic to represent our fictional software company and add our own identity to the installation. In the properties window for the Welcome dialog, select Browse in the Bitmap property. When the dialog comes up, you can select a file in your project. However, this file is not part of our project yet. We can add the file to our project as well as select it for our bitmap property at the same time. Select the Application Folder from the combo box at the top of the dialog. Click the Add button to browse to and select your banner graphic file. Close out the dialogs, and you should be done with the banner. Repeat the process for all the remaining dialogs in the installation project. You won't have to browse for the file again, but you do have to select it from the Application Folder directory each time.
14. If you want, customize the copyright warning and the welcome text for the dialog through their properties. Notice that the default text uses a bracketed variable to represent the product name. There are other variables that you can use throughout the installation to refer to all kinds of information. Hit the Help system to find out what's available.
15. It's time to add a custom dialog to our application. It will contain a single check box that enables the user to indicate whether the readme file should be installed. Begin by highlighting the Start group in the UI editor tree. Right-click it and select Add Dialog. Select Check Boxes (A) from the context menu. This adds the dialog into the tree structure, at the end of the Start group. However, we want it to occur in a different place. It should come between the Welcome and Installation Folder dialogs. Simply drag it to the new location in the tree. Note that although you can change the order of the dialogs, any custom dialogs such as this one must come before the Installation Folder dialog.
16. There are lots of properties for the new dialog that we need to change to make it look like we want it to. The simple ones are listed here. Go ahead and make these changes.

BannerBitmap. Set this to the custom image we loaded earlier.

BannerText. This is the title of the dialog. Set it to Readme File.

BodyText. This is the text in the dialog. Set it to the following text: If you would like to install the readme file, please make sure the box below is checked.

CheckBox1Label. This is the text next to the check box. Set it to Install ReadMe.

CheckBox1Property. This is essentially a global variable that can be referenced at other places in the installation. Set its value to INSTALLREADME. We use it later in a condition.

CheckBox1Value. This is the default value for the first check box. Set it to a value of checked.

CheckBox2Visible. There are four check boxes by default on this customizable dialog. We need only one, so we need to turn the rest of them off. Set the CheckBox2Visible property to False. Do the same for the other two check boxes.

17. Now that we have the custom dialog in place, we need to make use of the check-box value we got from the user. Pop over to the File System editor and select the readme file we added earlier. In the Properties window, enter the following text in the Condition property:

```
INSTALLREADME = 1
```

This allows the installer to drop the readme file conditionally. If the check box in our custom dialog is set, the property we entered for that check box is set to 1. If it's set to 1 in our condition for this file, the user checked the box, and we drop it. Otherwise, it is ignored.

18. At this point, our UI and setup are just about done. However, we want the users to register their software at our company Web site. To do this, we install a canned Web page that we can launch after the installation, which provides a link to the (fictitious) company registration page on the Web. We do this with a custom action. First, we need to build the functionality ourselves.

19. Create a new class library project in Visual Studio .NET. Name it RegisterWeb. When it comes up, delete the default Class1.vb from the Solution Explorer. Now add a module to the project: right-click the project name and select Add, Add Module from the context menu. In the module, add the following code, which launches a Web page located in our application directory in Internet Explorer:

```
Module RegisterModule
    Public Sub Main()
        Dim sPath As String
        sPath = System.Reflection.Assembly.
```

```
                GetExecutingAssembly.Location
            sPath = Left(sPath, InStrRev(sPath, "\"))
               & "BDSreg.html"
            Shell("C:\Program Files\Internet Explorer
               \iexplore.exe " & _
                 sPath, AppWinStyle.NormalFocus, False)
        End Sub
  End Module
```

20. Open the Properties dialog for the project. Change the Output Type to Windows Application, and then set the Startup Object to Sub Main. We now have a program with no UI that launches our support registration Web page. Compile the program and note its location.

21. Close the RegisterWeb project and open our deployment project again. In the File System editor, right-click in the right pane and select Add, Assembly from the context menu. When the dialog appears, click Browse and locate the RegisterWeb.exe assembly that we just created. Close out all the dialogs. As long as we're adding files, add the registration Web page and any files it needs. We have provided one on the companion Web site that you can use if you like. Add the files BDSLogo.jpg and BDSReg.html. The editor has a few files in it now and should look something like Figure 20.19.

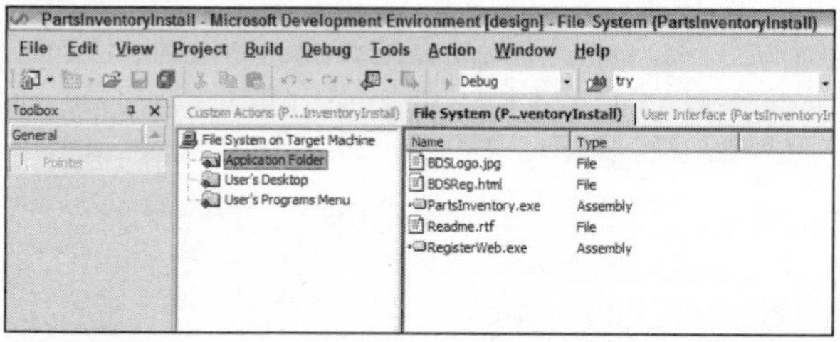

Figure 20.19 All our files are added to the deployment project.

22. Now we need to make use of the custom registration functionality we've built and added to our project. Open the Custom Actions editor by clicking its toolbar icon at the top of the Solution Explorer. Right-click the Commit item in the tree and select Add Custom Action from the context menu. Double-click the Application Folder and select the RegisterWeb.exe file that we recently added to the project. That adds it to the tree. With the executable selected, change the InstallerClass property to False. (You could have your custom action functionality launch at any of the four stages listed in the Custom Actions editor. We chose the Commit action because we wanted it to launch at the end of the installation, but you could just as easily have launched it during uninstall or rollback.)

23. Select Build, Build Solution from the studio menu. If everything goes well, it completes successfully. If you navigate to the project directory on your disk, you will find the MSI file that was built for you. Double-click it to run the installation. Figure 20.20 shows the starting dialog, with our custom banner graphic.

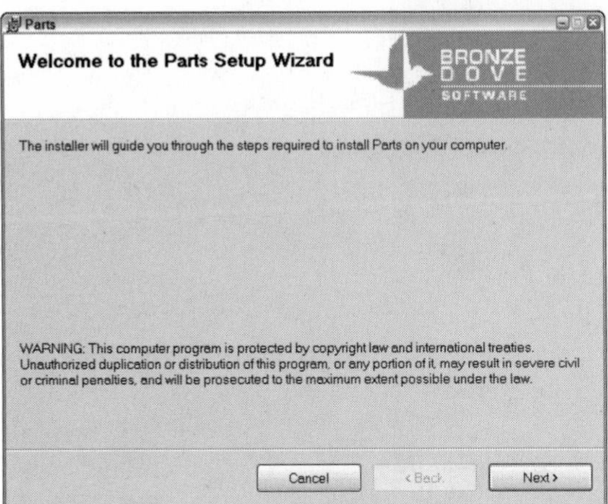

Figure 20.20 Our custom banner professionally personalizes the installation welcome screen.

24. Click the Next button to move on to the next panel (see Figure 20.21), where we put our custom dialog asking if the user wants to install the readme file.

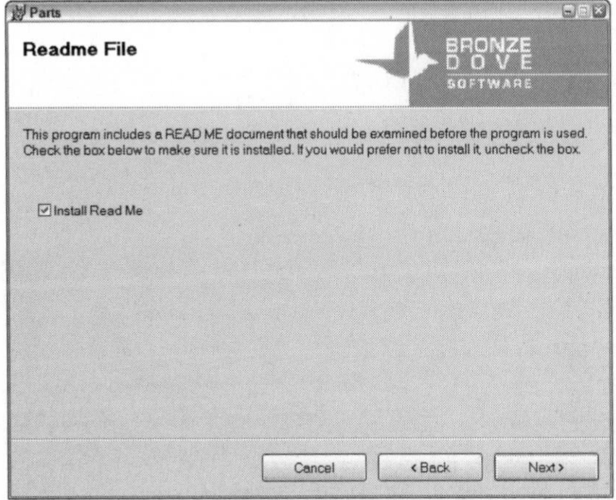

Figure 20.21 Our custom dialog is an example of the flexibility of the new installation system.

25. Click the Next button to navigate to the directory selection panel, shown in Figure 20.22. This is a canned dialog that we did not modify, although it looks good. It even has a button to show disk usage of the program (not shown in the figure) for the user's convenience.

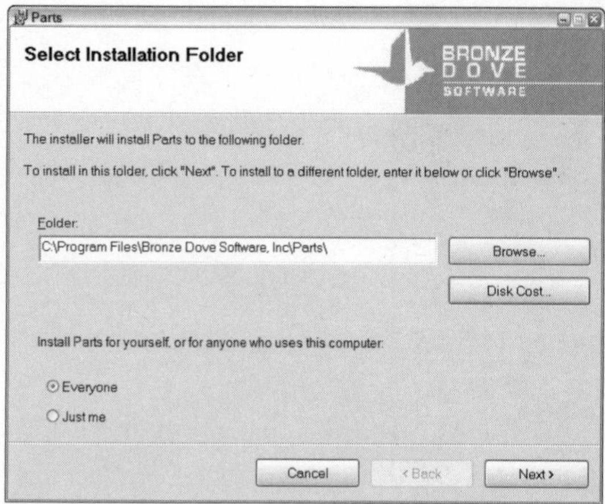

Figure 20.22 We did not modify the directory selection panel, but it looks good on its own.

26. Click the Next button to move to the next panel, which shows a summary of the installation options chosen. Click Next to begin the installation. The next panel has a status bar that updates as the installation proceeds (see Figure 20.23).

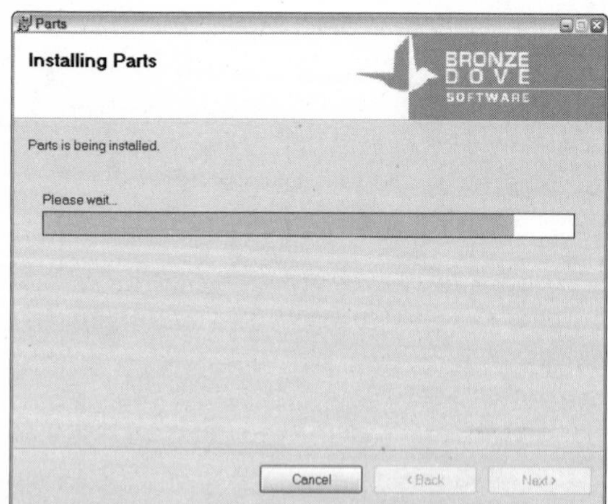

Figure 20.23 Installation progress is indicated with a standard progress bar.

27. When the installation is finished, two things happen. First, the final panel of the wizard is displayed, telling us that everything is done. Second, our custom action is launched, and a Web browser is fired up with our registration Web page, as shown in Figure 20.24.

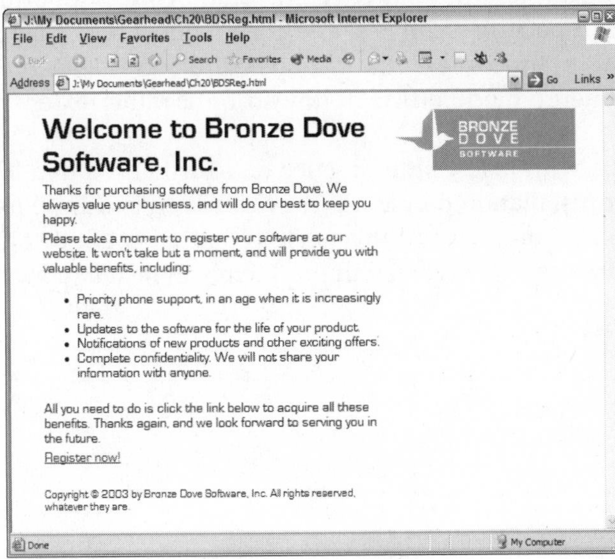

Figure 20.24 Our custom action functionality is launched on commit.

28. Now that the installation is complete, verify that it worked correctly. The default installation directory is Program Files\Bronze Dove Software\Parts. You can see that the executable is there, as are the data access component, our Web page files, and the readme file. You can even try out the uninstall feature by either using the Add/Remove Programs feature of Windows or running the installation again (it knows the program is already installed and starts up in Remove/Repair mode).

In this pair of labs, we've seen a fair amount of the installation capabilities of the new tools provided by Visual Studio .NET. They should handle most of your installation needs. However, there is much more to explore in these tools, so dig around to see what else is there.

Summary

This chapter introduced you to most of the capabilities of the new Microsoft Installer and the Visual Studio .NET installation tools. It showed the various types of installations available to you and covered some of the supporting technologies, such as namespaces, assemblies, and the manifest. The chapter went through the installation process and the various editors available in the tool set, and we built a merge module first, followed by a rather extensive application installation.

These installation tools, with just a little practice and further exploration, can solve almost all your installation problems. They can even be fun to use. The only drawback for programmers (and this is viewed as a benefit by anyone else) is that there is little coding involved in producing an installation.

Review Questions

1. Which operating systems support the Microsoft Installer natively?
2. What is a manifest? What is the easiest way to view one?
3. Where does a .NET application look for its dependent assemblies?
4. What is a merge module used for? What might be a benefit or two of using one?
5. Why would you create a standalone installation project instead of including the installation project in your main solution?
6. How do you add your own functionality to an installation?
7. What is the purpose of the Administrative installation section in the UI editor?
8. Are all the editors available all the time, or are some of them turned off occasionally?
9. What is the application database?

Answers to Review Questions

1. The Microsoft Installer is part of Windows Me, Windows 2000, and Windows XP. You can include the engine as part of the installation if your target platforms include Windows 95, Windows 98, or Windows NT.
2. A manifest is a list of all the items contained in an assembly. It includes the name and version of the assembly, as well as a list of all the files that make up the assembly. It also contains a list of external files upon which the assembly depends. The easiest way to view a manifest is using the ILDASM utility.
3. An executable looks first in its own application directory. If it can't find what it needs there, it checks the GAC, a home for shared components.
4. A merge module is an installation package that lays down components and has no UI. It is meant to be used by other installations. If you are building a component or set of components that could be used by more than one application, a merge module allows you to build an installation package for them once and then simply include it in other installations as needed.
5. Creating a standalone installation has the benefit of allowing one person to work on the installation project while other engineers work on the target program. It is also useful if you don't have access to the original source for the installation target.
6. Add your own functionality to an installation by creating a custom action in the editor. You can launch any sort of Windows executable you want, including full-blown programs. Useful examples might include a configuration program, a registration utility, or even launching the installed program itself.
7. The administrative section allows an administrator to install an image to a server, from which users can install the program on their local machines. The section in the UI editor enables you to customize the standard install to accommodate changes required for the administrative install.
8. The editors are all available in standard application installation projects. However, some are disabled in other project types. For example, the UI editor is disabled in Merge Module projects because they have no UI to edit.
9. The application database is where Windows stores information about all the applications installed on the system. It is of particular use to the uninstall process, which uses the database to determine what files to remove.

APPENDIX

A

Installing .NET

The installation of .NET can be quite simple or rather monotonous depending upon a small number of choices. This appendix lets you avoid the setup issues related to .NET and not have to worry about missing components or inability to create Web-related projects.

Installing .NET

A .NET installation can be accomplished in much less time than you might have been led to believe or have experienced if you follow a few simple steps. To begin, let's look at what you need.

What You Need

To install .NET, you need the following software:

- Windows OS CD (I recommend 2000 or XP)
- The 4 Studio .NET CDs (Visual Studio .NET)
- The Component Update CD
- Microsoft Word (viewer at least) to view the many .doc files that ship with the .NET SDK

Quick Installation Tips

The following tips will greatly reduce the time spent installing .NET and reduce the possibility of installation errors to nearly zero.

- Perform the installation as a member of the Administrators group.
- Make sure there is an administrator-level account that has a password and allow the Windows Component Update to run logged in as that account. (There is a check box for this when you launch the installer.) Depending on your operating system and previously installed components, Windows Component Update could reboot several times. If it has an account to use, it will log itself in and continue the process each time, saving you the trouble of manually logging on at each step.
- When you are faced with a selection of check boxes for adding features to .NET, just deselect and then reselect the top-level box to make sure everything is selected; trust me, it avoids a number of potential problems later.
- Before installing .NET, make sure that IIS is installed (with Front Page Server Extensions configured) on the machine you will be developing on, even if you think you won't be doing Web development.
- If you XCopy all five .NET CD contents to a network directory for performing installations, you can avoid quite a few CD swaps.

Installing .NET alongside Visual Basic 6 is perfectly fine because Visual Basic 6 components use the Registry, and Visual Basic .NET components are GAC-installed assemblies.

.NET Installation Procedure

After installing an appropriate operating system and logging on as a member of the Administrator group, you can begin installing .NET. Perform the following steps:

To install Microsoft Internet Information server:

1. Click Start, Settings, Control Panel, Add/Remove Programs.
2. Click Add/Remove Windows Components.
3. Select the check box for IIS.
4. Select the check box for Script Debugger.
5. Click Next to start the Windows Component Wizard.

6. Click Finish to end.
7. Restart the computer.
8. Verify Front Page Server Extensions have been configured.

To install Windows Component Update:

1. Place the .NET CD1 in the drive and wait for the setup screen to appear.
2. Click Windows Component Update, enter the Windows Component Update CD when asked, and then click OK.
3. Click *I accept*, Continue, Continue.
4. Indicate that you want to use the Administrator account, and enter the password (twice as indicated).
5. Click Install Now.
6. Click Done to finish.

To install Visual Studio .NET:

1. When you have returned to the setup screen following the installation of Windows Component Update, the second item will now be displayed. Click Visual Studio .NET to start the installation process. (You might have to pop the CD1 for .NET back in the drive to get this screen if the CD-ROM was removed.)
2. Select I Accept the Agreement.
3. Enter the Product Key.

The product key is most likely imprinted on CD1. On some high-color resolution laptop screens, you may actually have to adjust the angle of your screen to even *see* the product key boxes; no, I'm not kidding.

4. Click Continue.
5. Deselect and reselect the first check box (Visual Studio .NET Professional) to ensure that all options possible for .NET will be installed.
6. Click to start the installation.
7. Click Done, Exit.

APPENDIX

B

About the 60 Minutes Web Site

This appendix provides you with information on the contents of the Web site that accompanies this book. On this site, you will find information that will help you with each of the book's chapters.

This Web site contains:

- Streaming video presentations that introduce you to each chapter of the book. These presentations are intended to provide late-breaking information that can help you understand the content of the chapter.
- Sample code that is used throughout the book. The sample code presented can be easily copied and pasted into your Visual Studio .NET project.

To access the site, visit www.wiley.com/compbooks/60minutesaday.

System Requirements

Make sure that your computer meets the minimum system requirements listed in this section. If your computer doesn't match up to most of these requirements, you may have a problem using the contents of the Knowledge Publisher Studio.

- PC with a Pentium processor running at 266 MHz or faster with Windows NT4, Windows 2000, or Windows XP.
- At least 256MB of total RAM installed on your computer; for best performance, we recommend at least 512MB.
- A high-speed Internet connection of at least 100K is recommended for viewing online video.
- Internet Explorer 6.0 or higher.
- Browser settings need to have Cookies enabled; Java must be enabled (including JRE 1.2.2 or higher installed) for chat functionality and live Webcast.
- Screen Resolution of 1024x768 pixels.

60 Minutes a Day Presentations

To enhance the learning experience and further replicate the classroom environment, *Visual Basic .NET in 60 Minutes a Day* is complemented by a multimedia Web site which aggregates a streaming video and audio presentation. The multimedia Web site includes an online presentation and introduction to each chapter. The presentation, hosted by Bruce Barstow, includes a 10- to 15-minute video segment for each chapter that helps to deliver the training experience to your desktop and to convey advanced topics in a user-friendly manner.

Each video/audio segment introduces a chapter and highlights the important concepts and details of that chapter. After viewing the online presentation, you are prepped and primed to read the chapter.

Upon reaching the companion site that contains the video content for this book you will be asked to register using a valid email address and self-generated password. This will allow you to bookmark video progress and manage notes, email, and collaborative content as you progress through the chapters. All video content is delivered "on demand," meaning that you can initiate the viewing of a video at any time of the day or night at your convenience.

Any video can be paused and replayed as many times as you wish. The necessary controls and widgets used to control the delivery of the videos use strict industry standard symbols and behaviors, thus eliminating the necessity to learn new techniques. If you would like to participate in a complete five-minute online tutorial on how to use all features available inside the presentation panel, visit http://www.propoint.com/solutions/ and click on the DEMO NOW link on the left side of the Web page.

This video delivery system may be customized somewhat to enhance and accommodate the subject matter within a particular book. A special effort has been made to ensure that all information is readily available and easy to understand. In the unlikely event that you should encounter a problem with the content on the site, please do not hesitate to contact us at Wiley Product Technical Support.

Code and Bonus Content

In addition to the presentations, you can download the sample code files and view additional resources.

Troubleshooting

If you have trouble with the Web site, please call the Wiley Product Technical Support phone number: (800) 762-2974. Outside the United States, call 1 (317) 572-3994. You can also visit our Web site at www.wiley.com/techsupport. Wiley Publishing, Inc., will provide technical support only for installation and other general quality control items; for technical support on the applications themselves, consult the program's vendor or author.

APPENDIX

C

Glossary

ADO (ActiveX Data Objects) Replaced DAO and RDO and provided the best of both specifications. ADO was replaced in Microsoft .NET with ADO.NET.

ADO.NET Differs from ADO in several areas but primarily in the concept that almost all data access is disconnected. ADO.NET provides relationships between tables in a DataSet object that can be created from multiple, disparate data sources. Unlike its predecessors, XML is ingrained in ADO.NET.

API (Application Program Interface) Those portions made public by an application so that external applications can utilize functionality or interact with the application.

ASP (Active Server Page) Microsoft's implementation of server-side code for Web sites. ASP was replaced by ASP.NET.

ASP.NET The .NET improvement over ASP, compiled instead of interpreted and runs about four times faster overall than ASP, with development integrated with the Visual Studio IDE.

ATL (Active Template Library) A set of Windows development libraries used by C++ programmers in Windows prior to .NET.

CLS (Common Language Specification) Not a Microsoft specification but rather a multicorporation venture to describe what a common language should look like. MSIL is Microsoft's implementation of that specification. CLS is concerned with portability, so external type members are of keen concern. For instance, not all languages support unsigned variables, so they are not allowed as public members of a class.

COM (Component Object Model) A Microsoft standard for development classes that makes objects created from those classes work in a way that is predictable in a Windows environment. *See also DCOM.*

COM+ (Pronounced COM Plus) The next version of MTS (Microsoft Transaction Server). COM+ is Microsoft's solution to enterprise application architecture. It provides object brokering, transaction support, and resource management for COM components to provide a scalable system.

Common Language Runtime Responsible for everything in .NET. It compiles initial code to IL (intermediate language) format, acts as an interpreter for IL, manages calls to the .NET Class Library, handles COM interop, and even interacts with all the supporting systems such as the GC.

Component Usually synonymous with *Class library*. Class libraries are typically represented at the file level as DLLs. In Visual Basic 6 and C++6, these could be COM, DCOM, or COM+ components. In .NET, COM, DCOM, and COM+, components are placed inside .NET assemblies, don't use the registry at all, and are still referred to as class libraries; also known as components. The term *component* has also been used frequently to refer to anything in an assembly, including an EXE.

CTS (Common Type System) .NET languages share common base classes for all their types. For instance, Visual Basic .NET's Integer and C#'s int are both actually System.Int32 and are depicted as such in ILDASM after initial compilation.

DAO (Data Access Objects) A data access library (language) for accessing databases using the ODBC standard. DAO didn't work well over a network, so RDO (Remote Data Objects) was later introduced. RDO was replaced with ADO, and ADO was extended in the Microsoft .NET arena to ADO.NET.

Declare To declare a variable is to use a data type keyword and a name with the expectation that a location in memory with the size of the type specified will contain a value of that type and can be referenced using the name specified.

DLL (Dynamic Link Library) A library of classes (or maybe even just functions) that can be linked into your application to extend your application's capabilities and to avoid rewriting common code. The Win32API is a set of DLLs exposed by Windows.

DLL Hell A term that refers to the nightmarish issues of dealing with versioning of DLLs in the Windows environment (prior to .NET assembly versioning) due to the registry. One application can install itself and mydll version 2.0, and a second application can install itself and mydll version 3.0, thereby breaking the first application. There are many other issues, but this is one of the most significant. In .NET, the described scenario would work properly.

Event An OOP term that represents a member of a class, whose purpose is to receive messages on behalf of that object and perform some action on such receipt. The most common event for objects in Windows development is the Click event. The user clicks at some position on the screen, Windows intercepts that click and passes a message to the foreground application, which in turn sends a message to any event handler for the actual object that was clicked. The concept of delegates in .NET is closely related to the concept of an event procedure.

GAC (Global Assembly Cache) The place where all public assemblies are installed (they don't use the registry as do COM components). The utility gacutil is used to install assemblies into the GAC. Assemblies must be signed before they can be placed in the GAC, whose location is c:\winnt\assembly (adjusting for installation differences, of course). Looking at this directory from within Windows will bring up only a shell that provides limited information about the installed assemblies. To view more complete information about assemblies installed in the GAC, view it from the .NET command prompt.

GC (Garbage Collector or Garbage Collection System) A system in .NET that is responsible for managing heap memory.

GUI Graphical user interface.

HTTP (Hypertext Transfer Protocol) The protocol over which Web pages are requested and sent. Its major limitation is that it's all text (no persistence of type information), but it is more than widely accepted as the standard.

IDE (Integrated Development Environment) A program you can use to develop applications. The Visual Studio .NET development environment you use to build applications is an IDE.

ILDASM (Intermediate Language Disassembler) A tool that ships with the .NET SDK for viewing compiled applications in their IL form.

Initialize Initialization refers to the assignment of an initial value to a variable. In fact, whether it's the initial or subsequent value, the act of giving a value to a variable is referred to as assignment.

Interface When a class has only declarations and no definitions, it is said to contain only *interface* in C++, but in .NET we have an actual keyword *interface*, which creates the equivalent of a purely abstract class in C++. When a class derives from another class, we may or may not keep the inherited members public. If the base type is an interface, however, we must publicly implement all members defined in the interface. One important distinction is that a class can *inherit* from a class but *implement* an interface.

IO (Input/Output) The sending and retrieving of data to and from files and/or the screen.

Jet The driver for the Microsoft Access Database.

JSP (Java Server Pages) Similar to ASP pages, but written in the Java programming language. The most popular server-side scripting mechanism for Java-based systems.

Member An OOP term that means anything that is part of a struct or a class. Members of a class include methods, properties, delegates, indexers, structs, enums, and other classes.

Method A public member of a class. A class called *printer* may have methods named print(), DisplayStatus(), FormFeed(), and so on. Methods represent functionality for an entity.

MFC (Microsoft Foundation Classes) The standard classes that C++ Windows developers (prior to .NET) could use to simplify building Windows applications. MFC is actually one of the project types available in .NET, although for compatibility/migration reasons.

MSDN (Microsoft Developer Network) Provides total support for all Microsoft products; it is like one massive SDK. Can be installed or found at msdn.microsoft.com/library.

MSI (Microsoft Installer) A utility for creating setup packages for Windows applications.

Object A rather interesting concept in .NET. The traditional concept of an object is an entity that is completely self-contained in all of its methods, fields, properties, events, or whatever you make for the class. Structs and classes both create objects that fit that description. In .NET, everything is considered an object (by that description), but objects come in two types. The first type, based on a struct, is the value type. These are always copied by value and exist on the stack. The second type, based on a class, is the reference type. Reference types are always created on the heap. Keep in mind that the most basic description of an object is an actual instance of a class or struct in C#.

OLEDB Replaces ODBC and is still used as the Data Consumer specification even in .NET. ADO (ActiveX Data Objects) and ADO.NET both use OLEDB Drivers to access databases. DAO and RDO both used ODBC. OLEDB and ODBC are always used as acronyms and are never spelled out.

OOP (Object Oriented Programming) The art of designing software with the approach that all entities should be represented as self-contained, reusable objects. Several things are required of an OOP language: Inheritance, polymorphism, abstraction and encapsulation are the most important features expected.

OS (Operating System) Windows, DOS, Unix, Linux, Macintosh, and so on.

Property An OOP term that refers to a public member of a class that holds state information (data) for that class. A property of a House object might be color, squarefeet, address, stories, owner, and so on. Properties don't seem to "do" anything. They just seem to hold data. You will find in .NET that properties are actually implemented as a unique looking method that often abstracts private data members known as fields.

Protocol A method of communication that encapsulates the rules for that communication. TCP, IP, SOAP, and HTTP are all protocols.

RAD (Rapid Application Development) The ability to build an application very quickly. This usually comes with the price of speed of execution or language flexibility.

RDO (Remote Data Objects) A database access library/language replacing DAO and providing optimization for remote database connections. RDO was replaced with ADO and ADO was extended in the Microsoft .NET arena to ADO.NET.

SDK (Software Development Kit) Usually a collection of tools that ship with a product to support development. The .NET SDK is freely downloadable and has tools, documentation, help, samples, and so on.

SOAP (Simple Object Access Protocol) A protocol that can be used to invoke methods in remote objects without prior knowledge of the objects being used. SOAP is ingrained in Microsoft .NET technology in its use of Web services.

SQL (Structured Query Language) (Pronounced *sequel*.) The standard language for performing database operations on relational databases. Microsoft SQL Server is Microsoft's premier relational database.

STL (Standard Template Library) A pre-.NET library for C++ developers replaced by common language runtime base class libraries in .NET.

Transaction A transaction in the English language and what it is to a programmer are a little different. Both describe a transaction as a unit of work that may require multiple steps, for example, a banking transfer. A transfer transaction consists of a debit from one account and a credit to a second account. What if after making the debit, an error occurred and the money was not credited in the second account? Someone would be quite unhappy. To solve this issue the programmer's version of a transaction ensures that all steps in a transaction occur successfully or they all are rolled back (undone). *Rollback* is a common transactional-modeling term whose opposite is *commit*.

UI (User Interface) Also referred to as a GUI, or graphical user interface. The UI in *n*-tier methodology exists at the presentation layer and encompasses everything the user sees and interacts with.

Visual Basic A rapid application total development environment. Visual Basic 6 is still the most widely used language in the world but is technically superseded by Visual Basic .NET.

Visual Studio Microsoft Visual Studio. NET is version 7 of Microsoft's development suite of tools and includes primarily C# and Visual Basic .NET.

Win32 (API Windows 32-bit Application Program Interface) Refers to the Windows functions that can be called from Windows applications to avoid having to reinvent that same functionality. The primary DLLs in the Win32 API are kernel32.dll, user32.dll, and GDI32.dll. The common language runtime base libraries in .NET should be called from .NET to ensure that all our code is managed by the common language runtime. These base classes wrap the functionality in the Win32 API classes for .NET developers.

Index

G

H

I

J

K

L

U